NAKED IN CYBERSPACE

How to Find Personal Information Online

NAKED IN CYBERSPACE

How to Find Personal Information Online

Carole A. Lane

Edited by Helen Burwell
and Owen B. Davies

Wilton, CT
1997

 Printed on recycled paper.

PRINTED WITH SOY INK™
Trademark of American Soybean Association

This book is dedicated to the most important people I know:

Barry Wang, for his support and faith in me, and Skylar Wang,

for regularly interrupting my work for a cuddle.

I adore you both infinity times infinity.

Contents

About Links to Sites and Staying Current

The world of personal information online changes with each blink of the eye. While continuing improvements in the technologies that allow for the capture, storage and sharing of data are tremendously important to online information searchers, perhaps no current trend promises a greater impact—at least in the near-term—than the pace at which public records and proprietary databases are being made available on the Internet.

The limitations of any print volume covering Internet resources may be rather obvious: new sites appear every day, other sites are expanded to include new or enhanced databases, and still other sites disappear without a trace. In regard to the coverage of Internet resources in *NAKED IN CYBERSPACE,* the challenge for the author and publisher is to offer you—the reader—a way to keep abreast of new sites, databases and developments.

Our approach is to offer you at our World Wide Web site a regularly-updated directory of key Internet resources—including, wherever possible, active links to sites (you must have an Internet connection and WWW browser to utilize these links). This directory is designed to help you pinpoint sites offering specific types of information, and to keep you up-to-date on the trends and issues relevant to personal online research. It is being made available beginning in June 1997 at no charge to you as a valued *NAKED IN CYBERSPACE* reader. Please be sure to read the important disclaimer that appears at the bottom of this page.

To Access Internet Resources And Links:

1. Go to the *NAKED IN CYBERSPACE* WWW page at **www.onlineinc.com/pempress/naked**

2. Click on the "LINKS TO SITES" icon
   TIP: use your browser's bookmark feature to simplify reaching links in the future

3. Browse the descriptions and click on the links that interest you. Please send feedback, including information about new or non-working sites, by email to *bookauthor@onlineinc.com*

DISCLAIMER (please read carefully)
Neither publisher nor author make any claim as to the results that may be obtained through the use of the above mentioned links to Internet sites and resources, which are maintained by third parties. Neither publisher nor author will be held liable for any results, or lack thereof, obtained by the use of any links, for any third party charges, or for any hardware, software or other problems that may occur as a result of using any links. This program of Internet resources and links is subject to change or discontinuation without notice at the discretion of the publisher.

Foreword

On the one hand, we love our privacy. On the other, we want information, and we want to find it as quickly and conveniently as possible. However, if we can uncover the details of other people's lives, they can just as easily intrude into our own secrets...

The conflict between these two interests—privacy versus easy access to information—has been big news during the past few years. Radio and television tell us of the promise, and threat, of the Information Age. News series often choose an individual and shock us with the details that a search of computer databanks has revealed about the person's life. (This exposé in turn becomes searchable information because transcripts of daily news reports, documentaries, and other shows now may be retrieved from a variety of electronic sources.) These programs, presumably intended to inform, have sometimes scared viewers into wondering whether we have lost all semblance of privacy in our daily lives. It is a valid question.

Even commercials have begun to heighten this anxiety. Television advertisements now offer to locate anyone in the United States by searching through the information available online—for only $59.95! Radio stations across the country have begun to air advertisements for companies that will help us to check out potential household help, to prevent such possible tragedies as hiring a nanny with a criminal record to care for our children. These are useful services, but the underlying message is clear: In a world of networked information, there is nowhere to hide.

State and federal statutes guarantee citizens access to much of the information collected by government. Those of us who spend our days gathering information regularly cite these laws in our search for data that, occasionally, others might have preferred to keep hidden. The Open Records Act, the Access to Public Records Act, the Freedom of Information Act all give us entry to government files.

More informally, all sorts of groups, from senior citizens chatting over morning coffee at a neighborhood gathering place to Baby Boomers or Generation X-ers attending business meetings or social events, argue that "it is a free country" or words to that effect. They, too, want access to information.

Some of us have known for years that we could go down to the local courthouse, hall of records, or other government offices to obtain information about lawsuits, real property, businesses, and some other matters. We could call the state capital to request certain other information by telephone. But since the revolution—the information technology revolution, that is—things have changed dramatically!

Computers have revolutionized record-keeping. Not long ago, federal, state, and local government offices stored their information by hand. It could take weeks for new records to find their way into the files. Some were misfiled. Others were lost completely. And once in the files, most records just gathered dust. For all but the most pressing purposes, it was far too much trouble to search them out and pull the paper from among the hundreds or thousands of file cabinets. Suddenly all those records can be filed simply by typing them into a terminal, and they can be retrieved in seconds.

Computer networks have made them even more accessible. More and more states and counties are making information available via computerized dial-up systems. Others are selling computer tapes to entrepreneurs who have created searchable databanks containing hundreds of files. Voter records, real property transactions, incorporation records, and many other forms of government data now are available online and on CD-ROM. Large and small vendors of public information have sprung up across the country. Some have made it possible to search all of their files simultaneously to find all existing links to a company or individual, from several different counties or states.

Though such information has grown increasingly available for more than a decade, very few people have known of these computerized archives until fairly recently. We all know that computers and other electronic technology have changed the way we live, often in important ways. Yet we take much of this transformation for granted, without realizing that information, in its various forms, has contributed to these changes.

Public records are only one piece of a complex puzzle comprised of the many lists on which we find ourselves. Our birth and death are recorded. So are our addresses, telephone numbers, contributions, political persuasion, education, employment, spending and bill-paying habits, and on and on. These records can be compiled, searched, reorganized, and manipulated, so that valuable information emerges from them.

Organizations that have gathered vast files of data in the process of marketing and servicing their products may give them away or sell their lists to others. These businesses then use the information to develop new products or services, or to help in making good business decisions. Depending upon our own need for information at any given time, we may be for or against in the debate about public access to information that might be considered personal.

Enter the Internet. The Information Highway has been a driving force as the number of personal computers in American homes races to catch up with the population of television sets. We even hear that new technologies soon will merge these devices into a single do-all information appliance. And as interest in the Internet explodes, so does the quantity of information available over the Net. Both government and the private sector are making billions of bytes of data available through the World Wide Web. Some of it is free, and some is available for a fee.

The Internet is quickly changing our lives, far more dramatically than most of us yet recognize. This is especially true of our relationship with what some people would consider personal information. We offer our thoughts and ideas on listservs or chat groups. Huge archives store the contents of these discussions for future searching. Although in some cases members may specify that their comments should not be archived, most people either do not know this or do not bother to specify "Do not archive." Their views are not only available to their intended recipients, but are preserved for all to see.

Much other personal information is finding its way onto the Internet.

Some college students are required to set up their own home pages on the World Wide Web. These Web pages often contain photos, likes and dislikes, and other details that once might have remained private. Historical associations and others interested in genealogy have made available electronic files, which may contain information about our ancestors. Consultants, authors, and other professionals put up pages of professional credentials. Newspapers and magazines, which often contain profiles of small-town celebrities, are available in electronic format. All these resources contain the personal details of individual lives.

All of this information can be located by search engines, some of which index every word on the page! We now hear of "meta" search engines, which provide search results covering multiple search engines simultaneously. If personal information exists on the Internet, it can be found by anyone who is interested enough to go looking for it.

In addition, the major commercial database vendors are creating World Wide Web sites that will allow customers to search their databases over the Internet. This means that photographs and other data can be downloaded and printed at the desktop. Although some vendors allow only subscribers to use their databases, others are offering inexpensive searches on demand.

So it goes. Each week, information becomes easier to obtain. This trend will continue for the foreseeable future. Given the rapid improvements in technology during the past five years, and expected during the next five, who knows where it will lead?

In creating *Naked in Cyberspace*, Carole Lane looked at the vast universe of electronic information already available. As her work progressed, she found it necessary to add new data sources to the already long list. Eventually, so many of them appeared that they outgrew any practical book, and Online Inc. found it necessary to archive a more complete list on the company's Web site. Each day the project continued, it became steadily more obvious that users of electronic information needed a tool to guide them through the growing maze of databases, CD-ROM titles, and Internet sites that contain information about individuals.

Naked in Cyberspace serves many purposes. Some readers will find it a valuable introduction to personal information searching. Others will use it as a reference tool, to be consulted chapter-by-chapter, as they need specific information. For almost everyone, it will point to useful new resources to be consulted in doing one's job.

Readers from attorneys to apartment leasing agents will find that this book offers new opportunities to find information about people. Even law enforcement personnel, who already rely on specialized databases, are likely to discover novel data sources here.

For those engaged in genealogy or similar pursuits, the tips found here may help to reveal the missing link that will solve a puzzle or to locate an elusive ancestor.

For librarians or other information professionals who must keep up-to-date with information sources, there are surely a few unfamiliar products or services mentioned. These sources may be useful in handling future reference questions or research projects.

They are only the beginning of what could become a lifelong quest. The listings of books, publications, and organizations, together with the archive at Online's Web site (**www.onlineinc.com/pempress/naked**), will guide you to resources for further learning about the many topics discussed in the following pages.

For some, reading this book will be an eye-opening adventure. As we learn about the various information sources now open to us, many readers will find themselves bubbling with ideas for using them at work and in their daily lives.

This book also may raise troubling questions about our own privacy.

Have we been mentioned in the newspaper? Do we have a personal Web site? Are we an officer, director, or major stockholder in a business? Recently divorced or married? Have we purchased property, been involved in a lawsuit, started a business, registered to vote, or applied for a professional license? If the answer to one or more of these questions is "Yes," then most likely we are, as Carole Lane declares, "naked in cyberspace!"

Helen Burwell
Burwell Enterprises
Dallas, TX
1997
Email: helen@Burwellinc.com
Web Address: http://www.Burwellinc.Com.

Acknowledgments

I would like to acknowledge all of the brilliant and supportive people in AIIP (the Association of Independent Information Professionals) who taught me well, encouraged me, and were never further away than my computer and modem. Special thanks to:

Marjorie Desgrosseilliers, for the brainstorming that started this book, suggesting ideas for the cover, and the ongoing (and sometimes daily) support.

Helen Burwell, my wonderful technical editor, for her endless patience and keen insight.

Mary Ellen Bates, who advised and encouraged me, and took me under her wing from my first dumb question on Section 0.

Colin McQuillan, a gifted writer who inspired a writer in me.

Reva Basch, for not laughing when I told her that I wanted to follow in her footsteps, and instead introduced me to her publisher.

Thanks to Owen Davies for his superb line editing, to Holly Pivor for her meticulous copyediting, and to Christine Watts for her endless patience and support as the manuscript evolved into a book under her direction.

Thanks to Richard Hammond and Fernando Escobar for the wonderful original cover art, to Iris and Cliff Miller of Pacific HiTech for getting Richard and Fernando involved, to Greg Mursko and Matt Kornhaas for their outstanding cover design, and to Production Manager Sharon Peck for putting it all together. I also want to thank Online Inc.'s Webmaster, Paula Westwood, for her ongoing efforts to build and maintain a great Internet site for the book.

Thanks to Lisa Glandon and LEXIS-NEXIS, and to the folks at Knight-Ridder Information, Inc. and DataStar, who all allowed me time and access to their databases so that I could find real examples that illustrate various types of records, and the power of their databases. Also, thanks to Gale Research Inc. and SilverPlatter Information, who provided the Gale Directory of Databases, a wonderful resource which was absolutely essential to my efforts at identifying databases. Thanks also to Stuart Sandow, NIA Academy of Public Records Research, and Robert Heibel, Director, Research/Intelligence Analyst Program, Mercyhurst College, both of whom provided invaluable input on key chapters.

My sincere gratitude goes to my supporters and cheering squad, without whom this book would not be possible, and nothing else would be nearly as much fun: Melissa Sands, Tish & Dave Duesler, Hamideh Fatemi, Carlos Neucke, Liza Solis-Reyes, Bill Plachy, Doris Alvarez-Ramirez, Rachelle and Mike Garcia, Jana and Rich Beeson, Mark and Gina Jennings, Tom Garcia, David Agoff, Anne Peters, Amy Thiessen, Elizabeth O'Hara, Jack Hurwitz, Patricia Cordova, everyone at CHR, the wonderful women of the North County Association of Female Executives (NCAFE), and the rest of my family—the Santiagos, Lanes, Wangs, Goodwins, Zamichielis, Fromsons, Sands, Reyes, and Cannucciaris.

Finally, thanks to John Bryans and Jeff Pemberton, who made this book a reality.

Carole A. Lane
Oceanside, CA
1997

I.

INTRODUCTION TO PERSONAL RECORDS IN CYBERSPACE

Welcome to Cyberspace
(Check Your Clothes at the Door)

Sitting here in my home office, what could I find out about you? What could you learn about me? How deeply could we probe into each other's private lives? And how many of our own closely held secrets are truly shielded from the prying keyboards of skilled data searchers? Those questions are the seeds from which I have grown a busy research firm, tapping the wealth of online data to help my clients learn what they need to know about people, companies, and markets. They also are the seeds from which this book has grown. The answers will probably startle you.

In a few hours, sitting at my computer, beginning with no more than your name and address, I can find out what you do for a living, the names and ages of your spouse and children, what kind of car you drive, the value of your house, and how much you pay in taxes on it. From what I learn about your job, your house, and the demographics of your neighborhood, I can make a good guess at your income. I can uncover that forgotten drug bust in college. In fact, if you are well-known or your name is sufficiently unusual, I can do all this without even knowing your address. And, of course, if you become a skilled data searcher, familiar with the online resources available to us all, you will be able to learn much the same things about me, or almost anyone else who attracts your curiosity.

Whether you seek information about others or simply want to protect your own privacy, you need to know about finding personal information online because there is not a lot of real privacy left, and what little remains is disappearing fast. Very soon, we will all be "naked in cyberspace."

For most of us, that is a somewhat scary thought, and no one can be blamed for wishing to keep their private lives private. Yet the growing availability of personal information has benefits that can be as important as the obvious potential dangers. There are many perfectly valid reasons to seek information about others.

If you have ever been curious about your ancestors or about lost relatives, you are a prime candidate for using some of the most common personal databases, the genealogical records compiled by churches, hobbyists, and historical societies around the world. Many of these archives are still available only as books and paper files. Yet a growing number of them can be obtained on CD-ROM, and some can be tapped directly by computer. These may be the most common and extensive non-commercial databases now available. For many people, genealogy provides a fascinating and comparatively easy introduction to the vast universe of online information.

Most parents already know what it is like to help a child find information for a school report. Most of these home information searches begin with a few minutes of thumbing through the nearest encyclopedia. This is a good way to begin and one that cultivates research skills children will find useful throughout their lives. However, you may often find yourself making an unexpected trip to the library, where you, your child, and a helpful librarian sort laboriously through card files, reference works, and computerized indices to search out relevant books and magazine articles. These days, it can be faster, easier, and far more effective to tap into a few online databases, where the facts are readily available on almost any subject you can name. Professional writers and journalists use these resources daily as the most efficient means of gathering information for their books and articles.

In business, uses for online information abound. If you have applied for a job, sought credit or insurance, tried to rent an apartment or buy a house, or even made a substantial donation to charity, you almost surely have been the subject of many online information searches. Many employers routinely screen job applicants, and computerized databases now supply much of the information they need. Financial institutions such as banks, credit card companies, and collection agencies use personal records to track assets, debts, and investments; identify potential clients; weigh credit risks; and locate "skips," debtors who move in the hope that creditors will be unable to find them. Insurance companies use personal records to screen out risky applicants, set rates, process claims, and investigate possible fraud. Landlords use them to check out potential tenants. Attorneys use them to locate experts who can testify in civil and criminal trials and to find witnesses to crimes. Charitable organizations even use them to identify likely donors. And, of course, if you run a small business, own a house with a rental apartment, or contribute your free time to raise funds for a local charity, you will find the same personal records just as useful as these organizations did when they checked up on you.

Today most large institutions would be paralyzed without computerized personal records. The medical industry uses them to track and evaluate medical treatment, to match organ donors with patients who need a transplant, and to study illnesses and health risks. Government uses personal records in many thousands of computerized databases to assess taxes, dole out benefits, locate deadbeat parents, and carry out many of its other activities. Law enforcement uses personal records to identify and track criminals and witnesses to crimes. And while privacy laws justifiably restrict access to many of the records used by medicine, government, and law enforcement, many institutional databases are available for at least limited private use.

It also is possible to make a business of research itself. I have done it. A few of the people who read this book may well join me. You could be one of them. Many information brokers (also known as information professionals or researchers) mine personal records to compile biographical information, gather competitive intelligence, or provide information in support of clients both in industry and in private life. List brokers use personal records to identify new markets, potential investors, or groups of people with common interests or characteristics that mark them as likely customers for specialty retailers. Private investigators use personal records to locate information about people, their assets, and their activities. Often, when someone vanishes "without a trace," they can be located without ever leaving the office, just by searching through the appropriate databases. By the time you finish this book, you should have begun to master the basic skills needed to build a career finding information for clients in any of these fields—and gained the ability to provide for your own information needs.

Whatever your goal in searching for personal records, you will find it much easier to accomplish than it would have been twenty years ago, when most personal records existed only on paper. Your searches probably will be much more productive as well.

One reason is the sheer mass of information that is generated, and that others collect about us, as we pass through life. From the day we're born, our personal records begin to accumulate—in the hospital, perhaps at an obstetrician's office. Our birth certificate follows quickly and soon is filed down at City Hall. Then there are school records, supplemented by Social Security records, a driver's license, tenant records, voter registration, professional licenses, employment records, and tax records. Even the least active life today generates records at every turn.

When we actually *do* something, still more records appear. Most of us get married, rent a living space, establish some credit, buy a vehicle, subscribe to magazines. Many people get divorced, serve in the armed forces, commit crimes, write for publication, are interviewed, sue someone or are sued by them, join associations, answer ads for free goods or information, start businesses, make investments, or file for bankruptcy. Some, such as politicians and celebrities, spend nearly all of their time in the limelight and have every accomplishment, failure, or even rumor about then documented by the press. It all leaves a paper trail. Even if we remain in the shadows, comfortable within the illusion of our anonymity, almost everything we do leaves a "paper trail." We can be tracked by almost anyone who chooses to go looking for it.

Today, paper trails have given way to "vapor trails;" far more of our records exist in the memories of computers than in paper files, much less the fallible memories of human beings. The availability of all those computerized databases is the second reason that data searching is so much easier and more productive today.

Before starting my research business, I worked as a systems analyst for many years. My job was to design computerized databases. It did not take me long to recognize that once information is entered into a database, it takes on a strange new life of its own, with benefits for searchers that go far beyond mere convenience. Computerized records are not just easy to call up and read; they can be manipulated, compared, and used to generate information that simply was not available before.

For example, consider a telephone book. When you use the printed version, you look up a person's name to find their address or phone number. That's about all there is to it. Put that same information into a computerized database, and suddenly it is transformed. You can still use a person's name to locate their address and phone number, but it does not end there. Now you can enter an address to find all the people or businesses with a telephone there, along with their phone numbers. If you have only a telephone number, you can enter it to find out whose it is and where they live.

But that is just the beginning. It takes 10,000 or so telephone books to store all the numbers for all the phones in the United States, far more than you would ever want cluttering your home or office. Yet a national telephone directory can be compressed into a few CD-ROMs that take up no more shelf space than a paperback book. If you do not want to buy all of that rapidly changing information, you can dial into a telephone database and look up names, numbers, and addresses (paying as you go) without ever storing a single telephone book.

That convenience brings with it opportunities no printed directory can offer. If your search subject has an unusual name, you can search for their surname in a computerized directory and locate possible relatives across town or throughout the country. Much more sophisticated research is just as easy. Once you have found your subject's address, you can ask for a range of addresses on either side and find the names and phone numbers of their neighbors. You can use a telephone database to learn how common a surname is within the United States or within a specific region. You can find out how many "Main Streets" there are in the U.S.A., how many cities are named "Lafayette," and exactly where to find "Success." (It's in Arkansas, of course.) All this from the stodgy old telephone book!

When information gets into a computer database, it can be indexed, searched, compared, summarized, shuffled, sliced, and diced almost any way you want, at lightning speeds and often from a terminal half-way around the world. It is this combination—thousands of vast, all-inclusive databases containing hundreds of millions of personal records, equipped with search facilities no mere book or filing cabinet can equal—that allows us to discover so much about each other without ever leaving our desks.

In the next few hundred pages, you will learn what these exciting, and occasionally troubling, new research tools can do for you. I will show you how to search online databases for the information you want, introduce you to the most important archives of personal records, and provide a reference guide to several thousand databases that can sometimes offer up exactly the information you need. Before you finish reading, I hope you will feel ready to try a few online searches yourself.

How This Book Is Organized

The five chapters of the Introduction are intended to give you a good general background on personal records—what is recorded in the world's databases and, in brief, how to go about finding it.

Database searching itself is introduced in Chapter Two. This is meant as a primer for those unfamiliar with the process of searching a database. In this chapter, you will discover some of the ways in which indices can help you to find the information you need.

Chapter Three offers a look at the Internet and how it can be used to locate personal records, along with such consumer-oriented systems as CompuServe, America Online, and Prodigy. You will also find that many specific Internet sites are mentioned throughout this book; these references will point you to specific types of personal records that can be accessed on the "Net."

Three typical searches form the substance of Chapter Four. Here, the reader gets into the real-world practice of locating information. You will find that this is a kind of free-form exercise, rather than a fixed procedure. At each step, the information found guides the choice of the next database to try, the next question to ask. Experience also helps in making these choices, of course. As in computer programming, water skiing, or any other skill, you will get better with practice.

A discussion of privacy issues in Chapter Five rounds out Section I. While not directly related to the "how-to" of searching, this is a subject that will influence many of the searches you perform. Much of the information that could theoretically be found online is off-limits to outside researchers, and there are tough laws to enforce these strictures. Whether they are tough enough, or restrictive enough, is still being debated. You may well see more limits enacted to control the kind of searching you are about to do.

Although *Naked in Cyberspace* can be read cover-to-cover, it is not necessary to do so. Readers should complete this introductory section. Even if you have had a little experience with online databases, these pages provide valuable information specific to searching for personal information. After that, Section II, "How Personal Records Are Used" supplies details of how to proceed with searches for certain kinds of personal information.

What Type of Research Interests You?

If you are looking for a lost love, a friend, or someone who owes you money, Chapter Six will help you learn more about locating people.

Chapter Seven will provide the information you need for pre-employment screening and if you manage a business, Chapter Eight will tell you where to find potential employees online. Depending upon the types of position you hire for, Chapter Twelve may also be useful; it can guide you to experts in a wide variety of fields.

If you own or manage a rental property, see Chapter Nine for tenant screening.

If you think you've already found your "one and only," but want to check them out before giving your heart, soul, and half your assets, see Chapter Ten for information on asset searching and Chapter Fourteen for private investigation. If you haven't found Mr. or Ms. Right, and if money will influence your choice, Chapter Thirteen, "Prospect Research (Fundraising)" can be used to figure out who has the money, and Chapter Fourteen can help you find out if they are already married.

As a business person, you may need to size up the competition, as well as job applicants. Begin with Chapter Eleven, which describes how personal records can be used in competitive intelligence research. Chapter Seven, on pre-employment screening, can help you to uncover valuable information about potential partners and others with whom you might be considering some type of financial arrangement. So can Chapter Ten, on asset searching, and perhaps even Chapter Fourteen, on private investigation, depending upon the situation.

If you are an attorney or involved in a lawsuit, an asset search can help you to decide whether your opponent has enough money to be worth suing or to finance a protracted court battle. See Chapter Ten. And if you need an expert's testimony, Chapter Twelve can be of help in finding the right expert witness.

Colleges and universities, nonprofit organizations, and volunteers hoping to raise funds for local charities should read Chapter Thirteen for information on the use of personal records in prospect research.

Anyone interested in private investigation will find that Chapter Fourteen provides a solid introduction to how personal records are used in this field. Professional investigators, however, will want to read all the chapters in Section II. Depending upon their clientele and specialties, private investigators may find themselves carrying out an asset search, trying to locate a missing person, seeking an expert, or looking for almost any other kind of personal information.

Each of these chapters will refer you to other parts of the book, where further explanation and assistance can be found.

Types of Personal Records

The third section of *Naked in Cyberspace,* "Types of Personal Records," describes and illustrates the many types of personal records available in databases. Some of these records are open to everyone, and you may choose to gain access to them and use them in your research. Others are restricted by law or held in proprietary databases. You may qualify for access to them, or you may just want to know more about them in order to understand how much of your own life has been recorded in someone's computer files. In most cases, you have the right to obtain records about yourself, so many of these chapters also provide instructions for requesting your own records.

Adoptees seeking birthparents and birthparents seeking the children they once gave up for adoption should refer to Chapter Thirty-two.

Genealogists should jump directly to Chapter Thirty-four for information on the types of genealogical records that can be found online. Chapter Six provides information on locating people, which should be helpful to genealogists as well.

Where Can I Find More Information?

Section IV "Where Can I find More Information?" lists resources for the personal records researcher. Books addressing various types of research are listed first, followed by periodicals, and then organizations. Frankly, none of these chapters is exhaustive. Although you will find a great deal of information about personal records in *Naked in Cyberspace,* this book may not contain "all you ever wanted to know" about any particular subject, much less about all of the many kinds of records held in the world's computers or about every type of search that can now be carried out in cyberspace. I have tried to include all of the most important resources available, but filling the book with lesser materials would easily have doubled its size, and price. And even then the book would have been incomplete, since new resources are added almost every day.

The appendices contain listings of databases that contain information about people. Many are available online, while others can be had on CD-ROM. These are followed by listings of adoption registries, major bulletin-board vendors, public records producers and vendors, and other database vendors. Databases and vendors listed in these appendices are referred to throughout the book.

The appendices suffer from the same limitations as the reference material in Section IV. No list of databases or database vendors can ever be complete, since new resources appear almost daily. Nonetheless, this final section of the book will provide a great many resources with which to begin your search for personal information.

For an updated selection of databases and vendors, turn to *Naked in Cyberspace's* site on the World Wide Web. Go to the home page at: **www.onlineinc.com/pempress/naked**, and click on the appropriate link. This site provides a comprehensive listing of personal records resources now available.

Database Searching

There is nothing terribly difficult about finding information in a database. Whether online or on CD-ROM, electronic media invariably offers search facilities more sophisticated and convenient than anything a bound book or library could hope to provide. The real problems are knowing which databases to search and how to phrase your inquiry narrowly enough to avoid having all the useful information buried in mounds of dross. Those are the real subjects of this book. Before we get to them, however, there are some technical details to consider.

Equipment and Software

For some applications, like video editing, you really want the biggest, fastest, most expensive computer you can buy. Database searching is not like that. All that you really need is a computer capable of running software designed to work with the databases that interest you. For the Internet, however, a fast modem can make the difference between your loving and hating the time you spend online. For most online databases, any communications software will do. Generic packages such as ProComm or SmartCom will work fine. Since communications software is made for nearly any operating system, whatever computer you have almost surely can be used to access many online databases.

There are exceptions, however. Some databases can be searched only through software that is custom-made for a particular vendor's products. In that case, access is limited to the types of computer for which the vendor provides software. Even databases that can be searched through generic communications software often also offer custom programs that are more user-friendly or have features built in to save time and money or to track the cost of your searches. Database vendors such as LEXIS-NEXIS, NewsNet, and Dow Jones News/Retrieval have come a long way to make accessing their systems easier by developing Windows software that even novices can use to navigate their systems.

When building custom software, database vendors and third-party developers often create their products first for the Windows operating system, their largest market. Editions for the Apple Macintosh usually follow later, or may not be released at all. Of course, when software is improved or debugged, vendors follow the same priorities. Macintosh users can face long waits for Mac-compatible software, and they may be left out in the cold. This can be even more of a problem for those with machines still farther from the IBM-inspired mainstream.

If you plan to buy a computer for the sake of working with online databases, it makes sense to begin by learning whether the databases that interest you require any specific software. Then find out whether software upgrades for the different operating systems are released in any particular order. This may help you to choose your operating system and thereby narrow the list of computers suited to your task.

When compiling information for this book, I was tempted to ignore CD-ROM databases in order to concentrate on online systems. I realized along the way, however, that the CD-ROM databases are increasingly being moved online, while older online records are appearing on CD-ROM. Furthermore, with the right equipment, it is possible to search a CD-ROM database as though it were an online database. I also could not ignore some of the exceptional personal records offerings now available only on CD-ROM. For these reasons, I decided to include CD-ROM databases in this book.

The same arguments apply to putting a CD-ROM drive in your computer. The drive you select does not have to be the fastest on the market, but if you use it frequently you will long for all the speed this technology provides. If you cannot afford to buy the CD-ROM drive of your dreams and yours proves to be so slow that it tests your patience, you may want to upgrade to a faster drive when you have the opportunity.

A few databases are available on diskette, but since the space on a diskette is extremely limited, only the smallest databases are available in this format. (Since these databases usually are of interest only to specialists within very narrow fields and seldom are widely marketed, they are not covered in this book.) Many databases previously offered on multiple diskettes are now being moved over to CD-ROM, so the role of diskettes in this field is shrinking rapidly.

Some databases also are available on magnetic tape, but modems and CD-ROM drives are far more common in both offices and homes today, and nearly all of the databases most of us will ever wish to use are available in at least one of these formats. If your interests are highly specialized and one of the products you need requires the use of magnetic tape, you should make sure that you can add a tape drive to your computer. This should not be a problem for most business systems.

TYPES OF DATABASE VENDORS

Boutique Services

Some database vendors provide access only to their own databases. These stand-alone systems sometimes are referred to as "boutique" services. One example of a boutique service is Burrelle's Broadcast Database, which offers transcripts of television broadcasts such as "60 Minutes" and transcripts from presidential press conferences, news documentaries, and radio broadcasts. Such a specialized service has much to offer, even though it does not include the databases of other companies. Most public records vendors also qualify as boutique services. Boutique services can offer lower rates than might otherwise be the case, since they avoid an additional tier of resellers who make their profit by charging for access to the database. On the other hand, a boutique can also be a very expensive place to shop if its offerings are unique.

Multi-Producer Database Vendors

Some of the larger database vendors, such as Knight-Ridder Information, Inc. (formerly DIALOG Information Systems, Inc.), offer not only their own databases, but also those of other companies. This strategy allows Knight-Ridder to include over

400 databases in its service, including news, business and industry information, book catalogs, patent and trademark filings, scientific literature, and so on. Most of the databases offered by Knight-Ridder are actually compiled by other companies.

A provider can make its database available through multiple vendors, thereby broadening access to the database without having to provide the marketing or support that a large market otherwise would require. For example, Experian (formerly TRW) Business Credit Profiles are available through several database vendors, including CompuServe, NewsNet, NIFTY-Serve, and Knight-Ridder, as well as directly through Experian Business Credit. If individuals have only occasional need for a Experian Business Credit Profile, they are less likely to sign up for direct access through Experian, but may find the reports through one of the other systems to which they subscribe.

Although you must pay the database vendor for access to the information, in addition to the database provider, signing up with a large database reseller can save you the time and expense of signing up with many different providers, not to mention the inconvenience of having to keep track of separate user IDs and passwords for every company that you deal with, and how to search each system efficiently.

Gateway Services

These database or bulletin-board vendors provide access both to their own products and to the products of other database vendors. For example, CompuServe offers gateways to American Airlines; Computer Products Directory, Ltd.; CUC International, Inc.; Investment Technologies, Inc.; IQuest; Knowledge Index; Official Airline Guides; Paper Chase; Spear Securities, Inc.; and ZiffNet Information Service.

CompuServe's Knowledge Index includes over 100 of the databases available from Knight-Ridder Information, Inc. Access through the Knowledge Index service can actually be less expensive than direct access to Knight-Ridder; however, use of the Knowledge Index for commercial purposes is strictly prohibited, so professional researchers must access these databases directly through Knight-Ridder.

Another gateway service from CompuServe is IQuest, which provides access to some Knight-Ridder databases and to products from many other suppliers. Among the companies whose wares are distributed through IQuest are Ovid Technologies, NewsNet, Inc., and DataStar. Although IQuest may be used commercially, searching on IQuest is generally more expensive than direct access through the database vendors.

If a gateway service accesses a tape of the data, rather than the producer's actual database, the data available through the gateway may also be less current than what exists on the producer's or vendor's database. For only occasional use of a database, a gateway provides the convenience of ready access without having to sign up with another vendor. For regular use, it is usually more cost-effective to sign up directly with the database vendor, rather than with a gateway service.

Information professionals (IP) often use a combination of databases, signing up with larger multiproducer vendors for a variety of databases, with some boutique services for specialized information, and gateway services for occasional use.

Types of Data

Although several vendors may offer a given database, this does not mean that they offer all of the same data. Sometimes a database is carried with full text, meaning that when you find the article or report you need, you will be able to read it all directly from the database, download it to your computer or hard drive, or print it out.

Bibliographic or indexing databases provide information about articles or reports available for your research topic and sometimes include abstracts or citations that give more details about the information from the text. However, they do not provide the full text itself. When a citation is found, it usually is necessary to order the text separately or to visit a library or courthouse to review the full record.

Some databases include a combination of bibliographic citations and full text.

Directory or dictionary databases provide specific, limited information about a subject. The telephone directory is the classic example, but many product listings and professional directories follow the same general format. This type of database may also include some text about the company or product.

Numeric databases consist of tables or statistics. Although numeric databases may also carry some text, their primary purpose is to provide statistical data.

Sometimes a database producer or vendor will add value to a product by offering additional information not originally provided on a database or by merging several databases together. Alternatively, they may choose to split the data from one database into several, offering information products tailored to more specific needs, sometimes at a lesser cost than for the full database.

The currency of data may vary from one vendor to another. Some databases are updated daily, others weekly, monthly, or at longer intervals. Some are even updated "periodically," which can mean anything. At times, it is not the currency of information that matters, but how far back the records go. This varies from database to database and vendor to vendor.

For any of these reasons, you may find that you prefer accessing a database through one vendor rather than another, even if the contents are based on essentially the same information.

Search Languages

Databases usually are organized to allow searching in certain fields that have been indexed. A given database may also be searchable by using terms found in the citations or abstracts of the articles. If the full text is available, it sometimes may be searched as well, but one cannot assume this simply because the full text of the article is available. Database producers and vendors may have their own unique indexing system, or they may use one that is shared by other information providers. All of this contributes to the complexity of searching a database.

Many databases allow searching based on Boolean logic. In its simplest form, Boolean logic allows the researcher to narrow a search by asking that the items retrieved have more than one thing in common (connecting search terms with the word AND), to broaden the search by asking that the items have at least one of the characteristics being requested (using OR), or to exclude undesired items from the set retrieved (using NOT). An example of a Boolean search would be:

(HUBCAP? AND ((RECREATIONAL(1w)VEHICLE?) OR RV)) NOT IMPORT?

This search would retrieve articles in which both HUBCAPS and RECRE-ATIONAL VEHICLES were mentioned, as well as those mentioning HUBCAPS and

RVs, but would exclude those in which IMPORT, IMPORTS, or IMPORTED were also found. It also would reject the word IMPORTANT. The question mark is used in this example as a "wildcard," which takes the place of other characters. Any word that begins with IMPORT will be excluded from this particular search. Some databases use other symbols as wildcards, such as !, $, or *. Sometimes these symbols indicate that only one character may take the place of each wildcard, while in other cases, the wildcard substitutes for any number of letters. The term (1w), in this example, means that RECREATIONAL must appear within one word of VEHICLE, in the given order. This type of proximity operator also will vary from one database to the next. Proximity operators can be used to indicate that given words must be found near each other in any order, in a given order, or within the same paragraph, depending upon the search software.

Each database provider and vendor has its own search language. The following are examples of some of the most common database search and retrieval functions and some of the commands used by database vendors.

Database Function	Knight-Ridder Command	LEXIS-NEXIS Command	NewsNet Command
Select a database	BEGIN or B	.cl (change library) or .cf (change file)	(none)
Find	SELECT or S	(none)	SEARCH or SE
Display	TYPE or T	.fd (first document)	READ (full text) or SCAN or SC (headlines)
Display one screen	DISPLAY or D	.fp (first page)	PREVIEW or PRE
Save/Deliver later	PRINT or PR	.pa (print all)	(none)
Sign-Off	LOGOFF or DISC or LOG or LOGOUT or OFF or BYE or QUIT or STOP	.so (sign off)	OFF

Of course, these are simple examples. There are many more commands that accomplish variations of these and other search and retrieval tasks. There also are custom software packages built for searching these systems, each offering a different interface with its own menus and options. Many vendors have also developed more sophisticated software that can help you to locate hard-to-find items, sort sets of retrieved data, eliminate duplicate articles, rank them for relevance, and otherwise assist in your searches. The more sophisticated commands are rarely available through gateway systems, which is one more reason that information professionals often choose direct access.

Some databases also provide less sophisticated menus for searching. These commonly are menu-driven and are geared toward the novice or occasional user. Gateway systems and public records vendors usually offer this type of search software. Public records vendors often provide menu-driven software, which makes it relatively simple to search for individual records, but may make it difficult or impossible to find groups of records with common characteristics or otherwise to construct a set of data in an automated way.

Before searching a database, especially through an expensive online service, it is important to obtain the manuals that document its use, to learn the procedures for searching out and retrieving data from it. If the database is not of the simplified, menu-driven variety, you also would do well to attend training classes offered by the producer or vendor. You will not only learn the basic search commands, but also may pick up some search tips that can save you a fortune in online costs.

When you are ready to begin your search, it pays to work out the most efficient search strategy, using the best commands available for that particular database, BEFORE logging on. When you are being charged by the minute, you have no time to waste looking up commands.

Make sure that you know the cost before ordering, displaying, or printing any of the documents you find online. Some vendors provide a command that allows you to check the cost before placing an order or issuing the print command. Sometimes this is found in a separate printed pricing guide. Also be aware of how long you are spending online, and of the cost-per-minute charges. Some systems offer a command to give you a minute-by-minute estimate. Others do not tell you until you logoff, which is too late to avoid unpleasant billing surprises. More detailed information on costs associated with the use of online databases appears later in this chapter, under "Online Database Pricing."

Database searching, like most other skills, gets easier with practice. Some database vendors provide practice databases, practice user IDs, or free time on their systems so that you can get used to searching their databases. When these are provided for free, or at relatively low cost, they are great ways to get some inexpensive search practice. Some libraries offer access to databases, though these usually offer CD-ROM products rather than online databases. If a library near you offers a CD-ROM database for which the online search commands are the same (which is not always true), you might be able to get comfortable with a database without incurring the expense of the CD-ROM product or the online costs.

Some database vendors now are also offering a flat-fee option in which one can pay a single monthly fee for unlimited access to their databases. For inexperienced searchers or those who expect to make a great deal of use of those particular databases, this can be another cost-saving option.

In addition to practice databases and classes, several other resources can help you to become an efficient online searcher. There are books about searching, organizations for information professionals, information industry publications, and online and database conferences, all of which provide learning experiences and can assist you in keeping up-to-date with the latest search techniques and software.

If you do not have the expertise or the time or inclination to learn to search databases efficiently, you can also hire an information professional to perform the searching for you, so you do not have to do all this on your own. I will offer more thoughts about this option later in this chapter.

Delayed Retrieval

CD-ROM databases provide virtually instant access to the data included in them, slowed only by the speed of the computer used to access them. Online databases may also provide immediate access to even more vast amounts of data. On the other hand, they may serve only as an ordering mechanism by which to request a report. The actual data may not be delivered to you for a couple of hours, a day, a week, or even longer. This type of delayed retrieval is particularly common of public records systems. In fact, on some systems, you locate the report that you want through an online index, type in the command to retrieve the document, and then twiddle your thumbs while someone on the other end of the system either writes a letter to the agency (court, Department of Motor Vehicles, etc.) where the actual record is located or sends someone out to retrieve the document and eventually mails it back to you. But this beats the alternatives—doing without the information or hopping a plane to go to the agency in person.

Some bibliographic databases do not provide a way to order the full-text document you need. Where this is the case, you will have to track it down yourself or call a document delivery company to locate it and deliver it to you.

When comparing databases, it is important to distinguish whether the data is actually accessible online, whether there is any delay in retrieving it, and whether the vendor provides any way to order documents that are not available online.

Database Pricing and Fees

Have you ever tried to figure out which long-distance carrier really gives you the best telephone rates once you add in all the incentives and discount plans? Figuring out the cost of database research makes even that task look easy. The best adjective that I have heard used to describe database pricing is Byzantine. Database fees can be unreasonably complex, and many change in structure and form at random intervals. After the change, they may seem to cost less, while new hidden fees actually raise your bill. Database fees take you through a labyrinth where every turn hides a toll bridge. On the upside, if you do not like the way a database vendor prices its products, the fee structure probably will change and change again before you have had time to figure the old one out. Of course, you may not like the new pricing any better.

Each database vendor offers a pricing structure that combines its own unique selection of several basic patterns. Comparing them in order to decide which database will charge the least for a given article or report is more convoluted than comparing apples and oranges; it's more like comparing Irish setters, fire engines, and grapefruits.

Bear in mind that a database that seems to have lower prices can actually end up costing more if the vendor's search engine lacks the commands that let you extract your results in an efficient manner.

Some database vendors offer several pricing structures or options, so it may be necessary to compare pricing not only between vendors but also among the options offered by each vendor.

CD-ROM Database Pricing

One might think that at least the pricing of CD-ROM databases would be relatively straightforward—after all, there is a physical object to be bought—but that is not always the case. Although many CD-ROM databases can be purchased with unlimited use, several variations on CD-ROM pricing can make this simple fee structure more complex. In some cases, actual costs become difficult to anticipate or compare.

Some CD-ROM databases may only be leased, rather than purchased. In that case, one must return the discs in order to get the updates. They may even be programmed to disable the database automatically after the lease expires. That can be a serious drawback if obsolete records are important to you. Many private investigators, for example, rely on old telephone directories to tell them where their quarry has been. For them, an inexpensive database that must be leased may end up costing more than an expensive one that can be bought outright.

Other CDs carry metering software that keeps track of your usage in order to levy additional fees. Metering programs may even disable the database after a given number of uses, bringing research to a halt until the user has bought more time and the vendor has re-enabled the system.

Some CD-ROM databases are charged at one rate for single users, but at a higher rate if put on a network for multi-user access.

Other vendors offer volume discounts. Software wholesalers may offer a lower price, and some institutions such as libraries or hospitals may receive preferential rates. Prices normally drop right before a new version of a CD-ROM database is released, so if you are quoted a price that seems too good to be true, be sure that you are receiving the current version; you may also want to check with the vendor for a release date on the next edition.

Like other types of software, CD-ROM databases can also enter the market at an attractive price, only to have the price raised later, when the database becomes popular.

Online Database Pricing

Although CD-ROM database pricing may seem a bit confusing, it is nothing compared with the tangled mass of online database charges. For a newcomer to online searching, flat-fee subscriptions can be an excellent choice, if only for their simplicity. Unfortunately, not all database vendors offer this option, and among those who do, many are priced too high for the occasional user.

Many, perhaps most, online database vendors charge a sign-up (or initiation, or membership) fee for access to their databases. These fees may be as little as $15 or $20, and may even be refunded in the form of usage credits. Some are more expensive. Sema Group InfoData AB, Rattsbanken, a vendor from Sweden, charges an initiation fee of $500! Many variables can change the initiation fee that some vendors charge.

After the signup fee come subscription fees, which may be charged monthly or at longer intervals. Again, these may be only a few dollars each month, or they may be quite expensive. Online Computer Library Center, Inc., (OCLC) charges $6,500 per year for some of its databases.

Instead of a subscription fee, or sometimes in addition to it, some vendors charge minimum usage fees. No matter how little you use the database during a given period, you will be charged at least that minimum fee. If you do use the database, the charges count against that minimum; when it is reached, additional charges begin to accrue. For low-volume users, a pay-as-you go plan can be a much better choice, even if the rates per hour and per report are somewhat higher. However, that option is not always available.

Most vendors charge an hourly fee for the use of their databases. A few services may be free, while many more are only a few dollars an hour. However, some are expensive. The highest charge I have encountered is $300 per hour. Additional fees usually are charged for the information you find, view, or print. Discounts are sometimes available for high-volume users or for those who pay in advance for a set number of hours. Vendors with multiple databases may charge a different rate for each one, or the databases may be grouped into several pricing levels. If several vendors carry the same database, each one will have its own pricing structure and hourly rate. They may not all carry exactly the same data, and they may or may not provide an index that permits efficient searching for the type of data you need.

The list of possible charges goes on.

Many databases offer a choice of preformatted reports, each of which carries a different fee. You pay for exactly the information you want, and no more. The smallest unit of print may be the database record (or accession) number. Another common format is the KWIC (Keyword-In-Context) print, which provides a few lines of type surrounding the keywords that match your search request. Sometimes it even is possible to select exactly the fields you wish to see displayed. There are further variations, depending on the vendor and database, on whether you view the record on the screen or have it emailed, faxed, or mailed to you. For Dun & Bradstreet Financial Records, fees exceed $100 per report.

Add in copyright fees, which may be included in the cost of the database or billed separately, telephone and network charges, and a host of other charges, which mutate as vendors think up new ways to bill for their data.

All these variables make it even more important to compare prices among the various database vendors whose services you may wish to use. Unfortunately, they also make it nearly impossible to be sure which vendor's options will give you the most data for the most reasonable price. This is one area in which you must struggle along as best you can.

Copyright and Resale

Simply because information is available on a database does not mean that it can be used freely, without concern for copyright. If you buy or lease a CD-ROM database, copyright, use restrictions, and proprietary rights may all be defined on the packaging or within the database itself. For telephone directory databases, I have seen restrictions limiting use for commercial direct mail or telemarketing to no more than 250 listings per month. Alternatively, some telephone directory databases may be purchased with unlimited use, while others ban commercial use entirely.

Almost without exception, it is a severe violation of copyright for you to download records from one database to sell to another, or to resell any individual record to multiple users.

Online database vendors normally include copyright and use agreements in their contracts. Copyright statements are also found in the system documentation and on individual database records and reports.

If documents are ordered through a document delivery company, it usually charges a copyright fee, which is passed on to the publisher. If you go to a library and make copies of an article, you may already be in violation of a copyright. You may be able to pay the copyright directly to the publisher in order to remain in compliance. Rather than having to track down individual publishers yourself, it is also possible to set up an account with the Copyright Clearance Center in order to pay them the copyright fees for individual documents, which they will then distribute to the publishers for you.

Again, it is important that you become very familiar with copyright law if you plan to use databases or any other type of information for a commercial purpose.

Errors and Omissions

There is something uncommonly convincing about the information found in databases. Just as people once assumed that stories in the newspaper would not have been published if they were untrue, it is easy to believe that the information downloaded is valid. And yet you know that you cannot believe everything you see on TV or read in the paper. In the same way, you can't believe everything that you obtain from a database.

Some sources are more suspect than others. Information that is downloaded from a publicly accessible database, such as those created through voluntary contributions of their users, is particularly unreliable. However, even on proprietary databases errors may be found. Some errors are introduced at the time the data is created. For example, a news article can contain errors which are not corrected or improved in any way by moving the article to a database. Some database records are based on information that individuals or companies contribute about themselves. These may be incorrect or incomplete, or at least present the information in an unrealistically flattering light. Some individuals will also go to great lengths to mask their identities, using pseudonyms, altering key identifying information, such as their birthdates, and otherwise making their records difficult to locate or to verify.

When moving the data from its original form to a database, additional errors may creep in. Typists can make mistakes while entering records. Records can be overlooked or indexed incorrectly, making them difficult to retrieve. This is extremely important to remember when searching for public records. One cannot guarantee that an individual has no criminal history simply because no criminal record was found. The record may not be available online, the vendor may not cover the geographic area or court where the record exists, or the record may be indexed incorrectly and impossible to retrieve. The vendor's software even may miss the record due to a program bug.

Many chapters in this book contain more specific warnings about certain kinds of information, but one rule applies to all database records: evaluate them as you would information obtained from any other source. Consider the source, the reputation of the vendor, and the possibility that the record may contain errors that must be reconciled through other sources or by ordering copies of original documents when conflicts are found or when validation of the information is extremely important.

Information Professionals or Brokers

You may have heard the term "information broker" (IB) or "information professional" (IP). Many other names also have been applied to this profession: freelance librarian, researcher or freelance researcher, cybrarian, finder, information consultant, information manager, information specialist, infopreneur, library consultant, and online researcher.

On occasion, much to the dismay of the profession, the press has written of "information brokers" when describing data thieves and others who break into computer systems or office file cabinets, pay off insiders, or otherwise obtain information illegally in order to sell it. As a result, some brokers who provide professional, legal, and ethical business or personal services avoid the title of "information broker" in order to avoid being tainted by the unsavory reputations of the dishonest and unethical, but newsworthy, minority. When I mention information brokers in this book, I will be referring to professionals and not to those who steal information or use it illegally.

Whatever the term, information brokers or professionals can be loosely defined as people who provide information for a fee and charge for their services. I will use IB and IP interchangeably throughout this section. Information broker is a bit of a misnomer, however, because it is not actually the information that an IB is normally selling. The information itself usually belongs to the database vendor. What the IB sells is expertise and the time it takes to locate whatever information the client requests.

Many IPs have a background in library science, but the advent of the "information age" has attracted people to the information field from nearly every profession and background. An information brokerage often operates as a sole proprietorship, but many are partnerships or corporations and some even serve as contracting agencies for many independent brokers.

An IP can provide the search expertise that a client needs but may not have the time, resources, or inclination to acquire. Database searching can be complex and expensive, and not everyone loves to do it. It sometimes makes more sense for a researcher to contract with someone else for this service, so that they can focus their attention and resources on other areas of their business.

If a company makes frequent use of databases or other types of research, it then may be more cost-effective to have researchers on staff and provide them with the ongoing training and resources to do their job efficiently. In-house researchers sometimes make use of IBs to handle business requests outside their field of expertise, or to locate information or search databases to which the company does not have access.

IBs do not offer exactly the same services. Some are subject specialists who offer a wide range of expertise and services from asset location to biomedical or engineering-literature research. Others are generalists who will undertake many different forms of research. There are even IPs who do no online searching at all, whose expertise may be in telephone research, market analysis, teaching research, or some other specialty within the information arena. IPs such as these often contract with other IPs to obtain the information they need from online databases.

Information professionals charge according to their own pricing structures, at various rates. For small units of information, such as credit headers, it is not uncommon to see fees charged at a flat rate per report. Other types of information merit an hourly charge, which may range from $40 per hour to $250 per hour. Online and other expenses are often passed through to the client, with or without a mark-up. (Some database vendors prohibit information professionals from marking up their online fees, to avoid the perception of inflated online rates.) There are IBs who offer a not-to-exceed estimate, limiting their research efforts to your budget or to the charges they expect to incur. Others will give a range within which the expenses will fall. Still others may quote a maximum number of hours and/or reports to be devoted to the project. IBs sometimes work on retainer, offering a certain amount of research or labor during a given period at a set rate.

If you are looking for an information professional to perform research on a contract basis, there are a couple of good resources for finding them. *The Burwell Directory of Information Brokers* (published by Burwell Enterprises, Inc.) is an annual, international directory that lists IBs by specialty, geography, services offered, and other criteria.

Another resource is:

Association of Independent Information Professionals
234 W. Delaware Avenue
Pennington, NJ 08534
609/730-8759
609/730-8469 Fax
73263.34@compuserve.com

AIIP is a nonprofit organization whose "regular" members are all owners of information brokerages. (AIIP also includes "associate" members who either work for others or are interested in the profession.)

The Internet, Bulletin Board Systems, and Personal Information

---

B y now, virtually everyone knows what the Internet is: a globe-spanning array of interlinked computer networks through which growing millions of people and companies exchange messages that range from scientific reports to singles ads. However, to those still unconverted, it may not be clear why the rest of us think the Net is so important. For anyone who needs personal information, it is a significant question.

The notion of a new communications medium, a new way to get information from one place to another, may not seem very profound. Neither the telephone nor the radio seemed all that important at one time either—Alexander Graham Bell imagined that his invention would be used primarily to carry music from the orchestra to distant listeners—yet each of these technologies changed the world. The Internet (along with the competing bulletin board systems) is the first truly new communications medium to appear since television.

It is a medium with advantages.

Like the telephone, the Net carries private messages from person to person and company to company. However, these "email" messages are written, rather than spoken, and they can be sent and picked up from nearly anywhere at any time. For people who are on the move or who work unusual hours, this convenience can be important.

Also, Net messages are cheap, often far cheaper than the equivalent telephone call. For most people in many countries of the world today, Internet access is just a local phone call away. With the Net, that local call can carry your message to Singapore for the same price as a phone call to the house next door. One colleague who lives in a small New Hampshire town reports that a one-minute call to the next town, less than four miles away costs $.75 during peak hours, while the call to send an email message around the world is free!

In some ways, the Net is a lot like postal mail, known to Net citizens, or netizens, as "snail mail." The main difference is that messages flash around the world at the speed of light, rather than waiting to be carried by hand, truck, and air transport. This gives online messages a more conversational tone, with people often exchanging thoughts several times a day. ("Live" conferences also are possible on the Internet, but most Internet messages are posted and read at the participants' convenience.)

Like radio programs and newspaper articles, Internet messages also can be broadcast publicly to groups of people with common interests. Everyone who looks in on a Usenet newsgroup can read everyone else's messages and reply to whichever they wish. New bulletin boards are created whenever enough people declare their interest. Unlike the radio or newspaper, however, virtually anyone can join in to reply, offer their own opinions, and share their ideas.

In a very real sense, everyone on the Internet is a potential advertiser or publisher. Thus, one can find home pages that promote nearly any type of business, topic, hobby, or interest. Companies all over the globe are setting up home pages on the World Wide Web, which often include information about the company, its history, annual reports, press releases, and other items formerly available only in print or in proprietary research databases. Larger works are also published on the Internet, including magazines, directories, and even complete books.

All these are examples of what the Internet has to offer, and to some extent what it all "means" must be inferred from these new and fast-changing resources. Yet it is too early to confidently predict where the Net is ultimately headed. Although the Internet is over twenty years old, it began as a United States Defense Department network, used to support military research. Later it grew to include other government agencies, universities, and colleges, but it remained closed to the general public. Only in the last few years has the Internet opened to the general populace.

Fifteen years or so ago, while the Internet itself was still a government preserve, free enterprise networks began to appear as well. Over the years, they have grown into CompuServe, America Online, Prodigy, and other consumer-oriented bulletin board systems, each offering its own constellation of online databases and information services. In recent years, these online worlds have begun to merge, as the consumer systems have provided gateways into the Internet, and the online population has exploded from a few hundred thousand to an estimated 40 million. It is clear that some "critical mass" has been reached, that there now are enough people online to create a viable new community that stretches across the entire world.

The Internet is a global conference call, virtually free (depending upon where you're calling from), and with just enough structure to keep it all from disintegrating into chaos. Online, people with any interest or expertise can find each other and exchange ideas all across the world as easily as they talk with their neighbors. They can discuss any topic, read and understand each others' views, and have their voices heard as well. Thus, they can build on each other's knowledge and reach new levels of understanding. Already, a new global culture is emerging. What shape it will take remains to be seen.

What the Internet Is Not

While the Internet is a fascinating and often useful means of communication, it is not the be-all, end-all panacea for all information needs. At least, not today.

Although billions of bytes of information flow across the Internet each day, the vast bulk of it is personal mail, discussion, or opinions shared by Internet users. Some of the information is valuable and may be found nowhere else, but much of it, from the researcher's point of view, is pure garbage. Putting information on the Internet does nothing to improve its quality, and it is often unclear whose opinions are being heard or who authored any particular article or file that can be found and downloaded onto your computer. It is much like listening to the talk on the street, but the Internet neighborhood extends around the world. For some of us, the simple fact that information is found on a database or accessed via a computer gives it greater authority. Where the Internet is concerned, this is particularly unwise. For example, if you were attempting to obtain information about the reputation of an "expert" via the Internet, you might unknowingly find yourself talking with one of the so-called expert's close friends, or even with your candidate. For privacy, and sometimes for other reasons, many people use another name (or gender) while online, so you may not know who you're really talking to.

Another problem is that so much information is now accessible through the Internet that it can be virtually impossible to weed through it all to locate any specific fact. One needs a minimum of software to access the Internet (which is available free from many online vendors, or included in a variety of magazines on the newsstand); after that, dozens or hundreds of utilities and ancillary software can be found online to help with navigating and searching the Net. However, the treasures that can be accessed through the Internet can be stored nearly anywhere, and many are not indexed. Despite the variety of search tools available, information can remain so well hidden that even the most experienced searchers cannot find it without knowing the address. Without knowing where something is, there are sites that may never be discovered without a great stroke of serendipity.

The Internet is not yet subject to the same constraints that govern advertising on television or the radio, or in the newspaper. Nearly anyone can create a WWW home page, making it easy to invent a company on the Internet, add a directory naming oneself as a top executive, fabricate company history and press releases, and make any claim at all about that fictitious company, its products, and services. Since no one owns the Internet, no one is responsible for policing it, and it will take a while before the laws regulating truth in advertising catch up with this new medium. Today, using Internet home pages, online zines, or other information published on the Internet to verify information about a person is risky, at best. Although information found on the Net may prove entirely correct, it should be verified through other sources if its accuracy is important to you.

One more thing: given all the free data that now is available over the Net, it is sometimes easy to forget that unique or otherwise valuable information is still worth charging for. The growing number of vendors that now allow access to their databases via the Internet have not suddenly decided to provide access for free. Some of the most useful databases that can be tapped through the Internet remain just as expensive as they were before they moved to the Net. Professional database vendors continue to require subscriptions and charge fees for access to their data. Using the Internet to access those databases has not changed that.

What Kinds of Personal Information Can You Find on the Internet and Commercial Bulletin Board Systems?

Many types of personal records can be found on the Internet. For example, if you are interested in tracking down your ancestors, the Internet should be your first stop.

Through the Internet (as well as CompuServe's Roots forum, GEnie's Genealogy Round Table, and similar bulletin boards on other systems), genealogists are linking their lineages and contacting other researchers who will share their records around the globe. Many databases that genealogists find useful have found their way onto the Net. Others (such as census indices, marriage record indices, land records, and various collections) have been placed on CD-ROM, while cataloged on the Net so that individuals can order them for their own use. There are hundreds of genealogical sites on the Internet, with many simply dedicated to indexing all of them. Along with a great deal of lineage information, one can find a searchable death index, rosters of civil war combatants and a searchable database of civil war soldiers and sailors, medal of honor citations, an index to British, German Loyalist officers of the American revolution, and a French and Indian War site, providing the names of French soldiers who went to Canada from 1755 to 1763. More recent collections include a Korean War KIA/MIA Database and the Vietnam Era Prisoner of War, Missing In Action Database. (Further information about genealogical records can be found in Chapter Thirty-four.)

Many bulletin board systems offer online encyclopedias, which can be a good source for biographical information on historical as well as contemporary figures. (Further information about these databases can be found in Chapter Fifteen.)

The commercial bulletin board services also have some unique offerings for the personal records researcher. For example, CompuTrace (a service of CDB Infotek), provides a searchable file of information about living individuals, a similar file about the deceased (based on Social Security Administration files), and a file of information about corporations and limited partnerships. These all are available through CompuServe. CompuServe also provides a gateway to many professional research databases.

Many recruiters and employers seeking potential new hires consider the Internet one of their most important resources. If you are looking for a job, putting your resume on the Net will make your availability known to recruiters and employers alike. Forums for certain interest groups, such as computer consultants and data processing professionals, already carry hundreds of resumes and job offers. Similar resources now appear for professions unrelated to computers. (More information about recruitment and job searching can be found in Chapter Eight.)

Before looking for work at one of these sites, you should understand that anyone at all can read the information you include—not just those who might offer you a job. Your current employer might even see it. You should also be aware that anyone might be following the trail of your search, to find out what your interests are, and what you're posting. Services such as Deja News (found on the Internet at: **http://www.dejanews.com**) index Usenet newsgroups and even go so far as to provide an index of all of the messages that you post to any newsgroup. A recent *New York Times* article noted that through this service, it was discovered that a highly regarded privacy advocate had posted 527 messages to Usenet in the last year-and-a-half, with postings to 32 different newsgroups, such as the Cyberpunk mailing list, a beer newsgroup, and a fan group for Debbie Reynolds. If you knew where someone spent his online time and had an index to finding all of the messages that were posted, you might learn more about an individual than ever imagined possible, and all of this can be accessed on the Internet without a person's knowledge. You would do well not to post more personal information online than you want the world to know; you never know who's listening.

If you were seeking information about someone who might reasonably use the Internet to search for a job, you might be able to locate a resume online as well. It could contain the person's home address and telephone number, educational background, family members, and personal interests, as well as employment history.

Many Internet accounts include a free or low-cost home page, so even netizens without a business to advertise are creating personal home pages, where they tell the world who they are and what interests them, sometimes including everything from their favorite recipes, hobbies, or music to picture of their families and pets. Before spending time and money using expensive databases to find information about someone, it makes more and more sense to see whether the individual has a home page, either personally or professionally, where the very information needed may already be posted.

If you are trying to locate someone, the Internet and its commercial offshoots offer telephone directories, such as the "Phone*File" on CompuServe, "White Pages" on America Online, "Switchboard" at: **http:/www.switchboard.com/**, and dozens of other telephone directories on the Internet. Netscape at: **http://home.netscape.com** has a "People" icon, which provides various searches for addresses, phone numbers, or email addresses of people and companies. There is also a reverse phone number search available there, a United States Toll-free Number directory, and index to Personal Home Pages, a WhoWhere Edgar search, and a link to international phone directories. Yahoo!'s "People" search at: **http://www.yahoo.com/search/people**, Lycos' PeopleFind at: **http://www.lycos.com/pplfndr.html**, and Excite's People Finder at: **http://www.excite.com/Reference/people.html** each provide searchable telephone directories, and others can be found throughout the Net. With these resources, the person you seek may be no more than a search or two away. (Further information about telephone directories can be found in Chapter Seventeen.)

Other Internet search tools are designed specifically to help you find people who use the Internet. Finger and Whois are used to find out whether the person you are seeking has an Internet account, and the results of a search may even include a home address. Some of the consumer networking services also make it possible to search member directories. For example, America Online allows you to search member "profiles," which include whatever information a member chooses to divulge. This may or may not include the subject's name. CompuServe allows searching by name, which may also be narrowed geographically. (Further information about finding people who are online can be found in Chapter Six.)

There are also dozens of general-purpose search engines and Internet indices:

- a2z (**http://a2z.lycos.com/index.html**)
- Alta Vista (**http://www.altavista.digital.com/**)
- c/net's Search.com (**http://www.search.com/**)
- Excite (**http://www.excite.com/**)
- Galaxy (**http://www.einet.net/**)
- Hot Bot (**http://www.hotbot.com/**)
- Infoseek (**http://www.infoseek.com/Home**)
- Infospace (**http://www.infospace.com/**)
- Internet Sleuth (**http://www.isleuth.com/**)
- Lycos (**http://lycos.cs.cmu.edu/**)
- Magellan (**http://www.mckinley.com/**)
- Peekaboo (**http://www.peekaboo.net/**)
- WebCrawler (**http://www.webcrawler.com/**)
- World Wide Web Yellow Pages (**http://www.mcp.com/newriders/wwwyp/**)
- Yahoo! (**http://www.yahoo.com**)

along with their growing legion of competitors—which can be used to search for the name of a person or company among the millions of World Wide Web pages, gopher sites, FTP files, and Usenet newsgroup postings. Unfortunately, names are often one of the least individual things about us, so searching for a particular "John Smith" among the millions of Internet users may turn up so many matches that it would take days to go through them all, with no guarantee that your subject was among them. If a person's name is uncommon, it is worth trying several of the search tools to see what they come up with; as each conducts the search in a different way. However, if you do not find the person you seek fairly quickly, do not waste too much time reading through all of the possibilities. (Refer to Chapter Six for further explanation of problems with names.)

Even a company may share its name, but so many firms of every size are putting up their own home pages on the Internet that it is definitely worth a search or two if you are looking for someone who owns his own business. Employees are also sometimes listed on company home pages. Profiles of key executives can be found, as well as annual reports, which usually list the members of the board and the top executives. On one of the corporate home pages I looked at recently, I even found profiles of the company's top scientists, along with lists of their inventions and contact information for each. I have found speeches by key executives that I would not have located on high-priced databases, and it is not at all unusual to find a company's recent press releases included on its home page. (Refer to Chapter Eleven for information on gathering competitive intelligence on companies and individuals within companies.)

Students may also be listed in an Internet student directory for their college or university, or perhaps in an Internet fraternity house or sorority directory. Even some high school directories can be searched on the Net. People who have already graduated often can be found in an alumni directory. Associations are creating their own Web sites, many of which include searchable member directories. There also are directories of experts, consultants, faculty, attorneys, and other professionals that can be searched on the Net. (Further information about staff, professional, and other directories can be found in Chapter Eighteen.)

Adoptees and birthparents seeking one another can use the Internet to register their names with the Adoption Information Registry. If their names are matched, they will be put in contact with one another so that a reunion can be arranged. There are also Usenet newsgroups in which adoptees and birthparents provide assistance and advice to one another, including search assistance, and adoptee/birthparent classifieds are being compiled on the Internet as well. Similar help can be found through nearly all of the consumer data services. On America Online, the keyword is "Adopt." On CompuServe, you will find adoption search assistance in the Issues Forum. On Delphi, it's in Heritage. The Family Round Table on GEnie carries this information, and on Prodigy, you can look within the Genealogy bulletin board. (For further information on adoption records, refer to Chapter Thirty-two.)

For entertainers, sports heroes, and almost any type of celebrity, fans are compiling databases on the Internet. There are show business roundtables, soap opera, sports, and rock forums, photo libraries, and bulletin boards for fan clubs. These often include screen and television credits, upcoming concerts and appearances, fan reviews, photo libraries, and trivia. Fans also share stories of their personal encounters, opinions, and collective adoration with other fans through Usenet newsgroups and online mailing lists. Some television shows host their own forums in which they invite feedback on their episodes and take suggestions for future programs. It may even be possible to converse online with your favorite celebrities, as online vendors arrange "live chats" with rock stars, sports heroes, authors, stars of stage and screen, politicians, and other celebrities. If you need information about someone famous, the Internet can be a great resource. (For further information on celebrity records, refer to Chapter Thirty-three.)

Other databases being assembled by netizens deal in quotations (some you might recognize, some you might not) and obituaries (of the famous, as well as of the compilers' friends and family members). (More about quotations can be found in Chapter Twenty-two, and information about obituaries and deaths can be found in Chapter Twenty-eight.)

Missing children also are listed on the Net, along with their photos, in the hope that someone will recognize them as a neighbor or schoolmate and contact the authorities. Registered sex offenders are also listed in order to notify communities of their presence. (Information about these databases can be found in Chapter Twenty-one.)

If you want information on a political figure, you can find Congressional directories, candidate profiles, political speeches, and many other valuable resources for political research on the Net. Information about political figures is common to many of the consumer data services. The biographies and voting record of incumbent officeholders can be found on the Political Profiles database on Prodigy. Congressional Tracking, on CompuServe, also provides information about how any member of Congress has voted recently. (Further information about political records can be found in Chapter Thirty-five.)

Public records are slowly coming to the Internet. For example, in some areas, court record indices may be found on the Net. Although most public records are still within the domain of commercial public records vendors, many of these vendors are now offering access to their systems through the Internet, or allowing people to order records through their Internet Web sites. (Further information about public records can be found in Chapter Thirty-one.)

Some full-text books are accessible through the Internet, including some biographical works, and more are being uploaded each day. (Refer to Chapter Fifteen for further information.)

Original magazines are being published on the Net, where they are referred to as "zines," and print magazines and newsletters are setting up Web sites that carry part of their contents or provide extra information about the articles that have appeared on paper. Many of these publications carry articles about individuals. For personal research, alumni magazines can be particularly helpful, as their news items usually list marriages, births, deaths, and accomplishments of the alumni.

Television, radio, and news programs have also set up Web sites, and some of these include recent stories about individuals. On more than one occasion, I have caught part of a news story on a television newscast and gone to the news program's Web site for additional details. Some of the newswire services also are providing their broadcasts through the Internet, sometimes linked to the home pages of companies that are mentioned in them. (Further information about news sources and transcripts can be found in Chapter Twenty.)

If you know something about a person's interests, you may be able to find a Usenet newsgroup in which this person participates or where a colleague, friend, or family member can be found. The more you know about your subject, the easier it will be to gather additional information. If you believe in the theory that that there are only six degrees of separation between all of us, it probably makes intuitive sense to you that one key to finding information about a person is to locate someone who knows someone, who knows someone, until you reach the circle of people who actually know the individual in question. With more people visiting the Internet every day, the chances get better all the time that people you are looking for, or at least someone who knows them, will be found online.

Finally, the Internet includes whatever information people care to share about themselves. This can be considerable. Companies wishing to market to people with particular interests gather names and Internet addresses of those participating in key newsgroups in order to target them for mailing lists and other marketing ventures. Although the online community generally frowns on this, it does illustrate that people are gathering information about us through our participation on the Net. (Further information about mailing lists can be found in Chapter Nineteen.)

You will find Internet addresses for sites mentioned previously, as well as many others, listed throughout this book and at the *Naked in Cyberspace* WWW site (**www.onlineinc.com/pempress/naked**). This list can never be complete, and even if I had been able to include every site that a personal records researcher might find useful, the list still would have been inaccurate a week after it was finished. The Internet is evolving quickly. New sites appear daily, while old ones vanish or are transformed almost beyond recognition. No list of Net resources can ever be one-hundred percent accurate, but the sites in this book were updated continuously throughout the writing and production process, and the online version will be updated on a regular basis. I invite you to use the email link to let me know of any promising resources you think I should include—as well as any obsolete ones.

When I started writing this book, I planned only a small section for the Internet, as there were few Internet resources for personal research. That has all changed. As the online community has grown, so have the personal records resources on the Internet, which today is an extremely valuable tool for locating people, adoption searches, competitive intelligence, and many other types of research that rely on personal records.

A Few Sample Searches

A ny personal records search begins with assessing the information at hand and determining the goals for the search. In this chapter, I will present three sample searches which illustrate how personal records are used with various pieces of starting information and different goals. More information on these and other types of searches can be found in Section II "How Personal Records Are Used," but these samples will give you a good idea of how you can put personal records to use in your own life.

Locating a Person

The first sample represents the most universal type of search using personal records. Nearly everyone has someone that they would like to locate—an old friend, a first love, a lost family member, or someone who owes them money. I have performed searches such as this for creditors, attorneys trying to locate a witness, people looking for old friends and estranged family members, as well as locating many of my own old friends.

Each location search is somewhat unique, but they all start out with a list of the information at hand. (In Chapter Six, you will find the form I use to list all of the information known about the subject of a search.) In this case, it was an adoption search, and there were several good leads.

I had been contacted by a pre-adoptive mother (we'll call her Diane) who wanted to track down the birthmother and birthfather of her infant to expedite the adoption. Diane's attorney had advised her that the adoption would go more smoothly if she obtained written consents from the birthparents directly. There was also a twist. The birthmother had been married to someone other than the birthfather at the times of the conception and birth, so Diane also wanted to locate the birthmother's husband to obtain his consent as well.

Diane had received the birth certificate for her infant. It contained the full name and birthdate of the birthmother. The birthfather's first and last name were listed as well, but his birthdate was unknown. (They had actually only met once, in a bar, so the spelling of his name was also in question.) Diane had received a copy of the marriage certificate for the birthmother and her husband, which contained their full names, dates of birth, names of their parents, and a 14-year-old address. With this much information, it was a relatively simple matter to track down the birthmother.

To make things even simpler, the birthmother and her husband had an unusual last name. I used an online phone directory (Phone*File, which is available through CompuServe) and searched for anyone with that last name in California. Only eight listings were found. None of the listings matched their first names or first initials, but one listed a first initial that matched the husband's middle name. I ran an Address Update (which you can request through a public records vendor, if you do not have accounts with the credit agencies) and found that it was the husband's address; the record matched his full name and date of birth. I ran another Address Update for the birthmother, using that same address, and found that she had moved to a new address, which was provided. Both of their Address Update reports provided an additional piece of valuable information—their Social Security numbers. With that information, Diane would be almost guaranteed success in tracking them down again in the future, should she need to, such as in a medical crisis.

I searched the online telephone directory for the birthfather, but found no matches at all in California. This seemed odd because even if he was not listed, it seemed reasonable to assume that in a state as large as California there should be at least one person with the same surname. The failure made me question the spelling of his name all the more. Upon contacting the birthmother, I found that she had one more piece of information about the birthfather which proved valuable. She had an old phone number for him. Using the telephone number, I went back to the online phone directory and searched for a match. I found a listing for a woman whose last name sounded much like the one on the birth certificate, but was spelled differently. (It turned out to be the birthfather's mother, whom Diane did not wish to contact.) With the corrected spelling, I was able to run another Address Update report against the address found in the telephone directory and obtain the birthfather's current address.

Many other search procedures could have been used to obtain the same results, and this search could have taken other directions, depending on the information uncovered at each step. This was a best-case scenario, and some searches are more difficult. However, this straightforward example demonstrates how easy personal records can make it to solve a problem that at first glance might seem all but impossible. It also illustrates how simple it can be to locate a person when you begin with good identifying information.

Searching for Assets

Our second example illustrates an asset search. You may wonder why you would ever need to conduct such a search. In fact, many people today use asset searches in different ways. Let us look at just a few.

People who are weighing a possible partnership or other financial arrangement sometimes worry about con men and women. Even if they do not doubt the basic honesty of their proposed partner, they feel better if they have first verified that the person they are dealing with has a realistic view of their assets. This can include anyone considering marriage!

Anyone who is being sued may wish to size up the resources of their opposition. Similarly, those considering suing someone can perform an asset search to determine whether it is worth the expense of a lawsuit to go after what the other party owns. (It does little good to win a costly suit if the other party has nothing to pay you.)

Even charitable agencies have used asset searches to figure out where the big money is before targeting their fundraising efforts.

The asset searches that I typically perform are for financial businesses—companies that lend a great deal of money and want to know exactly what their debtors have to offer before going after them in court. In fact, many of their cases never make it to court because the information that they bring with them to the deposition convinces the debtor that the company plans to go after *all* of their assets—and knows where to find them. A recent search went something like this.

As always, I started by looking over the information my client had provided. In this case, it amounted to credit reports from all three credit agencies (Equifax, TransUnion, and Experian). These reports provided a list of the debts owed by the subject, as well as his full name, date of birth, Social Security number, current and previous addresses, employer, and public records including a bankruptcy, a judgment, and two federal tax liens. Notable among the debts were real estate loans, which meant that there was most likely property to go after.

Having read and organized all of the data received on the credit reports, I ran my first search—an "Info:Probe," offered through one of the public records vendors (CDB Infotek). When used to identify someone's assets, this service includes a search of this vendor's Bankruptcies, Liens and Judgments file, Civil Filings, Corporations and Limited Partnerships, FAA Aircraft Ownership, Fictitious Business Names, General Index, Judgment Docket & Lien Book, Real Property Ownership, Uniform Commercial Code Searches, and U.S. Coast Guard Watercraft File. An Info:Probe provides an inexpensive way to find out whether this public records vendor has any records on file for your subject before you spend the time and money to search individual files. In this case, a search of records for the Western states revealed the following matches:

1 AZ Real Property Ownership Search By Name (Statewide)
2 CA Real Property Ownership Search By Name (Statewide)
3 NV Real Property Ownership Search By Name (Statewide)
4 UT Real Property Ownership Search By Name (Statewide)
5 CA Real Property Ownership Search By Buyer/Seller (Statewide)
6 WA Real Property Ownership Search By Buyer/Seller (Statewide)
7 CA Real Property Ownership Search By Lender (Statewide)
8 CA UCC Summary/Detail Search by Debtor Name
   Data Available From 01/04/65 Thru 07/17/96
9 OR UCC Summary/Detail Search by Debtor Name
   Data Available From 08/09/63 Thru 04/08/96
10 UT UCC Summary/Detail Search by Debtor Name
   Data Available From 12/01/65 Thru 06/24/96
11 CA San Diego County Superior Court Divorce Filings
   Data Available From 01/01/87 Thru 01/15/96
12 CA Los Angeles County Superior Court Civil
   Data Available From 01/01/79 Thru 05/28/96
13 CA Orange County Superior Court Civil Filings—Summary/Detail
   Data Available From 01/01/89 Thru 05/31/96
14 CA Riverside Superior Court Civil Filings—Summary/Detail
   Data Available From 01/01/85 Thru 03/31/96
15 CA Sacramento Superior Court Civil Filings
   Data Available From 01/01/37 Thru 03/29/96
16 CA San Mateo Superior Court Civil Filings—Summary/Detail
   Data Available From 01/01/78 Thru 01/31/96
17 CA Ventura Superior Court Civil Filings—Summary/Detail
   Data Available From 01/01/73 Thru 12/31/93
18 CA Los Angeles County All Municipal Court Civil—Plaintiff/Defendant
   Data Available Thru 06/10/96
19 CA Orange County All Municipal Court Civil Filings
   Data Available From 01/01/90

20 F.A.A. Aircraft Owners Search—By Owner Name
    Data Available Thru 06/30/96
21 CA Los Angeles Fictitious Business Name Filings by Owner Name
    Data Available From 01/01/81 Thru 06/30/96
22 CA Orange Fictitious Business Name Filings by Owner Name
    Data Available From 01/01/84 Thru 08/31/95
23 CA Riverside Fictitious Business Name Filings by Owner Name
    Data Available From 01/01/85 Thru 04/12/95
24 CA Corporation & Limited Partnership Records—By Registered Agent Name
    Data Available Thru 07/19/96
25 CA Corporation & Limited Partnership Records—By Officer/Director Name
    Data Available Thru 07/19/96
26 UT Corporation & Limited Partnership Records—By Officer/Director Name
    Data Available From 01/01/01 Thru 04/03/96
27 CA Bankruptcies, Liens, Judgments & Notice of Default (LOC)
28 ID Bankruptcies, Liens & Judgments (LOC)
29 NV Bankruptcies, Liens & Judgments (LOC)
30 OR Bankruptcies, Liens & Judgments (LOC)
31 UT Bankruptcies, Liens & Judgments (LOC)
32 CA Los Angeles County General Index
    Data Available From 04/07/85 Thru 04/19/96
33 CA San Francisco County General Index
    Data Available From 06/16/85 Thru 07/27/95

End of probe.

I then pulled each of the individual reports resulting from the Info:Probe search and read them over to determine which applied to my subject, and which were for someone with the same name. (CDB Infotek has placed a cap on the cost of the searches that result from an Info:Probe, so instead of costing several hundred dollars to pull all of these reports individually, the total was only $100.) Some of the records available online, such as those for real property, are fairly complete and require little further explanation. For example:

—··—··—··—··—··—··—··—··—··—··—··—

OWNERSHIP INFORMATION:
—··—··—··—··—··—··—··—··—··—··—··—

Owner(s): JT	BRONSOM JAMES D & FRANCESCA N
Mailing Address:	2235 S JORDAN CANAL RD SALT LAKE CITY, UT 84118-1454
Property Address:	2235 S JORDAN CANAL RD. SALT LAKE CITY, UT 84118-1454
Owners Phone No.:	
Parcel No.:	23-51-327-002-0000
County:	SALT LAKE
Municipality:	

Sale Information:	Assessor Information:	
Sale Date:	Exemption(s):	NONE
Sale Recording Date:	Taxes:	$1,227
Book No.:	5509 Land Value:	$27,200
Page No.:	1022 Improvement:	$68,400
Sale Amount:	Total Value:	$95,600
Sale Amt Indicator:	Percent Improved:	71%
Mortgage Amount:		
Mortgage Rate:		
Mortgage Term:		
Mortgage Type:		
Assumable Mort. Amt:		
Multi/Split Ind:		

Property Characteristics

Land Use:	SINGLE FAMILY
Property Ind:	SINGLE FAM.RES
Acres:	.900

Other records, such as Uniform Commercial Code filings (UCCs), are merely indices:

1 Filing Number:	91276700
Document Type:	UCC1—Financing Statement
File Date/Time:	02/20/1991 14:03
Debtor:	BRONSOM JAMES D
	522 WEST 1500 SOUTH
	SLC, UT 84115
Secured Party:	JOHNSTONE FINANCIAL SERVICES
	P O BOX 3292
	PORTLAND,OR 97208
Collateral:	A,A/R,EQ,FU,FX,INV,BILLS+
Microfilm:	822
Expire Date:	02/20/1996

The preceding UCC record does not provide the details of the debt or the collateral that was pledged, so I used the filing number to order copies of the records from a public records retriever. (You could also order them directly from courts in most cases.) The records arrived a day or two later, listing many additional assets that had been pledged against various debts.

I ran Info:Probe searches against each company name with which the subject was affiliated (which I found listed in various records, such as the Fictitious Business Name filings and Corporations and Limited Partnerships). This turned up additional UCC and Bankruptcy filings. I ordered copies of the files, and found full financial statements including bank accounts, tax records, and many other undisclosed assets.

I repeated the whole process using the wife's name (which I found on their joint real property records), and found assets which were under her name alone.

Then I went after vehicles registered under their names or their businesses. The necessary searches are offered by many public records vendors.

Business credit profiles (offered through many professional research databases, but also available on Prodigy, CompuServe, and so on) were pulled on all of the businesses linked to the husband or the wife. This search provided several other public records for areas of the country not covered by the public records vendor. Copies of those documents were also ordered.

I searched news databases for further information about the husband, wife, and every business that they were affiliated with. Some newspapers publish a weekly column that lists properties sold in their area, and these uncovered still more properties which the couple owned. This search revealed no press releases or other news articles about their companies. When such records are found, they sometimes include announcements of important partnerships, contracts, or other significant changes in their business that can affect their financial position.

Finally, I looked on the Internet to find out whether the subjects or any of their companies had a Web site. In this case, they had not, but in other cases, I have discovered annual reports, press releases, and other important information. It is always worth a check.

Since a great deal of money was at stake, my client probably would still plan to send someone out to conduct surveillance on the debtor. The investigator might sift through their trash, find out who they were meeting with, and otherwise attempt to locate assets, such as off-shore accounts, which would not show up in the news or in the public records. What I provided from my computer would be the majority of what my client took to court, however, and would serve as the basis for further investigation. In many cases, such as when determining whether someone is worth suing or whether Prince Charming really owns a castle, the information that you can gather using your computer will be more than sufficient.

A Background Profile

For the last sample search, I will show you how to construct a background profile from online sources. This particular case demonstrates the way a reporter or campaign worker might use personal records to learn about a political candidate. The template used in this example (beginning on the page that follows) is important and, before you begin any background profiling of your own, you may wish to create your own form using the elements included here. The idea is to bring together as many relevant details as possible in order to create a comprehensive overview of the individual.

For this example, some simple Internet research was done on industrialist and presidential candidate H. Ross Perot. The actual work reported here is just a first step. An exhaustive search dealing with a subject as active and well-known as Perot could easily take months of work, but I will map out a reasonable path for continuing this effort. The same principles would guide any such background research you might wish to undertake.

My first step in this search was to find out what information the Perot Campaign headquarters had published about him. I began with the Ross Perot for President Official World Wide Web site on the Internet (**http://www.perot.org/**). There I found a detailed biography, which provided plenty of information from which to start an investigation. Speeches, a campaign schedule, view papers, the text of his infomercials, and many other relevant topics were supplied for the consumption of both the press and anyone else interested in Perot or his views. With only the information published on Perot's own Web site, I was able to gather the following data:

SUBJECT PROFILE

FULL NAME, ALIASES, NICKNAMES, MAIDEN NAME, MARRIED NAME: Ross Perot

GENDER: M

BIRTHDATE AND/OR AGE: June 27, 1930, in Texarkana, TX

SOCIAL SECURITY NUMBER: No data provided at Web site

PHYSICAL DESCRIPTION: Many photos available; Audio & video also available.

DESCENT: No data provided at Web site

LAST ADDRESSES: Ross & Margot Perot live in Dallas

EDUCATION: Attended public schools and Texarkana Junior College

> He entered the United States Naval Academy in 1949 and graduated in 1953. While at the Naval Academy, he served as class president, chairman of the honor committee, and battalion commander. He told his parents his goal was to attend Annapolis and he did, and was elected class president.

OCCUPATION/EMPLOYMENT: Beginning at age seven, Perot worked at various jobs throughout his boyhood, including breaking horses, selling Christmas cards, magazines, and garden seeds, buying and selling bridles, saddles, horses and calves, delivering newspapers, and collecting for classified ads.

> As his family grew, he envisioned a new kind of computer business, selling fully-operational hardware and software systems to manage business information. He took his new idea to his bosses at IBM. They liked the concept but the giant company wanted to stay focused on hardware sales and declined. Driven to make the idea of a fully-operational computer system a success, in 1962 he borrowed $1,000 from his wife Margot, named his mother, his sister and his wife his corporate directors, and EDS (Electronic Data Systems) was born. The company's only employee, Ross Perot. After 78 sales calls, he closed his first contract, and the company took off, solving complex problems for the nation's and the world's largest corporations. He built a team that would transform one man's dream into a company of 95,000 employees and 12.4 billion dollars in revenue that it is today.

> Perot accepted another challenge in 1984 when he sold EDS to General Motors for $2.5 billion. The ownership that he retained in the company made him GM's largest individual stockholder and a member of the board of directors. After major disagreements over the quality of GM automobiles, Perot resigned from the GM board in 1986. In 1988, he started a new computer service company, Perot Systems. Today this company operates in the United States and Europe.

> Perot '96 Campaign Headquarters, 7616 LBJ Freeway, Suite 727, Dallas, TX.

ORGANIZATIONS, AFFILIATIONS & AWARDS: In 1969, when President Nixon asked for Ross' help in pressuring the North Vietnamese for better treatment of our POWs, Ross embarked on a three-year campaign to end the injustice (according to Infomercial 4). (Another slant on this statement is found on Perot's Web site, where it states: In 1969, the U.S. government asked Perot to determine what action might be taken to improve the brutal treatment our POWs were receiving in Southeast Asia.) He worked on this project for the next four years, placing himself and his family at considerable personal risk, until the prisoners were released in 1972 at the end of the Vietnam War. In recognition of his efforts, Perot received the Medal for Distinguished Public Service, the highest civilian award presented by the Department of Defense.

In 1979, when revolutionaries in Iran took two of his employee hostage, Ross took action. The U.S. government said there was nothing that could be done. Nevertheless, Ross pledged to get his people out and he did, committing his company's resources and risking his own life to lead the successful rescue mission.

When two EDS employees were taken hostage by the Iranian government in 1979, Perot directed a successful rescue mission composed of EDS employees and led by Colonel Arthur 'Bull' Simons. Perot personally went into Iran and inside the prison where his associates were held. Noted author, Ken Follett, wrote a best selling book, On Wings of Eagles, about the rescue. An NBC TV miniseries was later made about this event.

Later that same year, the governor of Texas requested Perot's help in dealing with the growing problem of the use of illegal drugs in the state. Perot led the Texans' War on Drugs Committee that proposed five laws to make Texas the least desirable state for illegal drug operations. All five bills were passed by the legislature and signed into law.

In 1982, another Texas governor asked for Perot's assistance to improve a deteriorating situation—the quality of public education in the state. Recognizing that a first-class educational system is the foundation for economic improvement, Perot led the effort to reform the school system. This program resulted in major legislative changes and improvements in Texas public schools.

Perot has been the recipient of numerous awards and honors, including:

The Winston Churchill Award. Perot was the third recipient and the only businessman to receive this award, given to those who best exemplify the imagination, boldness, and vigor of the late British prime minister. The presentation was made by Prince Charles in 1986.

The Raoul Wallenberg Award. As the first recipient of this award, Perot was honored for a lifetime of service that embodies the spirit, courage and dedication of Raoul Wallenberg, the Swedish diplomat who saved more than 100,000 Hungarian Jews from the Nazis during World War II.

The Jefferson Award for Public Service.

The Patrick Henry Award. Perot was the first recipient of this award given to an American for outstanding service to his country.

The National Business Hall of Fame Award.

The Sarnoff Award for contributions to the electronics industry.

The Eisenhower Award for support of our Armed Forces.

The Smithsonian Computerworld Award. As the first recipient of this award, Perot was recognized for his contributions to the computer industry.

The Horatio Alger Award. This award is presented to individuals who overcome obstacles to achieve significant success in their careers.

In 1984, Perot purchased the only copy of the Magna Carta that has been allowed to be taken out of Great Britain. It has been placed on loan to the National Archives in Washington, D.C., where it is displayed alongside the U.S. Constitution and the Bill of Rights.

Reform Party candidate for President for 1996.

Founder of the Reform Party of Kentucky.

RELIGION: No data provided at Web site.

MILITARY BACKGROUND: Honorable discharge from the Navy in 1957.

After graduation, Perot served at sea for four years on a destroyer and an aircraft carrier.

LICENSES: No data provided at Web site.

HOBBIES: No data provided at Web site.

RELATIONSHIPS (FAMILY MEMBERS, FRIENDS): Ross and Lulu May Perot, parents.
Mother was dying of cancer when he went to Iran to rescue his employees.

Bette, sister

In 1956, Ross married Margot Birmingham from Greensburg, Pennsylvania, whom he met while a midshipman at the Naval Academy. Margot taught school during the early years of their marriage. Ross and Margot have been married for forty years. Margot is a direct descendent of Benjamin Fell, a friend of George Washington, as well as a shoemaker, and a patriot.

Ross and Margot live in Dallas and have five children—Ross, Jr., Nancy, Suzanne, Carolyn, and Katherine. The Perots currently have nine grandchildren.

One grandson is named Benjamin Fell Mulford.

Dr. Pat Choate, running mate—A political economist, think tank strategist, populist spokesman and author, Pat Choate is one of America's most widely recognized authorities on U.S. competitiveness, management practices, and public policy.

Colonel Bull Simons, the retired war hero who led Perot's employee team to rescue his 2 employees from captivity in Iran.

Bill Gaylord, an executive working for Ross' company in Iran in 1978 who was arrested (along with another employee), held in prison, and later rescued by Perot's employee team.

"Paul," the other employee who was taken prisoner.

PUBLICATIONS:
Books:
United We Stand
Not for Sale at Any Price
Save Your Job, Save Our Country
Intensive Care, We Must Save Medicare and Medicaid Now
Preparing Our Country for the 21st Century
The Dollar Crisis, By Ross Perot and Sen. Paul Simon
Ross Perot: My Life and the Principles for Success

SUBSCRIPTIONS (MAGAZINES): No data provided at Web site.

FINANCES (ASSETS): The Perot family is actively involved in charitable and civic activities. They have given over $100 million to various causes.

LAW HISTORY: No data provided at Web site.

BANK ACCOUNTS: No data provided at Web site.

POLITICS: Many of his views are published on his Web site, as well as in speeches and the news.

CREDIT CARDS: No data provided at Web site.

You will note that I was not able to fill in every element of the profile template from this one source, and you can easily understand why Perot's own Web Site would not offer some of this information. Using any of the currently available Internet search engines and simply entering "Ross Perot," you can begin to fill in some of the blanks. There are hundreds if not thousands of sites and documents on the Net that mention, discuss or quote Perot. For instance:

A Fact Sheet on H. Ross Perot
http://www.competition96.com/perot/fact.htm

The text of various speeches by Perot, including:
- Port Huron Northern High School Graduation—June 7, 1995 where Mr. Perot revealed that his father had to drop out of high school when he was 14, and had to work as a Texas cowboy because his father had died. His mother was able to finish high school, but could not afford to go to college. (**http://www.competition96. com/perot/schoedule/s6-7-95.htm**)
- Ross Perot's Speech—Lando Lecture, Kansas State University—January 24, 1995 (**http://www.competition96.com/perot/schedule/s1-24-95.htm**) where Mr. Perot stated that his sister and he were the first in their family's history to be able to attend college.
- Pat Buchanan on Ross Perot's Radio Show—May 7, 1995 (**http://www.buchanan. org/rosspat.html**)
- Transcripts on Perot, H. Ross (a site offering a list of 891 transcripts available for a fee from Journal Graphics, updated May 2, 1996) (**www.tv-radio.com/~kelsy/ topics/perothro.htm**)
- A Power Mini Report from The Story of Your Life for Ross Perot (an astrological analysis) (**http://www.adze.com/bios/pols/perot.html**)
- The Perot Periodical—An Unauthorized Quarterly (**http://www.brainlink.com/ ~nota/**)

Searching the Web for clues about Mr. Perot's religious convictions, I also found accusations of Pat Choate's ties to Jew-Haters.
(http://www.jdl.org/perot.html)

In case you haven't realized it already, the biggest problem you will encounter in searching the Internet for information about a public figure like Perot is an overabundance of data. To wade through everything posted online about Perot, and then tackle the all-important task of verifying what is fact and what is fiction, is simply not practical. Therefore, if I were in charge of Perot's campaign, or the opposing one, or an investigative reporter writing a piece on the candidate, I would search Internet sites and documents only to the point where I felt all the elements listed in my template were addressed in reasonable detail. I would then take this data and draw up a timeline, attempting to cover every period of his life. Friends, family, and associates would be placed in the appropriate time slots. So would employers, significant events in Perot's life, and so on.

To verify the data, and continue to round out the profile, I'd gather up all biographies on Perot available, including the autobiography listed in the subject profile under "Publications." I would search online biographical book directories, biographical index directories, and biographical directories (such as Who's Who in American Politics, which is available online). Given Perot's renown, additional biographical information might also be found in encyclopedias (searchable online, as well as on CD-ROM and in print). Many additional political databases could be searched (such as Political Profile on Prodigy and CQ Info on CQ Washington Alert Service), providing information about candidates.

I would also want to know who had contributed to Perot's presidential campaigns, and whether he had contributed to any Political Action Committees. This information could be found in several databases and publications that are searchable online.

My next search would include news databases, where I would flush out further biographies and details to place into my subject profile and timeline. One of the things an investigative reporter would look for in the timeline are gaps. If there is a gap in the subject's employment, or a time period when the subject's whereabouts are not accounted for, that period would be targeted for further investigation. Conflicts in the information could also signal a potentially important area for investigation.

News articles about people in the political arena, or others who have gathered a great deal of press, usually save me quite a bit of time in my own research, since I can quickly gather information that others may have taken weeks or months to uncover. In the case of Ross Perot, news articles would report that Henry Ross Perot was born to Gabriel Ross Perot (known as "Big Ross," although he was only about five feet tall, born 1899, died 1955) and wife Lulu May (born 1897, died 1979), pillars of the First Methodist Church. Big Ross was a cotton broker who traded horses as a hobby, and Lulu May was a leader of the Ladies Garden Club. They were members of the country club, financially comfortable, sending their children to private schools. Much has been written about their son's belief in the principles of the Scout handbook, his years in military service (with some speculation about how he was able to cut short his stint), and the building of his billions in the computer industry (starting at IBM until he formed his own company, EDS). Many articles and one very successful book have been written about his rescue of two of his employees who were held hostage in Tehran. More intimate details can also be found in the news, including the address of his childhood home, and his parents' loss of their first child (Ross Jr.). You could find H. Ross Perot's height (5'6"), accounts of his love for Norman Rockwell paintings, and his charitable works (reportedly giving away $100 million to projects for education, battered women, and the homeless since 1969), among many other personal details that have already been divulged or discovered about this very public figure. Of course, I would still want to gather further documentation to verify the news reports, but first I would read everything I could get my hands on that was already in print.

I would also want to start following Perot's paper trail, both manually and online, hoping to verify or disprove all of the information found. I would send public record retrievers out to gather records that are not yet available online, starting with Henry Ross Perot's birth certificate, while I ran online searches of public records systems and retrieved any record for Ross Perot, H. Ross Perot, Henry Ross Perot, Margot Perot, Margot Birmingham, or any other alias found, starting in the Texas area and then branching out nationally and even internationally. These searches would include driving records, criminal records, civil records, real property records, and so on. Similar searches could be conducted for all known family members and could even extend to friends and business associates.

An asset search, such as the one in the previous example, would seek out personal and business assets, which, in this case, amount to billions of dollars. I would also expect to find some of this reported in the news, since Mr. Perot has been a political candidate and there has been considerable interest in his wealth.

Normally, I might not care too much about a candidate's pedigree, but since his wife, Margot, claims to be a direct descendent of Benjamin Fell, I would want to obtain details on Margot's lineage, if only to make sure that there was no discrepancy in this claim. The Internet could be very helpful in locating others who had information on this family tree and who might be willing to share whatever records they had gathered.

An investigative reporter would likely want to contact many of the people whom this process identified as friends, family members, and associates, in order to gather first-hand information and uncover new facts, as well. All of this background work done on the computer could be used to lay the groundwork for interviews, uncover discrepancies or gaps in a person's history, and help to target certain areas for more intense investigation.

Similar background profiles can be created for those who are not well-known, starting with the information at hand rather than published biographies (an employment application in the case of a job applicant; a residential history in the case of a potential tenant). Although little or no information about your subject may have appeared in the news, and while you might find nothing at all on the Internet, use every tool at your disposal in searching for additional information. You may be surprised how much you can find out online about "ordinary people" through a concerted effort and by your willingness to use multiple sources of public records.

The key to research is in understanding the types of records that are available, and then conducting a methodical search, carefully documenting the information found, along with its source, questioning discrepancies, verifying all data before accepting it as fact, and looking for loose ends. You will find this true of genealogical research, locating people, biographical research, or any other type of research, including all of the many types of research that are based on personal records.

If you find any of these searches alarming or upsetting in their intimacy, please go on to the next chapter, where privacy is discussed.

A Word About Privacy

Before moving on to the core of this book to discuss where personal records may be found and how they can be used, one more subject must be considered. This is a concern, not only when learning to search through personal records, but every time personal research is undertaken. It is the matter of privacy. It probably has occurred to you already. I have given talks on the subject of "Personal Records Online" from one end of the country to another, and on each occasion someone in the audience has raised questions of privacy.

This is a subject that invites an emotional response. Few of us relish the fact that others have access to a great deal of personal information about us, or could have it with surprisingly little effort. However, most of us would claim the right to investigate the background of others, at least under certain circumstances—for example, if we were hiring a nanny to care for our children, an accountant to handle our investments, or a live-in companion to watch over an elderly parent. Much as we all wish to protect our own right to privacy, we all accept that this right is not absolute. Whether it is appropriate for us to invade someone's privacy, or for them to invade ours, sometimes calls for delicate judgment. In some cases, the question has been answered for us.

Privacy Laws

Legislation offers our privacy some protection. There are laws restricting access to personal information, such as the Privacy Act of 1974 (Public Law 93-579, 5 U.S. Code 552a), which sets limits on the collection and transfer of personal data by government agencies and lets citizens sue agencies that violate the act. Other laws guarantee access to personal information. For example, the Information Practices Act (California Civil Code 1798-1798.76), a California law, gives the right to see otherwise confidential personal information in records concerning oneself. Federal law restricts access to credit information to those with a legitimate need for it, such as banks to which we have applied for a loan. State laws restrict access to many different kinds of personal information, while some records are protected in one state, but not in another. Our medical records are somewhat protected from use without our permission. However, much of our personal information is simply unregulated.

Even where laws do protect our privacy, they are a fragile barrier. Science has long sought to define the natural laws that govern the world around us and sometimes help us to predict the future. I would propose a similar theory that may someday prove to be a law of information:

If information exists in one place, it exists in more than one place.

Credit information provides a good example. Access to personal credit information is regulated by the Fair Credit Reporting Act (Public Law 91-508) and is generally considered to be one of the more private areas of our personal records. Yet it is not as difficult to obtain credit information as many people probably believe. Assuming that:

- the credit agencies do their part in protecting credit information and allow access to it only with a legally "permissible purpose;"

- a computer hacker does not illegally break into the credit agency's computer system;

- an employee of the credit agency does not illegally obtain or sell the information;

where else might someone also find the information held by credit agencies?

Credit card companies have records that include your credit card numbers, anything that you voluntarily filled in on the credit application, your credit limit and balance, and the details of each credit transaction and payment. Only part of their information is sent to the credit agencies, where it can be used by stores and others in deciding whether to extend credit or make a loan. Before issuing a credit card, a credit grantor undoubtedly will have pulled a copy of your full credit report, which will later be stored in the company's files. An employee probably will have reviewed your credit application and credit report in order to decide whether or not to extend credit to you; in that case, the information may also exist in the memory of at least one employee at every business from which you have requested credit. Another credit report may be pulled later in order to assist the company in deciding whether to raise your credit limit or cancel your card. Again, some of the individuals involved in this process become familiar with your credit history. All this information may be placed on file by each company or agency that pulls your credit report.

Others may become aware of your spending by observing whom you pay for what. If you are famous, such observations may be more memorable; they may even be profitable for the observer. Even for those of us who are not celebrities, our family members, friends, and anyone who happens to be nearby may watch when we sign our credit card receipts. A stranger may not care how much you spend, but if your face later appears on the front page of their newspaper, it may take on greater significance. You need not have become implicated in a major scandal or crime to trigger this sort of recollection. All it would take is the local newspaper's photograph of you singing with the church choir or setting out on a camping trip with the local Cub Scouts. Although this will not provide a complete picture of your credit history, it could supply a valuable clue.

Store clerks, waiters, mail-order business staffers, and many others put through your credit transactions, keeping copies for their establishments. Not only does the employee have information about your purchase, but others in the company have access as well. Duplicate copies of credit slips may also be found in their trash.

Speaking of trash, what would yours tell us? Many people, if not most, drop credit card receipts, bills, bank statements, and other revealing information into their own trash without shredding them. Others gain legal access to all that information the moment you place it on the curb. These scraps of paper all can reveal small pieces of your credit history.

Another source of information may be current, previous, or even prospective employers. Employment applications often include a clause requesting your permission to obtain your credit history. Once received from the credit agency, this information may be attached to your employment application or kept in your employee file.

Whether you rent or own your home, you probably have given your permission to obtain your credit history before moving in. It probably is still on file for your current home, and perhaps even for previous dwellings.

Law enforcement agencies may also have reason to track your purchases or to obtain copies of your credit report. Your records may even be subpoenaed to court as part of a case that involves you, your family, or your associates, and if you have ever been divorced, goodness knows what types of financial information will make its way into the proceedings. All of it may become part of the public record, available to anyone who takes the trouble to find it.

So you see, information about you that may be protected by the credit agencies also exists in many other places, all of which are generally unregulated. This is true not only for credit records, but for most types of personal information.

For that reason, I am amazed when I read articles in the newspaper stating that someone has been found to be paying someone off for "inside" information. I am almost amused to find that some of these cases involve ridiculously high payments for information that can be legally obtained elsewhere for much less money, and often even free, by simply looking through sources such as public records. Is it laziness, ignorance, or both? A little imagination would go a lot further in finding legal avenues to nearly any type of information.

I do not advocate obtaining any type of information illegally. In this book, you will not find instructions on how to hack into systems or gain illegal access to protected information. *Naked in Cyberspace* serves as an inventory of the computer databases that store information about us and a textbook of how to use them. By the time you finish it, you should understand the many sources of personal information, whether public or private. After that, it is up to your own imagination to find legal sources, rather than seeking out illegal ones, or to go through the proper legal channels to request copies of records that are privately held—or to protect your own records to the limited extent that still is possible.

Technology and Personal Information

As computers have made it easier to search for personal records, they have eroded our privacy. This process can only accelerate in the years to come.

Many of the personal records available today have been available for many years. However, they have been relatively inaccessible. This includes public records, which theoretically have always been open to inspection, but for many purposes were too inconvenient to obtain. Just a few years ago, acquiring public records meant going to the effort and expense of traveling to the courts, records halls, and other buildings where the originals are stored, only to spend further hours sifting through archives or waiting in long lines for copies. This was enough to discourage most people from undertaking any but the most critical investigation.

Even in the early days of the Computer Age, information searching remained inconvenient. Records existed only on large, expensive mainframe computers, and they could be accessed only from a terminal in the same building. It still was necessary to visit the repository or to order records and wait for them to arrive by mail.

The long, broad trail of records that we all leave behind remained difficult and tedious to follow.

Today, computers are networked, and information that exists in a database in Maryland or California is no farther away than your desktop PC in Texas or Illinois. With a notebook computer, it is right there in your lap. Hardware and software costs have fallen so dramatically that an estimated 50 percent of American households now own at least one computer; in business, personal computers are all but universal. So is access to information. Today, simple curiosity is motive enough for some people to investigate their neighbors, friends, and associates. Our beloved privacy is largely an illusion.

Other technologies are further eroding the walls around our lives. Powerful databases now can be developed on a PC, and massive amounts of data can be stored there on a CD-ROM or hard disk. As a result, sensitive information now is stored routinely in small computers distributed throughout a business, in what is known as client-server architecture. Putting the information at the client's site—in the end-user's small computer rather than the corporate mainframe—can reduce the security of the data. Rather than being locked inside one system whose access was closely controlled and monitored, information often exists at many sites, where it may be relatively unprotected.

High-speed networks now allow computers to send and receive information from town to town or half-way across the world within seconds. Systems like America Online, CompuServe, and Prodigy are bringing these networks into the home, and the Internet is linking them all into a single, globe-spanning super-network. Growing millions of individuals throughout the world are gaining access to vast quantities of information stored at universities, government sites, and many other institutions.

As these networks have grown, "hackers" have made a sport of breaking into distant computers electronically and exploring their contents at will. We often think of hackers as electronic muggers or terrorists who may secretly alter the records on computer systems, erase data or programs, or even bring whole networks to a halt. Frightening as this image can be—can you imagine the chaos a hacker could cause by attacking an air-traffic control system?—hackers who destroy records or make it impossible to access them do little to harm our privacy.

Not all hackers are destructive, however. Many "sport hackers" pit their wits against computer security systems for the pure intellectual thrill of defeating the security measures that defend computers and networks. Ironically, hackers intent only on amusement pose a greater threat to our privacy than their destructive colleagues. In addition to peeking into the records they find on the databases they "crack," hackers have been known to share their victories, posting telephone numbers, passwords, and break-in strategies on electronic bulletin boards so that others can admire their expertise. In this way, even beginning hackers have picked up the information necessary to invade our private information.

Somewhere between the sport hackers and the destructive hacker lies the data thief. These specialists break into computer systems for the specific purpose of obtaining the information stored inside. They may not harm the data or the computer systems that they invade; it usually is in their interests to leave no trace of their activities. However, they do invade our privacy and steal information to which they have no right.

There is no way to quantify exactly how seriously the various forms of hacker threaten our privacy. No one really knows how many hackers there are, nor how capable they may be, and new security measures are making it more difficult to gain unauthorized access to computers. However, it is clear that technology is also putting our records at greater risk.

Databases now can store information in one format and almost instantly translate it to another. Thus, it is becoming easier to combine or compare data from different sources. Information collected, and perhaps even volunteered, at different times and for different purposes can now be bought, sold, traded, and manipulated to offer new information products, identify new markets, and otherwise expand its use. Privacy no longer means quite so much when someone can manipulate information freely, pass it to others, and use it for purposes we never approved.

Not all databases are easy to use. Even some that are publicly accessible or are available by subscription can be terribly complex and difficult to navigate. Today, it still may prove impossible to find a certain piece of information in an efficient or cost-effective manner. This has stopped some from acquiring data that they otherwise would seek. But this obstacle is shrinking all the time. To make their products easier for unskilled researchers to use, database vendors are developing sophisticated new "front ends" for their systems. Some allow clients to phrase their inquiries in "natural languages" that approach everyday English. Others use the point-and-click menus familiar to almost anyone with a personal computer. The need to learn Boolean logic and sophisticated search commands is passing quickly. One more defense around our personal information is being stripped away.

Artificial intelligence (AI) software allows computers to mimic some of the decisions by which human experts do their jobs. In the near future, it may enable any novice researcher to ferret out information as efficiently as the most skilled professional can today. AI also is being used to develop "intelligent agents," software that someday may help us all to navigate the vast array of computers and databases linked to the world's networks.

As all this is taking place, multimedia accessories and software are making computers easier and more exciting to use, and network theoreticians have long promised that computers would merge with television. The result will be interactive TV, which promises to open vast new quantities of information to fast, easy access. The first stage of this development can be seen as Web TV.

In years to come, it may be possible to request information from anywhere in the world and have it delivered to our televisions. It will not be mere data anymore, but graphs, charts, timelines, images, and video with all the simplicity and impact of TV. This remarkable new access to knowledge will revolutionize our educational systems, communication, and the way we view information in general.

A *Last* Word about Privacy

By now, it should be clear that Lane's First Law of Information has a corollary:

If information exists anywhere, no matter how carefully guarded, it exists somewhere else, where virtually anyone can gain access to it.

If privacy is important to you today, you must understand what personal records are being stored, how they are used, and who has access to them. You will find that information in the pages to come. Where possible, I have also included instructions for obtaining copies of your own records from the agencies that store them and for removing your records from their files. You can find a list of books about privacy in "Books," the first part of Section IV, "Where Can I Find More Information?" You may also wish to subscribe to periodicals that specialize in issues of privacy or even to join organizations involved in defining or protecting privacy. Lists of these resources too are available in Section IV. Many online resources also can help you learn more about your privacy rights. Indices to these resources are available on at least two Internet sites:

http://www.yahoo.com/Government/Law/Privacy/

and the Privacy Rights Clearinghouse home page at:

http://www.privacyrights.org/

The old brand of privacy, the kind we enjoyed because people simply could not find our records, is almost history. In just a few years, we will no longer be able to control our information, nor even to restrict access to it effectively; neither will anyone else be able to control theirs. As a result, we will be forced to develop new standards, new laws, and a whole new way of viewing privacy and access to information.

In practical terms, all that really is left for us is to learn to use this new, almost universal access to its best advantage, and perhaps to play a rear-guard defensive action on behalf of our own records. By the time you finish reading *Naked in Cyberspace*, you should be more prepared to do both.

II.
HOW PERSONAL RECORDS ARE USED

Locating People

Many of us have wished at one time or another that we could locate someone. Almost everyone has lost track of an old friend, a relative, or an old flame, and who would not wish to locate someone who owed them money? This personal need to find people is one shared with many professions, all of which are growing to depend more and more on the use of personal records now available online.

Law Enforcement—Members of the law enforcement community routinely need to locate people who are witnesses to crimes, previous victims, criminals, and so on.

Attorneys—With the criminal justice system chronically overburdened, under-funded, and short of manpower, a criminal case can take months or more before it gets to court; a civil suit can take even longer. By that time, key witnesses may have moved away or been lost, and they must be located prior to the court date.

Probate attorneys must sometimes locate heirs before a will can be executed. If someone wishes to obtain rights to something (a patent, trademark, or mineral rights), an attorney can assist a client by tracking down the owner and obtaining the necessary signatures.

In the most dramatic example, a capital murder case, attorneys may need to locate people from a person's past, perhaps all the way back to the person's childhood. They may want to provide character witnesses or "re-construct" a person's life, in order to convince a judge and jury that their client should not receive the death sentence. Under these most dire of circumstances, locating a person could actually mean the difference between life and death.

Attorneys routinely use private investigators, process servers, information brokers, and even paralegals to locate people.

Process Servers—Process servers are hired by attorneys or the court to locate persons who are ordered to appear in court.

Skip Locators—When someone moves without notifying creditors, a skip locator may be called to track the person down. Skip locators can also be hired to locate people who have jumped bail. This is probably the most dangerous type of work in locating people. It can also be the most difficult. Unlike most of the people one might need to find, the skip locator's quarry deliberately leave as few clues to their whereabouts as possible.

Private Investigators—Private investigators are hired not only by attorneys, but also by businesses and individuals to locate people for many reasons.

Creditors—Creditors and collection agencies often need to locate people who owe money and move unexpectedly. This includes people who must track down a former spouse or lover in order to collect on child support payments.

Information Brokers/Researchers—During the course of research, an information broker sometimes needs to locate an expert in order to gain information about subjects being researched or to update previously published findings.

Employers and headhunters (employment agencies) sometimes hire an information broker to locate someone in order to make a job offer. Even when the current employer is known, it is sometimes best to locate the person's home and approach him or her there, rather than at the job, when making a competitive offer.

Holders of patents, trademarks, and copyrights must also be found and contacted in order to purchase the property or to negotiate the rights to use it.

Although many other types of professionals need to locate people, they do not all have the expertise or experience to perform database research efficiently. In that instance, an information broker can be a valuable ally to other professionals who need to locate people. Information brokers are often hired by attorneys, process servers, skip locators, private investigators, and others to locate people or to provide the part of the picture that can be found on databases or through other types of research.

Adoptees and Birthparents—Birthparents sometimes wish to locate an adoptee in order to assure themselves that the adoptee is well or to reunite with this person. Adoptees also often wish to locate their birthparents in order to obtain information such as family medical history or in hopes of a reunion. Natural siblings and other relatives also initiate such searches at times.

Alumni Associations—Alumni associations often attempt to locate their members in order to plan high school and college reunions. They also search for former students in order to solicit funds from them.

Family Members—It is not unusual today for people to marry more than once, to have children with more than one partner, or to blend their families through remarriage, forming stepfamilies and all of the resulting relationships. When families break apart, for whatever reason, people can lose touch with natural and stepfamily members, and later they may wish to locate them in order to re-establish those relationships.

Friends and Other Loved Ones—Nearly everyone has lost track of a friend or former loved one at some point in their lives. Faced with the need to find someone, many people will hire a private investigator or information broker to find the individual. Others can do so on their own. This is becoming easier for those who know how to make use of computer databases and bulletin boards.

Getting Started

The first and most important task in locating a person is to document all of the information you have, and all that you gain on each step of your search. I use the form which follows to assist me with this task. Some of the questions on this form may not seem relevant to your particular search, but they can all provide leads to additional resources that might be used to locate the subject. All documents and notes from each contact or search are attached to the profile, which is updated as new information is received until all avenues have been fully explored, the budget has been exhausted, or the subject has been found.

From this point forward, each search is unique. There is no exact formula for which databases are searched first or how many are examined. I wish that I could lay out some methodical search procedure so that one would always succeed, or at least be certain that any possible clues have been unearthed, but in fact there is some luck involved in locating people, in addition to one's analytical and search skills.

I had, for example, occasion to search for a niece of a client, who had not been seen by her father's side of the family since she was 2 years old. At the time of the search, the subject was approaching the age of 30. Prepared for a long and arduous search, I started with one of the earliest pieces of information that I received. I contacted the medical records department at the hospital in which the subject had been born. A kindly clerk let it slip that the subject had been a patient of the hospital until she was in her teens, which was a leap forward by many years. This alone was a stroke of luck because the family believed that she had moved to another state at the age of two.

Pleased with that information, I went out to dinner. By the time I returned, the subject of the search had called and left a number where she could be reached. Upon contacting her, I found out that the medical records clerk had, of her own volition (and against hospital policy), called the emergency contact on the subject's admission records. The contact turned out to be an aunt on the mother's side of the family, who called her niece and passed on my number. The niece was thrilled to be put in contact with her two aunts and grandmother, whom she had always wanted to find, but whom she had not known how to locate.

The only database search that I performed for that project was to check a telephone directory to locate the hospital. I hope that this illustrates the following points. First of all, don't overlook any detail that you have in front of you; any lead may prove to be important when it is explored. Second, don't expect all of the answers to be found on a database. Although wonderful resources, computers and databases are still just tools, and a telephone is every bit as important in research. Third, enlist allies whenever possible. If you are courteous when requesting information on the telephone, you will be more likely to receive assistance and even advice, which may be just the tidbit you need to track the person down.

SUBJECT PROFILE

FULL NAME, ALIASES, NICKNAMES, MAIDEN NAME, MARRIED NAME:

GENDER:

BIRTHDATE AND/OR AGE:

SOCIAL SECURITY NUMBER:

PHYSICAL DESCRIPTION:

DESCENT:

LAST ADDRESSES:

EDUCATION:

OCCUPATION:

ORGANIZATIONS:

RELIGION:

MILITARY BACKGROUND:

LICENSES:

HOBBIES:

SEARCH REASONS:

RELATIONSHIPS (FAMILY MEMBERS, FRIENDS):

SUBSCRIPTIONS (MAGAZINES):

POSSIBLE LOCATION (ANY IDEAS YOU MAY HAVE):

FINANCES (ASSETS):

LAW HISTORY:

BANK ACCOUNTS:

POLITICS:

CREDIT CARDS:

The Problems With Names

Before spending money for an online search, there are a few potential problems that you should be aware of. Finding people by scanning through personal records often requires more background information than simply knowing their names.

1. Names are not unique—A name by itself will rarely provide a positive identification. In the telephone book for a community of only 50,000 people, I recently counted no fewer than 11 men named David Smith and 12 named Robert Johnson. Literally dozens of names were shared by two or three men or women, many with the same middle initial. Where the subject's location is unknown, the problem of duplicate names is far worse.

2. Nicknames may be used—When searching for someone in a database, you should be aware that your subject may be listed under a nickname. You probably would automatically search for Robert under Bob, Bobby, Rob, and Robbie, and even his initials, but you may have no way of knowing that a particular Robert is known as Moose or ChooChoo, so a database search may miss these records entirely. Likewise, a person known as Al at work may actually sign his proper name, Elvyn, on legal documents, while the newspaper article about his softball team may list him as Doc, as he is known to his teammates. You might not find him at all without this knowledge.

3. Aliases—People sometimes also use more than one name. While often thought of in connection with a criminal seeking to evade the law, there also are many legitimate reasons individuals adopt other names. For example, women (and very rarely men) often take on their spouse's surnames after marriage. Some continue to use their maiden names. Some women continue to use their maiden names professionally, but socially use their spouse's surname.

Adoptees usually take on the adoptive parent's surname. Often the first name is changed as well, if the adoption occurs early in the child's life. Adult adoptees frequently are given the option of choosing which name they would like to use, and can select an entirely new name if they wish.

People sometimes change their names simply because they don't like their given names, or because they wish to avoid the notoriety that their names carry. For example, you may recall that Jeff Gillooly, Olympic skater Tonya Harding's ex-husband, went to court to change his name after his release from prison.

A writer may also use an entirely different pen name. For instance, Stephen King has written several books under the name Richard Bachman.

An actor or actress may take on a screen name. Some will go to court to have their names changed legally, while others will continue to use their given names everywhere except on the screen, in order to maintain whatever privacy is available to them offscreen.

4. Middle Names—Some people commonly use their middle names, but still sign legal documents with their proper names. A database may list either or both.

5. People, particularly women, compound their own last names at times, using both their maiden and married name. On some databases, the first last name is entered as a middle name. On others, the two last names are run together. On still others, a hyphen may appear between the names. Sometimes one of the last names is simply dropped.

6. First names also are sometimes abbreviated, as in F. Scott Fitzgerald. If a database lists F as the first name, a search for the full first name (i.e., Francis) may not turn up a single match, even though there are many records dealing with your subject. Some database software is sophisticated enough to cope with these situations. Much is not.

7. Misspellings and typographical errors are not as uncommon as one would hope. People entering names or other information into a database sometimes make mistakes which make it difficult, if not impossible, to locate the record.

When a database is indexed, the indexer can also make mistakes, confusing a last name with a middle name, and so on. You've probably heard the expression "Garbage In, Garbage Out" (or GIGO). That pretty much says it all.

8. Common names are sometimes handled differently than uncommon names by the application software. When a common name is entered, the application software may require that other identifiers match as well before returning the record in question, especially if they were designed with privacy in mind. Without additional information, it sometimes is not possible to reach the threshold of certainty at which the system will return the matching record. For example, a match to a person's name alone is not sufficient for locating a credit record. Other matches to home address, Social Security number, birthdate, spouse's first name or initial, and so on are also all considered in determining whether the person on the database does in fact match the inquiry that was entered.

9. Ethnic variations sometimes can make it challenging to locate a record. For example, there are countries in which a woman commonly uses her mother's maiden name, rather than her father's surname. This can lead to some confusion when the woman enters the United States. You may find some records under one surname, while others are listed under the other.

Vietnamese, Chinese, and other names with sounds that are unfamiliar to some Americans often confuse those entering the information into the database, as well as those searching for it. It is not unusual to find first and last names transposed in such cases, or to find variant spellings. For example, former Chinese Premier Zhou Enlai might be found under the more common spellings Chou En Lai or Chou En-Lai, in which case the last name might be indexed as Chou, Lai or En-Lai.

10. Indexing variations—Some databases do not have a standard convention for indexing names. In those cases, it may be necessary to search for the name in several ways. Variations that I have found include:

Surname, First Name
Surname, First Name, Middle Initial
Surname, First Name, Middle Name
Surname, First Initial
Surname, First Initial, Middle Initial
Surname, First Initial, Middle Name
First Name, Surname
First Name, Middle Initial, Surname
First Name, Middle Name, Surname
First Initial, Surname
First Initial, Middle Initial, Surname
First Initial, Middle Name, Surname

On databases that charge per search, trying all of these variations could be expensive. If a combined search is possible, that would certainly be preferable, but not all databases allow a combined search.

Some databases do not index the names at all, making it necessary to search the text of the article, rather than a defined field.

11. Most databases cannot discern the difference between Doe (as in John Doe) and DOE (the acronym for the Department of Energy). When news databases are searched for names such as these, a good many misses may be found before a real hit is identified.

Excluding articles in which the term "energy" is used may inadvertently drop some of the hits that you wanted. Even excluding articles with exact matches on "Department of Energy" may drop an article that names John Doe from Albuquerque in the same article that happens to mention someone from the DOE. LEXIS-NEXIS does have a command for searching for words in capitals (i.e., ALLCAPS(DOE)), so that these can be excluded, and another command to identify words with only one capital (i.e., CAPS(DOE), which will identify instances of Doe), but in being able to discriminate among these subtleties, this system is an exception.

These problems with names usually can be overcome, but you should be aware of them before conducting a database search.

Databases Used

Many factors influence the choice of databases that one uses to locate a person. Nearly any type of personal record can be useful under the right circumstances. Section III of this book, "Types of Personal Records," describes the types of database records used in personal research.

The following questions and explanations will illustrate how some of the choices of databases are made. When reading them, try to imagine that you are looking for someone, and that these questions are being asked by someone who will help you to select the databases to be searched.

What Do You Know About the Person?

I am always surprised when a former spouse or lover does not even have the Social Security number of someone he or she was married to or had a child with. Good identifying information is the key to locating a person. When unique or complete identifying information is available, it may take only a single search to locate the person. When it is not, many searches may be necessary in order to fill in these gaps before the final search is possible. Some of the best identifiers are Social Security number and date of birth. Although it is possible to find a person without these, having them can shorten a search considerably. Knowledge of these identifiers also makes it possible to verify whether any of the records found actually belong to the person that you're looking for.

Armed with a Social Security number, the first thing that I would do would be to run a search for it through the credit agency databases. In many cases, this is all that is needed to locate a person who is not hiding, and uses a credit card, holds a mortgage, or uses some other form of credit.

Is the Name Unique?

If I were looking for a person with a name as uncommon as Engelbert Humperdink's, I would begin by searching a telephone directory. The odds would be pretty good that any Engelbert Humperdinks found would either be the person I was searching for, or at least a close relative who might know his whereabouts.

For unique surnames, it may be worthwhile to use a telephone directory database to locate all of the people in the country who share that surname in order to locate family members of the person being sought.

How Long Has It Been Since You Knew Where This Person Was?

When looking for someone who has recently moved, several databases might provide an address update. The Postal Change of Address or Publisher's Change of Address searches offered by some of the public records vendors would be excellent choices.

An online telephone directory (as opposed to a CD-ROM telephone directory) might have the updated record before it could be found elsewhere. Whether online or on CD-ROM, a telephone directory that allows for address searches could also be used to identify former neighbors who might know where the person had moved to.

The consumer credit databases might have been updated by a creditor who was notified of the change of address. In that case, an Address Update (or Finders) search could provide the new address and possibly the telephone number. Even if creditors have not been given a new address, if the subject is shopping for a new car or applying for more credit, recent inquiries on the subject's credit profile might lead you to his approximate whereabouts.

When many years have passed since the person's location was last known, I am more likely to try one of the "wild card" searches offered by a public records vendor, such as the People Locator: Info:Probe, offered by CDB Infotek. A search such as this can save much time and money by combining several searches into one, and hopefully turning up at least a lead or two.

Is the Person Hiding?

The problem often becomes more difficult when someone is known to be in hiding, perhaps from creditors. In this case, I might not search the records that the dividual would be likely to know about, such as telephone directory listings and real property records, or I might search these sources using the names of children, spouse, or associates. I would also look for voter registration records, not only in the subject's name, but the names of the spouse and any adult children, who might reside at home, or use their home address for voting purposes if they were away at school.

I might also try more obscure public records, such as fishing and hunting licenses. A person who is keeping a low profile may not be so careful about these types of records, as the person might not understand that these can now be searched online.

Is the Person Famous? An Expert?

If a person is famous, I would be more likely to check news databases for information about the individual's whereabouts. I would also check professional directory databases such as BASELINE—Celebrity Contacts, for information on how to contact the celebrity, or other professional directories to find out where this person worked.

For an expert, I might look for anything that this person might have written or anything that might have been written about this person in order to find his or her affiliations. A database such as the LC MARC: Name Authorities database (available from the U.S. Library of Congress Information System) could be useful in this respect, as it identifies names listed by the Library of Congress.

For people who are well-known in their field, I might also put a message on an online bulletin board (such as an Internet Usenet newsgroup), in an area visited by their fans or colleagues, if the search was not confidential.

Are There Friends or Relatives Who Might Be Located as an Alternative?

When a person is hard to locate, it is often worthwhile locating his or her parents, children, or other close relatives who may be able to tell you where the person is. Even former spouses can be helpful, especially if they have children in common.

Once I was trying to locate a client's lost uncle, who had not been seen in over 20 years. Although elderly, he was not listed on any of the death indices that I checked, and I had no reason to believe that he was dead other than that he had not reconciled with his family for so many years. I knew that he was divorced and that he and his former spouse had adopted a child. It was believed that he and his ex-wife may have reconciled later. Unable to find the uncle, I looked for his ex-wife and found that she was listed on the death index. This led me to send for her death certificate. It did not list the uncle (her husband), but their son was listed as next of kin, along with his address. Upon contacting him, I learned that his father had died many years before in a traffic accident. I could have been looking for the subject for a very long time if I had not branched out to look for family members instead.

How Old Is the Person?

If the person that you're seeking is elderly, it is important to rule out death before proceeding to other searches. Refer to Chapter Twenty-eight—Death Records for databases that can be used to assist you in this task. Even a young person may have died, so this possibility can never be completely overlooked.

A person's age might also be considered in determining the likelihood that he would be credit-active. A person who is young or aged would be less likely to have active credit than a person in his twenties through sixties, so a search of the credit records could be more productive for that age group. When a person in this thirties or forties does not turn up on the credit files, I begin to wonder whether there is some problem with the information I've been given, or whether there is some likelihood that the person is living on the streets.

If the subject is of driving age, I would want to check for a driving record. Even in states that do not routinely release home addresses (such as California), it would help narrow my search by determining that the subject is licensed within a state.

For someone old enough to pursue a profession, professional licenses might also be checking. People in their mid-years might also show up in marriage and divorce or other civil suits, or even have a criminal record, all of which might be found on property records should also be explored for people in their thirties (and young through their sixties (and older), and since these are available statewide for many states (rather than at only the county level, as many other public records are), it is possible to cover a broad area fairly quickly. There are many additional public record indices available online, any of which may contain information about the individual that you're seeking. These are important resources for people who need to locate others.

If the person you're seeking is of college age, he or she may belong to a fraternity or sorority. Some fraternities and (far fewer) sororities now maintain online sites, especially on the Internet. One Internet site that is attempting to link all of the fraternities and sororities online can be found at:

http://www.greek.com/

The home pages linked to this address normally include the location of the sorority or fraternity (which can be used to contact the organization and inquire whether the student you're seeking is a member), along with a brief list of officers and advisors. Some of these sites also include a list of their full roster, which may be all that you need to track down the student you're looking for.

University students who are not members of a fraternity or sorority can also sometimes be found online because student directories are springing up online at many colleges and universities, both in the United States and abroad. A list of college and university home pages can be found at the following site:

http://www.mit.edu:8001/people/cdemello/univ.html

A searchable list of American Universities can also be found at:

http:/www.clas.ufl.edu/CLAS/american-universities.html

For a person who has already graduated from a college or university, many additional Internet sites might be worth reviewing. There is no shortage of alumni associations who now have home pages on the Internet. Many of of them list brief biographies and contact information for individual alumni. Some of these sites also carry alumni publications that list marriages, babies, promotions, and other types of alumni news.

Although many others exist, the best Internet site that I've found that indexes university alumni associations is at:

http://weber.u.washington.edu/~dev/others.html

As of this printing, over a hundred colleges and universities are linked to this site, but dozens more may be added by the time you read this. One would have to go online to find out if a particular school is included.

High school alumni associations are also creating home pages on the Internet, so people of any age beyond the early teens might be found at such a site. Since more people do graduate from high school than college, such sites may grow into an even more valuable resource in the future. One Internet site that indexes both college and high school alumni associations can be found at:

http://www.yahoo.com/Education/Organizations/Alumnae_i_Associations/

Reunions can also be searched at that site, so you may even be able to plan a rendezvous once you've found your favorite alumnus.

Age can also help you to decide whether the subject may have served or be serving in the military. The Military Personnel/Base LOCATOR (available on CD-ROM from Staff Directories, Ltd.) could be used to locate active personnel. If it's possible that the subject died in the Vietnam War, the USA Wars: Vietnam database (available on CD-ROM from Quanta Press, Inc.) would provide dates of birth and death, military rank, branch of service, for each individual whose name is inscribed on the Vietnam Veterans Memorial in Washington, DC.

If your subject is a minor, it may be easier to locate parents or older relatives. If you are searching for a missing child, law enforcement should, of course, be notified in order to gain the assistance of both their personnel and their databases. The Missing Children Database (on CompuServe) might also have information about the person, and the last place that he or she was seen, although not his or her whereabouts. The Missing Children Database can also now be found on the Internet at the following National Center for Missing and Exploited Children site:

http://www.missingkids.org/search.html

Resources for Families of Missing Children can also be found at:
http://www.att.com/tobesafe

What Is Your Relationship to the Person? Why Are You Looking for Him or Her?

Access to certain databases will depend upon your purpose for the search. For example, if you are a creditor, you probably have a signed authorization allowing you to retrieve the full credit profile of the subject, and you have permissible purpose according to the Fair Credit Reporting Act. If you have neither permission nor permissible purpose, you may not have access to all the details provided on the credit report, but you can use the credit headers to provide location information.

In California, the Department of Motor Vehicles, in most cases, will not provide home addresses of individuals; however, if you are a process server and are pursuing a subject for a legal case, you may be able to gain access to this information directly from the DMV (online or in person).

If you are a friend or relative, you can expect more cooperation from your subject's other friends and relatives than a creditor would receive. On the other hand, if you are a creditor, you can expect more cooperation from ex-spouses (who might be located online), other creditors (found on the credit report), and other people who have sued the subject (which you can find on the civil records).

If you are looking for long-lost relatives for genealogical purposes, the less expensive resources should probably be utilized, as there is generally no rush for the information. If there is a life-or-death purpose for the search, no expense can be spared, so the choice of databases will be wide open.

If you are an adoptee searching for a birthparent, adoption registries may already have records of a parent who is looking for you; likewise, these registries can aid birthparents searching for the offspring that they gave up for adoption. These should certainly be considered first.

If you are looking for someone that you plan to sue, or who might run away if this person knew you were looking for him or her, more discretion would be called for. Posting online messages asking for anyone with information to contact you, or otherwise enlisting help from others, may not be an option. It is just possible that the person that you're looking for may also use the system where your message is posted, or a friend or relative may tip the person off.

If you would like to find out whether someone is a member of one of the online systems, it is possible to search the membership directory on some of the services. For example, CompuServe allows members to search the membership directory by name and will return the city, state, and email address of those persons found whose names match. On the Internet, there are also tools for searching for a person, including the "WHOIS" server, which can lead you to the system that the person is accessing the Internet from:

http://www.rs.internic.net/cgi-bin/whois/

or

http://rs.internic.net/cgi-bin/whois

There is also a "finger" server, which searches for matches on email addresses and returns real names. A list of "finger" gateways can be found at:

http://www.yahoo.com/Computers_and_Internet/Internet/
World_Wide_Web/Gateways/Finger_Gateways/

You can also find similar search capabilities provided by many of the Internet telephone directories. Please refer to Chapter Seventeen for further information.

A "horton" server provides a list of real names and email addresses for people who have recently used a site, and there are several other tools that can be useful in locating people on the Internet. Further information about the use of these tools can be found on the UCSD Science and Engineering Library—People and Organizations page, located at:

http://scilib.ucsd.edu/people-org/people.html

There are also Missing Persons sites on the Internet, at which anyone can enter the information that they know about someone they're seeking, in hope that someone will see it and offer information. Some of the people listed are old friends, some are parents, and so on. Sites such as these can be found at:

Instant Technologies Missing Persons Pages:

http://www.instantech.com/cgi-win/missing32.exe/open

There are other sites that are listed as Missing Person sites, that are referral services for detective agencies, or the agencies themselves. If you are not able to locate the person you're seeking on your own, you might find one of these services are able to help you.

Summary

Although I cannot cover every possible scenario for how a person might be located, I hope that you have already begun to understand how the many types of records available online and on CD-ROM can make the task easier, and that these examples have sparked your imagination. Each situation is unique, and a great deal of your success will depend not only on your knowledge of the resources available, but on your analytical and research skills as well. As I have said, there is also some luck involved, and it certainly helps to have good instincts and intuition.

You should also recognize that not everyone can be located (e.g., labor leader Jimmy Hoffa has been missing since the late 1970s). For those who can be located, the time and budget for the search are not always sufficient to complete the task. Although there is an impressive list of database resources available, sometimes surveillance or legwork can prove more productive, in which case, you may want to hire a private investigator rather than take on such a task by yourself.

On the other hand, there are many people who can be located with no more in hand than a national telephone directory database, which can sometimes be found at your local public library. If you decide to pursue a search on your own, many organizations can provide assistance and advice, and they may also share database resources among their members. Organizations focused on adoptee/birthparent searches, genealogical research, private investigation, process serving, public records research, and skip tracing all participate in locating people from their own perspectives. You can find listings of all of these types of organizations in Section IV "Where Can I Find More Information?—Organizations."

There are search guides for adoptees, birthparents, and genealogists, as well as books about public records research and some specifically written about locating people. Listings of all of these can also be found in Section IV "Where Can I Find More Information?—Books."

Last of all, many periodicals can help you to keep up with changes in the technology, new databases being introduced, advice, and techniques for locating people. Such periodicals may focus on adoptee/birthparent searches, genealogical research, investigative journalism, or private investigation. Listings of many of these periodicals are also included in Section IV "Where Can I Find More Information?—Periodicals."

Good luck and happy hunting!

Pre-Employment Screening

If you are not screening job applicants, you probably have been screened as one. If you are in a responsible position and likely to attract the attention of corporate headhunters, you may go through some level of pre-employment screening even if you have not applied for a job, most likely without ever becoming aware of it. Not so many years ago, someone could make almost any claim on a job application, secure in the near-certain knowledge that the lie would never be found out. It was simply too much trouble to check most claims, so relatively few employers did more than a cursory follow-up; many did not even bother to call former employers to confirm the applicant's job history. In the last decade, this situation has changed dramatically. We live in a less trusting society today, and thanks to computers, information is much easier to come by. At most major companies and many smaller ones, pre-employment screening is now routine, and it is likely to be increasingly comprehensive.

Prospective employees are screened in order to protect a company. At a basic level, no employer wants to get stuck with an employee who has lied about his (or her) work history or capabilities, and cannot do the job. It is much easier and less expensive to screen out such people as applicants than to fire them later.

Company assets also can be put at risk when someone is hired under a false identity, or when the person has ulterior motives for seeking employment. Employers risk embezzlement and fraud by employees who have access to company funds. Customer funds may similarly be put at risk by a thieving or inept investment counselor, banker, accountant, or anyone else given the responsibility for or access to their money.

Trade secrets can be just as vulnerable when an unscrupulous employee is hired. A company's reputation can suffer at the hands of an employee who does not deal well with customers, or is out to sabotage the company. An unskilled programmer can bring a company's information systems to a halt if his or her code fails to operate, or degrades the system's performance, and it might even damage the existing systems. A company that cannot access its own information could be shut down in a matter of days.

These risk factors may seem to be limited to those involving key executives, but even a maintenance person or janitor often receives a master key to an apartment building or office complex in order to clean up or make necessary repairs. They then could steal tenants' belongings or gain access to untold amounts of proprietary information.

Moving up to the top of the risk hierarchy, lives can be put in danger by a poor hiring choice. A pilot or bus driver need only suffer a momentary lapse in order to cause massive destruction and loss of life. Someone with drug or alcohol problems or a medical condition which might cause them to black out would be a poor choice for such a position, and I wouldn't want to see them in the operating room, or entrusted with the care of a child. A building contractor who uses poor quality materials or cuts corners, an elevator repair person who does not properly inspect and maintain all of the elevators, a security guard who falls asleep on the job—there are any number of cases in which a single unqualified person could endanger the lives of employees, customers, and the public at large.

Violence in the workplace is also a very real danger today, and one for which employers must assume some responsibility. When a new hire covers up a history of mental instability or violence, fellow employees, customers, employers, and the public could be put at risk. If a violent incident does occur, the employer will have to answer for it, and not only to the employees, customers, and families who have suffered. They may also find themselves in a court of law, accused of criminal negligence in hiring such an individual.

Although an employer may not wish to be suspicious of job applicants, or to intrude upon their privacy, the safety and well-being of other employees and customers, as well as the good of the company, must all be weighed in deciding how much pre-employment screening to perform. This is balanced against the amount of risk they are comfortable in shouldering.

What Is Pre-Employment Screening?

Pre-employment screening can take many forms. The employment application is normally the starting place. At a bare minimum of screening, employers usually call to verify information provided on a job application. Even if all of that information checks out, this is far from a thorough employment screening, as only the information volunteered by the applicant will then have been confirmed.

Merely calling telephone numbers supplied on a job application can make it exceedingly simple for someone to fake a work history. After all, the employer may not really know who they are calling. There are companies which, for a fee, will verify whatever a customer asks them to, pretending to be the previous employer and providing a glowing review of their work history. An applicant's friends may be willing to do the same.

Even legitimate employers often are far from candid when they receive a call to verify the person's work experience. Most will verify the dates of employment, salary, and job title. Fewer will provide an evaluation of their work performance, job responsibilities, whether the employee left on good terms, and whether they are eligible for re-hire, and this information is becoming more difficult to obtain. Many employers now fear being sued by former employees who are refused a job because of negative information provided for a pre-employment screening. Such suits are surprisingly common and occasionally are successful.

At least one online vendor/public records search service advertises that it can shield employers from such suits if they provide negative information on a former employee. This is because the vendor has credit bureau status, which allows it to ask such questions without fear of a lawsuit.

This is not to say that references should not be called. In fact, not calling to verify the references given could be considered negligent. However, when these calls are made, the telephone numbers should be looked up or obtained from Directory Assistance (or an online telephone directory), and the Personnel or Human Resources office should be requested, rather than the name of the person that the applicant has provided. This probably will not uncover a company that has been set up as a phony reference shop, but one might be able to catch someone who has named their best friend as a former employer, or someone waiting at home for your call to XYZ Corporation. However, even when the proper connections are made to a real former employer, one shouldn't expect too much from the calls, and most employers should not stop there.

A number of databases can assist in pre-employment screening, and some of them can reveal important information that the job applicant failed to divulge.

Professional Licenses

For fields in which a person must maintain a professional license, the applicant may be asked to supply a copy of the license. For some employers, this may be sufficient verification of licensing; however, a real con artist may go so far as to forge a license. Without obtaining verification from the licensing authority (the Department of Consumer Affairs, Department of Health Services, Department of Professional Regulation, Division of Consumer Affairs, Bureau of Professional and Occupational Affairs, or other licensing bureau, which varies from state to state), an employer may not be able to detect a forgery.

Licensing authorities can often be contacted directly to verify a license. Some public records vendors also provide access to databases of professional license holders, which can be used to verify the status of a license. For example, CDB Infotek offers a search that can verify licenses held by an individual in various fields, which can include many of the following fields, depending upon the state:

Accountant/Public Accountant
Acupuncturist
Air Conditioning Contractor
Alarm Contractor
Animal Health Technician
Appliance Repair
Architect
Asbestos Consultant/Contractor
Athletic Agent
Athletic Trainer
Auctioneer
Audiologist (Speech Pathologist, Language, Hearing)
Barber
Behavioral Science
Building Contractor
Business Broker
Certified Public Accountant
Certified Real Estate Appraiser
Certified Shorthand Reporter
Chiropractor
Cinerator Registration
Clinical Psychologist

Clinical Social Worker/Social Work Practice
Collection Agency
Contractor
Cosmetology (Hairstyling)
Dental Auxiliary
Dental Conscious Sedation Permit
Dental Examiner
Dental General Anesthetic
Dental Hygienist
Dentist
Deputy Pilot
Detection of Deception Examiner
Dietitian/Nutritionist
Direct Disposer
Dispensing Optician
Drywall Contractor
Electrical Repair/Contractor
Embalmer
Employee Leasing
Engineer and Land Surveyor
Engineer Business
Funeral Director

Funeral Home
General Contractor
Geologist
Geophysicist
Hearing Aid Dispenser/Dealer
Home Furnishing—Dry Cleaning
Home Furnishing and Thermal
    Insulation
Hypertrichologist
Interior Designer
Land Sale Registration
Land Surveyor
Landscape Architect
Marriage Counselor
Marriage/Family Therapist
Mechanical Contractor
Medical
Medical Board (of California)
Medical Corporation
Medical Examiner
Medical Group Clinic
Medical Practice
Mental Health Counselor
Mortuary Science
Motor Vehicle Sales
Naturopath
Navigation Commission (Delaware)
Nurse Midwife
Nursing Home Administrator
Nutrition Counselor
Occupational Therapist
Occupational Therapist Assistant
Ophthalmic Dispenser/Technician
Optical Shop
Optician
Optometric Practice
Optometrist
Osteopath
Pharmacist
Pharmacy Practice
Physical Therapist
Physician
Physician Assistant

Plumbing Contractor/Master Plumber
Podiatrist
Pollutant Storage Contractor
Pool Contractor
Private Investigator/Detective, Alarm,
    Security
Professional Boxing
Professional Wrestling
Professional Engineer
Professional Land Surveyor
Professional Planner
Professional Service Corporation
Psychiatric Technician
Psychological Examiner
Psychologist
Public Mover
Radiographer (X-ray Technician)
Real Estate Agent
Real Estate Appraiser
Registered Nursing
Respiratory Care Therapist/Practitioner
Roofing Contractor
Sanitarian
Sheet Metal Contractor
Shorthand Reporter
Social Worker
Specialty Contractor
State Pilot
Structural Engineer
Structural Pest
Sub-Surface Sewer Cleaner
Sub-Surface Sewer Installer
Surgeon
Talent Agent
Tax Preparer
Therapist
Underground Utility Contractor
Veterinarian (Veterinary Medicine &
    Surgery)
Vocational Nurse
Warehouseman
Wholesale Drug Distributor

Not all of these licenses are included for any one state, and this vendor currently offers various combinations of licenses for only seven states; however, other vendors offer their own combinations of licenses for a variety of states, so many employers may find that they're able to perform all license verification for applicants in their field conveniently from their own computers.

Licenses also appear in biographical databases and professional directories, but I would not recommend these as a means of pre-employment verification, as this information may have been supplied by the job applicant, and it seems unlikely that anyone would update it when a person's license has lapsed.

Professional license searches are also beginning to appear on the Internet. For example, Nebraska private investigator and detectives licensing records, and collection agency licensing records can all be searched at:

http://www.nol.org/home/SOS/

Utah real estate, occupational, and professional licenses can be searched at:
http://www.commerce.state.ut.us/web/commerce/admin/licen.htm

Motor Vehicle Records

A company may also use motor vehicle records in their employee screening, and these may be obtained online as well. Certainly a clean driving record and a valid driver's license would be desirable for anyone who will be driving as part of their work responsibilities. Employers should know of any limitations on the applicant's ability to drive (such as restrictions on night driving or the types of vehicles that they may operate) in order to make sure that the appropriate accommodations can be made, if necessary.

If the employee will be supplied with a company vehicle, the employer may feel that it's important to know if there are accidents on their record, and if so, who was at fault.

If a company's group insurance policy excludes pre-existing conditions, a company may also choose to check motor vehicle records for evidence of personal injury accidents, which may be excluded from their coverage for a period of time after employment.

FAA Airmen

If an applicant is being hired as a pilot, a search of the FAA Airmen Directory can be executed online through many public records vendors, in order to verify a pilot's license.

Some of these vendors are accessible on the Internet as well, including National Credit Information Network, which does offer this search at:

http://www.wdia.com/ncihome.htm

Consumer Credit Records

The credit agencies offer a variation on their normal credit report for use specifically in pre-employment screening (usually dropping the birth date, and containing other slight variations in content and format), but employers may also pull the regular credit report. Both reports require the permission of the job applicant. The credit and employment reports are used by many employers to determine whether a prospective employee has been responsible about their own finances. For employees being hired in the financial arena, this may take on greater importance. After all, would you want to hire a financial advisor who had a history of bad debts?

A person who will be given access and authority over company funds or customer accounts may be required to have a squeaky clean credit record and low debt ratios in order to be entrusted with that type of responsibility and authority.

The credit record can also be used as a means to verify some of the information given by the job applicant. For example, the Social Security number often appears on the credit report header. The number is not normally verified with the Social Security Administration when a person is obtaining credit, so verifying the number on the job application against that on the credit report will only show whether the applicant is consistent with the number that they have given others, and not that it is correct. If several Social Security numbers are found on the credit report, and they do not appear to be a result of a creditor's transposition or typing errors, one may wonder why the applicant is using various numbers, and may suspect some type of fraud. If the Social Security number is completely invalid, meaning that it falls within a range not yet issued by the Social Security Administration, the credit record may also contain a warning to that effect.

Previous employers' names and addresses also sometimes appear on a credit or employment report. If the information displayed does not correspond to that on the job application, the discrepancy should be resolved with the job applicant. If the applicant's reported employment history implies that he lived in one part of the country at a given time, but the credit record shows addresses in other areas, this again should be resolved.

A company may also perform a Social Security number search against the credit files in order to identify any other names used by the individual, as well as anyone else who may be using the same Social Security number to obtain credit. When several individuals are using the same Social Security number and appear to be living at the same address, one possibility is that the Social Security number may be shared by a group of individuals who are in the country illegally. If only one other, apparently unrelated, person is using the same Social Security number, either that individual or the applicant may be doing so in error. This is not uncommon, but it should be cleared up. A Social Security number may also display as invalid or belonging to a deceased person on the credit file. Calling this to the attention of the applicant may prompt them to re-check their number and correct it, as they may simply have forgotten the number, rather than attempted to perpetrate any kind of fraud.

It's important that employers who use credit records to pre-screen employees remember that what appears on the credit report is not necessarily correct. As explained in Chapter Twenty-five—Consumer Credit Records, mistakes can be made and records from more than one individual can be erroneously combined. With this in mind, one should not assume that an applicant is lying when a discrepancy is found, but discrepancies should be followed up on and resolved to the employer's satisfaction.

Consumer Credit Records may be obtained online from the three national credit agencies, or through any of the hundreds of credit bureaus, or public records vendors, some of which may be found on the Internet.

An Alternative Social Security Number Screening Device

Even without access to consumer credit records, anyone can perform a crude type of Social Security number screening, using a software tool found on the Internet or other bulletin boards. From time to time, I have run across Internet sites which, when given a Social Security number, will return the state and approximate year of issuance. I have seen similar software available for downloading from online forums on CompuServe and other bulletin board systems. With a little searching (in forums for genealogy, private investigation, and locating people) one can often obtain a copy of this type of software online.

Although this type of search does not verify that the Social Security number belongs to any given person, it can be used to verify that the Social Security number is within a range issued by the Social Security Administration. It may also raise questions if a person's Social Security number was issued before that individual was born or in a state in which that person had never lived.

Earnings History

A company may also choose to obtain verification of an applicant's earnings history from the Social Security Administration (SSA). This can be particularly useful when the information cannot be verified by an employer, such as when they have gone out of business or their records have been destroyed in a fire or other accident. Although a company cannot directly access the SSA database to screen their applicants, earnings information from the SSA is made available, with the applicant's consent, by at least one employment screening company:

Edge Information Management Inc.
One Harbor Place
1901 South Harbor City Boulevard
Suite 401
Melbourne, FL 32901
(800) 725-3343
(800) 780-3299 Fax

Not all earnings are reported to the SSA. There is a maximum amount that an employer must report for an employee, and the maximum has increased from year to year. When the Social Security Administration opened for business in 1937, the maximum was only $3,000. By 1966, this figure more than doubled to $6,600. A decade later (1976), the maximum was $15,000, and by 1990, the maximum had increased to $50,400. Although these maximums may cover a majority of Americans, the earnings records will not encompass many CEOs, top entertainers, or others at the high end of the earnings spectrum.

The earnings history from Edge Information Management Inc. can be ordered online, but the records are not immediately accessible. The information obtained by Edge is uploaded to their system at a later date, and may then be accessed by the employer.

Education Verification

An employer may want to verify the applicant's educational background. The first check should be to verify that the school is a legitimate college or university. A search of Peterson's College Database (available online through OVID, CompuServe Information Services, Inc., CompuServe Knowledge Index, Dow Jones News/Retrieval, and Knight-Ridder Information, Inc., as well as on CD-ROM from SilverPlatter Information, Inc.) can be performed to locate the school if it is a legitimate one. For a graduate school, a search of Peterson's GradLine (available online through CompuServe Knowledge Index and Knight-Ridder Information, Inc. and on CD-ROM from SilverPlatter Information, Inc.) can also be used to verify its legitimacy. If the school is not found on one of these databases, it may be necessary to contact the regional accrediting association to make sure that the degree claimed is not from a diploma mill. (For information about the six regional accrediting agencies, contact the Council on Post-Secondary Accreditation).

If the school is legitimate, the employer would then want to verify the years of attendance and degrees attained by the applicant. I have not yet seen a system that makes it possible to access school records databases directly; however, some companies offer online systems through which an educational verification can be ordered. After the information is obtained from the school, it is uploaded to their system and accessed by the client. Some schools require the consent of the applicant, whereas others do not.

There are printed directories that list educational institutions, and one of the directories from BRB Publications also provides instructions for obtaining educational data. To contact BRB Publications for a current list of their directories, you can call (800) 929-3764, or write to:

BRB Publications
1200 Lincoln #306
Denver, CO 80203

Employment History

Employment verification usually is performed on the telephone, but may also be ordered online through some of the employment screening companies. After the information is obtained from the former employer, it is uploaded to the employment verification system and can then be accessed by the prospective employer.

Worker's Compensation History

An employer may wish to obtain details of any previous worker's compensation claims filed by an employee before hiring them. They may wish to spot an applicant who has filed frequent claims or who seems to be particularly accident prone, as well as to identify pre-existing injuries which their group insurance company may wish to know about.

Many states will release information about previous worker's compensation claims. Some require the applicant's authorization, while others do not. A few will not release the information even with authorization.

For many states, a worker's compensation claims history may be ordered online through some employment screening companies. After the information is obtained from the state or district office, it is uploaded to the employment verification system and can then be accessed by the employer.

For further information about worker's compensation records, please refer to Chapter Thirty—Medical and Insurance Records.

Occupational Safety and Health Administration (OSHA) Records

Records on industrial inspections and accidents are obtained from the U.S. Department of Labor, Occupational Safety and Health Administration, and sold by many public records vendors (such as CDB Infotek). Employers may wish to obtain information on accidents involving an applicant, just as they would worker's compensation records.

For further information about Occupational Safety and Health Administration records, please refer to Chapter Thirty.

Medical Records

Medical records are usually confidential; however, insurance companies are routinely given access to medical histories of millions of Americans. Employers who self-insure their employees may also have access to the complete medical records of their employees through firms such as the Medical Information Bureau (MIB). For further information about this company, please refer to Medical Insurance Databases in Chapter Thirty.

Public Records

Public records can also be used in pre-employment screening. A criminal records check in each county where an applicant has lived, going back several years, might reveal a history of violence, embezzlement, or other crimes that could have a direct bearing on an applicant's employment.

Some employers will wish to check the credit headers to determine whether the applicant has lived in other states or counties where a previous criminal record might be located.

For employment in criminal justice, federally chartered or insured banking institutions or securities firms, or state or local government, the National Crime Information Center (NCIC) database may also be used to check for criminal records nationally. Please refer to Chapter Twenty-six—Criminal Justice Records for further information about this database.

Civil records could also reveal a suit involving a previous employer or fellow employee, which could be of interest no matter which side was doing the suing. If a prospective employee has been sued for fraud, this would be a definite red flag for most employers. Before hiring the applicant, the employer would need to be completely satisfied with the explanation for such a suit.

Personal injury lawsuits might also be found in the civil records, which might be used to identify pre-existing injuries, which the employer's group insurance company may wish to know about.

A great deal of additional information might be gleaned from public records. For further information, please refer to Chapter Thirty-one—Public Records.

Combined Pre-Employment Searches

Public records vendors and pre-employment screening companies often offer combined pre-employment screening packages. These may include any combination of the reports listed earlier.

Other Pre-Employment Databases

Employers also sometimes use proprietary databases to screen their employees. For example, EMA-SPA (Employers Mutual Association United/Stores Protective Association), in Simi Valley, California, is a not-for-profit company that keeps private files on previous employees of their member companies (which include Circuit City, Reno Air, department stores, and other companies, for a total of approximately 150 firms). These "incident files" catalog people who were fired because their bosses concluded that they were stealing, using drugs, or harassing co-workers while on the job, among other things. Shoplifters caught by department stores are also named.

Most of the estimated 200,000 people on file with EMA-SPA do not know that their names are on file, and many (if not most) have never been arrested for their purported wrongdoings. This means that they may have had no opportunity to defend themselves, and yet, their future employment opportunities at any of the member firms may be impacted by their presence on this database. I would not be surprised to see the demise of this and similarly "private" databases as their existence becomes more widely known.

Summary

An employer has a variety of means for pre-screening potential employees, and many databases can help with the process. Not all pre-screening work can be accomplished on a computer, however. No database can entirely remove the need for an interview with the applicant, and not all types of records are available online. Military records, for example, cannot be obtained online, but may be obtained for use in the pre-screening process by submitting the appropriate request form to the service in question. There are also aptitude tests and technical interviews specific to many occupations.

A thorough screening depends in large part on the information supplied by the applicant, and the employer's ability to verify each pertinent fact and find any holes in the information supplied. The application should account for all periods of time since they began working (or at least several years), including where they were living and working at all times. Gaps in their residential or employment history could indicate a problem period and should be discussed with the applicant.

Employers may also use other screening devices, such as integrity and honesty tests, drug tests, handwriting analysis, psychological assessment, and physical exams, in hopes of further reducing their risk of hiring a problem employee. Although there has been some controversy over the effectiveness of these methods, some employers do feel that administering these tests does, at the very least, discourage potential employees from applying for a job if they know that they have something to hide.

There are legal limitations on the types of records that can be used in pre-employment screening, and, in some cases, the age of the records that can be considered is regulated. The Fair Credit Reporting Act, for example, limits the employer to considering only the last seven years for most types of credit records used in pre-employment screening. It also requires that an applicant be told when they are rejected for a job because of information on their credit report or investigative consumer report. A patchwork of other state and federal laws (including civil rights acts and laws barring discrimination against the disabled) govern pre-screening in various areas of the country. It is incumbent on the employer to be aware of these laws and to adhere to them in all pre-screening of prospective employee. The Legal Information Institute at Cornell Law School provides a couple of Internet Web sites that might be worth examining for this type of legal information.

U.S. Employment Law:
http://www.law.cornell.edu/topics/employment.html

U.S. Employment Discrimination Law:
http://www.law.cornell.edu/topics/employment_discrimination.html

These sites may also lead you to other legal or employment sites where further information can be found.

Of course, one should always consult an attorney for interpretation of the laws and how they apply to one's own situation.

Again, please remember that databases do contain errors, so no pre-screening process should rely solely on the computer. Employers should obtain authorization from applicants before delving into their backgrounds and should discuss any findings with them. Only in this way can an employer avoid unfairly denying employment to a qualified individual.

For further information on pre-employment screening, books that include additional sources and methods are listed among the Background Research/Investigative Reporting Books and Public Records Research Guides, which appear later in Section IV "Where Can I Find More Information?" Organizations of employers sometimes also provide information on screening potential employees. You might also consider subscribing to periodicals such as those listed under Pre-Employment Screening and Recruitment Publications, also found in Section IV.

On the Internet, you can also locate companies that perform pre-employment screening or sell reports that can be used for this purpose, as well as Usenet newsgroups and mailing lists on which such issues are discussed. One site that I ran across recently indexes some of these Internet resources, and is listed as Employee Relations Web Picks at:
http://www.nyper.com/

Recruitment and Job Searching

A few years ago the only reason to use a computer when searching for a job was in writing up a resume. Recruiters hardly needed a computer at all. That is no longer true. In the last year or two, the job hunting and recruiting scenes have changed considerably.

Online job postings are now routine, and job-seekers upload their resumes to online bulletin boards, employment services, and directly to companies at an ever-increasing rate. In another year, it may be difficult to imagine finding a job in some industries (such as in data processing/computers) or at professional or executive level positions without the use of online resources or databases.

Savvy recruiter Mark Jennings, of Jennings & Associates, Inc. (in Rancho Cucamonga, California, and at: **recruiting@earthlink.net**) describes the influence of the Internet on the recruiting industry as "dramatic and permanent." He credits the Internet with opening new doors to business that he would never have seen otherwise, as well as allowing him to work nationally, in cooperation with recruiters around the country. (Mr. Jennings also believes that the Internet has heightened the ethics of the recruiting field, as it has given recruiters a mechanism for communicating with colleagues, discussing issues, and policing themselves. He explained that anyone who experiences a problem with another recruiter can spread the word very quickly online, so recruiters have a greater incentive for treating others ethically.)

In a recent conversation, Jennings compared the use of online services to the use of fax machines. He said that recruiters were forced to get fax machines around 1987 in order to stay in business. "Today," he added, "if a recruiter is working on placement of professionals or executives, you're either doing business online or you're not in business."

Applicants once sent resumes containing detailed work histories and personal information directly to companies who advertised their job openings in the newspapers. Now a resume may travel far beyond those bounds, being downloaded from online services by executive search firms, company recruiters, and others who can use the information to size up their competition.

Job applicants, company recruiters, executive search firms, and businesses are all continuing to adjust to this new employment arena. Let us look at some descriptions and examples of the employment information now available and how it is being used.

Job Seekers

People seeking employment have always had to reveal personal information such as home address and telephone number. Their resumes have often included information such as employment history, responsibilities, professional accomplishments, salary history, educational background, professional association memberships, awards received, and references.

Today, resumes are being uploaded to online bulletin boards and databases, where they can be accessed not only by a particular company that interests the applicant, but in some cases by nearly anyone with a computer and the willingness to pay the database vendor's fees, if any.

General Resume Databases

Many of the online systems offer resume databases. Following are a couple of examples of general resume databases (or databanks) that can be used to seek out prospective employees:

- The National Resume Bank (available online through The National Resume Bank) contains qualifications summaries submitted by those seeking work in many employment sectors.

- Resumes on Computer (available online through HRIN, The Human Resource Information Network) contains professionally produced resumes of people actively seeking employment.

(Refer to Appendix N for these database vendors.)

Many other resumes are available online through the bulletin board services. Since it seems that nearly everyone in the world has their own Internet home page (okay, I am exaggerating—slightly), resumes can also be found at individual Internet sites as well as in collections of resumes found all over the Internet. When I performed a recent Internet search for "Resumes" (using an Internet search tool, the WebCrawler), 4,042 sites were identified. Among these sites were companies that can assist a person in developing an online resume, complete with graphics and hypertext links, as well as many commercial services that for a fee will store people's resumes online. The Internet Professional Association (IPA) maintains an Internet Home Page at:
http://www.ipa.com/

The IPA Employment Networks includes the IPA Journal, the Recruiters Online Network (RON), StaffNET and the Global Employment Network (GEN). The IPA offers free posting of resumes to their members through the IPA—Recruiters Online Network at:
http://www.ipa.com/careers/resumemail.html

Various recruitment resources can also be found at:
http://www.ipa.com/resources/index.html

Another Internet site, the Internet's Online Career Center (OCC), claims to be the Internet's first and most frequently accessed career center. This center offers listings of jobs, resumes, career fairs and events, among other things. The OCC can be found at:
http://www.occ.com/occ/

The Monster Board accepts resumes, employer profiles, job postings and information on career fairs. This board can be found at:
http://www.monster.com/home.html

The JobCenter offers a service to send matching job ads each day to people who submit their resumes. Both resumes and job ads are also searchable at this site:
http://www.jobcenter.com/

Intellimatch On-Line Job & Career Services provides a site in which a "WATSON Structured Resume" can be entered, and employers can search resumes using "Holmes Searches." This site is located at:
http://www.intellimatch.com/

A couple of the additional Internet resume sites that index and link many others can be found through:

U.S. Resume:
http://www.usresume.com/ushome.htm

The Virtual Job Fair Resume Center:
http://www.careerexpo.com/pub/Rsubmit.html

Jobs Sought Within a Geographic Area

Those seeking a position within a specific geographic area may find that there is an online service specifically designed to suit their needs. For example, those who have been "downsized" in the Indianapolis area may wish to add their resumes to the Regional Re-Careerment Center at:
http://www.iquest.net/reg-recar/

Jobs Sought Within an Industry

People looking for work in a particular industry can upload their resumes to online bulletin boards that are focused on that industry, where their resume can be read by employers and others who may be able to point them to a job opening. Not all bulletin boards will allow this type of upload, so before uploading, it is best to spend some time there in order to become familiar with the etiquette of a forum or send a message to the system operator (or Sysop) in order to find out if this is allowed.

I have noticed that some people upload the same resume that they might have previously mailed to an employer, including their home address, telephone number, and salary information. This always startles me. Would you want to post this personal information on, say, a grocery store bulletin board? Putting it on an Internet newsgroup or Web site is every bit as public. My own approach would be to note that salary and reference information is available upon request, and substitute an email address for the home address. This would maintain at least some level of privacy and perhaps keep them off of some mailing lists for "opportunity seekers" and other get rich quick schemes. (Remember that anything that is uploaded to an online bulletin board can be read by people in other industries who also feed off personal information.)

Databases of resumes for people seeking employment in particular industries include, for example:

- Capsule Job Listings (available online through Publications and Communications, Inc.) which includes the Action Hot List, providing information on job seekers in the contract (temporary) technical services industry
- Travaux Publics de France (available online through Centre de l'Industrie Francaise des Travaux Publics) which includes, among their 11 files, a file called Repertoire d'Offres et Demandes d'Emploi, containing references to job opportunities and jobs sought in public works

(Refer to Appendix N for these vendor addresses.)

Other databases for particular industries, such as these, may also be found on the Internet. Some of the general resume databases mentioned here maintain sections for specific industries as well.

Minorities Seeking Employment
A few databases contain only resumes of job seekers from minority groups. Examples are:

- HispanData, also known as the National Hispanic Resume Databank (available online through Hispanic Business, Inc.) which contains resumes of Hispanic professionals and recent college graduates who are seeking employment with Fortune 500 corporations (A fee is charged to the person adding a resume to the databank.)
- Minority Graduate Database (available online through HRIN; The Human Resource Information Network) which contains information on college graduates from some 350 schools who are members of minority ethnic groups and are seeking employment

(Refer to Appendix N for these vendor addresses.)

Military
For resumes of enlisted personnel, warrant officers, commissioned officers and persons separated from the National Guard and Reserve forces, who will soon be leaving the military and seeking employment as civilians, one can look to:

- Military in Transition Database (available online through HRIN, The Human Resource Information Network and MILITRAN, Inc.)

There is also a database containing information on more than 1,000 job fairs available to U.S. military personnel entering the civilian work force and firms interested in hiring them:

- JFAIR (available online through HRIN, The Human Resource Information Network)

College Students Seeking Employment
For resumes of college students or recent graduates, there are many databases available, including:

- CareerNet—New York University's database of part-time and full-time jobs for current students, also lists resumes of NYU students seeking employment.

- College Recruitment Database (available online through HRIN, The Human Resource Information Network) contains resumes of undergraduate and graduate students in a wide range of disciplines.

- CVPRO (available online through SUNIST) contains references to French college students and recent graduates seeking employment, and to employment and training opportunities.

- kiNexus (available on CD-ROM from kiNexus, Inc.) contains resumes of new and recent college and university graduates, representing 1,850 academic institutions, as well as some experienced college graduates wishing to find new employment.

(Refer to Appendix N for the addresses of these vendors.)

Hot Prospects

Recruiters can use resumes posted online to locate hot prospects for job openings. They may also use professional and staff directory databases, such as those listed in Appendix D and described in Chapter Eighteen—Staff, Professional, and Other Directories, in order to identify individuals in key positions, who may have the required experience and expertise for a position they are trying to fill.

News databases can be used to identify the movers and shakers in an industry. Mergers and acquisitions, executive changes, and other events taking place within companies are often detailed in the news. Recruiters and competitors can use this information to determine when the time is ripe for spiriting away key employees with a better offer.

Additional information and resources for identifying hot prospects for recruitment can be found in Chapter Twelve—Identifying an Expert, as much of that information can also be applied to recruitment.

Job Openings

Not every job seeker may want to upload their resume to a database or online service, where their current employer might see it. For those job seekers who would like to use databases and other online resources to locate their own jobs, job openings can also be found on some Internet sites.

Additional databases and bulletin boards can be used by job seekers to find open positions. Examples of these can be found at:

http://www.isleuth.com/empl.html

The U.S. Department of Labor, in coordination with state public Employment Service Agencies, sponsors American's Job Bank at:

http://www.ajb.dni.us/

The Career Mosaic J.O.B.S. Database also holds job openings at:

http://www.careermosaic.com/cgi-bin/rotate-jobs.pl/

CareerWEB job listings can be found at:
http://www.cWeb.com/

The E-Span Employment Database Search is located at:
http://espan.com/

Following are additional databases and online sources in which specific types of job opening may be found. Many include various instructions for sending resumes and applications to prospective employers.

Classified Ads

Although there are many news databases available online and on CD-ROM, most news databases omit the classified ads. An exception to this rule is the Job Ads USA Database (available online through HRIN, The Human Resource Information Network), which provides listings of current job openings advertised in newspaper employment classified sections throughout the United States.

Many Internet sites also contain classified ads for jobs. In fact, using the Internet search engine Alta Vista, I searched for "EMPLOYMENT CLASSIFIED" and turned up over 100,000 sites as of July 1996.

Other databases that include job openings among their listings are:

- Business NewsBank PLUS (available on CD-ROM from NewsBank, Inc.—see Appendix A for their address) contains full-text articles and includes a feature called Job Search, which provides access to job opportunities by city and state (which is updated monthly, by subscription).

- CVPRO (available online through SUNIST—see Appendix N for this address) includes a file called Businesses, which contains employment and training offers from business people.

- E-Span Job Search (available online through America Online, CompuServe Information Service, and GEnie—see Appendix L for these addresses) provides descriptions of job openings listed by subscribing organizations.

- Jobs Database (available online through American Institute of Physics (AIP), PINET (Physics INformation NETwork)—see Appendix N for this address) contains job listings for positions in academia, industry, and government, especially in the fields of geophysics, astronomy, and materials research.

Openings Within an Industry

Some databases are focused on jobs in a particular industry. Examples of these include:

- Capsule Job Listings (available online through Publications and Communications, Inc.), which contains current job openings in the contract (temporary) technical services industry

- IBISCUS (available online through SUNIST), which contains, among other things, a list of employment opportunities for development specialists

- ISA-NET (available online through International Society of Appraisers (ISA)), which contains among other things, descriptions of employment opportunities as personal property appraisers

- Online Hotline News Service (available online through CARL Systems Network and on CD-ROM from Information Intelligence, Inc. (III)), which includes the JOBLINES* file, providing descriptions of employment opportunities from potential employers in the library automation and online database searching fields in the United States and Canada

- Travaux Publics de France (available online through Centre de l'Industrie Francaise des Travaux Publics), which includes, among their 11 files, a file called Repertoire d'Offres et Demandes d'Emploi, which contains references to job opportunities and jobs sought in public works

(Refer to Appendix N for these database vendors.)

Similar information can be found on the Internet. For example, physicians can find information about practice opportunities on the Medical Practice Opportunities home page, located at:

http://worldmall.com/mpo/

Jobs in radio and television can by found at the Corporation for Public Broadcasting Employment Outreach Project, at:

http://www.cpb.org/jobline/index.html

The Navy Jobs Home Page is at:

http://www.navyjobs.com/

The Monster Board offers the ability to search for job openings by discipline. Job discipline information can be found at::

http://www.monster.com:80/job_disciplines.html

Those seeking jobs in the academic arena can also visit the Academic Position Network, which is searchable by state, and located at:

http://www.umn.edu/apn/

Online bulletin boards focused on a particular industry often list both job openings and the resumes of job seekers. Many such bulletin boards are found on CompuServe, Prodigy, and the Internet. For example, the Computer Consultant's forum on CompuServe has both Positions Wanted and Positions Available sections where data processing professionals often share their employment needs.

Online mailing lists can also be used to notify people of openings in their field. For instance, the Special Libraries Association (SLA), San Diego chapter, maintains an Internet mailing list to which association and industry news is frequently sent. Contributors to this mailing list include SLA's Employment Chairperson, who sends announcements of job openings for corporate librarians in the Southern California region (and in particular San Diego), as a service to their membership. Other organizations provide similar online mailing lists.

Openings Within Specific Companies or Agencies

Many companies and various branches of government now maintain their own online job bulletin boards, which applicants can use to find openings for which they are qualified. More and more of these are appearing on the Internet. In fact, when I used Alta Vista, I searched for "company" "job opportunities" and came up with over 30,000 listings, many of which are for individual companies! I could continue to look up other terms such as "jobs," "classified ads," and specific company names, using any of the Internet search engines, and find a great variety of additional sites.

Other databases contain information on many companies, such as those listed in Appendix C. Some databases have been developed specifically for job seekers to learn more about prospective employers, including:

- DISCovering Careers & Jobs (available on CD-ROM from Gale Research Inc.) which contains, among many other things, essays on the 100 most important companies, which might be considered prospective employers

- National Association for Law Placement Directory of Legal Employers (available online through WESTLAW) which contains information on employers of legal professionals.

(Refer to Appendix N for these vendors' addresses.)

Openings Within a Geographic Area

Some online bulletin boards list job opportunities within a geographic area. An example is Los Angeles Job Fair (available online through LA ONLINE), which contains information on career opportunities in technical and non-technical fields at Los Angeles-area companies. Databases such as these can also be found on the Internet. Some of the employment bulletin boards also offer the ability to search by geographic area, including the Monster Board at:

http://www.monster.com/

Openings for College Students

Some colleges and universities assist their students by maintaining databases of local job openings. An example is CareerNet, New York University's database of part-time and full-time jobs and internships available for current students. Students can access this database through the CareerNet location or by logging onto a school mainframe from campus kiosks, by modem, or by plugging their computers into wall jacks in their residence hall rooms. Listings from this database are also made each week and sent to graduating seniors and alumni.

Newsletters

Newsletters, some of which can be found online, are sometimes used to advertise job openings. One example is Corporate Jobs Outlook!, a newsletter about career opportunities at 500 leading corporations (available online through HRIN, The Human Resource

Information Network). Other newsletters that focus on a particular industry can also provide information valuable to job seekers.

Career Magazine is an Internet site that contains not only news articles, but job openings and resumes. It is located at:

http://www.careermag.com/

Summary

The ways in which jobs are advertised and applicants are recruited have been transformed in the last few years. The economy, technology, and the availability of online (and particularly Internet) access have all played a part in the changing employment scene.

Job hunters in many fields will operate at a growing disadvantage if they lack access to the online resources used by companies and recruiters who are looking for them. Recruiters who cannot take advantage of the online bulletin board systems, databases, and the Internet will similarly be operating at a disadvantage.

This chapter has provided only an introduction to the many online resources available to job seekers and their would-be employers. Additional online sites can be found on America Online and various other bulletin board systems. Many publications, such as those listed under Pre-Employment Screening and Recruitment Publications (see Section IV "Where Can I Find More Information?—Periodicals"), may contain useful information for navigating some of the online resources available for recruitment, and may also explain the legal issues involved in recruitment and hiring. Still more resources are listed in the comprehensive database of personal information resources available at the *Naked in Cyberspace* Web site (**www.onlineinc.com/pempress/naked**).

For many workers seeking jobs, employers offering jobs, and recruiters trying to pair the two, online systems have already become essential. This will ultimately affect the nature and volume of personal information floating around cyberspace.

Tenant Screening

I f you have ever rented a house, condominium, apartment, or any other type of real property, you probably already know that landlords (and property management companies) almost always screen prospective tenants in some way before allowing them to take possession of a property. Some of this screening may take place on the telephone, calling references such as an employer and previous landlords and verifying whatever information the prospective tenant supplied on the rental application. Many databases also can alert property owners and managers to additional information that a would-be renter may not have volunteered.

Credit Records

Probably the most common online resource used for tenant screening is a credit database. A credit profile can be used to show a person's history of good credit, which will reveal whether they are responsible about their debts and will be likely to pay their rent. It can uncover a history of late payments and bad debts, which might make them a less desirable tenant.

Use of a credit profile will not allow a landlord to foresee all possible problems that they might have with a tenant, nor provide information on all past rental problems. Most of the information on the credit files relates to credit cards and loans, so things like late rental payments are not normally reflected.

You should also know that the records carried by the three national credit agencies vary in significant ways, as described in Chapter Twenty-five—Consumer Credit Records. Landlords who routinely pull a credit report from only one agency should be aware that one of the other credit agency databases may offer additional information on their prospective tenant.

A landlord may choose to deal only with the credit agency that is the most established (has the most reporting companies on file, better coverage of public records, etc.) in their area of the country; however, when screening tenants from other regions, another credit agency's report may be more complete. It can be expensive to pull credit records for each prospective tenant from all three agencies; yet failing to do so can increase the risk of renting to a bad debtor.

Public Records

Public records can also provide information on a person's rental history. For example, civil records can include suits by previous landlords to recover payment for property damage inflicted by the prospective tenant. Real property records can include foreclosures under the applicant's name. Criminal records may show a history of violence, possibly even involving previous neighbors or landlords, or current members of their household. These are all problems that any landlord might want to know of when deciding between several prospective tenants.

Tenant Databases

Many databases have been built specifically for tenant screening. In fact, hundreds of companies maintain proprietary tenant screening databases across the country. Trans Registry Limited (TRL) is an automated computer service which links these databases, allowing property managers access to landlord-tenant court records from approximately 200 courthouses nationwide. This service also allows access to credit reports, landlord-reported tenant histories, wanted fugitive searches, skip tracing, risk scores, and many other services designed for the property management industry. For additional information about this database, contact:

Trans Registry Limited (TRL)
11140 Rockville Pike #1200
Rockville, MD 20852
(301) 881-3400
(301) 984-7312 Fax

Summary

Tenant screening involves legal issues , which can vary from one state to another. For example, a landlord may not have the right to consider certain records as part of their tenant screening process, or there may be limitations on how many years of history may be considered for particular types of records such as bankruptcies. Landlords who screen prospective tenants should become thoroughly knowledgeable about the laws governing tenant screening in their area.

For information on landlord-tenant laws, you might wish to visit the Legal Information Institute (of Cornell Law School) on the Internet. Among their sites, U.S. Landlord-Tenant Law can be found at:

http://www.law.cornell.edu/topics/landlord_tenant.html

And the Plain-Person's Guide to Minnesota Landlord-Tenant Laws is available at:
http://www.olen.com/rentlaw/index.html

For further information, many publications regularly carry articles that discuss resources for tenant screening, along with legal issues for landlords and property management companies. Some of these are included later in this book under Property Management Publications in Section IV "Where Can I Find More Information?—Periodicals." On the Internet, you can also peruse TenantNet, the Online Resource for Residential Tenants' Rights at:

http://tenant.net/

An electronic newsletter for landlords is available from The Rental Property Reporter at:

http://www.teleport.com~rpr/

Real estate-oriented resources can also be found at RealtyGuide at:
http://www.xmission.com/~realtor1/

There are also bulletin board forums such as the Home & Real Estate RoundTable on GEnie, where such discussions regularly take place.

In addition, property management organizations such as those listed under that heading later in Section IV "Where Can I Find More Information?—Organizations" can provide still more information and publications in this field.

On the Internet, you can also find many sites for companies that perform tenant screening, attorneys specializing in landlord rights, and commercial property information.

Landlords should also be aware that any type of database can carry errors, and denying housing to someone should not be taken lightly, nor based solely on a problem surreptitiously discovered on a database. I strongly advise obtaining written permission from prospective tenants before performing any type of tenant screening, and if a problem is discovered, discussing the results with applicants before ruling them out as tenants. It is possible that a bad debt can be explained or that a record found belongs to another individual entirely. (This is not an uncommon occurrence.) Unless a landlord discusses possible problems with rental applicants, the applicants may have no way to explain or correct the problems and may be unfairly denied housing.

Asset Searches

Performing an asset search may be the furthest thing from your mind today, but there are a few instances in which almost anyone may find themselves needing to do just that. So, just who needs an asset search?

Anyone Who Is About to Sue Someone

At some point in your life, you may have occasion to sue someone. You may have an ironclad case, miles of proof, and all of the reasons in the world for wanting to sue someone. You may even be 100% sure that you'll win the case—hands down.

Before spending big bucks on legal fees, it might be wiser to spend a few dollars finding out whether the person that you're suing has anything worth suing for. If you are suing because someone owes you money, it is entirely possible that they don't have it to pay you. In that case, your sense of satisfaction upon winning your case may vanish when you realize that there is no way for you to satisfy the judgment and that you now have legal fees to pay as well.

If it turns out that the person you're suing is wealthy, that information could also be valuable if a settlement is offered.

If you decide to go ahead with the suit, and you win, knowledge of your opponent's assets might also make it easier to satisfy the judgment, and recoup your expenses.

Anyone Being Sued

If someone is suing you, it might also pay to know your opponent's financial position. This might help you to gauge their seriousness at pursuing the suit or the likelihood of their accepting an out-of-court settlement. If, as part of the suit, they claim that you have damaged their financial position, you may also want to gather evidence to the contrary.

Anyone Going Into Business With Someone

If you're about to go into business with someone, especially someone whose financial backing you'll be relying on, you would do well to obtain as full a picture of their financial position as possible. If they are committing to sharing the business' ongoing expenses in exchange for partial ownership, investigating whether they are in a position to fulfill their end of the agreement may save you from hardship later.

Anyone Extending a Substantial Amount of Credit to Someone

If someone asks you for a loan, or asks you to perform any type of service now in exchange for payment to be made at a later date (i.e., after they liquefy some funds, after they get paid for the project that they're working on, after the cow jumps over the moon), they may not be telling you that several other people already are waiting in line for the money or that the IRS has already filed a tax lien on their future assets. An asset search can help you to weigh the situation before putting your own assets at risk.

WHAT TYPES OF RECORDS ARE AVAILABLE?

Real Property—A home represents the largest asset many Americans will ever own. Real property records will identify homes owned by an individual as well as land and business properties. These can be found online for many areas of the country.

You should also be aware that people who are trying to hide their income sometimes pour money into an existing asset such as their home equity, thereby paying down the mortgage while protecting the funds (if their property is protected by homestead law).

Bank Accounts—Banks do not give individuals or private investigators access to lists of their account holders or to their account information online. Public records can, however, sometimes lead you to identify bank accounts. Some of the Company databases also sometimes list the name of the bank or banker, which can help you to locate their bank accounts, as explained in Chapter Twenty-three—Bank Records. Examples of databases that include this banking information for at least some of their company records include:

- ABC Europe Production Europex (available online through DataStar and FIZ Technik)
- Business Who's Who of Australia (available online through AUSINET)
- COMLINE Japanese Corporate Directory (available online through DataStar and NEXIS)
- Company Intelligence (available online through DataStar, Knight-Ridder, and NEXIS)
- Dun & Bradstreet Swiss Companies Full Financial Data (available online through DataStar)
- Dun's Market Identifiers (available online through CompuServe Information Service, DataStar, Dow Jones News/Retrieval , and Knight-Ridder; Refer to Appendix L for the address of CompuServe, and Appendix N for the others)
- Dun's Million Dollar Directory (available online through Knight-Ridder and NIFTY-Serve)
- Hoppenstedt Germany (available online through DataStar, FT PROFILE, GENIOS Wirtschaftsdatenbanken, Gesellschaft fur Betriebswirtschaftliche Information mbH (GBI), Knight-Ridder, and QUESTEL•ORBIT)
- KOMPASS Israel (available online through Infomart Online)
- Standard & Poor's Register—Corporate (available online through CompuServe Knowledge Index, Knight-Ridder, LEXIS, and NEXIS)
- Taiwan On-Line Business Data Services (available online through F.B.R. Data Base Inc.)
- World Trade Center NETWORK (available online through GE Information Services (GEIS))

(Refer to Appendix N for the addresses of these vendors, except where otherwise noted.)

Bank loans may also be found on credit records. Since people often obtain loans from banks where their accounts are held, any loan from a bank found on a credit report may warrant further investigation.

Motor Vehicles—Department of Motor Vehicle records can be used to locate motor vehicles, including automobiles, trucks, trailers, commercial vehicles, motor homes, buses, motorcycles, off-road vehicles and snowmobiles. Many public records vendors, as well as some of the DMV's themselves, offer online searching of these files.

Boats—The DMV also registers motorized boats in their vessel registration files, and many of these can be searched online. Watercraft of 27 feet or more, or 5 net tons or more, can also be found on the U.S. Coast Guard Watercraft file offered by some of the public records vendors, including LEXIS.

Aircraft—The Federal Aviation Administration registers all individuals and businesses who own aircraft throughout the United States. Some public records vendors also offer these records.

Business Assets—Along with such personal assets as a home and car, people may own very significant business assets. Corporate and Limited Partnership records, Fictitious Business Name Statements (or DBAs—Doing Business As), and Uniform Commercial Code filings (in which they may promise business assets as collateral for a loan) can all point you to businesses in which a person has a financial interest. These are all offered by public records vendors.

Many, many company databases list principals and key executives of businesses. The persons named may have financial interest in the companies that they operate as well.

Stock Ownership—Many databases identify owners of more than 5% of a publicly held company, information that must be declared on Form 13D of the Securities and Exchange Commission. Some of these databases also identify the holdings of company officers, directors, and principals owning 10% of a firm's equity.

Company databases also sometimes list shareholders. Examples of databases that include names of shareholders are:

- Analysis (available online through ARK Information Services)

- CIFARBASE (available online through GENIOS Wirtschaftsdatenbanken and NEXIS)

- COMLINE Japanese Corporate Directory (available online through DataStar and NEXIS)

- Company Credit Reports (available online through COSMOSNET)

- Company Intelligence (available online through DataStar, Knight-Ridder, and NEXIS)

- Datastream Company Accounts (available online through Datastream International Ltd.)

- DATEX (available online through Kiwinet)
- Dunsmarketing (available online through QUESTEL•ORBIT)
- FP Corporate Survey (available online through Infomart Online)
- GEOSOC (available online through O.R. Telematique)
- INFOCHECK (available online through DataStar and
  The Infocheck Group, Ltd.)
- Insider Trading Monitor (available online through CDA/Investnet, and
  Knight-Ridder)
- Jordans Shareholder Service (available online through Jordan & Sons Ltd.)
- Mergers and Acquisitions Database (available online through
  The Infocheck Group, Ltd.)
- NEEDS-COMPANY (available online through NEEDS
  (NIKKEI Economic Electronic Databank System))

(Refer to Appendix N for the addresses of these vendors.)

Some public records vendors, such as Information America, also offer a stock owner-ship search among their asset searching services. Information America's stock search details stock transaction and holding information for directors, executive officers, and shareholders who control at least 10% of stock in a public company. Proposed sales notices of restricted securities are also included.

For more information on this subject, see also Chapter Eleven—Competitive Intelligence.

Charitable and Political Contributions—Large contributors to political candi-dates can be found in the news, as well as on many databases (as explained in greater detail in Chapter Thirty-five—Political Records).

Philanthropists can also be found in the news, and on the fundraising databases described in Chapter Thirteen—Prospect Research (Fundraising).

People who make large contributions to charitable or political causes usually have substantial assets behind those contributions, so this type of information can help you to gauge the size of the assets that you're going after.

Civil Records—During civil suits, business holdings and personal assets often become part of the public record. Detailed information that would not otherwise be public may be subpoenaed by the courts or found in the discovery process by the attorneys involved in the case.

During a divorce, assets of both parties are normally presented to the court, and agreement is reached as to how they can be split most equitably. A spouse may be aware of hidden assets that they wish to share in, so they may present this evidence in court, where it again becomes public knowledge. They may have even hired a private investi-gator to locate offshore accounts, penthouses purchased for mistresses, or money earned through illicit activities. In the worst divorce cases, scandalous amounts of information can be uncovered.

The civil record indices offered by public records vendors can point you to the location of civil suits, which may then be obtained from the court or records building in order to find out what has already been uncovered in previous cases.

Criminal Records—If a person has been tried for fraud, grand theft, embezzling, or other crimes, it is possible that many of their financial dealings and assets may be documented in the criminal records. Although this level of detail won't be found online, the criminal record indices offered by many public records vendors can point you to the existence and location of this information.

Probate Records—If a person has inherited money, jewelry, art, real property, or other valuable items, this may be found in probate records, which sometimes can be searched online through public records vendors. Again, the online records are only an index to the actual records, which exist at the county court or records building.

Tax Liens, Bankruptcies, and Judgments—Detailed financial records are normally introduced during bankruptcy proceedings. Tax liens and judgments can also provide records of assets and debts. All of these can be found online in many areas of the country through public records vendors.

Some databases offered by more mainstream business, financial, or news database vendors focus on business litigation or personal and corporate bankruptcies. Suits, judgments, satisfaction, bankruptcies, and foreclosures all can be found on databases such as these. Examples of databases of this type include:

- Bankruptcy (available online through Securities Data Company, Inc., Financial Database System) provides information on companies that have filed for bankruptcy.

- Canadian Bankruptcy File (available online through Infomart Online) which contains summary data on approximately 280,000 personal and business bankruptcy filings in Canada, as well as data on approximately 900 trustees (i.e., parties who administer bankruptcies).

- Dun's Legal Search (available online through Dun & Bradstreet Business Credit Services) which contains public record information for businesses in all U.S. states.

- SANP, also known as Italian National Archive of Protests or Italian National Defaulters File (available online through CERVED International, S.A.) contains default information on individuals and corporations, from the official default bulletin of local Chambers of Commerce.

- SCRL Defaillances (available online through DataStar and QUESTEL•ORBIT) contains announcements of current liquidation and bankruptcy judgments by French commercial courts prior to their publication in the Bulletin Officiel des Annonces Civiles et Commerciales (BODACC).

(Refer to Appendix N for the addresses of these vendors, except where otherwise noted.)

Company databases also frequently carry legal information about companies, including bankruptcies, civil suits, and judgments. Refer to Appendix C for examples of company databases.

News articles and newswires also describe financial difficulties encountered by some businesses, including bankruptcies and judgments. They also record profits, business mergers, and other such information. Federal Filings Business Newswire (available online through Dow Jones News/Retrieval) is one newswire that often contains financial information. This database provides proprietary news, financial data, and investment research from the U.S. Securities and Exchange Commission (SEC), other federal government agencies, Capitol Hill, and bankruptcy courts.

One publication carried online is focused specifically on bankruptcies. *National Bankruptcy Reporter* (available online through NewsNet) contains the complete text of the publication *National Bankruptcy Reporter,* which provides in-depth coverage of bankruptcy filings. This publication/database includes the name of the company, principals/contacts, and their addresses and assets and liabilities.

Some news database producers have also separated bankruptcy and other financial notices into their own searchable databases. For example:

- CAPA (available online through BELINDIS) contains more than 96,000 citations to public notices appearing in the *Moniteur Belge*, the Official Journal of Belgium. It covers persons and companies declared bankrupt or who have applied for a deed of arrangement with creditors, as well as persons deprived of certain rights (i.e., legally disabled) or placed under guardianship.

- *The Daily Reporter* (available online through DataTimes) contains bankruptcies, liens, notices (e.g., bidding, circuit court, city), and permits (e.g., building, burial) listed in *The Daily Reporter* (Milwaukee, Wisconsin) newspaper.

(Refer to Appendix N for the addresses of these vendors.)

Credit records list such public records as bankruptcies, liens, and judgments on personal and business credit profiles. The credit agencies also sometimes offer additional databases for searching business litigation as well. One such database is the Business Litigation Database, offered by Trans Union Credit Information Company. This database contains court records on companies from New York and New Jersey, including information on: suits, judgments, satisfactions, bankruptcies, foreclosures (for New Jersey only), and federal, state, and city tax liens.

Credit Information—Debts are not the only thing you can find on credit records. A loan from a mortgage company may indicate that your subject is paying for property, which may be listed under another name. Vehicle loans or inquiries from car dealers may lead you to other vehicles owned by an individual, even though they may not be registered in your subject's name.

When someone has a great deal of credit card debt but indicates that they have no assets, one can't help but wonder where the money was spent. This may cause you to do more digging into their assets or lead an attorney to request additional documentation to corroborate their story of where the money went.

As noted earlier, public records also are sometimes included on credit records.

Although all three national credit agencies offer credit records online, along with numerous credit bureaus throughout the country, anyone wishing to access personal credit information must have a legally permissible purpose, as defined by the Fair Credit Reporting Act. For further information, please refer to Chapter Twenty-five—Consumer Credit Records. However, the FCRA does not restrict access to business credit records.

Uniform Commercial Code (UCC) Indices—UCC Filings can be very helpful in documenting assets that have been used as collateral for loans. The online indices do not contain detailed asset information, but they do allow you to locate the records, so that the full detail can be obtained from the courts. Please refer to Chapter Thirty-one—Public Records for additional information about these records.

Assets in the News—Additional personal and business assets are sometimes discovered in the news. A magazine or newspaper article may cover a fundraiser being held on someone's yacht or their purchase of fine art at a Sotheby's auction. At times, the news reveals even detailed financial information.

For example, an article from the June 26, 1990 edition of the *New York Times,* entitled, "Quick: Who'd Have Trouble Living on $450,000 a Month?" listed some of the huge expenses paid by Donald Trump each month. It also mentioned several of his assets, including:

- his personal 727 jetliner
- his 282-foot yacht
- his $2,000 suits
- three homes, including Mar-a-Lago, in Palm Beach, Florida; a 118-room residence; and his 50-room penthouse triplex in Manhattan's Trump Tower, which comes complete with an 80-foot living room, bronze-edged floor-to-ceiling windows overlooking Central Park, and a 12-foot waterfall.

Additional articles discussing his various business assets might also be found through a search of news databases.

WHAT'S MISSING?

Bank Accounts—A person may have funds in banks from one end of the country to the other. Although some public records can point to bank accounts, there may still be funds held in many bank accounts that you won't discover online.

Insurance Policies—Unless an insurance policy is discovered as an asset in a public record (such as a divorce settlement), you may not be aware that the subject is insured. One reason these can be important is that a person might prepay a policy (especially one that gathers interest) in order to hide assets there.

Assets in Areas That Are Not Online—Many counties, courts, and other agencies have not yet made their records accessible online. Even when a public records vendor offers a statewide search, the fine print often notes that the search accesses all available counties. This can leave broad gaps in what is actually searched.

If records are gathered in a haphazard manner, the vendor may well miss some records when they are entered into the online system. For example, a public records vendor may actually go to the county court, pick up, and scan a stack of new files every Friday. This procedure can easily miss a file that is being used in court on that day or is sitting on someone's desk.

When records are scanned or manually entered into a system, some of the writing on the records may not be legible or can be misread. In that case, the record may be indexed in such a way that it will never be found online.

Assets Held Under Aliases or Unknown Associates—Although you may be able to anticipate some of the names under which assets are hidden (i.e., names of relatives, close friends, business associates, and businesses), and perform searches under them, assets may still elude you if they are listed under aliases or have been transferred to associates that you're not aware of.

One way to uncover some of these assets is to perform an online search for real estate whose taxes are billed to a person's mailing address, but even this precaution will overlook real estate that is not linked to an individual through any known address or name, just as it will miss other assets that remain hidden.

Money—If a person is trying to hide his or her assets, he or she may purchase savings bonds, cashier's checks, or just keep cash in a home safe or hiding place. Database searching alone will seldom help much in discovering this.

Off-shore Holdings—If a person is sending money to offshore accounts, you may have no way to discover it online. For this reason, attorneys will sometimes subpoena telephone and telefax records, overnight delivery receipts, passports and travel agency records, and hotel receipts (which often note telephone calls made.) This sometimes can reveal suspicious activities, such as calls to Switzerland or trips to the Cayman Islands.

Summary

Although many assets can be discovered online, it may still be necessary to hire a private investigator specializing in asset investigation, and/or to subpoena additional records from the individual, in order to gain a full assessment of their financial status. Database searching skills are becoming increasingly important, and can make an asset search more efficient and thorough, but investigative skills, analytical skills, and experience still are of greatest importance.

For additional information on performing asset searches, consider reading books on background research and investigative reporting; many are listed later in this book in Section IV "Where Can I Find More Information?—Books." You may also find books specifically on asset searching or private investigation, which should also be included on your reading list.

Organizations that you can learn from include those focused on asset searching, debt collection, fundraising/prospect research, legal research, private investigation, and public records research. Lists of these types of organizations are also included in Section IV under "Organizations."

Publications focused on competitive/business intelligence, fundraising/prospect research, investigative journalism, and private investigation can also provide information on different perspectives on asset searching. See "Periodicals" in Section IV.

Competitive Intelligence

C ompetitive intelligence is loosely defined as gathering information about one's business competitors. It includes collecting knowledge of one's industry and anything that can affect the industry or the business. This can encompass factors such as technological developments, shifts in the economy, changes in legislation and regulations, and mergers and acquisitions. Databases can make the task of tracking all of these areas much more manageable.

On the personal side, competitive intelligence includes knowledge of the people involved in the industry. Businesses are made up of people, and changes in that composition can have dramatic effects on businesses and industries.

Who's Who?

In order to track personnel, you must first identify them. You can find the names of some key players in any industry mentioned in the news whenever articles are written about their companies.

There are also dozens of company/business databases that include the names and positions of key personnel and company contacts. A list of business credit and financial databases that include personal information can be found in Appendix C.

One more way to identify key personnel is to search business and professional directory databases online and on CD-ROM. (Refer to Appendices D and E for listings of these databases.)

The Internet is becoming increasingly useful as a source for this type of information. A growing variety of companies, both large and small, now maintain their own World Wide Web home pages on the Internet. Many of these sites include press releases and the names of key individuals within a company. At the least, these listings include the names of the CEO, president, or other spokesperson. Sometimes the names of scientists, or those responsible for important developments within the company are also listed. A few Web sites give access to the entire corporate directory. These are not standard listings, or necessarily searchable as a database would be, but they can add details that would not easily be found otherwise.

Corporate Musical Chairs

The departure of a company president or chief executive officer is quite newsworthy and will often coincide with some type of shake-up in the company, frequently taking the form of a reorganization. The classic move for the new management is to streamline the operation, cutting costs, eliminating functional redundancies, and sometimes replacing the old guard with their own trusted people.

Companies looking for a clear opportunity to get a jump on their competition can take advantages of times like these, hoping that the upheaval taking place inside their competitor's company will delay the introduction of new products and services into the market. Continually scanning the news (newspapers and newswires) for announcements of the departure of key executives and appointments of new executives is vital to companies whose market position is dictated by their ability to get a product to market first. For public companies, a change of key executives may also cause the generation of an SEC filing, which can also be searched online.

Current Awareness

Current Awareness, Alert Service, Selective Dissemination of Information, and SDI are all names for the continuous monitoring of a particular subject or set of subjects. This is a common practice in competitive intelligence research, where the need for information never ends and seldom is limited to any single topic. Some of the database vendors have automated current awareness searches. They make it possible to enter search terms along with a search interval—daily, weekly, bi-weekly, monthly, and so on. The system then repeats the search automatically at the stated interval and sends the results into the researcher's online mailbox. This saves the time required to perform the same search repeatedly, and it often costs less. Not all systems can automate Current Awareness searches yet. To use the rest, the searcher must re-run the query by hand as often as necessary.

For competitive intelligence, it is important to set up the Current Awareness parameters to search not only for company and personnel names, but for appointments, promotions, resignations, retirement, and other significant changes in personnel that can affect competitors. When the target company is a subsidiary of a larger corporation, the important changes may be made at another, higher level of the organization, so one must be sure to also include the parent company and other affiliated companies in the search.

Where Have They Been? What Have They Done?

Once you have identified the key players in an industry, you will want to know more about them in order to try to predict what they might do next. Databases can assist you in locating or developing your own biographical dossier on each person. Some of the best predictors of future actions can be found in their past, so you will want to know where they have worked, and what they have accomplished before. Executives with a history of turning companies around and making them profitable can be considered important adversaries; they should be watched closely.

You may also be able to identify their previous business associates, who might be able to provide insight into their character and work style. In a close-knit industry, it is sometimes possible to find a friend of a friend who knows the former business associate and can set up an interview. It is also possible that some former associates are already on your own staff.

There are executives who, although extremely successful, are difficult to work with. News articles have been known to go on at length about a successful, albeit demanding, explosive, or domineering personality. Executives with a history of sexual harassment, drunk driving, or other problems that can affect the workplace are also sometimes exposed in the news. All this information may be found through a database search reaching back several years. Former associates can also provide this type of information.

This kind of problem personality can create hard feelings among colleagues and subordinates. When one is identified at another company, it may be possible to take advantage of that information by courting and then pirating away some of the competition's best people. This can have the dual effect of improving one's own business and crippling the opposition.

What Are They Thinking?

Listening closely to the competition is important, as they will sometimes explain their plans for their company in great detail. Their predictions for the future of the industry often reveal the direction in which their company is moving. Interviews with key executives, or articles or books by them, should always be read with this in mind.

CEOs and high-level executives are frequently called upon to give speeches, which reveal their assessment of the industry, along with their predictions for the future. They may even have occasion to testify before Congress; if so, their names will appear in such sources as *Congressional News,* which is searchable online. (Refer to Chapter Thirty-five for information about political records.)

Impressions and summaries of speeches often make their way into the news, but the most important competitive details, and the context of any statements made, can sometimes be lost in these synopses. In fact, the article may offer little more than the speaker's name, the topic, and where the speech took place. When this is the case, it may still be possible to contact the organization that sponsored the speech and order a copy of the conference or meeting materials handed out to the attendees.

On the other hand, when a speech is attended by a knowledgeable business analyst, the ensuing article can include not only key points made in the speech, but further analysis and insights into the speaker's impact on the industry.

Excerpts of notable speeches by prominent businesses can sometimes be found online in the newsletter *The Executive Speaker,* available through NEXIS.

The complete text of speeches can also be found in a few of the databases. The *Wall Street Transcript,* available online through DataTimes, contains verbatim speeches by chief executive officers to security analyst groups. *General Meetings Speeches,* available online through Gesellschaft fur Betriebswirtschaftliche Information mbH (GBI), contains the complete text of speeches made at the general meetings of German companies.

Predictions also are sometimes found on a company's home page on the Internet. The full text of speeches are sometimes included, and annual and interim reports also sometimes contain this kind of information.

There's nothing like seeing your competition in action. If you'd like to attend a meeting which an important executive will be attending, or where he or she will be speaking in order to draw your own conclusions, and possibly even have the opportunity to question him or her directly, you can find scheduled conferences, events, trade fairs, and meetings listed on many databases. Three of the most prominent are FAIRBASE (available online through OVID, DataStar, FIZ Technik, and Gesellschaft fur Betriebswirtschaftliche Information mbH (GBI)); Federal News Service Washington Daybook (available online through News-Net), and Global Meeting Line (available online through Global Meeting Line, Inc.)

A call to the conference registrar can often confirm whether any of the executives that you are tracking will speak or attend. If you cannot attend an upcoming conference or meeting, tapes, transcripts, or other handouts can frequently still be obtained, sometimes even before the event.

Transcripts from radio and television broadcasts, many of which can be found on databases, also can offer an excellent chance to find out what an executive is thinking.

Stock Ownership

As part of their compensation package, many executives receive stock in their company. They may also purchase shares on their own. There is nothing unusual or particularly revealing about that. What can be telling is a change in the ownership patterns. For example, if several members of a company's board were to dump all of their stocks suddenly, you could bet that something was brewing. If a company executive regularly accrued a given number of stocks each year and then uncharacteristically sold them all at once, that might be a step toward leaving the company. If a company president immediately sold off all the company stocks received each year as part of their compensation package, one might also question their emotional investment or faith in the company.

Several databases can be used to monitor the purchase and sale of company stocks by key executives and major shareholders. Please refer to Chapter Ten—Asset Searches for examples of these.

Business Predictions Hidden in Public Records

Sometimes public records can reveal a company's plans. For example, when a company buys real estate, there may be a plan to expand or relocate. If they wish to keep that information confidential, they may purchase the property under the name of an executive or the corporate attorney.

A company may also hide public transactions under a separate name that has been set up for this purpose. Searching for fictitious business name statements (or DBAs—Doing Business As) under the names of key executives can sometimes reveal the existence of another business being operated under an executive's name. Corporation and Limited Partnership records can also expose this.

When a company is having financial or legal difficulties, the principals also will sometimes start a new corporation before declaring bankruptcy and/or closing the old business. For competitive intelligence research, the formation of a new corporation under the names of a competitor's key executives should at least cause one to investigate further.

Inventions and new products developed by scientists or others within a company may be patented in the name of the inventor or employee rather than in the company's name. Searching the patent databases under the names of key personnel as well as companies can alert you to an impending change in products or reveal new products that they may plan to introduce to the market. Likewise, they may trademark the names of new products before they are introduced to the marketplace, and a search of the trademark databases can be helpful in discovering them.

If executives purchase property a fair distance from their employers, one might also suspect that they are planning to move on. Of course, there are other possibilities, such as a vacation home or an investment, so one shouldn't jump to conclusions based on this type of information alone.

As a last example of the usefulness of public records, when an executive is in trouble due to drunk driving, assault, or other criminal convictions, it does not take too much of a leap to conclude that changes in the company will result from a conviction.

Summary

Companies that regularly research their competitors have found databases to be of tremendous assistance in this task. This is not only because of the depth and breadth of the information available, or the convenience of accessing it from their offices, but also because database vendors will keep their interest in their target companies confidential.

Competitive intelligence, however, does not normally stop at database research. Primary research, such as talking with people in the industry and with their competitors, suppliers, and customers, is another important part of developing a complete picture of an industry.

Companies that want information about their competitors can discreetly search the databases in order to track both developments in the industry and the activities of their competition; however, calling the competitors and finding someone willing to talk, send information, or provide their insights into the business and the industry are tasks usually best handled by a third party, such as a market research firm or information brokerage. After all, how much time would you be willing to spend educating your competitors?

For further information on competitive intelligence, you can learn from professional research organizations such as the Society of Competitive Intelligence Professionals (SCIP), which is listed in Section IV "Where Can I Find More Information?—Organizations."

The Information Professionals Institute offers a seminar on "Finding Competitor Intelligence Online—Commercial and Internet Sources." IPI's Web site is:

http://www.ipn.net/ipi

Books on background research and investigative reporting should also shed some light on the subject, and periodicals focused on competitive and business intelligence, investigative journalism, and private investigation may also give you additional insight into this type of research. These are all listed in Section IV.

Two excellent Internet Competitive Intelligence sites include those of Fuld & Co. at:

http://www.fuld.com

and at:

http://www.cipher-sys.com

Identifying an Expert

There are many definitions of an expert. Webster defines an expert as "having, involving, or displaying special skill or knowledge derived from training or experience." Oscar Wilde had another definition: "An ordinary man away from home giving advice." The first time I was paid to travel 3,000 miles to give a speech, I knew that I officially qualified as an expert, by Oscar Wilde's definition if not by Webster's.

There are many reasons to need an expert and just as many definitions under which one might qualify. In order to find the right expert, you need to know how the experts special knowledge will be used.

Preparing a Legal Case

Attorneys frequently rely on experts to testify in court. Forensic experts may be needed to explain a type of testing or to validate or dispute a test result being used as evidence. A medical expert may testify to the likelihood of a person coming out of a coma intact, when the family is petitioning to turn off life support.

Not all experts are from scientific fields. An expert from law enforcement may be called upon to explain the proper administration of a choke hold or how to subdue a person under the influence of PCP. Pyrotechnic experts may testify to the inherent dangers of using fireworks and the proper procedures for avoiding accidents. A financial expert may be asked to explain what a junk bond is and how risky this type of investment is in financial terms.

Experts such as these often are called into court to testify in hopes of lending further credence to the attorney's argument before the judge or jury. In these cases, the expert's credentials (degrees, positions held, years of experience, membership in professional associations, and awards won), previously published opinions, experience testifying in court, agreement with the attorney's position, ability to express ideas clearly and succinctly, ability to stand up to cross-examination, willingness and availability to testify in court, personal warmth before a jury, and many other factors may be weighed in seeking the ideal expert witness.

Planning a Meeting

A conference planner may need to identify many experts for any given meeting. One may be needed to give the keynote speech, others to serve on panels, and still others to lecture on a variety of topics. In order to attract greater attendance, more renowned experts will often be preferred, especially as the keynote speaker.

When a panel of experts is to appear at a conference, it usually is best that they hold a variety of opinions or can speak from various perspectives or experience in order to ensure a lively discussion. A debate may also be planned, in which one expert is needed to present the pro argument, while the other presents the con. In other conference sessions, a speaker may be sought to teach a basic or advanced class on a topic requested by the previous year's attendees.

Conference planners must often balance the need for big names with the desire to present certain topics that are of most interest to the attendees.

Recruiting New Employees

Recruiters, or "headhunters," as they often are called, are frequently asked to find prospective employees with a given level of expertise in a specified field. In some cases, the best candidates hold similar positions in competing organizations and must be identified. In other cases, a company may wish to pursue a new venture and needs someone who can advise them, possibly on a contract basis. The recruiter must normally rely on the employer to define criteria that the candidate must meet and then find prospects who fit the profile.

Pursuing the Unknown

Nearly all researchers must sometimes locate experts. Information brokers or researchers, such as myself, often find that an expert can cut through a great deal of information quickly, explaining the most significant points and providing insight and direction that can cut a research project's life cycle in half. The expert may be a scientist or technician who can put complex ideas into simpler language, or it may be an industry insider who can bring a historical perspective to current events in the business or help to read current signals for indications of what might happen next.

Scientific researchers also need to locate experts in order to discuss previous research findings, determine whether additional research is underway, but not yet published, or even to bring these experts in to collaborate on a project with other experts.

The expert's experience and accomplishments may be irreplaceable. In choosing an authority to consult, these may be given more weight than other credentials, such as degrees and current professional associations.

Producing a Talk Show

The recent explosion of talk shows appearing nearly every hour on several competing television stations, not to mention radio, brings up an obvious question: How in the world do the producers find enough guests who are worth watching? For some programs, it is not terribly difficult. There seems to be no shortage of people eager to talk about how they cheated on their spouse with another family member, got more than one woman pregnant at a time, or hate their twin. Other talk shows focus on celebrities, so their need for outside experts may also be small. However, some talk shows invite experts on to educate and enlighten us, to debate political issues, or at least to provide perspective or glib repartee on sensational topics.

Each talk show has its own criteria for what makes both an expert and a good talk show guest. It may not be enough to be the author of a new book, president of a university, the victorious attorney from a famous legal case, the head of a nonprofit organization, or even a Nobel prize winner. Guests must also be able to speak up, keep pace with the show, and perhaps mix in just the right amount of humor and entertainment value.

Writing an Article, Book, Play, or TV Show

Journalists often seek out experts for interviews or quotes. They sometimes also need to find experts on each side of an argument, in order to present both sides fairly, so the experts' published opinions can help narrow the field.

Authors of books and screen plays also consult with experts in order to obtain facts and anecdotes that can add texture to a story, opinions on whether something reads realistically, or sometimes just to learn the language that a character might use.

Television writers on shows like "ER" and "Chicago Hope" have experts on the set who teach the actors how to do everything from taking a temperature to performing open heart surgery, or at least how to appear as if they can. Cop shows often use consultants from law enforcement as well. Even soap opera writers call in experts to advise them about a story line from time to time, such as when a character will be struggling with drug dependence or AIDS.

In these cases, the expert's ability to tell a story, or relate to the story being told, adding anecdotes and nuances that make the tale ring true, may be their most valuable assets. Their experience and knowledge are essential, but their title or credentials will be more important to a journalist than to a screen or soap opera writer who is gathering information, rather than quoting the source. Experience as a consultant on a television or movie set (especially on a successful film or series) may also weigh heavily in establishing them as an expert. The entertainment industry does, after all, understand film credits.

HOW CAN YOU IDENTIFY AN EXPERT?

Expert Witness Directories—Attorneys have the advantage of being able to turn to directories of experts when they need an expert witness. The individuals listed in these directories have normally established themselves as experts within their fields, as well as having indicated their willingness to appear in court to testify. Any of the following directories, all available online, might be used in order to locate expert witnesses:

- ExpertNet (available online through West Publishing—WESTLAW) contains information on physicians available to serve as expert trial witnesses or consultants to attorneys in medical malpractice and personal injury cases.

- Forensic Services Directory (available online through LEXIS and West Publishing—WESTLAW) contains the names of scientific, medical, and technical experts available to serve as expert trial witnesses or consultants to attorneys, corporations, and the government.

- Technical Advisory Service for Attorneys (available online through West Publishing—WESTLAW) contains information on individuals in a variety of occupations available to serve as expert witnesses or as consultants to attorneys.

(Refer to Appendix N for the addresses of these vendors.)

Professional directories are another source of experts. Directories for many professions are available online and on CD-ROM; many are listed in Appendix D. The advantage a database directory offers over the same information in book form is that it usually can be searched by not only a person's name, but by their field of expertise, geographic location, degrees, and many other useful criteria. This makes it possible to review the credentials of a known expert as well as to discover other potential experts based on your own criteria. Some of the professional directory databases that are most useful in identifying an expert include:

- BEST Great Britain on CD-ROM (available on CD-ROM from Longman Cartermill Ltd.) includes BEST Great Britain—which contains qualifications for scientists and researchers in U.K. public sector institutions.

- BEST North America (available online through Cartermill Inc.) which contains information on research and development activities at major North American universities and research institutions. One of the six files included in this database is Expertise, which provides information on researchers, scientists, engineers, physicians, and others in the research community.

- Information USA (available online through CompuServe; refer to Appendix L for their address) which contains information on free or low-cost information, grants, or other resources available from U.S. state and federal government agencies. Among other things, this database includes names and telephone numbers of some 9000 experts in various fields.

- Management Experten-Nachweis (available online through Gesellschaft fur Betriebswirtschaftliche Information mbH (GBI)) which contains information on corporate and individual management experts in the fields of science, marketing, business, and business consulting in Austria, Germany, and Switzerland.

- SVERKER (available online through BYGGDOK) contains information on Swedish senior civil engineers available to advise younger colleagues.

- Texas Faculty Profiles (available online through Knowledge Express and Texas Innovation Network System (TINS)) contains profiles of experts at some 50 public and private Texas universities in all science and engineering disciplines, as well as medicine, agriculture, arts and humanities, and business.

(Refer to Appendix N for the addresses of these vendors, except where otherwise noted.)

Association Directories—Associations are an important resource for any researcher. Associations often maintain libraries of information that might otherwise be impossible to tap into. There is an association for virtually any trade, hobby, or interest in the world. If you doubt it, stop by a library and peruse a print copy of the *Encyclopedia of Associations*.

Associations also are a valuable resource for locating experts, who know everything you ever wanted to know about ferrets, yo-yos, aircraft commutators, natural childbirth, or almost any other subject. Databases of associations that are available online or on CD-ROM include:

- Consultants and Consulting Organizations Directory (available online through HRIN, The Human Resource Information Network) which contains information on organizations and individuals available as consultants to business, industry, and government

- Deutsche Unternehmensberater (available online through GENIOS Wirtschaftsdatenbanken) which contains biographical profiles of 300 members of the German Association of Consultants

- Directory of Associations in Israel (available online through Israel National Center of Scientific and Technological Information (COSTI)) which contains information on scientific organizations, technical associations, industrial laboratories, and research institutes in Israel

- DIRLINE (available online through MEDLARS) which contains information on organizations that provide information in their areas of specialization

- Encyclopedia of Associations (available online through Knight-Ridder, OCLC EPIC, and OCLC FirstSearch Catalog) which provides detailed descriptions of international and United States national, regional, state, and local membership organizations in all fields

- Encyclopedia of Associations CD-ROM (available on CD-ROM from SilverPlatter Information, Inc.) which provides detailed descriptions of international and United States national, regional, state, and local membership organizations in all fields

- Encyclopedia of Associations: National Organizations of the United States (available on CD-ROM from Gale Research Inc.) which contains detailed descriptions of national organizations

- Information Sources in the UK (available on CD-ROM from Aslib, The Association for Information Management) which contains information on organizations that provide subject-specific information free of charge or on a fee basis

- NRCM Database (available online through United States Library of Congress Information System) which provides information on organizations that are qualified and willing to answer questions or provide information in their areas of specialization

- Soviet Public Associations Directory (available online through Gesellschaft fur Betriebswirtschaftliche Information mbH (GBI), MagnaTex COMMUNICATE!, and SovInfoLink) which contains information on associations, institutions, and organizations in the Commonwealth of Independent States (C.I.S.)

- Verbande, Behorden, Organisationen der Wirtschaft (available on CD-ROM from Verlag Hoppenstedt GmbH, Wirtschaftsdatenbank) which contains profiles of German and international institutions and associations

- Yearbook of International Organizations on CD-ROM (available on CD-ROM from Bowker Electronic Publishing) which contains information on organizations in 225 countries

(Refer to Appendix N for the addresses of these vendors, except where otherwise noted.)

Company Directories—Company directories can be another good source of experts. Almost anyone in a key position of an important company could be assumed to have some expertise and insight into the industry. In a smaller or close-knit industry, it is not too unusual to find a company insider who has also worked for the competition and has something to say about them as well.

Business credit and company financial databases, such as those found in Appendix C, often are indexed by position, making it easy to identify company presidents, some senior executives, corporate attorneys, and a variety of other positions, which vary from one database to the next.

Staff directories of politicians and those in the political arena can also be found online and on CD-ROM. (Refer to Political Directories in Chapter Thirty-five for further information on this.)

Some companies have also set up their own bulletin boards or databases that are accessible online. To find out whether there is such an online site, it is usually necessary to check with the company directly and request instructions for dialing into their system. More and more of these resources are now found on the Internet, however, and can be located through any of the standard Net search tools without first contacting the company. Any of these sites may contain a company directory.

Biographical Databases—Biographical directories in print are seldom very useful in identifying experts because the entries are usually listed in name order and may not be indexed by specialty, experience, or other useful criteria. Once converted to computer media, however, biographical databases take on whole new dimensions. Suddenly it becomes possible to find experts by a combination of indexed fields and free-text searching, which can help to pinpoint the people with the attributes you need. Examples of biographical databases can be found in Appendix A.

Articles That Cite An Expert—Another way to identify an expert is to take another expert's word for it. If writers of articles in respected trade journals often cite someone as an expert, that person may at least be worth consideration and further research.

Some databases, such as SciSearch on Knight-Ridder, have defined fields for cited authors, cited inventors, and cited references. This makes it much easier to determine how important a cited work is, or how often an expert is cited, without confusing the author of a given article with writers who are cited within the article.

Knight-Ridder's search software offers a command that allows one to RANK the results of a field. RANK cited authors, and it provides a list of authors according to the number of times other writers have cited their publications, providing the number of citations for up to 50 authors. If you need the most-cited authors in articles over the last two years, you can first narrow your set by date before RANKing the results. When looking for experts, the RANK command can be very useful.

Articles By An Expert—Expertise in a field can also be narrowed down by their published works. When a potential expert is identified, you can look at what they have written in order to find out whether their publications touch on subjects of interest and to gain some understanding of their work and opinions.

Authors who have written a great deal about a subject can also be identified through use of the RANK command (on Knight-Ridder), by RANKing the author field.

For example, using the PsycINFO database on Knight-Ridder, I searched using the descriptor code for Multiple Personality, which is 32480. (Many other search terms could be used, but for the sake of the example, only this one was chosen.) This search resulted in 602 matching articles. I narrowed the sample by selecting only those articles published between 1990 and 1995; this left 296 hits. RANKing that set by author resulted in a listing of the top 50 authors, ten of which are included here:

DIALOG RANK Results

RANK: S5/1-296 Field: AU=File(s): 11
(Rank fields found in 296 records—322 unique terms)

RANK No.	No. Items Ranked Term
1	14 ROSS, COLIN A.
2	11 COONS, PHILIP M.
3	10 KLUFT, RICHARD P.
4	7 PUTNAM, FRANK W.
5	7 BOWMAN, ELIZABETH S.
6	6 VAN DER HART, ONNO
7	6 FRASER, GEORGE A.
8	6 LOWENSTEIN, RICHARD J.
9	6 MILLER, SCOTT D.
10	5 BOON, SUZETTE

Be aware that even writers who have published a great deal on a given subject may turn out to be journalists, rather than practitioners. If you are looking for expert practitioners rather than expert journalists, some of the entries found may need to be discarded.

Of course, not all publications are available online, so an expert who writes for airline magazines and other publications found only in print may not be located through an author search.

Encyclopedias can also be useful for identifying experts: Simply find out who wrote the section that pertains to your field of interest. The author will be an expert, almost by definition. Refer to Appendix F for a list of encyclopedia databases available online or on CD-ROM.

Award Winners—People who win awards may also be considered experts in their fields. Announcements of awards can often be found in trade journals, newsletters, and even newspapers and newswires. Many of these news publications can be found online. You might pay particular attention to newspapers in the geographic area of the organization that is bestowing the awards, in order to find an announcement or list of the winners.

If you anticipate an upcoming competition or annual awards ceremony, you might also ask the organization that will be giving the awards to send you the announcement of the winners as soon as possible, or find out from them where the announcement will be released. The awarding organization should also be able to provide contact information on all winners and contestants.

Transcripts From Other Legal Cases—When looking for expert witnesses (or experts to be interviewed), one useful technique is to look at similar legal cases and find out who testified in them. Legal databases such as LEXIS and WESTLAW can provide for this type of information. For example:

Jury Verdict and Settlement Summaries (available online through LEXIS and WESTLAW) contain summaries of personal injury jury verdicts and settlements. For each case, this database provides verdict or settlement amounts, case type, state and county where the case was tried or settled, party names, attorney names, expert witness names, and other factual information. (Refer to Appendix N for the addresses of these vendors.)

When you know that the opposing counsel plans to call an expert witness of their own, legal databases can also reveal cases where their expert has testified before, in order to find out how well they have done, whether they are likely to stand up under cross-examination, and whether their statements in court have been consistent with the information they will be presenting in your case. Of course, it makes sense to check out your own expert witnesses in this way as well.

Other background information, such as professional history and published works, can be important. In some cases, a complete background check may be warranted in order to avoid unpleasant surprises that could discredit your expert witness in court.

Experts Who Have Testified Before Congress—You will find more than politicians in Congress. Depending upon the issue being debated, you might find witnesses from nearly any industry or background. For example, the late musician Frank Zappa once testified before Congress rather eloquently on the subject of censorship.

If you agree that a person who has testified before Congress should be considered an expert, several databases may be helpful. The following include the names of witnesses who have testified before Congressional committees:

- A Matter of Fact (available online through OCLC EPIC and OCLC FirstSearch Catalog) which, among other things, contains materials, with accompanying comparative statistical content, extracted from testimony presented at Congressional hearings by witnesses considered to be experts in their field

- Congressional Information Service, Inc. (CIS) (available online through Knight-Ridder) which, among other things, contains abstracts of testimony given by individual witnesses or groups of witnesses

- Congressional Masterfile 2 (available on CD-ROM from Congressional Information Service, Inc. (CIS)) which, among other things, contains abstracts of testimony given by individual witnesses or groups of witnesses

- CQ Committee Action Votes & Rosters—Committees Database (available online through CQ Washington Alert Service) which provides comprehensive analysis of all committee and subcommittee action and votes, and includes, among other things, a witness list for each action

- CQ Committee and Floor Schedules (available online through CQ Washington Alert Service) which provides schedules for the U.S. House of Representatives, Senate, joint committees, conference committees, and floor votes for the next day up to three months ahead, and includes names and affiliations of witnesses for each meeting or hearing

- Statistical Abstracts from the A Matter of Fact Database (available on CD-ROM from SilverPlatter Information, Inc.) which, among other things, contains materials, with accompanying comparative statistical content, extracted from testimony presented at Congressional hearings by witnesses considered to be experts in their field.

(Refer to Appendix N for the addresses of these vendors.)

Transcripts From Talk Shows—If you are looking for an expert with experience on talk shows, you should be aware that transcripts from many television shows and radio broadcasts can also be found online. Several are described in Chapter Twenty—News.

You can also search book directory databases (such as those listed in Appendix B) in order to locate additional sources for talk show hosts. One of the best, the Yearbook of Experts, Authorities & Spokespersons (also known as the Talk Show Guest Directory), published by Broadcast Interview Sources, is available on the Internet at:
http://www.yearbook.com/

Online Bulletin Board Systems (Internet et al)—There is no shortage of expertise represented on the Internet. Using Alta Vista (one of the many Internet search engines), I searched for EXPERTS and found 351,651 Web sites (as of July 1996). HotBot (another Internet search engine) reported 221,235 sites for CONSULTANTS. I selected sites at random and found a mix of commercial services, companies involved in expert systems, lists of experts in particular fields, and searchable databases, among other things. Usenet newsgroups, Internet mailing lists, telnet and gopher sites, and World Wide Web pages all could help to identify and locate an expert in a particular field.

Lists of Usenet newsgroups for almost every conceivable topic can be found through the indices at:
http://www.yahoo.com/News_and_Media/Usenet/Newsgroup_Listings/

Bulletin boards and forums offered by other vendors (such as America Online, CompuServe, and Prodigy) can also contain a wealth of information, along with the advice of experts or contact with the experts themselves.

Appendix L contains a list of the main bulletin board vendors. Each of these services has an online directory, which is updated frequently as new forums and services are added. The best way to keep up with the ever-changing canvas of the Internet is to become familiar with the various search tools that can be used to navigate the Internet and discover current sites. The next best method is to rely on Internet books and directories such as the many varieties of "Internet Yellow Pages" and the various magazines that provide information about the Internet, lists of sites, and ways of using the Internet for research. Some of these can be found in Section IV "Where Can I Find More Information?—Periodicals."

There are many Internet sites and databases that I have found interesting for locating experts. One such database, Speakers Online, contains biographical information on many authors, celebrities, and other speakers who can be hired as speakers. An example of the type of information that you'll find at this site follows for Mike Ditka:

Mike Ditka

As a player, as a coach, and as a spokesman, Mike Ditka has firmly established himself among pro football legends.

After being named the 10th coach in Chicago Bear's history on January 20, 1982, Ditka led the Bears to an overall mark of 107-57. The Bears 52 regular season wins, between 1985-1988, are the most ever by an NFL team in any four year span. Ditka ranks second among Bear Coaches, in both tenure and victories, trailing only his first pro coach, George Halas, the team's founder and coach for 40 seasons.

During his coaching tenure Ditka guided the Bears to six NFC Central titles, three appearances in the NFC title game, and a Super Bowl victory. In 1985, the Bears posted an 18-1 record, a total matched only by the 1984 San Francisco 49ers. The Bears 1985 campaign was highlighted by a 46-10 Super Bowl victory over the New England Patriots. That same year, The Sporting News, Associated Press, and the pro football writers named Ditka Coach of the Year. Ditka is the only Bear coach to lead his club to five straight post season appearances.

Ditka was once again named Coach of the Year following the 1988 season during which the Bears compiled a 12-4 regular season record, topping the NFL. Chicago beat Philadelphia in the divisional playoff (20-12) before falling to the eventual Super Bowl champion San Francisco 49ers in the NFC title game at Soldier Field.

Ditka was the 21st Bear to be inducted into the NFL Hall of Fame (July 30, 1988).

Ditka is an NFL and PGA commentator for NBC Sports.

Additional speaker bios from this database, such as one for author and business expert, Tom Peters, along with information for contacting Speakers On-line can be found at:

http://speakers.com/

Faculty experts can be found from:

Brandeis:
http://www.brandeis.edu/news/experts/introduction.html

Clark University:
http://www.clarku.edu/resources/communications/experts/Introduction.html

USC:
http://www.usc.edu/dept/News_Service/experts_directory.html

Expert faculty sites such as these can be found for many other universities as well. They often are set up by the university public affairs office to assist the press in locating faculty experts.

A list of college and university home pages can be found at the following site. Many of these institutions maintain databases of experts on staff:

http://www.mit.edu:8001/people/cdemello/univ.html

The Community of Science Database is a searchable database of first-person expertise records from leading universities and R&D organizations in North America. Its purpose is to provide a comprehensive directory of faculty researchers and scientists and to connect academic and corporate researchers via the Internet and other electronic platforms. This type of database can be a valuable resource for locating experts who might otherwise not be identified, but you should consider a database of first-person accounts much like the Yellow Pages. If anyone can declare their own expertise in the database, as they would in an advertisement, you must carefully evaluate their credentials and qualifications in order to determine whether you agree with their claim of expertise. The Community of Science Database can be found at:

http://best.gdb.org/

The National Institute of Health Internet Web site includes a directory of scientific staff members, other key individuals, and guest researchers who had been at NIH for a year or more as of January 1, 1994. This Web side can be found at:

http://www.nih.gov/

There are many indices for biologists located at:

http://muse.bio.cornell.edu/misc/directories

Organizations with expertise in artificial intelligence can be found at:

http://www.aaai.org/Organizations/ai-organizations.html

One of the Internet sites set up specifically to help you find people with particular interests can be found at:

http://scilib.ucsd.edu/people-org/people.html

Summary

After reading this chapter, it should be clear that there are many definitions for an expert, and nearly limitless ways to identify them.

After identifying an expert, one normally must still locate them and speak with them in order to determine whether they are really suited to your purpose, whether they are willing to assist you, and whether they are available at the time needed. You can refer to Chapter Six—Locating People for further information about how to find them.

After identifying an expert, evaluating their qualifications, locating them, and interviewing them, the final decision of who is the best suited for the job often is a subjective one. The database resources available should help to identify prospective experts in nearly any area, but the final decision should not be left to a database.

For further information on identifying experts, there are publications such as the newsletter, *The Expert and the Law* (available online through NEXIS), which covers the application of scientific, medical, and technical knowledge to litigation, along with the Online Research and Database publications listed later in Section IV "Where Can I Find More Information?—Periodicals." The magazines *ONLINE* and *DATABASE* also have carried excellent articles on the use of databases in order to locate experts. Organizations, like the professional research organizations and the legal research organizations listed in Section IV "Where Can I Find More Information?—Organizations," can also be good sources of additional information.

Prospect Research
(Fundraising)

Another way that personal records are used is for prospect research, which is one piece of the fundraising effort. When an organization is looking for donations, it seldom makes sense to spend their limited resources sending mailings or contacting people who do not have much money. Rather than going after a few dollars from many people, some organizations find it more productive to go after larger sums from fewer donors. Prospect research seeks to identify those people who are most likely to donate funds.

Prospect research typically involves more than personal records. Businesses, foundations, and even the government can also be good prospects for donations or grants.

Prospect researchers also normally use more than database resources. Print directories, newspapers, and magazines that are not yet online can be just as useful. Personal knowledge of the who's who or social elite, or the aid of someone traveling in wealthy social circles may be the most valuable resources that an organization can have in obtaining funds.

Nonetheless, databases can help to identify many people who have the resources and possibly the willingness to donate large sums to a good cause.

News

News databases can be of great assistance to a prospect researcher. Articles talk of people's assets and personal wealth every day. News articles even rank the wealthiest people in America, or the wealthiest people in computers or other industries.

When a celebrity speaks out for a cause, it can bring them to the attention of organizations supporting it. For example, talk show host and actress Ricki Lake was sentenced to community service after being arrested for participating in a protest against the use of fur, during which property damage took place. Animal rights organizations could have added her to their lists of prime candidates for donations as a result.

Large donations can also be found in the news, such as when someone pays to add a new wing to a hospital. Even organizations with unrelated causes may add these donors to their lists simply because of their wealth and their demonstrated willingness to give to a good cause.

Campaign Contributions

Information about campaign contributions can also identify individuals who have money and may be willing to donate it. For further information about campaign contributions, please refer to Chapter Thirty-five—Political Records.

Public Records

Public records can sometimes aid in assessing wealth. Real property records, for example, can reveal whether someone is a renter or owns a particular home, and whether the home is an expensive one. Performing a search using a person's name, it is also possible to locate all of the homes and real property that they own in a state. The geographic coverage for this type of searching varies from vendor to vendor, but some statewide searches are available.

Most public records systems require a name or an address in order to perform a real property search, so searching by the value of the home in order to locate all of the expensive homes within an area is seldom possible. There are a couple of exceptions to this rule though. DataQuick Information Systems and TRW REDI can both provide this type of information. (Refer to Appendix M for their addresses.)

Telephone Directory Databases

Even telephone directories can be used to locate wealthy prospects. When one rich person is found, a telephone directory database able to search by address can reveal any neighbors who have listed telephone numbers. Public records vendors sometimes offer "neighbor" searches that provide similar data. It is possible that a wealthy person's neighbors may be renters and others who may not be wealthy. After all, not every rich person lives among the rich. However, there are neighborhoods in which riches are the rule, rather than the exception, and telephone directory databases can be used to scour these neighborhoods, street by street, in order to locate candidates who are at least suspected of having wealth.

Motor Vehicle Records

Sometimes the department of motor vehicles sells lists of people who own a particular type of vehicle. Car dealers often use these lists in order to send out coupons for repairs or to make other offers. These databases could also be very useful in locating wealthy individuals: Rolls Royce owners seldom are poor.

Not all DMVs in all areas of the country sell this information, and access sometimes is restricted to the vehicle industry. In this case, fundraisers cannot obtain these records directly from the DMV.

Mailing list companies sometimes can provide this type of information as an alternative, which may come from other sources, such as warranties and questionnaires.

Mailing Lists

Mailing lists of wealthy individuals and philanthropists can be purchased on diskette. Though sometimes costly, this is probably the quickest, easiest way for an organization to acquire a database of hundreds or thousands of wealthy prospects. Some of these individuals have donated large amounts in the past. Some mailing lists target people who have donated to a particular type of cause or who have made multiple donations. Others consist of people who own expensive cars, or have almost any type of interest or hobby, or profession. People with an expensive hobby or a well-paid profession might be wealthy or at least have sufficient income to consider them as prospects.

For further information on mailing lists, please refer to Chapter Nineteen— Mailing Lists.

Foundations and Grants Databases

There are foundations and grants databases such as the Foundation Directory, Foundation Grants Index, GRANTS (all available online and on CD-ROM through Knight-Ridder), and Prospector's Choice (available on CD-ROM from The Taft Group). Rather than identifying individual philanthropists, these databases list organizations that provide money to worthwhile causes. For additional information about foundations and grants, some home pages on the Internet index numerous other sites. These include:

The Foundation Center's Home Page at:
http://fdncenter.org/

Information about the Grants Database can be found at:
http://www.oryxpress.com/grants.htm#grntdb

Summary

Although many databases assist a prospect researcher or organization in seeking funds, most prospect researchers supplement them with other information sources. When prospective contributors are identified, some must still be located. Contact must then be made with them. This can take many forms, and if not done tastefully, eliciting sympathy and conveying the necessary information inoffensively, even the best prospect list may produce few contributions.

Fundraising must include not only research skills and experience, but marketing savvy, public relations, and great people skills, in order to obtain the best results.

For further information on prospect research and fundraising, please refer to Section IV "Where Can I Find More Information?" for listings of periodicals and organizations. Information about additional publications can be found on the Internet, including:

Philanthropy News Digest:
http://fdncenter.org/phil/

Foundation News & Commentary:
http://int1.cof.org/fnc/

You can also find the Council on Foundations Publications Catalogue at:
http://int1.cof.org/docs/printed.html

A few more Internet sites that may be of interest to prospect researchers follow:

The Philanthropy Journal, including Philanthropy-Related Links:
http://www.philanthropy-journal.org/

Association of Professional Researchers for Advancement Home Page:
    http://weber.u.washington.edu/~dlamb/apra/abtapra.htm

Virtual Prospect Research:
    http://members.aol.com/Marthamur/murphy/index.html#table

The Office of Development Research at Northwestern University:
    http://pubweb.acns.nwu.edu/~cap440/

The Grantsmanship Center:
                            http://www.tgci.com/

GrantsWeb:
                http://web.fie.com/cws/sra/resource.htm

    Several fundraising books and directories can be found at:
                    http://www.oryxpress.com/books/

Private Investigation

Private investigation involves more than database searching. Investigators are also called upon to provide protection and security, surveillance, and other "hands on" services that cannot be performed from behind a desk. Insurance companies and attorneys both commonly rely on private investigators (PIs). Businesses and individuals turn to private investigators as well.

Many private investigators use subterfuge (or pretense), disguises, inside contacts (in the police department, telephone company, or banks, for example), and electronic devices in their assignments. These all are far beyond the scope of online research and will not be covered here. However, many private investigators are coming to rely on the use of online and CD-ROM databases as important components of their investigative toolbox.

Public Records

Private investigators have always relied on various types of public records. This used to involve spending hours or days digging through physical records at county court houses and records buildings. This is still necessary in some cases, but online indices to public records are now available for many areas of the country. This allows an investigator to do a more thorough job of locating public records, while reducing the need to travel from one court house to another or to hire investigators in other areas to search for records that may not even exist. When a record appears in an online index, the investigator can then visit the court house or send someone to pick up a copy of the full record. Sometimes it even is possible to order a physical copy through the online system.

The ability to search for records across an entire state, or even nationwide, and to search through civil, criminal, probate, and other records at one time has made online databases much more cost effective than old-fashioned "legwork." The bottom line is that a private investigator can do a more thorough job in less time, for less money, and dedicate more of the budget to other types of investigative work. (Refer to Chapter 31 for further information about public records.)

Motor Vehicle Records

Many private investigators also rely heavily on motor vehicle records. Private Investigators who provide surveillance need to be able to identify people who come and go from a watched location, as well as who is seen with their target. The ability to run a quick database search to learn who owns a vehicle makes it possible to perform this task much more efficiently. (Refer to Chapter 27 for further information about motor vehicle records.)

Telephone Directories

Telephone directories also are extremely useful in investigative work, but PIs often require information that standard phone books cannot supply. Often, the investigator must perform a reverse directory search; instead of simply looking up someone's telephone number, it is necessary to begin with a number or an address and find a name. Sometimes old telephone directories are more helpful than the current version. Until recently, this forced investigators to store old phone books from across the country. Even then, searching through dozens of bound directories was never easy.

CD-ROM telephone directories make it possible to store phone directories from the entire country in an inch of shelf space, or less. They also make it far more convenient to search for someone across a wide geographic area, to locate everyone with a given surname in order to track down relatives, to search by address in order to find out who lives at a given location, and to search by address range in order to locate a person's current or former neighbors.

Some CD-ROM telephone directories are available exclusively by lease, with upgrades provided only after the previous discs are traded in. These may be an attractive choice for other professions, but they are not generally as useful to investigators who are not disposed to giving up old phone directories, whatever their form. Not all CD-ROM databases allow different types of reverse directory search. Some vendors charge a premium for their databases with all of these capabilities, and a lesser price for their databases that provide only a name search. These factors often influence an investigator's choice of telephone directory databases. (Refer to Chapter 17 for further information on telephone directories.)

Not All Private Investigators Use Databases

Not all private investigators use databases. This depends in part on the PI's specialty. Although I can't think of a single area of investigation that would not benefit from the availability of additional information, some private investigators do not feel that they need database research. Some simply are not inclined to spend the time or expense in developing database research skills. Others do not get along with computers, do not want to spend any more time than necessary in the office, or are not interested in becoming proficient at database searching, for whatever reason. For these PIs, information brokers/researchers can provide this service, thereby freeing them to pursue other areas of investigation.

Researchers can search not only public records, but business, news, and legal databases, filling in company and industry financial information, news, product announcements, names of key executives, information on expert witnesses, and other pieces of the investigative puzzle. Even investigators who are loathe to touch a computer can benefit from the databases now available through an intermediary. Information brokers offer a valuable resource to many private investigators, while other P.I.s are honing these skills themselves in order to expand their investigative capabilities.

Bulletin Boards

The development of online bulletin board systems is also changing the investigator's trade in some ways. Private investigators who had previously worked alone now may find a wide range of colleagues available to help them in all areas, at any time of the day or night. Investigative techniques and resources can be shared, friendships forged, referrals made, and partnerships formed, all through the use of online bulletin board systems. When investigators need help in a distant city, or even another country, or need someone with special expertise, or access to resources that they lack, one of their online colleagues often can supply just what they need.

On CompuServe, one place that private investigators meet is in the Investigators section of the Crime Forum. Investigative resources also are springing up on the Internet. A list of them can be found at The Private Investigation Home Page:

http://165.247.199.212/pihome/index.cgi

The Internet also carries Usenet newsgroups, such as alt.private.investigator. A mailing list for both private investigators and information professionals (i.e., information brokers) is also available on the Internet. Information about this mailing list, and the email address with instructions for joining, can be found at:

http://www.ipn.net

The PI Mall is described by its sponsor, the National Association of Investigative Specialists (one of the largest national PI associations and also publisher of *PI Magazine*), as "a one-stop shop for finding a Private Investigator on the World Wide Web." At the PI Mall, you can view different Private Investigator Web sites, search for a PI in your state, and shop for PI shirts and books. If you are interested in becoming a PI, the PI Mall offers encouragement and resources. Find the PI Mall at:

http://www.pimall.com

The Bodyguard Home Page, offered by International Association of Personal Protection Specialists & Executive Protection Associates, Inc., can be found at:

http://www.iapps.org/

The Cyber Bounty Hunter Home Page, offered by Western States Bail Recovery Association & Asset Recovery Group, Inc., is located at:

http://www.bounty-hunter.org/

There is also no shortage of private investigators who have put up their own home pages on the Internet. Visiting these, or the sites noted above, will lead you to an almost unending chain of additional sites of interest to private investigators.

Further Information

Many books address particular aspects of investigation, such as surveillance, fraud investigation, background investigation, and public records research. A list of books on public records research and another list on background research and investigative reporting are both included in Section IV "Where Can I Find More Information?—Books."

If you are serious about investigation, you might also consider joining one of the organizations for private investigators. A list of some of these also appears later in this book.

Finally, many publications can teach you more about the field of private investigation. These include not only magazines about private investigation, but also publications dealing with competitive/business intelligence, investigative journalism, online research, and databases. Lists of these types of publications are also provided in Section IV "Where Can I Find More Information?—Periodicals."

III.
TYPES OF PERSONAL RECORDS

Biographies

For "one-stop-shopping" on the personal information superhighway (to borrow a much over-used phrase), biographies are a great place to start, and there are many from which to choose.

Biographical Book Directories

Biographical books often contain information that it has taken someone else years to dig out. Autobiographical books may include personal revelations and a perspective that could be found nowhere else.

Although many directories can be used to search for books about a person, a single database search can scan through many of these directories at once, providing a list of the books in print, as well as those out of print.

For example, the Books in Print database, produced by the R. R. Bowker Company, includes all of the information in the most current printed editions of all of the following publications:

- *Books in Print*
- *Subject Guide to Books in Print*
- *Forthcoming Books*
- *Subject Guide to Forthcoming Books*
- *Books in Print Supplement*
- *Scientific and Technical Books in Print*
- *Religious and Inspirational Books in Print*
- *Medical and Health Books In Print*
- *Books Out-of-Print*
- *Paperbound Books In Print*
- *Children's Books In Print*
- *Subject Guide to Children's Books In Print*

A search of this database for Marilyn Monroe renders 170 listings, one of which is:

DIALOG(R) File 470:Books In Print
(c) 1994 Reed Reference Publishing. All rts. reserv.

1400382 1631960XX STATUS: Active entry
TITLE: My Story
   AUTHOR: Monroe, Marilyn
   PUBLISHER: Madison Bks UPA PUBLICATION DATE: 07/1986 (860701)
   LCCN: N/A
   BINDING: pap.—$3.50
   ISBN: 0-8128-8283-0

VOLUME(S): N/A
ORDER NO.: N/A
IMPRINT: Scrbrough Hse
STATUS IN FILE: New (87-05)
SUBFILE: PB (Paperbound Books in Print)

LIBRARY OF CONGRESS SUBJECT HEADINGS: MONROE, MARILYN, 1926-1962 (00312968)
PAPERBOUND BOOK SUBJECT HEADINGS: BIOGRAPHY-GENERAL (00000255)

If I were interested only in those books in which the name Marilyn Monroe appears in the title, another search could narrow the list to 54 books, including such listings as:

- *Marilyn Monroe: Photographs 1945-1962*
- *The Murder of Marilyn Monroe*
- *Norma Jean: My Secret Life with Marilyn Monroe*
- *Goddess: The Secret Lives of Marilyn Monroe*
- *Joe & Marilyn: The Tragic Love Story of Joe DiMaggio & Marilyn Monroe*

I could search further for books in which Marilyn Monroe was the subject, regardless of the title, finding additional listings such as "The Birth of Marilyn: The Lost Photographs of Norma Jean."

Reviews of the books can also be extracted from this database, making it possible to evaluate them before deciding which to order or to track down. This type of database can be of great assistance when researching what has been written by or about someone.

Refer to Appendix B for a listing of additional book directory databases.

Biographical Books

Actual books are now being placed online and on CD-ROM, and some of them are biographical works. For example, if you consider the Bible, the Book of Mormon, or the Koran to be biographical works, versions of each can be found in full text on a database either online, on CD-ROM, or on both. These can also be found in full text on the Internet.

Other biographical works available on the Internet include:

- *My Bondage and My Freedom* and *Narrative of the Life of Frederick Douglass* (American writer, orator, abolitionist and former slave) by Frederick Douglass
- *Letters of a Woman Homesteader* by Elinore Pruitt Stewart
- *The Autobiography of Benjamin Franklin*

For listings and locations of other online books, you can visit the The Online Books FAQ (Frequently Asked Questions) Page on the Internet:

http://www.cs.indiana.edu/metastuff/bookfaq.html

or Alex, A Catalog of Electronic Texts on the Internet:

http://www.lib.ncsu.edu/stacks/alex-index.html

Encyclopedias are another example of books available online, as well as on CD-ROM.

Encyclopedias

Encyclopedias have probably been used to study historical figures since the first was invented in the year 961. (I got that from an encyclopedia!) Putting today's encyclopedias into databases has had a number of benefits, aside from the adding the excitement of sound bytes and video action.

First, an encyclopedic database is likely to have much better search capabilities than any printed volume can. Searching for a name can point out all of the places where it occurs in the encyclopedia, so you're less likely to miss a citation.

Second, CD-ROM encyclopedias may be updated more frequently than the print version, and may contain relatively current information about people and events. An online encyclopedia may be updated even more frequently, so encyclopedias should rightfully be considered even when researching contemporary persons and events.

Third, CD-ROM encyclopedias are often relatively inexpensive compared to the print version, and access to the online version often is included with subscriptions to services such as America Online or Prodigy. A CD-ROM encyclopedia is sometimes thrown in when purchasing a CD-ROM player or a computer.

A last benefit is that a whole set of encyclopedias can fit onto a single CD-ROM or can be accessed through online services. For those for whom space is a problem, this represents a change for the better.

Refer to Appendix F for a listing of additional general encyclopedia databases.

Biographical Index Directories

Many companies produce biographical directories. These may be general directories, containing information about notable people from virtually any walk of life, or they may target specific groups, such as attorneys, women in science, or Asian Americans. So many biographical works are now available in electronic form that there are databases that index the directories themselves.

Biography Master Index (BMI), produced by Gale Research Inc. (and available online through Knight-Ridder as File 287), is a master key to biographical information on over 3,000,000 persons who have distinguished themselves in hundreds of fields. BMI indexes approximately 630 biographical dictionaries and directories, including current works such as:

- *Who's Who in America*
- *The International Authors and Writers Who's Who*

and retrospective sources such as:
- *Medieval Women Writers*
- *Biographical Dictionary of American Science, 17th-19th Centuries*

A search of BMI for Walter Cronkite renders extensive listings of 91 citations for Mr. Cronkite. Some excerpts from these listings follow:

DIALOG(R) File 287: BIOGRAPHY MASTER INDEX
(c) 1994 Gale Research Inc. All rts. reserv.

9274946
Cronkite, Walter 1916-

Authors in the News. A compilation of news stories and feature articles
from American newspapers and magazines covering writers and other
members of the communications media. Volume 1. Edited by Barbara
Nykoruk. Detroit: Gale Research, 1976. (auNews 1)

Celebrity Register, 1990. Detroit: Gale Research, 1990. Biography Contains
portrait. (CelR 90)

Childhood in Poetry. A catalogue, with biographical and critical
annotations, of the books of English and American poets comprising the
Shaw Childhood in Poetry Collection in the Library of the Florida State
University. First Supplement. By John Mackay Shaw. Detroit: Gale
Research, 1972. (ChhPo S1)

Contemporary Heroes and Heroines. Detroit: Gale Research, 1990. Use the
Index to locate individuals found in group biographies. Biography
contains portrait. (ConHero)

Contemporary Theatre, Film, and Television. A biographical guide featuring
performers, directors, writers, producers, designers, managers,
choreographers, technicians, composers, executives, dancers, and
critics in the United States and Great Britain. Volume 6. Detroit: Gale
Research, 1989. Earlier editions published as "Who's Who in the
Theatre." (ConTFT 6)

Encyclopedia of Twentieth-Century Journalists. By William H. Taft. Garland
Reference Library of the Humanities, vol 493. New York: Garland
Publishing, 1986. (EncTwCJ)

The Facts on File Encyclopedia of the Twentieth Century. Edited by John
Drexel. New York: Facts on File, 1991. Biography contains portrait.
(FacFETw)

The Lincoln Library of Social Studies. Eighth edition. Three volumes.
Columbus, OH: Frontier Press Col., 1978. Biographies begin on page 865
of Volume 3. (LinLib S)

Political Profiles. "The Johnson Years." Edited by Nelson Lichtenstein.
New York: Facts on File, 1976. (PolProf J)

Who's Who in the World. Fourth edition, 1978-1979. Wilmette, IL: Marquis
Who's Who, 1978 (WhoWor 78)

The World Almanac Biographical Dictionary. By the editors of "The World
Almanac." New York: World Almanac, 1990. (WorAlBi)

Journalists of the United States. Biographical sketches of print and
broadcast news shapers from the late 17th century to the present. By
Robert B. Downs and Jane B. Downs. Jefferson, NC: McFarland & Co.,
1991. (JrnUS)

Who's Who in America. 47th edition, 1992-1993. Two volumes. New
Providence, NJ: Marquis Who's Who, 1992. (WhoAm 92)

Who's Who in the East. 24th edition. 1993-1994. New Providence, NJ:
Marquis Who's Who, 1992. (WhoE 93)

Please note that these are only excerpts; many additional Cronkite citations are
available on BMI. As this demonstrates, this type of search can guide you to many of
the biographical directories and dictionaries that contain information about a person.

Other databases used to index biographical works include: Wilson Biography Index,
EPIC and FirstSearch Catalog (both from OCLC), and Biography & Genealogy Master
Index CD-ROM (from Gale Research Inc.). These databases contain references to information in biographies, autobiographies, memoirs, journals, diaries, biographical fiction, critical studies, juvenile literature, and periodicals, publications like *Who's Who*,
major biographical dictionaries, handbooks, and directories.

On the Internet, there is also an Index to Biographies from the MacTutor History of Mathematics archive can be found at:

http://www-groups.dcs.st-and.ac.uk/~history/Alphabetical.html

Biographical Directories

After searching the biographical index directories, the next step is to search the indexed directories. Unfortunately, not all biographical directories are available on databases yet, so you may have to track down some of the sources manually. However, a great many are available online or on CD-ROM, and the number is always increasing.

One of the biographical databases now available is Marquis Who's Who. It contains over 97,000 profiles drawn from:

- *Who's Who in America, 42nd edition*
- *Who's Who in America, 43rd edition*
- *Who's Who in America, 44th edition*
- *Who's Who in Frontiers of Science and Technology, 1st edition*
- *Who's Who in Frontiers of Science and Technology, 2nd edition*

The individual biographies in this directory range in length from a few lines to a few pages, and may list not only a person's professional accomplishments, but personal information about the subject's family, home address, and more. Since the subjects themselves provide the information collected in many of these directories, they may volunteer facts that would not otherwise be found or be public knowledge. However, information may also have been concealed or presented in an unrealistically favorable light.

A search of the Marquis Who's Who database (via Knight-Ridder) for auto magnate Lee Iacocca renders the following listings:

DIALOG(R) File 234: Marquis Who's Who
(c) 1994 Reed Reference Publishing. All rts. reserv.

00260218 Record provided by: Biographee
Iacocca, Lido Anthony (Iacocca, Lee)
   OCCUPATION(S): former automotive manufacturing executive
   BORN: Oct. 15, 1924 Allentown, Pa.
   PARENTS: Nicola and Antoinette (Perrotto) I.
   SEX: Male
   FAMILY: married Mary McCleary, Sept. 29, 1956 (dec.); married Darrien
     Earle, March 30, 1991; children- Kathryn Lisa Hentz, Lia Antoinette
     Nagy.
   EDUCATION:
     ME, Princeton U., 1946
     BS, Lehigh U., 1945
   CAREER:
     chmn. bd. chief exec. officer, Chrysler Corp., Highland Park, Mich.,
     1979-93
     pres., chief operating officer, Chrysler Corp., Highland Park, Mich.,
     1978-79
     pres., Ford N.Am. automobile ops.

pres., Ford Motor Co. (Ford div.), 1970-78
exec. v.p. of co., Ford Motor Co. (Ford div.), 1967-69
v.p. car and truck group, Ford Motor Co., 1960
gen. mgr., Ford Motor Co. (Ford div.), 1960
v.p., Ford Motor Co.
vehicle market mgr., Ford Motor Co., 1960
car mktg. mgr., Ford Motor Co., 1957-60
truck mktg. mgr. div. office, Ford Motor Co., 1956-57
dist. sales mgr., Ford Motor Co., Washington, 1946-56
successively mem. field sales staff, various merchandising a, Ford
Motor Co., Phila.
With, Ford Motor Co., Dearborn, Mich., 1946-78
CAREER RELATED:
bd. dirs. Chrysler Fin. Corp.
CREATIVE WORKS:
Author: Iacocca: An Autobiography, 1984, Talking Straight, 1988.
CIVIL/POLITICAL ACTIVITIES:
Past chmn. Statue of Liberty-Ellis Island Centennial Commn.
AWARDS:
Wallace Meml. fellow Princeton U.
MEMBERSHIPS:
Mem. Tau Beta Pi.
CLUBS AND LODGES: Detroit Athletic

As you can see, this record is noted as "Provided by Biographee." In other words, Mr. Iacocca provided this information, so you may find details that would be difficult and time-consuming to dig out elsewhere. These listings can also sometimes note political and religious affiliations, avocations, and even home addresses.

The information can be very detailed and extremely helpful when researching a famous person, but you will also find many lesser known and unknown people in these directories. Although Carole A. Lane is far from a household name, I received applications from several of the biographical directories shortly after starting my research business, so you never know who will turn up in one of these, or what they will divulge.

Refer to Appendix A for a listing of additional databases that contain biographies.

Biographical Newspaper Articles

Hundreds, if not thousands, of newspapers are now available online and on CD-ROM databases. These range from national papers such as the *New York Times* to local papers such as *Grants Pass Daily Courier*. Some of these papers are carried with the full text of the articles, while others are only indexed or carry abstracts of the articles, which can be ordered separately.

Magazines, journals, and newsletters also are available in databases, providing coverage of nearly every interest under the sun.

Any of these news sources may contain biographical articles. Some of the database vendors segment biographical articles into separate databases or database sections in order to simplify search and retrieval. Others provide search indices on persons named in the articles, while still others must be searched in their entirety in order to locate information about a person.

A few examples of biographical databases taken from news sources are:
- The *Associated Press* Candidate Biographies
- *Los Angeles Times* Biographical Stories
- *New York Times* Biographical File
- *The Washington Post* Biographical Stories

Other Biographical News

In addition to newspapers, some magazines and journals publish biographical articles, many of which are available as databases, either online or on CD-ROM. Television programs also feature biographical pieces on personalities from all fields, and transcripts from some of them are now available online. News of upcoming programming of the television show "Biography" can also be found on the Internet at http://www.biography.com/watch. Refer to Chapter Twenty for further information about news sources.

Bulletin Board Services

Bulletin board services are a growing resource for biographical research. According to the *Encyclopaedia Britannica 1996 Book of the Year,* by the end of 1995, the Internet had at least 20 million users, and perhaps as many as 30 million. Millions of additional people use other bulletin board systems, such as America Online, CompuServe, and Prodigy, and many million more have at least visited online.

Within these online systems are sections where people meet to talk about specific topics or interests. These sections are often referred to as forums, newsgroups, discussion groups, or bulletin boards.

If you are looking for biographical information about a famous individual, there may well be a forum dedicated to storing and exchanging facts and opinions about that one person. A few examples found on the Internet:

- Walt Disney
- Albert Einstein
- Terry Pratchett
- William Shakespeare
- Wodehouse

Of course, anyone newsworthy can generate enough interest for a group of netizens to create another Usenet newsgroup. If your subjects are appearing in the news, you can use one of the Internet search engines in order to find out if there are newsgroups that are discussing them.

One caveat: The information found on the bulletin boards may be best characterized as opinion. There are experts on the forums whose opinions you might not have access to otherwise, and a great many learned people do participate. You may even find the neighbor or childhood friend of the person you're interested in. That said, much misinformation is also shared over these forums, and you should consider the information at best as hearsay, to be verified elsewhere if it is important to you.

General Indices

W henever you look for information, a general index search can provide an excellent starting place. An index can guide you to other files or databases (usually offered by the same vendor) containing information about your subject. One example of a general index is Knight-Ridder's Dialindex (File 411).

Dialindex

A search of Dialindex points you to other databases on Knight-Ridder's system in which your search terms were found. In the following example, I searched all of Knight-Ridder's files (using SET FILES ALL) to locate databases that contain information about actress Marisa Tomei (searching for MARISA within two words of TOMEI). No fewer than 93 different databases on this system contained one or more matching records. I have listed some of the resulting records here:

Your SELECT statement is:
   a marisa (2n) tomei

Items	File	
205	727:	Canadian Newspapers_1990-1995/Mar 15
133	647:	Magazine ASAP(TM)_1983-1995/Mar W2
109	638:	Newsday/New York Newsday_1987-1995/Mar 14
99	746:	Time Publications_1985-1995/Feb 27
97	630:	Los Angeles Times_1985-1995/Mar 16
94	484:	Newspaper & Periodical Abstr._1988-1995/Mar 14
91	703:	USA Today_1989-1995/Mar 14
40	88:	Academic Index(TM)_1976-1995/Mar W1
32	613:	PR Newswire_1987-1995/Mar 16
30	648:	Trade & Industry ASAP(TM)_1983-1995/Feb W3
29	260:	UPI Newx_Apr 1983-1994/Jan
28	611:	Reuters_1987-1995/Mar 16
27	16:	PTS Promt(TM)_1972-1995/Mar 15
19	570:	PTS Mars(R)_1984-1995/Mar 16
16	649:	Newswire ASAP(TM)_1995/Mar 15
14	111:	Natl. Newspaper Index(TM)_1979-1995/Mar
13	545:	Investext(R)_1982-1995/Mar 15
9	610:	Business Wire_1986-1995/Mar 16
8	299:	Magill's Survey of Cinema_-1995/Feb
8	715:	Christian Sci.Mon._1989-1995/Mar 13
7	636:	PTS Newsletter DB(TM)_1987-1995/Mar 15
5	614:	AFO English Wire_Jun 1991-1995/Mar 15
5	615:	AFP Intl French Wire_Aug 1991-1995/Mar 14

5	622:	Financial Times Fulltext_1986-1995/Mar 15
4	635:	Business Dateline(R)_1985-1995/Mar W1
4	15:	ABI/INFORM(R)_1971-1995/Mar W1
3	211:	Newsearch(TM)_1995/Mar 15
3	148:	Trade & Industry Index(TM)_1981-1995/Feb W3
3	261:	UPI News_Feb 1994-1994/May 23
1	541:	SEC Online(TM) Annual Repts_1995/Feb W4
1	287:	BIOGRAPHY MASTER INDEX_1980-1994
1	234:	Marquis Who's Who_1990-1994/Oct
1	621:	PTS New Prod.Annou.(R)_1985-1995/Feb W4
1	726:	S.China Morn.Post_1992-1995/Mar 16

93 files have one or more items; file list includes 396 files

As you might expect, many of the files that contain mentions of this actress are news files. You might be surprised to see that many cross into the financial arena, as the names of the actors and actresses in a film will often be mentioned when box office numbers and profits are tallied. Some biographical databases also contain information about Ms. Tomei.

When you are looking for a person of less renown, a DIALINDEX search sometimes can also point you to an article in a local newspaper where a person may be mentioned for participation in a group such as the Chamber of Commerce or the PTA, or where their promotion or wedding has been announced. One should not assume that indices such as these are useful only for researching the famous.

The previous example also turned up a few articles in the financial files, including File 542: SEC Online 10-K Reports and File 545: Investext. One might have overlooked these files when searching for information about Ms. Tomei, and this illustrates one of the ways in which a general index search can be particularly useful. General indices can point you to information that you would not have suspected otherwise, or take you in new directions after you have exhausted other possibilities.

Since the search criterion in this case was imprecise (searching for the word MARISA within two words of TOMEI), you also should be aware that the articles found may have nothing to do with the actress. References to JAMES TOMEI AND MARISA SMITH or JOHN MARISA OF TOMEI INTERNATIONAL, would also meet this search criterion. When searching for someone whose name is as unusual as Marisa or Tomei, I would use this imprecise kind of search and take the chance of a few poor matches.

When many references are found or when a subject's name is common, I would suggest adding other terms to your search criteria to screen out poor matches. The danger is that you may miss valuable information if your search criteria are too stringent or exclusive. You must balance these two factors in your search strategy. A search for Bob Dole, for example, would identify a great many pointers to other databases (and even more if one included references to Robert Dole), but some references would be for persons other than the former Republican Senator and Presidential candidate. Because his name is so common, one must either use more specific search criteria or retrieve and sift through a great many poor matches in order to uncover the occasional gem.

FamilyFinder Index

There are many CD-ROM databases that are produced for genealogical research. You can find quite a few (if not the majority) of them at the Family Tree Maker Online home page on the Internet at:

http://www.familytreemaker.com/

If you are interested in researching a person's lineage, there is a general index called the FamilyFinder Index which can be searched on the Internet, in order to indicate whether any of the Family Archive CD-ROM databases contain the name that you're seeking. The FamilyFinder Index contains approximately 115 million names from census records, marriage records, social security death records, actual family trees, and more. Approximately 20% of the people who have ever lived in the United States are listed there. This index currently includes:

World Family Tree CDs
World Family Tree: Vol. 1, pre-1600 to present
World Family Tree: Vol. 2, pre-1600 to present
World Family Tree: Vol. 3, pre-1600 to present

Family History and Pedigree CDs
Family Pedigrees: Everton Publishers, 1500-1990 (#15)
Family Pedigrees: GENTECH95 & ARI, 1500-1989 (#108)
Family Pedigrees: United Ancestries, 1500-1950 (#100)
Family History Collection: Virginia Genealogies #1, pre-1600 to 1900s (#162)

Marriage Index CDs
Marriage Index: LA, 1718-1925 (#1)
Marriage Index: IL, IN, KY, OH, TN, 1720-1926 (#2)
Marriage Index: AL, GA, SC, 1641-1944 (#3)
Marriage Index: MD, NC, VA, 1624-1915 (#4)
Marriage Index: AR, MO, MS, TX, 1766-1981 (#5)
Marriage Index: AR, 1779-1992 (#6)
Marriage Index: AZ, CA, ID, NV, 1850-1951 (#225)
Marriage Index: GA, 1754-1850 (#226)
Marriage Index: Selected States, 1728-1850 (#227)
Marriage Index: IL, IN, 1790-1850 (#228)
Marriage Index: KY, NC, TN, VA WV, 1728-1850 (#229)
Marriage Index: Selected Counties of Ohio, 1789-1850 (#400)
Marriage Index: Selected Areas of New York, 1639-1916 (#401)

Census Index CDs
Census Index: OH, 1880 (#20)
Census Index: Ireland, 1831-1841 (#197)
Census Index: Western PA, 1870 (#285)
Census Index: Eastern PA, 1870 (#286)
Census Index: NY City, 1870 (#287)

Census Index: Baltimore, Chicago, St. Louis, 1870 (#288)
Census Index: NC, SC, 1870 (#289)
Census Index: VA, WV, 1870 (#290)
Census Index: GA, 1870 (#291)
Census Index: Colonial America, 1634-1790 (#310)
Census Index: U.S. Selected Counties, 1790 (#311)
Census Index: U.S. Selected Counties, 1800 (#312)
Census Index: U.S. Selected Counties, 1810 (#313)
Census Index: U.S. Selected Counties, 1820 (#314)
Census Index: U.S. Selected Counties, 1830 (#315)
Census Index: U.S. Selected Counties, 1840 (#316)
Census Index: U.S. Selected Counties, 1850 (#317)
Census Index: U.S. Selected States/Counties, 1860 (#318)
Census Index: U.S. Selected States/Counties, 1870 (#319)
Census Index: U.S. Selected States/Counties, 1880 (#320)

Other
Social Security Death Index U.S., 1937-1995 (#110)
Military Records: U.S. Soldiers, 1784-1811 (#146)
State Index: Upstate NY, 1685-1910 (#160)
Mortality Index: United States, 1850-1880 (#164)
Cemetery Records: Salt Lake City, 1848-1992 (#168)
Land Records: AR, FL, LA, 1812-1907 (#253)
Land Records: MI, 1700-1908 (#254)
The Complete Book of Emigrants (#350)

Searching the FamilyFinder Index for genealogist and author Alex Haley, I found the following records:

Name	Est. Date	Location	Archive Type
Haley, Alex	b1800-1899	Unknown	World Family Tree
Haley, Alex ??? Negro	1850-1880	United States Mortality	CD 164
Haley, Alex Palmer	1500-1990	Worldwide Pedigree	CD 100
Haley, Alexander	1728-1850	KY,NC,TN,VA,WV	Marriage CD 229
Haley, Alexander	1789-1850	OH Marriage	CD 400
Haley, Alexander	1830	MD Census	CD 315
Haley, Alexander	1830	VA Census	CD 315
Haley, Alexander	1840	MACensus	CD 316
Haley, Alexander	1840	MD Census	CD 316
Haley, Alexander	1840	NC Census	CD 316
Haley, Alexander	1850	MA Census	CD 317
Haley, Alexander	1850	MS Census	CD 317
Haley, Alexander	1850	NCCensus	CD 317
Haley, Alexander	1850	NY Census	CD 317
Haley, Alexander	1860	MD Census	CD 318
Haley, Alexander	1860	NY Census	CD 318
Haley, Alexander	1870	MD,IL,MO Census	CD 288
Haley, Alexander	1870	MN Census	CD 319
Haley, Alexander	1870	New York City Census	CD 287

Haley, Alexander	1880	TX Census	CD 320
Haley, Alexander	1937-1995	Private	United States Social Security
Haley, Alexander		Private	World Family Tree
Haley, Alexander Chandler	b1860-1869	Unknown	World Family Tree

As you can see, this index points to the Family Archives CDs with records containing the name Alex Haley. As I know that author Alex Haley's name is actually Alexander Palmer Haley, I would suspect that the third record might pertain to a CD containing a pedigree either contributed by this same person, or one in which he was named. Since Mr. Haley was not born until 1921, I would rule out many of the other records as not directly pertaining to him, but they could provide information about a relative. Any of the remaining records could also refer to this author, another relative with the same name, or someone completely unrelated. I would need to check the corresponding CD to investigate this further. (The actual CDs can be ordered for your own use, but may also be found in the collections of some genealogical libraries or associations.)

Refer to Chapter Thirty-four for further information on genealogical records.

PUBLIC RECORDS INDICES

Public records vendors sometimes offer general indices that can point you to their other databases of public records. These are extremely useful in locating people or information when you have only a name, and no starting place for your search. Examples of public records general indices include Information America's Wizard and CDB Infotek's InfoPROBE. Refer to Appendix M.

A slightly different type of public records index is offered in CDB Infotek's Compu-Trace, available through CompuServe. This database does not guide you to CDB Infotek's databases, but instead points to areas of the country in which public records refer to your subject's name.

Information America's Wizard

Information America provides a system-wide search called Wizard. Wizard allows you to search all of Information America's online products simultaneously in order to identify where further information about your subject can be found. It then lists each of their databases with a Yes/No indicator stating whether matches were found.

Further information about Information America can be found on the Internet at:
http://www.infoam.com/welcome.htm

CDB Infotek's Info:PROBE Searches

CDB Infotek offers several general index searches called Info:PROBE searches, for use in locating information on individuals or businesses. These probes do not provide the actual records. Instead, they provide a list of records in which information exists matching a name that is entered. Their Info:PROBE searches include the following:

People Locator Info:PROBE
searching over 300 nationwide, regional, and local databases:

Nationwide Consumer Reporting Agencies
People Tracker
National Address Changes
Publishers' Mailing Lists
Motor Vehicle Records
Online Telephone Directories
County Assessor Records
Household Census Lists
Secretary of State Information
Professional Licensing Indexes
Registered Voter Profiles (Commercial States Only)
Dun & Bradstreet Full Business Reports
Bankruptcies, Liens & Judgments
Uniform Commercial Code Indexes

Individual and Business Asset Finder Info:PROBE
searching over 500 nationwide, regional, and local databases:

Motor Vehicle Ownership Searches
Real Property Ownership Records
Fictitious Business Names
Federal, State and County Tax Liens
Dun & Bradstreet Full Business Reports
UCC Filings
Bankruptcy Filings
Civil Court Judgements
Real Property Refinance, Construction Loan & Seller Carry-Back Information
Watercraft Searches
Tax Liens

Background Info:PROBE
searching over 600 nationwide, regional, and local databases:

Background On-line which provides nationwide access
Nationwide Felony & Misdemeanor Criminal Court Filings and Case Reviews
Driving Histories
Nationwide Upper and Lower Court Civil Court Filings
Nationwide Social Security Number Tracks
Professional Licensing
Dun & Bradstreet Full Business Reports
Consumer and Credit Reports
Business Market Identifiers
OSHA Searches
Bankruptcies, Liens & Judgments
Neighborhood Searches
Corporate/Limited Partnership Records
UCC Filings

Insurance Info:PROBE
searching over 400 nationwide, regional, and local databases:

Individual and Business Background Info:PROBE searches over 600 nationwide, regional, and local databases
Background On-line which provides nationwide access to criminal filings, drivers' records, Consumer Credit
    Employment Records, Social Security Tracks, Bankruptcies, Liens, Judgments, and more
Nationwide Social Security Number Tracks
Driving Histories
Death Records

> Bankruptcies, Liens, and Judgments
> Real Property Records
> Corporate/Limited Partnership Records
> UCC Filings
> Nationwide Felony & Misdemeanor Criminal Court Filings and Case Reviews
> Nationwide Civil Court Filings
> Professional Licensing
> OSHA Searches

Due Diligence Info:PROBE
searching over 600 databases:

> Bankruptcies, Liens, and Judgments
> Real Property Ownership Records
> Corporation & Limited Partnership Records & Document Retrieval
> UCC Filings & Document Retrieval
> Nationwide Civil Court Filings
> Nationwide On-Site Criminal Court Searches
> Dun & Bradstreet Full Business Reports
> Business Credit Reports
> OSHA Searches
> Professional Licensing

Individual and Business Pre-Trial Preparation Info:PROBE
searching over 400 databases:

> Nationwide Civil Court Filings
> Nationwide On-Site Criminal Court Searches
> Bankruptcies, Liens, and Judgments
> OSHA Searches
> Real Property Ownership Record
> Corporation & Limited Partnership Records
> Dun & Bradstreet Full Business Report

After performing an Info:PROBE search, you can search the actual databases found, at a discount from the normal search price. In fact, there is now a price cap on the searches performed as the result of an Info:PROBE, which can account for substantial savings over the per-search price.

For further information about CDB Infotek's databases, you can find them on the Internet at:

http://www.cdb.com/

CDB Infotek's CompuTrace

CDB Infotek's CompuTrace is offered on CompuServe. It contains a Living Individuals File, a Deceased Individuals File, and a Corporations/Limited Partnerships File.

The CompuTrace Living Individuals File contains information on over 140 million individuals nationwide whose names appear in telephone white pages directories, publishers' mailing lists, postal forwarding information, real estate files, and registered voter files. This information is updated quarterly. The Living Individuals File will normally provide name verification and the city, state, and ZIP code of the last reported residence for living individuals.

To illustrate how one might use this file to locate information about a person, I chose actor and comedian Kevin Kline. As his name is fairly common, it should come as little surprise that the search resulted in dozens of matches, or "hits." Since I knew that Mr. Kline was married to actress Phoebe Cates, I thought that her name might be less common and performed the following search:

COMPUTRACE—LIVING FILE INPUT

Enter LAST NAME : cates

Enter FIRST NAME : phoebe

COMPUTRACE—LIVING FILE INPUT

COMPUTRACE—LIVING FILE
AVAILABLE STATES MENU

1. ALABAMA	19. LOUISIANA	37. OKLAHOMA
2. ALASKA	20. MAINE	38. OREGON
3. ARIZONA	21. MARYLAND	39. PENNSYLVANIA
4. ARKANSAS	22. MASSACHUSETTS	40. RHODE ISLAND
5. CALIFORNIA	23. MICHIGAN	41. SOUTH CAROLINA
6. COLORADO	24. MINNESOTA	42. SOUTH DAKOTA
7. CONNECTICUT	25. MISSISSIPPI	43. TENNESSEE
8. DELAWARE	26. MISSOURI	44. TEXAS
9. DIST OF COLUMBIA	27. MONTANA	45. UTAH
10. FLORIDA	28. NEBRASKA	46. VERMONT
11. GEORGIA	29. NEVADA	47. VIRGINIA
12. HAWAII	30. NEW HAMPSHIRE	48. WASHINGTON
13. IDAHO	31. NEW JERSEY	49. WEST VIRGINIA
14. ILLINOIS	32. NEW MEXICO	50. WISCONSIN
15. INDIANA	33. NEW YORK	51. WYOMING
16. IOWA	34. NORTH CAROLINA	52. ALL
17. KANSAS	35. NORTH DAKOTA	
18. KENTUCKY	36. OHIO	

Select First STATE (1-52) OR ? for menu : 52

You have entered the following search criteria for the LIVING file search.

    Last Name—CATES
    First Name—PHOEBE
    States—52 ALL

Is the entered information correct? (Y/N) : y

Processing request. Please wait.
    1 LIVING file records were found that matched the search criteria.

and retrieved the following details:

CDB INFOTEK
COMPUTRACE—LIVING FILE SEARCH

NAME: CATES PHOEBE B
CITY OF LAST RESIDENCE: GARRISON
STATE OF LAST RESIDENCE: NEW YORK
ZIP CODE OF LAST RESIDENCE: 10524

Last page !

Hoping that Mr. Kline might also be noted on the record in question (perhaps a marriage license or real estate purchase), I re-ran his name, choosing this time only New York records rather than all states. This allowed me to narrow my results down to 8 records, including the following record:

CDB INFOTEK
COMPUTRACE—L!VING FILE SEARCH

NAME: KLINE KEVIN S
CITY OF LAST RESIDENCE: GARRISON
STATE OF LAST RESIDENCE: NEW YORK
ZIP CODE OF LAST RESIDENCE: 10524

Last page !

In order to gather more detailed information, my next step would be to use one of the public records vendor systems, such as CDB Infotek, LEXIS, or Information America to check for marriage licenses, real estate filings, or other records in Garrison, New York under the names Phoebe Cates or Kevin Kline.

Since this search did not identify which types of records or how many exist, additional searching is necessary, but at $15 per hour (or $.25/minute), I was able to complete both searches for under $2. This is quite a bargain when you need a good starting place for a search.

Telephone Directories

T elephone directory databases would seem to be pretty self-explanatory. They contain names, addresses and telephone numbers. So why are there over fifty telephone directory databases available online and on CD-ROM?

Geographic Differences

As might be expected, one factor that differentiates the various telephone directory databases is geography. For example, the Base de Dados Mope database (available online) includes listings for Portugal, the Azores and Madeira Islands, and Cape Verde. TwixTel (on CD-ROM) covers Switzerland.

The online and CD-ROM databases typically cover a wider geographic coverage than the print editions. Many American directories include all the the United States, for example. Some of the directories combine several countries, such as the EuroPages which includes sixteen.

Residential Versus Business

Another difference between telephone directory databases is that, like print telephone directories, some carry residential listings while others list businesses. Some include both.

Subject Area

Telephone directory databases, especially those for businesses, may also concentrate on specific industries. For example, an online database called Academy Online lists educational institutions in the United States and Canada.

The directory producers may take other slices of the data as well. The North American Facsimile, for example, includes only businesses in the United States, Canada, and Mexico that have facsimile (fax) numbers, and lists fax numbers instead of voice telephone numbers.

Currentness

When selecting a CD-ROM or online telephone directory database, the data must be up-to-date. Whether online or on CD-ROM, the directory data may be updated semi-annually, quarterly, monthly, or on an ongoing basis. This could mean as often as hourly for an online database.

This does not mean that someone dealing with personal records would necessarily want the most current database. Private investigators have been known to hang onto old telephone books in order to locate where people "used" to be, as well as for use in verifying names or places, and CD-ROM products present an excellent alternative to print versions for this reason, as well as saving quite a bit of space.

A few producers of telephone directories do not sell their products, but only lease them. These companies require customers to return previous versions of their discs in order to receive more current versions. This makes their products somewhat less attractive for investigative work.

One should not assume that an online system is more current solely because it theoretically could be updated dynamically. Although online databases may be updated from one minute to the next, some are actually revised less often than the CD-ROM versions. If records are updated only once every quarter, or even less frequently, some records will be out-of-date, and newer records will be missing.

Accuracy

One telephone directory may claim to list 11 million businesses, while another claims 10 million, and another 9.2 million. The numbers alone do not tell the complete story. The accuracy of the data may also vary.

Because some directories are created directly from tapes from the telephone companies, the data in them may be cleaner. Other directories may be created from multiple sources, making them more complete, but some of their sources could also be less accurate.

If directory producers wish to add numbers, they may not remove old listings. Instead, they may replace an old listing only when a new record is received, thus leaving the database littered with out-of-date entries.

At the other end of the spectrum, some database producers contact each business at least once each year to verify their listings. You can expect to pay a premium price for this level of accuracy.

Added Content

Business telephone directories may contain a great variety of added content in order to make them more usable and valuable. One of the most frequent additions is the Standard Industrial Classification (SIC), which identifies the primary industry, and sometimes the secondary, or additional industries in which each business operates. For some businesses, the SIC code can be very clear. For others, especially those which manufacture a variety of products or whose services are not clearly identified by a single SIC code, the code may be less valuable, or even confusing. The SIC code may be supplied by the business itself or assigned by the telephone directory producer, so the same business may be coded differently on various databases.

Added content may also include the number of employees, names of owners, directors, executives, staff, or key personnel, yellow page category, size of yellow page advertisement, and year in which the business was first listed in the directory.

Contents may vary even among residential telephone directories. People Finder, for example, lists not only the names, addresses, and telephone numbers for individuals, but includes dates of birth, residence type, length of residence, family members and their dates of birth.

Older versions of the CD-ROM telephone directories sometimes included unlisted telephone numbers, which were acquired from public records and sources outside of the telephone companies. In later versions, most producers have omitted unlisted numbers from their telephone directories.

Search Capabilities

Among the most important features of any database are its search capabilities. Telephone directories are no exception. For residential listings, some of the options available include searches by name, address, a range of addresses, telephone number, Soundex code, and partial names and indices. Alternative search capabilities can dramatically increase the value (and often the price) of telephone directory databases.

For example, assume that you have checked a printed telephone directory for someone, but your subject has since moved away and you cannot locate a new listing. If you can extract names and addresses of people living nearby (through a range of address search), one of their former neighbors may help you to locate your subject. With a partial name search or index, you can locate others with the same surname, and thereby find relatives in other areas of the country or even beyond.

Consider how a telephone number search can be used in concert with Caller-ID. When someone calls, Caller-ID displays their telephone number on a small screen. When you call an 800 or 900 number for information (or any number, for that matter), you may think that you are doing so anonymously. In fact, the vendor on the other end of the line may be using Caller-ID to log your telephone number. The number can then be used to search a telephone directory database in order to find your name, address, and possibly additional information. You may never even know that this is happening. If you begin to receive mail offers or telephone solicitations after calling a company from your home or business, this is one way that you may have ended up in their database.

Not all telephone systems send the Caller-ID yet. You can call your local telephone company to find out if yours does. If so, and if you wish to reclaim your telephone anonymity, you can buy another device that blocks your telephone number from being sent to Caller-ID, or your telephone company may block Caller-ID for you.

Use Restrictions

Most telephone directory databases restrict the use of their data in one way or another. One of the most basic restrictions is that you cannot download all of their data and sell it as your own product. (This is true of almost any database on the market.) A product may also carry the restriction that it may be used only by the purchasing end-user, and may not be loaned, rented, put on a network, or otherwise made available to or shared with others.

A telephone directory database producer may restrict its product from use in generating commercial mailing lists or telemarketing. One of the ways that it enforces this restriction is to pepper the databases with a false listing here and there. When a solicitation is received under the false listing, the producer discovers which company is making the offer. Violators are easily caught.

Further restrictions may include the number of records that you can download in any given period. For example, PhoneDisc USA Residential limits use of its data for commercial direct mail or telemarketing to 250 listings per month.

Some telephone directory databases carry no such restrictions and allow unlimited downloads and use. If you intend to create mailing lists, be sure to verify that there are no use restrictions before purchasing a CD-ROM product or signing up with an online carrier.

Price

One last factor that differentiates the various telephone directory databases is price. Like other databases, telephone directories carry many different pricing structures. Some online databases require hourly and/or per search charges, while CD-ROM products entail the cost of purchase or lease. One unusual thing about telephone directory prices is that the same data can be charged at the most dramatically different rates I've seen, depending upon how you access it.

An example of this is Metromail. When Metromail residential data is accessed through CompuServe's Phone*File, the charge is only $15 per hour. An annual subscription to the Metromail's MetroSearch Library on CD-ROM, (with business and residential coverage of all 4 regions of the U.S., semi-annual updates, and AT&T 800 numbers listed), costs $9,995. Although the subscription does contain additional data, it still would be much cheaper to buy a business directory (for under $200) and use the AT&T Toll-Free Internet Directory, which is free on the Net.

Pro CD offers many telephone directory products on CD-ROM, but for those with infrequent need, it makes more sense to access Pro CD's records via America Online (keyword White Pages), where the fees are included in one's monthly subscription.

Using telephone directory databases for personal research often requires more than one product, so some comparison shopping can be important. It may be useful to own a CD-ROM database (many of which are currently priced in the $100 to $150 range) and dial into an online database as a secondary source. If you have an ongoing need for this type of information, you may also find that alternating your CD-ROM purchases and updates between two or more vendors provides greater coverage.

Telephone Directories on the Internet

Telephone directories can also be found on the Internet, and most are accessible for no more than the hourly cost of your Internet connection. For example, you can search the Switchboard for business and residential listings at:

http://www.switchboard.com

The Four11 Directory can be found at:

http://www.four11.com/

The Bigfoot Directory can be found at:

http://www.bigfoot.com/

InfoSpace offers several white and yellow page directories, as well as government directories, a fax directory, an 800 directory, and a set of world directories, at:

http://www.infospace.com/

American Directory Assistance is at:

http://www.abii.com/lookupusa/adp/peopsrch.htm

The Ultimate White Pages, containing several telephone directory searches, can be found at:

http://www.infochase.com/ref/ultimates/

World Pages, offering telephone directories for countries all over the world, can be found at:

http://www.worldpages.com/worldsearch

A reverse telephone directory (searchable by phone number rather than name) is available through 411 Locate at:

http://www.411locate.com/

Housernet is a home page directory, allowing searches by birthday, marital status, age range, and/or sex:

http://www.housernet.com

An electronic yellow pages called ComFind can be found at:

http://comfind.com

As stated earlier, the AT&T Toll-Free Internet Directory is available on the Internet. It contains only national 800 numbers, but you can't beat the price. It's free. For information about this directory, you can send email to: **tollfree@attmail.com;** or call (800) 562-2255. The address for this service online is:

http://att.net:80/dir800/

Other telephone directories lie hidden within additional Internet sites. Many such directories list university faculty and students. For example, the telephone book for the University of St. Gallen Student Association in Switzerland can be found at:

http://www-students.unisg.ch/telefonbuch/index.html

Other telephone directories can be found at Internet sites all over the world. One site that can help you to identify many of them can be found at Yahoo—Reference:Phone Numbers:

http://www.yahoo.com/Reference/Phone_Numbers/

For Further Information

This book offers several additional sources of information about specialized telephone directories. Refer to Appendix J for a listing of telephone directory databases. Refer to Appendix C for business credit and company financial databases that include personal information. Refer also to the Appendix D listing professional and staff directory databases and Appendix E for other directory databases containing employee information. The databases listed in each of these sections may also be used as telephone directories.

Staff, Professional, and Other Directories

W hen you need information about people, professional and organizational directories have much to offer.

Staff Directories

Staff directories list personnel who belong to a single organization. These directories may serve as telephone books for the organizations, or may actually contain detailed information about the personnel on staff.

An example of a staff directory is the Military Personnel/Base LOCATOR, available from Staff Directories Ltd. This database provides listings of military and civilian personnel, with biographical and other information included in many cases.

Another example, Staff Directories on CD-ROM, includes a Congressional Staff Directory, Judicial Staff Directory, and Federal Staff Directory.

There are many staff directories for government offices and educational institutions available on the Internet as well. These include:

Arkansas State Directory (state agencies)
http://www.state.ar.us/dcs/ar_dir.htm

The State of Florida Telephone Directory
http://fcn.state.fl.us/teldir/help.html

North Star Minnesota Government Directories
http://www.state.mn.us/dir/index.html

Washington State Department of Information Services (includes state agencies, educational institutions, and many local government organizations)
http://dial.wa.gov/

CSU (Connecticut State University) Telephone Directory
http://www.csu.ctstateu.edu/sysoff/csu_teldir.html

Electronic Telephone Directory for University of Copenhagen
http://garm.adm.ku.dk/phone-e.html

UPMC (University of Pittsburgh Medical Center) Telephone Directory
http://www.upmc.edu/upmc/tele.html

University of Sussex (UK)
http://www.susx.ac.uk/SFgate/phone.html
Refer to Appendix D for additional examples of staff directories.

Professional Directories

Professional directories may concentrate on a specific occupation or a range of occupations. One example is COSMOS 3, a database containing biographical information on corporate executives, bankers, and other prominent business leaders in Japan. For each person, this Japanese-language directory provides name, address, date of birth, education, occupation, employment history, and current position.

Some professional directories available online and on CD-ROM target executives, physicians, physicists and astronomers, and attorneys, as well as members of many other professions.

The Martindale-Hubbell Law Directory, available online and on CD-ROM, is one of the best-known professional directories. Martindale-Hubbell contains information about lawyers and legal services. Listings for attorneys include the attorney's name, firm name and address, telephone number, date of birth, college of first and additional degrees, law school, fields of law, court admissions (e.g., local, state, federal), scholastic and legal honors, Martindale-Hubbell rating (when available), membership(s) in bar associations, clients, languages, biography, firm size, and legal services. The Martindale-Hubbell Law Directory is also now searchable on the Internet as the Martindale-Hubbell Lawyer Locator at:
http://www.martindale.com/

If I were a prosecuting attorney about to face famed lawyer Johnnie Cochran in court, a quick search of the Martindale-Hubbell would certainly help me to size up the competition. One can hardly imagine an attorney who has received more awards than Mr. Cochran, as you can see from the following listing taken from the Martindale-Hubbell on LEXIS:

Copyright 1995 by Reed Elsevier Inc.
MARTINDALE-HUBBELL ® LAW DIRECTORY

Practice Profiles Section

JOHNNIE L. COCHRAN JR.
Law Offices of Johnnie L. Cochran, Jr. A Professional
Corporation
4929 Wilshire Boulevard, Suite 1010
Los Angeles, California 90010
(Los Angeles County)
Telephone: 213-931-6200
Fax: 213-931-9521

RATING: AV

POSITION: Member

ADMITTED: 1963, California; 1966, U.S. District Court, Western District of

Texas; 1968, U.S. Supreme Court

LAW-SCHOOL: Loyola University of Los Angeles (Now Loyola Marymount University) (LL.B.)

COLLEGE: University of California (B.S.)

TEXT: Recipient: Criminal Trial Lawyer of the Year, Los Angeles Criminal Courts Bar Association, 1977; Pioneer of Black Legal Leadership Award, Los Angeles Brotherhood Crusade, August 1979; Trial Lawyer of the year, won. Leon Miller Award, John M. Langston Bar Association, 1982-1983; Equal Justice in Law Award, Legal Defense Fund, National Association for the Advancement of Colored People; Distinguished Alumni Award, UCLA Black Alumni Association, March 1988; Outstanding Criminal Defense Attorneys, Southern California, July 1989; Trial Lawyer of the Year, The Los Angeles Trial Lawyers Association, January 1991; Trial Lawyer of the Year Award, Criminal Courts Bar Association, 1977; 1990 Trial Lawyer of the Year; Kappa Alpha Psi, 1991; Civil Rights Lawyer of the Year Award, L.A. Chapter of the NAACP Legal Defense Fund; Presidential Award, L.A. Chapter of the NAACP; Lifetime Achievement Award, Pasadena Branch, NAACP, 1991; Man of the Year, Los Angeles International Airport Kiwanis Club, 1991. Deputy City Attorney, Criminal Division, City of Los Angeles, 1963-1965. Assistant District Attorney of Los Angeles County, 1978-1982. Former Adjunct Professor of Law: Trial Tactics and Techniques, UCLA School of Law and Loyola University, School of Law. Member, Board of Directors: Los Angeles Urban League; Oscar Joel Bryant Foundation; 28th Street Y.M.C.A., L.A. Family Housing Corp.; Los Angeles African American Chamber of Commerce; Airport Commissioners City of Los Angeles; American Civil Liberties Union Foundation of Southern California; Lawyers Mutual Insurance Company. Special Counsel, Chairman of the Rules Committee, Democratic National Convention, June 1984. Special Counsel, Committee on Standard of Official Conduct (Ethics Committee) House of Representatives, 99th Congress. Lawyer Representative, Central District of California, Ninth Circuit Judicial Conference, August 1990. President, Black Business Association of Los Angeles, California, 1989. Member: State Bar of California (Co-Chair, Board of Legal Service Corps., 1993); American College of Trial Lawyers. Fellow, American Bar Foundation. (Certified, Criminal Law, The State Bar of California Board of Legal Specialization)

Born: October 2, 1937, Shreveport, Louisiana

Maintains law offices at more than one place

West's Legal Directory, as well as Simon's European Law Directory, are also both available on the Internet at:

http://www.westpub.com/WLAWInfo/world.htm

Other examples of professional directories found on the Net include:

Health Source Professional Directory (professionals/practitioners of natural or alternative healthcare):

http://www.healthcsource.com/hsource/directories/profess.htm

The Complete Directory of Law Officer's Personal Home Pages:
http://www.officer.com/officers.htm

And at least one site provides indices to various professions:

Professional Net (Your Internet Guide to the Professionals and Where to Find Them) at:
http://www.profnet.co.uk/profnet/

Refer to Appendix D for additional examples of professional directories.

Ancillary Directories

Other directories also sometimes include employee information. Examples of these can be found among company and business directories, available online and on CD-ROM. Many contain listings of key personnel, management, executives, contacts and sometimes even shareholders.

A less obvious database in which you might find information about your subject is the Archaeological Sites Database. Though primarily devoted to the archeological sites of Arizona and adjoining areas, it also provides information about management, architects, and builders.

Refer to Appendix C for business credit and company financial databases that contain personal information. Refer to Appendix E for additional examples of other directory databases containing employee information.

Mailing Lists

D o you receive catalogs, telemarketing calls, junk mail? If so, your name is on a mailing list database, and probably more than one. Direct marketing companies buy, sell, and trade your name and "profile" to companies who hope that you may be interested in their products or services. More than 10,000 lists of data about individuals are now available for rent. This is a multibillion dollar industry.

If you are interested in mailing to a particular segment of society, be it people of a certain religion or financial status, people suffering from any illness or ailment you can name, those who enjoy cross-stitch or hockey, who buy into "get rich quick" schemes, or hold certain political beliefs, mailing list brokers can provide mailing lists of these individuals from their databases. Some will even supply it on diskette, so that you can form your own database or easily load it into your contact management software or spreadsheet.

Along with mailing lists available for rent, there are databases (some online, but more on CD-ROM) from which you can extract your own mailing list data.

You may wonder how mailing list companies know so much about you, your beliefs, and your spending habits. There are actually more sources of mailing list information than you've probably ever imagined, and those sources range from the innocuous to some that might be thought of as either inventive or invasive, depending upon your perspective.

Telephone Directories
Telephone directories represent one of the most innocuous sources for mailing lists. The only personal information that one might guess when compiling a mailing list from a telephone directory is a person's sex, and not even that is certain any more.

If you have read Chapter Seventeen, you know that some telephone directory databases now include date of birth, residence type, length of residence, other family members and their birthdates. This makes it possible, using this single source, to develop a mailing list targeting a much more specific marketing group.

If you plan to develop your own mailing list from a telephone directory database, be sure to check it over thoroughly before buying. Many of the telephone directories that include residential listings strictly prohibit their use in mailing lists. (If, on the other hand, you wish to develop a mailing list of companies, you should have little difficulty finding a telephone directory database to accommodate you, either online or on CD-ROM.)

One CD-ROM residential telephone directory database, Address Maker, lists residents of Japan and allows you to print mailing labels for the Japanese market. Another database, OzOnDisc, lists both residences and businesses in Australia; it also enables the creation of mailing lists and labels. Phonedisc New York and New England includes businesses, residences, and government offices served by the New England Telephone and New York telephone companies in Connecticut, Maine, Massachusetts, New Hampshire, New York, Rhode Island, and Vermont; it is also a mailing list tool. Other examples can be found, but limitations vary from vendor to vendor and version to version, so you'll need to evaluate them before buying.

One step away from extracting your own data is Donnelley's master file (an online database). It contains data on 84 million households, and can be accessed remotely from another computer, allowing you to obtain list counts based on your own parameters. You can then order mailing labels for a geographic or custom-defined market area, rather than extracting the data yourself. (Refer to the listing for CONQUEST/DIRECT in Appendix J for information about accessing this database).

Refer to Appendix J for other examples of Telephone Directory databases, many of which are used to produce mailing lists.

Other Directories

With a little help from professional or trade directories, it is easy to compile mailing lists based on occupation. American Book Trade Directory, which lists bookstore owners and managers, is used for this purpose. The Martindale-Hubbell Law Directory is used to produce mailing lists of attorneys (selectable by legal specialty, gender, age, geographic area, or school of graduation), as is the Directory of Intellectual Property Attorneys. The Directory of Engineering and Engineering Technology Undergraduate Programs contains information about undergraduate engineering and engineering technology deans and is sold as a mailing list. Various hospital directories are used to compile databases of specialists in many medical fields. The Rocky Mountain Petroleum Directory, and like ones from the Mid-continent, Northeast, and Gulf states, provide information for mailing lists of professionals in the petroleum field. Many additional examples can be found for other professions and industries.

School directories are used to compile mailing lists of high school and college students, who make up additional marketing groups.

If you want a mailing list from any of these sources, a mailing list broker should be able to assist you in locating the one you want. Do ask about any licensing restrictions before buying or renting any lists. Some lists allow unlimited use, but most do not. If the list you want is available on diskette (many are not), its use may be limited to one year after the purchase date. Some lists allow only one-time use, and you must pay for each subsequent mailing. In order to discourage multiple uses, many companies will not even provide the data on diskette. A list with one-time use may be prohibitively expensive if you plan to send several mailings to the same people over the coming year. I have been told that it takes four exposures before prospective clients recognize a company's name. If that is true of your industry, I suggest you either buy a list that allows unlimited use for a period long enough to allow at least four mailings, or budget to re-purchase the list four times. If you can send only a single mailing, you may be wasting your money.

Some directory databases can be accessed directly to compile your own mailing lists. The Capital Source (available online and on diskette) is one. It lists persons and organizations in the United States government, corporations, media, and professional organizations located within the metropolitan Washington, DC area. For each person or organization, this database provides name, department or organization name, contact name and title, office or business address, political party, street address, city and state, ZIP Code, and telephone number. The software makes it possible to generate mailing labels. Another database, Aviation Compendium (available on CD-ROM), contains names and addresses of Canadian and United States aircraft registrants, airmen, pilots, air traffic controllers, airport facility owners, facility managers, mechanics, inspectors, medical examiners, and air taxi operators. This database can also be used in developing mailing lists.

Appendix C contains business credit and company financial databases which also identify individuals within the companies, and many of these databases can also be used to create mailing lists. Appendices D and E contain other examples of directory databases, many of which can be used in developing your own mailing lists.

Magazine Subscriptions

If you subscribe to almost any magazine today, you can bet that your name is being sold on their mailing list. What you read can be very telling, as so many magazines are tailored to very specific audiences and tastes.

Artists, antique collectors, auto mechanics, auto racing enthusiasts, business owners, children, classic car collectors, aviation enthusiasts, brides-to-be, Corvette owners, the elderly, entrepreneurs, expectant and new mothers, the gay and lesbian community, off-road vehicle owners, parents, people of any race, religion, and ethnicity, sailing enthusiasts, step-parents, and women all are targeted for mailing lists, based on the magazines that they subscribe to.

Magazine publishers each have a composite image of their target readers. They may sell their lists of subscribers based on those composites, which will typically include the percentage of women versus men, average income, median age, and many additional details. For example, you could undoubtedly guess that nearly all of *Black Enterprise Magazine*'s subscribers are African Americans, but the publishers also know that 56 percent of its subscribers are men, and their median age is 42, making those subscribers a target audience for particular types of goods and services.

Another type of mailing list that can be created from magazine subscriptions is a "new mover" list. When you or a third party, such as the post office, notify a magazine that you subscribe to of your new address, that type of information can be used to create such a mailing list. New movers could be good targets for grocery and video stores, insurance companies (for either renters' or homeowners' policies), restaurants, gardeners, and a variety of other consumer-oriented retail businesses.

Associations and Membership Groups

Ramada business card members earn points for each stay in a Ramada Inn or Hotel. They also earn their place on another mailing list. Restaurants sometimes sell lists of children's names and birthdays when they are signed up for birthday clubs or kids clubs, and they may do the same for adult membership groups. Frequent Flyer programs can be great sources for locating people who may be interested in hotel discounts, new luggage, or other travel bargains.

Many trade associations also sell their membership lists. The American Dental Association and the American Pharmaceutical Association sell mailing lists of their members. So do the American Vocational Association (for vocational educators) and the Special Libraries Association (for corporate librarians). If you want to market to attorneys, the American Bar Association and the Los Angeles County Bar Association both sell their membership lists. The American Academy of Family Physicians, the Institute of Packaging Professionals (IOPP), and the Society of Decorative Painters all sell their membership lists for use in mailing lists.

Even B'nai Brith, a cultural and fraternal Jewish organization, sells its membership file.

So do many fan clubs.

In theory, you can ask the organizations you join not to sell your name as part of a mailing list. However, one member of a national dating service opted out of having her personal information and single status sold to the masses, and was later distressed to receive a flurry of offers for singles. The dating service explained that an ex-employee had stolen a copy of its membership database and sold it to a mailing list firm. This type of theft is always possible when there is a profit to be made. Even the most private membership information can turn up in a mailing list at some point.

Call-Ins/Write-Ins/Buyers

Have you ever written or called to buy something that was offered on the television or radio or in a mailing? Have you ever entered a contest or purchased anything at all through the mail? Of course you have, and these are other sources of mailing lists.

One mailing list of this type includes individuals who watch live opera from the Met on public TV. Another lists those who watch E! Entertainment Television. Do you wonder how anyone knows what you're watching? They are not monitoring your television signal, although cable companies could probably do that. The people on the Met's list responded to an offer for a sample of the Met's Teleguide that had been advertised during the broadcast. E! Entertainment Television ran a sweepstakes on their cable station and then sold a mailing list of the contestants. These are just two of many ways in which TV stations can gather information on who is watching. People who send videos into "America's Funniest Home Videos" also are placed on a mailing list, whether or not they actually are accepted as contestants on the show.

Radio Shack asks for name, address, and telephone number at the time of each purchase, even when you pay cash, and then uses this information to build its own mailing list.

If you have ever bought advertising space of any kind, there is a better than even chance that you've been added to at least one advertisers' list by now.

Buyers are sometimes asked to complete questionnaires about their interests and will provide information about their "lifestyle characteristics" and demographics, such as sex, age, occupation, marital status, home ownership, credit card usage, ages of children at home, geography, income, and political party. Unlisted telephone numbers are routinely volunteered. Questionnaires may even collect information such as the type of breakfast cereal that customers eat, their make of car, the brand of diapers their baby wears, and more. Quaker Oats once offered buyers of its Cap'n Crunch cereal "high value" coupons and a wristwatch for filling out this type of questionnaire. Among other things, Quaker Oats wanted to know consumers' opinions on firearm ownership, school prayer, and mandatory drug testing. If not for use on mailing lists, what in the world would a cereal manufacturer want with that kind of information? I can't imagine how it might have helped in any of their advertising campaigns, but that is the only other possibility that I've come up with.

Asking people to fill out questionnaires in order to receive "free" information can also provide facts that would be hard to compile otherwise. These questionnaires sometimes become mailing lists for single mothers, heads of households, divorcees, widows, and other consumer groups.

Did you know that mailing lists even single out people with particular ailments? These are sometimes compiled when you request treatment information, fill a prescription, or fill out a survey or questionnaire. The following list contains selections available from the "ailments" database of only one company, along with their record counts:

	QUANTITY
Allergies	4,936,091
Alzheimer's Disease	18,789
Angina	113,947
Arthritis and Rheumatism	113,429
Asthma	56,580
Back Pain	129,713
Bladder Control and Incontinence	67,157
Bleeding Gums and Gingivitis	151,649
Blindness	107,496
Diabetes	107,872
Emphysema	19,420
Epilepsy	10,017
Frequent Headaches	209,107
Frequent Heartburn	242,682
Gastritis	121,701
Hearing Impaired	170,958
Heart Disease	44,780
High Blood Pressure	44,983
High Cholesterol	274,942
Migraines	34,049
Motion Sickness	58,753
Osteoporosis	20,143
Parkinson's Disease	3,903
Sensitive Skin	376,225
Sinusitis	246,266
Thinning Hair and Baldness	682,134
Ulcer	47,451
Yeast Infection	77,528

(Could you ever have imagined that a yeast infection or gingivitis could make your name valuable to a direct marketing firm?)

Book clubs typically sell their lists of their customers, sometimes creating separate lists such as "coffee table book purchasers." Other catalog companies do likewise, separating their customers into groups such as those who purchase children's goods. Some credit card companies also segment their customers into broad spending tiers such as "Rodeo Drive Chic," "Fifth Avenue Sophisticated," "Fashion Conscious," and "Value

Seeker," based on spending habits. This segmentation makes their mailing lists more marketable, as they target more and more specific spending groups.

If you participate in online discussions on the Internet or other bulletin board systems, you should be aware that posting your address or telephone number can also make that information available to mailing list vendors and others, and there are companies that regularly troll the online bulletin boards hoping to pick up this type of information in order to compile their lists. (You never know who is listening when you're talking online.)

Other information can be *inferred* from your purchasing habits. For example, a purchaser of a ship-to-shore radio probably also owns a boat or a yacht, so buying one may place you on a list of boat owners, whether you actually own a boat or not. Other things can also be gleaned from sales data, and not just by the marketing firms. One car rental company that sold its list later received many complaints from customers whose spouses drew an entirely different inference when they received a mail order offer declaring that their recent rental of a car entitled them to a discount from another company. If you rent a car in hopes of sneaking around on your spouse, you might want to reconsider that plan.

Some companies place newspaper or magazine ads offering free goods or information, or "too good to be true" products or ideas. Some of these companies simply want to get your name and address in order to sell it on their mailing lists. "Opportunity Seeker" lists can be compiled this way. For instance, a company can place an ad offering a way to make millions for a mere $20 investment. If you send in your check, you may have not only bought their "get rich quick" scheme (which may not be worth the price of the stamp), but also paid to have your name added to an "Opportunity Seeker's" list. If you continue to answer similar ads, marketers may elevate your status from "Opportunity Seeker" to "Sucker," and the offers will *really* start to pour in!

If you want to find out how long it takes your name to circulate from one contact to the world, try this little experiment. When filling out personal information, alter the way your name is listed by adding or deleting a middle name, changing a middle initial, or making some other slight variation that you can recognize, yet that will not make it impossible to deliver your mail. You can then track the time that it takes this new identity to spread from one company to another.

Warranty Registration Cards

Another source for mailing lists is warranty registration cards that are filled out when one makes a purchase or receives a gift. For example, if you have ever purchased a Black & Decker appliance and sent in the warranty card, you may have been placed on one of several mailing lists, depending upon the product you registered. Minolta, the maker of photographic equipment, sells the information from its warranty cards as well.

The facts requested on warranty registrations can be quite detailed, including information about other products that you own and sometimes even a whole questionnaire of personal questions. One type of question that makes your name and profile very saleable involves what you *plan* to purchase in the future. If you were selling microwave ovens, wouldn't you like to have a list of people who plan to purchase one in the next few months? If you fill out a warranty card checking off the box that states that you plan to buy a new VCR, computer, washing machine, or anything else in the next six months, and you are suddenly deluged with offers for them, you can bet that it is no coincidence.

As I understand it, you do not actually even need to send in warranty cards in order for your purchases to be covered under warranty. However, I have not yet been able to bring myself to believe this, so I still fill them out and send them in. I fill them out imaginatively, however, picking and choosing the interests for which I would like to receive catalogs in the future.

If you have a relative or client who plays golf and you do not, you might consider checking off golf as one of your interests anyway, in order to receive free golfing catalogs and other offers that you can pass on to them, or to use the catalogs to buy gifts for them. If the warranty card asks whether you play occasionally or frequently, you can bet that marketers are interested in each group. Perhaps a golf shop has found that those who play occasionally seldom have their own clubs, shoes, or various golf goodies, so they may send their catalogs to the "occasional" group. Maybe a golf resort has found that their target group is only those who play frequently, so they will send their discount coupons and brochures to the "frequent" group.

If you can imagine how the information that you give out might be used, you stand a better chance of receiving the types of offers that you will actually enjoy.

Friends and Family

You may not be the only one volunteering information that places you on a mailing list. Mailing lists are also created from information volunteered by your associates. When MCI Communications Corp. started the Friends & Family discount calling plan, it was not the first company to ask for referrals to other prospective customers. For years, mail order companies have been asking their customers to provide names and addresses of others who might want their catalogs. The record, CD, and book clubs even offer free merchandise if you can convince your friends to sign up for a membership.

Telephone Inquiries

As noted in Chapter Seventeen, merely placing a phone call may land you on a mailing list, even when you do not give out your name or address. This can happen while you listen to a recorded message, without speaking to a soul. With Caller-ID, the company at the other end of the phone may be able to capture your telephone number and then use a reverse telephone directory (indexed by telephone number rather than name) to add your name and address to its database.

Companies may also call and request your participation in a survey, and then use the information gathered in creating mailing lists.

Attendees

If you attend a gallery opening or special exhibition, a class or workshop, a beauty show, computer show, or other trade show, you've guessed it by now. These are also sources of mailing lists.

Donors

If you have contributed to any type of cause—to back a political candidate, support an environmental protest, or to help cure a disease, for instance—you probably have noticed a significant increase in the number of requests you receive. A donation can be "the gift that keeps on giving." The recipient may continue to make money by selling your name and profile to others who also would like a bit of your cash.

Politically-based donor lists include the Beer-Bellied Reactionary Republicans list (contributors said to be dedicated to preserving "American ideas and traditions"), and the Blue & White Jewish Donors list (donors to pro-Israel candidates). Others include Taxpayers for Government Reform (donors to the balanced budget amendment, line item veto, tax reduction and other congressional reform issues), and the Fund for the Feminist Majority Donors (donors to an organization founded to promote feminist issues and leadership for women in government, business, education, law, media, and medicine).

There are many, many lists of donors who contribute to animal protection causes: Animal Activist Donors, Anti-Cruelty Donors, Animal Legal Defense Fund donors list, In Defense of Animals Donors, International Wildlife Coalition Donors, People For the Ethical Treatment of Animals Donors, Save the Whales Donors, Super Ocean Activists donors list, World Wildlife Fund Donors, and the ASPCA donors list are among them.

Lists of donors to health causes also are plentiful. Among the causes whose donors can be found on mailing lists are the Arthritis Foundation, cerebral palsy, heart research, Alzheimer's research, the International Eye Foundation, the March of Dimes, Paralyzed Veterans of America, and the SIDS (Sudden Infant Death Syndrome) Alliance. There are many others. One list includes people who have formerly donated to the Epilepsy Foundation of America. The Muscular Dystrophy Association markets several specialized lists of its contributors, including Catholic, Hispanic, and Jewish donors, "mail responsive donors," donors who have contributed more than once, and those who have responded to the organization's annual telethon. Additional lists include donors to any one health cause, and those who have contributed to more than one, or who have contributed more than once to any similar cause. These sometimes are called "sympathetic donor lists," or something of the sort.

Government Agencies

Government agencies also provide information for mailing lists. If you own any type of aircraft, the Federal Aviation Administration (FAA) may have sold your name and profile. Your state Department of Motor Vehicles (DMV) may have done so when you registered a car, truck, or trailer. The Coast Guard may have sold your information when you registered a boat with them, and the Federal Communications Commission (FCC) may have done the same when you registered your ship to shore radio.

Technically they may not have "sold" your information. When "selling" is prohibited, they might instead charge for the effort that it takes to compile the information and then give the data away free. What it nevertheless comes down to is that the year, make, and model of your aircraft, car, truck, motorcycle, boat, or yacht may be listed in a database, along with the information it will take to contact you.

Most of us give the Post Office change-of-address forms when we move. They then contract with several companies to process changes of address so that our mail will continue to get to us after we've moved. This is another source for "new movers" lists.

State licensing boards for pharmacists, surveyors, marriage and family therapists, and other professions are yet another source. State insurance departments license agents and agencies to sell property, casualty, life, and disability insurance, and can be a source for mailing lists specifying agents licensed to sell any of these.

Public Records

Although it is possible to compile mailing lists from public records, this process can be extremely labor-intensive to do on your own using court documents. For most types of records, one would have to collect the records one at a time, read through them, locate the names and addresses, and scan or input them into a computer or type them onto mailing labels.

Some of the public records databases available online could be useful in compiling specialized lists, but most public records vendors allow searching only record by record, using personal names rather than parameters such as ALL DIVORCEES IN CLEVELAND DURING 1995, which would be more useful for compiling mailing lists. This may be good news for those of you who were hoping that such intimate details as your divorce would remain somewhat private, but it probably is only a matter of time before these are all automated and the search capabilities are improved.

This is not to say that there are no public records databases suitable for use in building mailing lists. One database convenient for this purpose is Real Estate On CD-ROM. This database includes four sets of tax assessor data and map information on real estate in various United States county and city jurisdictions. Users can search by address, map/parcel number, sales price, date of title transfer, year built, tax amount, properties owned by lender, and absentee owner, and can print mailing labels for selected groups of owners. A similar database, The Massachusetts and Connecticut Real Estate Transfer Database and another, RealScan Systems (containing data on commercial, industrial, and residential property for three counties in Florida) can also be used for generating mailing lists. Refer to Appendix M for information on public records producers and vendors.

If you are hoping to build a mailing list based on a type of public record that cannot yet be searched easily online or on CD-ROM, you may have better luck renting an existing list rather than starting from scratch. One such mailing list is the New Bankruptcies/Judgments/Tax Liens list (available from New Residata Marketing Services, Inc.). This list includes people who are suffering from difficult economic times. It is compiled from many public records sources across the country and includes individuals who have filed for bankruptcy, incurred federal and/or state tax liens or who have legal judgments levied against them. (Refer to Section IV: "Where Can I Find More Information?—Books"—for additional sources of Mailing List Directories.)

Online Mailing Lists

Online mailing lists (or listservs, as they're known on the Internet) used to represent one of the few areas in which people had some control over whether their name remained on it. Members who did not wish to remain on an online list could usually have their names removed before they were passed on or sold for the creation of other lists. Many online vendors prohibit the sending of unsolicited junk mail online (referred to as "spamming") or advertising on online bulletin boards. Even where these practices are not prohibited they can result in loss of online privileges if the vendor receives many complaints against a particular person or company.

As of late, the spamming rate on many of the online systems seems to be on a sharp increase (for the Internet, CompuServe, and especially America Online, if my email is any indication). Mailing list vendors are using software to capture data about individuals and their interests as they travel through cyberspace. Email address lists are being compiled, sold and re-sold daily. Software such as Floodgate reports to make it possible to send 50,000+ emailings in less than a half hour, costing less in time and expenses than a fraction of what similar postal mail would cost. Given these factors, I would not predict much slowing of this type of advertising.

Online vendors are attempting various methods of controlling the spamming rate, blocking email being received from certain parties, requesting that members return any message that they find offensive to the sending party, or sending copies of solicitations to their vendor for follow-up.

Although the Internet is not regulated by any one vendor, Internet users have developed their own ways of controlling the Net's use as an advertising medium. Members can make their wishes abundantly clear when they find themselves spammed (the recipients of unwanted junk email), or when advertisers use public bulletin boards (Usenet newsgroups) to post their advertisements, rather than placing them in permissible areas. One or more members may "flame" (publicly denounce) the offending company or person, letting everyone who reads their messages know what they think of the solicitations. If the junk email continues, extremely irate members may set up their computers to send repeated messages to the offending company or person, letting them know their feelings in no uncertain terms. These messages may even number in the thousands each day, filling the online advertiser's mailbox and making it difficult if not impossible for them to receive any orders or inquiries. If those who are offended also send complaints to the advertiser's Internet access provider, many access providers will drop such offenders from their services. The advertiser can go to another provider to set up a new account, but probably will have lost orders in the meantime, incurred charges for obtaining the new account, and suffered other inconveniences. Thus far, this has been successful in stopping most advertisers and marketers from spamming on the Net, advertising online in places where it is not permitted, or keeping names on their mailing lists after their removal has been requested.

Now that email can be transferred from one online service to another, advertisers are finding ways to circumvent the prohibitions of the online service providers. Efforts continue to be made on behalf of the members to slow or stop advertisers from deluging members with unwanted solicitations.

Mailing List Swapping

Companies who own their own mailing lists sometimes trade them with other firms, in order to expand their marketing reach. If a company says that it does not sell its mailing list, this does not always mean that it does not trade it or give it away, either free or for the price of processing the data.

Finding an Existing Mailing List

If you are interested in renting an existing mailing list, rather than compiling one of your own, you might want to use a directory to search through the tens of thousands of lists now available. One of the most comprehensive mailing list directories in print is SRDS Direct Marketing List Sources, from Standard Rate and Data. Oxbridge Communications, Inc. has its own database called the National Directory of Mailing Lists, reported to contain information on some 20,000 mailing lists. Their minimum order is 1,000 lists, which makes this an option for serious mailing list brokers only. The company also produces a print directory of the same name. (Refer to Section IV: "Where Can I Find More Information?—Books" for additional sources of Mailing List Directories.)

You can even locate information on some of the available mailing lists through an Internet search. One site, Direct Marketing World, contains a List Locator. Direct Marketing World can be found at:

http://www.dmworld.com/

Their current list of mailing list categories includes:

Accounting	Fashion, Women's	Manufacturing Companies
Banking	Finance	Men
Boating	Fishing and Hunting	Millionaires
Book Buyers	Food and Gourmet	Music
Business Executives	Gamblers	Nurses
Business to Business	Gay and Lesbian	Opportunity Seekers
Canadian	Gifts	Pet Owners
Children	Government Agencies	Professional
Clothing	Government Officials	Publications
Collectibles	Health	Residential
Computers	High Technology	Schools
Consumer, General	History	Self Improvement
Crafts and Hobbies	Hospitals	Senior Citizens
Credit Seekers	Households	Singles
Doctors	Insurance Industry	Software
Donors	International Lists	Sports
Education	Investors	Students
Engineers	Jewish	Transportation
Entertainment	Law Firms	Travel
Environmental	Lawyers	Video
Ethnic	Libraries	Wealthy Individuals
Farmers	Lottery Players	Women
Fashion, Mens	Mail Order Buyers	Women Executives

If you do decide to search the Internet for available mailing lists, be sure to search for "data card" as well as "mailing list," which should provide many links to available lists and the companies that provide them.

A mailing list broker should be able to help you locate or sort through the mailing lists available to find one that will fit your needs. You can find mailing list brokers listed in the telephone book yellow pages of any large city. One print directory that includes mailing list brokers, along with their specialties, is Direct Marketing Market Place: The Networking Source of the Direct Marketing Industry, published by National Register Publishing.

Mailing List Expenses

Vendors usually charge a base price (a price per thousand records) for their lists, with further charges that depend upon the type of output requested (cheshire labels, pressure-sensitive labels, magnetic tape, diskette, or 3x5 cards), shipping costs, and additional selection criteria (such as telephone numbers, age, gender, geography, and income level). If the list is unique, the charges will be higher, and marketers usually charge a premium for re-use of the list, if multiple uses are allowed at all.

Each vendor sets its own minimum number of records (often 5,000) that may be rented or a minimum charge for use of its lists. Many vendors also place restrictions on how their lists can be used, often requiring the right to approve any piece before it is mailed.

Stopping the Junk Mail and Telemarketing Calls

If junk mail and telephone solicitors are driving you crazy, you may want to have your name removed from their lists. The only way to get rid of all junk mail and telephone solicitations is to pay off all of your bills, close out all of your accounts, cancel all of your credit cards, and move without having any of your mail forwarded. You might also need to change your name in order to keep them from tracking you down. From that point on, ride only public transportation to keep your name out of the DMV, and do not buy any other type of transportation that requires a license or registration (such as a motorcycle, boat, or aircraft). Do not maintain any type of professional license, or take part in a profession where you might be listed in a directory. Make all purchases in cash, do not request anything through the mail or respond to any type of solicitation, and just to be on the safe side, don't get a telephone. You probably will have to give up your friends and family as well.

Short of this, you can take somewhat more reasonable steps that at least should significantly cut down on your junk mail and telephone solicitations.

DON'T:

- Send a change-of-address form to the Post Office, as that probably will add your name and address to a "new movers" list, as well as provide a mechanism for all of the companies currently sending you junk mail to receive updates. Notify friends, family members, and business contacts directly instead.

- Give out personal information to everyone and anyone who asks.

- Print your telephone number on your checks or give it out any more than necessary.

- Fill out warranty registration cards. If you must send them in, do not provide any more than the minimum required information identifying the product purchased, its serial number, and your name and address.

- Participate in birthday clubs, buyers' clubs, or membership organizations.

DO:

- Get a new unlisted telephone number to cut down on telemarketing calls, or at least omit your address to cut down on new mail solicitations. According to the federal Telephone Consumer Protection Act, all telemarketers in the United States (except for nonprofit, tax-exempt organizations and charities) must maintain a "do not call" list of those who do not wish to be contacted. This still allows them to call you once each year before you can take legal action against them, but it may help.

- Tell telephone solicitors that you want to be put on their "do not call" list.

- Tell mail order companies, 800 and 900 number operators, and other companies that you call, in answer to television, radio, magazine and newspaper advertisements, that you do not wish to be put on any mailing lists, to have your telephone number or name sold, or to receive calls from them.

- Call to place telephone orders for products or goods from a pay phone or from your office, rather than from home.

- Write to each company that sends you an offer, and ask to be taken off of its mailing lists.

- Let charities that you contribute to know that you do not want your name or information sold or released; or make all donations anonymously.

- Contact each of the major companies that compile street-address directories and asked to be removed from their present and future listings:
  - R.L. Polk & Company
  - Haines & Company Inc.
  - Reuben H. Donnelley Corp.

(Refer to Appendix O for these companies.)

In New Zealand, Parliament passed legislation mandating that direct marketers may not buy, sell, rent or exchange personal information without permission from the individual. Violators are subject to a fine of up to $30,000 per violation. In Canada, consumers are given the opportunity to have their names removed from lists at least once every three years. In the United States, there is little to stop anyone from buying, selling, or trading consumer names, addresses, and profiles for use in mailing lists, but you are not completely on your own.

You can sign up with the Direct Marketing Association's Telephone Preference Service to have your name and phone number added to their "do not call" list. This will only get your message to members of the Direct Marketing Association, but it will cut down on what you receive. (Refer to Appendix O for their address.)

You may also consider joining one of several privacy groups that will list your name in their directories and send it to hundreds of companies, threatening legal action if they solicit you. This will not eliminate all junk mail, but it will reduce the burden. One such group is Private Citizen, Inc. (PCI). Another organization that will help you to contact some of the country's largest mailing list compilers is the Stop Junk Mail Association. Buyer's Choice also allows you to specify what types of direct mail and what lists you want to opt out of. Refer to Appendix O for the addresses of these associations.

Opting out of mailing lists will take some time, effort, and continued diligence on your part, and it is doubtful that you will ever stop receiving junk mail entirely or permanently. As long as junk mail remains an effective advertising medium, companies will continue to fill your mail boxes with offers and advertisements.

News

Spies are of no use nowadays. Their profession is over.

The newspapers do their work instead.

—*Oscar Wilde*

Most of us probably would select the news as one of our first resources when look-ing for information about a prominent person. However, the news can provide information about virtually anyone. With the various news media churning out story after story, day in and day out, even the most obscure topics and least famous peo-ple can find their way onto a talk show or into a magazine or newspaper story.

News Directories

Online and CD-ROM databases are rich with news information culled from news-papers, newswires, magazines (and their online equivalent "zines"), journals, and even television and radio broadcasts. So many sources for news are available online that entire directories are dedicated to tracking and cataloging them. Fulltext Sources Online from BiblioData tracks just publications that are carried in full text, and their listings number in the thousands. Internet addresses are included in the listings. (This directory is also searchable online through DataStar.)

Another directory, Books and Periodicals Online by Nuchine Nobari (published by Library Alliance), tracks both books and periodicals that are carried online.

Many additional news directories are available. Some are dedicated to tracking newsletters or periodicals only, while others contain a combination of news sources, many of which are not yet online in any form. (Appendix G lists news directories that are searchable online or on CD-ROM.)

Although news directories will not guide you to individual articles in which a given person is mentioned, they can be very useful in pointing you in the right direction. For example, if I were looking for information about a person whom I knew lived in Hungary, I might search Fulltext Sources Online to find publications that could be searched online in full text. This search results in five possibilities:

- *Budapest Business Journal*
- *Budapest Sun*
- *Hungarian Financial Revue*
- *Invest in Hungary*
- *MTI Econonews*

If a person were known in the food industry, I could use a news directory database to locate dozens of food publications in which I might find information about or by them. If my subject specialized in ice cream, I might want to go straight to:

- *Ice Cream Reporter*

or to any of the following:

- *Frozen and Chilled Foods*
- *Frozen Food Age*
- *Frozen Food Digest*
- *Milk Products*

Other directories can be similarly used to locate industry publications or local newspapers, and to find out which of them can be searched online.

For publications that cannot be searched online, you might then call the publisher, which often can be found by a search of online publications directories. Many keep an in-house index or database that could reveal whether they have written about your subject. Alternatively, you might visit a university library that carries back issues of the magazine or journal or microfiche of the newspaper.

For European publications, if you don't know who the publisher is or you don't know which publications to contact, you might also try searching the following Internet site for a list of the top 250 European daily newspapers, which includes circulation figures:

http://mediator.pira.co.uk/newsfocus/top250/content.html

Another good source for the text of newspapers or local business journals not available online is the library in the publication's home town, which you can find using a telephone directory database. The reference librarian may be able to help in searching back issues for you or may arrange to lend microfiche of their back issues to a library near you, so that you can search through them yourself.

Newspapers

Newspapers can supply information about virtually anyone. Most carry the "big stories," as you would expect, but smaller newspapers also routinely mention people who are involved in local groups, such as the PTA or the Girl Scouts. Anyone who gets married, is promoted, or dies may be listed among their announcements. Local business people are mentioned for their involvement in the Chamber of Commerce, the Rotary Club, and similar groups, and are sought for quotations when events could affect their businesses or the local economy. Traffic accidents, county fairs, and dozens of everyday events can make their way into newsprint. Even children may be mentioned or featured for winning at spelling bees or science fairs or for bringing in a prize lamb at the 4-H Club.

Something else one can find in smaller newspapers is information about arrests. Although not generally newsworthy by big-city standards, the arrest of a local citizen for solicitation or drunk driving can be big news in a small town. In fact, some communities have taken to publishing the names of all "johns" caught for solicitation of prostitutes in the local papers, in order to shame their citizens into better behavior.

If you wish to search through newspapers for articles about someone, there are a few variables to consider. First, not all newspapers are yet available online or on CD-ROM, so you may need to use a news directory (online, on CD-ROM, or in print) to locate the papers in the subject's region and learn how you can best access them.

Some newspapers are found online or on CD-ROM only as citations and abstracts. This is useful for locating the articles that interest you, but you may then need to contact the newspaper, a local library, or a document delivery company to obtain a copy of the full article. Some database vendors also allow for online ordering of the articles.

Databases have been compiled from selected biographical articles appearing in the *Los Angeles Times, New York Times,* and *Washington Post.* Segregating this information into its own database (as LEXIS-NEXIS has done for each of these papers) makes searching it much more convenient.

DataTimes, Dow Jones News/Retrieval, Knight-Ridder Information, Inc., LEXIS-NEXIS, and NewsNet all offer large numbers of newspapers online. When you do not know where the information might be found, online systems such as these allow you to search across dozens of newspapers at once, which can save a great deal of time and expense. Newspapers may also be found on the Internet through sites such as:

Newspapers Accessible on the Internet:
http://isis.iah.com/wysenet/papers.html

Top:News and Media:Newspapers:
http://www.yahoo.com/News_and_Media/Newspapers/

Top:Business and Economy:Companies:Media:Newspapers:
http://www.yahoo.com/Business_and_Economy/Companies/Media/Newspapers/

Campus Newspapers on the Internet Web & Gopher:
http://beacon-www.asa.utk.edu/resources/papers.html

Electric Library:
http://www2.elibrary.com/id/28/177/search.cgi

Some databases also combine news sources, drawing from newspapers, newswires, magazines, journals, and television and radio transcripts. Examples of these can be found later in this chapter under "Combined News Databases."

Newswires

Newswires are a good place to look for business information such as press releases, product announcements, legal actions, company acquisitions, announced earnings and dividends, and expansion plans; civic, cultural, and scientific events; and developments in politics and government. Source organizations include public and private companies, associations, political parties, unions, sports and entertainment organizations, educational and scientific institutions, and government agencies.

Personal data that can be gathered on the wires typically includes announcements of promotions and changes in management, especially in the upper ranks of large corporations. News about celebrities, politicians, sports stars, and others in the news are also found there. One newswire database, Associated Press Candidate Biographies (available on LEXIS-NEXIS as APBIO), contains the text of biographical newswires about political candidates.

Nearly anything that anyone cares to put in a press release and pay a newswire company to broadcast may be found in a newswire database. Newswires can even include photographs.

The information on the newswires tends to be brief, but full feature articles sometimes follow, if the story is picked up by other news media. That is often the hope of those issuing press releases on the wires.

Some newswires carry only a certain type of news. The Catholic News Service Wire (available through NewsNet, Inc.), for example, covers news and developments within the Catholic church, including papal actions, election and confirmation of church officials, and summaries of official developments relevant to the Catholic church. If you were looking for recent information about the Pope, or another clerical official, this newswire could be a good source. Similarly, E-Wire (available through Newsnet, Inc., CompuServe Information Service, and America Online) contains news releases covering environmental topics. There are many financial and economic newswires, such as Federal Filings Business Newswire (available through Dow Jones News/Retrieval and as part of several other databases) and Japan Economic Newswire Plus (JEN) (available through Knight-Ridder Information, Inc., NEXIS, and Dow Jones News/Retrieval, and as part of LEXIS Country Information Service).

Several newswires carry a broader spectrum of news. One of the best known is UPI News, from United Press International. UPI News (available through Knight-Ridder Information, Inc., CompuServe Knowledge Index, AT&T FYI News Service, NewsNet, Inc., and NEXIS, and as part of Futures World News Network) includes national and international news; current events; the political scene at the federal and state government levels; business; financial and sports news, columns and commentaries; and standing features. Gannett News Service (available online through DataTimes Corporation) is another example, carrying national and international news, features, finance, and sports stories, with an emphasis on state and regional stories. Kyodo News Service (available online through NewsNet, Inc. and DataStar, and as part of: Newswire ASAP) covers Japan's current events, internal politics, governmental news, economics, and business; it also includes coverage of American and European dealings with Japan, and news from the Pacific Rim.

All these newswires are available as databases. In addition, a number of databases combine several newswires into one service. For example, IAC Newswire ASAP (available online through Knight-Ridder Information, Inc.) provides access to certain date ranges of the following fourteen newswire services:

- Agencia EFE
- Business Wire
- Comtex
- Deutsche Press-Agentur
- Federal News Service
- Japan Economic Newswire
- Kyodo News Service
- Market Consensus Surveys
- Newsbytes News Service

- PR Newswire
- TASS
- Tokyo Financial Wire
- United Press International
- Xinhua News Agency

Current newswires can also be found now on the Internet, and it is not unusual for companies to republish their press releases on their own Web pages. Thus, the Net is becoming a great place to start your search for news on top executives of a company.

Some of the newswires that you'll find on the Internet include:

Canada NewsWire:
http://www.newswire.ca/

Cole's Newswire:
http://colegroup.com/nw/

Conrail Newswire (for railroad employees):
http://www.conrail.com/news/

PR Newswire:
http://www.prnewswire.com/

SportsLine USA Newswire:
http://www.sportsline.com/

You can search for other newswires on the Net through the Electric Library at:
http://www2.elibrary.com/id/28/177/search.cgi

Magazines

Hundreds of magazines can be found online and in CD-ROM databases. Like the newswire databases, some magazine databases are dedicated to a single publication. For example, there are databases such as *AutoWeek, BYTE, Canadian Mining Journal, Fortune, LIFE, Public Utilities Reports,* and *The Washington Quarterly.*

If you know or suspect that one of these publications contains an article about someone you are researching, you should be able to locate and extract the story within a few minutes if it exists on one of these databases.

Other databases include many magazines among their sources. For example, CMP Publications Computers File includes:

- *Computer Reseller News*
- *Computer Systems News*
- *Network Computing*
- *UNIX Today!*
- *VARBUSINESS*

and Time Publications includes:

- *Entertainment Weekly*
- *Fortune*
- *LIFE*
- *Money*
- *People*
- *Sports Illustrated*
- *Time International*
- *TIME*

Another database, Magazine ASAP, contains articles from more than 100 selected general-interest periodicals.

Additional databases include articles from magazines and from other news media, such as newspapers and newswires. Examples of these can be found later in this chapter.

Many magazines also maintain a Web site or other presence on the Internet. Such a site may include past or present issues, or portions of either. Many Internet sites index magazines along with other news sources that can be found on the Net. Please refer to "Combined News Databases" later in this chapter for examples of these sites. One Net site that is dedicated to magazines (although some online zines are mixed into their listings) is Starting Point—Magazines, which can be found at:

http://stpt.com/cgi-bin/magazine/magazine.cgi

Additional magazines can be found on the Internet at site such as:

Top:News and Media:Magazines:
http://www.yahoo.com/News/Magazines

Online Commercial Magazines:
http://digital.net/magazine.html

Campmor Outdoor Magazines on the Internet:
http://www.campmor.com/outdoor.magazines.html

Senior Com From Gus's NewsStand: Magazines on the Net:
http://www.senior.com/mags.html

You can search for other magazines on the Net through the Electric Library at:
http://www2.elibrary.com/id/28/177/search.cgi

Journals

Do you remember the commercial in which a group of women in an office building breathlessly ogle a shirtless hunk of a construction worker while he drinks a can of Diet Coke? This ad raised a bit of a furor in advertising circles and caused some controversy between people who found the ad to be sexist and those who were amused to see men treated as sex objects.

If you were starting an advertising agency and decided to find and recruit the genius who created this ad, you would not have to look far. Hundreds of trade journals are available online, and several among them address the advertising industry. *Adweek,* for example, is available on NEXIS, as well as within the Marketing and Advertising Reference Service (MARS) database on DataStar, Knight-Ridder Information, Inc., NEXIS, and FT PROFILE. A quick search of *Adweek* reveals far more than the name of the person who created the Diet Coke ad. Writer Ann Cooper turned out an entire article about him for the April 11, 1994, Eastern Edition. Within the article, you could obtain the following information to aid in your recruiting efforts:

Name: Lee Garfinkel
Age: 39 (at the time the article was written)
Marital Status: Married
Father's Background: Shoe Salesman from 175th Street in the Bronx
Current employer:
    Lowe & Partners/SMS (a $500 million agency), since November 1992
    Located in the Grace Building, Sixth Avenue, New York (corner office)
Current position: Chief Creative Officer and Vice President
Salary: In the high six figures
Previous Employment: (in reverse chronological order)
    Star Copywriter at BBDO (for 3 years)
    Starting as Junior Copywriter, ending as Creative Director at Levine,
    Huntley, Schmidt & Beaver
    Stand-Up Comic
Business Associates:
    Andy Langer, CEO at Lowe & Partners/SMS
    Frank Lowe, Chairman at Lowe & Partners/SMS
    Martyn Straw, Head of Planning at Lowe & Partners/SMS
    John Hayes, President at Lowe & Partners/SMS
    Barbara Siegel, Copywriter at Lowe & Partners/SMS
    Peter Cohen, at Lowe & Partners/SMS and previously at Levine, Huntley, Schmidt & Beaver
    Todd Godwin, at Lowe & Partners/SMS and previously at Levine, Huntley, Schmidt & Beaver
    C.J. Waldman, at Lowe & Partners/SMS and previously at Levine, Huntley, Schmidt & Beaver
    Leslie Stern, at Lowe & Partners/SMS and previously at Levine, Huntley, Schmidt & Beaver
    Richard Ostroff, at Lowe & Partners/SMS and previously at Levine, Huntley, Schmidt & Beaver
    Bob Nelson, at Lowe & Partners/SMS and previously at Levine, Huntley, Schmidt & Beaver
    Amy Borkowsky, at Lowe & Partners/SMS and previously at Levine, Huntley, Schmidt & Beaver
    Tony DeGregorio, creative partner at Levine, Huntley, Schmidt & Beaver
Current Agency Accounts:
    Diet Coke (a $70 million account)
    Hanson, a bricks-and-chemical conglomerate
    Grey Poupon
    Fresca
    Sprite
    Smirnoff (handled out of the London office)
    Cinzano
Accounts That Got Away:
    Thom McAn shoes
    Comedy Central
    Burger King
Previous Agency Accounts:
    Pepsi, for which Mr. Garfinkel won awards (at BBDO); worked on M.C. Hammer's "Feelings" commercial, "Logo" (the ad with Cindy Crawford), and "Shady Acres"
    Matchbox Toys at Levine, Huntley, Schmidt & Beaver

Reading this article, you could also find out a great deal about Garfinkel's personal management style and reputation, his manner of dress, and even details of his office decor, including a rubber donkey's head! If you were planning to recruit him, this article would provide a wonderful starting place for your background research. You might find that you have business associates in common who might provide an introduction or additional background information. You could identify Garfinkel's current and previous ads to get a better understanding of his creative capabilities. If you knew anyone who worked for any of the accounts that got away, you might find out why they did. All of this information could give you an advantage in recruiting or negotiating.

This type of article could also be extremely useful for companies providing competitive intelligence to other advertising agencies. One may think of trade journals as being rather dry and lifeless reading, but from the perspective of a researcher, I consider this type of article quite full of juicy details.

Many journals can also be found on the Internet. Please refer to the "Zines" section of this chapter, as well as the "Combined News Databases" section for examples of sites indexing journals found on the Net.

Zines

Zines, sometimes called e-zines or e-journals, are online publications. They may be published as online editions of familiar magazines (such as *HotWired,* the online edition of *Wired*), or may be entirely new publications that exist only online.

Because anyone can publish a zine and add it to the Internet, zines can have a considerably different look and feel than the print publications you are used to. You may find information in them that you would not find elsewhere. You may also find strong language and even stronger opinions. Be aware that many zines lack the credibility of print publications, and the writers and publishers could even take pains to maintain their anonymity while publishing pure lies. If you read something about someone in a zine, always consider the source.

The online medium also lends itself to the exchange of views between readers about the publications, sometimes including online discussion with the authors or the publisher. This type of interchange is much more immediate and interactive than the "letters to the editor" section of print publications, and it adds another dimension to the zines.

Many zines are free to the reader, but some are emailed only to paying subscribers. Unlike print publications, it would be possible for a zine publisher to offer partial purchase, so that a subscriber could pay for only the parts of the zine that interest them.

There are so many zines being published that several Internet Web sites are dedicated to keeping track of them and/or reviewing their work. Many of these sites include news. Please refer to "Combined News Databases" later in this chapter for examples of those sites. One site that is dedicated to indexing only zines is Zine Net—The Place for Zines on the Web. It can be found at:

http://www.zine.net/

Searching zines for articles about a particular individual can be an arduous task, especially if the publisher has not indexed the publication with the searcher in mind. Thus, the researcher can easily miss these sources.

Other sites on which you can find additional zines include:

E-Zine-List:

http://www.he.net/%7Ebrumley/dir/magazine.htm

Directories of Electronic Journals (from Hyper Journal):

http://www.gold.ac.uk/history/hyperjournal/director.htm

Electronic Journals:

http://rourier,dur.ac.uk:8000/journals.html

Online Publications:Zines:

http://www.etext.org/Zines/

Scholarly Journals Distributed Via the World Wide Web (from the University of Houston Libraries):

http://info.lib.uh.edu/wj/webjour.html

Newsletters

These days, it seems like almost every organization is publishing a newsletter. These can provide valuable information on current topics in any field of research. They can be filled with recaps of meetings, elections, and events, including the names of many of their members. People who do not otherwise write professionally can sometimes have their arms twisted to contribute an occasional article to a newsletter.

Some newsletter databases combine more than one newsletter. One of the largest, combining more than 650, is Newsletter Database, from Information Access Company (IAC). Dozens of others cover one or more newsletters. NewsNet is a good source for many, including some very expensive ones and some which are exclusive to this service. Newsletters provide more avenues for finding information about individuals participating in organizations, associations, or professions.

Many additional newsletters can be found on the Internet. Some of the best sites indexing these can be found within Yahoo!, such as:

Business and Economy: Companies: Newsletters:

http://www.yahoo.com/Computers_and_Internet/Internet/Newsletters/

Government: Law: Newsletters:

http://www.yahoo.com/Government/Law/Newsletters/

Science: Astronomy: Newsletters:

http://www.yahoo.com/Science/Astonomy/Newsletters/

Arts: Performing Arts: Drama: Newsletters:

http://www.yahoo.com/Arts/Performing_Arts/Drama/Newsletters/

A search of Yahoo! for "Newsletters" will provide indices to a great many more newsletters, categorized by subject.

Television and Radio Transcripts

If you have watched any news or talk shows lately, you've probably heard the announcement at the end of the program telling where to call or write for transcripts of the show. The same companies often make those transcripts available online as well. Transcript databases are useful in locating people who have appeared on talk shows or on the radio. They also can help you to find out what has been said about someone. If it is your job to book talk show guests, transcript databases can tell where else someone has appeared and what they have talked about. You can also use these databases to find out whether other shows have recently covered the topic that you are planning. If you know or even suspect that the person that you are researching has written a book or been involved in anything controversial, there is a good chance that a transcript database will help you to identify any live interviews on television or radio. Talk show transcripts often appear in one of the following databases:

- Burrelle's Broadcast Database and Burrelle's TV Transcripts
- TRANSCRIPT (See Appendix I for the address.)
  (Note that TRANSCRIPT contains only citations and abstracts, although copies of the transcripts may be ordered online.)

LEXIS-NEXIS also carries several transcripts databases within their News library. Theirs include not only news transcripts, but same-day transcripts for newsworthy trials, such as those involving O.J. Simpson.

For international news, you might also consider:
- BBC Monitoring Summary of World Broadcasts
- CNN News Transcripts (See Appendix I for the address.)

(Refer to Appendix N for addresses of these vendors except where otherwise noted.)

A few additional online databases are somewhat more limited or subject-specific in the transcripts that they offer. The MacNeil/Lehrer Newshour database carries transcripts of that program. Network Earth Forum carries information from the TBS television program. Reuter Transcript Report provides word-for-word record transcripts of Washington, DC political news and events. Wall $treet Week (WSW), carries transcripts of the Public Broadcasting System television program of the same name.

At least two transcript databases are available on CD-ROM as well:
- Broadcast News on CD-ROM
- CNN Newsroom Global View

Television and radio transcripts can also be found on the Internet, although these are often limited to the most current news. Some television stations are indexed at:

Yahoo!—Business and Economy:Companies:Media:Television:Networks:
http://www.yahoo.com/Business_and_Economy/
Companies/Media/Television/Networks/

Many television and radio programs also maintain their own presence now on the Internet, America Online, CompuServe, or Prodigy. This often is announced during or after their broadcast. These sites sometimes include transcripts or information about recent broadcasts and usually include an email address where further information can be requested.

Another site that indexes Television, Newspaper and Movies is the Entertainment & Miscellaneous Links at:

http://www.tcac.com/%Esteveb/ent.html

You can search for TV & Radio Transcripts on the Internet through the Electric Library at:

http://www2.elibrary.com/id/28/177/search.cgi

Examples of these sites include:

The Rosie O'Donnell Show:

http://www.rosieo.com/

Politically Incorrect with Bill Maher:

http://www.abctelevision.com/pi/index.html

Home & Family:

http://www.homeandfamily.com/

Late Night with Conan O'Brien:

http://www.nbc.com/entertainment/shows/conan/index.html

Ricki Lake

http://www.spe.sony.com/Pictures/tv/rickilake/ricki.html

Many additional show sites can be found on the Internet, while others maintain sites on services such as America Online and CompuServe.

Combined News Databases

Many news databases combine a number of news sources, including newspapers, newsletters, newswires, magazines, journals, and television and radio transcripts. These databases may contain full text or only citations and abstracts of the articles or transcripts. Databases that cross many news media are an excellent choice for a fishing expedition when you do not know whether any information is available about a person.

Combined news databases can be subject-specific, such as:
- Computer ASAP, which concentrates on the computer industry
- Ethnic NewsWatch, which focuses on ethnic and minority newspapers, magazines, and journals
- PROMT (Predicasts Overview of Markets and Technology), concentrating on companies, markets, products, and technologies for major international, national, and regional manufacturing and service industries.

Some databases combine just a couple of types of these news sources. Examples of these include:

- The Business Library, which includes business, trade and industry publications

- McGraw Hill Publications Online, which includes a selection of magazines and newspapers

- Reuter TEXTLINE, including major daily and financial and business newspapers and journals

- Trade & Industry ASAP, taken from business and trade periodicals and newswires

Similar databases can be found on CD-ROM. Not all databases carry full text online or on CD-ROM. Some, like Reuter TEXTLINE, mix citations and abstracts with full-text articles.

Some Internet sites also index multiple news sources. Examples of such sites include:

Online Magazines, which indexes both popular print magazines and zines found on the Internet:

http://www.ecnet.net/users/mupmw7/mags.htm

Journals and Magazines can be found through the searches available at:

http://www.lib.lsu.edu/epubs/journals.html

Magazines, Newspapers, Radio, Television Networks, and more can be found at:

http://www.nextek.com/mrhodes/HTTP/media.htm

Online Magazines, Newspapers and Radio Stations can be found through:

http://www.cyber.aus.net/ezine.htm

News Clipping Services, Current Awareness, and SDI (Selective Dissemination of Information)

If you are not able keep up with all of the news, but need to keep track of a competitor, a celebrity, or any other topic, news clipping services can provide a solution.

A News Clipping service can scan a set of publications or databases at regular intervals—daily, weekly, monthly, quarterly, or on any schedule you like. Search parameters are selected ahead of time, and the results may be delivered online, via fax, by overnight delivery, or via "snail mail," the U.S. Postal Service.

Many online vendors offer the ability to set up your own automated clipping or current awareness service. You can enter the search statements ahead of time, identify databases to be searched, set the interval at which you'd like to repeat the search, and specify your preferred delivery method. For complex searches or databases that you do not have access to, you might also consider using an information professional who can provide this service for you. For those publications that are not available online, it may be necessary for you to find a newsclipping service that specializes in the clipping of print publications.

A dozen or more vendors now offer free clipping services on the Internet. In some cases, headlines and "basic" articles are free, while the full text of some articles may be obtained only by subscribers who pay a monthly fee for access to "premium" publications or wire services.

Bulletin Boards

Online bulletin boards (sometimes referred to as forums, or roundtables, or Usenet newsgroups) are far more than the equivalent of their predecessors, the thumbtack bulletin boards of the past. Online bulletin boards now provide an international public forum for posting questions, opinions, and information and for holding discussions and debates between people around the globe.

Whatever the subject, there is probably a bulletin board where you can meet others with a similar interest and discuss issues near and dear to you.

When traveling among these bulletin boards, you will soon notice that there are different rules for different boards. The number one rule on most bulletin boards states whether or not advertising is allowed on the board. Another rule often states that re-publishing anything that appears on the board is prohibited; this can actually be a matter of copyright infringement. Other rules have to do with proper etiquette (or "netiquette") for any bulletin board. Typical netiquette rules may prohibit the use of offensive language or discourage personal attacks.

Large vendors of bulletin boards, such as America Online, CompuServe, and Prodigy, usually appoint or hire a system operator (Sysop), or host, for each board, to ensure that the rules are obeyed, to bar access for those who refuse to obey the rules, and to try to keep participation active on the board. (For systems that accept paid advertisements, the time you spend online can translate to advertising dollars for them.) The largest bulletin board system of all, the Internet, is more of a free-for-all, where individual members take it upon themselves to police the boards in which they participate.

A little time spent reading the participants' messages will quickly reveal the unique personality of each forum or bulletin board. Since each forum serves as a microcosm of diverse people with one or more similar interests that brought them to the board, one forum can have a very different feel or personality from another. On one, you may find a virtual community where members support one another, offering advice and assistance, forming friendships, doing business together, and otherwise becoming a somewhat cohesive group. Participants in these groups often remain with them for years. On another forum, members curse, debate, and harangue one another; pontificating on any given point or issue; and YELL AT EACH OTHER AT THE TOP OF THEIR LUNGS (by using upper-case characters) whenever they see a message they disagree with. Visitors to these groups often move on fairly quickly to less contentious neighborhoods.

Some boards serve as a meeting or messaging place for people who at other times meet face-to-face. On others, the members use aliases, maintain relative anonymity, and never meet or correspond in any other way.

Before becoming too involved in a bulletin board, it is best to spend a little time visiting to find out not only what the rules are, but whether the board offers a community or group of people that you want to converse with.

Appendix L contains a list of some of the major bulletin board vendors. On the Internet, there are reported to be as many as 20,000 bulletin boards, or Usenet newsgroups, as they are referred to on the Net. Boards come and go, often dying for lack of participation, so expect the list of available boards on any of these systems (and most especially on the Internet) to change continuously.

When you are looking for information about people, bulletin boards can help in a number of ways. First, there is the chance that the person you are looking for may also participate in a bulletin board, so you may be able to make direct contact. Some bulletin board vendors (such as CompuServe) allow online searching of their membership directories, providing at least an email address, and sometimes more. Although no single membership directory exists for the Internet, there are mechanisms for finding people using their names or email addresses. For those who value their privacy, there also are businesses and a few pro bono services that will relay any messages through their own email address in order to mask the original sender's identity.

If you know someone's interests, you might ask around in the forums that you think they would be most likely to join. Even if they do not participate in the forum, associates of theirs may, and they may be willing to put you in contact.

If you are looking for information about a celebrity, there may be a fan club forum that can fill you in on every film, commercial, or television show that they've appeared in; the names of their family members and friends; and their next scheduled appearance; and even what they eat for breakfast. The celebrity may even participate in the forum from time to time.

If you want information about a respected authority in any field—engineering, nuclear science, law, cardiology, astrology, or astronomy—a forum can often provide access to others who are very familiar with their work and who can point you to a wealth of information. It is possible to gather a great deal of information about an expert's professional reputation by posting your questions in a forum devoted to their field of expertise.

You may even find that you are talking to current or former neighbors or co-workers of your subject. Keep in mind that most forums are public vehicles, so this is not the place for gathering sensitive information about someone without their knowledge.

Again, exercise caution. Information found on a bulletin board should be taken with a grain of salt. After all, you probably do not even know for sure who you are talking to. It is best to use the forum to gather leads to more hard-core facts, rather than accepting what you hear as factual.

Photographic Images

A ny large newspaper receives hundreds of photographs each day. Among those photos are pictures of celebrities, politicians, and people from every walk of life. During the last few years, photography has begun to replace old-fashioned chemical film with digital imaging. This has enhanced our ability to capture, store, index, and manipulate photographs and to transmit them around the world. Digital cameras have become the tools of photojournalists and newspapers, advertising agencies, and even artists. Sophisticated equipment can already scan and store up to 100 images at one time. A single CD can store 3,000 to 4,000 thumbnail images (small low-resolution "condensations" of the digitized photographs) or approximately 100 high-resolution images, and developing technologies like DVD (Digital Versatile Disc) promise far greater capacity.

At the same time, computer programmers have developed software to capture photos from the wire services, along with their header and keyword information, and pull them into databases. Such a system can capture and file thousands of photographs each day.

Once on databases, photo editors can locate and retrieve their choice of images on nearly any subject. What used to take hours of paging through photographs can now be accomplished in minutes if the database is well indexed, and the search software is well designed. The pictures can then be cropped, sharpened, colorized, manipulated in dozens of ways, and scaled to fit the space available for them.

Photo Stock Agencies

Newspapers are not the only industry to take advantage of these developments. MPCA (Media Photographers' Copyright Agency, Inc.) and Applied Graphics Technologies (AGT) have joined to create MPCA in View, a completely digital stock agency. MPCA is a subsidiary of the American Society of Media Photographers (ASMP) and includes more than 500 "world-class" photographers.

Picture Network International (PNI) has developed Seymour, a natural-language search program for photographs. They reportedly now provide an online stock photography service with access to over a quarter million images from 35 of the world's top picture agencies. Participants include such leading photo agencies as Aurora, Bruce Coleman, Photo Network, Rainbow, Alaska Stock Images, AllStock, Archive Photos, and Black Star Publishing. Once an image is selected, information about it can be viewed, including rights and model releases. Many images can be licensed directly through PNI. A low-resolution version can be downloaded for placement in comprehensives or layouts. Images can be delivered online, on CD or by overnight delivery service.

For further information, you can reach PNI at:

Picture Network International
2000 15th Street North
Arlington, VA 22201
(703) 312-6210
(703) 558-7898 Fax

Other database products are designed to act as your own private photo stock. Products such as these can provide photographs of people involved in all types of activities. Most of the people pictured are somewhat anonymous. Celebrities, politicians, models, and other famous faces also are sometimes included. Examples of photo stock databases available on CD-ROM are:

- Comstock Desktop Photography
- ELECTRICIris Vol. 1, No. 1, People and Environments
- Image Folio
- Photo Gallery

Photo stock agencies that can be found on the Internet include:

Stock Market Photo Agency:
http://www.tsmphoto.com/

A directory of stock photo sources is included at:
http://www.creativedir.com/html/13.html

If you're on a limited budget, you will be pleased to know that some stock photos have become available as shareware, or available for free if credited properly to the photographer. The online medium has enabled even amateur photographers to share their work with the worldwide online community, so if you're looking for a photograph of anyone famous, or a picture of an anonymous person participating in just about any type of activity, there is a good chance that you can find unpublished shots from amateurs and professionals alike, using online photographic forums, fan sites, and photographers' Internet Web pages to locate and contact photographers who have photo stock to share.

News Services
Another online service, NewsCom, offers retrieval of text, photos, and graphics. This is fairly new for online services, as most text databases do not yet offer either photos or graphics. Some of the sources included in NewsCom's service are the *Wall Street Journal Report, TIME, U.S. News and World Report, USA Today, Gannett News Service, Barron's, the Times of London News Service, El Pas, The Christian Science Monitor News Service, Weather Services, Magellan Geographix,* and *Allsport.*

Although online news databases usually are more up-to-date than CD-ROM versions, one advantage of the disc version is that photographs and other graphics are more often incorporated into the stories, just as they originally appeared in print.

Business Periodicals and Magazines

Several business periodical and magazine databases available on CD-ROM incorporate text and photos, just as they appeared in the original publications. These databases can be useful if you want to find out what someone in a magazine or periodical looks like, but re-use of the photographs may be prohibited except by prior arrangement with the publisher. Examples of these products are:

- Business Periodicals Global
- General Periodicals Research II
- Magazine Express
- Time Almanac

Many publications have also produced online versions, on the Internet, as well as CompuServe and similar systems. It is possible to download the images that appear on the pages of many of these publications, just as you download the text of the articles.

Missing Children and Loved Ones

Photographic image databases now are being used to aid in locating missing children and other loved ones. CompuServe carries one such database; it provides descriptions and images of criminally-abducted children in the United States and Canada. Information provided by law enforcement agencies worldwide includes physical description, date of disappearance, and investigation information, including agency name, address, telephone number, investigating officer, agency case number, and the FBI's NCIC number. Photos in this database include a picture of each child before their abduction, and simulated age progression photos sometimes show how the child might look now. For information about the Missing Children Database, contact:

National Child Safety Council
Missing Children Division
4065 Page Avenue
P.O. Box 1368
Jackson, MI 49204
(800) 222-1464
(517) 764-6070
(517) 764-3068 Fax

Similar databases are being developed on the Internet and other systems, many through volunteer efforts of members. Some of the missing children's sites on the Internet include:

Missing Children (from the Phoenix Police Department):
http://www.ci.phoenix.az.us/MISSKIDS/missing.html

Missing Children from the greater Los Angeles Area:
http://www.at-la.com/children/

Missing Children's Network of Michigan
http://www.aliens.com/mcn/top.html

Missing Children Minnesota:
http://www.shadeslanding.com/missing/miss_pg2.htm

The Missing Children's Network Canada:
http://www.alliance9000.com/E/MCNC/

The Missing Children Database, from the National Center for Missing & Exploited Children:
http://www.missingkids.org/search.html

Info-Highway International's Missing Children's Directory:
http://www.gmcd.org/

Missing & Exploited Children (from GalaxyGate International Mall):
http://www.galaxygate.com/missing.htm

Child Quest International:
http://www.childquest.org/child_quest/cqmissingchildren.html

CRIMINALS

Alleged Abductors
Missing children databases may also carry photos of the child's alleged abductor, when known. One such site, the Abductors' section of the Child Quest International, Inc. database, can be accessed through:
http://www.childquest.org/cgi-bin/all_abductors.cgi

Registered Sex Offenders
There has been a great deal of controversy over whether and how communities are to be notified when registered sex offenders move into their neighborhoods. With the passing of the federal statute known as Megan's Law, states are required to find a way to notify communities of registered sex offenders living in their areas. There are many forms that this notification can take: alerting school administrators and neighborhood watch groups, issuing press releases, setting up 900-numbers which the public can call to find out if someone they suspect is registered, or even holding townhall meetings. Additional methods include the creation of CD-ROM databases containing information and photographs of registered sex offenders, which are now being made available upon request by some police and sheriff stations. By the time this book reaches your hands, the Internet will also be used to identify registered sex offenders. The Sex Offender site can be found at:
http://www.sexoffender.com/

The FBI's Ten Most Wanted Fugitives

If you want to know who the FBI's Ten Most Wanted Fugitives are, you needn't travel to FBI headquarters in Washington, DC, or even to your local post office. Pictures and background on the FBI's Ten Most Wanted Fugitives can now be viewed on the Internet at:

http://www.fbi.gov/mostwant/tenlist.htm

Photos Included in Other Databases

Photos are included in many other types of database, especially those on CD-ROMs. Multimedia encyclopedias are filled with photographs of scientists, inventors, and important figures in history. Additional CD-ROM databases that can help in tracking down a needed photograph include:

- The African American Experience: A History on CD-ROM
- The American Indian: A Multimedia Encyclopedia
- The Hulton Deutsch People Disc
- LDS Historical Library CD
- Middle East Diary on CD-ROM
- Time Traveler CD
- History on CD-ROM
- USA Wars: World War II
- World War II Archives on CD-ROM
- World War II Quiz Book

If you are looking for a picture of a Guinness record holder, you might be interested in The Guinness Disc of Records. Space buffs might like:

- Space Adventure
- Space Series: Apollo

Other CD-ROM databases can be found that target many other areas of interest. Any of them may contain photographs as well.

A new book, *Finding Images Online* (written by Paula Berinstein and published by Pemberton Press), will be a big help to anyone trying to find photographic images online.

You might also find that you can download the images you want from online forums (or bulletin boards), or from the Internet, or receive assistance there that will lead you to the photo that you're seeking.

Quotations

A s you know, public statements can be more telling than anything a biography or resume reveals. Consider Newt Gingrich's statements made in a lecture as part of the televised history course "Renewing American Civilization," which he teaches for Mind Extension University. If you were wondering where Speaker Gingrich stands on issues concerning gender differences, he shared his views that:

Women:

"Have biological problems being in a ditch for 30 days because they get infections."

Men:

"A male gets very, very frustrated sitting in a chair all the time because males are biologically driven to go out and hunt giraffes."

These curious revelations were quoted in many newspapers that can be searched online and were rebroadcast on television news programs. Anyone writing a biography or an investigative profile may find news sources well worth searching for quotes by the subject in order to reveal thoughts and motivations.

If you are looking at a historical or famous person, there is a good chance that a search through news files will unearth a quotation from an interview or a historical reference to something the subject is reported to have said. In addition to newspaper databases, there are news databases focusing on newswires and television and radio transcripts. Refer to Chapter Twenty for additional information about searching the news.

Speech Databases

If you wonder about an executive's statements or views, you might consider also searching sources such as "The Executive Speaker," which is published by a company of the same name. In this newsletter, available online through LEXIS-NEXIS, you can find a bibliography of speeches made by executives since 1980 and the organizations that heard them. Part of each speech is also available, but the full text of the speech must be ordered offline. "Executive Speeches," a full-text database of speeches offered by the same company, is included in the ABI-INFORM database carried by many database vendors including BRS, DataStar, Knight-Ridder, FT Profile, Info Globe, STN, and WESTLAW.

Quotations Databases

Many databases specialize in quotations. These quotations are generally brief, but they can provide a glimpse of the speaker's views. Consider persons as ultimately quotable as Albert Einstein or Oscar Wilde. During their lifetimes, many quotations were attributed to them on topics ranging from God to Mathematics, Art to Women.

Toolworks Reference Library (a CD-ROM product produced by The Software Toolworks) combines several reference works including *Webster's NewWorld Dictionary of Quotable Definitions*. A search for Albert Einstein provides 33 quotations, most of which reveal sober reflections, including one of my personal favorites:

"I remind myself that my inner and outer life depend on the labor of other men, living and dead, and that I must exert myself in order to give the same measure as I have received."

There are 180 quotations attributed to Oscar Wilde in this database. Although most are colored by his rapier wit, others reveal a more serious side of his views. A recurring theme involves his image of women as *"Picturesque protests against the mere existence of common sense."* Such quotations could cause a biographer to speculate on misogynist tendencies that may have biased his relationships, and following that theory, to concentrate much of a biography on exploring those relationships.

Refer to Appendix I for additional quotations databases.

Professional and Technical Papers Presented

If a presentation is given at a conference, a professional or technical paper may well provide essentially the same information. From it, you might find material worthy of quotation. One database that carries such papers is Ei Engineering Meetings, provided by Engineering Information, Inc.

This database includes bibliographic listings of approximately 756,000 professional and technical papers from national and international conferences in all areas of engineering. It covers about 900 conferences yearly and dates as far back as 1982. Database vendors now carrying this database include CAN/OLE (under EiM), and STN International (as MEET). It is also included in the Ei Compendex Plus database offered on Knight-Ridder and DataStar.

Published Articles

People's written words can also provide wonderful insight into their character and views. If someone has written articles for newspapers, magazines, journals, or newsletters, it is often possible to locate their work through a database search. Many databases provide bibliographic information, abstracts, or even the full text of articles.

An example is Academic Index, provided by Information Access Company. This database (carried as File 88 by Knight-Ridder) indexes more than 1,450 scholarly and general interest publications starting in 1976, and provides full-text articles from 250 journals dating back to January 1993.

Many similar databases focus on scientific journals, popular magazines, newspapers, and newsletters. Refer to Appendix G for directories of other news databases.

Published Books

To locate books written by a particular author, check with databases such as Books In Print, produced by R.R. Bowker, which provides information about them. Refer to Appendix B for a list of databases that index books.

You may also find relevant quotations in biographies written by others about the person. Refer to Chapter Fifteen for further information about searching for biographical books.

As entire books are slowly being placed on the Internet and on CD-ROM, it is possible, in some cases, to search entire texts for the best or most telling quotations.

When searching the Internet for additional quotation sites, I recently ran into The Commonplace Book at Web site:

http://sunsite.unc.edu/ibic/Commonplace-Book.html

The Commonplace Book is described as "an edited collection of striking passages noted in a single place for future reference." Anyone with Internet access can submit favorite passages with proper attribution, and once verified, they may become part of this virtual book of quotations.

Political Speeches

Many historic U.S. speeches and addresses are now available on the Internet. Chapter Thirty-five provides further information about these documents.

College Dissertations

If you need quotations from someone's doctoral thesis, you may be in luck. One bibliographic database indexes virtually every American dissertation granted at accredited North American universities since 1861. Dissertation Abstracts Online is produced by Dissertation Publishing, UMI, and is carried by Knight-Ridder (as File 35). Selected masters theses have also been included since 1962. Abstracts to the doctoral records have been included since July 1980, and those for masters theses have been included since Spring of 1988. Since 1988, the database also has included citations for dissertations from 50 British universities. Although the full dissertation is not available online, a copy can be ordered online.

Canadian masters and doctoral theses are microfilmed, published, and cataloged by the National Library of Canada. A bibliography of Canadian theses is available through DOBIS Canadian Online Library System from National Library of Canada. Refer to Appendix N for the address.

Quotations Bulletin Boards

If you are very interested in quotations, you may also want to visit loQtus, which can be found at:

http://pubweb.ucdavis.edu/Documents/Quotations/homepage.html

This Web site, administered by Jason R. Newquist, seeks to link all of the quotations resources available on the Internet. It currently includes links to a quotations Usenet group: **alt.quotations,** as well as a quotations listserve, and a quotations FTP site. You will also find links to collections of quotations that have been compiled by many individuals, some centering around certain topics, and some more eclectic.

Yahoo also has indexed quotation sites, which can be found at:

http://www.yahoo.com/Reference/Quotations/

On the Internet, a list of useful resources related to quotations may be found at:
http://www.starlingtech.com/quotes/links.html

Another excellent site, the Quotations home page, includes many types of quotes, a list of quotation reference books, and magazines, and links to other Internet quotation sites. The Quotations page can be found at:
http://www.lexmark.com/data/quote.html

Collections of quotations from famous authors and others, such as Dorothy Parker and George Bernard Shaw, can be found at:
gopher://gopher.ainet.com:70/11/Misc/Quotations/author.collections

If you're looking for David Letterman's latest Top 10 List, you can find it on the Late Night with David Letterman home page at:
http://www.cbs.com:80/lateshow/lateshow.html

or the Top 10 archive located at:
http://www.cbs.com/lateshow/ttlist.html

Some of these collections contain disclaimers stating that quotations have not been verified, so be sure to confirm them elsewhere if they are important to you.

Chapter Twenty-three

Bank Records

F or someone about to file a lawsuit, or to file for divorce, or in any other situation where they might wish to measure someone's financial standing, bank records can be a very telling information source. Because of this, they also are among the most closely guarded. Yet if bank records themselves are not readily-accessible, other personal records, both online and off, can still reveal a lot about the funds they hold.

Personal Bank Accounts

When speaking about personal records, I am often asked, "Can you find out about someone's personal bank accounts?" Of course you can, but not through a database.

Well, that is not entirely true. A database search might help in a few roundabout ways. Although public records will not provide direct access to bank accounts, they can put you on the trail of them, as well as other financial records.

For example, you can use a database search to locate divorces in the civil indices. You still must obtain a copy of the actual divorce documents, as the details of the divorce are not yet online. Somewhere within the paperwork of the divorce you often will find financial records of either or both parties. Other civil records include tax liens and civil suits, and the papers filed in these cases can also contain records of bank accounts. Bankruptcies and Uniform Commercial Code (UCC) filings found online can likewise lead you to legal documents containing bank account information. Even criminal records can contain banking information if a person's crime was embezzlement or some other type of theft. Of course, the funds may have been seized or spent before the information does you any good.

Other database searches may lead you to a person's business banking accounts and there is the possibility that their personal accounts are with the same bank.

If you have a legally permissible purpose for obtaining a credit report (such as when you are one of the creditors), you may find records of bank loans, bank credit cards, or credit inquiries from various banks listed on the credit profile. Any of these may point you to the bank where the subject's personal or business funds are maintained.

One database available online and on CD-ROM does contain personal banking information, but it is limited to listings of approximately 3,100 executives. It is Simmons Top Management Insights from Simmons Market Research Bureau, Inc. (Please refer to Appendix N for their address.) The information for the Simmons Top Management Insights database is collected through interviews and questionnaires, so bank account information is only there if the executive agrees to supply it. Many do not.

None of these methods or sources is guaranteed to turn up bank accounts, and even when they do, you still may need a subpoena to obtain the bank balances, or a court order to get at the funds. If you are looking for bank accounts in connection with a legal case, your attorney may be able to acquire the information through the legal discovery process or obtain proper legal authorization to gain the information from other sources, such as the person's accountant.

If someone promises to find personal bank accounts for you, they may be using methods that have nothing to do with databases. They may be paying off insiders in the banks for information, something I strongly recommend against trying or allowing anyone else to do on your behalf. They may be sifting through the person's trash, which can provide bank statements and receipts revealing not only account numbers, but the balances as well. Telephone records could reveal overseas calls to banks, which may be where the funds are hiding. "Garbacology" (the study of garbage) is legal in most places once the trash hits the curb, so be aware of what you throw away if you value your privacy.

Many other techniques have been used to locate bank accounts. One could follow a person around waiting for them to go to the bank, stand behind them in the supermarket, or even tail them through the shopping mall, hoping to watch over their shoulder as they write a check. Alternatively, send them a check for a few dollars, calling it a refund or prize of some type, and hope that they will deposit it into their personal bank account. Once it has been deposited, the bank information can be obtained from the back of the returned check. Some people have been know to engage in deception in order to elicit banking information. If someone calls you, claiming to be from your bank and asking to confirm information on your accounts, call them back at the bank before volunteering anything. Better yet, go to the bank to clear up any problems. It would be rare for a bank to call and ask for the very keys that would open your accounts to thieves and con artists.

These all are common means of finding information about a person's bank accounts, some legal, some not. What no individual can do is to dial directly into a database and access another's personal banking information without their permission. While banks must have this capability in order to transfer funds and cash checks, they do not produce such databases for individuals, nor do they produce mailing lists of their banking customers. Even check verification systems usually rely on a combination of records of past bad checks and telephone calls to banks, in order to verify that the checks that you write will be good.

If someone "guarantees" that they can provide personal banking information, this is a red flag. If this person cannot tell you what his sources are, there is the chance that the methods are illegal, and I recommend steering clear of this individual. I would not even consider putting my business or myself at risk by unknowingly being involved with anyone else's illegal activities, or purchasing stolen data. There are legal means of obtaining banking information as noted earlier, but none of them bring "guaranteed" results.

Business Bank Accounts

If you are looking for a business' banking information, rather than an individual's, a quick database search may provide a pointer to their accounts.

There are business databases that list bank references or affiliations. Examples of such databases are:

- ABC Belge pour le Commerce et l'Industrie
- ABC/Dienstverleners
- ABC Europe Production Europex

- ABC Germany
- ABC Luxembourgeois pour le Commerce et l'Industrie
- ABC voor Handel en Industrie
- Base de Dados Mope
- BISNES Plus
- BizEkon News—Soviet Business Directory
- Business Who's Who of Australia
- COMLINE Japanese Corporate Directory
- Company Intelligence
- COMPUSTAT
- Dati Anagrafici di Imprese Lombarde
- DBRISK
- Domanda e Offerta Nazionale e Internazionale
- Dun & Bradstreet Swiss Company Information
- Dun's Market Identifiers
- Dun's Market Identifiers Australia
- Dun's Million Dollar Directory
- DunsPrint Canada
- DunsPrint Worldwide
- Hoppenstedt Germany
- ICC Full Text Accounts
- INFOCHECK
- INFOTRADE Belgian Company Financial Data
- Kompass Far East
- KOMPASS-FRANCE
- KOMPASS Israel
- Luxemburgs ABC voor Handel en Industrie
- SDOE
- SICE: Foreign Trade Information System
- Standard & Poor's Register—Corporate
- Taiwan On-Line Business Data Services
- Teikoku Japanese Companies
- TRW Business Credit Profiles

Sometimes CD-ROM databases contain business banking relationships and affiliations. Examples of these include:

- ABC der Deutschen Wirtschaft
- ABC EUROPEX
- Australian Business Compendium
- Business Who's Who of Australia

- Dun's Middle Market Disc
- Dun's Million Dollar Disc
- Hoppenstedt Directory of German Companies
- Japanese Company Factfinder: Teikoku Databank
- Kompass France on Disc
- ProFile Canada
- REACH: Review and Analysis of Companies in Holland
- Standard & Poor's CORPORATIONS

Although all of these databases have fields for bank references, this information is not always provided. You may find it in one database, but not another, and the bank listed in one database may disagree with that provided in another. Annual reports or financial statements, available either online or directly from the company, may provide further banking information; bank balances may even be included.

Uniform Commercial Code (UCC) filings found on public records databases can also point to records that contain business bank accounts, as can bankruptcies, tax liens, and judgments. Just as when looking for personal banking information, the actual case documents must be acquired from the courts in order to obtain this level of detail. (Refer to Chapter Thirty-one for further information on UCC filings.)

If someone offers to provide business banking information for you, although easier to acquire through legal means than personal banking information, it would still be wise to ask about their sources. Along with database searches, both legal and illegal means can be used to obtain banking information, and you should be aware of which you are paying for.

For further information about business financial records, please go on to Chapter Twenty-four.

Business Credit and Company Financial Records

Many business financial records are widely available on databases that are found online, as well as on CD-ROM. Some databases contain only information on publicly-traded companies, while others list both public and private companies. Certain databases address particular industries exclusively, such as banks or manufacturers. Others cross industry boundaries. Sources, details, and currentness also vary. Some contain hidden treasures for anyone seeking personal information.

Appendix C lists business credit and company financial databases. This list has been limited to databases of this type that also contain information about individuals. Others, such as Experian's Business Credit database, are also useful when assessing a business owner's assets. When a company is a sole proprietorship, its assets and debts may represent a large portion of the individual's finances as well.

Business credit and company financial databases can help to identify business relationships, as they will often list key personnel including executives and officers, auditors, attorneys, bankers, and others.

Along with business associates within a company, these databases can at times help one to identify principal suppliers and customers of a business. People at each of these companies could be interviewed for further information if one were attempting to compile a complete dossier on an executive, business owner, or company.

Something occasionally found in company financial databases, such as INFOCHECK, is salary information. A few of the company databases also list the main shareholders, along with their holdings.

Biographical information may also be stored on company financial databases. Biographies such as these are normally limited to the principals of the companies.

Public Records

Databases such as Dun's Legal Search contain public record information, including parties to lawsuits. Parties to a suit are not necessarily limited to the principals of the company, so almost any employee could conceivably turn up on such a database.

Other business databases limit their public records to a single type of record, such as the Bankruptcy DataSource (available online through LEXIS), which is self-explanatory.

Business credit databases often list Uniform Commercial Code (UCC) filings, which can include property owned by the company that has been used to secure a loan. Alternatively, a UCC could also be filed when the company lends money or extends credit to one of its own customers or associates.

Sources of Business Financial Information

Annual and quarterly reports, and other business financial data may be filed with the U.S. Securities and Exchange Commission (SEC). This information is accessible on various databases, as well as on the Internet at http://www.sec.gov/. Additional financial reports can often be found on company Web pages.

When assessing a person's wealth based on their company's value, you should be aware that the company itself may have provided the information. It may give an overly optimistic view of the firm's position, or a strongly negative picture if that serves the company's purposes. Without independent verification or some insight into the company and the industry, one could easily be misled.

For some of these databases, company financials have been audited by independent accounting firms. This lends more credibility to their figures.

Financial information can also be independently gathered, using combinations of sources such as the company's creditors, stock value, news, public records, and independent analysis. This provides a composite of the company's financial position, reputation, and expectations for future growth or decline.

When a person's finances are primarily tied up in their business, researching their business's finances takes on much greater importance.

Chapter Twenty-five

Consumer Credit Records

B efore discussing consumer credit records themselves, there are some important restrictions to be aware of. Because people are so protective of their financial information, consumer credit databases are among the most heavily regulated in existence. There are stiff penalties for their misuse.

The Fair Credit Reporting Act (FCRA)

The Fair Credit Reporting Act (Public Law 91-508) ensures that consumers are treated fairly and that information disseminated about their credit standing is accurate. If you use the credit files, it is imperative that you become familiar with its content and abide by it.

Copies of the FCRA can be found at any law library or on the Internet. For example, I obtained a copy from:

http://www.camel.com/initial.htm

and noted other sites carrying the same information in various formats.

Section 604 of the FCRA details "permissible purpose" for obtaining consumer credit reports as follows:

604—Permissible Purpose of Reports

A consumer reporting agency may furnish a consumer report under the following circumstances and no other:

- In response to the order of a court having jurisdiction to issue such an order

- In accordance with the written instructions of the consumer to whom it relates

- To a person which it has reason to believe—

  - intends to use the information in connection with a credit transaction involving the consumer on whom the information is to be furnished and involving the extension of credit to, or review or collection of an account of, the consumer; or

  - intends to use the information for employment purposes; or

  - intends to use the information in connection with the underwriting of insurance involving the consumer; or

  - intends to use the information in connection with a determination of the consumer's eligibility for a license or other benefit granted by a governmental instrumentality required by law to consider an applicant's financial responsibility or status; or

  - otherwise has a legitimate business need for the information in connection with a business transaction involving the consumer.

Credit Databases

First a little background. There are currently three national credit agencies in the United States. They are Equifax, TransUnion, and Experian (formerly TRW).

Hundreds of credit bureaus offer information from these three agencies. As explained previously, the FCRA regulates who can access consumer credit histories and for what purpose. In order to abide by these regulations, each credit agency sets up criteria that applicants must meet in order to subscribe to their system. These criteria may include a physical inspection of the premises, in order to verify that those requesting access to the credit files appear to be operating a legitimate business. If you believe that you are eligible to subscribe, refer to the end of this chapter for information about contacting the credit agencies.

Each agency has built a database repository for information that is reported by creditors (such as Sears and American Express) and third parties (such as companies that go to the courts to collect public records). Like some other database vendors, credit agencies own little of the information they sell. Most of it belongs to the creditors who report it or to the public, via the courts that maintain the public records.

Information is not reported to the credit agencies in an entirely uniform manner. Although each agency requests the most complete information available to identify each consumer with certainty, not all creditors collect all types of identifying information. For instance, companies that built their customer databases in the 1970s often neglected to store the customer's Social Security number because privacy issues then made it seem unlikely that they would be allowed to do so. Thus, the most useful means of identifying one individual's records often is unavailable.

Most larger creditors, such as credit card companies, department stores, and banks, report their information to all three agencies. Smaller creditors, such as jewelry stores, smaller lending institutions, and public records providers may not. Each of the national credit agencies has distinct strengths within certain regions of the country, due largely to reports from thousands of smaller creditors and reporting agencies.

Another issue is "depth of file," technical jargon that indicates how long creditors have reported to an agency. One credit agency may have more depth of file than another within a certain part of the country.

Each agency has developed its own unique, proprietary algorithm or matching system for determining which records (among billions) belong to each consumer. This secret formula is held almost as tightly as the recipe for Coca Cola. As a result of their matching system, credit reports from one agency will include more records—some of which may not belong to the subject. Another agency will err on the side of caution, showing only records that meet more stringent matching criteria.

The last factor differentiating credit agencies is price. Each charges a stiff fee for becoming a subscriber, monthly minimum fees regardless of use, and record fees that vary with volume. If you pull only an occasional report or a few each month, you will be charged top dollar for them. Those prices could drop to pennies if you regularly pull large volumes of reports. If you only have occasional need for credit reports, it would probably be to your benefit to go through a third party in order to retrieve credit records. There are credit bureaus all over the country, many of which access all three credit agencies. Some will pull records without charging sign-up fees or minimum monthly quotas of reports, and for the occasional user this could represent significant savings.

Searching the Credit Files

Due to the need to protect credit history information about individuals, access to the credit databases is restricted to certain "inquiry types" or standard types of search. An individual may not search across the records in order to identify groups of individuals with similar characteristics. This process is meant to provide access to singular records, on a one-by-one basis only.

This is not to say that records for multiple individuals will never appear as the result of a single inquiry. At times, more than one person's records match the inquiry criteria. For example, if a father and son had the same name and lived at the same address, it is likely that one inquiry would call up records for both individuals, especially if the date of birth was not included on the inquiry. With some credit agencies and bureaus, it is also possible to enter a dual or joint inquiry in order to access the combined records of a husband and wife. However, credit agencies generally intend to restrict searches so that only one individual's records are accessed and displayed for each inquiry processed.

For this reason, you will not find the "wild card" search capabilities that are available with other databases. In other words, one cannot enter SMITH, J to retrieve credit records for all of the Jane, John, and Joe Smiths in the database. Neither can one enter a name without an address. If the minimum necessary information for the inquiry type is not complete, the system will return an error message, rather than a credit report.

Even if the minimum information is entered, the system may require further data. This can occur if the name is as common as Smith or Jones, or Rodriguez or Sanchez, or the address is as common as Main Street or a post office box. A search may also fail if the matching system weighs any part of the data less heavily, for whatever reason, and the remaining details do not meet the credit agency's matching threshold. In these cases, the system may not be able to determine whether the record is for the same person, and it may not display the information.

Unfortunately, entering too much information can also bring negative results. For example, if you enter a date of birth, middle initial, or Social Security number that conflicts with information reported by the lender, the credit agency's matching system may determine that it probably is not for the same person.

As you can see, the way the inquiry is entered can affect the results of the search, and there may be additional factors about a single inquiry that can make the process more complex, depending upon each credit agency's matching system.

As noted earlier, the matching system or algorithm for each of the credit agencies is unique, and one of their most carefully held secrets. Thus, it is not always apparent why the same inquiry can yield different results from one credit agency reporting system to another, or why entering slightly different inquiries into the same system bring more or less complete results. This can occur not only because of differences in the data held within their files, but due to differences in how the inquiry is processed and the data is matched. For these reasons, one credit agency's system is sometimes preferable to another, given a specific inquiry. It may also be necessary to enter more than one inquiry for a single individual in order to gain the most complete information possible.

Credit Agency Reports

Several types of reports are generated from the credit databases. Some contain credit information and are thereby regulated by the Fair Credit Reporting Act. Others contain what is considered "identifying" information only, without credit information, and are, therefore, unregulated.

The information contained on the credit agency reports can be considered unverified. In other words, the credit agency stores the information on its files, but does not generally confirm it unless the consumer disputes the facts of their credit history.

If the consumer fills out a credit application and notes an employer on the form, that information may be entered into the system as part of an inquiry by a lender who is considering extending credit to the individual. The employer's name may then appear in the consumer's file and will be displayed on subsequent reports, although no one has verified that the consumer is actually employed.

There also are occasions when one person's identifying information is similar to another's and their credit histories become mixed.

For these reasons, if a credit report is being used as part of a credit granting or employment decision, it is best to verify all information with the subject, or with independent sources such as creditors and employers.

Consumer Credit History (a.k.a. Profile or AcroFile or Focus Form 2000) Reports

The consumer credit report contains credit information for an individual. It may also contain certain public records such as bankruptcies, liens, and judgments against a consumer. In addition, some identifying information appears about the consumer. Certain identifiers can always be expected:

- Inquiry information (the information that you entered in order to request the credit report)
- Consumer name
- Consumer address

Several other pieces of identifying information also may be displayed. It should be noted that not one of the three credit agencies stores or displays all of the following information:

- Age
- Year of birth
- Date of birth
- Home telephone number
- Previous addresses
- Employer's name
- Employer's address
- Position
- Salary
- Date on which the employment was first reported
- Date employed

- Date on which the employment was verified
- Previous employer's name
- Previous employer's address
- Marital status
- Number of dependents
- Spouse's first initial or name
- Spouse's Social Security number
- Spouse's employment information

Warning messages may appear for a number of reasons, including suspicion of fraud. They may be displayed if the person has been reported deceased, if the Social Security number lies outside the valid range, or if the address is known to be non-residential, such as a hospital or jail. Refer to "Fraud/Alert/Prevention/Detection" later in this chapter for further explanation.

If there is credit information on file for the consumer, the credit information displayed may include:

- Reporting credit grantor's name
- Credit grantor's identifier
- Consumer's account number
- Type of account
- Terms of account
- A code to identify the consumer's relationship or association with the account (sometimes referred to as the Equal Credit Opportunity Act code, or ECOA code)
- Date the account was opened
- Balance date
- Date of the consumer's last payment
- Original amount of the loan
- Credit limit
- High balance amount
- Charge-off amount
- Current balance
- Monthly payment amount or estimated monthly payment amount
- Account status
- Status date
- Amount past due
- Payment history
- Collateral

- Original creditor
- Oldest opening date of an account
- Newest reporting date of an account
- Names of those who have inquired about the consumer, their identifier, their account number, date of the inquiry, type, terms, and amount of their credit line to the consumer
- Name, address, and telephone number of the credit agency office or credit bureau nearest the consumer's home address (so that the consumer can be referred there to clear up any errors appearing on the report)
- Report messages: these may warn of a variation in the identifying information (such as a transposition in the Social Security number), warn of an invalid ZIP Code, or contain a statement from the consumer (such as when an account is in dispute)
- Summary counts, which may include the number of trade lines displayed, number of public records, total balance of installment loan accounts, total balance of real estate loans, total balance of revolving charge accounts, recent inquiries for the given Social Security number, recent inquiries for the given address, number of times the accounts have been delinquent, total dollars past due for each loan type, and total percentage of revolving credit available to the consumer
- Risk scores (used for evaluating the risk of extending credit to the consumer)
- Names of lenders who appear on the report, their identifiers, their addresses, and telephone numbers

If there is public record information on file for the consumer, the public record information displayed may include:

- Court name
- Case number
- Filing date
- Plaintiff
- Court code
- Amount
- Type of public record

Employment (a.k.a. Employment Insight, Persona, or PEER) Reports

The employment report may be essentially the same thing as a credit report. It may or may not appear in a different format, depending upon the credit agency.

A few of the items on the normal credit report are suppressed from the display when the report is pulled for employment purposes:

- Age
- Year of birth

- Date of birth
- Marital status
- Number of dependents
- Account numbers

The credit agency may offer additional pre-employment screening, such as drug testing or employment verification, in addition to this report. This varies by agency.

Collection Reports

The collection report is essentially the same thing as a credit report. It contains the same information as the credit report, in addition to a code indicating that the consumer is repaying their bills through debt counseling.

Consumer Reports

Consumer reports are essentially credit reports that are issued to consumers about their own credit history. Refer to the end of this chapter for instructions on requesting a copy of your own credit report.

Address Update (a.k.a. Finders, Return Mail, Credit Header, Atlas, or FACT) Reports

When Address Update reports do not contain credit information, they normally can be purchased without meeting FCRA criteria for permissible purpose. I say "normally" because this seems to lie in a gray area and may be interpreted differently by each of the credit agencies, depending upon what they display on their report. In fact, FCRA standards have at times been applied when Address Update reports have been requested for famous persons, such as highly-placed elected officials.

This Address Update report is used to locate people who have moved. It is used by creditors, alumni, and charitable associations, along with other organizations. To order this report, you must enter a consumer's name and last known address in order to determine whether there is a more current address on the credit agency's file. The consumer's full identifying information will appear if found.

This report may also include the addresses and phone numbers of people living near the consumer's current residence. It may include a list of creditors (without the details of the tradelines), an indicator noting that there are public records on file, an indicator indicating that a bankruptcy is on file.

Following is an example of a Finders (or Address Update) report. I have taken the liberty of condensing and changing many of the details.

```
03-22-96 12:16:56 INQUIRY NUMBER: 114 DEPARTMENT: 1 OPERATOR: CAL
NM-LANE, CAROLE,A.
CA-9222,MAIN,ST,OCEANSIDE,CA,92057.

* 210 EQUFAX CREDIT INFORMATION SERVICES,        P O BOX 740241,
        5505 PEACHTREE DUNWOODY RD STE 600,ATLANTA,GA 30374-0241,404/612-2585

*LANE,CAROLE,A SINCE 12/29/82 FAD 03/01/96        FN-305
```

9222,MAIN,ST,OCEANSIDE,CA,92057,TAPE RPTD 08/91
3919 MESA DR 555,OCEANSIDE,CA,92056,TAPE RPTD 4/90
3919,MESA,DR,SAN DIEGO,CA,92056,TAPE RPTD 4/90
AGE-30,SSS-055-32-5784
01 ES-PRESIDENT,TECHNOSEARCH INC
02 EF-SR SYSTEMS ANALYST/DATA ADMIN, TRW

TRADE LINE INFORMATION

ACCOUNT NUMBER	DATE RPTD	MEMBER NO.	FIRM NAME	TYP	TELEPHONE NO.	LAST ACTV
	03/96	444ON12348	ATT UNIVSL	R	(800) 423-1423	02/96
	03/96	906DC23455	J C PENNEY	R	MAIL ONLY	02/96
	02/95	906BB67895	CITIBANK	R	MAIL ONLY	11/94
	02/95	155BB87657	DISCVR CD	R	MAIL ONLY	02/95
	01/95	906OC65434	CHEVRON	O	MAIL ONLY	01/95
-xxxxxxxxxx	08/93	180FF09283	CSLFC	I	MAIL ONLY	08/93

END OF REPORT EQUIFAX AND AFFILIATES—03/22/96   SAFESCANNED

Address Verification (a.k.a. Report Card) Reports

Address Verification reports do not contain credit information and are, therefore, unregulated.

This report often is used by mail order and catalog companies that ship goods to people who place orders using credit cards. The consumer's name, address, and credit card number are entered on the inquiry. A verification message is returned indicating whether the address and credit card number match those on the credit agency's file, and the consumer's full name and address appears if found.

If the consumer has recently moved, the addresses may not match, so this does not necessarily indicate that any type of fraud is being perpetrated. If a match is not found, the shipper is advised to contact the consumer and verify their information prior to shipment.

Social Security Number Search (a.k.a. DTEC or TRACE) Reports

Social Security Number Search reports do not contain credit information and are, therefore, unregulated. This report is used in locating people, especially those who have changed their names, due to marriage or other circumstances. Upon entering a Social Security number, the credit agency returns a report listing names and addresses of consumers that it links to that number, along with the rest of their identifying information.

Following is an example of a DTEC (or Social Security Number Search) report. I have again taken the liberty of condensing and changing many of the details.

03-22-1996 12:17:16 INQUIRY NUMBER: 115 DEPARTMENT: 1 OPERATOR: CAL
DTEC-055-32-5784

SSN ISSUED -72 STATE ISSUED-CA

M1 OF 1 NM-LANE,CAROLE.A CA-9222,MAIN,ST,OCEANSIDE,CA,92057,01/95
     FA-3919 MESA DR 555,OCEANSIDE,CA,92056,08/91 ES-PRESIDENT,TECHNOSEARCH INC
     SS-055-32-5784   AGE 30 &

END OF REPORT EQUIFAX AND AFFILIATES—03/22/96

Fraud Alert/Prevention/Detection (a.k.a. FACS+, Safescan, Fraud Detect, HAWK, HAWKeye) Reports

The fraud detection report may be combined with the credit report, or it may be ordered separately. If ordered separately, it does not contain credit information and is, therefore, unregulated.

When requesting the fraud detection report, the consumer's name and address is entered, along with their Social Security number, if available. The credit agency checks the address against its files of addresses belonging to hospitals, jails, mail drops, and businesses. It also checks the address against residential addresses that have been used for fraudulent purposes in the past.

If received on the inquiry, the Social Security number is checked to verify that it is within the range issued by the Social Security Administration, that it is a valid number (one that does not contain invalid combinations of digits, such as -00- in the 4th and 5th positions), and that the Social Security Administration does not show the holder as deceased.

Employment information may also be checked against that on file. The telephone number may be checked against a file of invalid or fraudulent numbers.

Counts are also displayed for the number of recent inquiries against the Social Security number and against the address.

Following is an example of a FACS+ (or Fraud Detection) summary that was excerpted from a consumer credit report.

```
FACS+ SUMMARY:
    INPUT SSN ISSUED 1972-1974
    FROM 06-01-94 # OF INQS WITH THIS SSN=0
    FROM 06-01-94 # OF INQS WITH THIS ADDR=4
```

Examples of Additional Credit Services

The credit agencies offer additional services for the financial industry. The services offered vary from agency to agency, and the following list is not exhaustive. The agencies often add new services to match or improve on those of the competition.

- A Skip Locator (or Locate or Watch) service can be activated to notify a creditor if one of their accounts applies for credit elsewhere or if a new address is placed on the file for them.

- A Bankruptcy service can be activated to notify a creditor if one of its accounts declares bankruptcy.

- A Signal (Alert, Monthly Portfolio Review, or SENTRY service) service continuously monitors accounts according to the creditor's own criteria in order to notify creditors when a consumer's account requires action, such as raising or lowering their credit limit.

Similarly, the credit agency may scan its entire credit files (under services such as Customer Portfolio Review, Quest, SOLO, or SILHOUETTE service) according to the lender's criteria and identify consumers who will then be offered credit. (That is why you may receive offers for pre-approved lines of credit from time to time.) These lists may be further screened by matching against other lists, and psychographic characteristics, in order to identify a targeted market for a company's services or goods.

- Collection letters (Smart letters, Advantage letters) may be sent to delinquent consumers on the creditor's behalf.

- A Credit Watch (or Credentials) service regularly provides consumers with a copy of their own credit report and/or notifies them if someone inquires about their credit or reports a derogatory line of credit for them.

- An instant update (or Repo Hotline) service allows a creditor to flag an account immediately when a problem arises.

- A Positive ID service is offered (to public utility companies) to verify the identity of a consumer. If the Social Security number is not found or matched, the Department of Motor Vehicles records may be accessed for verification. A G.A.D. (Government Agency Disclosure)/Motor Vehicle Report may also be offered (to investigative companies) to verify identity.

- Tenant screening services are offered to landlords and property management companies.

- Insurance personal property claim records are used to assist insurance under-writers in processing claims and detecting fraud.

- One service (Verifind) helps to locate owners of unclaimed assets—lost depositors, shareholders, and policyholders.

Credit Bureaus

As mentioned earlier, hundreds of credit bureaus offer information from the three national credit agencies. Many have access to reports from all three agencies. In order to make these reports easier for their clients to read, some bureaus edit the credit information into a standard format, so that their clients do not have to learn to read the differing reports from Equifax, TransUnion, and Experian.

Another option that credit bureaus sometimes offer is to pull credit reports from one, two, or all three credit agencies and combine them into a single report, in order to furnish a more complete credit profile.

Credit bureaus may also collect credit or public record information, provide independent verification services such as employment or education verification, or in other ways add value to the information provided by the credit agencies.

Consumer Rights

If you are concerned about your credit records, you can request a copy of your credit reports by contacting each of the credit agencies and following their procedures. If you have recently been denied credit, employment, or insurance, they will each furnish a copy of their report for free.

If you see an error on your credit record, you may contact the credit agency, which will then verify the information by checking with the source. If whoever reported the information agrees that there has been an error, the record will be deleted from your credit report. If they insist that the information is correct, you may either take your dispute to the creditor for resolution or write a short statement explaining the dispute to the credit agency and ask that it be placed on your credit record.

REQUESTING A COPY OF YOUR CREDIT REPORT

Equifax: If you have been denied credit, employment or insurance within the last 60 days, you may request a free copy of your Equifax credit report by calling (800) 685-1111, and following their instructions for automated or mail-in requests. Mail-in requests should be sent to:

Equifax
P.O. Box 105873
Atlanta, GA 30348
http://www.equifax.com/

You will need to furnish your full name, Social Security number, date of birth, current address (and previous address if you have recently moved), and a copy of your driver's license, utility bill, and Social Security card. (Be sure to sign your request.) I still suggest calling first, as the company's voice system provides specific instructions, and their mailing address does change periodically. This information should be verified before sending your request.

If you have not been denied credit recently, you may request a copy of your Equifax credit report by writing to the preceding address, furnishing the same information, and including the required fee. This fee varies from $3 to $8, depending upon the state, so you will need to call to verify the amount before sending in your request. If your spouse would also like a copy of their report, this must be requested separately.

TransUnion: If you have been denied credit, employment, or insurance within the last 60 days, you may request a free copy of your TransUnion credit report by calling (316) 636-6100 and using their request line to answer the necessary questions.

If you have not been denied credit recently, you may request a copy of your Trans-Union credit report by writing to:

TransUnion Corporation
Consumer Disclosure Center
P.O. Box 390
Springfield, PA 19064-0390
http://www.tuc.com/

Furnish your full name, full address, previous addresses for the last two years, Social Security number, date of birth, current employer, and telephone number. Be sure to sign your request, and include a check for $8. A joint report for you and your spouse may be obtained by supplying all of the same information for your spouse and paying a double fee of $16. You can call TransUnion Corporation, Consumer Disclosure Center at (216) 779-7200 to verify or update these instructions before sending your request.

Experian (formerly TRW): If you have been denied credit, employment, or insurance within the last 60 days, you may request a free copy of your Experian credit report by calling (800) 831-5614 and answering the necessary questions.

If you have not been denied credit recently, Experian will supply one complimentary credit report to you each year upon request. You may request a copy of your Experian credit report by writing to:

Experian National Consumer Assistance Center
P.O. Box 949
Allen, TX 75013-0949
http://www.experian.com/

You must furnish your full name (including generation such as Jr. or III, if applicable), your spouse's first name (if applicable), your Social Security number, your year of birth, your current address, previous addresses for the last 5 years (including ZIP Codes), and proof of your identity, such as a current bill from a major credit card company, a utility bill, or a valid driver's license. Be sure to sign your request. If your spouse would also like a copy of their report, it must be requested separately.

Foreign Consumer Credit Records

There are credit agencies that operate outside of the United States. For example, Equifax and TransUnion both maintain separate credit databases in Canada, Equifax de Mexico Sociedad de Informacion Crediticia S.A. and National Credit Bureau (BNC) both offer credit record in Mexico, and Central Communication Bureau (CCB) maintains credit records in Japan.

In order to obtain foreign credit records, one can call or write to the foreign credit agency, or to the credit agency that they use in their own country, in order to have them obtain and send the records. Gaining online access to foreign credit systems is seldom possible from within the United States. Neither do the United States credit agencies allow direct access to their systems from outside of the United States. However, they will send credit records upon request, so long as the inquiry meets the permissible-purpose requirements of the FCRA.

Limitations on the Records Displayed on Credit Reports

There are legal limitations on what can be included on a credit report, and the length of time that it can appear. These limitations are defined in the Fair Credit Reporting Act. They include the following:

- Bankruptcies (under Title 11) must not remain on the report for more than ten years after the date of adjudication or order for relief.

- Lawsuits and judgments must not remain on the report for more than seven years after the date of entry or until the governing statute of limitation expires, whichever is longer.

- Paid tax liens must not remain on the report for more than seven years after payment.

- Collection or charged-off accounts must not remain on the report for more than seven years.

- Records of arrest, indictment, or conviction of a crime must not remain on the report for more than seven years after the date of disposition, release, or parole.

- Any other adverse item must not remain on the report for more than seven years.

However, the FCRA does make some exceptions to these rules.

Other factors may also limit the information displayed on a credit report. For example, smaller creditors may not report to any of the credit agencies, or may report to only one or two rather than all three. Some do not report all of their accounts on a monthly basis, instead reporting only those accounts that are late or unpaid. If a credit agency believes that a creditor's records contain too many errors, it may choose not to accept records from that creditor. In an effort to assure that the date limitations of the FCRA are adhered to, a credit agency may choose to purge records at some time before the required date.

Public records may not be collected from certain courts or jurisdictions and, therefore, are not represented on the credit report. Human errors are also sometimes made when these records are collected, and some may be missed as a result. There also may be a delay in the collection of these records or in placing them on the credit files.

Summary

Although credit reports provide a great deal of valuable information, they do not represent a complete picture of a person's worthiness for credit, employment, or insurance. Studies have shown that as many as 50 percent or more of the credit reports pulled contain errors. For these reasons, any information shown on a credit report should be verified before a decision is based upon it.

Criminal Justice Records

According to the FBI's Uniform Crime Reports, approximately 13.9 million crime index offenses were committed in 1995; 21,597 people were murdered; 97,464 forcible rapes occurred; there were 580,545 robberies and 2.6 million burglaries; and 1,099,179 aggravated assaults took place. An estimated 15.1 million arrests were made during this period.

Every one of these crimes triggers a long and complex series of procedures designed first to catch and then to convict the criminal, documenting the process at every step of the way. At the crime scene and in the following hours and days, investigators gather evidence, take statements from witnesses, weigh the results of forensic tests, and search through criminal histories contained in computerized databases to find possible suspects. Physical evidence such as fingerprints, hair, body fluids, and fibers may be gathered and can even be computer matched against other samples already on databases from prior arrests. From the arrest, through pretrial hearings, perhaps a grand jury hearing, the trial itself, and sentencing, each agency involved in the case may start its own file, search databases for records at the local level as well as in the state repository and possibly even the FBI's Interstate Identification Index, and draw its own conclusion. When the convict is committed to prison, and when s/he is eventually released, still more records are created.

Although some of these databases are accessible only to law enforcement personnel, your knowledge of them will give you a better idea of the types and amount of personal information that are being gathered in databases. Many of the records created throughout the criminal justice processes are matters of public record and can be accessed by anyone for any reason. For example, court documents are, for the most part, public records. When looking for criminal records, you will find Court Dockets and Criminal Record Indices are available online for many areas of the country. Case Transcripts and Case Summaries may also include details of criminal cases. Please refer to Chapter Thirty-one—Public Records for further information about these records and databases. Additional information on criminal cases may also be found in the news. Please refer to Chapter Twenty for information on news databases. Although criminal court records are not typically made available online in full text, computer indices to these records are very useful when searching for records of past crimes and seeking the location of the physical files.

CRIMINAL JUSTICE DATABASES

The Department of Justice is a huge organization, made up of over forty smaller agencies, and describing the databases used within its framework is no small task. In fact, Information Resource Management (IRM) normally accounts for 6 to 8 percent of the department's total budget ($10.9 billion in Fiscal Year 1994), or nearly $900 million. This tremendous expenditure pays for administrative functions, but most of it is spent on information systems and databases that are primarily used to gather information about people.

During the course of our lifetimes, there is a fairly good chance that at least one of these systems will contain some information about almost all of us. Even the most law-abiding citizens can experience the theft of a vehicle or a home break-in, or witness other crimes. We are all candidates for inclusion in a criminal justice database. This does not mean that any single database holds information about all of us, however. Thus far, each law enforcement agency maintains its own systems, and information passes between them only under narrowly controlled conditions.

Many criminal justice systems use proprietary technology that makes it difficult to exchange information. Much information is exchanged manually by copying and sending documents, making telephone calls, or meeting with other law enforcement personnel. In order to streamline operations, and provide greater efficiency and effectiveness, information systems are now being developed with interoperability in mind.

What follows is a partial list of databases used in law enforcement that contain personal records, emphasizing those in general use, those with far-reaching impact on criminal justice, and those I found to be the most interesting in my search for personal data.

Advance Passenger Information System (APIS)

The Advance Passenger Information System allows inspectors to conduct computer queries on U.S.-bound passengers while their flights are still en route. This system is supported by the Interagency Border Inspection System (IBIS), which links databases of several inspection agencies.

Automated Fingerprint Identification System (AFIS)

Fingerprints are scanned into the Automated Fingerprint Identification System, where ridge details and other identifying characteristics are digitized in such detail that the system can find a match among the millions of fingerprints previously scanned. Card-scan devices can be used to scan standard inked fingerprint cards into the system. Live-scan devices can capture fingerprint images directly from subjects' fingers, which are rolled onto scanning pads. The AFIS equipment can also lift a latent fingerprint at a crime scene. These advances make it possible to capture, scan, and transmit fingerprints from a squad car or crime scene to the AFIS, match the prints against those in the database, and transmit the results back to the officer in the field.

Booking Logs

Law enforcement agencies normally create daily written records of suspects who are booked. These records may show up in the local newspaper, in a police database, or even on the Internet. For example, the Booking Log for San Diego County, providing name, sex, race and date of birth of all suspects who are booked can be found at:
http://www.co.san-diego.ca.us/cnty/cntydepts/law/sheriff/bookingname.html

Central Repository

All 50 states, Puerto Rico, and the District of Columbia have established central repositories for their criminal history records. These repositories are state databases used to maintain criminal history records of those arrested for felonies or serious misdemeanors. (The definition of a felony and a serious misdemeanor can vary from state to state, so reporting is not always consistent.) According to a survey conducted by SEARCH for the

Bureau of Justice Statistics, more than 47.3 million individual offenders were included in state central repositories at the end of 1992. Records of reportable arrests and their eventual disposition are maintained within the central repositories. Disposition data can include decisions by the police to drop all charges, the prosecutor's decision not to prosecute, court decisions such as convictions and sentences, confinement in a correctional facility, or release from incarceration.

Each central repository includes a Master Name Index (MNI) which has been automated in many states. The MNI identifies each individual whose criminal records appear in the repository. Some contain a felony flag, which indicates whether the individual has arrests or convictions for felony offenses. When the MNI contains a felony flag, it can be especially useful for such purposes as presale firearm checks, criminal investigations, or bailsetting.

Federal regulations exclude traffic violations and certain other petty offenses from these "criminal history records" in systems built or operated with federal funds, so few state repositories maintain them. Juvenile offenses were omitted until 1992 (except where the juvenile was tried as an adult), but they are now included in some of the state repositories. Neither records of federal offenses nor records from other states are included. When a local agency requests a national record check, the request is routed from the central repository to the FBI.

Consolidated Asset Tracking System (CATS)

CATS is a new multi-agency computer system, under development by the Executive Office of Asset Forfeiture (EOAF), for tracking the assets of accused criminals. CATS provides a consolidated asset forfeiture database. Participants in CATS will be all DOJ law enforcement components, the Internal Revenue Service, the U.S. Postal Service, the U.S. Park Police, the U.S. Secret Service, and the Bureau of Alcohol, Tobacco, and Firearms.

Consolidated DNA Identification System (CODIS)

CODIS consists of national and regional DNA databases that assist in investigating sex offenses and violent crime. This is a combined effort of the FBI and state DNA laboratories.

DNA can be obtained from a wide range of body fluids and other materials, including blood, semen, mouth swabs, body hair, and many other materials. DNA extracted from one of these samples is unique to an individual, with the exception of identical twins, and it remains unchanged throughout a person's lifetime, unlike fingerprints and other identifying characteristics. The CODIS databases consist of data representations of DNA profiles; no medical samples are stored. They may eventually be merged into "NCIC 2000," a planned upgrade to the National Crime Information Center system.

A similar database, Phoenix, has been developed in Europe. The Criminal Justice and Public Order Act 1994 empowered British police to take biological samples from people charged with, or reported for, recordable offenses including murder, attempted murder, manslaughter, sexual offenses, and other crimes. In the future, CODIS and Phoenix may be able to exchange information in order to expand the capabilities of both systems.

Counterdrug Information Indices System (DRUGX)

DRUGX is the uniform drug intelligence database, which serves as a pointer to enable investigators in federal agencies to obtain and share information on drug-related cases.

Crime Information Network (CINet)

The Crime Information Network (CINet) is a cooperative effort by academia, law enforcement and the private sector to provide law enforcement managers, investigators and intelligence analysts (I/IAs) with a timely open source overview of regional, national and international organized criminal activities and terrorism. When fully operational on the Internet, it will provide full public access to its terrorism section, while access to the law enforcement section will be limited to certified law enforcement agencies. The goals of CINet are to create an awareness of the scope of crime, generate opportunities for I/IAs to apply open source information to their work, and to overcome the "islands of information" syndrome which frequently stifles the sharing of information of common value in law enforcement.

http://pscusa.com/cinet/criminfo.html

Criminal Records

Court records of criminal cases are stored throughout the courts and record halls of America. An increasing number of these records are now indexed on databases, making it possible for anyone to locate them using the databases of a public records or legal database vendor. Background checks and employment screening typically include searches of criminal records for each county in which a subject is known to have lived. As not all of these records are yet automated, it may still be necessary to conduct manual records searches and to order copies of the original case documents in order to gain a full understanding of the details of a case. Please refer to Chapter Thirty-one—Public Records for further explanation of criminal records that are accessible to the public.

Many courts have created Internet sites on which you can find instructions for obtaining records. Record indices may also be searched through these sites in the future. There is an index to court WWW sites, which can be found on the Internet at:

http://www.ncjrs.org/courwww.htm

EPIC (El Paso Intelligence Center) Database

For over 20 years, the El Paso Intelligence Center has maintained the Drug Enforcement Agency's database of drug dealers and traffickers, used by federal, state and local law enforcement agencies. EPIC has agreements for data exchange and analysis of information with other federal agencies involved in reducing the flow of drugs with all 50 States, the District of Columbia, Guam, Puerto Rico, and the U.S. Virgin Islands, as well as 20 foreign countries.

Inmate Logs

Of course, police agencies maintain records of who they have incarcerated, but you may not have realized that some of these agencies have posted them on the Internet as well. One such site, Who's In Jail—Sheriff's Inmate Log for San Diego, California, allows searching by inmate name or inmate number, and provides name, sex, race and

date of birth of the inmate. You can find this site at:
http://www.co.san-diego.ca.us/cnty/cntydepts/law/sheriff/whosin.html

INS Automated Fingerprint Identification System
The Immigration and Naturalization Service Fingerprint Identification System is designed to counter the threat from criminal aliens.

INS Passenger Accelerated Service System (INSPASS)
INSPASS, first introduced in 1993, uses biometric technology to speed the inspection of frequent travelers who enroll in the system and receive a special card. This is intended to speed the flow of legal traffic through U.S ports-of-entry.

Integrated Automated Fingerprint Identification System (IAFIS)
The FBI currently processes up to 36,000 fingerprint cards each day. IAFIS is an FBI program (including a database) used to provide a paperless and prompt nationwide system which law enforcement agencies can access to identify known and wanted criminals. With the new system, the FBI estimates that it will process 73,000 cards per day. Fingerprint identification of arrestees is expected to be reduced from 21 days to an average of 2 hours.

Interagency Border Inspection System (IBIS)
The IBIS is an automated lookout system that links the databases of several inspection agencies, including airports, land border ports, and seaports. This is aimed at strengthening the country's security against terrorists, drug traffickers, and criminals. IBIS also supports the Advance Passenger Information System.

The INTERPOL-U.S. National Central Bureau System
INTERPOL maintains an interrelated electronic and computerized communications system, which is spread across the United States and around the world. INTERPOL's U.S. National Central Bureau has developed a system in which known felons who have been indicted in U.S. District Courts for distribution of narcotics or money laundering, but who have evaded prosecution by fleeing the country, can be entered into the INTERPOL network in order to assist in locating them and returning them to the United States.

Interstate Identification Index (III)
The FBI's Interstate Identification Index holds information about persons arrested for felonies or serious misdemeanors under state or federal law. The index includes identifying information, FBI Numbers, and State Identification Numbers (SIDs) from each state or federal file holding information about an individual. States that do not participate in the III may still voluntarily submit records to be stored in the FBI files, which may then be searched as part of the III process.

When a III inquiry is received and a matching record is found, the III automatically sends a record request to the state repository holding the information about the person.

The III deals only with criminal justice inquiries at this time. Non-criminal justice inquiries are handled by the individual states, or by the FBI from the state files that have been voluntarily contributed.

According to the Bureau of Justice Statistics, 29 states were members of the Interstate Identification Index at the end of 1993. Several changes are needed before the remaining states can fully participate in the Interstate Identification Index. Some are technology changes, as not all states have automated their records completely enough to be incorporated into the III. Some state laws prohibit non-criminal justice use of their records, which is in conflict with other states that may inquire about their data. These conflicts also must be resolved if state records are to be uniformly available at the Federal level. These changes are now under way.

One more change will add a flag called the Felon Identification for Firearm Sales (FIFS) to the records of all felons listed in the III, as well as those pending a felony arrest. This is the first stage of developing a National Instant Criminal Background Check System (NICS), which will make it possible to perform an instant felony check for those wishing to purchase firearms. NICS must be in place by November 30, 1998, as mandated by the Brady Handgun Violence Prevention Act.

A National Fingerprint File (NFF) will also be added to NCIC as one more way to index the records by fingerprint. The NFF will contain fingerprints of federal offenders and the first-arrest set of fingerprints taken on any offender within any state. When an inquiry is received, and a matching index record is found, a record request can automatically be sent by the III to the state or federal agency holding information about the offender. This will help to identify and gather more complete criminal histories of those using aliases or other identities.

In the future, it is hoped that complete, accurate, and immediately accessible records will allow states to:

- more effectively track movement of felons from state to state
- quickly access criminal histories when individuals previously convicted of felonies are re-arrested or attempt to purchase firearms
- ensure that persons responsible for child care, elder care, or care of the disabled do not have prior disqualifying convictions
- more easily identify criminal offenders subject to "three strikes" laws
- identify individuals who have a criminal history of domestic violence or stalking, and determine whether individuals are subject to civil restraining orders arising out of domestic violence incidents
- immediately identify individuals with prior criminal records in any state
- make better and more informed decisions relating to pretrial release and detention of offenders, career criminal prosecutions, and appropriate correctional confinement

Motor Vehicle Records

Law enforcement officers regularly use driver's license data, driving histories, motor vehicle registrations, and other MVR data. For further information on this data, please refer to Chapter Twenty-seven—Department of Motor Vehicles.

National Crime Information Center (NCIC)

First established by the FBI in 1967, the National Crime Information Center is a system used by all branches of law enforcement, as well as criminal justice agencies. The NCIC system contains information about wanted, missing and unidentified persons (such as children, amnesia victims, and unidentified dead bodies). These records are used for criminal history searches, which may be included in the pre-employment screening process for criminal justice employment, employment by a federally chartered or insured banking institution or securities firm, or by state or local governments. NCIC is also used as part of the background screening process for licensing pursuant to a state statute approved by the U.S. Attorney General.

The National Child Search Act of 1990 requires that law enforcement agencies immediately accept all reports concerning a missing child and enter a record with the child's description into NCIC. That information then becomes available to all of law enforcement throughout the United States, Puerto Rico, the U.S. Virgin Islands, and Canada.

NCIC also includes several other types of records. It catalogs burned, decomposed, and skeletonized remains in order to provide a central clearinghouse for unidentified remains found by different agencies, and to aid in the identification of victims in the event of a catastrophe. It records stolen items, including vehicles, license plates, boats, guns, articles of personal property, and securities. It contains a file of Canadian warrants as well. Since 1991, NCIC has also carried warrants of deportation for wanted criminal aliens. The Secret Service protective file (also part of NCIC) provides information on individuals who may pose a threat to the President or other authorized protectees.

Further developments will allow the storage of images in the database, as part of "NCIC 2000." The images are expected to include mug shots of suspects, tattoos, crime scenes, evidence, and fingerprints, which will enhance law enforcement's ability to convey and access these types of information whenever and wherever needed.

National Drug Pointer Index System (NDPIX)

NDPIX is a pointer system developed by the Drug Enforcement Administration (DEA) to allow participating federal, state, and local agencies to determine whether other jurisdictions have information related to their ongoing drug investigations.

National Fingerprint File (NFF)

Please refer to the Interstate Identification Index (III) discussed earlier in this chapter.

National Incident-Based Reporting System (NIBRS)

NIBRS is a long-range effort to modernize law enforcement data collection in order to provide a truer, more complete picture of crime. It is currently being used in several states and is being tested in others, but is not expected to be completely online until 2010.

According to J. Harper Wilson, chief of the FBI's Law Enforcement Support Section, the FBI currently receives 1.6 billion records a year—a number that is expected to rise to more than 50 billion once NIBRS goes online. The 52 distinct data elements to be collected under NIBRS will include much more detailed information about the criminal offense, the victim, the offender and any property involved. These records are expected to give law enforcement a broader view of criminal activity in the United States because NIBRS will also collect data on 22 crime categories instead of the eight serious offenses that now make up the FBI's Crime Index.

The FBI will use this data to analyze certain types of offenders and crimes, such as drug-related robberies, hate crimes, domestic violence, and crimes in which alcohol was a factor.

National Instant Criminal Background Check System (NICS)

Please refer to the Interstate Identification Index (III) discussed earlier in this chapter.

Regional Information Sharing System (RISS)

The Regional Information Sharing System (RISS) is an innovative, federally-funded program to support law enforcement efforts to combat organized crime activity, drug trafficking, criminal gangs and violent crime. The six regional projects of RISS—MAGLOCLEN, MOCIC, NESPIN, RMIN, ROCIC and WSIN—provide member law enforcement agencies in all 50 states with a broad range of intelligence and investigative support services. For more information, you can visit the RISS Internet site at:

http://www.iir.com/riss

Violent Gang and Terrorist Organizations File (VGTOF)

The Violent Gang and Terrorist Organizations File will contain information on members of violent gangs and terrorist organizations, and pointers to other contacts within law enforcement who can share further information. This is being developed by the FBI and will become part of the NCIC system.

OTHER USES FOR CRIMINAL RECORDS

Criminal history records can be extremely important in many aspects of police work. For example, when police officers stop someone for as little as a traffic violation or loitering, knowledge that the person is wanted for a crime, has a history of violence, is an escapee from prison, or has failed to comply with the terms of their parole, probation or bail, will better prepare the officers before approaching the person, which can sometimes even save their lives. When a firearm or other dangerous weapon is found in the possession of a felon, that represents another felony, for which the police can arrest the person. The availability of complete, updated criminal history records to officers in the field is vital to police work.

Criminal records are also used to perform pre-employment background checks.

INTERNATIONAL CRIMINAL JUSTICE ORGANIZATIONS AND DATABASES

In addition to the databases used within the United States criminal justice system, some international databases are shared by multiple countries, in order to coordinate their criminal justice efforts. Information about some of these cooperative efforts follows.

Europol

The European Community nations are moving to establish a joint police organization known as Europol. The Treaty on European Union defines the functions of Europol as support for national criminal investigation and security authorities; database development and maintenance; central analysis and assessment of information; collection and analysis of national prevention programs; and measures relating to further training, research, forensic matters, and criminal record keeping.

INTERPOL and TREVI

The International Criminal Police Organization (INTERPOL) and TREVI are the two main mechanisms of multinational police cooperation in Western Europe. INTERPOL has a Police Coordination Division, which manages police cooperation among countries; an Administrative Division, which operates the telecommunications systems; and the Research Division, which collects and analyzes crime information of interest to INTERPOL members. National Central Bureaus in each member country are the contact points for coordinating international criminal investigations.

The U.S. bureau, one of the largest and most active, is a separate agency within the U.S. Department of Justice. The U.S. bureau can identify and obtain foreign assistance for virtually any investigative problem in any legal jurisdiction. This is often accomplished through INTERPOL's interrelated electronic and computerized communications system spread across the United States and around the world.

CRIMINAL JUSTICE BULLETIN BOARDS AND NETWORKS

There are many bulletin boards on which criminal justice information, techniques, and experience are shared. Some are accessible by the public, such as the American Society of Law Enforcement Trainers (ASLET), found within the SafetyNet forum on CompuServe, and A.L.E.R.T.: A Law Enforcement Round Table found on GEnie. The Consular Affairs Bulletin Board (from the U.S. Department of State, Bureau of Consular Affairs) provides a forum for the exchange of information dealing with security and crime problems abroad.

Others are proprietary, such as FOPNet, operated by the Fraternal Order of Police and IACP NET, operated by the International Association of Chiefs of Police.

The INTERPOL Network links police agencies around the world for cases that involve state and local authorities working in conjunction with their federal counterparts. It is administered by the U.S. National Central Bureau (USNCB).

The National Criminal Justice Reference Service (NCJRS) operates an electronic bulletin board system that provides up-to-date information about NCJRS publications, products, and services. Moreover, the bulletin board provides information about Office of Justice programs, project funding opportunities, national and international criminal justice news, legislation, criminal justice conferences, and other criminal justice services and organizations. For further information, please refer to their Internet site at:
http://www.ncjrs.org/

The National Law Enforcement Technology Center (NLETC, which is part of the National Institute of Justice) is developing bulletin board access and databases to help law enforcement agencies share information about products that they wish to purchase, or that they can borrow from one another.

Many courts have their own independent bulletin boards, as do police and sheriff's departments. Law schools also sometimes operate independent bulletin boards, although these are increasingly seen on the Internet now. A few additional examples of bulletin boards used within the Criminal Justice system include those dedicated to Air Patrol, Customs Service, Department of Justice, the Federal Bureau of Prisons, and Immigration Law.

ADDITIONAL CRIMINAL JUSTICE DATABASES AND SYSTEMS

The databases listed earlier do not represent all of the criminal justice databases used to store or track information about people.

Neither do they come close to representing all of the databases used within the criminal justice system, as many additional databases are used that do not contain information about individuals at all, or contain such information only incidentally. For example, litigating organizations within the criminal justice system also use legal research databases, such as those offered by JURIS, LEXIS, and WESTLAW. Other examples include databases used to catalog stolen art or spent ammunition.

There are also technological developments that can be combined with the criminal justice databases and systems, in order to provide more efficient access to criminal justice records or simplify the booking process.

FOR FURTHER INFORMATION

For further information about databases used within the criminal justice system, many additional resources are available.

Publications

Many databases provide indices to criminal justice publications. For example, the National Criminal Justice Reference Service maintains a database of abstracts for more than 130,000 criminal justice books, documents, and reports published by the U.S. Department of Justice, other local, state, and federal government agencies, international organizations, and the private sector. Users can search the database using Knight-Ridder Information, Inc. in the Criminal Justice Periodical Index (File 171), or can obtain this information on CD-ROM through NCJRS at (800) 851-3420.

The directory of NCJRS publications can also be searched on the Internet at:
http://www.ncjrs.org/catalog.htm

NCJRS' newest service, the Justice Information (JUST INFO) electronic newsletter, is designed to provide criminal justice professionals with accurate, current, and useful information about criminal and juvenile justice. There is no cost to participate in this service, but users must have access to Internet email. Further information about this newsletter can be found at the NCJRS Internet site mentioned earlier in this chapter. (Information about joining other electronic mailing lists, such as the JUVENILE JUSTICE (JUVJUST) Electronic Mailing List can also be found at that site.)

Additional databases that index criminal justice publications include:
- Criminal Justice Abstracts (available online through WESTLAW and on CD-ROM from Willow Tree Press, Inc.) which contains citations, with abstracts, to journals, reports, books, dissertations, magazines, and newspapers covering criminal justice topics

- CINCH: The Australian Criminology Database (available online through OZLINE: Australian Information Network) which contains more than 26,000 citations, with some abstracts, to Australian literature on criminology

- Criminology and Penal Jurisdiction (available online through IZUM ATLASS/COBISS) which contains bibliographic information on articles, books, Congress and other materials from the field of criminology

- Index to Legal Periodicals (available online through CDP Online, LEXIS, OCLC EPIC, OCLC FirstSearch Catalog, WESTLAW (ILP), and WILSONLINE and on CD-ROM from H.W. Wilson Company, WILSONDISC, SilverPlatter Information, Inc., and CD Plus Technologies) which contains citations to articles selected from legal periodicals, including journals, yearbooks, and annual reviews
- INFO-SOUTH Latin American Information System (available online through Knight-Ridder and INFO-SOUTH Latin American Information System) which contains citations, with abstracts, to periodical literature relating to the contemporary social, political, and economic situation in Latin America
- JURISST (available online through Commission de la Sante et de la Securite du Travail du Quebec (CSST), Services Juridiques) which contains citations, with abstracts, to Quebec jurisprudence relating to occupational safety and health
- Law Enforcement and Criminal Justice Information Database (available online and on CD-ROM through International Research and Evaluation (IRE)) which contains citations, with some abstracts, to the literature on law enforcement and criminal justice
- Legal Resource Index (available online through CARL Systems Network, CompuServe Knowledge Index, DataStar, Knight-Ridder, LEXIS, WESTLAW) which contains citations, with selected abstracts, to articles published in key law journals, bar association publications, and legal newspapers
- LegalTrac (available on CD-ROM from Information Access Company) which contains citations, with selected abstracts, to articles published in key law journals, bar association publications, and legal newspapers

There are magazines and newsletters that one can subscribe to, such as the Law Enforcement Bulletin. Recent issues of this publication can be found on the Internet at:
http://www.fbi.gov/leb/leb.htm

Information about publications from the Office of International Criminal Justice can be found on the Internet at:
http://www.acsp.uic.edu/index.htm

Tables of contents and selected articles from recent issues of several publications can be found at this site, including those from:

CJ On-Line—Europe
CJ On-Line—International
CJ On-Line—The Americas

CIA publications can be found at:
http://www.odci.gov/cia/publications/pubs.html

The National Clearinghouse for Criminal Justice Information Systems operates an automated index of more than 1,000 criminal justice information systems used by state and local governments, and operates the Criminal Justice Information System Bulletin Board. Their number is (916) 392-2550.

Many additional publications track specific types of laws, cases filed, and their progress. Examples include:

- BNA Antitrust & Trade Regulation Daily (available online through HRIN, The Human Resource Information Network, LEXIS, and WESTLAW) which provides comprehensive reports on legislative, regulatory, and judicial developments affecting restrictive trade practice law

- BNA California Environment Daily (available online through LEXIS, NEXIS, and WESTLAW) contains information on legislative activities, regulations, and standards affecting California environmental law

- Breast Implant Litigation Reporter (available online through NewsNet Inc.) which provides current information on developments in breast implant suits nationwide, including coverage of civil and criminal actions, significant discovery proceedings, actions taken by the U.S. Food and Drug Administration, the public disclosure of documents, and detailed coverage of trials and appellate proceedings from the most important cases

- Business Law Brief (available online through FT PROFILE and NEXIS) which contains the complete text of *Business Law Brief,* a monthly newsletter on significant developments in international business law

- CAN/LAW (available online through Infomart Online, LEXIS, and QL Systems Limited) which contains the complete text of Canadian legal publications covering various points of law

- Money Laundering Alert (available online through NewsNet, Inc., as well as the Newsletter database on Knight-Ridder and PROMT) which contains the complete text of Money Laundering Alert, a monthly newsletter covering legislative, regulatory, enforcement, and international developments in the area of money laundering controls and asset forfeiture

- Weekly Criminal Bulletin (available online through Infomart Online, LEXIS, and QL Systems Limited) which contains more than 32,000 summaries of judgments in criminal cases tried in the federal and provincial courts in Canada.

Other Criminal Justice Resources

There are many other Internet sites dedicated to criminal justice, such as the index found at:

http://www.ncjrs.org/other.htm

and the international index found at:

http://www.ncjrs.org/intlwww.htm

and The United Nations Crime and Justice Information Network (UNCJIN):

http://www.ifs.univie.ac.at/uncjin/mosaic/

The Central Intelligence Agency Home Page, which now contains a warning that it may be used only for authorized purposes, and that you are consenting to monitoring and auditing by use of this site:

http://www.odci.gov/cia/

The Department of Justice:

http://www.usdoj.gov/

The FBI Home Page:

http://www.fbi.gov/

The FBI Home Page contains information about the mission of the FBI, along with information about the top crimes that the FBI is currently investigating. You can also find information about the FBI's Ten Most Wanted Criminals at:

http://www.fbi.gov/mostwant/tenlist.htm

Dozens of additional sites for individual police departments can be found on the Internet, and they are rapidly multiplying in number. To locate an up-to-date listing of these sites, search for subjects such as "criminal justice" or "law enforcement" with WebCrawler, Alta Vista, or one of the many other Internet search utilities.

The Police Officer's Internet Directory can also provide links to many other Internet sites of interest to police officers. This site can be found at:

http://www.officer.com

Department of Motor Vehicles

The Department of Motor Vehicles (DMV) in each state maintains several types of records on individuals. These include identifying information, the status of driver's licenses, records of violations, license suspensions, and accident records. The DMV also maintains vehicle and vessel registrations and histories.

Identifying Information on Individuals

The DMV maintains identifying information on individuals, for use on drivers licenses and identification cards. This information typically includes:

- Driver's license or identification card number (in some states, the Social Security number is used)
- Driver's full name
- Aliases (AKAs, maiden names)
- Residential address
- Mailing address
- Birthdate
- Sex
- Height
- Weight
- Color of eyes
- Color of hair
- Photo

All of this information, except for the photo, is available online for nearly all states. However, many states restrict who has access to the records. This is explained in greater detail at the end of this chapter.

Driver's License Data

In addition to the identifying information, driver's license data also includes:

- Status (valid, expired, suspended, revoked)
- Class of license (single vehicle, 3-axle house car, motorcycle, etc.)
- Date issued
- Expiration date
- Extension code (out-of-state, renewal by mail, military, etc.)
- Restriction code (corrective lenses required, may not drive on weekends or holidays, court restrictions, artificial limb required, under seat cushion required, must be accompanied by licensed adult, etc.)

- Duplicate issuance date
- License held code (surrendered by the court, withheld by DMV, etc.)

Driving Records

Accident and violation information is not only used in hiring a chauffeur or delivery person. It has also been used to locate individuals and track their whereabouts on a given date. If one were being sued for damage to another's vehicle or for personal injury resulting from a fender bender and the claim appears suspicious, it could be worth obtaining a copy of the plaintiff's driving record in order to find out whether damage to the vehicle has been reported before or the person appears to be particularly "accident prone." For the full details of an accident, one would still want to request the full accident report from the jurisdiction noted on the record, as the online information is brief, and valuable details may be hidden in the paper documentation.

A driving record may also include any of the following data:
- Violation or accident date (up to seven years for major violations; up to three years for minor violations)
- Abstract of the court's record indicating a conviction
- Court case disposition code
- Court docket or citation number
- Assigned code number
- Location of court
- Accident involvement
- Financial responsibility file number
- Coded report numbers
- License plate number
- Notice of failure to appear in court (FTA)
- Notice of failure to pay a court-imposed fine (FTP)
- Conviction date
- Statute(s) violated (number)
- Statute abbreviation
- Departmental action
- Date departmental action order was mailed
- Effective date of departmental action
- Vehicle code number authorizing departmental action
- Ending date of departmental action
- Reason for departmental action
- Date of service of departmental action
- Code for service of departmental action
- Financial responsibility file number

Vehicle Registrations

The DMV registers vehicles including automobiles, trucks and commercial vehicles, trailers, motor homes, buses, motorcycles, off-road vehicles, and snowmobiles. Registration records make it possible to identify vehicles owned by an individual or company. This is useful for asset searches, especially where expensive vehicles are involved. Spouses and other relationships also sometimes appear on vehicle registration records as co-owners.

Vehicle registration records are not only useful for law enforcement, but are particularly helpful for surveillance work. Vehicle license plate numbers can be taken down at a surveillance site and later used to identify whose vehicles were coming and going from the location. Of course, the driver may be someone else altogether, and some of the vehicles may turn out to be rental vehicles, but these records often do provide invaluable leads.

Vehicle registrations include a Vehicle Identification Number (VIN). For vehicles manufactured since 1981, the VIN has been standardized into the following format:

- Digit 1—nation of origin
- Digits 2-3—manufacturer and make or model
- Digits 4-8—car or truck line, series, body type, restraint system, engine, or other information as defined by the manufacturer
- Digit 9—check digit (used to validate the VIN)
- Digit 10—year of manufacture
- Digit 11—assembly plant
- Digits 12-17—production number
- Legal owner
- Residential address
- Mailing address
- Abbreviation of vehicle make
- Ownership certificate issue date
- Owner as-of date
- Vehicle weight

Vessel Registrations

The DMV also registers motorized boats and vessels. Vessel registration records are used for asset searches when it is suspected that the subject may own a boat. Vessel registrations include:

- Vessel identification number
- Manufacturer
- Hull number
- Year of manufacture
- Length measurement of vessel

- Hull material code
- Vessel hull type code
- Body type model abbreviation
- Type of propulsion
- Legal owner
- Residential address
- Mailing address

Vehicle/Vessel Histories

In addition to current registration information, vehicle and vessel histories reveal where a vehicle or vessel came from. Vendors sometimes offer different pricing, depending upon how many years you want to go back when checking a vehicle/vessel history.

Vehicle histories can be used to show a relationship, such as when one party purchases a vehicle or vessel from another. They can also be used to show how someone has hidden their assets, as when they transfer vehicles and vessels to other family members and friends.

Problem Driver Pointer System (PDPS)

The Problem Driver Pointer System (PDPS) is an electronic database allowing users to identify drivers who have DUI (driving under the influence) and other major traffic convictions, or who have suspended or revoked licenses due to serious violations in any state. The PDPS is managed by the National Driver Register, which maintains an index of the records and pointers to the corresponding state records. It is not managed by the state DMV.

The PDPS is used by government and employers to screen prospective employees. It is not open to investigators. Individuals may submit requests for information about themselves directly to the National Driver Register.

How to Access DMV Records Online

Some vehicle records that are available online must be acquired in two steps. First they are ordered online; they cannot actually be retrieved until a day or two later, after DMV employees have had time to search them out manually and the vendor has time to type them into their own system. Other vendors purchase tapes from the DMV and allow access to their systems or sell CD-ROMs of the data, which quickly become obsolete unless they are updated regularly. In some states, it is also possible to retrieve online data directly from the DMV.

Many public records vendors offer DMV records as well. For example, CDB Infotek offers driving records for 47 states, searches of vehicles by owner name in 37 states, and searches by license plate or VIN number in 47 states. New York records are returned immediately, but in most other states, records are returned in one or two business days.

Many additional online vendors offer DMV data, not just those which trade in public records. Some, like CARFAX in Virginia, DATEQ in Georgia, Explore Information Services in Minnesota, Pollock & Co. in Connecticut, and Experian Target Marketing Services in Texas, specialize in DMV data, and offer records for several states. Some companies, such as Database Technologies, Inc., in Florida, provide complete records for law enforcement and offer private citizens access to only a portion of the records. Some companies, such as Intelligence Network Inc. in Florida, offer records for a single state. Even companies with only limited public records offerings sometimes provide access to some DMV records. CompuServe, for example, provides an online gateway to Florida DMV records.

Regulations on Accessing DMV Records

Regulations for access to DMV records vary from state to state. For example, Massachusetts is one of about 30 states that offer complete driving records, home addresses, and vehicle records to anyone willing to pay the copy fee. Some state DMVs will even sell copies of their entire files to marketers. In California, however, home addresses are not generally available to anyone without a commercial-requester account with the DMV, a $50,000 bond, and a permissible purpose for obtaining the record.

California's restriction originated in 1990, when state legislators adopted a law barring release of home addresses except under special circumstances. This law was passed after the murder of actress Rebecca Schaeffer, who was shot by an obsessive fan who obtained her home address from the DMV with the assistance of a private investigator. DMV address information from vehicle registrations has also been used to track down doctors who perform abortions, as well as women who visit their clinics, to harass them, threaten them, or incite violence against them.

These facts spurred Senator Barbara Boxer from California to introduce an amendment entitled the "Protection of Information in State Motor Vehicle Records," which she attached to the Crime Bill (Omnibus Crime Control Act). The amendment would extend restrictions on DMV information to all states. At the same time, Representative Jim Moran from Virginia introduced a similar bill in the House of Representatives. In September 1994, Congress passed the Omnibus Crime Control Act with the amendment. This law restricts access to name, address, telephone number, and other personal information held by each state DMV.

Several exceptions are contained in the law, allowing access for government use, insurance industry claims and underwriting purposes, driver safety disclosures, and employment verification. People are also allowed to request that their information not be made available to firms collecting data for mailing lists or for building their own databases.

The states have until September 1997 to comply with the Protection of Information in State Motor Vehicle Records law. Before full compliance is obtained, there may be challenges to the law, so the final outcome is not yet certain.

Death Records

D eath records today are widely available in several computerized forms. This has made it efficient and relatively inexpensive to locate information on the computer about someone who has died.

Although examples supplied in this chapter deal with people whose names you may recognize, the death records databases contain records for millions of people, few of whom are famous. Anyone who has died may be included.

Social Security Records

The primary source of automated death information is the Social Security Administration (SSA). The SSA has kept records of deaths in the United States since the late 1920s. The SSA usually learns that a person has died when someone claims a death benefit or when the agency is notified to stop Social Security payments to a person. Although they do not have records of all deaths, their records do approximate 50 million names. Thus, this agency is a rich resource for genealogists and others.

The Social Security Administration licenses its records to several vendors. Each of these vendors sets their own price for access to the records, and the prices vary widely. For example, a "nationwide death search" can cost $75 for a single online search, $15/hour for as many searches as you like, $45 for a CD-ROM database containing all of the records from 1937 to 1995, or can be free on the Internet. There are many other prices for this same data, depending upon the vendor.

Which of these options you choose should depend on how often you expect to search these files, and how important current records are to you. Some systems require the name and Social Security number for searching, whereas others require only one or the other. If you need death information for genealogical purposes and you expect to search often for additional records, the CD-ROM version may be the best bargain. You may even find that a library, family research center, or local genealogical association owns a copy of the CD that you can use. If you only have occasional need for these records, CompuTrace may be your best bet. More information about this system appears later.

For the most current information, you may need to look at services that combine SSA records with other types of records, as most (if not all) vendors receive update tapes from the SSA only on a quarterly basis. These combined services often carry a much heftier price tag per search.

CDB Infotek's CompuTrace

CompuTrace (a product of CDB Infotek) is available online as one of CompuServe's premium services. The CompuTrace deceased data is purchased from the Social Security Administration. On this system, the cost for searching is $15/hour, and there is no "per-search" charge. The data is more current than the CD version. CompuTrace claims to include information about over 40 million individuals who died after 1928.

All individuals contained in this file were United States citizens residing anywhere in the United States (including Puerto Rico and the Virgin Islands), areas under United States administration (Canal Zone, Canton Islands, Mariana Islands—except for Marshall Islands, Midway Islands, and Wake Island), or in one of the following countries or continents at the time the death was reported:

Africa	Guam
American Samoa	Mexico
Asia	Oceania (Australia & Pacific Islands)
Canada	Philippine Islands
Central America & West Indies	South America
Europe	

For example, a search for actress Greta Garbo displayed the following record:

CDB INFOTEK
COMPUTRACE—DECEASED FILE SEARCH

NAME: GARBO GRETA
DATE OF BIRTH: 09/18/1905
SOCIAL SECURITY #: 558-66-0000
STATE SSN ISSUED: CALIFORNIA
YEAR ISSUED: 1962—1963
CITY OF LAST RESIDENCE: MILLTOWN
STATE/COUNTRY OF LAST RESIDENCE: NEW JERSEY
ZIP CODE OF LAST RESIDENCE: 08850
ZIP CODE OF LUMP SUM PAYMENT: N/A
DATE OF DEATH: 04/00/90

Last Page !

Please note that CompuTrace does not provide the full Social Security number. It does appear when the records are accessed directly through CDB Infotek, rather than through CompuServe, however.

Social Security Death Records Index (CD110)

The Social Security Death Records Index (CD110) is a two-CD set containing over 50 million names of deceased individuals who had Social Security numbers. Included in the 50 million names are approximately 400,000 railroad retirement records from the early 1900s to 1950s. The records consist of:

- The individual's name and Soundex code (Refer to Chapter Thirty-four for explanation of Soundex codes.)

- Dates of birth and death

- Social Security number and state where it was issued

- State of residence at death

- ZIP Code of last known residence and the primary location it is associated with (for approximately 77% of the records)
- ZIP Code of the address where the death benefit payment was sent and the primary location it is associated with (for 15% of the records)

This CD-ROM set from Automated Archives, Inc. (now owned by Banner Blue, which has been acquired by Brøderbund), is available as part of the Family Tree Maker's Family Archive collection. Further information about these products can be found on the Internet at:
http://www.familytreemaker.com/facds.html

A similar Social Security Death index is also now available on the Internet as a free service from Ancestry Search at:
http://www.ancestry.com/SSDI/Main.htm

A search of this database for early civil rights leader and congressman, Adam Clayton Powell, produced the following results:

POWELL, ADAM 109-03-4579 (NY) b. 29 Nov 1908 d. Apr 1972

POWELL, ADAM 208-09-9013 (PA) b. 14 Dec 1887 d. May 1973lr. 15234

POWELL, ADAM 379-05-7528 (MI) b. 22 Dec 1900 d. Dec 1980lr. 48503 (Flint, Genesee, MI) lp. 48504 (Flint, Genesee, MI)

POWELL, ADAM 409-16-3416 (TN) b. 10 Dec 1903 d. Apr 1971lr. 38242 (Paris, Henry, TN)

POWELL, ADAM 424-10-6754 (AL) b. 04 Dec 1897 d. Oct 1973lr. 36587 (Semmes, Mobile, AL)

POWELL, ADAM 426-90-5340 (MS) b. 30 May 1943 d. Aug 1984lr. 60644 (Chicago, Cook, IL)

POWELL, ADAM 451-28-5636 (TX) b. 15 Nov 1887 d. Oct 1968lr. 77363 (Plantersville, Grimes, TX)

POWELL, ADAM 453-36-6140 (TX) b. 20 Apr 1924 d. Oct 1979 lp. 77868 (Navasota, Grimes, TX)

Knowing Congressman Powell's date of birth, I am able to identify the first record as the correct match, so you see, having some good identifying information can help at every stage of researching a person.

Public Records Vendors

Many additional public records vendors offer searches of Social Security Death Records, often under trade names such as "Decedent Trace" and "National Death Search." The date ranges, update schedules, and prices for these searches can vary significantly. In most cases, the vendors allow a search on only one name at a time, using pre-defined fields, and charging a fee for each search attempt.

A notable exception is the Social Security Number Death Master File search on LEXIS. This search includes only the records from 1962 to the most recent quarter, but LEXIS allows the same search capabilities as on the firm's other databases. It is possible to search for a range of names, or even a combination of names (such as Robert or Bob) in the same search. The content of LEXIS' Social Security number Death Master File is listed as:

- Name of deceased individual
- Social Security number
- Date of death

- Date of birth
- State/country of residence
- ZIP Code of last residence
- ZIP Code of recipient of death benefits

Not all of the information is necessarily present for each record. For example, a search for actor River Phoenix displayed the following result:

SOCIAL SECURITY ADMINISTRATION DEATH MASTER FILE

* * * THIS DATA IS FOR INFORMATION PURPOSES ONLY * * *

NAME: PHOENIX, RIVER

SOCIAL SECURITY NUMBER: 571-61-9058

DATE OF DEATH: 10/31/1993

DATE OF BIRTH: 06/23/1970

As you can see, this record omits the State/Country of Residence and the ZIP Codes. The full Social Security number does appear, however.

Public records vendors may also offer death records indices from other sources, as well. CDB Infotek, for one, offers death records indices from the California and Texas Departments of Health.

Fatality Reports

Details of occupation-related fatalities in Canada can be found online in the Fatality Reports database, produced by the Canadian Centre for Occupational Health and Safety. The records in this database include date and place of inquiry, date and place of accident, name and occupation of deceased, industrial sector, cause of death, manner of death (e.g., accidental, preventable), accident description, and recommendations of the reviewing agency. This database also includes some 500 reports compiled by the Farm Safety Association of Ontario summarizing farm fatalities in Ontario. Sources include reports completed by coroners, medical examiners, government ministries, police investigators, and workers' compensation boards.

The Fatality Reports database is available from:

Canadian Centre for Occupational Health and Safety (CCOHS)
CCINFOline
250 Main Street East
Hamilton, ON, Canada L8N 1H6
(800) 668-4284
(905) 570-8094
(905) 572-2206 Fax

CEMETERY RECORDS

Cemetery caretakers usually keep records of the names and death dates of those buried, as well as maps of the grave sites. They may also keep more detailed records, including the names of the deceased's relatives. In addition to these paper records, there are tombstones, which can provide information such as birth and death dates and the names of other family members. The best place to find cemetery records are in the cemeteries. Often, if there is no longer a caretaker of the cemetery, records can be found in the holdings of local libraries, archives, or historical societies. Some of this information can also now be found on CD-ROM databases, and online.

Salt Lake City Cemetery Records (CD168)

The Salt Lake City Cemetery Records is a CD containing burial information of many of the early pioneers to the Great Basin area. It covers the period of September 1848 to November 1992. Although many of the Mormon pioneers and their descendants were buried in this cemetery, there are also early Protestant and Catholic families buried here. The information contained on this compact disc includes name, birth date, birthplace, death date, death place, burial place, and burial location in the cemetery. This CD-ROM from Automated Archives, Inc. (now owned by Banner Blue, which has been acquired by Brøderbund), is available as part of the Family Tree Maker's Family Archive collection. Further information about these products can be found on the Internet at:

http://www.familytreemaker.com/facds.html

Also refer to the Roll of Honor: Civil War Union Soldiers (CD351) in Chapter Thirty-four for additional cemetery records.

USA Wars: Vietnam

If you believe that someone you are looking for may have died or been declared missing in action in the Vietnam War, this database may contain exactly the information you need. The USA Wars: Vietnam CD contains information about U.S. involvement in the Vietnam War. This CD includes special and general operations orders, a chronology of battles, histories of major units, order of military ranks, medals and awards, references to congressional hearings, and participants missing in action (MIAs), a glossary, and bibliographic references. For each individual whose name is inscribed on the Vietnam Veterans Memorial in Washington, DC, this CD lists their name, date of birth and death, military rank, branch of service, and a wall panel locator. The USA Wars: Vietnam CD-ROM database is available through:

Quanta Press, Inc.
1313 Fifth Street S.E.; Suite 223A
Minneapolis, MN 55414
(612) 379-3956
(612) 623-4570 Fax

MORTALITY RECORDS INDICES

Mortality schedules counted the number of deaths that occurred in the year before the census was taken. They exist for the 1850 through 1880 censuses. This means that there are only four schedules currently available for the U.S. census. A mortality schedule lists:

- The individual's name
- Age
- Sex
- Occupation
- Cause of death
- Date of death
- Place of death by county

Mortality schedules are now available on CD-ROM as part of the Family Tree Maker's Family Archives.

Mortality Records Index: United States—Family Archive (CD164)

Source: Mortality Records, created by the Bureau of the Census during census years, document the deaths of individuals who had been recorded in the previous census. This CD indexes the Mortality Records of the following states: Alabama, Arkansas, Arizona, California, Colorado, Connecticut, District of Columbia, Dakota Territory, Delaware, Florida, Georgia, Idaho, Illinois, Indiana, Iowa, Kansas, Kentucky, Louisiana, Michigan, Minnesota, Mississippi, Montana, Nebraska, Nevada, New Hampshire, North Dakota, Ohio, Oregon, Pennsylvania, South Dakota, Tennessee, Texas, Utah, Vermont, Virginia, Washington, West Virginia, and Wyoming.

Date Range: 1850-1880

Further information about these can be found on the Internet at:
http://www.familytreemaker.com/facds.html

Texas 1860, 1870, 1880, 1890 Mortality Schedule (CD49)
This CD (also available from AAI) contains approximately a million mortality records for 137 counties in 1860, 135 counties in 1870, 196 counties in 1880, and 180 counties in 1890. The Social Security Death Benefits records for Texas are also included.

Demografiska Databasen
This online database (in English and Swedish) contains historical demographic and social data on 365,000 individuals listed in 19th century Swedish church records and other historical sources. Records date from 1800 to 1895, with some coverage extending back to 1700. Typical data items include parish catechetical examination register, register of births, register of deaths, register of marriages, register of migration, date of birth, place of birth, name(s), legitimate or illegitimate birth, and twinship. Also included are demographic events data such as date of death, date of marriage ceremony, change of residence within parish or across border, previous and later domicile, trade (profession), social status, civil status, and position in family household. Kinship relations data

including parents, spouses, children, and source of information is also included. Demografiska Databasen is available from:

Umea Universitet
S-901 87 Umea, Sweden
90 166740
90 166958 Fax

Deaths in the News

When the famous die, one can expect to find information about them and their deaths in newspapers, magazines, and often even television or radio transcripts. News of a celebrity's death is often accompanied by information summarizing their accomplishments and events in their lives. (Refer to Chapter Thirty-three for further information about celebrity deaths.)

The news also contains articles about the deaths of less-celebrated individuals. People who die in accidents or who suffer violent deaths are often featured in news stories. Even those who die under normal circumstances may be mentioned within other articles or may be featured in an obituary. Obituaries usually also list surviving family members, which can provide a lead to further information about the subject.

News database vendors sometimes make it simpler to search for the deceased by coding obituaries in such a way that they are easy to locate. For example, Dow Jones News/Retrieval uses the code N/OBT to identify obituaries in their Press Release Wires.

Genealogists are also interested in obituaries, so there have been some efforts made at compiling obituary databases from newspapers. For example: Obituaries listed in Denver, Colorado newspapers can be found on the Internet at:

ftp://ftp.cac.psu.edu/pub/genealogy/text/data

in the file: **den-1993.arj**

An alphabetical list of obituaries from the *Houston Chronicle* can also be found at the same address in the file: **houobit1.zip**.

There also are sites for people to register obituaries for their own loved ones on the Internet, including:

The Virtual Memorial Garden:
http://catless.ncl.ac.uk/VMG

The Obituary Page 1994- at:
http://catless.cl.ac.uk/Obituary

The World Wide Cemetery:
http://www.cemetery.org/

Public Record of Death

Several public records databases contain records of death. One such database is offered by CDB Infotek. CDB's databases include the Department of Health Death Records Index online for California. A search of this database may provide the date of death, county registrar number, state file number, county of filing, and Social Security number, if reported. Of course, you may still wish to obtain a copy of the full death certificate in order to locate next of kin, and the decedent's resting place.

CDB Infotek also offers an online Superior Court Probate index for California, that provides a file date, file number, and case title. Although not particularly telling in itself, you may use this information to order the full probate record from the court. Probate records (not yet online) include wills, financial and property information, lists of next of kin, lists of claims against the estate, personal information about the deceased, and details of how the decedent's property was distributed.

The Occupational Safety and Health Administration (OSHA) maintains records of workplace accidents and fatalities, which are indexed and searchable online through several public records vendors including WESTLAW, Information Resource Services Company (IRSC), and CDB Infotek. CDB allows searching of these records nationally by accident victim name. Basic information is available online, but for an additional fee, CDB will supply further details, including the victim's age, injury information, part of the body, events and factors causing and contributing to the accident, and so on.

Wrongful deaths (motor vehicle and other types) may also be found online in the civil records, offered by many public records vendors. Criminal records may also contain murder, manslaughter, self-defense, and accidental deaths as well.

Genealogical databases may also carry deaths among their vital records, such as on the Territorial Vital Records (CD J2) database, available from Brøderbund, The New South Wales Pioneers Index, The Tasmanian Pioneers Index, Western Australia Pioneers Index, and The Victorian Pioneers Index, all available through the Royal Melbourne Institute of Technology (RMIT). For further information about all of these databases, please refer to Chapter Thirty-four—Genealogical Records.

Deaths in Other Databases

Many other databases offer death records, both online and on CD-ROM . Some are covered in other chapters of this book. For example, biographical databases (discussed in Chapter Fifteen) contain the date or at least the year of death for thousands of persons, few of whom are famous. Some of the quotations databases (discussed in Chapter Twenty-two) also contain the year of death for persons who are quoted. Encyclopedias normally carry this information as well, when referring to someone now deceased.

Some databases that you might not think of for death records can prove surprisingly informative. One such is ADEC International Art Prices CD-ROM. In addition to information about art, this CD includes information about the artists including birth date, death date, and nationality, among other details. ADEC International Art Prices CD-ROM is available through:

Gordon & Lawrence Art Reference, Inc.
1840 8th Street South
Naples, FL 33940
(800) 726-2665
(813) 434-6842
(813) 434-6969 Fax

Tax Records

I t may either disappoint or relieve you to know that the Internal Revenue Service does not release federal income tax records to online searchers simply for the asking. However, this does not mean that income tax information can never be found through the use of online systems.

Franchise Tax Records

Franchise tax records include both personal and business tax returns. Although most of the information on these returns is considered confidential, some states do make at least some of it available online. This can help in determining the standing of a domestic or foreign corporation.

This non-confidential information can include the name of the corporation, address, phone number, date opened for business within the state, officers and directors, corporation number, tax year, filing date of return, name and title of person signing the return, tax due date, and amount of delinquent taxes.

Board of Equalization Records (or State Sales Tax Board)

State sales tax records may be found online for some states. In California, for example, the state Board of Equalization values state assessed property, oversees local property tax assessment, hears appeals from the Franchise Tax Board, and collects a wide variety of business taxes. These taxes include the Alcoholic Beverage Tax, Cigarette Tax, Emergency (911) Telephone Users Surcharge, Energy Resources Surcharge, Hazardous Waste and Substance Taxes, Insurers Registration Tax, Motor Vehicle Fuel Tax, Private Railroad Car Tax, Sales and Use Tax, Solid Waste Disposal Fee, Timber Yield Tax, and Use Fuel Tax.

If someone wishes to avoid paying sales tax on goods bought for resale (paying tax on their sales instead), they must apply for a Sales and Use Tax permit. Records such as these are kept by the State Sales Tax Board or a similar agency. For some states, these permits can be found through an online search of the state Board of Equalization records, which are provided by some of the public records vendors.

Property Tax Records

Real property records contain property tax information and, for many counties, can be found online through public records vendors. This information normally is collected from the county assessor's office.

The county assessor's office also collects taxes on unsecured property such as aircraft and boats, but that information is not generally available online. Real property tax records from County Assessors in selected states are now available on WESTLAW from Experian REDI Property, with more states to be added as available.

Although not available online as real property records, one may search Federal Aviation Administration (FAA) records for aircraft registrations through public records vendors, or the U.S. Coast Guard Watercraft database for merchant and recreational vessels weighing five net tons or more (approximately 27 feet or more). In some states, the Department of Motor Vehicle records include information about smaller boats. Florida Department of Natural Resources Boat Registrations can also be searched online. However, none of these records indicate the value of the craft nor the amount of taxes paid. That information must still be obtained from the county assessor's offices, which have not yet made this information available online.

Income Tax Records Within Public Records

If one fails to pay taxes, a federal, state, or county tax lien may be filed. Public records vendors routinely offer online tax lien indices, sometimes grouped with bankruptcies and judgments into a single search. When a matching record is found, only the basic information will be listed online, but you can then request a copy of the actual records from the court. These may provide more detailed tax records for an individual or a business.

Bankruptcies can also be expected to include detailed financial records, including tax returns, which can be requested from the court or records center once you have located the case online.

Another great place to find income tax records is in the records of a civil suit, particularly for tax-related cases. If a person has a dispute with the IRS settled in court, details of the person's financial affairs may all be found in the court documents.

Divorce cases, child custody, and support actions all are found to be good sources for tax returns and other financial information. Online civil records indices are available from many public records vendors, and again, the full record can then be requested in order to obtain details of a person's financial position, frequently including income tax records.

Uniform Commercial Code (UCC) indices also are available online. Their presence indicates that a financial statement is on file with the Secretary of State, which may be available at the county level as well. Income tax records are sometimes included in the financial statements. For more information on UCC filings, please refer to Chapter Thirty-one—Public Records.

Medical and Insurance Records

"Whatsoever things I see or hear concerning the life of men,
in my attendance on the sick or even apart therefrom,
which ought not to be noised abroad,
I will keep silence thereon,
counting such things to be as sacred secrets."

—*An excerpt from the Hippocratic Oath*

Are medical records private? People probably would like to think so. Of all the matters you may consider to be "sensitive information," your health is among the most personal. Have you had a facelift? Lost a breast to cancer? Had a venereal disease? For most people, information about these and many, many other types of personal health matters are expected to remain private.

The truth is that despite their sensitivity, medical records are not as discreetly held as individuals would hope. Let's take a few minutes to consider how medical information is processed today.

Databases of medical records exist in doctors' offices, hospitals, pharmacies, and medical facilities of all types. Some of these databases are standalone systems. Many others are part of integrated systems that link the records of one department or medical facility to those of another. In Wisconsin, this concept has grown into the Wisconsin Healthcare Information Network, or WHIN, which transmits laboratory results, transcribed medical reports, patient demographics, and insurance claims between doctors' offices, hospitals, and insurance companies throughout the state.

Linking medical databases lets patients' medical records follow them throughout a hospital stay, and potentially throughout their lives. This is more efficient than maintaining independent records, and by giving doctors and nurses more information about the patient's medical history and condition, it can improve medical care itself. This added knowledge can eliminate redundant tests and treatments, and it can be especially important in an emergency. Information about past treatments, medical conditions, current prescriptions, and allergies can save a patient's life.

Take the simple case of a physician administering a new medication. If the patient is not questioned, is unconscious or disoriented and unable to answer, or for whatever reason does not report taking a medication, the doctor could unknowingly administer conflicting medications or treatment. This could further endanger the patient's health. Better access to the patient's medical history can prevent such mishaps.

Healthcare information is being automated in large and small ways today. Even companies outside of the healthcare field are getting involved. Physician Computer Network, Inc. (PCN) has computer access to the patient records of over 90,000 office-based doctors.

(This represents about 27% of the physicians in the United States, according to PCN, while they continue to expand.) PCN offers doctors computerized billing and electronic links to hospitals, labs, and insurance companies.

On March 15, 1995, Equifax held a major news conference to announce that it had launched a new business in healthcare information. The company is forming a strategic alliance with AT&T and Consort Technologies, Inc., to develop "paperless" patient records. The new computerized system automates the creation of complete patient records, automates prescriptions and laboratory tests, checks for allergies and drug interactions, and can access all required information at the point of care. These are examples of how healthcare systems are being linked today.

Medical Registries

On an even larger scale, there are databases that track the incidence and results of particular types of injury, disease, or treatment. These medical registries also identify patients to be contacted for research into their illnesses.

Cancer registries were among the earliest types of medical database developed, and they remain the most numerous and highly detailed registries in operation today. In the United States, local hospital databases were consolidated during the 1950s and '60s into several regional and state cancer registries. The National Cancer Act of 1971 marked the beginning of the "war on cancer." Among many other provisions, it instructed the United States National Cancer Institute (NCI) to create a continuous system of national cancer surveillance. Two years later, the NCI established the Surveillance, Epidemiology, and End Results (SEER) program, which operates as a network of cancer registries for state and regional populations. The SEER program does not attempt to monitor all types of cancer, nor does it cover all populations. SEER data is accumulated from selected areas of the nation, currently 11 population-based registries, accounting for approximately 12 percent of the United States population. Data from the SEER registry is used today to estimate national rates of cancer incidence and patient survival. Key staging and prognostic data are monitored, and this information has been used to distinguish early-stage from late-stage cancer, stimulating opportunities for early detection and control of cancer.

Many other medical registries in the U.S. track such disorders and conditions as:

- AIDS
- Angiofollicular Lymph Node Hyperplasia (AFH)
- Congenital Malformations
- Coronary Artery Surgery
- Endocarditis Prophylaxis Failure
- Epidermolysis Bullosa (EB)
- Eye Trauma
- Football Head and Neck Injury
- IDDM (Insulin-Dependent Diabetes Mellitus)
- In Vitro Fertilizations
- Mushroom Poisoning

- Percutaneous Transluminal Coronary Angioplasty (PTCA)
- Tuberculosis
- Trauma

An Alzheimer's Disease registry is being developed by CERAD, the Consortium to Establish a Registry for Alzheimer's Disease.

International registries also are beginning to appear. The Caitlin Raymond Registry of Bone Marrow Donor Banks combines the resources of independent regional bone marrow registries in the United States with those of other registries. As an international registry, it has access to the names of more than 300,000 people. Similarly, the International Fetal Surgery Registry is accumulating data that may determine the efficacy and safety of the various surgical procedures performed on fetuses.

Medical registries have proved to be remarkably valuable in this kind of research. Since the first computerized trauma registry opened at Cook County Hospital in Chicago in 1969, hospital trauma registries have been used primarily to assess the quality of medical care and to pinpoint necessary changes in treatment. Data from the National Eye Trauma System Registry has also helped to identify ways to prevent occupational eye injuries, such as wider use of safety glasses and improvement of engineering controls. In Virginia, a legislative subcommittee used data from the Virginia Statewide Trauma Registry to support a bill to regulate the use of all-terrain vehicles.

Organ, bone and tissue donor registries operate as waiting lists for those needing a transplant, as well as tracking patients who have received them. For example, the Scientific Registry of the United Network for Organ Sharing, established in late 1987, has tracked over seven thousand cardiac transplant procedures since its inception. Its data revealed that patients face greater risk of death in heart centers that seldom perform a transplant than they do in centers where doctors get more practice in the procedure. These statistics could be used to justify closing some cardiac treatment centers in order to keep the remaining centers busy or, alternatively, to justify changes in training or procedures at the less active centers.

One of the best known successes of registry-based medical research came from the National Football Head and Neck Injury Registry. Established in 1975, this database tracks serious injuries of the cervical spine caused by participation in football. Analysis of registry data revealed that so-called "freak accidents" in which football players were paralyzed by neck fractures were primarily caused by the use of a tackle in which the player strikes his opponent with the top of his helmet, much like a battering ram. As a result of this work, game rules and coaching techniques were changed to eliminate the use of this tackle. This has dramatically reduced the incidence of quadriplegia since 1976.

Despite these and many other successes, American medical registries are still in the embryonic stage. One reason for this is the lack of unique medical identifiers for each U.S. citizen. For many reasons, registry operators would like to key each person's medical records to an individual code that would follow people throughout life, much like the Social Security number. However, this raises privacy concerns, as well as the fear that identifiers will in some way make medical care more impersonal. Part of the controversy over the United States National Healthcare Reform Initiative in 1994 centered on this issue.

Norway and Sweden have used this kind of identifier for decades now. In Norway, each citizen is assigned a national identification number shortly after birth. The number is structured so as to link the baby's records to the mother's records and, in most cases, to the father's. This becomes part of the Medical Birth Registry, which records all live births and stillbirths with a gestational age of at least 16 weeks. Registration is compulsory and is performed by midwives. As of 1994, about 1.5 million births had been registered. Future medical treatments are tracked by the birth registry number. This code is also recorded on death certificates, making computer linkage of birth and death certificates simple and direct.

Sweden has a Medical Birth Registry similar to Norway's. Over 99 percent of births in Swedish hospitals have been recorded since this registry was established in 1973.

Privacy issues aside, the assignment of unique identifiers makes it possible to track people's health throughout their lives. Research that would be difficult, costly or even impossible using American medical registries is little more than a database search in Sweden and Norway. For example, in Sweden and Norway physicians can perform a search to find out what percentage of AIDS patients also have cancer. The link between birth and death records makes it easy to extract longevity figures for patients who received fetal surgery. Even more fundamentally, doctors can determine how many people in the general populace suffer from any given malady. Because medical registries in the United States are generally limited to patients who have experienced one specific illness or treatment, it is nearly impossible to correlate their data. Such comparisons can sometimes identify factors common to several disorders or prove that a factor often seen in one disease also occurs among patients not afflicted by the illness. This can provide clues that could lead to the development of a vaccine or even a cure. Because American medicine does not use personal identifiers, you may well be overlooked for life-saving new medical treatments.

Of course, we must weigh these benefits against the need for privacy. No one is likely to suggest that you be given unrestricted access to another's medical histories. What the medical profession struggles to achieve is a balance that respects privacy, yet makes it possible to use individual medical data to find cures for disease, prevent injuries, and improve medical care. I hope that in the near future that balance will be found.

Access to Medical Records

Physicians, nurses, and other medical professionals are trained to treat patient records with the utmost confidentiality. Although they sometimes must discuss a patient's condition or share a patient's records, those circumstances are supposed to be limited to professional medical consultation or discussions with insurance carriers.

However, many others also have access to a patient's medical information: admissions staff, laboratory personnel, X-ray technicians, pharmacists, insurance billing personnel, medical records transcriptionists and filers, and personnel from virtually every other department or office in a hospital or physician's office. Private and public review organizations and auditors may look at medical records in order to assess the level of care offered by a hospital or a physician, to investigate possible healthcare fraud, or to improve the efficiency or reduce the cost of healthcare.

Still more people routinely handle sensitive medical records. Insurance companies receive copies in order to process payment claims. Government agencies receive the records in order to process claims on their services. Some of these agencies contract with third parties, companies like Computer Science Corporation, in order to process the claims. In this case, a third party receives the medical records as well. The Health Care Financing Administration in Washington manages Medicare and Medicaid claims, with computer databases now processing more than half of its claims electronically. Private insurance companies also are automating their claims processing. In 1993, the Chicago-based Blues Association teamed up with IBM and Medical Management Resources Inc. (MMR), a subsidiary of Blue Cross and Blue Shield of Kentucky, to launch EDI-USA. This is said to be the nation's largest electronic network for claims processing and is estimated to save $1.5 billion a year in transaction costs. Such electronic systems may reduce the chance for claims processors to look through patient records, but they may provide greater opportunity to break into the records electronically.

According to an October 1994 *Consumer Reports* article, Physician Computer Network reserves the right to copy patient information from the computers of all doctors who use its service to its own computer, and to sell that information to other companies. According to PCN's contract with doctors, the company can collect only aggregate data and cannot identify any individual patient or doctor. Nonetheless, in effect, they can rummage through the patient databases of approximately 10 percent of the physicians in the United States.

Employers may also receive full access to the medical records of their employees. When a company insures its own employees rather than paying for outside coverage, each medical treatment is reported to the employer in order to process the insurance claims. Rather than the relative anonymity of an insurance company, the treatment records and medical information may be processed by a co-worker. This could raise "office gossip" to a whole new level.

Medical Insurance Databases

In an effort to stop fraudulent insurance claims, some insurance companies have even created their own databases of medical records. Perhaps the largest of these databases is that of the Medical Information Bureau (MIB), a non-profit company founded in 1902 by the medical directors of fifteen insurance companies. Today, MIB maintains up to seven years of medical records on approximately 15 million people in the United States and Canada. Not everyone who applies for a life, health, or disability insurance policy is recorded in MIB's database. Insurance companies decide whether or not to file a report with MIB and, if so, what should be in it. Serious medical conditions generally are reported, along with other factors that might affect someone's life expectancy, such as a poor driving record or a taste for dangerous sports. This information may come from the individual's insurance application, a physical examination, a physician, or the insurer's own investigation, which may include a search of public records.

If you have been rejected for insurance, or charged a higher premium, you might do well to request a copy of your MIB report from:

Medical Information Bureau (MIB)
160 University Avenue
Westwood, MA 02090-2307
(617) 329-4500
(617) 329-3379 Fax

If there is a report on you, it will usually arrive about a month after you send in MIB's request form. If the report contains errors, notify the bureau so that they can tell you how to make a correction.

PUBLIC RECORDS

Any system so complex as the one that now distributes medical records far and wide allows the possibility of abuse. Most physicians today are extremely sensitive to the ethical issues that surround patient confidentiality. On rare occasions, a doctor might slip and discuss a patient's medical condition inappropriately, but such transgressions probably are more rare in medicine than in most other professions, with the possible exception of the clergy. However, the farther medical records circulate, the greater the risk that they will be released improperly. To prevent this, individuals depend both on handling procedures and on the ethical sense of the people who handle them. This system works surprisingly well.

Nonetheless, private investigators sometimes can uncover surprising amounts of medical information about you. Does this mean that they have broken into medical facilities, computer systems, or insurance companies, or paid informants to breach confidentiality? Not necessarily. While they may have followed their subject in and out of the doctor's office or found medical receipts in their garbage, there often are ways to learn medical secrets that are both legal and easier than "dumpster diving." Medical information can also overflow into public records.

Civil Records

Lawsuits can uncover a great deal of information about specific incidents in a person's medical history. Personal injury suits often describe a particular accident in great detail, and many discuss other facts relating to a person's health. Product liability suits may describe injuries that the plaintiff believes were caused by a poorly designed or defective product. Suits against a health insurance company may provide itemized lists of treatments, along with details of a patient's medical condition. Malpractice suits certainly would describe a patient's condition and treatment. Even judgments granted to a physician or hospital for nonpayment of medical bills can provide details of a patient's care.

A physician's notes may be subpoenaed to court as part of a case, and these notes sometimes extend beyond description of the incident in question (such as a traffic accident). They may describe mental health, the health of other family members, and provide a transcription of everything else that the patient and physician have ever discussed.

When income tax returns make their way into the public record—which can happen in any lawsuit, including divorce—large deductions for medical expenses can reveal the existence a possibly serious medical condition.

Public records vendors provide some online indices to lawsuits, but it is necessary to request a copy of the case file itself in order to review the details.

A company in Chicago found a niche in the public records arena by offering a database to physicians which allowed them to search for malpractice suits filed by any given patient. It is unclear how this information was used: whether physicians discussed their findings with the patient or in some way took precautions against future malpractice suits. If they used information about prior suits to deny patients treatment, this in itself might lead to future litigation. Perhaps that is why I can no longer verify the existence of this company.

Motor Vehicle Records

Some additional information can also be gleaned from the state DMV. A driver's license may note driving restrictions, such as the need for glasses. A driving history including drunk driving incidents may suggest a problem with alcoholism. If accidents are noted, description of a serious injury may also be included.

Worker's Compensation Records

Companies such as Avert and Informus Corp. provide databases of Worker's Compensation filings. These filings include information such as:

- Name of employee
- Employee's Social Security number
- Type of injury
- Nature of injury
- Extent of injury
- Part of body
- Accident type
- Relevant dates
- Name of employer
- Insurance carrier

(Refer to Appendix M for listings of these companies.)

News

Searching the news databases may uncover stories about traffic or industrial accidents, assaults, and other incidents that involve injuries. When a patient is famous or a ground-breaking medical procedure is performed, intimate details of the person's health may be reported as well.

Although not a primary source of medical information, anything can turn up in the news. Before the advent of news databases, searching each individual newspaper for the unlikely event that such an incident might be mentioned was not efficient. The news databases now make it easy and efficient to search broad spans of newspapers, newswires, and television and radio transcripts.

For further information about news databases, please refer to Chapter Twenty.

Mailing Lists

There are mailing list companies compiling lists of people with ailments ranging from arthritis to Parkinson's disease, broken down by age, sex, income, marital status, and as many other factors as one could name.

These mailing lists may be compiled from information obtained directly from the patients, such as the Hillsdale-High Blood Pressure Sufferers list, which is compiled from direct mail questionnaires. People who subscribe to specialty publications, such as *Diabetes Self-Management* magazine, will find themselves on a specialty mailing list, where it is assumed that they are diabetic. Anyone who purchases a diet or exercise product by telephone or mail may end up on one of the many diet and fitness lists. Some lists are even more specific, such as the Jewish Vegetarians list offered by R.C. Direct, Inc., which includes "buyers of books, as well as inquirers about Jewish Vegetarianism and the humane treatment of animals and the Jewish approach to diet and health." Experian Target Marketing Services even offers a list providing height and weight of individuals.

Huge mailing lists are compiled through responses from questionnaires inserted in packages, as well as mailings and magazine and television ads that offer information about medications to people who call or write. A few years ago, half a million viewers in sixteen states called a toll-free number given on a television commercial to find out the pollen count in their ZIP Code area. As a result, many of the callers received sales pitches for allergy medication from Warner Lambert, the ad's sponsor.

Even some pharmacies and physicians now sell information from their databases to drug-makers or mailing list companies.

Major drug companies such as Merck, SmithKline Beecham, and Eli Lilly, are engineering corporate takeovers of companies that distribute drugs to consumers. The hottest targets are companies that administer corporate prescription benefit plans and those that sell prescription drugs by mail. Eli Lilly's recently proposed acquisition of PCS Health Systems, for example, would give the pharmaceutical company direct access to 50 million patients.

For further information about mailing lists, please refer to Chapter Nineteen.

OSHA Records

Reports from the Occupational Safety and Health Administration (OSHA) are available online through CDB Infotek and some of other public records vendors. These reports detail information such as:

- Accident descriptions
- Address
- Business or establishment name
- Federal region
- Inspection type and scope
- Number and type of violations
- Number of employees
- OSHA area office
- Penalties
- Standard Industrial Classification (SIC) Code
- Union status

Some of these reports include the details of accidents, including the names of people involved in them. However, vendors may index them by business name, making it more difficult to search for information about an individual. It may be necessary to search for each business that the person has worked for in order to find out whether they have ever been involved in an accident that was reported to OSHA.

These records are also carried by legal database vendors, such as WESTLAW. In this case, searching for individuals may be simpler.

Although OSHA records are not a primary source for medical information, they do remain another possible location for details of a person's medical condition.

Concern for the Future

The technology is already in place for tracking your purchases at the supermarket. After your groceries are scanned at the checkout counter, you may have scanned in your own debit or check-cashing card, thereby linking those purchases to your identity. Today, this may do no more than make you the happy recipient of a tailor-made set of store coupons, and few would argue against that innocuous use, but, it soon will be possible to extract more intimate information from such data. Suppose insurance companies paid supermarkets a premium for access to that information. (This could be quite a profit center for the supermarkets.) Insurance companies could then determine who smoked too much, who ate too much junk or fatty foods, who might have a problem with alcohol, whose diet relied too heavily on beef or dairy products, and so on. This type of information could be used to define high-risk groups, assessing premiums, or even denying insurance coverage.

If you knew that your next purchase of a pint of Ben & Jerry's Chunky Monkey ice cream would send up a red flag at your insurance carrier, would that change your buying decision or would you merely start paying cash?

Just a little food for thought.

Public Records

P ublic records include hundreds of types of records which are kept in order to protect the public's interests. For example, real property records are stored in order to establish the legal owner of a property. This is important not only to the person claiming the property, but to potential buyers. If legal title could not be established in this way, none of us would have protection from con artists who sell a property they do not own, or sell a property to more than one buyer.

Corporate and limited partnership records exist so that the owner(s) of a business can be identified, and legal liability can be established. This is meant to assist one in pursuing legal satisfaction when a company is involved in fraudulent activities or other wrongdoing, or if their products are found to do harm.

You not only have a right to public records, but you actually already own them. Americans have established laws determining which types of records must be kept; who must create, store, and maintain them; and under what circumstances, if any, the government may deny access to those records. In most cases, you do not need a reason for wanting the records. It is none of the government's business why you want to know who owns a home or a business, what it is worth, or any other matters of public record. As taxpayers, you pay for the storage and retrieval of public records, and you pay the salaries of the public employees who assist in this process. In most instances, the government must provide free access to the records to anyone who asks; it may only charge a fee if someone wishes to obtain copies.

Today, many types of public records are available online through public records vendors and court records systems. These records can be extremely useful to those in various areas of personal research.

Limitations of Online Public Records

There are several limitations to the public records now available online. First of all, only a small portion of all public records information can yet be found online. This situation is improving, but it will be some time before you will be able to use a personal computer to tap into all the public records that you might wish to use in personal research.

Most online files of public records today consist of indices, rather than detailed records. It often is necessary to locate the records through the indices and then order copies of the physical documents to learn what you need to know.

Some jurisdictions and courts still have not automated their records or even their indices, so you will not find those online. Others may index only particular types of records. Even when public records vendors offer a "statewide" or "nationwide" search, they may mean that it includes all counties or courts that provide online access to that type of record, rather than all courts. This is not always clear in vendor advertising or documentation.

As with any other type of database, errors can also occur when the public records indices are built. Many of these difficulties are discussed in Chapter Six—Locating People.

Records can also be missed when the indexing takes place. If physical records are scanned in order to make them available online, a file may be out of place when its turn arrives and miss the indexing process altogether.

Public records vendors normally sell more current records than older ones, and some older records may not legally be used in pre-employment or credit screening. Some public records vendors begin collecting their records as of a given date and never fill in the earlier data. For these reasons, it is often difficult to locate older public records online.

In addition, collection methods can delay the availability of some recent records. If the online vendor or court records system offers direct access to the database at the city, county, state, or federal agency where the records are actually stored, the records that one accesses will be as up-to-date as possible. Anything less than that will introduce lag-time between the agency's records (which may already be backlogged) and the vendor's database. This delay may vary from one jurisdiction to another; some records may be delayed for three months or more.

Records filed in a municipality may not appear in the county records until much later. Cities may report to counties monthly, or only semi-annually, and the counties may not report to the states until much later. Information may even be held at the local level because the people involved are the record-keeper's friends or relatives.

Many public records vendors offer limited search capabilities. The sophisticated search engines found on some of today's online services are rarely encountered in the public records arena. In fact, many vendors allow only the most elementary menu-driven searches, with nothing even close to Boolean logic (AND, OR, and NOT) capabilities. One seldom finds a public records database that can be searched for groups of individuals with similar characteristics. An exception to this is LEXIS, which provides the same search capabilities for public records as for their news and legal databases.

This is not to say that a single inquiry will never result in the display of records for more than one individual. At times, several records match the inquiry criteria and are displayed. Some vendors will display a warning message when this occurs, or a summary of the possible record matches so that you can select the ones you wish to see in detail, rather than pay for all of them.

As for court record systems, in most states, PACER provides access to civil and criminal records from United States District Courts, as well as bankruptcy records. The actual case record content varies and is determined by each local district. Some districts keep all open and closed cases on their databases, whereas others maintain only open cases and purge records after cases are closed. Similar court records systems include NIBS-BRASS, CHIP, ACES (Appellate Court Electronic Services), and EDOS (Electronic Dissemination of Opinions System). Others are emerging in courts throughout the country, each with its own content and search capabilities.

All of these circumstances can omit public records from online systems and make useful information more difficult to obtain. These are imperfect processes, so the current online public records systems should still be viewed as evolving tools, rather than final solutions.

TYPES OF PUBLIC RECORDS AVAILABLE ONLINE

Arrests

Although records of arrests may be viewed on the blotters sitting in police stations across the land, arrest records are not generally available through online public records systems. This is probably for the best, as arrests are not convictions and under the criminal justice system should not be held against the accused. Furthermore, certain minorities clearly have been subject to arrest in certain areas due only to their ethnicity, and not their activities, so consideration of arrests could bear unfairly on those groups.

This does not mean that arrests never show up online. You can also find a few police blotters accessible through the Internet, such as those listed by *The Orion Online Newspaper* found at: **http://orion.lab.csuchico.edu/** and by *The Stute Online* (the weekly newspaper of the Stevens Institute of Technology) at: **http://stute.jacobus.stevens-tech. edu/**. Some newspapers routinely print the whole police blotter, especially in smaller towns. Celebrity arrests may be featured in all news media as well. For example, references to Paul Reuben's (a.k.a. Pee-Wee Herman's) arrest continue many years after the fact, and any time a celebrity is arrested for a run-in with the paparazzi, it is sure to receive a great deal of news coverage. (Please refer to Chapter Twenty for further information about coverage of arrests in the news.) Unfortunately, a subsequent release, dismissal, or acquittal may go unreported in the same news databases that are filled with stories of the arrest.

With these factors in mind, one should be very cautious about the use of arrest records.

Articles of Incorporation

The Articles of Incorporation is the legal instrument which creates a corporation, pursuant to the general corporation laws of the state. Please refer to the discussion of corporate and limited partnership records later in this chapter.

Bankruptcy Records

Bankruptcy is a legal process under federal law intended to not only insure fairness and equality among creditors, but also to help debtors by enabling them to start anew with property exempted from their liabilities, unhampered by the pressure and discouragement of previous debts. A person is not bankrupt until adjudicated bankrupt under federal law. A corporation is not bankrupt until it performs an "act of bankruptcy" or proceedings in bankruptcy have been instituted by or against it.

Bankruptcy information can be found on many public records systems and court records systems, as well as on consumer credit reports, business credit reports, and company financial databases. Bankruptcies can include voluntary and involuntary adjudication of a debtor under Chapter 7, Chapter 11, or, Chapter 13; as well as relief of the debtor by reorganization and readjustment, which is under Chapter 11. Chapter 12 bankruptcies, which apply to family farmers, can also be found online.

When Susan "Stop the Madness" Powter filed for bankruptcy in 1995, she called a press conference in order to make the announcement. Had she not done so, her filing probably would have appeared in the press anyway, as bankruptcies are a matter of public record. What follows is Susan Powter's California bankruptcy record, as provided by the LEXIS system:

UNITED STATES BANKRUPTCY COURT
CENTRAL DISTRICT OF CALIFORNIA—LOS ANGELES

In Re POWTER SUSAN J

PETITIONER: POWTER SUSAN J
000-00-0000
1875 CENTURY PARK EAST #23
LOS ANGELES, CA 90067

NUMBER: LA9510009

FILED 01/03/1995

TYPE: Chapter 11

FIRST MEETING DATE: 02/15/1995

ATTORNEY: THOMSEN YOUNG
310-277-6910

FIRM: PACHULSKI STANG ZIEHL & YOUNG PC

(In the actual record, her Social Security number appears in the place of 000-00-0000, but it seemed only courteous to leave her a tiny bit of privacy in what otherwise is a very public life.)

When a bankruptcy record such as this is located, many more details usually are available on file at the court. It would still be necessary to obtain copies of those records in order to gain a complete picture of the bankruptcy, or a person's finances.

Business Public Filings

Although sometimes grouped as Business Public Filings, these include bankruptcies, tax liens, and judgments on businesses. Please refer to those reports individually elsewhere in this chapter.

Campaign Contributions

Please refer to Chapter Thirty-five—Political Records for information about tracking campaign contributions.

Case Transcripts

Copies of actual court transcripts can be ordered online through services such as WESTLAW and LEXSEE on the LEXIS service. These services typically require a case citation in order to retrieve a document. Thus, it is sometimes necessary to search the court indices for this information before retrieving copies of the actual case transcripts.

Case Summaries

Summaries of cases, details of verdicts, and settlements can be found in the legal journals, such as those in the LEXIS Verdicts Library. Records such as these can be very helpful in obtaining a quick synopsis of a case, as well as in locating and checking the credentials of expert witnesses and attorneys. Attorneys use such information to size up the competition and to gather fodder for the impeachment of witnesses.

Certificates of Listings or Secretary of State Filings

A certificate of listing, from the Secretary of State, lists the types of records that are on file for a specific corporation. Typical records would include:

- Corporate identification number
- Corporation name
- Type(s) of document(s) on file

Certificates of Merger

A certificate of merger, from the Secretary of State, indicates that two or more corporations have merged. Typical records include:

- Corporate identification numbers
- Corporation names

Certificates of Name Reservation

A company may reserve a business name with the Secretary of State for a period of 60 days, during which time they are incorporating under that name or changing the previous corporate name. These records can provide clues as to what a competitor is planning. Typical certificates of name reservations include:

- Business name to be reserved
- Name of party reserving business name
- Address of party reserving business name

Certificates of Non-Filing

A certificate of non-filing indicates that there are no records on file with the Secretary of State for a given corporation, either active or inactive. This is useful in fraud investigations, as well as for those companies wishing to find out whether a corporation name has been used within a state. (Note that an unincorporated company may still be using the name). A typical certificate of non-filing record will list only the corporation name.

Certificates of Status

A certificate of status from the Secretary of State indicates the existence and current standing of a corporation doing business within a state. Typical records include:

- Corporate identification number
- Corporation name
- Corporate status

Civil Court Indices

Civil court indices can be obtained from the superior, supreme, district, justice, municipal, small claims, city or circuit courts, as well as the court of common pleas. Online civil records may include indices to civil, probate and family law (such as dissolution of marriage—divorce, legal separation, nullity, dissolution with Uniform Child Custody Act, and summary dissolution) cases. Civil court indices can be used to locate court minutes, court dockets, and civil case files. They are available from public records vendors as well as court records systems. As an example, I searched the California Civil Case Indices for Madonna (Ciccone), using the LEXIS system. Six cases were found. One of the records follows:

LOS ANGELES COUNTY SUPERIOR COURT CIVIL CASE INDEX

CASE NAME: MARKHAM SMITH IAN v. AIRCOA CORP, et al

CIVIL CASE NUMBER: C 567609

FILING DATE: 09/27/85

DISTRICT: CENTRAL (LOS ANGELES)

CASE TYPE: CIVIL

PARTY:

PLAINTIFF	DEFENDANT	COMMENT
MARKHAM SMITH IAN	AIRCOA CORP	
MARKHAM SMITH IAN	CICCONE MADONNA LOUISE V	
MARKHAM SMITH IAN	HEMDALE LEISURE CORP	
MARKHAM SMITH IAN	MADONNA	
MARKHAM SMITH IAN	ORION PICTURES CORP	
MARKHAM SMITH IAN	PENN SEAN	
MARKHAM SMITH IAN	WARNER BROS INC	

As you can see, these indices do not reveal why the suits were filed, but they do provide enough information to locate case transcripts or actual court documents for further research.

It is worth noting that civil suits sometimes can also be found in the news, especially if any of the parties involved are well-known. Smaller newspapers and local radio and television stations may also carry stories of lawsuits when the local citizenry is involved. (Please refer to Chapter Twenty for further information about news databases.)

Consumer Public Filings

Although sometimes grouped as consumer public filings, such filings often include bankruptcies, tax liens, and judgments for individuals. Please refer to those reports individually elsewhere in this chapter.

Corporate and Limited Partnership Records

Public records vendors typically obtain articles of incorporation and limited partnership records from the Secretary of State. These records aid in locating the name of the registered agent in order to serve process on a company, and make it possible to obtain the legal name of a business when conducting a fraud investigation. Other uses include asset searching and even locating people.

CDB Infotek has now made its Corporations/Limited Partnerships File available online to CompuServe users (as part of their CompuTrace service), as well as to those who subscribe directly to CDB Infotek. The CompuTrace version is abbreviated and omits such details as the agent of service, which can be found on the full record through CDB Infotek, as well as through other public records vendors. The following example for one of movie mogul George Lucas' businesses was obtained from the CompuTrace service:

CALIFORNIA SECRETARY OF STATE DATE 05/02/96
PROVIDED BY CDB INFOTEK

THE DATA IS FOR INFORMATION PURPOSES ONLY, CERTIFICATION CAN ONLY BE
OBTAINED THROUGH THE OFFICE OF THE CALIFORNIA SECRETARY OF STATE

SEARCH CRITERIA: LUCAS

BUSINESS NAME: LUCASFILM LTD.
ADDRESS: PO BOX 2009
SAN RAFAEL CA 94912
CORPORATION TYPE: ARTICLES OF INCORPORATION
STATUS: ACTIVE
PRESIDENT: GORDON RADLEY

Corporate Document Listings or Corporate Records

Although sometimes grouped as corporate document listings or corporate records, these can include certificates of acquisition, mergers, and name changes.

When looking for examples using LEXIS' Secretary of State file, I searched for records of director/producer Steven Spielberg and found 11 records. A listing for one of these companies, Amblin' Entertainment, Inc., follows:

CALIFORNIA SECRETARY OF STATE, CORPORATE RECORD.

NAME: AMBLIN' ENTERTAINMENT, INC.

TYPE OF CORPORATION: ARTICLES OF INCORPORATION (DOMESTIC)

CORPORATE STATUS: ACTIVE

DATE OF INCORPORATION/QUALIFICATION: 04/01/1980

MAILING ADDRESS: 10345 OLYMPIC BLVD
                   LOS ANGELES, CA 90064

REGISTERED AGENT: MICHAEL RUTMAN

REGISTERED OFFICE: 10345 OLYMPIC BLVD
                     LOS ANGELES, CA 90064

PRESIDENT: STEVEN SPIELBERG
             10345 OLYMPIC BLVD
             LOS ANGELES, CA 90064

STATEMENT OF OFFICERS FILED NUMBER: 189456

STATEMENT OF OFFICERS FILE DATE: 04/29/91

TAX-BASIS: STOCK

CORPORATE NUMBER: 955752

HISTORY:
        DATE:07/14/1983
        TRANSACTION:CERTIFICATE OF AMENDMENT
        COMMENT:NAME CHANGED FROM: AMBLIN' ENTERPRISES
        OTHER CORP NO:00955752
        AMENDMENT NO:A0268275

OTHER CORP NO: 01353337
        AMENDMENT NO:A0381973

        DATE:12/15/1989
        TRANSACTION:MERGER
        COMMENT:SURVIVOR-MERGED IN C1381376 AMBLIN' MERCHANDISING CORPORATION
        OTHER CORP NO:01381376
        AMENDMENT NO:A0381973

        DATE:12/15/1989
        TRANSACTION:MERGER
        COMMENT:SURVIVOR-MERGED IN C1208012 MOON SONG PRODUCTIONS, INC.
        OTHER CORP NO:01208012
        AMENDMENT NO:A0381973

The other ten records found include Amblin' Merchandising Corporation and On Ramp Films, Inc., which have both been merged out; 86 Amblin' Television, Inc. and 86 U-Drive Productions, Inc., which have both been dissolved; and Amblin' Productions, Inc., Amblin' Television, Inc., Diamond Lane Productions, Extra-Terrestrial Productions, Inc., Nighttime Films, Inc., and U-Drive Productions, Inc., all of which are still active.

As you can see, this type of search can be very useful in locating assets or backgrounding an individual. It conceivably could even help someone in searching for a job. After all, if my dream were to work for Steven Spielberg, a quick online search could point me to seven companies where I could begin my job search.

Corporate Tax Records
Corporate tax records typically include:

- Corporate filename
- Current year's tax assessments
- Current year's payments
- Previous year's tax assessments
- Previous year's payments

Court Dockets
A court docket lists the cases on a court's calendar. Court docket information is now available online through several court records systems, such as the PACER (Public Access to Court Electronic Records) system, NIBS-BRASS, CHIP, ACES (Appellate Court Electronic Services), and EDOS (Electronic Dissemination of Opinions System).

Criminal Records
Criminal records are created, stored, updated, and tracked throughout the criminal justice system. When criminal cases reach the courts, they normally become a matter of public record. (An exception to this is for juvenile cases, which usually are sealed from public view.) Criminal court records can be filed at the municipal, superior, or federal courts. Typical criminal records found on public records systems include:

- Court
- Case or file number
- Case title
- Date filed
- Close date
- Defendant name
- Defendant date of birth
- Additional or cross-defendant name or plaintiff name
- List of charges
- Violations

Please refer to Chapter Twenty-six—Criminal Justice Records for information about how these records are used in the criminal justice system.

Death Records

Please refer to Chapter Twenty-eight for information about death records and to Chapter Thirty-three for celebrity deaths.

Divorce Records

Divorce records can be found in the Civil Court Indices, or sometimes separated into their own databases. CDB Infotek, for example, offers a divorce index for Nevada, and another for Texas. Please refer to the discussion of civil court indices mentioned earlier in this chapter for further information about divorce records.

Federal Tax Liens

A federal tax lien is a lien of the United States on "all property and rights to property" of a taxpayer who fails to pay a tax for which that person is liable to the federal government. It reaches not only all property owned by the taxpayer when the lien arises, but also property that otherwise would be exempt by state law from the reach of creditors. Please refer to the discussion of tax liens later in this chapter, which also deals with state and county tax liens.

Fictitious Name Statements

Fictitious Name Statements (a.k.a. Doing Business As, DBAs, Fictitious Business Names, or assumed names) provide information on filings that reflect the intent of an individual or company to conduct business under a fictitious name. These can be very useful in competitive intelligence research, and are also used to locate people and to determine an individual's business affiliations. The information provided typically includes:

- File number
- File date
- Business name
- Business address
- Owner name

An example for "the Hollywood Madam," Heidi Fleiss, follows:

LOS ANGELES COUNTY, CALIFORNIA, FICTITIOUS BUSINESS NAMES

DBA NAME: HEIDI

BUSINESS ADDRESS:1999 AVE OF THE STARS #2800
                 LOS ANGELES, CA 90067

OWNER: FLEISS HEIDI

OWNER ADDRESS: 1999 AVE OF THE STARS #2800
                 LOS ANGELES, CA 90067

BUSINESS TYPE: INDIVIDUAL

FILING DATE: 11/04/1993

FILE NUMBER   93-2161429

These records are also important because they can assist one in identifying the real owner of a business, and reveal a person's relationship to other businesses. This is useful in fraud investigation, competitive intelligence research, background checking, and asset searching.

Franchise Tax Board Status Letters

The Franchise Tax Board Status Letter is the official certificate from the State Franchise Tax Board which reveals a corporation's ability or inability to transact business within the state. Typical online indices to these records include:

- Corporate identification number
- Corporation name
- Status
- Actions taken by the Franchise Tax Board (as a result of unpaid tax liability)

These records can typically be found through a search of corporate and limited partnership records.

Grantor/Grantee Indices

Grantor/grantee records, maintained by some counties, can be a catch-all place for various types of records. They may include abstracts of judgment, death distribution decrees, deeds, property transfers, fictitious name filings, financing statements, homesteads, liens, notices of default, powers of attorney, reconveyances, satisfactions of judgment, UCC financing statements, and up to 400 document types. Some public records vendors carry an index to grantor/grantee records, although they may contain only certain types of these records, such as property transfers.

Hospital Liens

Hospital liens may appear as part of a Judgment Docket & Lien Book search, grouped with bankruptcies, liens, and judgments, or otherwise appear in some type of online lien index. Please refer to the discussion of liens later in this chapter for further information.

Judgments

A personal judgment, usually referred to simply as a judgment, is rendered against an individual or an entity such as a corporation for the payment of money damages. Typical judgment indices include:

- Case or lien number
- Creditor name
- Debtor name
- Filing and release dates
- Liability amount

Lawsuits

Please refer to the discussion of court dockets, civil court indices, case transcripts, and case summaries earlier in this chapter.

Liens

Liens may include hospital liens, mechanic's liens, and sidewalk liens. A public records vendor may offer each of these as separate searches, or grouped together into one search. Online vendors sometimes group liens into a "Liens and Judgments" search, or Judgment Docket and Lien Book search. For example, CDB Infotek offers the New York State Supreme Court Judgment Docket & Lien Book, which includes civil judgments, hospital liens, mechanic's liens, building loans, lis pendens, sidewalk liens, and federal tax liens. Typical records include the following information:

- Attorney name
- Creditor name
- Debtor address
- Debtor name
- Effective date
- Expiration date
- Filing type
- Judgment or lien amount
- Satisfaction date
- Third party

Records such as these are used in fraud investigation, background searches, skip-tracing, asset searching, and so on.

Please refer also to the discussion of tax liens later in this chapter for additional information.

Limited Partnership Records

Please refer to corporate and limited partnership records discussed earlier in this chapter.

Lis Pendens

Lis pendens are pending lawsuits. Notices of lis pendens are required in some jurisdictions to warn others (such as prospective purchasers) that the title to a property is in litigation, and that they will be bound by any judgment. Lis pendens may also appear in the Judgment Docket & Lien Book. Please refer to the discussion of liens earlier in this chapter for further information.

Marriage License Indices

Marriage license information is very useful for locating people. Women may not appear on other records because their names have changed with marriage. Marriage license indices can be used to identify the new surname. A copy of the marriage license can also be ordered, which may provide the actual address at the time of the marriage. Typical marriage license index information includes:

- Registration or file number
- State file number (or book and page number)
- Name of bride
- Name of groom
- Age of bride
- Age of groom
- County of record
- Filing date

It also is sometimes possible for a couple to obtain a "confidential" marriage license. These marriage licenses do not require a blood test, as they are offered only to couples who are already cohabiting. These licenses may be missing from the marriage indices, as it is assumed that the couple would want to protect the fact that they cohabited prior to marriage. Thus, the fact that no marriage license is found does not prove that none exists. Please refer to Chapter Thirty-four—Genealogical Records, for additional marriage record information available on CD-ROM.

Mechanic's Liens

A Mechanic's Lien is "one created for the purpose of securing priority of payment of the price or value of work performed and materials furnished in erecting or repairing a building or other structure, and as such attaches to the land as well as buildings and improvements erected thereon." Please refer to the discussion of liens earlier in this chapter for further information.

Notice of Default/Notice of Sale

A Notice of Default (sometimes referred to as a Notice of Sale) identifies a failure to discharge a duty or make payments on a loan. This most often refers to a failure to make payments on a mortgage loan. These records are filed at the county recorder's office, but some of the public records vendors offer them online. These records typically include:

- Filing date
- Filing number
- Debtor name(s)
- Debtor address
- Court location
- Document information
- Tax assessor's parcel number
- Tax assessor's lot number
- Tax assessor's map number
- Actual street address of property

Occupational Safety and Health Act (OSHA) Records

In 1970, Congress passed the Occupational Safety and Health Act to prevent employees from being injured or contracting illnesses in the course of their employment. This empowered OSHA to inspect business premises and to impose civil and criminal injunctions and penalties where safety violations are found. Some public records vendors have obtained OSHA records from the United States Department of Labor, Occupational Safety and Health Administration, and make them available online. These records can help in competitive intelligence research, background investigations, and sometimes in locating people. Typical records include:

- Accident information
- Accident victim name
- Administrative payment information
- Business address
- Business name
- Company debt on file with OSHA
- Failure to abate history
- Hazardous substances found during inspection
- Hours spent in inspection
- Inspection office
- Inspection officer
- Number of employees
- OSHA file entry date
- Penalties assessed
- Reason for inspection
- Scope of inspection
- SIC Code
- Total number of violations cited

Probate Records

Probate records (wills and the documents proving their legality and validity) are indexed online in some jurisdictions. Typical records include:

- Case title
- File date
- File number
- Name of decedent

Real Property Ownership

Real property records, usually obtained from county recorder and tax assessor records, are available on many public records systems. In fact, several systems (like

Damar and DataQuick) have been designed specifically for real property records and are used extensively by real estate and title agents. These records are also very useful for asset investigation, as a home represents the largest asset for many people.

Real property ownership records may include not only ownership information and property transfers, but refinances, construction loans and seller carry-backs (in which the seller of the property is also the lender). Searches by owner name, property address, and mailing address are all available through public records systems, some at the county level, and others combining several counties or "statewide" (with the limitations explained earlier). These searches are performed in order to locate all of the properties owned by a person or business, as well as the history of ownership and current title of a property.

Real estate systems can also offer searches using other property characteristics, such as the number of bedrooms and bathrooms, price, and area. Typical real property records may include any of the following, depending upon the system and the type of record:

Assessed land value	Number of units
Basement	Pool/spa
Buyer address	Property parcel number
Document date	Property tax amount
Document number	Property use description (i.e., single family
Document type	residence, vacant land, etc.)
Elevator	Sale amount
Garage size	Sale date
Garage type	Seller address
Improvement value	Situs (property) address
Interest rate	Square footage of lot
Lender address	Square footage of structures
Loan amount	Stories (of building)
Loan type	Style (of building)
Number of baths	Total number of rooms
Number of bedrooms	Total value for each parcel
Number of buildings	Type of air conditioning
Number of exterior walls	Type of foundation
Number of fireplaces	Type of heating
Number of partial baths	Type of roof
	Year built

Real estate systems may contain additional information, such as the listing agent's name and asking price. Searching the LEXIS system for real property records in Illinois for talk show host and actress Oprah Winfrey, I found 9 records, some indicating that she had sold properties and others that she had purchased properties. One of these records follows:

PROPERTY TRANSFER RECORD FOR COOK COUNTY, IL

Buyer: WINFREY, OPRAH G; OPRAH G WINFREY DECLARATION OF TRUST,Trustee

Buyer Mailing address: 180 E PEARSON, UNIT 5603, CHICAGO, IL

Seller: AMERICAN NATIONAL BK&TR CO OF CHICAGO (Trustee/Conservator); TRUST

Seller Mailing Address: 33 N LASALLE, CHICAGO, IL

Property Address: 180 E PEARSON, UNIT 5602, CHICAGO, IL

*********************** SALES INFORMATION *************************

Sale Date: 11/2/1993

Recorded Date: 11/3/1993

Sale Price: $ 1,500,000 (Full Amount Computed From Transfer Tax)

County Transfer Tax: $ 750.00
City Transfer Tax: $ 11,250.00
Total Transfer Tax: $ 1,500.00
(Note from author: I recognize that these numbers do not add up, but this is how the information that was downloaded appeared.)

Document Number: 93889433

Deed Type: TRUSTEE's DEED

Assessor's Parcel Number: 17-03-226-065-1160

Legal Description: MULTIPLE LOTS; LOT: 4-18; UNIT: 5602; SUBDIVISION: CANAL
TRUSTEES SUBDIVISION; SEC/TWN/RNG/MERIDIAN: SE4 S03T39NR14E 3P

Brief Description: UNIT #5602 IN LOTS 4 TO 18 & LOTS 7-A TO 7-F 11 A & 11 B IN
MARBAN RESUB PART OF BLK 20 IN CANAL

************************ PROPERTY DESCRIPTION ************************
Land Use: CONDOMINIUM

Please refer to Chapter Thirty-four—Genealogical Records, for land records and CD-ROM collections of property ownership records.

Sales and Use Tax Permits

Sales and Use Tax Permits, from the State Board of Equalization or Comptroller's Office, represent information about individuals and companies who pay sales tax and have either an active or inactive taxpayer ID assigned. Files include corporations, limited and general partnerships, and sole proprietors. Information listed from these permits includes:

- Taxpayer name
- Taxpayer address
- Type of business
- Outlet information

SEC Reports

Securities and Exchange Commission (SEC) Reports are available through many online systems, such as the DISCLOSURE database on Knight-Ridder. SEC filings are not found on as many public records systems as on other, more mainstream systems, but they may be found on either. SEC Reports include various SEC Filings, Company Profiles, Quarterly Financials, and Annual Financials. They are useful in asset investigation, competitive intelligence research, and can even be used in locating people. Records can include any of the following information, derived from annual reports, 10-K forms, 20-F forms, 10-Q forms, and proxy statements, or any other SEC filing:

Annual assets and liabilities	Legal counsel
Auditor company name	Market value
Balance sheet	Names of 5 percent owners
Company address	Names of insiders
Company telephone number	Names of officers, directors, nominees
Current dividends	Net income
CUSIP number	Number of employees
Dun's number	Number of shareholders
Earnings per share	Outstanding shares of stock
Exchange symbol	Previous dividends
Fiscal year and date	Shares held by officers and directors
Five year summary of sales	SIC Code
Forbes number	Stock transfer agent
Forms filed with the SEC (with dates)	Subsidiaries
Fortune number	Ticker symbol
Latest annual data date	Trade dates
Latest quarterly data date	Trade highs/lows/closing prices
Latest weekly data about prices	Trade volume

Some SEC reports can also be found on EDGAR, the Electronic Data Gathering, Analysis, and Retrieval system. EDGAR performs automated collection, validation, indexing, acceptance, and forwarding of submissions by companies and others who are required by law to file forms with the U.S. Securities and Exchange Commission.

Not all documents filed with the Commission by public companies will be available on EDGAR. Companies were phased into the system over a three-year period that ended on May 6, 1996. As of that date, all public domestic companies are required to make their filings on EDGAR, except for filings made to the Commission's regional offices and filings made on paper because of a hardship exemption. Third-party filings with respect to these companies, such as tender offers and Schedules 13D, are also filed on EDGAR.

Electronic filing is banned for some documents, and consequently those records will not be available on EDGAR. Other documents may be filed on EDGAR voluntarily, but are not mandatory, and consequently may or may not be available on EDGAR. For example, Forms 3, 4, and 5 (security ownership and transaction reports filed by corporate insiders), Form 144 (notice of proposed sale of securities) and Form 13F (reports filed by institutional investment managers showing equity holdings by accounts under their management) may be filed on EDGAR at the option of the filer. Similarly, filings by foreign companies are not required to be filed on EDGAR, but some of these companies do so voluntarily.

Since January 1994, EDGAR filings can be found on the Internet at the following address:

http://www.sec.gov/edgarhp.htm

Sidewalk Liens
Please refer to the discussion of liens earlier in this chapter for further information.

Statements and Designations by Foreign Corporations and Amendments
Corporations doing business in one state while incorporated in another may be found in the Statements and Designations by Foreign Corporations and Amendments. Typical records include:
- Corporate identification number
- Corporation name

As you can see, very little information is provided on this type of index; however, it is sufficient to obtain copies of the actual records, where details may be found.

Statements of Domestic Stock Corporations
Please refer to corporate and limited partnership records discussed earlier in this chapter.

Tax Liens
Tax liens can include federal, state, and county tax liens. Typical tax liens found online include:
- Court
- Lien number
- Tax board certificate number
- Date of lien
- Debtor name
- Doing Business As (DBA)
- Cross-debtor name

- Secured party/plaintiff name
- Amount of lien

A search on LEXIS for actress Kim Basinger turned up a couple of county tax liens in Los Angeles. One of these tax liens has been included to illustrate the type of information that one can find on these documents:

JUDGEMENTS AND LIENS
STATE OF CALIFORNIA

LA COUNTY / RECORDER OF DEEDS

DEBTOR: BASINGER KIM

ADDRESS: 10390 SANTA MONICA BV
         LOS ANGELES, CA 90025

CREDITOR: COUNTY OF LOS ANGELES

AMOUNT: $ 1,031

NUMBER: 94576835

TYPE: COUNTY TAX LIEN

ENTERED: 03/24/1994

A search for the late rapper Tupac Shakur turned up four state tax lien records. Two are liens, and two are releases. One of the releases follows:

JUDGEMENTS AND LIENS
STATE OF CALIFORNIA

LA COUNTY / RECORDER OF DEEDS

DEBTOR: SHAKUR TUPAC

ADDRESS: 23236 LYONS 219 AV
         NEWHALL, CA 91321

SSN/TAX ID: 546-47-7539

CREDITOR: STATE OF CALIFORNIA

AMOUNT: $ 18,206

NUMBER: 9546953

TYPE: STATE TAX LIEN RELEASE

Certificate No. 94277005692

ENTERED: 11/14/1994

RELEASED: 01/12/1995

On many public records systems, tax liens are also included in a grouped search of bankruptcies, liens, and judgments. Tax liens can also be found on consumer credit and business credit reports. Please refer to liens discussed earlier in this chapter for further information.

Uniform Commercial Code (UCC) Indices

The Uniform Commercial Code was adopted to assure national uniformity when describing goods, timber or crops that are pledged as security for a loan. These filings offer protection against debtor bankruptcy, insolvency, or default.

If household goods or furnishings are pledged, these records are filed in the county where the debtor lives or where the goods are located. If timber or crops are pledged, these records are filed in the county where the timber or crops are grown. If business or farm equipment, accounts payable, inventory, or trust receipts are pledged, these records are filed with the Secretary of State or Department of Commerce.

UCC Indices typically include the following:
- File number
- File date
- Document type (original filing, assignment, continuation, etc.)
- Record location
- Debtor's name (person or business)
- Debtor's tax identification number
- Debtor's social security number
- Debtor's business address
- Debtor's home address
- Debtor's mailing address
- Lender's name (person or business)
- Lender's business address
- Lender's home address
- Lender's mailing address

COURT RECORDS SYSTEMS

In addition to the various public records vendors who are making public records accessible online, the federal courts have introduced services permitting online public access to court information. These services include ACES, PACER, and similar systems developed separately by various districts, operating under names such as NIBS-BRASS and CHIP.

Appellate Court Electronic Services (ACES)

First introduced in 1989, ACES is an electronic system of appellate court information and decisions. Records include slip opinions, court oral arguments, calendars, court rules, notices, press releases and reports. This service includes federal circuit courts, as well as some district and bankruptcy courts.

Public Access to Court Electronic Records (PACER)

Also introduced in 1989, PACER provides online access to court case information and court dockets. It includes U.S. Bankruptcy Courts, the United States Court of Appeals, and United States District Courts, and there are plans to include all federal, circuit, district, and bankruptcy courts. Some, but not all, of the PACER systems offer both civil and criminal dockets.

For further information about PACER, you can visit their Internet site at:
http://www.teleport.com/~richh/pacer.html

OTHER TYPES OF RECORDS AVAILABLE FROM PUBLIC RECORDS VENDORS

Business Credit Records

Dun & Bradstreet, Experian, and other vendors offer business credit records. These are provided directly by these vendors, but are also available on some of the mainstream systems, such as Knight-Ridder Information, and from public records vendors as well. Please refer to Appendix C for examples of business credit and company financial databases, and the systems that they are offered on. Additional information can be found in Chapter Ten—Asset Searches.

Consumer Credit Records

Many public records vendors offer consumer credit records, address updates, Social Security Number searches and other credit-based records. Please refer to Chapter Twenty-five—Consumer Credit Records for further information.

Death Records (from the Social Security Benefits Records)

The Social Security Administration is usually notified of a person's death when a beneficiary dies or the death benefit is claimed. These records are not public, but the Social Security Administration does make them available through many public records vendors. Please refer to Chapter Twenty-eight—Death Records for additional information about SSA records, as well as many other types of death records.

Federal Aviation Administration (FAA) Records

The Federal Aviation Administration (FAA) maintains records on all currently registered individuals or businesses who own aircraft throughout the United States, as well as an FAA Airmen Directory. Federal Aviation Administration Ownership information includes:

- Description of the aircraft
- Owner address

- Owner name
- Registration information

FAA Airmen Directory records include:
- Name of airman
- Mailing address of airman
- Certificate class
- Date of last medical exam

Fish and Game Licenses

Fish and Game Licenses may seem relatively trivial as public records go, but they actually can be very useful. For example, someone who is hiding from creditors may not realize that a fishing trip can leave an automated paper trail that others can follow from across the country, leading them directly to his or her location.

General Indices

Public records vendors sometimes offer a general index search, which allows one to search all, or a portion, of the vendor's databases at once. These indices identify which databases contain records matching the individual's name or other search criteria. Although vendors may levy an additional charge for this index search, the fee is sometimes credited against subsequent fees on searches that result from the general search. Please refer to Chapter Sixteen for further information about General Indices.

Military Locators

Public records vendors also sometimes offer a service whereby they provide the location of active military personnel and military retirees who are receiving benefits.

Motor Vehicle Records

Motor vehicle registrations, driving records, and driver's license information are offered by many public records vendors. Please refer to Chapter Twenty-seven—Department of Motor Vehicles for more information about these records.

National Address Search

National address searches can be as simple as a national telephone directory search (as described in Chapter Seventeen), or they may include several other searches, such as postal change of address, publishers' change of address, and even real estate. Please refer to these specific types of records elsewhere in this chapter for more information.

National (Postal) Change of Address (NCOA)

The U.S. Postal Service provides national change of address records through many vendors in order to expedite address updates. Some of the vendors who receive these records are public records vendors, who then sell the individual records upon request.

Professional Licenses

Professional license indices are available online through many public records vendors. The records are normally obtained from various individual licensing agencies,

and are sometimes combined into a multi-license search. Typical records include:
- License number
- License issue
- Expiration date
- License type
- Licensee name
- Licensee address

An example of a professional license, this one for Los Angeles County medical examiner Thomas Noguchi, follows:

CALIFORNIA PROFESSIONAL LICENSES—DEPARTMENT OF CONSUMER AFFAIRS

NAME: NOGUCHI THOMAS T

ADDRESS: 1200 N STATE ST RM2519
             LOS ANGELES, CA 90033
             LOS ANGELES COUNTY

BOARD: MEDICAL BOARD OF CALIFORNIA

LICENSE-TYPE: PHYSICIAN AND SURGEON

LICENSE-CLASS: PERSONAL LICENSE

LICENSE NUMBER: 00016263

STATUS: CLEAR—PAID RENEWAL

LICENSE ISSUE DATE: 06151955

LICENSE EXPIRATION DATE: 01/31/1997

LAST UPDATE TO LICENSE INFORMATION: 12/13/1994

Please refer to Chapter Seven—Pre-Employment Screening for additional information about professional licensing databases.

Publishers' Change of Address
Magazine publishers receive notifications of changes of address from their subscribers. Even those hiding from a creditor sometimes update the publishers of magazines in order to take their subscriptions with them to their new addresses. Some publishers sell these records to public records vendors, who then sell individual records upon request.

Telephone Directory Searches
Many public records vendors offer location or surname searches based on telephone directories. They sometimes also offer reverse directory searches, allowing one to look up a telephone number or address and find the person who owns it, and neighborhood searches, which provide a range of names and telephone numbers for the

homes surrounding a targeted home. Some vendors also use warranty card data, census information, and mailing lists to add length of residence and approximate income levels of occupants; one such service is Infoscan, offered by CDB Infotek. Please refer to Chapter Seventeen—Telephone Directories for more information on searching telephone directories.

Utility Company Records

You can occasionally find an individual's water, electric, sewer, cable, and gas company records available on a public record vendor's system. These records are not usually available to the public directly through the utility company, so their presence online represents an even more valuable resource for investigators.

Voter Registration Records

Voter registration records are available online through some of the public records vendors. These are particularly useful for locating people, as they provide a name and address, as well as a birthdate, which often is absent from public records and can help to identify individuals with common names.

Voter registration records typically include:
- Name of voter
- Address of voter
- Date of birth
- Party identification
- Registration date
- Voter identification number
- Voting district number

Watercraft Ownership Records

Watercraft ownership records from the U.S. Coast Guard can be found online through some of the public records vendors. These records contain information on merchant and recreational vessels weighing no less than five net tons (approximately 27 feet or more) that are owned by U.S. citizens or corporations. These records can be useful in locating assets of an individual or corporation. Data included in these records include:
- Certificate status
- Home port
- Official ID number
- Owner name
- Owner address
- Service type
- Trade indicator

- Vessel description
- Vessel name
- Vessel size
- Vessel weight

Worker's Compensation Records

Worker's Compensation Act statutes establish the liability of employers for injuries or sicknesses which arise out of and in the course of employment. Worker's Compensation records typically include:

- Date of birth
- Date of injury
- Filing date
- Injury duration
- Injury type
- Name of injured party
- Social Security number

Records such as these are offered by some public records vendors.

Grouped Searches

Public records vendors sometimes group their searches in various ways in order to make them more attractive or to provide a better value to the buyer. For example, a real property search might include several counties or states. Another vendor might group bankruptcies, tax liens, and judgments into a single search. A civil records search can include records from both municipal and superior courts. Several searches can also be packaged into a more general Asset Search or People Finder grouping. Some group searches may even include all public records that the vendor has on file. Many other varieties of grouped search can be found on public records systems. Although grouped searches are sometimes offered at a discount from the individual search prices, other vendors may charge a premium price for grouped search packages. As with most types of public records found online, wide price variations are common.

OTHER SERVICES AVAILABLE FROM PUBLIC RECORDS VENDORS

Document Retrieval

Although many databases found online supply only indices to the actual records, public records vendors sometimes allow customers to order an actual document to be retrieved from the court or records facility. The records may be available in a few hours, days, weeks, or even months, and may be delivered in a variety of ways, including online (on the public records system or through email), fax, overnight delivery, or the U.S. Postal Service.

On-Site Court Searches

Not all public records are even indexed online at this time. For those records that are not, some public records vendors let customers order a search, and then perform the actual search at the court or records building. At that point, the records may be delivered by any of the methods listed previously.

Screening and Verification Services

Public records vendors sometimes offer value-added services based in part on public records or database records. These may include pre-employment screening, tenant screening, or similar services which may also involve database searches, as well as calling previous employers, landlords, schools, or other agencies that have records that are not available online.

Services could even include administration of honesty test instruments, drug testing, or other pre-employment screening having little or nothing to do with database records.

Summary

Public records contain a wealth of information about individuals and their business dealings. Many types of personal research, such as asset searching, pre-employment screening, and locating people, are extremely dependent upon these records. As public records continue to be made more accessible, such research is becoming easier to do well.

What exists online today is a small portion of the public records that are actually stored. I do not expect all public records to become available online within my lifetime, but many more types will become available as the marketplace demands (and is willing to pay for them). How quickly a given record arrives online will also depend upon how it is collected and stored. In other words, some records will reach the online market because of demand, while others will become available simply because they are already automated and easy to load into a public records system. Online vendors are also beginning to offer foreign public records, both domestically and abroad. Eventually, this may make it possible to perform global asset searches, and to locate people who have left the country using online resources.

The process of selecting a public records vendor should include consideration of the geographic area that one anticipates needing records from, the types of records that one anticipates using, the searches and services available from the vendor (including online ease-of-use, document retrieval, and other factors influencing whether the records are accessible, and readable), and price (which may include online time, report fees, fees per printed line of information, fax fees, and on-site document retrieval charges).

In addition to the various public records vendors available by direct dial through your modem, there are fee-based public records databases accessible through the Internet in increasing numbers, such as:

KnowX (a service of Information America), offering state corporate and limited partnership records, UCCs, judgments, bankruptcy records and lawsuits, real property records, and other public information on companies and individuals:

http://www.knowx.com/infoam/infoam.exe?

National Credit Information Network (a division of W.D.I.A. Corporation, in Cincinnati, Ohio), allowing fee-based searches for death records, national changes of address, social security number searches, phone number searches, voter registration records, date of birth searches, vehicles owned by, FAA searches, real estate ownership, UCC record filings, and criminal history searches:

http://www.wdia.com/ncihome.htm

Public Data Corporation (PDC), offering an online database of New York City Public Records, including deed and mortgage records, UCC filings, bankruptcies, judgments, and mechanics liens:

http://www.pdcny.com

Superior On-Line Data, offering many types of public records such as civil suits, judgments, tax liens, foreclosures, bankruptcies, UCC filings, and corporate records, at:

http://www.cji.com/

Access Information Systems, offering many types of public records searches:

http://www.deepdata.com/search/

Many state public records and other government databases are also available through government office sites on the Net, including:

Alabama Secretary of State, offering corporate records:

http://www.alalinc.net/alsecst/al05000.htm%20

The Florida Department of Law Enforcement Missing Children Information and Registered Sexual Predators Databases, along with Florida's Most Wanted:

http://www.fdle.state.fl.us/

Illinois Gateway to the Secretary of State offering Corporate Name Availability searches:

http://www.sos.state.il.us/

State of Indiana—Sex Offender Registry:

http://www.state.in.us/cji/index.html

Missouri Secretary of State, offering corporate records:

http://mosl.sos.state.mo.us/bus-ser/corpdata.html

Nebraska Secretary of State, providing private investigator and detectives licensing records, collection agency licensing records, UCC searches, and corporate record searches:

http://www.nol.org/home/SOS/

New Mexico State Corporation Commission, which includes a corporate information inquiry:

http://www.state.nm.us/scc/

North Carolina Department of the Secretary of State, which includes corporation data:
http://www.secstate.state.nc.us/secstate/

Rhode Island Corporate Listings:
http://www.state.ri.us/submenus/corpindex.htm

Utah real estate, occupational, and professional licenses:
http://www.commerce.state.ut.us/web/commerce/admin/licen.htm

Indices to state vital (birth, marriage, divorce, and death) records can be found at:
http://www.inlink.com/~nomi/vitalrec/staterec.html

and at:

http://www.medaccessl.com/address/vital_toc.htm

There are additional Internet sites that link you to fee-based public records retrievers and services who can perform online searches for you, such as:

DAC Services (Transportation Information Services, Inc.):
http://www.dacservices.com/

Global Electronic Marketing (GEM), Inc., offering many public records searches:
http://www.geminc.com/bbs/index.html

Information Search Inc., providing various types of public records:
http://www.information-search.com/

Investigative Resource, Inc., offering many types of public records searches:
http://www.rsabbs.com/iri/main.html

National Document Retrieval (NDR), Inc. Public Records Research, offering many public records searches:
http://www.pihome.com/ndr/pubrec.html

Redi-Info Information Service, offering various types of public records:
http://cust.iamerica.net/rediinfo/

and services that offer online access directly to their systems (rather than going through the Internet), such as:

WESTLAW—in addition to legal information, WESTLAW carries public records data from Information America and Experian REDI (Experian's Real Estate division). Their home page can be found on the Internet at:
http://www.westpub.com/

LEXIS-NEXIS—similarly, LEXIS-NEXIS carries public records. The home pages is:
http://www.lexis-nexis.com/election96/public.html

Commercial Information Systems, Inc. (CIS):
http://www.cis-usa.com/services/

Datalink and Datafinder:
http://www.datafinder.com/datalink/search.htm

Hogan Information Services:
http://www.hoganinfo.com/prod.html

IRSC:

http://www.irsc:.com/

Opera Data Systems, Inc.:
http://www.realty-village.com/

To learn more about searching public records, several public records research guides are listed later in Section IV "Where Can I Find More Information?—Books," and public records research organizations appear in Section IV "Where Can I Find More Information?—Organizations." A list of public records vendors can be found in Appendix M.

Additional information about court records systems (such as ACES and PACER), can be found in the CompuServe Legal forum. Listings of the court telephone numbers and modem numbers are stored in their online library, along with instructions for accessing the systems, fees, and other useful information. This information can also be found through various sites on the Internet.

Adoption Records

A doption records are open and available in many countries, including Australia, Columbia, England, Finland, France, Holland, Israel, New Zealand, Scotland, and Sweden. In most of the United States, however, adoption records remain relatively confidential. The exact rules governing them vary from one state to another.

Adoptees, birthparents, siblings, and other relatives who wish to locate each other can and do use many of the available databases to aid in their search. Public records, telephone directories, and other databases can provide valuable clues, and sometimes will lead to the hoped-for reunion. Other databases have been built specifically for adoptees, birthparents, and others seeking reunions with lost relatives. How useful these resources are depends in part upon how much they know about one another.

Adoption/Reunion Registries

Adoption or reunion registries are databases in which a person registers (often for a fee) in order to help those who may be trying to find them. This type of database is normally passive; registry owners make no effort to locate a person beyond matching the name, date of birth, and any other known identifying characteristics to others on the registry who are seeking someone of that description. If both people seeking the reunion are matched on the registry, they are notified, and contact information is provided to both parties.

Some adoption and reunion registries are active registries, in which the agency actively searches for people on behalf of their registrants. This is normally a fee-based service, charged at a premium above the registry fee.

The grandmother of all reunion registries is the International Soundex Reunion Registry (ISRR). (Refer to Appendix K for the address and telephone number in Nevada.) The ISRR registers adoptees, siblings and birthparents, and also many others seeking reunions; runaways, kidnap victims, missing relatives, MIAs, POWs, and abandoned children are all candidates for inclusion in the system.

The ISRR can also be contacted on the Internet at:

http://www.plumsite.com/isrr/

Many other adoption and reunion registries are operated by private organizations, and some of these feed into the ISRR or other registries. Some states also operate adoption registries, as do some adoption agencies. For example, the New York State Department of Health has placed information and an application for joining the Adoption Information Registry on the Internet at:

http://www.health.state.ny.us/nysdoh/consumer/vr.htm

The following information describes how the New York Adoption Information Registry works, in the agency's own words:

ADOPTION INFORMATION REGISTRY: DESCRIPTION AND AVAILABLE INFORMATION

The Adoption Information Registry is a service offered by the New York State Department of Health to help adopted persons who want to learn about their birthparents. The services of the Adoption Information Registry are available to any person who was born and adopted in New York State and is at least 18 years old. The Adoption Information Registry also processes applications from birthparents who wish to consent to an exchange of information.

WHAT INFORMATION IS AVAILABLE?

There are two kinds of information available to adoptees who register: nonidentifying and identifying. Nonidentifying information can be given to the adopted person without the registration or consent of the birth parents. It may include the following details about the birthparents: ages at the time of the adopted person's birth; heritage, including their nationalities, ethnic backgrounds and race; education (number of school years completed); general appearance—height, weight, color of eyes, skin, hair; religion; talents, hobbies and special interests; occupations; health histories; facts and circumstances related to the adoption; name of the agency that handled the adoption, if any. However, all of this information may not have been recorded. Nonidentifying information can be given only to the adopted person. It cannot be given to the adoptive parents, birthparents, sisters or brothers, or anyone else.

Identifying information includes the names and addresses of the adopted person and his or her birthparents. Identifying information cannot be released unless the adopted person and the birthmother and father all register with the Adoption Information Registry. If only one birth parent signed the surrender agreement or consented to the adoption, then the consent of the other birthparent is not needed

It is against the law for the New York State Health Department to ask adopted persons or their birthparents to join the Adoption Information Registry, or to contact them in any way to obtain a registration.

HOW IS INFORMATION OBTAINED?

Information about birthparents is obtained from records that may be on file with the New York State Department of Health, the New York City Health Department, the court that handled the adoption and the agency, if any, that arranged the adoption.

Before identifying information is released, the NYS Department of Health will check to make sure that the adopted person and all required parents are registered. If so, each person will be contacted by the Adoption Information Registry to make sure that he or she still consents to the exchange of names and addresses. If even one of the necessary parties

has not registered, no on will be contacted; if even one of the
necessary parties does not give final consent, no identifying
information will be released. Usually, the agency that handled the
adoption will release the available information. However, if the
adopted person requests or if the adoption was not arranged by an
agency, release will be made by the New York State Department of Health.

New York State Department of Health   Date posted March 25, 1994

Registries such as these sometimes require the birthparents' consent for their natural children to have access to their records. When the adoptee contacts the agency, if the birthparent's consent is not on file, the request may be denied unless a court order requires the information in a medical emergency. Adoption registries may also require that adult adoptees give consent before releasing their location to their birthparents. A few state registries record confidentiality requests, rather than release consents.

Each registry sets its own requirements and regulations for matching persons. For example, there is often a minimum age requirement which varies from state to state. Minors usually are not given access to their birth records until they have reached the age of 18, 19, 21, or 25, depending upon the state. In some cases, the adoptive parent must give consent before the records are released, or the records can be released to a younger adoptee with parental consent. Some agencies require that both birthparents consent before the records are released, if both appear on the original surrender. In yet other cases, the agency must verify the consent with the person before their records are released. Laws surrounding adoptees' rights to their records are changing, so a person born on one date may be denied access to their records, while someone born in the same state a year later may be granted access, or vice versa.

Many additional reunion registries can be located and contacted on the Internet, such as:

BirthQuest Online International Searchable Database:
    http://www.access.digex.net/~vqi/top.html

Family Service of Greater Vancouver:
    http://familyforum.com/fsgv/adoption.htm

Manitoba, Canada Post Adoption Registry:
    http://ebula.on.ca/canadopt/mbgov.htm

Ohio Adoption Registry:
    http://www.ohiolife.org/adopt/ohregis.htm

Reunion Registry:
    http://www.absnw.com/reunions/

Seekers of the Lost International Reunion Registry:
    http://www.seeklost.com/index.html

Texas Voluntary Adoption Registry:
> **http://odin.mdacc.tmc.edu/~cyn/pat.molina.html**

West Virginia Mutual Consent Voluntary Adoption Registry:
> **http://www.adoption.org/ii9sgwv.html**

Birthparent Connection Registry

Another registry contains information about unwed mothers. The Home for Unwed Mothers Registry, in California, is used by birthmothers who stayed in the home to locate one another. It is also used by adoptees, who can ask to speak to birthmothers who were in the home at the same time as their own mothers. (Refer to Appendix K for the address.)

Bulletin Boards

As noted earlier, many online bulletin boards focus on adoption. Participants in these bulletin boards frequently offer information about state regulations, new legislation, search advice, and personal experiences. They often send out pleas for assistance to "...anyone who knows who my parents are..." and similar requests.

Adoption information can be found on all of the following systems:

America Online	keyword "Adopt"
CompuServe	Issues forum
Delphi	Heritage
GEnie	Family RoundTable
Prodigy	Genealogy bulletin board

Further information can be found on the Internet, at sites such as:

Adoptee Resources:
> **http://www.best.com/~savage/adopt7.html#adoptee**

Adoptees Mailing List Home Page:
> **http://psy.ucsd.edu/~jhartung/adoptees.html**

Adoption and Adoptees:
> **http://wwwmbb.cs.colorado.edu/~mcbryan/bb/712/summary.html**

Adoption Resources, Support, Information:
> **http://pages.prodigy.com/newadoptivemom/**

The Adoption Information Exchange:
> **http://www.halcyon.com/adoption/exchange.html**

Resources for Adoptive Parents:
> **http://www.adoption.com/Information.html**

These sites will point you to many others, where further adoption information is being shared.

Another bulletin board service, KinQuest, is dedicated to helping adoptees and birthparents find each other. This bulletin board not only includes legal information for each state, reading lists, and organizations, but also has a link to FidoNet, where adoptees' messages are sent though Echomail. KinQuest can be reached at:

KinQuest BBS
c/o William L. Gage
805 Alvarado Drive N.E.
Albuquerque, NM 87108
(505) 897-9239
(505) 897-0814; 8N1 14.4 baud
(505) 898-9215; 8N1 2400 baud

Adoption/Reunion Publications

There are an increasing number of publications on the Internet, and this now incudes adoption/reunion publications, such as

Reunions Magazine:

http://www.execpc.com/~reunions/

Seeker Magazine:

http://www.the-seeker.com/

Adoption Legislation

If you are about to embark on a search for your birthparent or a natural child who was given up for adoption, you might want to know about adoption laws in the state in which you were born or adopted or both. WESTLAW Family Law Library contains the complete text of United States federal court decisions, statutes and regulations, state court decisions, specialized files, and texts and periodicals dealing with family law. These resources include such topics as abortion, adoption, custody, divorce, juvenile delinquency, marriage, and minors' rights. A similar family law library can be found on LEXIS.

Search Master California Practice Library (available on CD-ROM from Matthew Bender & Company, Inc.) and California Family Law—Practice and Procedure, 2nd Edition cover all contemporary family law areas and offer guidance through all of the procedural and substantive laws arising in cases of dissolution, adoption, and other areas.

Listings and discussions of state laws can also be found on many of the bulletin board services previously noted.

Children Available for Adoption

For those seeking children to adopt, databases can definitely help. For example, the National Adoption Exchange (available online through National Adoption Center (NAC) contains information on approximately 1650 children with special needs available for adoption and 800 families seeking special children for adoption.

For further information, contact:

National Adoption Center
1500 Walnut Street; Suite 701
Philadelphia, PA 19102
(800) TO-ADOPT
(215) 735-9988
(215) 735-9410 Fax

The Jewish Children's Adoption Network maintains a similar registry of adoptable children needing Jewish homes, and a registry of Jewish families who are interested in considering children for adoption. Further information can be obtained from:

Jewish Children's Adoption Network
P.O. Box 16544
Denver, CO 80216-0544
(303) 573-8113

Celebrity Records

A ny type of record can include information about celebrities. The famous buy and sell property, go into business, use credit cards, and obtain medical care, much like anyone else. Of course, even routine events such as a day of work or a date can become a news event when a celebrity is involved, so news sources take on a higher priority when the people being researched are famous.

This chapter identifies some additional databases useful in researching celebrities. When seeking information on someone who is famous, these represent supplemental sources, which are often used in combination with conventional sources such as public records.

Biographies and Credits

As noted earlier in Chapter Fifteen—Biographies, much information about celebrities is contained in biographical and autobiographical form. Databases such as Marquis' Who's Who abound with facts on celebrities, as well as other people who are notable in their fields.

The contents of a record vary, depending upon whether the information was provided by the biographee or somebody else. A record sometimes contains a more complete list of honors and accomplishments if it was contributed by the biographee. For example, the record for composer Quincy Jones (reportedly contributed by the biographee) includes an extensive list of honorary degrees and an extremely impressive catalogue of creative works. His list of awards follows:

AWARDS:
Recipient 76 Grammy nominations, 26 Grammy awards, numerous Readers
Poll awards Downbeat Mag., Trendsetters awards Billboard Mag., Golden
Note award ASCAP, 1982, Image award NASCP, 1974, 80, 81, 83, 90, 91,
Hollywood Walk of Fame, 1980, Man of the Yr award City of Hope,
1982, Whitney Young Jr. award Urban League, 1986, Humanitarian of Yr.
award T.J. Martell Found., 1986, Lifetime Achievement award Nat.
Acad. Songwriters, 1989, Grammy Living Legend award, 1990, Grammy
award for Best Jazz instrumental, individual or group 1994 for "Miles
and Quincy Live at Montreux", Scopus award Hebrew U., 1991, Spirit
of Liberty award People for the Am. Way, 1992
named Entrepreneur of the Yr. USA Today/Fin. News Network, 1991
film biography: Listen Up: The Lives of Quincy Jones, 1990
(extracted from Knight-Ridder Information Services)

Frank Sinatra's record is equally impressive, but it was compiled by Marquis. Perhaps as a result, it also includes a list of ex-wives:

FAMILY: married Nancy Barbato, Feb. 4, 1939 (div.); children: Nancy,
Frank Wayne, Christine; married Ava Gardner (div.); married Mia Farrow,
1966 (div.); married Barbara Marx, 1976

This information might not have been provided if Mr. Sinatra had contributed the record. Although children from previous marriages often are found on these records, many biographees omit information about their former spouses.

When a record has been contributed by a biographee, Marquis' can be a good source for information about one's interests that you may not see elsewhere. Examples of celebrity interests include that for David Letterman, whose record lists:

Avocations: baseball, basketball, auto racing, running

For Jerry Seinfeld:

Political/Religious Affiliation: Jewish

Avocations: Zen, yoga

This does not imply that Marquis does not compile personal information on their own. For example, did you know that Jay Leno used to work as a Rolls-Royce auto mechanic and deliveryman? His record, compiled by Marquis', also includes his interest in antique motorcycles and automobiles. Of course, if you watched the "Tonight Show" for about a week, you would probably pick up this information there.

Another set of databases, these specifically used to track the entertainment industry, are BASELINE II, available online through NEXIS and BASELINE, INC. On NEXIS, the BASELINE II databases include:

- Box Office Grosses
- Celebrity Biographies
- Celebrity Contacts
- Company Profiles
- Film/TV/Theatre Credits
- In Production Credits
- Industry Personnel Credits
- Latest Grosses

The following biography for actress and talk-show host, Ricki Lake, is a good example of what you can expect from the Celebrity Bios database:

Copyright 1995 BASELINE II, INC.
Celebrity Bios

LENGTH: 185 words

NAME: Lake, Ricki

OCCUPATION: actor, talk-show host; also singer

BORN:
September 21, 1968

EDUCATION:
attended the Professional Children's School in New York

Ithaca College
left during her first year to take starring role in "Hairspray"

MILESTONES:
Raised in Westchester, New York

Began professional career singing in cabarets in NY

Appeared on "Kate and Allie" and in commercials

Had a singing role in the off-Broadway revue, "Five Dine, No Exaggeration"

1990: appeared in "A Girl's Guide to Chaos" at the Tiffany Theater in Los
Angeles

Lost 115 pounds over a 2 1/2 year period

1993-: hosted daytime talk show "The Ricki Lake Show"

FAMILY:
father
pharmacist

mother
house wife

sister
Lake, Jennifer
younger

COMPANIONS:
husband
Sussman, Rob
artist
born c. 1967

NOTES:
"I needed someone who was big and pretty and could act and dance. Ricki had a
great laugh and basically said 'I am Tracy, I can be that, I've always been that
type of girl. I've always been big, I'm not uptight about it and I've always
been a leader.' I'm very happy with her."—John Waters (in press release for
"Hairspray")
Lake also plays the flute, piccolo, clarinet and piano.

BIO:
After playing small parts on TV, came to prominence as Tracy Turnblad, the
irresistible hefty heroine of John Waters' camp classic, "Hairspray" (1988)
Although most of her work in "Working Girl" (1988) and "Cookie" (1989) was left
on the cutting room floor, Lake has subsequently starred in "Babycakes" (1989),
the TV remake of Percy Adlon's "Sugarbaby", was featured in Waters' mainstream
comedy "Cry-Baby" (1990), and became a regular on the TV series "China Beach"
(1990). After dropping over 100 pounds, Lake became the host of her own

daytime talk show, "The Ricki Lake Show", which debuted in the fall of 1993.
She also played one of Kathleen Turner's children in another outing with Waters.
"Serial Mom" (1994).

LANGUAGES: ENGLISH

LAST-UPDATE: January 27, 1995

LOAD-DATE-MDC: February 23, 1995

If one were about to interview a celebrity, it would also be very useful to have a list of their professional credits handy beforehand. BASELINE's Film/TV/Theatre Credits and Industry Personnel Credits files offer that information. The Almanac of Famous People is another biographical collection, which is included in Gale Biographies (available on NEXIS). This database is one more great place to start when researching the famous. It supplies pointers to many other biographical works that contain information about any given person.

There are other entertainment databases on which you can find film credits. They include:

- Cinemania (available on CD-ROM from Microsoft Corp.)
- Documentary and Film Database (available on CD-ROM from American Directory Corporation)
- Entertainment Systems International (available online through Dialcom)
- Hollywood Hotline (available online through America Online, AT&T FYI News Service, CompuServe, Delphi Internet News Service, and GEnie; refer to Appendix L for these addresses)
- Magill's Survey of Cinema (available online through CompuServe, CompuServe Knowledge Index, Knight-Ridder, NIFTY-Serve and Prodigy; refer to Appendix L for these addresses, with the exception of Knight-Ridder and NIFTY-Serve, which can be found in Appendix N)
- Television Programming Source Books on CD-ROM (available on CD-ROM from North American Publishing Company)
- Variety's Video Directory Plus (available on CD-ROM from Bowker Electronic Publishing, Reed Reference Publishing Group)
- VideoHound Multimedia (available on CD-ROM from Gale Research Inc.)

(Refer to Appendix N for addresses of these vendors, except where otherwise noted.)

Movie reviews can also provide film credits and cast lists. These can be found on:
- Hollywood Hotline's Movie Reviews (available online through CompuServe; refer to Appendix L for this address) which contains movie reviews written by Eliot Stein, including plot summaries, names of film companies, director, producers, stars, writers, and ratings.
- Mega Movie Guide (available on CD-ROM from Cineman Syndicate)

- Movie Reviews Database (available online through America Online, AT&T EasyLink, AT&T FYI News Service, BASELINE II INC., Delphi Internet Services Corporation, Dialcom, Dow Jones News/Retrieval, GEnie, and NEXIS, and as part of the BYTE Information Exchange (BIX)) which contains movie reviews written for syndication by film critic Jay A. Brown. (Refer to Appendix L for these databases, except for BASELINE, Dialcom, Dow Jones News/Retrieval, and NEXIS, which are listed in Appendix N)

- Roger Ebert's Movie Home Companion (available on CD-ROM from Quanta Press, Inc.)

- Roger Ebert's Reviews and Features (available online through CompuServe, which is listed in Appendix L) which contains the complete text of reviews of recently released feature films

(Refer to Appendix N for these vendors, except as otherwise noted.)

The Internet Movie Database is another collection of information, this one compiled with the help of many participants and submissions. It has become a commercial site, supported by advertisers, but searching the database remains free. The Internet Movie Database is available at the following two sites:

http://us.imdb.com/

and

http://uk.imdb.com/

Star biographies can also be found on the Internet at:

Mr. Showbiz Star Bios:

http://www.mrshowbiz.com/starbios/

and, of course, many fans have compiled biographies of their favorite stars on their own Internet sites, or on fan club sites that they contribute to.

Although this is a wonderful resource, whenever a database is assembled from voluntary submissions, you must always take extra care to verify the information found.

A similar database, the WWW Music Database, has been compiled covering music. It resides at:

http://www.cs.uit.no/Music/

Upcoming Projects

Back in 1994, I wondered what Tom Hanks was up to since winning his academy award for *Forrest Gump.* I found BASELINE's In Production (Inpro) file very useful for identifying projects in production, upcoming projects and appearances, and even rumors of future projects.

Tom Hanks was listed in the role of R9 in the film *Stranger in a Strange Land* and for a role in *Bolt,* both listed as in development (which also means that the name may change.) Another record noted that Tom Hanks had been mentioned to star in *The Postman,* which is in development. In another film in development, *The Passion of*

Richard Nixon, it is noted that Tom Hanks had been mentioned to play Richard Nixon. The animated film *Toy Story* was listed as lensing with Tom Hanks providing the voice of Woody. The American Film Institute Life Achievement Award was planning a Salute to Stephen Spielberg, filming on March 2, 1995, and Tom Hanks was listed as the host. Among the presenters at the "67th Annual Academy Awards Presentation" (TV special) on March 27, 1995, Tom Hanks was also listed. As you may deduce from this list, some of the listed actors do not end up playing the roles that they are linked to or rumored to be considering. Nonetheless, when researching a celebrity, it can be helpful for interviewers and others to know what roles, films, plays, and appearances are being planned or considered.

The Inpro database can be especially useful to those preparing to interview a celebrity. Records from this database typically include such information as:

- Film title
- Status
- Genre
- Location
- Production company
- Phone number
- Date on which shooting began
- Date on which shooting finished
- Distributor
- Producer(s)
- Director(s)
- Credits
- Cast
- Casting
- Publicity
- Synopsis
- Notes
- Language

Another source for information on upcoming projects of your favorite celebrities is to check with their fan clubs. A search of the Internet can provide contact information for hundreds of fan clubs, as well as information about their past, present and future projects.

Contact Information and Business Relationships

If you want to get in touch with your favorite celebrity, BASELINE's celebrity contacts database is a good choice. You will not find the stars' home addresses here; the contact provided is usually the celebrity's agency or management company. They can put you in touch with the celebrity if they feel that you have a valid reason to contact them, such as an interview or a role to cast, and they can tell you where to send your fan mail.

The following listing for actor Michael Richards is a typical example from this database:

Michael Richards

AGENCY: International Creative Management

AGENCY-PHONE: (310) 550-4000 (212) 556-5600

LANGUAGE: ENGLISH

LOAD-DATE-MDC: February 23, 1995

BASELINE Company Profiles can serve to provide additional background information about an individual in the entertainment industry. For example, if I wanted to know what businesses director/producer George Lucas was involved in, I could search Company Profiles to find Lucasfilm Ltd. This record could be used to identify business associates, such as Katherine Morris, Douglas Kay, and Jeff Ulin, any of whom might provide valuable insights for a profile of Mr. Lucas:

Lucasfilm Ltd

DIVISION:
LucasArts Digital Ltd
LucasArts Entertainment Company
Industrial Light & Magic (ILM)
LucasArts Licensing
THX Group Unit
Skywalker Sound
LucasArts Entertainment Co
Lucasfilm Business Group
Lucasfilm Commercial Productions (LCP)
New Media Group
Consumer Products

TYPE:
Production—Film
Production—Commercials
Production Services

PHONE:
Phone: (415) 662-1800
Fax: (415) 662-2460

PERSONNEL
Lucas, George
 Chairman
 CEO
Komisar, Sandy
 President & Chief Exec (LucasArts Entertainment Co)
Morris, Jim
 President (ILM)
Radley, Gordon
 President (Lucasfilm Ltd)
Morris, Katherine
 VP
 General Mgr (Lucas Digital Ltd)
Roffman, Howard L
 VP Licensing & THX divisions
Watts, Robert
 VP European Prod
Kessler, James
 VP Theatre Operations
MacPherson, Laurie
 VP
 General Mgr (THX Group Unit)
Kay, Douglas
 Chief Technical Officer (LucasArts Ent Company)
Friedman, Peter
 Exec Prod (LCP)
Rudnick, Ken
 Exec in Charge of Prod (LCP)
Goldman, Clint
 Sr Prod (ILM)
Blau, Patty
 Exec in Charg of Prod (ILM)
Townsend, Kevin
 Exec Prod (ILM)
Dashwood, Monica L
 General Mgr (THX Theatres & Consumer Products)
Strub, Kimberly
 Dir Mktg Theatre Operations
Fine, Deborah
 Dir Library Research
Ulin, Jeff
 Dir Business Affairs (LucasArts Ent Company)
Modray, Maxwell
 Dir (LCP)
Forrest, Matt
 Dir (LCP)
Money, Jim
 Dir (LCP)
Pasternack, Ellen
 Dir PR (Lucas Digital Ltd)
Vargo, Mark
 Dir (LCP)
Corey, Carl
 Dir (LCP)

Sharninghausen, William M
   Controller

PERSONNEL-NOTES:
Lindsley Parsons Jr, former President and COO of Lucas Digital Ltd, resigned
in mid-January 1994. (DV12/20/93.)

LAST-UPDATE: January 18, 1995

LOAD -DATE-MDC: February 23, 1995

News

Although any news database may provide information on celebrities, you might
want to focus on entertainment-related publications first. Some of the entertainment
news available online includes:

- *Billboard* (available online through DataTimes and NEXIS)
- *The Hollywood Reporter* (available online through DataTimes and NEXIS, as
  well as part of the PROMT database)
- *People Weekly* (available online through NEXIS, and as part of the Magazine
  ASAP database, as listed in Appendix G)
- *Rolling Stone Online* (available online through CompuServe, as listed in
  Appendix L)
- *Screen Digest* (available online through DataStar, DataTimes, Dow Jones
  News/Retrieval, FT PROFILE, GENIOS, Knight-Ridder, NEXIS, and
  WESTLAW)
- Time Publications (available online through Knight-Ridder), which includes
  *Entertainment Weekly, Fortune, Life, Money, People, Sports Illustrated, Time
  International,* and *TIME* magazines.

(Refer to Appendix N for these vendors, except as otherwise noted.)

Of course, since celebrities are involved, one might take a bit more skeptical look
at what appears in the news, as there are certainly mistakes, rumors that later prove
false, and even outright lies printed about celebrities every day.

Locating information on sport stars can also be assisted by searches of sport publications such as:

- *The National Sports Daily* (available online through DataTimes)
- *The Olympics Factbook* (available online through NEXIS and Prodigy; refer to
  Appendix N for NEXIS and Appendix L for Prodigy)
- *The Sporting News* (available online through DataTimes and NEXIS)
- *The Sporting News Multimedia Pro Football Guide* (available on CD-ROM from
  The Sporting News Publishing Company)
- *Sports Illustrated* (available online through NEXIS and as part of the Magazine
  ASAP and Time Publications databases, as listed in Appendix G)

- *Sports Illustrated CD-ROM Sports Almanac* (available on CD-ROM from Time Inc.)

(Refer to Appendix N for the vendors above, except as otherwise noted.)

Entertainment publications can also be found on the Internet, some in expanded versions. For example, TV Guide Entertainment Network includes an expanded version of *TV Guide Online,* a movie database, and live chats with celebrities and writers. It is located at:

http://www.tvguide.com

Sports celebrities may also be found in the online edition of *Sports Illustrated,* which can be found at:

http://pathfinder.com/si/

This site not only brings you to the current version of *Sports Illustrated,* but includes a photo gallery, a feature called "This Day in Sports," Reuters Sports News, and many other sports sites.

Other Databases

At least four foreign databases also cover aspects of the entertainment industry:

- Cinematografia (available online through Ministerio de Cultura de Espana, Secretaria General Tecnica, Puntos de Informacion Cultural (PIC)) contains information on films that have been made or distributed in Spain

- CSIRO Films (available online through OZLINE: Australian Information Network) contains full bibliographic descriptions of films, videotapes, and other audiovisual materials produced by CSIRO

- Film/Video Canadiana on CD-ROM (available on CD-ROM from OPTIM Corporation) contains English- and French-language descriptions of films and videos produced (or co-produced) by Canadian production companies and independent producers

- PIA Road Show Information (available online through NIFTY-Serve) contains current news on Japanese and other road shows

(Refer to Appendix N for these database vendors.)

Music databases also are available for researching musicians and their music. They include:

- RockNet (available online through America Online, CompuServe, and NIFTY-Serve; refer to Appendix L for America Online and CompuServe) which contains news of the rock music industry, including announcements and reviews of albums, concerts, and Music Television (MTV) events, as well as interviews with rock stars and radio and record industry personnel

- Don Och's Sound Library (available online through Knight-Ridder) contains information on vintage radio programs and music of the 1930s through the 1950s.

(Refer to Appendix N for these vendors, except where otherwise noted.)

If you are looking for information about a soap opera star, you might want to check out Soap Opera Summaries (available online through CompuServe). It includes cast lists, news, and gossip, addresses for writing the cast or fan clubs, cast birthdays, and plot highlights from one year ago.

The Hulton Deutsch People Disc (available on CD-ROM from ATTICA Cybernetics Ltd.) contains 10,000 images of 4,000 famous people, and many additional images can be found on other CD-ROM products, as well as on bulletin board systems.

Information about sports stars can be found on several databases. Some target a particular sport. For example, information on major league baseball can be found on:

- Microsoft Complete Baseball (available on CD-ROM from Microsoft Corp.)
- The Scouting Report (available on CD-ROM from Quanta Press, Inc.)

Soccer data can be found on:

- Futbol Internacional (available online through Ministerio de Cultura de Espana, Secretaria General Tecnica, Puntos de Informacion Cultural (PIC)), which provides information on Spanish national and international final matches
- TELESPORT (available online through SARITEL S.p.A.) which provides information about Italian soccer teams, athletes, and championships

(Refer to Appendix N for these vendors.)

Additional databases contain information and news on personalities from many sports, including:

- AGORA-SPORTS (available online through Europeenne de Donnees (ASPO))
- Computer Sports World (available online through Computer Sports World) which contains information on professional and collegiate sports
- News/Retrieval Sports Report (available online through Dow Jones News/Retrieval) which contains the complete text of sports news stories and statistics from the SportsTicker news service
- Sportel (available online through Sportel Communications Network)
- The Sports Network (available online through CompuServe and The Sports Network; refer to Appendix L for CompuServe) which contains news on professional and collegiate sports
- SportsAlert (available online through America Online, Bloomberg Financial Markets and GEnie; refer to Appendix L for America Online and GEnie)
- SportsTicker OnLine (available online through SportsTicker) which provides up-to-the-minute coverage of all professional and major college and international sports events
- Olimpiadas (available online through Ministerio de Cultura de Espana, Secretaria General Tecnica, Puntos de Informacion Cultural (PIC)) which contains results of more than 3,000 Winter and Summer Olympics events and other world championships

- Primeros Puestos del Deporte Espanol (available online through Ministerio de Cultura de Espana, Secretaria General Tecnica, Puntos de Informacion Cultural (PIC)) which contains information on approximately 1,000 medals and other honors won by Spanish athletes in international sports competitions

(Refer to Appendix N for these vendors, except as otherwise noted.)

Bulletin Boards

It sometimes is possible to converse directly with celebrities online. The Commercial Bulletin Board systems (America Online, CompuServe, Prodigy, etc.) often arrange for online conferences with actors, writers, or musicians, where individuals who participate are able to "talk" online with them.

For example, CompuServe has held online conferences with musicians Donald Fagen and Walter Becker of Steely Dan, Hootie and the Blowfish, Todd Rundgren, Jonathan Cain and Neal Schon of Journey, and singer/songwriter David Gates. Soap opera stars Linda Dano, Julia Barr, Walt Willey, Michael Swan, Diego Byrne, Randolph Mantooth, and Robin Strasser have all participated in online conferences. Jenny McCarthy, former co-host of MTV's show "Singled Out" and currently star of her own cable show, was the subject of an online conference, as were actors Jason James Richter and Jerry Doyle, teen model Allison Murray, and comedian Al Franken. Consumer advocate David Horowitz participated in another online conference, as did Nick Charles and Fred Hickman, co-anchors of "CNN Sports Tonight." The cast of Comedy Central's "Exit 57" has also been online in conference.

Some behind-the-scenes bigwigs have also participated in online conferences. Dan Hamilton, director of "As the World Turns," Chris Carter, creator and executive producer of "X-Files," and David Roehrig, producer for Fox, are all examples.

Authors Dean Koontz, and Susan Eisenhower (granddaughter of President Eisenhower), and science fiction writer Octavia E. Butler have held online conferences, and Vice President Al Gore has been in conference online as well.

Certain celebrities have found the online world to be a convenient medium for communication with friends and fans alike. During the filming of *The Net,* actress Sandra Bullock was interviewed on the set, where she said she spent all of her off-screen time on the Internet, talking with her friends. The convenience of being able to send messages to each other at any hour, from any location, can be a great help to people with irregular schedules, or who travel often.

Stars can also talk with people on a level that they may not be able to achieve any longer in the "real" world because they can meet and make friends without being recognized by fans. In fact, many celebrities have gone online under other names in order to listen in on what their fans were saying about them, or even to participate in critiquing their competition. From time to time, someone intent on "outing" the celebrities publishes a list of email addresses and pseudonyms of the famous and circulates it online. Many of the addresses and pseudonyms are then changed. This cat-and-mouse game continues.

A directory of celebrities on the Net can be found at:

http://www.four11.com/

The entries are categorized by:

- Actors
- Authors
- Business
- Entertainers
- Government
- Miscellaneous
- Models
- Music
- Sports
- Studios and Shows

Many other lists of celebrities can be found through Usenet newsgroups as well.

Many of the bulletin board systems provide online forums for fan clubs, show business, and music lovers, where information about any given celebrity may be shared. In July 1996, I used WebCrawler (an Internet search tool) to search for "fan club," and the system counted over 2,800 Internet sites containing these words. No doubt more have been added since.

Show Biz RoundTable, one prominent entertainment forum, is available online through GEnie. CompuServe has an Industry Canteen forum for entertainment industry professionals, as well as Soap Opera, Show Biz/Media, RockNet, Musik, Hollywood Online, and TV Zone forums. If I were searching for a celebrity's birthdate, someone participating in one of these forums might be of assistance. However, an even better bet would be to ask on one of the astrology forums, such as: **alt.astrology newsgroup** on the Internet.

There also are online forums for nearly any sport, where fans share information about sports stars. Examples of sports forums include the Sports Forum on CompuServe and Sports RoundTable on GEnie.

Many, if not most, television shows are also publishing their email addresses now so that fans can send fan mail, complaints, or ideas for shows. There are even whole online forums dedicated to particular shows, such as, "Baywatch" and "America's Funniest Home Videos," both now on CompuServe.

Since the entertainment industry is of such interest to so many people, new Internet sites spring up almost daily that contain information on actors, actresses, movies, television shows, and nearly anything else about the industry. Some of these sites are being indexed on the Internet at sites, such as:

Yahoo—Entertainment:Movies and Films
    http://www.yahoo.com/Entertainment/Movies_and_Films/

This index includes categories for:

- Actors and actresses
- Awards

- Box office reports
- Columns
- Companies
- Contests
- Events
- Exhibits
- Film festivals
- Film making
- Film music
- Film schools
- Genres
- History
- Home video
- Independent
- Interactive games
- Journals
- Laserdisc@
- Lists
- Magazines@
- Mailing lists
- Multimedia
- News@
- Organizations
- Parodies@
- People
- Personal pages
- Quotes
- Real-time chat
- Resources
- Reviews
- Screenplays
- Studios
- Theaters
- Theory and criticism
- This week's releases
- Titles
- Trivia
- Usenet

The Internet T.V. Resource Guide
> **http://www.teleport.com/~celinec/tv.shtml**

Yahoo—News and Media/Entertainment/Television
> **http://www.yahoo.com/News_and_Media/Television/**

INTERNET ENTERTAINMENT NETWORK
> **http://hollywoodnetwork.com/indexmain.html**

TV + Films:
> **http://boris.qub.ac.uk/edward/TV_Film.html**

Ultimate TV Show List
> **http://www.tvnet.com/UTVL/utvl.html**

I was curious to find out what type of information I might find using the Yahoo—Entertainment: Movies and Films: Actors and Actresses index, so I used it to look up information on actress Drew Barrymore. It provided the following sites:

A Drew World:
> **http://members.aol.com/drewbworld/dreworld.htm**

Club Drew:
> **http://www.geocities.com/Hollywood/3137/**

Drew Barrymore [geocities.com]:
> **http://www.geocities.com/Paris/8889/drew.html**

Drew Barrymore [Mr. Showbiz]:
> **http://www.mrshowbiz.com/starbios/drewbarrymore/index.html**

Drew Barrymore [Sam Haraldson]:
> **http://www.acm.ndsu.nodak.edu/~sharalds/drew.html**

Drew Barrymore [wfu.edu]:
> **http://www.wfu.edu/~david/drew/**

I Want to Be Drew!:
> **http://www-personal.umd.umich.edu/~melindab/Drew/drew.html**

More Barrymore:
> **http://www4.ncsu.edu/eos/users/r/rfbatcho/www/drew/**

Oh Drew!:
> **http://www.angelfire.com/ny/Medman/**

Ultimate Drew Barrymore Picture Gallery:
> **http://www.cbn.net.id/users/urdi/drew.htm**

The following Usenet newsgroup:
> **Usenet—alt.fan.drew-barrymore**

along with four links that no longer point to Drew Barrymore sites, and one more that is no longer being updated. This should give you some indication as to how changeable information on the Net is.

Along with a virtual Drew Barrymore photo gallery, these sites provided her date and place of birth, her real name (Andrew Barrymore), home town, names of relatives (including her ex-husband and current boyfriend), weight and height, descriptions of Drew's tattoos, a note that she's a vegetarian, a reference to her being bisexual, Drew's film and television credits, ratings for her latest films, awards she's earned, Drew quotes, an audio clip, a reference to the Melnik's song dedicated to Drew ("Drew Romance"), a poem about Drew, a book and magazine bibliography, upcoming appearances and projects, and pointers to other Drew Barrymore sites on the Net.

If I were to go back to the Yahoo site and look up Drew Barrymore in a week or two, the information might all have changed, with old sites dropped, addresses changed, and new sites added. These are simply the dynamics of the Internet, where information grows, evolves, and erodes as fast as the participants can post it.

Music resources are also being indexed at sites such as:

Worldwide Alternative Jukebox:

http://www.nbn.com:80/aaj/

JAMMIN REGGAE ARCHIVES Home Page:

http://orpheus.ucsd.edu/jammin/

Jazz Online:

http://www.jazzonln.com/

Yahoo's Music Resources:

http://www.yahoo.com/Entertainment/Music/

Sports information can also be found on the Internet, indexed through sites such as:

The Sports Network:

http://www.sportnation.com/

SportsLine USA (includes recent birthdays of those in sports):

http://www.sportsline.com/

Sports Illustrated:

http://pathfinder.com/si/

Yahoo's Recreation: Sports Resources:

http://www.yahoo.com/Recreation/Sports/

Celebrity Deaths

On the Internet, I have run across several sites that list celebrity deaths, including:

Dead People Server, which lists not only those celebrities who have died, but tells you which are alive whom you probably thought were dead:

http://www.scarletfire.com/dps/

The Obituary Page, which includes recent deaths of celebrities, and links to biographies of some:

http://catless.ncl.ac.uk/Obituary

The Death of Rock 'n Roll:

http://weber.u.washington.edu/~jlks/pike/DeathRR.html

Deceased Porn Stars:

http://www.xmission.com/~legalize/asm/dead-stars.html

Although it is not possible to offer a comprehensive list of information sources for celebrity research within a single chapter (in fact, it could fill an entire book at this point), the information presented here should give you some starting places for your research and illustrate the ways in which fans and vendors alike are compiling personal data about the famous. Many of the other databases presented throughout this book are at least as useful for researching the famous as they are for learning about the average citizen. With this many information resources available (in addition to "sources close to...," garbacologists, and the paparazzi), it is no wonder the tabloids are never at a loss for stories!

Please refer to Chapter Twenty-eight for additional sources for death records, which would also apply to celebrity records.

Genealogical Records

G enealogical research has come a long way. Although information about one's lineage is still frequently gathered from notes made in family Bibles and stories passed down from generation to generation, it is now just as likely to be collected online or from CD-ROM databases.

Genealogists often become masters of public records research and are some of the heaviest users of census, church, military, and burial records. They may also use most of the various other types of personal records described in this book. Libraries of genealogical information are available in print and on microfiche across the country and in many other parts of the world. Genealogists can utilize all of these in the quest for their roots.

Along with these resources, databases are produced specifically for genealogical research, and home-grown databases filled with family records, personal recollections, and research are copied and transmitted from one network to the next around the world every day. Many genealogical bulletin boards are extremely active, and they can be rich resources for advice and assistance, shared resources and research findings.

Software

Genealogists can choose from many computer programs with which to store their genealogical findings. Their choice of software is important because the use of standardized record formats read and written by the software can automate the process of sharing genealogical findings. This automation can make it possible to quickly locate whole branches of one's family, sometimes adding hundreds of relatives to a family tree within minutes. It can also link living relatives all around the world who are researching their shared heritage.

Before adding one's lineage to an online bulletin board, or submitting it for loading to a database, one must put records into the format required by that particular site. Although it may be possible to download lineage information from a database without any particular genealogical software program, having software that can accept and utilize the records in an automated fashion can assist a researcher considerably, especially when hundreds or thousands of records are downloaded at once.

Other factors influencing the genealogist's choice of software may include hardware requirements—Macintosh versus PC, 386, 486, Pentium; memory requirements, hard disk space requirements, CD-ROM versus diskette, etc.—maximum records allowed, types of relationships allowed (i.e., multiple marriages, step-families, adoptions, etc.), the software's ease of use, graphical capabilities, and price.

The list of software available for genealogical research is enormous. Just surfing around genealogical sites on the Internet and the ROOTS Forum on CompuServe, I ran across lists, reviews, discussions, and notes on over a hundred programs. Some are commercial programs, while others are available as shareware; copies can be downloaded on a trial basis, and if you like them, you can send the fee for a registered copy and receive technical support from the company.

For additional information on genealogical software, you can refer to the list of Genealogical Research Publications in Section IV "Where Can I Find More Information?—Periodicals," many of which carry reviews, announcements, comparisons, and articles about various genealogical software. *Computers in Genealogy* and *Genealogical Computing* provide this focus and might be good choices to start with.

You may also look to genealogical bulletin boards for discussions, reviews, and working copies of genealogical software. For example, CompuServe has split its genealogical forums, and now maintains a separate Genealogical Support Forum (GO GENSUP) for information about genealogical software. It is divided into the following nine areas:

- New England Historic Genealogical Society
- Wholly Genes Software (The Master Genealogist)
- Leister Productions (Reunion)
- Brothers Keeper
- CommSoft, Inc. (Roots IV)
- The Family Edge
- Everton Publishers
- National Genealogical Society
- Schröder and Fülling GbR (German-speaking ancestor research)

Employees of each organization monitor their respective sections of this forum, and offer assistance there. Other members also frequently jump in to answer questions about software and genealogy.

An Internet Usenet newsgroup is also available for genealogical software discussions:
soc.genealogy.computing

A list of Commercial Genealogical Sites, many of which are genealogical software companies, can also be found on the Internet at:
http://www.genhomepage.com/commercial.html

or at:

http://genealogy.tbox.com/genealogy/software.html

or on Yahoo! at:

**http://www.yahoo.com/Business_and_Economy/
Companies/Computers/Software/Genealogy/**

There are at least as many utility programs developed for (and often by) genealogists, and these can frequently be found online, posted on genealogical bulletin boards, and shared among genealogists. Many of these utilities convert genealogical data among the various formats which can be read by other genealogical software, spreadsheets, and word processing programs. There are also genealogical utilities that create all types of reports, timelines, and charts, define relationships between people, compute ages, search Personal Ancestral Files from the Church of Jesus Christ of the Latter Day Saints (LDS) library, generate Soundex Codes (which are often used on genealogical microfiche and databases; more about this later), compile statistics from genealogical databases, perform spell-checking, create all types of calendars, perform date conversions, check location names, translate between languages, and identify the state in which a given Social Security number was issued. Many of these utilities can be found on bulletin boards for little or no cost.

Maps, advice, archived discussions, software reviews, and other genealogical information can also be found on the forums and bulletin boards. For further information on genealogical bulletin boards (many of which are local systems, available for the price of a phone call), refer to Genealogical Networks, later in this chapter.

STANDARD GENEALOGICAL RECORD FORMATS

Before viewing genealogical records, you will need to know something about the format in which they appear. There are many formats for genealogical records which can make them more readable and useful to genealogists. Some of them have been standardized in order to automate sharing lineage data. The most common standardized formats for genealogical research include:

PAF (Personal Ancestral File)—PAF is the traditional format of the Church of Jesus Christ of the Latter-Day Saints.

Ahnentafel—An Ahnentafel is an ancestor table in which each position in a pedigree is given a unique number. This format is rarely used in online bulletin boards, but it is over a century old, and is still found in genealogical research.

Tiny-Tafel—The Tiny-Tafel format, first introduced in 1986 in *Genealogical Computing Magazine*, presents an abbreviated snapshot of a genealogical database. It is machine readable and used to match lineage information among databases that can utilize it.

The Tiny-Tafel contains one line of text for each family line, giving the surname, locations, and the time period represented by that line, along with codes that signify the researcher's degree of interest in receiving information concerning the ancestors or descendants of that line. Not all genealogical information fits into this abbreviated format, which is used for matching, rather than for storing or sharing full records. When a Tiny-Tafel is used to query other databases and a match is found, a copy of the full records from the matching database can be requested and sent in a more complete format, such as GEDCOM.

GEDCOM (GEnealogical Data COMmunications)—The GEDCOM format, introduced by the Church of Jesus Christ of the Latter-Day Saints in 1984, has evolved over the last decade, and several versions have been developed during that time. Today, GEDCOM is the most commonly-used format by genealogical software. However, this elongated format requires so much disk space and processing capacity that many genealogical bulletin boards prohibit its use. Some genealogical programs also have had difficulty interpreting this format due to inconsistencies between versions. The GEDCOM format nonetheless has become the standard for genealogical databases and is now the form most often used for exchanging lineage data.

One can also now find genealogical records posted on Internet Web pages in nearly any format imaginable. Further information about Internet sites can be found throughout this chapter.

Genealogical Networks and Bulletin Boards

At about the same time that the Tiny-Tafel format was being developed, around 1986, the idea of connecting the various genealogical bulletin boards around the country started to take shape. These connections would enable genealogists to exchange queries and genealogical data through an online network that would eventually reach around the world. (Although the Internet did exist at that time, it was not yet generally available to individuals outside of government or academia.) When the first two genealogical bulletin boards were connected later that year (using a program named Fido; hence, referred to as FidoNet), that was the beginning of the National Genealogical Conference. A list of existing FidoNet Echos can be found on the Internet at:

http://www.genealogy.org/~ngs/netguide/fidonet.html

Another Internet site lists genealogical bulletin board systems (GBBS) worldwide at Richard Cleaveland's GBBS, at:

http://www.genealogy.org/~gbbs/welcomet.html

Further information about genealogy and genealogical bulletin boards can be found through the National Genealogical Society (founded in 1903), which you can find on the Net at:

http://www.genealogy.org/~ngs/

Although genealogical bulletin boards appear on CompuServe, America Online, and other popular home systems, the Internet seems to be carrying an ever increasing load of the world's genealogical research traffic. In fact, there are so many genealogical sites on the Internet that many Web sites have been created simply to index them all. Such sites include:

The Genealogy Home Page:
http://ftp.www.genhomepage.com

The National Genealogy Society—Other Genealogy Home Pages:
http://www.genealogy.org/~ngs/otherhp.html

The National Genealogy Society—Genealogist's Guide to the Internet by George W. Archer:
http://www.genealogy.org/~ngs/netguide/welcome.html

Yahoo—Social Science:History:Genealogy:
http://www.yahoo.com/Social_Science/History/Genealogy/

Genealogy Listservers, Newsgroups & Special Home Pages:
http://www.eskimo.com/~chance/

Internet Guides and Genealogical Home Pages:
http://www.genhomepage.com/homepages.html

Genealogy Resources on the Internet:
http://www.umich.edu/~cgaunt/gen_int1.html

RAND Genealogy Club Home Page:
http://www.rand.org:80/personal/Genea/

USGenWeb Project:
http://www.usgenweb.com/

Cyndi's List of Genealogy Sites on the Internet:
http://www.oz.net/~cyndihow/sites.htm

One of the nicest things about doing genealogical research is that other researchers are usually happy to share their findings, advice, and sometimes their own research resources, even with strangers. It is not unusual for one researcher to look up information for another, send copies of their own records, or even to visit a church or cemetery to obtain information that a far-off correspondent otherwise would find difficult to acquire. Linking genealogists through online networks such as FidoNet and the Internet has broadened the research resources of genealogists around the world.

Commercial Databases

Along with the databases being developed and sent out on the networks by hundreds or thousands of individual genealogists, documenting their own family trees, there are databases for commercial use that contain records and collections that many genealogists find helpful. These represent some of the greatest bargains to be found in public records research. For example, the CD containing the U.S. Census Index for Ohio in 1880 contains approximately 800,000 entries from 87 counties, and sells for only $19.99. Of course, if a genealogist only needed one record from this region during this period, $19.99 might be quite a bit to pay for it, but for someone who expects to research many people who were in Ohio in 1880, this CD would be an excellent purchase.

Genealogical groups (such as those listed under Genealogical Research Organizations in Section IV "Where Can I Find More Information?—Organizations") sometimes make group purchases of commercial genealogical databases in order to provide greater research resources for their members. Family History Centers listed on the Internet at:

http://www.genhomepage.com/FHC/fhc.html

and

http://www.smartlink.net/~leverich/fhc.html

and public libraries that maintain genealogical collections may also make these databases available to the public.

There are several companies producing CD-ROM products for genealogists. At the forefront of these was Automated Archives, Inc. (AAI, which is now owned by Banner Blue, which was acquired by Brøderbund). AAI's CD-ROM products include census indices, marriage record indices, Social Security death indices, and various other other collections. Now sold as part of Family Tree Maker's Family Archive collection, you can find information about these and many other Banner Blue genealogical products on the Internet at:

http://www.familytreemaker.com/facds.html

and

http://www.everton.com/cdrom.html

Many of the CD-ROM collections are also listed later in this chapter. It should be noted that none claim to have comprehensive coverage of all records within a geographic area, or complete coverage of a time period, but they can be of tremendous assistance to beginning and professional genealogists alike.

Other companies providing genealogical CDs include:

Automated Research, Inc.:

http://www.aricds.com/

GenRef Inc.:

http://www.genref.com/product.html

Infobases:

http://mall.infobases.com/infobases/

Millisecond Publishing (Family Forest products):
http://www.FamilyForest.com/product.html

More are springing up, so an Internet search may provide additional links to companies with new products to assist you in your research.

There are also companies who will, for a fee, convert microfilm collections of your own records onto CD-ROM. As many of the existing large genealogical collections are still on microfilm, this is an important development which can be expected to expand the resources of genealogists, and make these records far more accessible and useful.

WHERE TO GET STARTED

Name Indices
When starting out your genealogical research, a name index can be an important resource. When you don't know where records for your family exist, a name index can point you to databases or sites where records may be found.

FamilyFinder Index is a name index, searchable on the Internet, which can point you to Family Tree's CD databases on which there are records with a matching name. This index can be found at:

http://www.familytreemaker.com/ffitop.html

I used the FamilyFinder Index to search for one of my ancestors, Valentine Eichenlaub (I just love that name), and found the following records:

Name	Est.Date Location	Archive Type
Eichenlaub, Valentine	1937-1995	United States Social Security
Eichenlaub, Volentine	1850 OH	Census CD 317

What this tells me is that there is further information about someone with this name on Family Tree's Social Security Death Index. I cannot be sure that this record is for my great-great-grandfather, as there could be more than one person with this name, but given how unusual this name is, it would be worth checking further.

This also tells me that there is someone listed as Volentine Eichenlaub in Family Tree's 1850 Census of selected counties of Ohio. As genealogical records are often taken from handwritten records, or even third party accounts, misspellings are not uncommon, so a name this close should be considered a likely match. My ancestor, Valentine Eichenlaub, was born in 1845, and died in Lima, Ohio, according to my family records, which makes a match on the 1850 Ohio census even more likely, so I would definitely want to obtain records from that census, in the hope of finding additional information, if not for my great-great-grandfather, perhaps for other family members.

One must keep in mind that genealogical records do contain errors. After all, reading and writing have not been common skills in all cultures at all times, so names on records may have been recorded as approximations of their phonetic sound. Soundex Codes can be very helpful in identifying various forms of the same name. (Further information about Soundex Codes appears later in this chapter.)

Another type of genealogical name index is used to locate other individuals who are researching the same family, in order to share their research findings. These surname indices can also be found on many bulletin boards. The information often, but not necessarily, takes the form of Tiny-Tafels (as described earlier in this chapter).

On the Internet, **soc.genealogy.surnames** is a Usenet newsgroup where genealogists have been posting their interest in specific surnames in recent years. Those messages have also been archived into a database, known as the Roots Surname List or RSL. Information about this database, searching it, and submitting information to it, can be found at:

http://www.smartlink.net/~leverich/rsl-index.html

The RSL can be searched through many search engines. Some of them can be found at:

http://www.rootsweb.com/rootsweb/searches

and at:

http://www.rand.org/cgi-bin/Genea/rslsearch.pl

Using one of the search engines to inquire into this database, I looked for the surname Goodwin (another branch of my family) in order to locate other researchers who are researching families with this surname. I found the following:

Surnames matching "Goodwin"

New entries are marked by a +, modified entries by a *, and expiring entries by an x. Clicking on the highlighted code words will give the name and address of the researcher who submitted the surname. (If no names are listed below this line, then none were found.)

Goodwin	1405		now ENG>MA>CortlandCo/OneidaCo,NY>OH,USA charliep
Goodwin	1465	1570	Blofield,ENG>Ranworth,ENG dearborn
Goodwin	1465	1602	ENG rwm
Goodwin	1510	1602	Blofield,NFK,ENG>Ranworth,NFK,ENG mcbride
Goodwin	1530	1746	ENG>ME,USA derwood
Goodwin	1544	1574	Blofield,NFK,ENG ckrause
Goodwin	1596		now ENG>MA>CT>MA,USA weymouth
Goodwin	1596	1773	ENG>HartfordCo,CT,USA schnell
Goodwin	1602	1602	ENG thoden
Goodwin	1640	1994	ENG>MA,USA>NB,CAN>BC,CAN jude
Goodwin	1662	1732	Stratford,CT,USA juli
Goodwin	1672		---- CT,USA aschmidt
Goodwin	1694		now PA>KY>IN,USA ole
Goodwin	1709	1860	AL,USA toma
Goodwin	1718		---- NJ>PA>IL>IA,USA cvillier
Goodwin	1745	1835	ME,USA phirl
xGoodwin	1750	1750	VA,USA holliday
Goodwin	1753	1851	Hamstead>Dunbarton>Portsmouth,NH,USA levenhag
Goodwin	1760	1870	SC>AL,USA aplynch
Goodwin	1790		now VA>IN>WA,USA dante
Goodwin	1800		now GreeneCo/WashingtonCo,PA,USA ggood
Goodwin	1800		now TYR,NIR>RI>NJ,USA loreem
Goodwin	1802	1937	NH>NY>IL>LA,USA burgoyne
Goodwin	1806	1937	MD>PA>OH,USA comcour
Goodwin	1808	1845	ON,CAN gmorin
Goodwin	1810	1930	NH>ME>MA,USA bobbim
Goodwin	1812	1861	Mapleton,DBY,ENG gek
Goodwin	1818		now Baltimore,MD,USA bjdeaver
Goodwin	1818	1900	HamiltonCo,OH>PutnamCo,IN>NortonCo,KS,USA paulette
Goodwin	1825	1880	FreemansReach,NSW,AUS raewyn
Goodwin	1826		---- TN>MO,USA kdunn
Goodwin	1829	1862	AYR,SCT>PA>MariposaCo,CA>YavapaiCo,AZ,USA tbgoss
Goodwin	1830	1894	DallasCo,AL>LauderdaleCo,MS>ChoctawCo,AL,USA rhead
Goodwin	1833	1981	MS>Lufkin,AngelinaCo,TX,USA hclark
Goodwin	1839	1930	UT>CO,USA kogle
+Goodwin	1850		---- IL>NE,USA julias
Goodwin	1850	1884	NY>DC>MD,USA qpgmr
Goodwin	1855	1910	PikeCo,OH>Clinton,IL,USA jparker
Goodwin	1857		now CarrollCo,MD>IL>NE>IA>MO>KingfisherCo,OK,USA aegok
Goodwin	1857	1993	SCT>AlleghenyCo,PA>WestmorelandCo,PA,USA mcilnay
+Goodwin	1875	1962	ENG>Trenton,MercerCo,NJ,USA blaines
+Goodwin	1876	1936	ENG>MN>OK>MN,USA slabot
+Goodwin	1882		now Bennettsville,SC,USA rarthur
+Goodwin	1885	1925	IsleOfWightCo,VA>Baltimore,MD,USA spratley

Goodwin	~1784	~1827	IRL>PA,USA dek
Goodwin	<1900		---- SFK,ENG johnb
Goodwin	c1580		now SFK,ENG>Kittery,ME>CA,USA karenjk
Goodwin	c1580	1632	BDF,ENG cacall
Goodwin	c1625		---- MA>NH,USA rickb
Goodwin	c1650	1770	YorkCo>NewKentCo,VA,USA arb
Goodwin	c1750		---- SussexCo,DE,USA nicklaus
Goodwin	c1770	c1860	LEI,ENG laurajt
Goodwin	c1780	1847	ENG>Sydney,NSW,AUS psherloc
Goodwin	c1789	1860	VA>GA>AL>GA>FL,USA mewexler
Goodwin	c1793	1904	KY>OH>IN>MO>ID,USA rogery
Goodwin	c1808		---- WGardiner,ME,USA smartzoo
Goodwin	c1820	1918	IL>WI>UmatillaCo,OR,USA mab
Goodwin	c1630	c1930	Rochdale,LAN,ENG>FallRiver,BristolCo,MA,USA xn
+Goodwin	c1850	now 1850	MA>NH>CA>NY>FL,USA ghahn
Goodwine	1793		now FL>SC>GA>PA>NY>MA>IL>SC,USA marqutta
Goodwine	1852	1905	IN>IL,USA pence

This provides the information and linkage that I would need to send electronic mail to other researchers who are interested in the Goodwin family, as well as indicating which period and geographic area each is researching so that I can decide which records are of most interest to me. This type of database can save a great deal of time and trouble when starting out your research, as you may find genealogists who have done most of the research on your lineage already, or who have unique family collections that would not otherwise be found.

Other surname indices can be found indexed on the Surname and Family Data section of the Genealogical Toolbox at:

http://genealogy.tbox.com/genealogy.html

This section of the Genealogy Toolbox provides links to the many family databases and surname information currently on the Internet. At this site, you can find links to database sites such as:

- General Family Resources
- Indexed Family and Surname Data
- Current Genealogy Toolbox Surname and Family Queries
- Genealogy Toolbox Surname and Family Query Archive

and General Family Resources such as:
- AdoptionNetwork Home Page
- British Royal Family Genealogy
- Distribution of Surnames within the United States; this page contains links to maps of the distribution of the 445 most common names derived from telephone white pages. It is maintained by Hamrick Software.
- Family Associations & Who To Contact
- Family History Collection at University of Kansas

- Family History Collection at UMS
- Family Periodical & Surname Publications
- GenServ Home Page
- German Nobility Database
- Information on the CANADIAN-ROOTS Mailing List.; this page, part of the Genealogy Resources on the Internet home page, contains information on the mailing list for the discussion of the Brother's Keeper genealogy program. The site is maintained by John Fuller.
- LaSalle County Genealogy Guild Surname Index
- Medieval Pomeranians 1503-1588
- Roots Surname List Name Finder
- Royal Genealogies
- Surname to Soundex Code
- Surnames: What's In A Name?; this site contains the history and origin of surnames in general, and of specific names including the area of origin and type of surname (patronymic, place, occupation, etc.). It is maintained by Larry Hoefling.
- Tiny Tafel Archive
- Traveller Southern Families
- U.S. Presidents Genealogy

Additional name indices can be used to point to books or other collections. For example, an index of Australians is available from White Room Electronic Publishing Pty. Ltd. This CD-ROM, The Australian Chronicles: An Index to Sources of Australian Biography, indexes a variety of sources, including Who's Who, biographical dictionaries, topical and local histories, and published local histories. Information about this product can be found at:

http://www.whiteroom.com.au/geneal.htm

Also, refer to Chapter Fifteen—Biographies, for Biographical Index Directories, and Chapter Sixteen—General Indices, for other databases that can be used as starting points for your research.

Soundex Codes

Genealogical records are frequently indexed using Soundex Codes, which are helpful in locating records containing variant spellings. (Although particularly common in genealogy, Soundex Codes are used for many other types of database as well.)

Assigning a Soundex Code is fairly simple. The first letter of the name is maintained, so, for example, with Eichenlaub, the first code is E. After the first letter, vowels are dropped, as are the letters h, w, and y, and any second consecutive occurrence of a letter. For Eichenlaub, this leaves CNLB. The remaining letters are coded according to the following assigned numbers:

1=B, F, P, V
2=C, G, J, K, Q, S, X, Z
3=D, T
4=L
5=M, N
6=R

For Eichenlaub, coding CNLB (the remaining consonants) would translate to 2541, so the total Soundex Code for that name would be E2541.

NAME   E I C H E N L A U B
SOUNDEX   E   2   5 4   1

Although a Soundex Code could have any number of characters, they are usually limited to 4, so E2541 would be shortened to E254. This could result in all of the following matches for Eichenlaub:

EAKENWALDER, EASHNAULT, EASNLAUFF, ECENHOWLER, ECHMALIAN, ECHONALS, **ECKENLAUB**, ECKENLE, ECKENLEVY, ECKENLEY, ECKENWALDER, ECKENWEILER, ECKENWELLER, ECKEN-WILDER, ECKENWILER, ECKMUELLER, ECKMUL, ECKMULLER, ECNELL, ECNOLS, EGENLAAD, EGEN-LAUF, EGENLER, EGENLRET, EGENOLF, EGGENWEILER, EGGENWELER, EGGENWILER, EGMALIN, EGNAEL, EGNAL, EGNALL, EGNEL, EGNELL,EGNYALOVICH, **EICHANLAUB**, EICHANLMOYER, EICHEN-HOLTZ, EICHENHOLZ, **EICHENLABU**, EICHENLAMB, EICHANLANB, EICHENLANG, **EICHENLAUB**, **EICHENLAUB X**, EICHENLAUF, EICHENLAUL, EICHENLAULE, EICHENLAUT, EICHENLIEB, **EICHENLOB**, **EICHENLOUB**, EICHENLOUF, EICHENMILL R, EICHENMILLER, EICHENMILLER, EICHENMUELLER, EICHENMULLER, EICHNALD, EICHNOLZER, EICHUNLAND, EICKENLAMB, EICKENLAND, **EICKENLAUB**, EICHENLOFF, EISENLOH, **EIGANLAUB**, **EIGANLUB**, **EIGENLAUB**, **EIKENLAUB**, EISENHELD, EISEN-HOLT, EISENLA, EISENLAHR, EISENLANE, EISENLARD, EISENLATH, EISENLAU, EISENLAUER, EISENL-EFFEL, EISENLEIMOR, EISENLERGER, EISENLISE, EISENLOAD, EISENLOEFFEL, EISENLOFFEL, EISENLOH, EISENLOHR, EISENLONE, EISENLOR, EISENLORD, EISENLOT, EISENLOW, EISENLREY, EISENMULLER, **EISHENLAUB**, EISMILD, EISMUELLER, EKHAML, EKMALIAN, EKNOWLES, ESCAMELLA, ESCAMILLA, ESCAMILLA II, ESCAMILLA MA, ESCAMILLA-CO, ESCAMILLAS, ESCAMILLIA, ESCAMILLO, ESCANELLA, ESCANELLAS, ESCANELLE, ESCANILLA, ESCANILLAS, ESCANUELA, ESCANUELAS, ESCHEMULLER, **ESCHENLAUB**, ESCHENLAUER, ESCHENLOHR, ESCHENWALD, ESCOMILLA, ESCONUELAS, ESENLY, ESHENWALD, ESHMAEL, ESHMALYAN, ESHMILLER, ESHMLE, ESKAMALEN, ESKENLOPH, ESKMULLER, ESMAEL, ESMAIELOF, ESMAIL, ESMAILKA, ESMAILZADEH, ESMAL, ESMEAL, ESMEL, ESMELE, ESMIEL, ESMIOL, ESMMEL, ESMOIL, ESMOLD, ESMUELT, ESMULLER, ESNAL, ESNAOLA, ESNAULT, ESNEALT, ESNEAULT, ESNELL, ESNEWALL, ESNLER, ESQUEMAULT, ESQUINALDO, ESQUINLIN, ESSANLOW, ESSENHOLM, ESSENLOHR, ESSIN/ELSIN, ESSMILLER, ESS-MUELLER, ESSMULLER, ESWINNEL, EUKENLHARGER, EUSMULER, EXAMILIOTIX, EYSAMLIN

Some of these (noted in boldface) are close to Eichenlaub, and might be attributed to misspellings, transpositions, typing errors, or variations or evolution of the same name, while others seem to have little relation to Eichenlaub at all. This demonstrates how Soundex can assist you in finding variant spellings, as well as a wide variety of mismatches.

Further information about Soundex can be found on the Internet at:
http://www.tip.washington.edu/bdm/genealogy/overviewofsoundex.html
and

http://www.firstct.com/fv/soundex.html

If you need help converting a name to its Soundex Code, there are Internet sites which you can use to convert the name for you, Examples of these can be found at:
http://www.gentech.org/soundex.html
and

http://orwant.www.media.mit.edu/soundex.html
and

http://www.dars.muohio.edu/~kaelbesa/coder.html

Similar software utilities for converting Soundex Codes may be found on other genealogical bulletin board systems.

Using Soundex Codes (rather than names) to search for records can save a genealogist countless hours reading name by name to find variations, especially when using a microfilm or microfiche reader, or printed records. Having a database with the ability to search both by name and Soundex Code is an important advance to genealogical research.

GENEALOGICAL REGISTRIES AND FAMILY PEDIGREES

Genealogical registries are used to collect family pedigrees, often contributed by many researchers and covering many families. Pedigrees can help a genealogist to identify relatives, locate existing records, and supplement what is already known about families, adding names, dates of important events, and links to other family members—even entire branches at once. (Some pedigrees on CD-ROM even contain supplementary notes and pictures.) When a residence or date of a family event is found on a pedigree, these can provide starting places to search for other records such as church records, vital records, or census records. One can contact local churches, archives, libraries, and county recorders to locate these original records, which may provide additional information about the individual. In addition, when the submitter's name is included in the registry or collection of pedigrees, a genealogist may be able to contact the individual who submitted the pedigree to obtain or share additional information.

Collections of pedigrees may take the form of private registries, maintained by genealogical associations. Others are sold as databases, while some are now accessible online. On the Internet, Yahoo! indexes family pedigrees at the following site:
http://www.yahoo.com/Arts/Humanities/History/
Genealogy/Lineages_and_Surnames/

As of the moment that I write this, there are already hundreds of Internet sites for particular surnames being indexed by Yahoo!, and more being added all the time.

Another site indexing genealogical databases online, including those indexed by surname can be found at:

http://www.gentree.com/

Another service called GenServ accepts submissions of GEDCOM data files on the Internet. It claims to have over 6 million names in over 4,550 GEDCOM databases on file. GenServ stores the GEDCOM files, and will provide a free access code for two months to those who have submitted their GEDCOMs. Otherwise, there are fees for subscribing to this database, and only those who contribute information are eligible to subscribe. Those with access codes can request a search. The data is not directly accessible, but a search may be requested, and a report of matching data will be returned. For further information about this service, visit the GenServ Home Page at:

http://soback.kornet.nm.kr/~cmanis/

There are also genealogical collections that have been contributed from individual genealogists, and made available on CD-ROM. Such collections include those being sold by Family Tree:

World Family Tree: Volume 1-7 (Pre-1600 to Present)

These CDs contain thousands of family trees contributed by Family Tree Maker customers and other family history enthusiasts. Millions of individuals are named, complete with event dates and family links where known. Some records contain additional source notes and biographical information. These CDs exclude information about living individuals except for their names, genders, and family links.

Family Pedigrees: Everton Publishers—Family Archive (CD 15)

Source: Family groupings from Everton's Family File 1 & 2 and "Roots;" Cellar Volume 1, provide information on about a million individuals. Most of these groupings are from the United States and Europe, but some are from Latin America, Canada, the Pacific Islands, and Asia.

Date Range: 1500-1990

Family Pedigrees: GENTECH95 & ARI (CD 108)

Source: This linked-relationship genealogy database contains individual records from 103 GEDCOM files. The files were contributed to GENTECH, Inc. by family historians attending the GENTECH95 Conference, and compiled into a linked database by Automated Research, Inc. Each one of the GEDCOM files includes documentation (source notes), which add to the reliability of the data. Such documentation, while highly desirable, is uncommon among other linked genealogy databases.

Date Range: 1500-1989

Family Pedigrees: United Ancestries (CD 100)

Source: All the pedigrees and family group sheets prepared by United Ancestries, Inc., and its predecessors over a 30 year period; these records were chiefly prepared by professional researchers for their clients and then linked into a single database. Most birthdates fall before 1850, and some select records date from before 1500. Many of the Royal lines of Europe are included.

Date Range: 1500-1990

Family History Collection: First Families of America (CD 114)

Source: This CD contains the text of the book *The Abridged Compendium of American Genealogy (Volume 1)*, Edited by Frederick A. Virkus, 1925. It includes records of over 200,000 individuals who appear in compressed lineages derived from thousands of individual family genealogies printed prior to 1925 (at which time there were approximately 6,000 U.S. genealogies in print). This volume of the compendium contains a representative number of the 3,929,214 individuals in the United States in 1790, along with their ancestries.

Family History Collection: GIS, Electronic Messages Volume 1 (CD 161)

Source: This CD contains approximately 400,000 electronic bulletin board messages referencing six million names of individuals from all over the world. Genealogical Information Systems, Inc., of Austin, Texas, has provided these electronic messages from FidoNet and from ten of its genealogy conferences. Messages date from February 1992 to August 1994, and have been enhanced to provide maximum research benefit.

Family History Collection: Family History Collection: Pennsylvania Genealogies #1 (CD 163)

Source: Images of the pages of all three volumes of *Genealogies of Pennsylvania Families* from *The Pennsylvania Genealogical Magazine,* as well as one volume of *Genealogies of Pennsylvania Families* from *The Pennsylvania Magazine of History and Biography*. The four volumes, originally published by the Genealogical Publishing Company, contain several hundred family history articles and Bible records, and reference approximately 62,000 individuals from Pennsylvania as well as the Delaware Valley. The articles from these four volumes touch on families of English, Welsh, Scotch-Irish, German, Dutch, and French origins, while the Bible records dwell on hundreds of additional families, many of them interrelated.

Date Range: Pre-1600 to 1900s

Family History Collection: Virginia Genealogies #1 (CD 162)

Source: This CD contains all five volumes of *Genealogies of Virginia Families* from *The Virginia Magazine of History and Biography,* originally published by the Genealogical Publishing Company, Inc. The family histories in these articles were compiled from 84 years' worth of family history articles. These articles reference approximately 65,000 individuals from all parts of Virginia. Most articles trace lines of descent through seven or eight generations, covering three or four centuries.

Date Range: Pre-1600 to 1900s

Further information about these CDs can be found at:
http://www.familytreemaker.com/

As noted earlier, there also are Internet newsgroups for sharing research on specific surnames. Lists of these can be found at:
http://www.eskimo.com/~chance/

http://news.hk.gin.net/newsgroup/soc.genealogy.html

http://www.meertech.demon.co.uk/genuki/newsgrou.htm

http://www.feefhs.org/newsgrps.html

http://www.vic.com/news/groups/soc.genealogy.html

http://eastman.freenet.mb.ca/sig/soc.genealogy_html

http://genealogy.tbox.com/genealogy/news/newlist.html

IMMIGRATION RECORDS
There are collections of immigration records available on CD-ROM. They include:

Complete Book of Emigrants (CD 350)
Source: With approximately 140,000 names, this CD is purported to contain the most comprehensive list ever published of the men, women, and children who emigrated from England to America between 1607 and 1776. It includes the texts of six books by Peter Wilson Coldham: *The Complete Book of Emigrants* (four volumes), along with *The Complete Book of Emigrants in Bondage* and its supplement. Peter Wilson Coldham, the foremost authority on early English emigration, compiled this data from a myriad of original English sources over several decades. The Genealogical Publishing Company in Baltimore, Maryland, provided Coldham's texts for electronic publication.

Date Range: 1607-1776

California Mennonite Historical Society—GRANDMA Database (GMV1)
Source: From the California Mennonite Historical Society; Low German Mennonites in the U.S., Canada, Russia, Prussia, Latin American and other places, from individual submissions, family books, church membership books, census records, family Bibles and private collections; generally, persons who trace their ancestry through the American Midwest back to Russia.

Date Range: Predominantly persons born prior to 1930

Further Information: http://www.fresno.edu/cmhs/gpc/cdrom.htm

You can also find the Emigration List for Bergen Hourbour (Norway) 1874-1924 on the Internet at:

http://www.uib.no/hi/1801page.html

CENSUS RECORDS

The first United States census was taken in 1790. It has been updated every ten years since, as provided for by the Constitution, in order to count America's citizens and apportion taxes among the states. A few limited censuses were also taken during colonial times, and interim head-counts have been taken in several states in between the national censuses.

Census records are the backbone of American genealogy. In fact, since data for individual households or persons is not published for 72 years (and is only available prior to that time to the government, the parties named, and, under certain circumstances, their descendants), individual census records remain almost the exclusive domain of genealogists.

The information gathered for the census has changed over the years. Between 1790 and 1840, the census included various statistics, but only the names of the heads of households were collected. That, along with the number of children, other adults, total persons in the household, and other counts, have been used by genealogists to validate other data, and provide leads to identifying additional offspring.

Since 1850, the names of all persons living in a household have been collected, along with their ages, sex, and race. The place of birth of each person in the household, and their relationship to the head of the household have been collected since 1880. In 1890, the length of each person's present marriage was added to the census, along with the number of children born and the number still living. For the genealogist, all of these details are golden, and since many people in past generations could not read or write, written records may not have existed before the census provided them.

Only eleven states participated in the first census. Additional territories and states were added over time. What follows is the first year that each of the listed states began participating in the census:

Year	State
1790	Connecticut, Maine, Maryland, Massachusetts, New Hampshire, New York, North Carolina, Pennsylvania, Rhode Island, South Carolina, Vermont
1800	Delaware, District of Columbia
1810	Kentucky, Louisiana, Virginia, West Virginia
1820	Georgia, Illinois, Indiana, Michigan, Mississippi, Ohio, Tennessee, Wisconsin
1830	Alabama, Arkansas, Florida, Missouri, New Jersey
1840	Iowa
1850	California, Minnesota, New Mexico, Oregon, Texas, Utah
1860	Kansas, Montana, Nebraska, Nevada, North Dakota, South Dakota, Washington, Wyoming
1870	Arizona, Colorado, Idaho
1890	Oklahoma
1900	Alaska, Hawaii

Arizona, Arkansas, California, Connecticut, Delaware, Florida, Georgia, Illinois, Indiana, Iowa, Kentucky, Louisiana, Maine, Maryland, Massachusetts, Michigan, Minnesota, Mississippi, Missouri, New Hampshire, New Jersey, New York, North Carolina, Ohio, Pennsylvania, Rhode Island, South Carolina, Tennessee, Texas, Vermont, Virginia, Wisconsin.

1840

Census Index: U.S. Selected Counties (CD 316)

Source: CD contains indices of census records that were gathered from various U.S. counties in 1840. The District of Columbia and the following 33 states are represented: Alabama, Arkansas, Connecticut, Delaware, Florida, Georgia, Hawaii, Illinois, Indiana, Iowa, Kentucky, Louisiana, Maine, Maryland, Massachusetts, Michigan, Minnesota, Mississippi, Missouri, New Hampshire, New Jersey, New Mexico, New York, North Carolina, Ohio, Pennsylvania, Rhode Island, South Carolina, Tennessee, Texas, Vermont, Virginia, Wisconsin.

1850

Census Index: U.S. Selected Counties (CD 317)

Source: CD contains indices of census records that were gathered from various U.S. counties in 1850. The District of Columbia and the following 38 states are represented: Alabama, Arkansas, California, Connecticut, Delaware, Florida, Georgia, Illinois, Indiana, Iowa, Kansas, Kentucky, Louisiana, Maine, Maryland, Massachusetts, Michigan, Minnesota, Mississippi, Missouri, Nebraska, New Hampshire, New Jersey, New Mexico, New York, North Carolina, Ohio, Oregon, Pennsylvania, Rhode Island, South Carolina, Tennessee, Texas, Utah, Virginia, Vermont, West Virginia, Wisconsin.

1860

Census Index: U.S. Selected States/Counties (CD 318)

Source: CD contains indices of census records that were gathered from various states and counties in 1860. The District of Columbia and the following 39 states are represented: Alabama, Arizona, Arkansas, California, Colorado, Connecticut, Delaware, Florida, Georgia, Idaho, Illinois, Indiana, Iowa, Kansas, Kentucky, Louisiana, Maine, Massachusetts, Minnesota, Mississippi, Montana, Nebraska, Nevada, New Hampshire, New Jersey, New Mexico, New York, North Carolina, Oklahoma, Pennsylvania, South Carolina, Tennessee, Texas, Utah, Vermont, Virginia, Washington, West Virginia, Wisconsin.

1870

African Americans in the 1870 Census (CD 165)

Source: CD contains federal census returns for areas of Georgia, North Carolina,

Pennsylvania, South Carolina, Virginia and West Virginia, as well as the counties containing the cities of Baltimore, Chicago, New York City, and St. Louis.

Census Index: Baltimore, Chicago, St. Louis (CD 288)
Source: CD contains indices of census records from three major cities: Baltimore, Maryland, Chicago, Illinois, and St. Louis, Missouri.

Census Index: Georgia (CD 291)
Source: CD contains census records from 132 counties in Georgia.

Census Index: New York City (CD 287)
Source: CD contains indices of census records from five counties that comprised New York City in 1870. These counties are Kings, New York, Queens, Richmond, and Suffolk.

Census Index: North Carolina, South Carolina (CD 289)
Source: CD contains indices of census records from 121 counties in North Carolina and South Carolina.

Census Index: Eastern Pennsylvania (CD 286)
Source: CD contains indices of census records from 19 counties in Eastern Pennsylvania.

Census Index: Western Pennsylvania (CD 285)
Source: CD contains indices of census records from 26 counties in Western Pennsylvania.

Census Index: Virginia, West Virginia (CD 290)
Source: CD contains indices of census records from 152 counties in Virginia and West Virginia.

Census Index: U.S. Selected States/Counties (CD 319)
Source: CD contains indices of census records that were gathered from various states and counties in 1870. The District of Columbia and the following 31 states are represented: Alabama, Alaska, Arizona, Arkansas, California, Colorado, Delaware, Florida, Georgia, Idaho, Illinois, Indiana, Iowa, Kansas, Kentucky, Louisiana, Maine, Minnesota, Missouri, Montana, Nevada, New Mexico, North Carolina, North Dakota, South Dakota, Texas, Virginia, Washington, West Virginia, Wisconsin, Wyoming.

1880

Census Index: Ohio (CD 20)
Source: CD contains indices of census records from 87 counties in the state of Ohio. It

was prepared by the Ohio Genealogical Society and represents all the Ohio counties that existed in 1880.

Census Index: U.S. Selected States/Counties (CD 320)

Source: CD contains indices of census records that were gathered from various states and counties in 1880. The following 14 states are represented: Alaska, Alabama, Arizona, Colorado, Idaho, Illinois, Nevada, New York, North Dakota, Ohio, South Dakota, Texas, Washington, Wyoming.

1910

Idaho (CD 335)

Source: CD contains records from the 1910 federal census of Idaho. While many census indices list only the head of each household, this census index attempts to list all individuals found on the 1910 federal census forms. (Please be aware that transcribers may have inadvertently omitted a few names however.)

There are also non-U.S. census indices available on CD-ROM:

Canadian Genealogy Index, 1600s-1900s (CD 118)

Source: CD contains over two million records referencing individuals from all regions of Canada, as well as early Alaska. The vast majority of the records fall between 1600 and 1984, although some records date before the 1500s. Gathered over twenty years of research from over one thousand different sources (including city directories, marriage records, birth records, land records, census records, and more), this collection of names represents one of the largest indices of historical Canadian records available.

Census Index: Ontario, Canada (CD 116)

Source: CD contains indices of census records from the 1871 census of Ontario, Canada. This CD indexes heads of household as well as individuals who had different last names than the head of household.

Census Index: Ireland, 1831-1841 (CD 197)

Source: CD contains indices of census records from two Irish counties: County Londonderry (from 1831) and County Cavan (from 1841).

Further information about these CDs can be found at
http://www.familytreemaker.com/

A Cornish Roots CD is also in the process of being compiled. Information about this project can be found at:
http://www.cornwall-net.co.uk/multimed/roots.htm

You can even find census indices posted on bulletin boards from time to time. For example, I have found the 1890 U.S. Census Index posted in CompuServe's Roots Forum library. The 1871 Ontario Census Heads of Households can also be found (in several compressed files all beginning with 1871) on the Internet at:

ftp://FTP.CAC.PSU.EDU/pub/genealogy/text/data

and it can be searched online at:

http://stauffer.queensu.ca/docsunit/searchc71.html

The 1830 and 1840 Census Index for Autauga County, Alabama can be found at:

http://www.tntech.edu/~beg/autauga/

The Census of Norway from 1801 is searchable on the Internet at:

http://www.uib.no/hi/1801page.html

The 1850 Census for Wyoming County, Virginia can be found at:

ftp://FTP.CAC.PSU.EDU/pub/genealogy/text/data/WyoCoWV1.850

Actual census records are also be found on CD-ROM in some cases, as filmed collections, rather than searchable databases. Further information about some of these products can be obtained from Census View, by Country Publishers, found on the Internet at:

http://www.galstar.com/

A catalog of microfilmed census schedules can also be found at:

http://www.genealogy.org/

BIRTH RECORD INDICES

Of course, what genealogist wouldn't want copies of all of their relatives' birth records? A birth record contains information such as the mother's full maiden name, the father's full name, the name of the baby, the date of the birth, and the name of the county where the birth took place. Many birth records also include other information, such as the birthplaces of the baby's parents, the addresses of the parents, the number of children that the parents have, the race of the parents, and the parents' occupations.

A birth record index can save a genealogist research time by revealing that a particular birth record containing an ancestor's name exists. Looking at the information in the birth index, which contains much of the information available on the original birth record, can help one to determine if the information is for a specific ancestor or just someone with the same name. It can also supplement what is already known about a family, allowing the genealogist to fill in missing information. Each birth record index usually provides the child's name, birthdate, and birth location. With this information, one can contact the county and get a copy of the original birth record or find a newspaper announcement, which may provide more details about the family.

Many of the Family Archive CD-ROM databases contain birthdates, but one of its CD-ROMs provides a birthdate index of all of them:

Birth Record Index: United States/Europe (CD 17)

Source: This CD combines birth information spanning nearly 1,000 years from four types of sources:

- Linked pedigrees from the World Family Tree and other databases
- Mortality Records from 1850-1880 for approximately 380,000 individuals (from CD 164)
- Social Security Death Records for millions of individuals born between 1800 and 1850 (from CD 110)
- Salt Lake City Cemetery Records of approximately 100,000 individuals born throughout the U.S., Europe, and elsewhere (from CD 168).

Date Range: 900-1880

MARRIAGE RECORD INDICES

Marriage records are also very valuable to genealogists. A marriage record can provide the bride's and groom's full names, the date of the marriage, and the name of the county where the marriage took place. Many marriage records also include other information, such as the names and birthplaces of the bride's and groom's parents, the addresses of the bride and groom, information about previous marriages, and the names of the witnesses to the marriage.

A marriage record index can reveal that a particular marriage record with an ancestor's name exists, thereby saving a genealogist much time and effort. The information in the marriage index can be reviewed to decide if the information is for a specific ancestor or just someone with the same name. It can also be used to add what is already known about a family. Each marriage index usually gives the county of marriage, marriage date, and the spouses' names. With this information, one can contact the county and get a copy of the original marriage record or find a newspaper announcement, which may offer more facts about the bride, groom, and their families.

Marriage Index: Alabama, Georgia, South Carolina (CD 3)

Source: CD contains indices of marriage records for selected years from 114 counties in Alabama (32) and Georgia (82). County records were not used for South Carolina; instead, other sources containing marriage records were compiled.

Date Range: 1641-1944

Marriage Index: Arizona, California, Idaho, Nevada (CD 225)

Source: CD contains indices of marriage records from selected counties in Arizona, California, Idaho, and Nevada.

Date Range: 1850-1951

Marriage Index: Arkansas (CD 6)
Source: CD contains indices of marriage records for selected years from 19 counties in the state of Arkansas.
Date Range: 1779-1992

Marriage Index: Arkansas, Missouri, Mississippi, Texas (CD 5)
Source: CD contains indices of marriage records for selected years from 161 counties in four states: Arkansas (11), Mississippi (83), Missouri (24), and Texas (82).
Date Range: 1766-1981

Marriage Index: Illinois, Indiana (CD 228)
Source: CD contains indices of marriage records from Illinois and Indiana.
Date Range: 1790-1850

Marriage Index: Illinois, Indiana, Kentucky, Ohio, Tennessee (CD 2)
Source: CD contains indices of marriage records for selected years from 222 selected counties in five states: Illinois (19), Indiana (52), Kentucky (67), Ohio (39), and Tennessee (45).
Date Range: 1720-1926

Marriage Index: Georgia (CD 226)
Source: CD contains indices of marriage records from 76 Georgia counties. The earliest records are for Effingham (1754), though most counties have records beginning in the 1800s. Counties not included are: Appling, Baker, Bryan, Burke, Clinch, Cobb, Dade, Gordon, Gwinnett, Heard, Lee, Lowndes, Macon, McIntosh, Twiggs, Walker, and Ware.
Date Range: 1754-1850

Marriage Index: Kentucky, North Carolina, Tennessee, Virginia, West Virginia (CD 229)
Source: CD contains indices of marriage records from 333 counties in five states. Some Tennessee marriage records are from newspaper collections. Some Virginia records are from ecclesiastical marriage collections. Some West Virginia records date from prior to its statehood.
Date Range: 1728-1850

Marriage Index: Louisiana (CD 1)
Source: CD contains indices of marriage records from 58 selected parishes (counties) in Louisiana. Records begin as early as 1718 in St. Helen's Parish. There are no records for any parishes for the years 1719-1727 and 1729-1733. After 1734, there is a general increase in records throughout the state, and the collection continues into

the mid-1900s. Most of these records were compiled from courthouse marriage records. For pre-1850 marriages, it is better to use Family Archive 227 because it is more comprehensive for that time period. Family Archive 227 does include everything that is available on Family Archive 1.

Date Range: 1718-1925

Marriage Index: Maryland (CD 224)

Source: CD contains an alphabetical listing of individuals who were married in Maryland between 1655 and 1850. Calvert County is not included since the courthouse burned in 1882 and most records were destroyed. In addition Garrett, Howard, and Wicomico Counties are not included since they were formed after 1850.

Date Range: 1655-1850

Marriage Index: Maryland, North Carolina, Virginia (CD 4)

Source: CD contains indices of marriage records for selected years from 180 counties in three states: Maryland (23), North Carolina (98), and Virginia (59). There is also one collection from the Maryland Historical Society (for Maryland), and from W.M.C. (for North Carolina).

Date Range: 1624-1915

Marriage Index: Selected Areas of New York (CD 401)

Source: CD contains marriage information from selected areas of New York and some of the earliest known church and government marriage information, from 1639, and continues through the 18th and 19th centuries.

Date Range: 1639-1916

Marriage Index: Ohio (CD 400)

Source: CD contains indices of selected marriage records from 85 counties in the state of Ohio. Fulton and Monroe Counties are not included, as records from these counties were destroyed by fires.

Date Range: 1789-1850

Marriage Index: Selected Counties of Arkansas, California, Iowa, Louisiana, Minnesota, Missouri, Oregon, Texas (CD 227)

Source: CD contains indices of selected marriage records from 227 counties in eight western states.

Date Range: 1728-1850

Further information about these CDs can be found at:
http://www.familytreemaker.com/facds.html

Marriage Indices can also be found posted on the Internet and other bulletin boards. For example, the Autauga County, Alabama marriage index for 1829-1898 can be found at:

http://www.tntech.edu/~beg/autauga/

There are searchable marriage indices found at:
http://www.ancestry.com/marriage

This site contains the following searchable databases:

- American Marriage Records prior to 1699
- Early Connecticut Marriages prior to 1800
- Early Massachusetts Marriages prior to 1800
- Early Virginia Marriages prior to 1824
- New York Marriages prior to 1784
- Pennsylvania Marriages prior to 1790

Marriages in the United Kingdom, Australia and New Zealand can be found at:
ftp://FTP.CAC.PSU.EDU/pub/genealogy/text/data

in a series of files beginning with "ukwit."

Marriage records can also be found in the New York Valley Quarterlies, Territorial Vital Records, combination databases for Australia, and ethnic records listed later in this chapter.

REAL PROPERTY RECORDS

Real property or land records in the Family Archives collection are from the General Land Office, Bureau of Land Management (BLM) and Interior, U.S. Department of the Interior in Springfield, Virginia. They include patents (deeds), homesteads, cash sales, miscellaneous warrants (purchases), private land claims, swamp lists, state selections, and railroad lists. Most titles were transferred through patents (deeds) from the federal government. Records of these patents are contained in huge tracts. They tell who obtained what land from the federal government and when.

Records on these CDs include:

- Patentee's name and Soundex Code
- State
- Accession number (directly relates a document image to the original hard copy document)
- Document number (used to order a copy of the original record from the BLM)
- Date the deed was signed
- Land office that handled the transaction

- Aliquot part reference
- Section number, block, township, range, and meridian/survey area
- Number of acres
- Act/treaty authorizing sale

Land Records: Alabama, Arkansas, Florida, Louisiana, Michigan, Minnesota, Ohio, Wisconsin (CD 255)

Date Range: 1790-1907

Land Records: Arkansas, Florida, Louisiana (CD 253)

Date Range: 1812-1907

Land Records: Michigan (CD 254)

Date Range: 1807-1908

Further information about these databases can be found at:
http://www.familytreemaker.com/facds.html

Land records can also be found on the Internet and other bulletin boards. For example, an index for land records in Autauga County, Alabama (1818-1878) can be found on the Internet at:
http://www.tntech.edu/~beg/autauga/

Refer to Chapter Thirty-one—Public Records for additional real property records available.

MILITARY RECORDS

Family folklore is filled with stories about relatives who were war heroes or who fought in famous battles. It is now possible to find military records on CD-ROM databases, as well as on the Internet and other bulletin boards in some cases. The following databases can be obtained on CD-ROM:

Revolutionary War Military Records: U.S. Soldiers (CD 146)

Source: Military service records of approximately 21,000 Revolutionary War Volunteers from 22 states and territories of the United States; the records are complete graphic reproductions of the actual records found on microfilm.

Date Range: 1784-1811

Roll of Honor: Civil War Union Soldiers (CD 351)

Source: CD contains images of the pages of all 27 volumes of the Roll of Honor as well as The Unpublished Roll of Honor. Originally published by Genealogical Publishing Company, these books reference the names of approximately 236,000 Union soldiers who were buried in over 300 national cemeteries, garrison cemeteries, soldiers' lots, and private cemeteries. The Roll of Honor is the only official memorial to the Union dead ever published, and in spite of its omissions and discrepancies, it remains the most comprehensive source of information on Civil War fatalities. For convenience and easy searching, an alphabetical name index of all 27 volumes and The Unpublished Roll of Honor is included on the CD.

Veterans' Schedules: U.S. Selected States (CD 131)

Source: CD contains an index of war veterans and veterans' widows who were enumerated on the special veterans' schedule of the 1890 United States census. Although the 1890 veterans' schedule was meant only to record information about Union soldiers and their widows, it also lists information about some Confederate soldiers, as well as soldiers who served in other wars, such as the War of 1812 and the Mexican-American War. States represented include Alabama, District of Columbia Illinois, Kentucky, Louisiana, Maine, Maryland, Michigan, Mississippi, Montana, Nevada, Nebraska, New Hampshire, New Jersey, New Mexico, North Carolina, North Dakota, Oklahoma, Oregon, Rhode Island, South Carolina, South Dakota, Tennessee, Texas, Utah, Vermont, Virginia, Washington, West Virginia, Wisconsin, and Wyoming. In addition, there are a few records from the states of California, Connecticut, Delaware, Florida, Georgia, Idaho, Indiana, Kansas, Massachusetts, New York, Ohio, and Pennsylvania.

Additional information about these databases can be found at:
http://www.familytreemaker.com/facds.html

Examples of military records available on the Internet include: The American Civil War—Rosters of Combatants & Regimental Histories:
http://funnelweb.utcc.utk.edu/~hoemann/warweb.html#rosters

This site includes rosters of the following:
- The U.S. Civil War Generals (from Kerry Webb; Union & Confederate)
- Civil War Units File: Unit Designations by States (Union & Confederate: version 3.8)
  - USA National & States A-I
  - USA States K-N
  - USA States O-W
  - CSA National & States A-M
  - CSA States N-V
- 43rd Georgia Volunteer Infantry, CSA
- 134th New York Volunteer Infantry
- 4th U.S. Infantry, Company C
- 32nd Indiana Volunteer Infantry
- 15th Mississippi Infantry Regiment, CSA
- 15th Iowa Infantry
- 1st Alabama Cavalry (USA) (includes reenactors' page)
- 10th West Virginia Volunteers, Company D

- 14th Virginia Cavalry, Company C
- Rosters of enrolled from Natchez and Adams County, Mississippi
- Belflowers in the Civil War (traces members of the Belfower family in various units)
- 23rd Alabama Volunteer Infantry Regiment
- 104th Pennsylvania Volunteer Infantry
- 10th Iowa Infantry
- Wisconsin 26th Infantry Volunteers
- 7th West Virginia Infantry Home Page
- 7th West Virginia Cavalry
- Patapsco Guard
- 1st Ohio Light Artillery, Battery L
- 8th Tennessee Cavalry, CSA
- 10th Regiment, Georgia Volunteer Infantry
- 2nd Ohio Volunteer Infantry
- 26th Mississippi Infantry, CSA
- New York 16th Regiment Infantry
- 2nd Regiment Veteran Cavalry—"Empire Light Cavalry"
- 16th Virginia Cavalry
- 29th Virginia Infantry, CSA
- Lawton-Gordon-Evans Georgia Brigade (CSA)
- 14th Kentucky Infantry
- 98th Regiment, Ohio Volunteer Infantry
- 15th West Virginia Volunteer Infantry (courtesy of Joy Gilchrist)
- The Electric Cemetery (contains Civil War section with pension record information)
- Virginia and Pennsylvania Units (searchable)
- 51st Virginia Infantry (via M.J. Loyd)
- The Iron Brigade of the West (via Carroll College)
- 20th Tennessee Cavalry, CSA
- Blount County, Alabama Genealogy Home Page (contains rosters and modern histories of Confederate Regiments)
- Alabama Regiments in the Army of the United States
- Overall Organization of Armies (Union and Confederate)
- Ideal Organization of Confederate Army c1863
- 22nd Kentucky Volunteer Infantry (via Becky Falin)
- 40th Kentucky Volunteer Mounted Infantry (via Becky Falin)
- 19th Alabama Regiment, Company H
- Pennsylvania Regiments

There is a full-text listing of Medal of Honor Citations now available on the Internet at:

http://www.army.mil/cmh-pg/moh1.htm

This includes the following sections:

- Civil War
- Indian Campaigns
- Interim 1866-1870
- 1871 Korean Campaign
- War with Spain
- Philippine Insurrection
- China Relief Expedition (Boxer Rebellion)
- Interim 1901-1911
- Action Against Outlaws—Philippines 1911
- Mexican Campaign (Veracruz)
- Haiti 1915
- Interim 1915-16
- Dominican Campaign
- World War I
- Haiti Campaign 1919-1920
- Second Nicaraguan Campaign
- Interim 1920-1940
- World War II Black Medal of Honor Recipients
- World War II (A-L)
- World War II (M-Z)
- Korean War
- Vietnam
- Somalia
- Special Legislation

An index of British, German, Loyalist officers of the American Revolution can be found on the Net at:

ftp://ftp.cac.psu.edu/pub/genealogy/text/data/.britmil.zip

Civil War Soldiers and Sailors System (CWSS) is a searchable database that is currently under development and contains names of Union and Confederate soldiers and sailors, plus the regiments that they served in. This database can be found at:

http://www.itd.nps.gov/cwss/

The French and Indian War site is dedicated to the French soldiers who went to Canada from 1755-1763 to fight in the French and Indian War:

http://web.syr.edu/~laroux/

The Korean War KIA/MIA Database can be found at:

http://www.onramp.net/~hbarker/casual.htm

The Library of Congress also offers a Vietnam Era Prisoner of War, Missing In Action Database. For further information about this database, you can visit the Internet site at:

http://lcweb2.loc.gov/pow/powhome.html

COMBINED RECORDS

Genealogical collections sometimes include combinations of records for a geographic area, an ethnic group, or some other subject area. Sources of genealogical records for ethnic groups can be found later in this chapter. An example of a geographic grouping includes:

State Index: Upstate New York (CD 160)

Source: This index of New York State records consists of references to city directories, tax lists, church records, military rosters, Bible records, and much more. These documents were all published in four upstate New York quarterlies dating from the late 1600s to the early 1900s: *The Capital, The Columbia, The Mohawk,* and *The Saratoga.* The index references approximately 300,000 individuals from the Hudson River Valley counties of Albany, Columbia, Fulton, Montgomery, Rensselaer, Saratoga, and Schenectady. The state records index provides the quarterly name, chapter title, volume number, and page on which the record appears so that one can order the quarterly and locate the record. The type of information provided by the quarterly will vary because these records come from many sources.

Date Range: 1685-1910

Further information about this database can be found at:

http://www.familytreemaker.com/facds.html

Other collections available on CD-ROM include those from Family Forest (products of Millisecond Publishing), which include:

- The Delaware Family Forest CD-ROM
- The Pittsburgh Family Forest CD-ROM
- Founders & Patriots Family Forest
- The Presidential Family Forest

Further information about these collections can be found at:

http://www.FamilyForest.com/product.html

ETHNIC RECORDS

There are genealogical collections based on ethnic groupings as well. Some are commercial databases, while others are compilations by groups of genealogists or individuals who have placed their data on bulletin boards for use by others. The following are examples of the ethnic genealogical records and files available, but this list is by no means comprehensive. Additional examples could be found for almost any ethnic group that could be named.

African and African-American Records

African-American Genealogy How-To from Family Tree Maker:
http://www.familytreemaker.com/00000360.html
The African American Genealogy mailing list:
http://ftp.cac.psu.edu/~saw/aagene-faq.html
African-American Genealogical Societies Around the U.S.A.:
http://www.everton.com/oe2-7/afamlist.htm
Afrigeneas:
http://www.msstate.edu/Archives/History/afrigen/index.html
Civil War Soldiers and Sailors System (CWSS) for U.S. Colored Troops:
http://www.itd.nps.gov/cwss/usct.html
Cyndi's List of Genealogy Sites on the Internet—African-American:
http://www.oz.net/~cyndihow/african.htm

Australian and New Zealand Records

The Australasian Genealogy Web Page:
http://www.vicnet.net.au/~AGWeb/agweb.htm
Convicts Transported to Australia:
http://www.ozemail.com.au/~jnelson/convict.html
Cyndi's List of Genealogy Sites on the Internet—Australia & New Zealand:
http://www.oz.net/~cyndihow/austnz.htm
Genealogy New Zealand:
http://www.voyager.co.nz/~ianclap/gennz.htm

The Royal Melbourne Institute of Technology (RMIT) also offers some combined databases for Australian genealogy. They include:

The New South Wales Pioneers Index 1788-1918

Source: New South Wales Registry of Birth, Deaths, and Marriages; 2 discs, each containing 2 million records: The Pioneers Series and The Federation Series. The New South Wales Pioneers Index includes index information on all birth, death, and marriage records between 1788 and 1918 held by the Registry of Births, Deaths and Marriages in New South Wales, Australia.

Date Range: The Pioneers Series 1788-1888; The Federation Series 1889-1918

The Tasmanian Pioneers Index 1803-1899

Source: From the Archives Office of Tasmania, it contains some 425,700 records on all birth, death, and marriage records held by the General Registry Office in Tasmania, Australia, and covers early church records for the years prior to 1838.

Date Range: 1803-1899

Western Australia Pioneers Index 1841-1905

Source: From the Registrar General's Office in Western Australia, it contains some 210,000 records on all birth, death, and marriage records held by the Registrar General's Office in Western Australia.

Date Range: 1841-1905

The Victorian Pioneers Index 1837-1888

Source: From the Archives Office of Tasmania, it contains some 1.74 million records on all birth, death, and marriage records held by the Registry of Births, Deaths and Marriages in Victoria, Australia, and covers early church records for the years before 1853 and civil registration records from 1853 to 1888.

Date Range: 1837-1888

For further information about the previous four Australian databases, please contact:

Royal Melbourne Institute of Technology (RMIT)
INFORMIT, RMIT Libraries
G.P.O. Box 2476V
Melbourne, VIC 3001, Australia
03 026 5667
03 663 3047 Fax

Belgian Records
Genealogy in Belgium:
> **http://win-www.uia.ac.be/u/pavp/genbel.html**

British/UK, English, Irish, and Welsh Records
The British Heraldic Archive:
> **http://www.kwtelecom.com/heraldry/**

Directory of Royal Genealogical Data:
> **http://www.dcs.hull.ac.uk/public/genealogy/royal/**

The Irish Family History Foundation home page:
> **http://www.mayo-ireland.ie/roots.htm**

The National Archives of Ireland:
> **http://www.kst.dit.ie/nat-arch/**

Royal and Nobel Genealogical Data on the Web:
> **http://www.dcs.hull.ac.uk/public/genealogy/GEDCOM.html**

The Scottish Genealogy Society home page:
> **http://pro1.taynet.co.uk/users/scotgensoc/**

UK+Ireland Genealogy Index:
> **http://midas.ac.uk/genuki/mindex.html**

Canadian Records

Canadian Genealogy and History Links:
>**http://www.islandnet.com/~jveinot/cghl/cghl.html**

Canadian Genealogy:
>**http://www.FreeNet.Calgary.ab.ca/science/genealogy/cdngene.html**

Canadian Genealogy Resources:
>**http://www.iosphere.net/~jholwell/cangene/gene.html**

Genealogy Resources on the Internet—Canada:
>**http://wwww-personal.umich.edu/~cgaunt/canada.html**

French Record

French-speaking Genealogy Page:
>**http://www.cam.org/~beaur/gen/welcome.html**

French Canadian/Cajun Records

The Acadian Genealogy Home Page:
>**http://tdg.uoguelph.ca/~ycyr/genealogy/**

Acadian Cultural Society Page de la Maison:
>**http://www.angelfire.com/ma/1755/index.html**

French-speaking Genealogy Page:
>**http://www.cam.org/~beaur/gen/welcome.html**

German Records

The German Genealogy Home Page:
>**http://www.genealogy.com/gene/index.html**

German Genealogy Sites and Organizations:
>**http://www.execpc.com/~kap/gene-de.html**

Internet Sources for German Genealogy:
>**http://www.bawue.de/~hanacek/info/edatbase.htm**

Indian Records

British Ancestors in India:
>**http://www.ozemail.com/au/~clday/**

Italian Records

The Italian Genealogy Home Page:
>**http://www.italgen.com**

The Arduini & Pizzo—An Italian Genealogy site:
> **http://home page.interaccess.com/~arduinif/**

Joe's Italian Genealogy Page:
> **http://www.phoenix.net/~joe/**

Jewish Records

JewishGen—Your Guide to Jewish Genealogical Research:
> **http://www.jewishgen.org/**

Jewish Resources:
> **http://pmgmac.micro.umn.edu/Jewish.html**

Latin American/Hispanic Records

Genealogy in Costa Rica:
> **http://www.nortronica.com/genealogy**

Cuban Genealogical Resources:
> **http://ourworld.compuserve.com/homepages/ee**

Hispanic Genealogy:
> **http://www.nortronica.com/genealogy**

Hispanic Genealogy Resources:
> **http://www.linkdirect.com/hispsoc/hispanic_links.htm**

Hispanic Genealogy Crossroads:
> **http://users.aol.com/mrosado007/cruces.htm**

Native American Records

NativeWeb—Tracing Your Roots:
> **http://web.maxwell.syr.edu/nativeweb/roots.htm**

Scandinavian, Norwegian, and Swedish Records

Scandinavian Genealogy Pages:
> **http://www.algonet.se/~floyd/scandgen/**

Swedish Genealogy:
> **http://sd.datatorget.educ.goteborg.se/**

Swiss Records

The Swiss Genealogy Page:
> **http://www.webcom.com/schori/swis.html**

The Swiss Surname List:
> **http://www.webcom.com/schori/swisname.stml**

Genealogy in French-speaking Switzerland:
> **http://www.unige.ch/biblio/ses/jla/gen/swiss-e.html**

Cyndi's List of Genealogy Sites on the Internet—Switzerland:
> **http://www.oz.net/~cyndihow/swiss.htm**

Ukrainian Records

Ukrainian Genealogical and Heritage Page:
> **http://ic.net/~ggressa/ukr.html**

Additional Ethnic Genealogical Resources

Many additional files can be found to assist with various types of genealogical research, and these resources often focus on particular geographic, religious, or racial groupings. Looking through CompuServe's Roots Forum library, I found many additional files concerning Jewish, Australian Jewish, Polish-Lithuanian, Puerto Rican, and Hispanic genealogy. Searching other genealogical bulletin boards would produce similar results. These files represent what has been uploaded to the online libraries, but this is only a small portion of the information that is actually passed on through online discussions taking place on the genealogical bulletin boards.

There are Internet newsgroups available for nearly any ethnic group as well. An index of Genealogy Listservers, Newsgroups and Special Home Pages can be found at:
> **http: //www.eskimo.com/~chance/**

Groups of ethnic and religious genealogical sites can also be found indexed on many Internet sites, such as:

Ethnic/Religious Genealogy Organizations:
> **http://ldsworld.com/links/fh-egs.html**

and

Yahoo! Genealogy Regional and Ethnic Resources:
> **http://www.yahoo.com/Arts/Humanities/History/**
> **Genealogy/Regional_and_Ethnic_Resources/**

Death Records

Genealogists can gain a great deal of information from death records. A death certificate not only details information about the death, but also provides dates of birth, and next of kin. Of course, genealogists recognize that the information is only as good as the knowledge of the person providing it, and since the decedent can't be consulted, errors are not uncommon. These mistakes can also be compounded by the same types of error found on other public records, such as those introduced when the records are transcribed from handwritten form to databases. It is the genealogist's challenge not only to locate valuable death records, but to identify errors in them and determine what the truth is.

Since death records are useful in so many types of research, I have dedicated a chapter entirely to them. Please refer to Chapter Twenty-eight for more information.

Genealogical Collections

The Library of Congress, America's national library, has one of the world's premiere collections of U.S. and foreign genealogical and local historical publications. The Library's genealogy collection began as early as 1815 when the government purchased Thomas Jefferson's library. Through generations of international giving, these family history collections today contain more than 40,000 compiled family histories and over 100,000 U.S. local histories. The Library also collects local histories from around the world. Researchers doing foreign research will find strong collections for western Europe, especially the British Isles and Germany. For further information, you can visit the library's Internet site at:

http: //www.loc.gov

Among other holdings, the U.S. National Archives maintains the original census records. For information about the genealogical holdings at the U.S. National Archives, you can find the National Archives Information Server at:

http: //gopher.nara.gov:70/1/

Summary

Not all information found on genealogical databases is necessarily accurate, so genealogists must do more than access databases. They must also research the information that they find, locate corroborative documentation to prove or disprove relationships and histories, weigh that evidence against their other data, and resolve any discrepancies and conflicts that are found. As new technology eases the process of gathering genealogical information, genealogists will be able to dedicate more time to evaluating and verifying the information they have amassed.

It should be noted that genealogical research is not limited to family ties from many generations past. Since most genealogists are acutely interested in tracing and documenting their own family histories, the contemporary records of family members are often quite complete. As this data is being shared at increasing velocity, it may even be useful in locating people or providing fodder for investigative journalists. Individuals trying to hide from creditors or guarding their privacy may not realize that their aunt, grandfather, or another relative is broadcasting information about them across genealogical networks around the world. The battle between the thirst for information and the right to privacy may take some interesting turns in the genealogical arena.

For additional information about genealogical records and research, many genealogical research guides are available, and some of them are listed in Section IV "Where Can I Find More Information?—Books." Other types of research guides, such as those for public records research can assist genealogists as well. Chapter Fifteen—Biographies offers additional avenues of genealogical research.

A partial list of genealogical periodicals also appears in Section IV "Where Can I Find More Information?—Periodicals." Many additional publications are available online on genealogical bulletin boards, which are indexed at some of the sites provided in this chapter.

There are hundreds of genealogical research organizations all over the world, filled with people who are glad to help others with their research, as well as to share their own research resources and findings. A list of genealogical research associations also can be found in Section IV "Where Can I Find More Information?—Organizations." Many of these fellow genealogists can also be found online on any of dozens of genealogical bulletin boards now available.

A genealogical television series, "Ancestors," began airing on PBS on January 28, 1997. The Internet site for this program provides an overview of each episode, the broadcast schedule, genealogical links, and other information about the program and genealogical research. This site can be found at:

http: //kbyuwww.byu.edu/ancestor.htm

Although no one could hope to provide everything you ever wanted to know about genealogical research in one chapter, or even one book, the resources listed in this chapter can take you well on your way to finding your own roots, or give you the tools that can lead you to them.

For additional information on genealogical research, you can't do better than to spend some time in the:

Family History Library of the Church of Jesus Christ of Latter-day Saints
35 North West Temple Street
Salt Lake City, UT 84150
(801) 240-2331
CompuServe: 75300,3123
GEnie Research Questions: F.H.Library
GEnie FamilySearch Questions: FamilySearch
America Online: FamHistLib
Prodigy: FHLS99B

In addition to the online and CD-ROM genealogical resources that are highlighted in this chapter, there are also microfilm collections available for genealogists, through the National Archives and Records Administration, which can be found on the Internet at:

http://www.nara.gov/nara/menus/genealog.html

Their collections include census records, military records, and immigration records. As microfilm has limited search capabilities, and requires hardware that is not common to most PC users, there are companies (such as ArchivalCD, at: **http://www.archivalcd.com/**; and GenRef, Inc. at: **http://www.genref.com/publish. html**) which can convert microfilm or personal record collections onto searchable CD databases for commercial or personal use. With these advancements, as well as the movement of genealogy onto the Internet and other bulletin board systems, genealogy has become a very exciting, high-tech hobby.

Political Records

I f you need to locate or research a political figure, there are dozens of databases to help you. Book directories can identify books written about politicians, past and present. Public records databases can supply information on their backgrounds, and genealogical records can provide details of their lineage and relations. Online political bulletin boards, such as the White House RoundTable (available online through GEnie), can also turn up valuable insights and leads to information about politicians, candidates, and events.

Political News

Since politicians live much of their lives in the public view, news databases can be rich resources for political research. Transcripts of the "MacNeil/Lehrer News Hour" (available online through NEXIS), "CNN News" Transcripts (available online through DataTimes and NEXIS), and other political radio and television programs may include discussions in which a politician who interests you has taken part or has been a topic of debate.

Political publications can also provide valuable insight. The online selections include such publications as:

- *The American Spectator* (available online through NEXIS)
- *BNA Washington Insider* (available online through HRIN, LEXIS, NEXIS, and WESTLAW)
- *California Journal* (available online through NEXIS and State Net)
- *Campaigns & Elections* (available online through NEXIS)
- *Common Cause* (available online through NEXIS)
- *The Cook Political Report* (available online through NEXIS)
- *CQ Government* magazine (available online through CQ Washington Alert Service)
- *CQ Weekly Report* (available online through CQ Washington Alert Service)
- *Department of State Dispatch* (available online through LEXIS and NEXIS)
- *The Evans & Novak Political Report* (available online through NewsNet)
- *Federal News Service Washington Transcripts*
- *National Journal* (available online through Legi-Slate, LEXIS, and NEXIS)
- *National Journal's Congress Daily* (available online through NEXIS)
- *National Minority Politics* (available online through NewsNet)
- *Roll Call* (available online through NEXIS)
- *Washingtonian* (available online through NEXIS)

- *Washington Post* (available online through CompuServe and CompuServe Knowledge Index, DataTimes, Dow Jones News/Retrieval, FT Profile, Knight-Ridder, Legi-Slate, and NEXIS)

- *Washington Times* (available online through DataTimes, Knight-Ridder, and NEXIS)

CD-ROM databases also provide some of this same information. One such database is Federal News on CD-ROM (available from National Information Services Corporation (NISC)). This disc includes the Washington Transcripts, Washington Daybook, and Kremlin Transcripts.

A search of regional and local publications can also be helpful. For example, if you were researching the Kennedys, you should search the *Boston Globe* in particular. It is available online through CompuServe, DataTimes, Knight-Ridder, and NEXIS.

Several newswire services have a political focus, and can be searched online. They include:

- The Associated Press-Campaign News (available online through NEXIS)

- Federal News Service (available online through Knight-Ridder and NEXIS)

- Federal Document Clearing House—Congressional Press Releases (available online through NEXIS)

- The Hotline (available online through American Political Network, Inc., NewsNet, NEXIS, and WESTLAW)

- Reuter Transcript Report (available online through CQ Washington Alert Service, NEXIS and Reuters Ltd.)

- States News Service (available online through NEXIS)

- State Capitols Report (available online through NEXIS)

- U.S Newswire (available online through DataTimes, LEXIS, NewsNet, and NEXIS)

Political Directories

A number of directories can be used to locate politicians and political staff members. Directories, such as: *The Capitol Source, The Congressional Staff Directory* (both available on NEXIS), *Staff Directories on CD-ROM,* and *The Congressional Staff Directory on Disk* (both available on CD-ROM from Staff Directories Ltd.) provide a "Who's Who" of Washington.

Other government directories can be found on the Internet at:
http://www.fedworld.gov/

Congressional Directories can also be found at:
http://www.fedworld.gov/legislat.htm

or at:
http://www.house.gov/Whoswho.html

The Library of Congress also provides access to a variety of Congressional directories at:

gopher://marvel.loc.gov/11/congress/directory

Links to Embassy staff directories and Congressional Foreign Affairs personnel can be found at:

http://www.embassy.org/

Congressional District/State Profile Reports contain profiles of each of the states and congressional districts, including listings of elected officials.

California Lobbyists/PACs Directory (available online through State Net) provides information on lobbyists, lobbyist employers, and political action committees (PACs) registered in the state of California.

Biographies

Who's Who in American Politics is included in the Bowker Biographical Directory database, which is available online through Knight-Ridder (File 236).

U.S. Presidents (available on CD-ROM from Quanta Press, Inc.) contains biographical and statistical information relating to the first 41 Presidents of the United States, from George Washington to George Bush. It also includes information about First Ladies and other interesting historical facts. The Presidents: It All Started With George (available on CD-ROM from National Geographic Society, Educational Services) also contains encyclopedic information on the Presidents, from George Washington to George Bush.

The Congressional Member Profile Report database (on LEXIS and NEXIS) supplies biographical information on members of the U.S. Congress. Each record includes name, party, elected office, terms served, birthdate, gender, religion, race, former occupation, education, and military service. CQ Member Profiles (available online through Congressional Quarterly Inc.) offers analytical biographies of all voting members of U.S. Congress. It provides personal data (birthdate, occupation, family, political career, military experience, and religious affiliation); descriptions of members' style at home and in Washington, with insight on their personality, influence, and priorities; state or district description and demographics; election and campaign finance history; party and presidential support ratings; committee assignments; key vote studies; and interest group ratings. Committee Membership Profile Report (available online through LEXIS and NEXIS) contains information on all U.S. Congressional committees and subcommittees. The Biographical Directory of the United States Congress 1774-1989 (available on CD-ROM from Staff Directories, Ltd.) presents biographical profiles of more than 11,000 men and women who served in the United States Congress from 1789 to 1989 and in the Continental Congress between 1774 and 1789.

Congressional biographies can also be found on the Internet at:

http://www.house.gov/MemberWWW.html

Biographies of presidents, congressional members, and state politicians can also be found on the Internet at:

http://www.vote-smart.org/

Staff members of the committees and subcommittees of the U.S. Congress are also found through the index at:

http://www.house.gov/CommitteeWWW.html

The Almanac of the Unelected (available online through LEXIS) contains information on the professional backgrounds, areas of expertise, and educational backgrounds of each staffer.

CQ INFO (available online through CQ Washington Alert Service) provides profiles of candidates running for federal office, lists of state governors, and the complete text of special reports and reference files on topics addressed by the U.S. Congress since the beginning of the 100th Congress. Political Profile (available online through Prodigy) provides biographies on political candidates in the U.S. AP Political Service (available online through DataTimes, LEXIS, and NEXIS) covers local, state, and national politics. One of the files included in this service contains biographies, including a biographical sketch, political history, and vital statistics. The Almanac of American Politics (available online through NEXIS and Legi-Slate) also provides descriptions and analyses of persons and events in American politics. This almanac can also be found on the Internet at:

http://politicsusa.com/PoliticsUSA/resources/almanac

The '88 Vote: Campaign for the White House (available on CD-ROM from ABC News InterActive) contains announcement and withdrawal statements of all 13 candidates, biographical information on each candidate, excerpts of key speeches from the Democratic and Republican conventions, and other information related to the 1988 presidential election.

Additional political speeches and addresses can be found on the Internet at:

gopher://wiretap.spies.com/11/Gov/US-Speech

Information on President Bush's nomination of Judge Clarence Thomas to the U.S. Supreme Court can be found on Nomine (available online through LEXIS and NEXIS). This database includes biographical information, news reports, and cases presided over and decisions by Judge Thomas during his tenure on the federal court, and as chairman of the Equal Opportunities Commission. The Clarence Thomas Hearings on CD-ROM is also available on CD-ROM from NewsBank/Readex.

Voting Records/Politics

The voting record of incumbent officeholders can be found in the Political Profiles database (available online through Prodigy), on the LEGI-SLATE database (available online through Legi-Slate), or on NAMNET: The Public Policy Electronic Network (available online through CompuServe).

Congressional Committee Vote Report (NEXIS) provides vote data for all full, joint, and select committees of Congress, and Congressional Committee Votes Archive (also from NEXIS) provides voting records of previous congresses. CQ Committee Action Votes & Rosters—Committees Database (available online through CQ Washington Alert Service) does the same.

Congressional Legislative Record (NEXIS) provides information on how members of Congress have voted recently. So does Congressional Tracking (available online through CompuServe). CQ Weekly Report (available online through CQ Washington

Alert Service) includes summaries of subcommittee work, investigations, hearings, and debates; reports of votes; and floor actions.

The Legi-Tech database covers voting records for members of the U.S. Congress and of the California, New York, and Washington state legislatures.

State Net 50-State Legislative Reporting (available online through State Net and WESTLAW) contains status information and summaries of bills currently before state legislatures and the U.S. Congress, along with name, address, telephone number, district, party affiliation, and committee memberships for all state legislators.

Telran (available online through Legi-Tech) is a legislative tracking service that contains histories of bills introduced during regular and special legislative sessions of the state legislatures in Arizona, Arkansas, California, Colorado, Florida, Illinois, Indiana, Louisiana, Michigan, Minnesota, New York, Ohio, Oklahoma, Tennessee, Texas, and the U.S. Congress. It also includes voting records.

State Net California Only (available online through State Net, from Information for Public Affairs, Inc.) is a legislative tracking service specializing in California politics. It includes state legislators' voting records. Legislation On A Disc: California (available on CD-ROM from Legi-Tech) also includes member voting records. A similar disc is available for New York.

There is also a national non-partisan, non-profit organization called Project Vote Smart which offers a database containing the voting records of presidents, members of congress, and state politicians. This database is accessible on the Internet at:

http://www.vote-smart.org/

Money

If you would like to know who has contributed to a candidate's campaign, how much money a politician has made for speaking engagements, or the financial history of a member of Congress, you can find this information from several online sources.

Congressional Member Financial Disclosures (available online through NEXIS) are annual reports filed by each member of Congress, detailing their financial histories.

Congressional Member Financial Report (available online through NEXIS) contains information on campaign contributions for each member and candidate from political action committees. Political Profiles (Prodigy) lists contributions received by political candidates, and contributions to political action committees. The Political Action Committee Report (available online through LEXIS and NEXIS) contains information on donations from political action committees to U.S. Congressional members. Federal Election Commission (FEC) Recent Releases (available on NEXIS) and Federal Election Commission Direct Access Program (available online through the U.S. Federal Election Commission) also include contributions of $500 or more to candidates for federal offices by supporters, including PACs and individual contributors.

The Federal Election Commission also provides a non-partisan federal candidate campaign money page on the Internet:

http://www.tray.com/FECInfo/

On this site, you can search by candidate name, by contributor name, or even by occupation, among other searches. Just for fun, I used the occupation search to look for contributions by actors and the result read like a Hollywood Who's Who. I might also have searched for Entertainer, Director, Producer, or other entertainment industry occupations to find out where the Hollywood elite are sending their contributions.

Seeing who a person contributes funds to can provide insight into political views and priorities. Seeing frequent contributions to certain types of candidates or political action committees, you might also infer that the contributor has a great deal of conviction and commitment toward certain causes. For example, what might you infer from the contributions made by Barbra Streisand?

STREISAND, BABRA
10/19/96 $500.00
BEVERLY HILLS, CA 90210
SINGER/ACTRESS -[Contribution]
FRIENDS OF MAX CLELAND FOR THE US SENATE
INC

STREISAND, BARBARA
10/23/96 $250.00
BEVERLY HILLS, CA 90210
ENTERTAINER -[Contribution]
FRIENDS OF TOM STRICKLAND INC

STREISAND, BARBARA
10/21/96 $250.00
BEVERLY HILLS, CA 90210
ACTRESS -[Contribution]
WALTER CAPPS FOR CONGRESS

STREISAND, BARBARA
1/9/96 $1,500.00
BEVERLY HILLS, CA 90210
ENTERTAINER -[Contribution]
HOLLYWOOD WOMEN'S POLITICAL COMMITTEE

STREISAND, BARBARA
10/22/96 $250.00
BEVERLY HILLS, CA 90210
ACTRESS/DIRECTOR -[Contribution]
CYNTHIA MCKINNEY FOR CONGRESS

STREISAND, BARBARA
2/28/96 $500.00
BEVERLY HILLS, CA 90210
ACTOR/PRODUCER/DIRECTOR -[Contribution]
SANDERS FOR CONGRESS

STREISAND, BARBARA
10/21/96 $250.00
BEVERLY HILLS, CA 90210
ENTERTAINER -[Contribution]
TOM ALLEN FOR CONGRESS COMMITTEE

STREISAND, BARBARA
10/22/96 $250.00

BEVERLY HILLS, CA 90210
ENTERTAINER -[Contribution]
SHERMAN FOR CONGRESS

STREISAND, BARBARA
8/6/96 $1,000.00
SANTA MONICA, CA 90401
ENTERTAINER -[Contribution]
BONIOR FOR CONGRESS

STREISAND, BARBARA
10/23/96 $250.00
BEVERLY HILLS, CA 90210
ENTERTAINER -[Contribution]
SAM GEJDENSON RE-ELECTION COMMITTEE

STREISAND, BARBARA
10/21/96 $250.00
BEVERLY HILLS, CA 90210
SINGER & ACTRESS -[Contribution]
LONGABAUGH FOR CONGRESS

STREISAND, BARBARA
10/21/96 $250.00

-[earmarked contribution]
DARLENE HOOLEY FOR CONGRESS

STREISAND, BARBRA
10/21/96 $250.00
LOS ANGELES, CA 90034
ENTERTAINER -[Contribution]
ELIZABETH FURSE FOR CONGRESS

STREISAND, BARBRA
6/18/96 $1,000.00
SANTA MONICA, CA 90401
SINGER/ACTRESS -[Contribution]
HARVEY GANTT FOR SENATE CAMPAIGN
COMMITTEE

STREISAND, BARBRA
9/6/96 $100.00
BEVERLY HILLS, CA 90210
-[contribution refunded to individual]
WELLSTONE FOR SENATE

STREISAND, BARBRA
8/29/96 $1,000.00
BEVERLY HILLS, CA 90210
ENTERTAINER -[Contribution]
WELLSTONE FOR SENATE

STREISAND, BARBRA
8/29/96 $1,000.00
BEVERLY HILLS, CA 90210
ENTERTAINER -[Contribution]
WELLSTONE FOR SENATE

STREISAND, BARBRA
4/12/95 $500.00
BEVERLY HILLS, CA 90210
ENTERTAINER -[Contribution]
WELLSTONE FOR SENATE

STREISAND, BARBRA
3/13/95 $1,500.00
BEVERLY HILLS, CA 90210
ENTERTAINER -[Contribution]
HOLLYWOOD WOMEN'S POLITICAL COMMITTEE

STREISAND, BARBRA
5/21/96 $1,000.00
BEVERLY HILLS, CA 90210
ENTERTAINER -[Contribution]
HOLLYWOOD WOMEN'S POLITICAL COMMITTEE

STREISAND, BARBRA
10/21/96 $250.00
BEVERLY HILLS, CA 90210
ENTERTAINER -[Contribution]
FRIENDS OF LANE EVANS COMMITTEE

STREISAND, BARBRA
9/26/95 $1,000.00
BEVERLY HILLS, CA 90210
ENTERTAINER -[Contribution]
FRIENDS OF SENATOR CARL LEVIN

STREISAND, BARBRA
7/23/96 $1,000.00
BEVERLY HILLS, CA 90210
ACTRESS/SINGER -[Contribution]
MCGOVERN COMMITTEE

STREISAND, BARBRA
4/11/96 $1,000.00
BEVERLY HILLS, CA 90210
ENTERTAINER -[Contribution]
FRIENDS OF SENATOR CARL LEVIN

STREISAND, BARBRA
6/21/96 $1,000.00
BEVERLY HILLS, CA 90210
ENTERTAINER -[Contribution]
CITIZENS FOR HARKIN

STREISAND, BARBRA
4/12/95 $500.00
BEVERLY HILLS, CA 90210
ENTERTAINER -[Contribution]
WELLSTONE FOR SENATE

STREISAND, BARBRA
2/27/96 $500.00
BEVERLY HILLS, CA 90210
ENTERTAINER -[Contribution]
BARRY GORDON FOR CONGRESS

STREISAND, BARBRA
4/13/95 $30,000.00
BEVERLY HILLS, CA 90210
ACTRESS/SINGER -[[Receipt--exempt from limits]]
DNC-NON-FEDERAL INDIVIDUAL

STREISAND, BARBRA
10/21/96 $250.00
BEVERLY HILLS, CA 90210
ENTERTAINER -[Contribution]
ARNESEN '96

STREISAND, BARBRA
10/25/96 $250.00
BEVERLY HILLS, CA 90210
ACTRESS -[Contribution]
TOM BRUGGERE FOR US SENATE

STREISAND, BARBRA
1/19/96 $1,000.00
BEVERLY HILLS, CA 90210
PRODUCER -[Contribution]
AMERICANS FOR FREEDOM OF CHOICE POLITI-
CAL ACTION COMMITTEE ("CHOICE PAC")

STREISAND, BARBRA
3/14/96 $1,000.00
BEVERLY HILLS, CA 90210
ENTERTAINER -[Contribution]
WYDEN FOR SENATE

STREISAND, BARBRA
2/13/96 $1,000.00
BEVERLY HILLS, CA 90210
DIRECTOR/ACTRESS -[Contribution]
KENNEDY FOR SENATE 2000

STREISAND, BARBRA
3/20/95 $2,500.00
BEVERLY HILLS, CA 90210
ENTERTAINER -[Contribution]
COLLEGE DEMOCRATS OF AMERICA INC

STREISAND, BARBRA
10/21/96 $250.00
BEVERLY HILLS, CA 90210

ENTERTAINER -[Contribution]
ADAM SMITH FOR CONGRESS

STREISAND, BARBRA
6/14/95 $1,000.00
BEVERLY HILLS, CA 90210
SINGER -[Contribution]
CLINTON/GORE '96 PRIMARY COMMITTEE INC

STREISAND, BARBRA
10/21/96 $250.00
BEVERLY HILLS, CA 90210
ENTERTAINER -[Contribution]
LYNN RIVERS FOR CONGRESS COMMITTEE 98

STREISAND, BARBRA
10/21/96 $250.00
BEVERLY HILLS, CA 90210
SINGER/ACTRESS -[Contribution]
FRIENDS OF FARR

STREISAND, BARBRA
5/30/96 $10,000.00
BEVERLY HILLS, CA 90210
-[[Receipt--exempt from limits]]
DNC NON-FEDERAL UNINCORPORATED ASSOCI-
ATION ACCOUNT

STREISAND, BARBRA
6/12/95 $1,000.00BEVERLY HILLS, CA 90210
ENTERTAINER -[Contribution]
FRIENDS OF BARBARA BOXER

STREISAND, BARBRA
4/13/95 $20,000.00
BEVERLY HILLS, CA 90210
ACTRESS/SINGER -[Contribution]
DNC SERVICES CORPORATION/DEMOCRATIC
NATIONAL COMMITTEE

STREISAND, BARBRA
10/1/96 $250.00
BEVERLY HILLS, CA 90210
THE J R 1992 TRUST -[Contribution]
FRIENDS OF MAURICE HINCHEY

STREISAND, BARBRA TRUSTEE
10/21/96 $250.00
BEVERLY HILLS, CA 90210
 -[Contribution]
CONNIE MCBURNEY FOR CONGRESS CAM-
PAIGN COMMITTEE

STREISSAND, BARBARA
9/20/95 $1,000.00
BEVERLY HILLS, CA 90210
SINGER/ACTRESS -[Contribution]
JOHN LEWIS FOR CONGRESS

The Legi-Tech database (available online through Legi-Tech) lists political contributions and lobbyist activities for members of the U.S. Congress and the state legislatures of California, New York and Washington. California State Campaign Finance Receipts and New York State Campaign Finance Receipts (both available online through NEXIS) contain the receipts of all candidates for state legislature. State Net California Only includes campaign contributions to state legislators. Legislation On A Disc: California and its counterpart for New York also cover political contributions.

Campaign contributions can also be found in publications, such as the *Political Finance* and *Lobby Reporter* (available online through NewsNet, NEXIS, and LEXIS).

The Congressional Honoraria Receipts Report (available online through LEXIS and NEXIS) contains information on fees paid to members of the U.S. Congress for speeches and personal appearances.

The Center for Public Integrity (CPI) has a set for four databases they call "The Buying of the President," which include assets held by various presidential candidates, organizations who paid honorarium for speeches given by presidential candidates, trips taken by presidential candidates while in office, and Arkansas state gubernatorial campaign finance records for President Clinton. These databases can be found on the Internet at:

http://essential.org/cpi/database.html

Events

Politicians do not hit the news only because of their actions. Sometimes their simple presence at a public event or private party may be considered newsworthy. This makes it relatively easy to identify their friends, relatives, business associates, and interests. The news databases can provide details of past events, but for upcoming events, there are several additional databases that you might want to try.

Reuter Washington Report (available online through NEXIS and Reuters Ltd.) provides coverage of events in Washington, DC, including press conferences, government hearings, speeches, demonstrations, the President's schedule, Congressional schedules, diplomatic events, and financial items. The calendar of daily activities in the U.S. Congress and the Office of the President can also be found in the BNA Presidential Calendar database (available online through Dialcom and WESTLAW) and in the Federal News Service Daybook (available online through NEXIS). Congressional Activities (available online through NewsNet) provides a calendar of forthcoming U.S. Congressional activities, with an emphasis on energy and environmental matters.

Congressional News (available online from CQ Washington Alert Service) provides a daily calendar of events on and off Capital Hill that influence legislation in the U.S. Congress.

CQ Committee and Floor Schedules provides schedules for the U.S. House of Representatives, Senate, joint committees, conference committees, and floor votes for the next day up to three months ahead. For each schedule, this database provides agenda, issue involved or bill number, chairperson, location and time, and names and affiliations of witnesses for each meeting or hearing. NAMNET: The Public Policy Electronic Network also includes Congress Schedule— containing a calendar of scheduled hearings, markups, and floor votes on industry issues. State Net California Only includes committee hearing schedules and floor agendas for the state legislature. Telran also covers committee assignments and floor and committee calendars.

Government Documents

If you would like to find out what bills a Congressional member has worked on, or glean some insight into a legislator's interests, some useful government documents can be located online. Congressional Information Service, Inc. (CIS, available online through Knight-Ridder) provides citations, with abstracts, to publications produced by the committees and subcommittees of the U.S. Congress.

Another database, Presidential Documents (available online through NEXIS and WESTLAW), contains the complete text of documents released by the Office of the President and published in the Federal Register.

Other government documents can be found on the Internet at:
http://www.fedworld.gov/

and an index of documents available through the Government Printing Office can be found through the Government Information Locator Service (GILS) at:
http://www.access.gpo.gov/su_docs/gils/gils.html

Over 10,000 government documents can also be found through the FedWorld File Transfer Protocol Search and Retrieve Service site at:
http://www.fedworld.gov/ftp.htm

We the People

Although this book is focused on locating information about individuals, it should at least be mentioned that many databases available online and on CD-ROM also compile information about groups of us. When information about an individual is not available, group records are sometimes used to extrapolate or make presumptions about individuals within the group.

For example, if you were trying to figure out whether a person was wealthy, and little information was available about the individual, census tract records might be used to determine the average wealth in the subject's neighborhood. It might then be reasonable to assume that the person should fit somewhere within the local range. This is far from a perfect method, but such inferences can be sufficient for certain purposes or as a preliminary screen to determine whether it was worth proceeding further.

Census Records

The United States Bureau of Census collects information on households and businesses throughout the United States, and has done so every 10 years since 1790. Data for individual households or persons remains confidential for 72 years under Title 44 of the U.S. Code. The older data is often used by genealogists in order to trace family lineage or gain information about neighbors or others living within a household as of a given point in time. Please refer to Chapter Thirty-four—Genealogical Records for more information on the older records.

More recent records are aggregated into groups and made available through many online and CD-ROM databases, including:

- Annual Demographic Update (available online through Catalyst) which contains 1990 data

- Catalyst (available online through Catalyst) which contains demographic data from the 1980 and 1990 U.S. national censuses, plus current-year estimates and 5-year projections

- CENDATA (available online through CompuServe, Knight-Ridder) which contains selected text and numeric data from Census Bureau economic and demographic reports, press releases, and new product announcements

- Census Information Service (available online through Dialcom) which contains the complete text of U.S. Census Bureau press releases based on reports presenting current statistics

- Census Reporting System (available online through HRIN, The Human Resource Information Network) which provides statistics from the 1980 Census

- Population Demographics (available online through Knight-Ridder)

- State Macroeconomic (available online through The WEFA Group)
- SUPERSITE (available online through CompuServe and DRI/McGraw-Hill)
- USA GeoGraph II—Spanish Edition (available on CD-ROM from MECC)
- USA GeoGraph II—The Multimedia Edition (available on CD-ROM from MECC)

(Note that the addresses for these and other database vendors mentioned in this chapter can be found in Appendix N.)

The main menu from the CENDATA database, on Knight-Ridder, appears as follows:

—CENDATA MAIN MENU

```
1   Census Bureau Products, Services, and Contacts
2   What's New in CENDATA
3   U.S. Statistics at a Glance (Including Economic Time Series Data)
4   Press Releases                     !———————————————————————————!
5   Census and You (Selected Articles  )! If you're a new or infrequent!
6   Product Information                ! user of the CENDATA menu!
7   CENDATA User Feedback              ! system, key HELP ,cr. to learn!
8   Profiles and Rankings              ! of the available short cuts in!
9   Agriculture Data                   ! using the system.  !
10  Business Data                      !===========================!
11  Construction and Housing Data      ! For a listing and a location!
12  Foreign Trade Data                 ! key of all Census Bureau !
13  Government Data                    ! reports contained in CENDATA!
14  International Data                  ! in whole or in part, key!
15  Manufacturing Data                 ! M1.3 <cr>!
16  Population Data                    !———————————————————————————!
17  Genealogical and Age Information
18  1990 Census Information
```

Selecting (16) Population Data brings the following choices:

16—POPULATION

```
1   Introduction to the Population Statistics Program
2    Population of the Counties: 1990 and 1980
3   Population Estimates and Projections
4   Household Estimates
5   Geographic Mobility
6   Households, Families, Marital Status, and Child Care
7   School Enrollment and Education Attainment
8   Labor Force, Income, Noncash Benefits, Pensions, and Poverty
9   Voting Patterns and Registration
10  Ethnic Data
11  Geographic Areas and Definitions
12  Other Population Topics
```

Selecting (3) Population Estimates and Projections from this menu provides:

16.3—POPULATION ESTIMATES AND PROJECTIONS

(See also menu 8.7, 1993 Metropolitan Areas, and menu 16.11.4, Geographic Areas and Definitions)

1 Estimates: Resident Pop. of States: July 1, 1990 to 1994
2 Estimates: National and State Estimates through 1993
3 Estimates: 1980-1990 Intercensal State Population Estimates
4 Estimates: Res. Pop. of States & Counties, April 1990 to July 1994
5 Estimates: Metropolitan Areas (MSA/CMSA) By Rank, 1992
6 Estimates: Metropolitan Areas (MSA/CMSA) By Rank, 1992 (Cont.)
7 Estimates: For Cities With Population Greater Than 100,000, 1992
8 Estimates: For Cities With Pop. Greater than 100,000, 1992 (Cont.)
9 Estimates: Resident Population of Puerto Rico Municipios: July 1, 1992
10 Projections: US (1993 to 2050)
11 Projections: States (1993 to 2020)

As you can see, the information is grouped and presented in many ways, but does not provide enough detail for anyone to know who lives in any given household, their race, age, educational level, employer, income, or any other specific details pertaining to an individual. Viewing information for a particular metropolitan area can be useful, however, in developing an understanding of the general populace of that area or neighborhood.

Several databases emphasize specific sections of the census data. For example, the following databases focus on population and housing information:

- Census Population Database (available online through HRIN, The Human Resource Information Network)

- American Housing Survey (available on CD-ROM from U.S. Bureau of the Census, Data User Services Division)

- AmericanProfile (available on CD-ROM from Strategic Mapping Inc.)

- ClusterPLUS (available on CD-ROM from Strategic Mapping Inc.)

- GraphicProfile (available on CD-ROM from Strategic Mapping Inc.)

- ONSITE (available online through STSC, Inc.) (1970 and 1980)

- ONSITE/PC (available on CD-ROM from Urban Decision Systems, Inc. (UDS))

- Population Statistics (available on CD-ROM from Slater Hall Information Products (SHIP))

- TargetScan (available on CD-ROM from Strategic Mapping Inc.)

- Population by Age, Sex, and Race (available online through GE Information Services (GEIS))

(Refer to Appendix N for these addresses.)

The county and city data collected by the Census Bureau are the focus of the following databases:

- County and City Compendium (available on CD-ROM from Slater Hall Information Products (SHIP))

- County and City Data Book, 1988 (available on CD-ROM from U.S. Bureau of the Census, Data User Services Division)

- County—City Plus (available on CD-ROM from Slater Hall Information Products (SHIP))

The Equal Employment Opportunity information collected by the census is the focus of these databases:

- Census of Population and Housing, 1990: Equal Employment Opportunity File (available online through HRIN, The Human Resource Information Network)

- EEO Data (available online through Catalyst)

(Refer to Appendix N for these addresses.)

Household Age/Income (available online through The WEFA Group) contains detailed time series of historical data on U.S. household income levels.

Senior Life (available online through Catalyst) contains data from the U.S. Census of Population and Housing, current-year estimates, and 5-year forecasts on persons aged 55 and older.

Colorado Economic and Demographic Information System (available online through Colorado State Data Center) contains demographic, financial, and employment time series data on Colorado local governments and all 50 states.

Census information is also available through the Internet. You can find their main index at:

http://www.census.gov/

Other Demographic and Statistical Databases

Many other demographic and statistical databases are available for the United States. These include:

- CACI Demographic Sourcebooks CD-ROM (available on CD-ROM from CACI Marketing Systems), which contains demographic data for residential ZIP Codes in the United States

- COMPASS (available on CD-ROM from Claritas), which contains items of demographic data and map boundary data for all census tracts, ZIP Code areas, counties, states, Metropolitan Statistical Areas (MSAs), Areas of Dominant Influence (ADIs), and Designated Market Areas (DMAs)

- ECONBASE: Time Series & Forecasts (available online through Knight-Ridder), which contains monthly, quarterly, and annual economic time series

- Fedstat/89-1 CD-ROM (available on CD-ROM from U.S. Statistics, Inc.), which contains U.S. demographic and economic statistics

- Income by Age (available on CD-ROM from Strategic Mapping Inc.), which contains demographic cross-tabulations of household income by age of head of household

- PCensus-USA (available on CD-ROM from TETRAD Computer Applications Limited), which contains demographic information on 3,141 counties in 50 states

- The Statistical Analysis and Retrieval System (available online through The Glimpse Corporation), which contains items of demographic and housing data for

U.S. geographical areas, including states, counties, minor civil divisions, census tracts, and ZIP Codes

(Refer to Appendix N for these addresses.)

One of the Internet sites used to index other federal statistical agencies can be found at: **http://www.census.gov/main/www/stat-fed.html**

A good many additional statistical and demographic databases have been created for marketing purposes. These are often compiled from many sources, including telephone directories, census information, surveys, and warrantee cards. Databases such as these can be used to determine the size of the target population before development of an ad campaign or to determine the best location for a new venture, such as a restaurant.

Census Projections

Projections of future census information are also available. They are included in some of the databases noted previously, as well as being the focus of the following databases:

- AmericanProfile Demographic Estimates and Projections (available on CD-ROM from Strategic Mapping Inc.), which contains current-year estimates and 5-year projections of U.S. population and households, including data on age, gender, and income
- Census Projections 1992-1998 (available online through HRIN, The Human Resource Information Network), which provides forecast information on occupational availability by race and gender based on projections of U.S., state, counties, and Metropolitan Statistical Area (MSA) labor force data
- New York Forecast Database (available online through The WEFA Group), which contains annual time series of forecast data for New York and New Jersey.

(Refer to Appendix N for these addresses.)

Foreign Census Records, Demographics, and Statistics

Census records, demographics, and statistical data are also available for other countries. The following databases are examples of those available for the following countries:

Australia

- AUSSTATS (available online through Australian Bureau of Statistics (ABS)
- CDATA 86: The 1981 and 1986 Australian Censuses (available on CD-ROM from Australian Bureau of Statistics (ABS))

Canada

- Alberta Statistical Information System (available online through Alberta Treasury, Statistics) for the province of Alberta and its census divisions and municipalities
- Canada 1986 Census Profiles (available on CD-ROM from OPTIM Corporation)
- Canada GeoGraph II—The Multimedia Edition (available on CD-ROM from MECC)
- CONQUEST/Canada (available on CD-ROM from Strategic Mapping Inc.)

France
- IGAMINFO (available online through SUNIST) for the French regions of Provence, the Cote d'Azur, and the Alps

Hong Kong
- SUPERMAP Hong Kong 1991 (available on CD-ROM from Huang Kwan & Associates Limited)

Italy
- Popolazione (available online through Istituto Centrale di Statistica (ISTAT))

Japan
- NRI/E Japan Economic & Business Database (available online through The WEFA Group)

New Zealand
- SUPERMAP2 (available on CD-ROM from Space-Time Research Pty. Ltd.)

United Kingdom
- CSO Macro-Economic Data Bank (available online through ADP Financial Services (UK) Ltd., Datastream International Ltd., DRI/McGraw-Hill, Reuters Information Services (Canada) Ltd., and The WEFA Group) for England, Scotland, Wales, and Northern Ireland
- National Online Manpower Information System (available online through University of Durham) for the U.K.

Many more international statistical agencies, such as: the Japanese Statistical Bureau, the Central Statistical Bureau of Latvia, and the National Institute of Statistics and Economic Studies in France can be found on the Internet, indexed at:
http://www.census.gov/main/www/stat-int.html

Demographic and Statistical Publications
Demographic and statistical information can also be found in many publications, including newspapers, magazines, books and journals. Some publications that focus on this type of information are available online as well. They include:

- *American Marketplace* (available online through NewsNet, Inc., and as part of the Newsletter Database and PROMT database)
- *The Numbers News* (available online through NEXIS)
- Statistical Abstracts of the United States (available online through the Internet at: **http://www.census.gov/stat_abstract/**)

IV.
WHERE CAN I FIND MORE INFORMATION?

Books

ADOPTEE/BIRTHPARENT SEARCH GUIDES

Adopted? Canadian Guide For Adopted Adults in Search of Their Origins
By Marcus, Clare
Published by: ISC Press, c1979

Adoption Newsletter Directory
Edited by: Hilborn, Robin
Published by: Adoption Helper
Toronto, Canada, Annual
ISSN: 1198-3906

The Adoption Searchbook: Techniques for Tracing People, 3rd, Revised Edition
By Rillera, Mary J.
Published by: Pure, Inc.
CA, 01/91
ISBN: 0-910143-00-5

Adoption Searcher's Handbook: A Guidebook for Adoptees, Birthparents & Others Involved in the Adoption Search
By Tillman, Norma
Published by: Diane Publishing, 03/94
ISBN: 0-7881-0513-2

The Adoption Searchers' Handbook
By Tillman, Norma
Published by: Diane Publishing, 04/94
ISBN: 0-7881-0714-3

Birthright: The Guide to Search & Reunion for Adoptees, Birthparents, & Adoptive Parents
By Strauss, Jean A.
Published by: Penguin Books

(Viking Penguin), 06/94
ISBN: 0-14-051295-0
LCCN: 93-036064

By Order of Adoption
By Downie, Jean A.
Published by: Distinctive Publishing, Inc., 1995

Faint Trails: An Introduction to the Fundamentals of Adult Adoptee/Birthparent Reunification Searches, Western States Edition
By Aigner, Hal
Published by: Paradigm Press, c1980
ISBN: 0937572004
LCCN: 80-153203 //r92

The Great Adoptee Search Book
By Strauss, Jean A.
Published by: Castle Rock Publications, 10/90
ISBN: 0-9627982-2-3

How to Search in Canada
By Marshall, Joan
Published by: SearchLine
ISBN 0-9694050-0-6

The ISC Searchbook
by Gallagher, Helen, Sitterly, Nancy, and Sanders, Pat
Published by: ISC Publications, c1986

Lifeline: The Action Guide to Adoption Search
By Klunder, Virgil L.
Published by: Caradium, c1991
ISBN: 1879499177, 1879499185;
LCCN: 90-85769

The Locator: The Complete Guide to Finding Family, Friends, and Loved Ones

(Adoption Search)
By Klunder, Virgil L.
Published by: Caradium Publishing, Annual

Official Alma Searchers' Guide for Adults: Supplement to Alma Search Workshops
By Clewer, Lisa Ray
Published by: Adoptees' Liberty Movement Association, c1982

Search: A Handbook for Adoptees and Birthparents, 2nd Edition
By Askin, Jayne and Davis, Molly
Published by: Oryx Press, 1992
ISBN: 0897747178
LCCN: 92-4210

The Search Consultant's Handbook
By Sanders, Patricia
Published by: ISC Publications, c1983

Searching in California
By Sanders, Pat
Published by: ISC Publications, c1982

Searching in Florida
By Robie, Diane C.
Published by: ISC Publications, c1982

Searching in Illinois
By Beckstead, Gayle and Kozub, Mary Lou
Published by: ISC Publications, c1984

Searching in Indiana
By Dimon Carty, Mickey
Published by: ISC Publications, c1985

Searching in New York
By Burke, Kate
Published by: ISC Publications,
c1987

Unlocking the Adoption Files
By Sachdev, Paul
Published by: Lexington Books,
c1989
ISBN: 0669209759
LCCN: 89-12300

**Where to Find Adoption
Records (United Kingdom)**
Published by: BAAF
Publications (British Agencies
for Adoption & Fostering)
London, England

BACKGROUND RESEARCH/ INVESTIGATIVE REPORTING BOOKS

*A Guide to Background
Investigations, 4th Edition*
By National Employment
Screening Services
Published by: Source
Publications, 1990

*A Journalist's Primer on
Locating Legal Documents*
Written and published by
American Bar Association
Commission on Public
Understanding about the Law
c1990

*A Public Records Primer and
Investigator's Handbook:
Newly Added—Libraries,
Chambers of Commerce,
Regional Newspapers,
Genealogical Libraries,
Sheriffs, Police, 1st revision*
By Ray, Don
Published by: ENG Press, c1991
ISBN: 0962955205
LCCN: 92-136162

Be Your Own Detective
By Fallis, Greg and Greenberg,
Ruth.
Published by: M. Evans and
Company, 1989

**Behind the Lines: Case
Studies in Investigative
Reporting**
By Patterson, Margaret Jones
and Russell, Robert H.
Published by: Columbia
University Press, 1986
ISBN: 0231060580
LCCN: 85-22422 //r87

**Business Information
Sources, Revised Edition**
By Daniells, Lorna
Published by: University of
California Press, 1985

Check It Out!
By Pankau, Edmund J.
Published by: Contemporary
Books, c1992
ISBN: 0809239450
LCCN: 91-39262

**Competitor Intelligence
Manual & Guide: Gathering,
Analyzing, & Using Business
Intelligence**
By Tyson, Kirk W.
Published by: P-H, 11/1989
ISBN: 0-13-155292-9 (1989/10)

**The Criminal Investigator's
Guide**
By Kernes, Steven T. and
Kuehn, Lowell L.
Published by: Thomas, c1982
ISBN: 039804693X
LCCN: 82-724

**The Detection, Investigation,
and Prosecution of Financial
Crimes**
By Nossen, Richard A.
Published by: Richard A. Nossen
and Associates, 1982

**Federal Law Enforcement
Training Center, Criminal
Investigator Training Division:**

Sources of Information
By U.S. Department of the
Treasury; available through the
Government Printing Office

**Financial Investigations: A
Financial Approach to
Detecting and Resolving
Crimes: Instructor's Guide**
By United States Internal
Revenue Service
Published by: Internal Revenue
Service: For sale by the U.S.
G.P.O., Superintendent of
Documents, 1994

**Get the Facts on Anyone, 2nd
Edition**
By King, Dennis
Published by: Macmillan,
04/1995
ISBN: 0-671-89301-7 (1994/10)
LCCN: 91-40513

**How to Investigate by
Computer**
By Thomas, Ralph D. et al.
Published by: Thomas
Publications, 1989

**The Investigation of White-
Collar Crime**
By Edelhertz, Herbert
Published by: Government
Printing Office, 1977

**Investigative and In-Depth
Reporting**
By Bolch, Judith and Miller, Kay
Published by: Hastings House,
c1978
ISBN: 0803834136; 0803834144
LCCN: 77-21100 //r87, 77021-100

**Investigative Journalism
Techniques**
By St. John, Mark
Published by: Research
Evaluation Program (Northwest
Regional Educational
Laboratory), National Institute
of Education (U.S.)
1985

Investigative Methods
By Buckwalter, Art
Published by: Butterworth
Publishers, 1984

Investigative Reporting: From Courthouse to White House
By Mollenhoff, Clark R.
Published by: Macmillan
Collier Macmillan, c1981
ISBN: 0023818700
LCCN: 79-25672 //r87

Investigative Reporting and Editing
By Williams, Paul N.1976
Published by: Prentice-Hall,
c1978
ISBN: 0135046629
LCCN: 77-4855 //r87

Investigative Reporting, 2nd Edition
By Benjaminson, Peter and
Anderson, David
Published by: Iowa State
University Press, c1990
ISBN: 0813801974, 0813801931
LCCN: 90-4361

Investigative Techniques in Complex Financial Crimes
By Kramer, W. Michael
Published by: National Institute
on Economic Crime, 1991

Investigator's Guide to Sources of Information
By Williams, David C.
Published by: U.S. General
Accounting Office, 1988

The Investigator's Handbook
By Strobl, Walter M.
Published by: Butterworths,
c1984
ISBN: 0409951366
LCCN: 83-15907

IRE 101 Computer-Assisted Stories from the IRE Morgue
By Scott, Andrew and
Investigative Reporters and
Editors, Inc.

Published by: Investigative
Reporters and Editors, Inc.,
c1993

The Modern Reporter's Handbook
By Jones, John Paul
Published by: Greenwood Press,
1970, c1949
ISBN: 0837139643
LCCN: 71-98233

The New Competitor Intelligence: The Complete Resource for Finding, Analyzing, & Using Information about Your Competitors
By Fuld, Leonard M.
Published by: Wiley, 11/1994
ISBN: 0-471-58508-4 (1995/02)

Open the Books: How to Research a Corporation
By Community Press Features
Published by: Urban Planning
Aid, Inc., 1974

Peace Officer Background Investigation Manual: Guidelines for the Investigator
By California Commission on
Peace Officer Standards and
Training
Published by: The Commission
on Peace Officer Standards and
Training, State of California,
1991

Perfectly Legal Competitor Intelligence: How to Get It, Use It & Profit from It
By Bernhardt, Douglas
Published by: Trans-Atlantic
Philadelphia, 1993
ISBN: 0-273-60153-9 (1993/06)

Preserving Corporate Confidentiality in Legal Proceedings
By Pitt, Harvey L. and Wachtell,
Herbert M.
Published by: Harcourt Brace
Jovanovich, 1980

The Private Investigator's Basic Manual
By Akin, Richard H.
Published by: Thomas, c1976
ISBN: 0398035202
LCCN: 75-33695 //r89, 75033-695

Raising Hell: How the Center for Investigative Reporting Gets the Story
By Noyes, Dan and Weir, David
Center for Investigative
Reporting (U.S.)
Published by: Addison-Wesley
Publishing Co., c1983
ISBN: 0201108593, 0201108585
LCCN: 83-11922 //r882

Raising Hell: A Guide to the Fine Art of Uncovering Corporate Secrets, Government Lies and Other Dirty Tricks, An Investigator's Handbook
By Noyes, Dan and Leishman,
David
Published by: Mother Jones, 1978

Reference Book for Criminal Investigator Logistics Management Orientation Course: (Procurement and R & D)
By United States Army Logistics
Management Center
Published by: U.S. Department
of Defense, Department of the
Army, Army Logistics
Management Center, 1975

Reporter's Handbook
By Florida Bar, Florida Press
Association, Florida Association
of Broadcasters
Published by: Public Relations
Division, The Florida Bar, 1981

The Reporter's Handbook: An Investigator's Guide to Documents and Techniques 2nd Edition
By Ullmann, John and Colbert, Jan
Investigative Reporters and
Editors, Inc.
Published by: St. Martin's Press,

c1991
ISBN: 0312051476, 0312004354
LCCN: 90-37266 //r94

Research Guide to American Historical Biography
By Muccigrosso, Robert and Niemeyer, Suzanne
Published by: Beacham Publishing, c1988-c1992
ISBN: 0933833091
LCCN: 88-19316 //r922

Take the Money and Strut!
By Faron, Fay
Published by: Creighton-Morgan Publishing Group, 1988

Techniques of Legal Investigation
By Golec, Anthony M.
Published by: Thomas, c1976
ISBN: 0398035229
LCCN: 75-34008 //r842

Telling the Untold Story: How Investigative Reporters Are Changing the Craft of Biography
By Weinberg, Steve
Published by: University of Missouri Press, c1992
ISBN: 0826208738
LCCN: 92-17674

GENEALOGICAL RESEARCH GUIDES

A Beginner's Guide to Hispanic Genealogy— Introduccion A La Investigacion
Genealogical Latino Americana
By Flores, Norma P. and Ludwig, Patsy
Published by: Western Book/Journal Press, 1993
ISBN: 0936029315
LCCN: 93-85298

A Genealogist's Guide to Arkansas Research

By Norris, Rhonda S. (Rhonda Shepherd)
Published by: Arkansas Genealogical Research, c1994
LCCN: 94-188985

A Guide to Genealogical Materials at the Rhode Island Historical Society Library
By Rhode Island Historical Society Library and Lamar, Christine
Published by: The Society, c1985

A Guide to South Carolina Genealogical Research and Records
By Holcomb, Brent
Published by: B.H. Holcomb, c1986
ISBN: 0913353073
LCCN: 87-102220

A Guide to Texas Research
Published by: Ericson Books, 1994, c1993
ISBN: 0911317554

A Key to the 1880 United States Federal Census Identifying Enumeration District Numbers and Microfilm Numbers of the National Archives and the Genealogical Library, 2nd Edition, Revised and Corrected
By United States National Archives and Records Administration, Church of Jesus Christ of Latter-Day Saints Genealogical Library
Published by: Heritage Books, 1986
ISBN: 0917890701
LCCN: 86-214697

A Practical Guide for the Genealogist in England
By Mellen, Rachael
Published by: Heritage Books, 1986
ISBN: 091789085X
LCCN: 86-186339 //r89

A Simplified Guide to Probate Jurisdictions: Where to Look

for Wills in Great Britain and Ireland, 3rd Edition
By Gibson, Jeremy Sumner Wycherley
Published by: Genealogical Publishing Co., 1986
ISBN: 080631155X
LCCN: 86-80613 //r90

The A-Z Guide to Tracing Ancestors in Britain
By Markwell, F. C. and Saul, Pauline A.
Published by: Genealogical Publishing Co., 1989
ISBN: 0806312521
LCCN: 89-80252

Acadian-Cajun Genealogy: Step by Step
By Hebert, Timothy
Published by: Center for Louisiana Studies, University of Southwestern Louisiana, c1993
ISBN: 0940984873
LCCN: 93-74254

Across the Atlantic and Beyond: The Migration of German and Swiss Immigrants to America
By Haller, Charles R.
Published by: Heritage Books, 1993
ISBN: 1556136978
LCCN: 94-114263

African-American Genealogy Workbook for Beginners, 2nd Edition
By Law, Nova
Published by: Legacy Publishing Co., 1993
ISBN: 1882804023
LCCN: 93-242066

Afro-American Genealogy Sourcebook
By Morton-Young, Tommie
Published by: Garland Publishing, 1987
ISBN: 0824086848
LCCN: 85-45112 //r94

Age Search Information
By Shepherd, JoAnn
United States Bureau of the
Census
Published by: U.S. Department
of Commerce
Bureau of the Census:
Superintendent of Documents,
U.S. G.P.O, distributor, 1990

*American Passenger Arrival
Records: A Guide to the
Records of Immigrants
Arriving at American Ports
by Sail and Steam, Updated
and Enlarged*
By Tepper, Michael
Published by: Genealogical
Publishing Co., 1993
ISBN: 0806313803
LCCN: 93-70370

*Ancestry's Guide to Research:
Case Studies in American
Genealogy*
By Cerny, Johni and Eakle,
Arlene H.
Published by: Ancestry Inc., 1985
ISBN: 0916489019
LCCN: 84-72694

*Ancestry's Red Book:
American State, County &
Town Sources, Revised
Edition*
By Eichholz, Alice
Published by: Ancestry
Publishing, c1992, 1989
ISBN: 0916489477
LCCN: 91-30311

*Beginning an Afro-American
Genealogical Pursuit*
By Scott, Jean Sampson
Published by: Eppress Printers,
c1985
LC Call No.: E185.96.536

Beginning Danish Research
By Carlberg, Nancy Ellen and
Keating, Norma S.
Published by: Carlberg Press,
c1992
ISBN: 0944878180
LCCN: 93-203107

Beginning Swedish Research
By Carlberg, Nancy Ellen
Published by: Carlberg Press,
1989
LCCN: 89-156347

*Beginning Your Family
History in Great Britain*
By Pelling, George
Published by: Genealogical
Publishing Co., 1989
ISBN: 080631253X
LCCN: 89-80251

*China Connection: Finding
Ancestral Roots for Chinese
in America, Revised 2nd
Edition*
By Low, Jeanie W. Chooey
Published by: J.W.C. Low Co.,
c1994
ISBN: 0963883518

*Civil War Records: A Useful
Tool: A Step By Step Guide to
the Availability and
Acquisition of Civil War
Records*
By Harris, Sherry
Published by: Shumway Family
History Services, c1990-c1993
LCCN: 91-182733 //r93

*Climb It Right: A High-Tech
Genealogical Primer, 1st
Revised Edition*
By Cosgriff, John Cornelius and
Cosgriff, Carolyn H.
Published by: Progenesys Press,
c1985
ISBN: 0917255011
LCCN: 85-3445 //r85

*The Encyclopedia of Jewish
Genealogy*
By Kurzweil, Arthur and Weiner,
Miriam
Published by: J. Aronson, c1991-
ISBN: 0876688350 (v.1)
LCCN: 90024-600, 90-24600

*Exploring Your Sephardic
Roots: A Resource Guide*
By Weiner, Miriam
Published by: M. Weiner, c1989

*The Family Historian's
Enquire Within 3rd Edition*
By Markwell, F. C. and Saul,
Pauline A.
Published by: Countryside Books
in association with the Federation
of Family History Societies, 1988
ISBN: 0907099777

*Family History and Local
History in England*
By Hey, David
Published by: Longman, 1987
ISBN: 0582005221, 0582494583
LCCN: 86-10329

*Family Record Extraction:
How to Extract Russian
Marriage, Birth, and
Christening Records, Field
Test Draft*
Written and published by: Church
of Jesus Christ of Latter-Day
Saints
c1992

*Family Roots: Discovering the
Past in the Public Record
Office*
By Colwell, Stella
Published by: C.E. Tuttle Co.,
c1991
ISBN: 080481774X, 080481774X
LCCN: 92-211267

*The Family Tree Detective: A
Manual for Analysing and
Solving Genealogical
Problems in England and
Wales, 1538 to the Present Day
2nd Edition*
By Rogers, Colin Darlington
Published by: Manchester
University Press, 1985
ISBN: 0719018455: (U.S.),
0719018463 (U.S.)
LCCN: 85-10531

*Finding Italian Roots: The
Complete Guide for Americans*
By Colletta, John Philip
Published by: Genealogical
Publishing Co., c1993
ISBN: 0806313935
LCCN: 93-79083

Finding Our Fathers: A Guidebook to Jewish Genealogy
By Rottenberg, Dan
Published by: Genealogical Publishing Co., 1986, c1977
ISBN: 0806311517
LCCN: 85082-512, 85-82512

Finding Your German Ancestors
By Smelser, Ronald M.
Published by: Ancestry, c1991
ISBN: 0916489515
LCCN: 91-8562

Finding Your People in the Shenandoah Valley of Virginia: A Genealogical Guide
By Good, Rebecca H. and Ebert, Rebecca A.
Published by: Hearthside Press, 1988
ISBN: 0945231008
LCCN: 88-14031

Finnish Genealogical Research
By Vincent, Timothy Laitila and Tapio, Rick
Published by: Finnish Americana, c1994
ISBN: 0963297562

Genealogical Guide to German Ancestors from East Germany and Eastern Europe
By Arbeitsgemeinschaft Ostdeutscher Familienforscher
Published by: Degener, 1984
ISBN: 3768610292
LCCN: 84-188380 //r85

Genealogical Historical Guide to Latin America
By Platt, Lyman De
Published by: Gale Research Co., c1978
LCCN: 78-75146 //r90

Genealogical Records in Texas
By Kennedy, Imogene Kinard and Kennedy, J. Leon
Published by: Genealogical

Publishing Co., 1987
ISBN: 0806311851
LCCN: 86-83384 //r87

Genealogical Research at the Library of Congress
By Library of Congress
Published by: U.S. Government Printing Office, 1993
LCCN: 93-246203

Genealogical Research Guide to Germany
By Palen, Margaret Krug
Published by: Heritage Books, 1988
ISBN: 1556131224
LCCN: 89-122287

Genealogical Resources in English Repositories
By Moulton, Joy Wade
Published by: Hampton House

Genealogical Resources in Washington State: A Guide to Genealogical Records Held at Repositories, Government Agencies, and Archives
By Washington State Archives and Washington State Historical Records and Archives Project
Published by: Secretary of State of Washington, Division of Archives, 1983
LCCN: 85-622980 //r92

The Genealogist's Address Book
By Bentley, Elizabeth P.
Published by: Genealogical Publishing Co., 1992
ISBN: 0-8063-1292-0

The Genealogy Beginner's Manual New Edition
By Ashton, Rick J., Sinko, Peggy Tuck, and Wolf, Joseph C.
Published by: Newberry Library, 1977
LCCN: 77-155716 //r85

Genealogy for Librarians, 2nd Edition
By Harvey, Richard

Published by: Library Association Publishing, 1992
ISBN: 0851574084
LCCN: 92-243238

Genealogy Online: Researching Your Roots
By Crowe, Elizabeth Powell
Published by: Windcrest (McGraw-Hill, Inc.), 1995
ISBN: 0-07-014749-3

Georgia Genealogical Workbook, 1st Edition
By Brooke, Ted O. and Davis, Robert Scott
Published by: Family Tree Copies from the Georgia Genealogical Society, c1987
LCCN: 87-70929

Going to Salt Lake City to Do Family History Research
By Parker, J. Carlyle
Published by: Marietta Publishing Co., 1989
ISBN: 0934153051
LCCN: 89-36914 //r91

Guide to Cuban Genealogical Research: Records and Sources, 1st Edition
By Carr, Peter E.
Published by: Adams Press, c1991
ISBN: 0963120905
LCCN: 91-90691

Guide to Family History Sources in the New Jersey State Archives
By Epstein, Bette Marie, Jones, Daniel P., Niederer, Karl J.
New Jersey Bureau of Archives and Records Preservation, New Jersey
Division of Archives and Records Management
Published by: New Jersey Department of State, Division of Archives and Records Management, 1987
ISBN: 0944313000
LCCN: 87-25025 //r94

The Handy Book for Genealogists: United States of America. Genealogical County Map of the United States of America 8th Edition
By Everton, George B. and Everton, Louise Mathews
Published by: Everton Publishers, c1991
LCCN: 91-209112

The Handy Book to English Genealogy 3rd Edition, Revised and Expanded
By Mellen, Rachael
Published by: Heritage Books, 1990
ISBN: 1556133596
LCCN: 91-107910

Hispanic American Genealogical Sourcebook, 1st Edition
By Byers, Paula K. (Paula Kay)
Published by: Gale Research, c1995
ISBN: 0810392275
LCCN: 94-37509

House Histories: A Guide to Tracing the Genealogy of Your Home, 1st Edition
By Light, Sally
Published by: Golden Hill Press, 1989
ISBN: 0961487615
LCCN: 88-83479

How and Where to Research Your Ethnic-American Cultural Heritage—Italian Americans
By Reed, Robert D.
Published by: R.D. Reed, c1979
LCCN: 87-403439 //r92
(Other volumes in this series are available for those of Black, German, Japanese, Polish, Russian, and Native American ancestry.)

How to Find Oregon Naturalization Records, Revised
By Lenzen, Connie
Published by: C. Lenzen, 1990

How to Trace Your Ancestors in Derbyshire
By Riden, Philip
Published by: Derbyshire Record Society, 1982
ISBN: 094632400X
LCCN: 83-211908 //r88

How to Trace Your Minnesota Ancestors
By Porter, Robert B.
Published by: Porter Publishing Co., c1985
ISBN: 0933565003

In and Around Record Repositories in Great Britain & Ireland
By Cole, Jean and Church, Rosemary
Published by: FTM, 1992

In Search of Hamish Mcbagpipes: A Concise Guide to Scottish Genealogy
By Goldie, Douglas Bruce
Published by: Heritage Books, 1992
ISBN: 1556135971
LCCN: 92-206056

In Search of the "Forlorn Hope": A Comprehensive Guide to Locating British Regiments and Their Records (1640-WWI)
By Kitzmiller, John M. (John Michael)
Published by: Manuscript Publishing Foundation, c1988
ISBN: 0961926058 (set), 0961926031 (v. 1), 096192604X (v. 2), 0961926058 (set)
LCCN: 89-190503

In Search of Welsh Ancestry
By Hamilton-Edwards, Savery, Gerald Kenneth
Published by: Genealogical Publishing Co., 1986
ISBN: 0806311223
LCCN: 85-70028

In Search of Your Canadian Roots

By Baxter, Angus
Published by: Genealogical Publishing Co., 1989
ISBN: 0806312505
LCCN: 88-83954

In Search of Your German Roots: A Complete Guide to Tracing Your Ancestors in the Germanic Areas of Europe
By Baxter, Angus
Published by: Genealogical Publishing Co., 1987
ISBN: 0806312009
LCCN: 87-80882

Irish Family History
By Yurdan, Marilyn
Published by: Genealogical Publishing Co., 1990
ISBN: 0806312742
LCCN: 89-82526 //r91

Jurisdictional Histories for Ohio's Eighty-Eight Counties, 1788-1985
By Phillips, W. Louis
Published by: Heritage Books, 1986
ISBN: 0917890817
LCCN: 86-183720

Lest We Forget: A Guide to Genealogical Research in the Nation's Capital, 4th Edition, Revised
By Babbel, June Andrew
Published by: Annandale, Virginia and Oakton, Virginia Stakes of the Church of Jesus Christ of Latter-Day Saints, c1976
LCCN: 66-29666 //r85

The Library: A Guide to the LDS Family History Library
By Cerny, Johni, Elliott, Wendy L. (Wendy Lavelle), Church of Jesus Christ of Latter-Day Saints. Family History Library
Published by: Ancestry Publishing, c1988
ISBN: 0916489213
LCCN: 87-70109, 87-70109 //r90

Looking for Your Mob: A Guide to Tracing Aboriginal Family Trees
By Smith, Diane (Diane Evelyn) and Halstead, Boronia
Published by: Aboriginal Studies Press, 1990
ISBN: 0855752092
LCCN: 90-226817

Marriage, Census, and Other Indexes for Family Historians, 3rd Edition
By Gibson, Jeremy Sumner Wycherley
Published by: Genealogical Publishing Co., 1989
ISBN: 0806312408
LCCN: 88-83493

Massachusetts Genealogical Research
By Schweitzer, George Keene
Published by: G.K. Schweitzer, c1990
ISBN: 0913857122
LCCN: 90-189937

The Matthews Method in African American Genealogical Research
By Matthews, Harry Bradshaw
Published by: H.B. Matthews, c1988
LCCN: 88-141111

Mexican and Spanish Family Research
By Konrad, J.
Published by: Summit Publications, c1987
LCCN: 87-410865

Mexico: General Research Guide
By Platt, Lyman De
Published by: Teguayo Press, 1993
ISBN: 1567879063

My Ancestor Was a Merchant Seaman: How Can I Find Out More About Him?
By Watts, Christopher T., Watts, Michael J., and Society of

Genealogists (Great Britain)
Published by: Society of Genealogists, c1986
ISBN: 0901878731
LCCN: 87-119007 //r94

My Ancestor Was a Migrant [in England Or Wales]: How Can I Trace Where He Came From?
By Camp, Anthony J.
Published by: Society of Genealogists, 1987
ISBN: 0901878944
LCCN: 89-108550

Ohio: "The History of Your Heritage" Series: History That Enables the Researcher to Understand and Expand His Genealogy
By Balhuizen, Anne Ross
Published by: Advanced Resources, 1993
ISBN: 187907902X

Our Quaker Ancestors: Finding Them in Quaker Records
By Berry, Ellen T. and Berry, D. A. (David A.)
Published by: Genealogical Publishing Co., 1987
ISBN: 0806311908
LCCN: 87-80356

Pennsylvania Line: A Research Guide to Pennsylvania Genealogy and Local History, 4th Edition
By Iscrupe, William L., Iscrupe, Shirley G. M., and Southwest Pennsylvania Genealogical Services
Published by: Southwest Pennsylvania Genealogical Services, c1990
ISBN: 0944128084
LCCN: 93-234725

Polish Genealogy & Heraldry: An Introduction to Research
By Hoskins, Janina W.
Published by: Library of Congress: For sale by the Superintendent of Documents,

U.S. G.P.O., 1987
ISBN: 0844406015
LCCN: 87-600087

Polish Roots—Korzenie Polskie
By Chorzempa, Rosemary A.
Published by: Genealogical Publishing, 1993
ISBN: 0806313781
LCCN: 93-77159

Probate Jurisdictions: Where to Look for Wills, 3rd Edition
By Gibson, Jeremy Sumner Wycherley
Published by: Genealogical Publishing Co., 1989
ISBN: 080631155X
LCCN: 89-128366, 86-80613

Relations in Records: A Guide to Family History Sources in the Australian Archives
By Australian Archives
Published by: Australian Government Publishing Service, c1988 (1989 printing)
ISBN: 0644068477
LCCN: 89-140510

Research Guide to Natrona County, Wyoming
By Natrona County Genealogical Society
Published by: Natrona County Genealogical Society, Publication Committee, 1986
LCCN: 87-151948

Research in Mexico City
By Platt, Lyman De
Published by: The Teguayo Press, c1992

Research in Oregon
By Lenzen, Connie
Published by: National Genealogical Society, 1992
ISBN: 0915156628
LCCN: 91-47195

The Researcher's Guide to American Genealogy 2nd Edition
By Greenwood, Val D.

Published by: Genealogical
Publishing, 1992
ISBN: 0-8063-1267-X
LCCN:89-081464

**Researching in Salt Lake
City**
By Carlberg, Nancy Ellen
Published by: Carlberg Press,
1994, c1993
ISBN: 0944878245
LCCN: 87-143463

**Rhode Island Sources for
Family Historians and
Genealogists**
By Sperry, Kip
Published by: Everton
Publishers, c1986
LCCN: 87-112341

**Roots and Branches: Ancestry
for Australians**
By Lea-Scarlett, E. J. (Errol J.)
Published by: Collins, 1979
ISBN: 0002164159
LCCN: 79-316125 //r86

**Searching for Your Ancestors:
the How and Why of
Genealogy, 6th Edition**
By Doane, Gilbert Harry and
Bell, James B.
Published by: University of
Minnesota Press, 1992
ISBN: 0816619905
LCCN: 91-32606 //r93

**Shaking Your Family Tree: A
Basic Guide to Tracing Your
Family's Genealogy, 1st
Edition**
By Crandall, Ralph J.
Published by: Yankee
Publishing, c1986
ISBN: 0899090885
LCCN: 85-40718

**Slave Genealogy: A Research
Guide with Case Studies**
By Streets, David H.
Published by: Heritage Books,
1986
ISBN: 0917890639
LCCN: 86-162912

Slovak Genealogy
By Kona, William
Published by: The Author, 1988

**South Carolina, A Guide for
Genealogists, 1st Edition**
By Hicks, Theresa M.
Published by: Peppercorn
Publications, c1985
LCCN: 85-238572

They Came in Ships
By Colletta, John Philip
Published by: Ancestry
Publishing, c1989
ISBN: 0916489426
LCCN: 89-17742

**Tracing Your Ancestors in the
Public Record Office, 4th
Edition**
By Cox, Jane, Bevan, Amanda,
Duncan, Andrea and Padfield,
Timothy
Great Britain, Public Record
Office
Published by: H.M.S.O., 1990

**Tracing Your English
Ancestors: A Manual for
Analysing and Solving
Genealogical Problems, 1538
to the Present, 1st USA Edition**
By Rogers, Colin Darlington
Published by: Manchester
University Press; Distributed in
the USA and Canada by St.
Martins Press, 1989
ISBN: 0719031729
LCCN: 89-8132

Tracing Your Family Tree
By Jean A Cole & Michael
Armstrong
Published by: Equation/Thorsons
Publishing Group, 1988
ISBN: 1-85336-035-X

**Tracing Your Irish Ancestors:
The Complete Guide**
By Grenham, John
Published by: Genealogical
Publishing Co., 1993
ISBN: 0806313692
LCCN: 92-74687

**Tracing Your Mississippi
Ancestors**
By Lipscomb, Anne S. and
Hutchison, Kathleen S.
Published by: University Press of
Mississippi, c1994
ISBN: 0878056971, 087805698X
LCCN: 94-13812

**Tracing Your Norwegian
Roots, Revised**
By Wellauer, Maralyn A.
Published by: Wellauer, c1986

**Tracing Your Scottish
Ancestors: A Guide to Ancestry
Research in the Scottish
Record Office**
By Sinclair, Cecil
Published by: HMSO, 1990 (1991
printing)
ISBN: 0114941181
LCCN: 92-176376

Tracing Your Scottish Ancestry
By Cory, Kathleen B.
Published by: Polygon, c1990
ISBN: 0748660542
LCCN: 92-247870, gb 89-49363

**Tracing Your Swedish
Ancestry**
By Olsson, Nils William
Published by: Ministry for
Foreign Affairs, 1987
ISBN: 9152002071

**Tracing Your Swiss Roots,
Revised**
By Wellauer, Maralyn A.
Published by: Wellauer, c1988
ISBN: 0932019021

**Unpuzzling Your Past: A Basic
Guide to Genealogy, 2nd
Edition**
By Croom, Emily Anne
Published by: Betterway
Publications, c1989
ISBN: 1558701117
LCCN: 88-34971

**Using Maps and Aerial
Photography in Your
Genealogical Research: with**

Supplement on Foreign Aerial Photography, Revised and Enlarged Edition
By Lind, Marilyn
Published by: Linden Tree, c1985
LCCN: 85-80941

Using Records in the National Archives for Genealogical Research, Revised 1990
Written and published by United States National Archives and Records Administration, 1990

Video Family History
By Sturm, Duane and Sturm, Pat
Published by: Ancestry Publishing, c1989
ISBN: 0916489442
LCCN: 88-35025 //r92

Vital Records Handbook
By Kemp, Thomas Jay
Published by: Genealogical Publishing Co., 1988
ISBN: 0806312203
LCCN: 88-80164

Vital Records Update, 1987 Edition
By Davidson, A. L. (Alvie L.)
Published by: A. L. Davidson, c1987

There are so many additional books and guides on genealogy that it was necessary to exclude books that pre-date 1985. This does not in any way reflect on their value or worthiness for study.

LOCATING PEOPLE

How to Locate Anyone Anywhere Without Leaving Home
By Gunderson, Ted L. with McGovern, Roger
Published by: The Penguin Group, c1989
ISBN: 0-525-24746-7, 0525484752, 0-452-26715-3
LCCN: 88-27093

How to Locate Anyone Who Is or Has Been in the Military: Armed Forces Locator Directory, 5th Edition, completely revised
By Johnson, Richard S.
Published by: MIE Publishing, c1993
ISBN: 1877639117
LCCN: 89-60697

The Locator: The Complete Guide to Finding Family, Friends, and Loved Ones (Adoption Search)
By Klunder, Virgil L.
Published by: Caradium Publishing, Annual

Secrets for Successful Searching: How to Locate Information and Find Almost Anyone
By Tillman, Norma
Published by: U.F.O., Inc., 1992
ISBN: 0-9634424-0-6

You, Too, Can Find Anybody
By Culligan, Joseph J.
Published by: Hallmark Press, Inc., 1991
ISBN: 0-9630621-0-7

MAILING LIST DIRECTORIES

Direct Marketing Market Place: The Networking Source of the Direct Marketing Industry
Published by: National Register Publishing, Database Publishing Group, annual
ISBN: 0-87217-327-5
ISSN: 0192-3137

National Directory of Mailing Lists
Published by: Oxbridge Communications, Inc.

SRDS Direct Marketing List Source

Published by: Standard Rates and Data
ISSN: 1071-4561

PRIVACY AND FREEDOM OF INFORMATION BOOKS; PROCEEDINGS, AND GOVERNMENT DOCUMENTS

A Citizen's Guide on Using the Freedom of Information Act and the Privacy Act of 1974 to Request Government Records: First Report
By United States Congress House Committee on Government Operations
Published by: U.S. G.P.O., 1993

A Framework for Identifying the Legal and Political Risks of Using New Information Technologies to Support Marketing Programs: Commentary
By Bloom, Paul N., Milne, George R. and Adler, Robert
Published by: Marketing Science Institute, c1992

An Act to Amend Title 18, United States Code, to Authorize the Federal Bureau of Investigation to Obtain Certain Telephone Subscriber Information
Published by: U.S. G.P.O.: Superintendent of Documents, U.S. G.P.O., distributor, 1993

An Act to Amend Title 5 of the United States Code, to Ensure Privacy, Integrity, and Verification of Data Disclosed for Computer Matching, to Establish Data Integrity Boards Within Federal Agencies, and for Other Purposes
U.S. G.P.O.: Superintendent of

Documents, U.S. G.P.O., distributor, 1994

**Anticipatory Breach
(Privacy and the Press)**
By Mustill, Michael J., Sir and
Lorenz, Werner
Published by: Butterworths, 1990
ISBN: 0406527024

**Civil Liberties and the
Electronic Frontier, Mapping
the Terrain: Conference
Report**
By Civille, Richard, Computer
Professionals for Social
Responsibility; Computers
and Civil Liberties Project;
Electronic Frontier Foundation
Published by: Computer
Professionals for Social
Responsibility, 1991

**Communications and
Computer Surveillance,
Privacy, and Security:
Hearing Before the
Subcommittee on Technology,
Environment, and Aviation of
the Committee on Science,
Space, and Technology, U.S.
House of Representatives, One
Hundred Third Congress,
Second Session, May 3, 1994**
By United States Congress House
Committee on Science, Space, and
Technology. Subcommittee on
Technology, Environment, and
Aviation
Published by: U.S. G.P.O.: For
sale by the U.S. G.P.O.,
Superintendent of Documents,
Congressional
Sales Office, 1994
ISBN: 0160445302
LCCN: 94-199342

**Compendium of State Privacy
and Security Legislation: 1989
Overview: Privacy and
Security of Criminal History
Information**
By United States Bureau of
Justice Statistics Search Group
Published by: U.S. Department of

Justice, Office of Justice Program,
Bureau of Justice
Statistics, 1990

**Compilation of State and
Federal Privacy Laws, 1992
Edition**
(Privacy Journal)
By Smith, Robert Ellis and
Sulanowski, James S.
Published by: Privacy Journal,
1992
ISBN: 0930072081

**Computer Crime: Phreaks,
Spies, & Salami Slicers**
Issues in Focus Series
By Judson, Karen
Published by: Enslow Publishers,
05/1994
ISBN: 0-89490-491-4
LCCN: 93-041198

**Computer Matching and
Privacy Protection
Amendments of 1990: Hearing
Before the Government
Information, Justice, and
Agriculture Subcommittee of
the Committee on Government
Operations, House of
Representatives, One Hundred
First Congress, Second
Session, on H.R. 5450,
September 11, 1990**
By United States Congress House
Committee on Government
Operations; Government
Information, Justice, and
Agriculture Subcommittee
Published by: U.S. G.P.O.: For
sale by the Superintendent of
Documents, Congressional Sales
Office,
U.S. G.P.O., 1991
LCCN: 91-601037

**Computer Matching and
Privacy Protection
Amendments of 1990: Report
(to Accompany H.R. 5450)
(Including Cost Estimate of
the Congressional Budget
Office)**
By United States Congress House

Committee on Government
Operations
Published by: U.S. G.P.O., 1990

**Computer Security & Privacy:
An Information Sourcebook**
By Greenia, Mark W.
Published by: Lexikon Services,
01/1994
ISBN: 0-944601-55-3

**Computers and Privacy: How
the Government Obtains,
Verifies, Uses, and Protects
Personal Data: Briefing
Report to the Chairman,
Subcommittee on
Telecommunications and
Finance, Committee on Energy
and Commerce, House of
Representatives**
By United States General
Accounting Office
Published by: The Office (distributor, 1990)

**Computers, Freedom &
Privacy: A Comprehensive,
Edited Transcript of the First
Conference on Computers,
Freedom & Privacy, Held
March 26-28, 1991 in
Burlingame, California By
Conference on Computers,
Freedom & Privacy (1st: 1991:
Burlingame, California)**
Warren, Jim C. Thorwaldson, Jay,
Koball, Bruce; Computer
Professionals for Social
Responsibility; Institute of
Electrical and Electronics
Engineers
Published by: IEEE Computer
Society Press, c1991
ISBN: 0818625651, 081862566X,
0818625678
LCCN: 91-75772 //r93

**Conference on Computers,
Freedom & Privacy, 1st
Edition**
Published by: IEEE Computer
Society, 1991
ISBN: 0-8186-2565-1
LCCN: 91-075772

Confidential Information Sources, Public and Private, 2nd Edition
By Carroll, John Millar
Published by: Butterworth-Heinemann, c1991
ISBN: 0750690186
LCCN: 91008-947, 91-8947

Constructing the Autonomous Legal Body: Privacy, Property, Inviolability
By Hyde, Alan, 1951- University of Toronto; Faculty of Law
Published by: Faculty of Law, University of Toronto, 1993

The Costs of Privacy: Surveillance and Reputation in America
By Nock, Steven L.
Published by: A. De Gruyter, c1993
ISBN: 020230454X, 0202304558
LCCN: 92-35480

Criminal History Record Information: Compendium of State Privacy and Security Legislation, 1992
By United States Bureau of Justice Statistics Search Group
Published by: U.S. Department of Justice, Office of Justice Programs, Bureau of Justice Statistics, c1992

Criminal Justice Information Improvement Act: Hearing Before the Subcommittee on Civil and Constitutional Rights of the Committee on the Judiciary, House of Representatives, Ninety-Ninth Congress, Second Session on H.R. 2129...July 16, 1986
By United States Congress House Committee on the Judiciary Subcommittee on Civil and Constitutional Rights
Published by: U.S. G.P.O.: For sale by the Superintendent of Documents, Congressional Sales Office, U.S. G.P.O., 1987
LCCN: 87-601200 //r90

Data Protection and the Media: Study
By Council of Europe, Committee of Experts on Data Protection, Council of Europe. European Committee on Legal Co-operation
Published by: Council of Europe Press, 1991
ISBN: 9287119376

Data Protection Law in Ireland
By Clark, Robert, LL.M.
Published by: Round Hall Press, c1990
ISBN: 0947686592
LCCN: 90-128325 //r93

Data Protection, Computers, and Changing Information Practices: Hearing Before the Government Information, Justice, and Agriculture Subcommittee of the Committee on Government Operations, House of Representatives, One Hundred First Congress, Second Session, May 16, 1990
By United States Congress House Committee on Government Operations Government Information, Justice, and Agriculture Subcommittee
Published by: U.S. G.P.O.: For sale by the Superintendent of Documents, Congressional Sales Office, U.S. G.P.O., 1991
LCCN: 91-600635 //r93

Data Transmission and Privacy
By Campbell, Dennis, Fisher, Joy, Center for International Legal Studies
Published by: M. Nijhoff; Sold and distributed in the U.S.A. and Canada by Kluwer Academic Publishers, c1994
ISBN: 0-7923-2713-6
LCCN: 94-000969

Domestic and International Data Protection Issues: Hearings Before the

Government Information, Justice, and Agriculture Subcommittee of the Committee on Government Operations, House of Representatives, One Hundred Second Congress, First Session, April 10 and October 17, 1991
By United States Congress House Committee on Government Operations, Government Information, Justice, and Agriculture Subcommittee
Published by: U.S. G.P.O.: For sale by the U.S. G.P.O., Superintendent of Documents, Congressional Sales Office, 1992
ISBN: 0160375541
LCCN: 92-187316

The Electronic Eye: The Rise of Surveillance Society
By Lyon, David
Published by: University of Minnesota Press, 01/1994
ISBN: 0-8166-2513-1; 0-8166-2515-8
LCCN: 93-035598

Employee Privacy
By Berenbeim, Ronald, Conference Board
Published by: Conference Board, c1990
ISBN: 0823703916
LCCN: 91-142969

Employee Privacy Law
By Hebert, L. Camille
Published by: Clark Boardman Callaghan, c1993-
LCCN: 93-14892 //r942

Ethical Issues in Journalism and the Media
By Belsey, Andrew and Chadwick, Ruth F.
Published by: Routledge, c1992
ISBN: 0415069262, 0415069270
LCCN: 92-4869

The Fair Health Information Practices Act of 1994: Hearings Before the Information, Justice,

Transportation, and
Agriculture Subcommittee of
the Committee on Government
Operations, House of
Representatives, One Hundred
Third Congress, Second Session,
on H.R. 4077, to Amend Section
552a of Title 5, United States
Code...April 20, May 4 and 5,
1994
By United States Congress House
Committee on Government
Operations, Information, Justice,
Transportation, and Agriculture
Subcommittee
Published by: U.S. G.P.O.: For
sale by the U.S. G.P.O.,
Superintendent of Documents,
Congressional Sales Office, 1994
ISBN: 0160462819

*FBI Authorization to Obtain
Certain Telephone Subscriber
Information: Report (to
Accompany H.R. 175)
(Including Cost Estimate of
the Congressional Budget
Office)*
By United States Congress House
Committee on the Judiciary
Published by: U.S. G.P.O., 1993

*Federal Employee Privacy
Rights and Standard Form 86:
Thirty-Second Report*
By United States Congress House
Committee on Government
Operations
Published by: U.S. G.P.O., 1990

*Federal Privacy of Medical
Information Act, H.R. 5935:
Summary, Justification,
Explanation, and Comparison
with Present Law: as
Approved by the Subcommittee
on Health, Committee on Ways
and Means*
By United States Congress House
Committee on Ways; Los Angeles
County Bar Association; Labor
Law Section
Published by: Regents of the
University of California, 1992
ISBN: 0892151781

*Freedom of Information Act
Guide & Privacy Act
Overview., Sept. 1992 Edition*
By United States Department of
Justice Office of Information and
Privacy
Published by: Office of
Information and Privacy, Office of
Policy and Communications,
U.S. Department of Justice: For
sale by the Superintendent of
Documents, U.S. G.P.O., 1992
ISBN: 0160405769

*From Cradle to Grave:
Government Records and Your
Privacy*
By Privacy Rights Clearinghouse
Published by: Center for Public
Interest Law, University of San
Diego, 1994

*Give Consumers a Choice:
Privacy Implications of U.S.
Postal Service National
Change of Address Program:
Forty-Third Report*
By United States Congress Com-
mittee on Government Operations
Published by: U.S. G.P.O., 1992

*Handbook of Personal Data
Protection*
By Madsen, W.
Published by: Stockton Press
(Groves Dictionaries), 04/1992
ISBN: 1-56159-046-0

*Health Data in the
Information Age: Use,
Disclosure, & Privacy*
By Institute of Medicine
Committee on Regional Health
Data Networks Staff
Published by: National Academic
Press, 04/1994
ISBN: 0-309-04995-4
LCCN: 94-002613

*Hearing on H.R. 1900, Privacy
for Consumers and Workers
Act of 1993: Hearing Before the
Subcommittee on Labor-
Management Relations of the
Committee on Education and*

*Labor, House of
Representatives, One Hundred
Third Congress, First Session,
Hearing Held in Washington,
DC, June 30, 1993*
By United States Congress House
Committee on Education and
Labor; Subcommittee on Labor-
Management Relations
Published by: U.S. G.P.O.: For
sale by the U.S. G.P.O.,
Superintendent of Documents,
Congressional Sales Office, 1994
ISBN: 0160448107

*Hearings on Emergency
Roadside Services and
Motorist Safety and
Department of Motor Vehicles'
Records, Privacy Versus Access*
By California Legislature,
Assembly Committee on
Transportation
Published by: Joint Publications
Office, 1990

*High-Tech Privacy Issues in
Health Care: Hearings Before
the Subcommittee on
Technology and the Law of the
Committee on the Judiciary,
United States Senate, One
Hundred Third Congress, First
and Second Sessions, October
27, 1993, and January 27, 1994;
High Tech Privacy Issues In
Health Care*
By United States Congress
Senate Committee on the
Judiciary; Subcommittee on
Technology and the Law
Published by: U.S. G.P.O.: For
sale by the U.S. G.P.O.,
Superintendent of Documents,
Congressional Sales Office, 1994
ISBN: 0160462746

*The Information Game:
Ethical Issues in a Microchip
World*
By Brown, Geoffrey
Published by: Humanities Press
International, 1990
ISBN: 0391035754
LCCN: 88-8289 //r942

Information Law Towards the 21st Century
By Korthals Altes, Willem F.
Published by: Kluwer Law and Taxation Publishers, 1992
ISBN: 9065446273
LCCN: 93-157155

Information Security and Privacy in Network Environments
By United States Congress, Office of Technology Assessment
Published by: Office of Technology Assessment, Congress of the U.S.: For sale by the U.S. G.P.O., Superintendent of Documents, 1994
ISBN: 0160451884
LCCN: 94-219217

Information Warfare: The New Frontier in Cyberspace
By Schwartau, Winn
Published by: Thunders Mouth, 05/1994
ISBN: 1-56025-080-1
LCCN: 94-002412

Interstate Identification Index Pilot Program: Hearing Before the Subcommittee on Civil and Constitutional Rights of the Committee on the Judiciary, July 30, 1992
By United States Congress House Committee on the Judiciary; Subcommittee on Civil and Constitutional Rights
Published by: U.S. G.P.O.: For sale by the U.S. G.P.O., Superintendent of Documents, Congressional Sales Office, 1993
ISBN: 0160401240
LCCN: 93-204854

The Introduction and Use of Personal Identification Numbers: The Data Protection Issues: Study by Council of Europe; Committee of Experts on Data Protection; Council of Europe; European Committee on Legal Co-operation
Published by: Council of Europe

Press, 1991
ISBN: 928711935X

The Law of Privacy
By Elder, David A. (David Andrew)
Published by: Lawyers Cooperative Publishing, 1991
LCCN: 91-60363

Lawyer's Guide to Computer Security & Privacy
Professional Reference Series
By Greenia, Mark W.
Published by: Lexikon Services, 01/1993
ISBN: 0-944601-73-1

Libel and Privacy, 2nd Edition
By Sanford, Bruce W.
Published by: Prentice Hall Law & Business, c1991-
ISBN: 0131091743, 0135296110
LCCN: 91-9284

Managing Privacy: Information Technology and Corporate America
By Smith, H. Jeff.
Published by: University of North Carolina Press, c1994
ISBN: 0807821470, 0807844543
LCCN: 93-33334

Misuse of National Crime Information Center Records: Joint Hearing Before the Subcommittee on Civil and Constitutional Rights of the Committee on the Judiciary, and the Subcommittee on Information, Justice, Transportation, and Agriculture of the Committee on Government Operations, House of Representatives, One Hundred Third Congress, First Session, July 28, 1993
By United States Congress House Committee on the Judiciary; Subcommittee on Civil and Constitutional Rights; United States Congress House Committee on Government Operations, Information, Justice,

Transportation, and Agriculture; Subcommittee Published by: U.S. G.P.O.: For sale by the U.S. G.P.O., Superintendent of Documents, Congressional Sales Office, 1994
ISBN: 0160461812

The Naked Consumer: How Our Private Lives Become Public Commodities
By Larson, Erik
Published by: H Holt & Co, 10/1992
ISBN: 0-8050-1755-0
LCCN: 92-014344

The New Faces of Privacy
By Ware, Willis H., Rand Corporation
Published by: Rand, 1993
LCCN: 94-145727

Nobody's Business: Paradoxes of Privacy
By Brill, Alida
Published by: Addison-Wesley Publishing Co., c1990
ISBN: 0201067455
LCCN: 90-623

Our Vanishing Privacy: and What You Can Do to Protect Yours
By Smith, Robert Ellis
Published by: Loompanics Unlimited, c1993
ISBN: 1559501006
LCCN: 93-77301

Oversight Hearing on the Use of Mailing Lists in Direct Marketing: Hearing Before the Subcommittee on Postal Operations and Services of the Committee on Post Office and Civil Service, House of Representatives, One Hundred Second Congress, First Session, October 10, 1991
By United States Congress House Committee on Post Office and Civil Service; Subcommittee on Postal Operations and Services
Published by: U.S. G.P.O.: For

sale by the U.S. G.P.O.,
Superintendent of Documents,
Congressional Sales Office, 1992
ISBN: 0160371813
LCCN: 92-219906

The Panoptic Sort: A Political Economy of Personal Information
By Gandy, Oscar H.
Published by: Westview, 1993
ISBN: 0813316561, 081331657X
LCCN: 92-37434

Personal Information: Privacy and the Law
By Wacks, Raymond
Published by: Clarendon Press;
Oxford University Press, 1989
ISBN: 0198256116
LCCN: 88-32109 //r93

Piercing the Paper Curtain: Gaining Access to Federal Records
By Reymont Associates
Published by: Reymont
Associates, c1992
ISBN: 0918734444

Privacy Act: An Office Consolidation and Index—Loi Sur La Protection Des Renseignements Personnels: Une Codification Administrative Et Index. Loi Sur La Protection Des Renseignements Personnels, 1991 Edition
By Privacy Commissioner of Canada
Published by: Privacy
Commissioner of Canada, c1991
ISBN: 0662584856
LCCN: 93-125650

Privacy and Data Protection: Issues and Challenges
By Tucker, G.
Organisation for Economic Co-operation and Development
Published by: Organisation for
Economic Co-operation and
Development, c1994
ISBN: 92-64-14096-4

Privacy and Human Rights: An International and Comparative Study, with Special Reference to Developments in Information Technology
By Michael, James
Published by: Dartmouth
Publishing Co., c1994
ISBN: 1855213818

Privacy and Publicity
By Kupferman, Theodore R.
Published by: Meckler, c1990
ISBN: 0887365086
LCCN: 89-31993

Privacy and Social Freedom
By Schoeman, Ferdinand David
Published by: Cambridge
University Press, 1992
ISBN: 0521415640
LCCN: 91-40062

Privacy Dimensions of Medical Record Keeping
By Ware, Willis H.
Health Records: Social Needs and
Personal Privacy (1993:
Washington, DC)
Published by: RAND, 1994

Privacy for Consumers and Workers Act: Hearing Before the Subcommittee on Employment and Productivity of the Committee on Labor and Human Resources, United States Senate, One Hundred Second Congress, First Session on S. 516, September 24, 1991
By United States Congress Senate
Committee on Labor and Human
Resources; Subcommittee on
Employment and Productivity
Published by: U.S. G.P.O.: For
sale by the U.S. G.P.O.,
Superintendent of Documents,
Congressional Sales Office, 1992
ISBN: 0160376580

Privacy for Consumers and Workers Act: Report Together with Minority Views (to Accompany H.R. 1218)

(Including Cost Estimate of the Congressional Budget Office)
By United States Congress House
Committee on Education and
Labor
Published by: U.S. G.P.O., 1992

The Privacy for Consumers and Workers Act: Hearing Before the Subcommittee on Employment and Productivity of the Committee on Labor and Human Resources, United States Senate, One Hundred Third Congress, First Session on S. 984, June 22, 1993
By United States Congress Senate
Committee on Labor and Human
Resources; Subcommittee on
Employment and Productivity
Published by: U.S. G.P.O.: For
sale by the U.S. G.P.O.,
Superintendent of Documents,
Congressional Sales Office, 1993
ISBN: 0160413087
LCCN: 94-117538

Privacy for Sale: How Computerization Has Made Everyone's Private Life an Open Secret
By Rothfeder, Jeffrey
Published by: Simon & Schuster,
c1992
ISBN: 0-671-73492-X
LCCN: 92-364

Privacy Implications of the U.S. Postal Service Address Correction Services: Hearing Before the Government Information, Justice, and Agriculture Subcommittee of the Committee on Government Operations, House of Representatives, One Hundred Second Congress, Second Session, May 14, 1992. Privacy Implications of the U.S. Postal Service Address Correction Services
By United States Congress House
Committee on Government
Operations Government

Information, Justice, and Agriculture Subcommittee Published by: U.S. G.P.O.: For sale by the U.S. G.P.O., Superintendent of Documents, Congressional Sales Office, 1994
ISBN: 0160434807
LCCN: 94-151568

Privacy in the Workplace: A Guide for Human Resource Managers
By Bible, Jon D. and McWhirter, Darien A. (Darien Auburn)
Published by: Quorum Books, 1990
ISBN: 0899304737
LCCN: 90-9075

Privacy of Social Security Records: Hearing Before the Subcommittee on Social Security and Family Policy of the Committee on Finance, United States Senate, One Hundred Second Congress, Second Session, February 28, 1992
By United States Congress Senate Committee on Finance; Subcommittee on Social Security and Family Policy
Published by: U.S. G.P.O.: For sale by the U.S. G.P.O., Superintendent of Documents, Congressional Sales Office, 1992
ISBN: 0160388732
LCCN: 92-222952

Privacy Project Report
By United States Internal Revenue Service
Published by: Department of the Treasury, Internal Revenue Service, 1994

Privacy Revealed: The Canadian Privacy Survey
By Graves, Frank L., Porteous, Nancy, Beauchamp, Patrick, Ekos Research Associates; Canada Department of Communications
Published by: Communications Canada, c1993

ISBN: 0662202538
LCCN: cn 93-99530

Privacy Rights of Employees: A Guide for California Businesses
By McPharlin, Linda Hendrix, California Continuing Education of the Bar
Published by: Continuing Education of the Bar, c1994
ISBN: 0881247545
LCCN: 94-621211

Privacy Rights of Federal Employees: Hearing Before the Legislation and National Security Subcommittee of the Committee on Government Operations, House of Representatives, One Hundred First Congress, First Session, November 15, 1989
By United States Congress House Committee on Government Operations; Legislation and National Security Subcommittee
Published by: U.S. G.P.O.: For sale by the Superintendent of Documents, Congressional Sales Office, U.S. G.P.O., 1990

Privacy: Individual Right Versus Social Needs Issue & Debate Series
By Gottfried, Ted
Published by: Millbrook Press, 10/1994
ISBN: 1-56294-403-7
LCCN: 93-026791

Proceedings: 1994 IEEE Computer Society Symposium on Research in Security and Privacy, May 16-18, 1994, Oakland, California
By IEEE Computer Society Symposium on Research in Security and Privacy (1994: Oakland, California); IEEE Computer Society Technical Committee on Security and Privacy; International Association for Cryptologic Research; Institute of Electrical and

Electronics Engineers
Published by: IEEE Computer Society Press, c1994
ISBN: 0818656751, 081865676X, 0818656778

Proceedings of the Second Conference on Computers, Freedom, and Privacy: L'enfant Plaza Hotel, Washington, DC, March 18-20, 1992
By Conference on Computers, Freedom & Privacy (2nd: 1992: Washington, DC); Hoffman, Lance J. Association for Computing Machinery; Special Interest Group on Computers and Society; Association for Computing Machinery; Special Interest Group on Communications; Association for Computing Machinery; Special Interest Group on Security, Audit, and Control
Published by: ACM; may be ordered from ACM Order Department, c1992
ISBN: 0897915534, 089791564X
LCCN: 93-191559

Protecting Privacy in Computerized Medical Information
By United States Congress Office of Technology Assessment
Published by: The Office: For sale by the U.S. G.P.O., Superintendent of Documents, 1993
LCCN: 94-125753

Protecting Privacy in Computerized Medical Information
Published by: Diane Publishers, 02/1994
ISBN: 0-7881-0446-2

Protecting Privacy in Computerized Medical Information
Published by: Gordon Press, 10/1994
ISBN: 0-8490-5769-8

Protecting Privacy in Surveillance Societies: The Federal Republic of Germany, Sweden, France, Canada, and the United States
By Flaherty, David H.
Published by: University of North Carolina Press, c1989
ISBN: 0807818712
LCCN: 89-4762 //r93

Protection of Personal Data Used for Payment and Other Related Operations: Recommendation No. R (90) 19 Adopted By the Committee of Ministers of the Council of Europe on 13 September 1990 and Explanatory Memorandum
By Council of Europe Committee of Ministers; Council of Europe Committee of Experts on Data Protection; Council of Europe; European Committee on Legal Co-operation
Published by: Council of Europe Press; Manhattan Publishing Co., distributor, 1992
ISBN: 9287119228

The Question of Privacy in Public Policy: An Analysis of the Reagan-Bush Era
By Sadofsky, David
Published by: Praeger, c1993
ISBN: 0275943003, 0275943968
LCCN: 93-6771

Recent Developments in Data Privacy Law: Belgium's Data Protection Bill & The European Draft Directive
By Dumortier, Joseph, 1950-
Interdisciplinary Centre for Law and Information Technology
Published by: Leuven University Press, 1992
ISBN: 9061864992

Regulating Privacy: Data Protection and Public Policy in Europe and the United States
By Bennett, Colin J. (Colin John)

Published by: Cornell University Press, 1992
ISBN: 0801426111
LCCN: 91-30559 //r93

Regulating Privacy: Data Protection & Public Policy in Europe & the United States
By Bennett, Colin J.
Published by: Cornell University Press, 04/1992
ISBN: 0-8014-2611-1; 0-8014-8010-8
LCCN: 91-030559

Resolved: That One or More U.S. Supreme Court Decisions Recognizing a Federal Constitutional Right to Privacy Should Be Overruled: Intercollegiate Debate Topic, 1991-1992: Pursuant to Public Law 88-246
By Library of Congress Congressional Research Service
United States Congress—House
Published by: U.S. G.P.O., c1991

Sale of Criminal History Records: Hearing Before the Subcommittee on Civil and Constitutional Rights of the Committee on the Judiciary, House of Representatives, One Hundred Second Congress, Second Session, July 30, 1992
By United States Congress House Committee on the Judiciary; Subcommittee on Civil and Constitutional Rights
Published by: U.S. G.P.O.: For sale by the U.S. G.P.O., Superintendent of Documents, Congressional Sales Office, 1993
ISBN: 0160401240
LCCN: 93-204854

Security & Privacy, Research in ('94 Symposium)
Published by: IEEE Computer Society, 1994
ISBN: 0-8186-5675-1

Social Insurance Numbers: Regulating Their Use, Revised

September 1992
By Johansen, David
Published by: Canada Library of Parliament, Research Branch, 1989, c1992
ISBN: 0660149117
LCCN: cn 93-73541

Tackling the Confidentiality Barrier: A Practical Guide for Integrated Family Services: A Special Report for New Beginnings
By Hobbs, Lola J. New Beginnings (Organization: San Diego, CA)
Published by: New Beginnings, 1991

Telecommunications Network Security: Hearings Before the Subcommittee on Telecommunications and Finance of the Committee on Energy and Commerce, House of Representatives, One Hundred Third Congress, First Session, April 29 and June 9, 1993
By United States Congress House Committee on Energy and Commerce; Subcommittee on Telecommunications and Finance
Published by: U.S. G.P.O.: For sale by the U.S. G.P.O., Superintendent of Documents, Congressional Sales Office, 1994
ISBN: 0160434130
LCCN: 94-149573

Telecommunications Privacy Principles. Principes De Protection De La Vie Privee Dans Les Telecommunications
By Canada Department of Communications
Published by: Communications Canada, c1992
ISBN: 0662593677
LCCN: ce 93-70701

Telephone Consumer Privacy Rights Act: Report, Together with Dissenting Views

(to Accompany H.R. 1305) (Including Cost Estimate of the Congressional Budget Office)
By United States Congress House Committee on Energy and Commerce
Published by: U.S. G.P.O., 1991

Telephone Privacy: Hearings Before the Subcommittee on Telecommunications and Finance of the Committee on Energy and Commerce, House of Representatives, One Hundred Third Congress, First Session, May 25 and June 24, 1993
By United States Congress House Committee on Energy and Commerce Subcommittee on Telecommunications and Finance
Published by: U.S. G.P.O.: For sale by the U.S. G.P.O., Superintendent of Documents, Congressional Sales Office, 1993
ISBN: 0160414601
LCCN: 93-235428

Telephone Privacy Act of 1990: Hearing Before the Subcommittee on Courts, Intellectual Property, and the Administration of Justice of the Committee on the Judiciary, House of Representatives, One Hundred First Congress, Second Session, on H.R. 4340, September 19, 1990
By United States Congress House Committee on the Judiciary; Subcommittee on Courts, Intellectual Property, and the Administration of Justice
Published by: U.S. G.P.O.: For sale by the Superintendent of Documents, Congressional Sales Office, U.S. G.P.O., 1991
LCCN: 91-600435

The Telephone Privacy Act of 1991: Report Together with Additional Views (to Accompany S. 652, as Amended)

By United States Congress Senate Committee on the Judiciary
Published by: U.S. G.P.O., 1991

Tools for Privacy: How to Outsmart the Phone, Fax, Cellular, & Computer Snooper!
By Block, Will and Lenard, Lane
Published by: Smart Publications (Health Freedom), 09/1994
ISBN: 0-9627418-4-1

Transborder Flow of Personal Data Within the EC: A Comparative Analysis of the Privacy Statutes of the Federal Republic of Germany, France, the United Kingdom, and the Netherlands and Their Impact on the Private Sector
By Nugter, A. C. M. (Adriana C.M.)
Published by: Kluwer Law and Taxation Publishers, c1990
ISBN: 9065445137
LCCN: 91-132837 //r93

Use of Social Security Number as a National Identifier: Hearing Before the Subcommittee on Social Security of the Committee on Ways and Means, House of Representatives, First Session, February 27, 1991
By United States Congress House Committee on Ways and Means; Subcommittee on Social Security
Published by: U.S. G.P.O.: For sale by the U.S. G.P.O., Congressional Sales Office, U.S. G.P.O., 1991
LCCN: 91-601255

Who Owns Information?: From Privacy to Public Access
By Branscomb, Anne W.
Published by: BasicBooks, c1994
ISBN: 046509175X
LCCN: 93-44348

Who's to Know?: Information, the Media, and Public Awareness
By Weiss, Ann E.
Published by: Houghton Mifflin,

1990
ISBN: 0395497027
LCCN: 89-26901 /AC

Whose Business Is It Anyway?: A National Opinion Survey on Workplace Decisions and Employee Privacy
By National Consumers' League
Published by: National Consumers League, 1990

Why We Ask Questions: Privacy Act Notification Statement of the Indian Health Service
By United States Indian Health Service
Published by: U.S. Department of Health and Human Services, Public Health Service, Indian Health Service, 1994

Without Consent: The Ethics of Disclosing Personal Information in Public Archives
By MacNeil, Heather
Published by: Society of American Archivists; Scarecrow Press, 1992
ISBN: 0810825813
LCCN: 92-16754

Workers' Privacy
By International Labour Office
Published by: International Labour Office, c1992
ISBN: 9221082512

Your Responsibilities as INS Employees Under the Freedom of Information (FOIA) & Privacy Act (PA)
By United States Immigration and Naturalization Service
Published by: U.S. Department of Justice, Immigration & Naturalization Service, 1990

Your Right to Federal Records: Questions and Answers on the Freedom of Information Act and Privacy Act
By United States General Services Administration;

Published by: U.S. General Services Administration: U.S. Department of Justice, 1992

Your Right to Privacy: A Basic Guide to Legal Rights in an Information Society
By Hendricks, Evan, Hayden, Trudy, Novik, Jack
Published by: Southern Illinois University Press, c1990
ISBN: 0809316323
LCCN: 89-21844

Your Rights and Instructions for Requesting Review of Adverse Determination Under The Privacy Act of 1974, Revised 1-91
By United States Internal Revenue Service
Published by: Department of the Treasury, Internal Revenue Service 1991

PUBLIC RECORDS RESEARCH GUIDES

A Journalist's Primer on Locating Legal Documents
By American Bar Association Commission on Public Understanding about the Law
Published by: American Bar Association, Commission on Public Understanding about the Law, c1990

A Public Records Primer and Investigator's Handbook: Newly Added—Highway Patrol, New Area Codes, Sheriff Substations, Public Records Act, 1993 California Edition
By Ray, Don
Published by: ENG Press, c1992
ISBN: 0962955213

Access to Public Information: A Resource Guide to Government in Columbia and Boone County, Missouri,

Revised Edition
By Davis, Aurora E.
Published by: Freedom of Information Center, 1990

British Archives: A Guide
By Foster, Janet and Sheppard, Julia
Published by: Macmillan

California Handbook: A Comprehensive Guide to Sources of Information and Action, 6th Edition
By Trzyna, Thaddeus C.
Published by: California Institute of Public Affairs, 1990

Check It Out!
By Pankau, Edmund J.
Published by: Contemporary Books, c1992
ISBN: 0809239450
LCCN: 91-39262

Cleveland State University Journalists' Handbook Series, Vol. II: Public Records Guide
By Jeffres, Leo W., et al.
Published by: Communication Research Center of Cleveland State University, 1988

Confidential Information Sources: Public & Private
By Carroll, John M.
Published by: Butterworth Publications, 1975

Disposition of Federal Records, Revised Edition
By Wire, Richard A., United States National Archives and Records Administration
Published by: National Archives and Records Administration, Office of Records Administration, 1992
LCCN: 93-246879

Federal Archives and Records Centers
By United States National Archives and Records Service

Office of Federal Records Centers
Published by: Office of Federal Records Centers, National Archives and Records Service, General Services Administration, 1979
LCCN: 79-601997 //r91

Federal Records Centres Users' Guide. Centres Federaux De Documents, Guide De L'usager, Revised reprint
By National Archives of Canada, Hubsher, Robert, Public Archives Canada Records

Management Branch Federal Records Centres Users' Guide
Published by: National Archives of Canada, 1991, c1990
ISBN: 0662547497
LCCN: 87-174582 //r92

Get the Facts on Anyone
By King, Dennis
Published by: Prentice Hall, c1992
ISBN: 0133518590
LCCN: 91-40513

Guide to New York City Public Records, 4th Edition
By Kronman, Barbara
Published by: Public Interest Clearinghouse, 1991

Guide to Public Records of Iowa Counties
By Dolan, John P., Jr. and Lacher, Lisa
Published by: Iowa Title Company, 1987

In and Around Record Repositories in Great Britain & Ireland
By Cole, Jean & Church, Rosemary
Published by: Family Tree Magazine, 1992

Investigator's 1990 State Records Access Directory

By Thomas, Ralph D.
Published by: Thomas
Publications, 1989

Paper Trails: A Guide to
Public Records in California
By Newcombe, Barbara T. and
Kaplan, David E.
Published by: Center for Investi-
gative Reporting; California
Newspaper Publishers
Association, c1990
ISBN: 0962179310
LCCN: 89-62720

Piercing the Paper Curtain:
Gaining Access to Federal
Records
By Reymont Associates
Published by: Reymont
Associates, c1992
ISBN: 0918734444

The Reporter's Handbook: An
Investigator's Guide to
Documents and Techniques,
2nd Edition
By Ullmann, John, Colbert, Jan,
Investigative Reporters and
Editors, Inc.
Published by: St. Martin's Press,
c1991
ISBN: 0312051476, 0312004354
LCCN: 90-37266 //r94

Sources of Information from
Abroad, Revised 2-93
By United States Internal
Revenue Service Office of
International Programs
Published by: Internal Revenue
Service, Assistant Commissioner
(International), Office of
International Programs, 1993
LCCN: 93-203481

The Urbana Municipal
Documents Center Manual
By Koch, Jean E., Grueneberg,
Howard C. and Schlipf,
Frederick A.
Published by: Urbana Free
Library, c1987
ISBN: 0960964665
LCCN: 86-51179 //r89

Where to Write for Vital
Records: Births, Death,
Marriages & Divorces
By U.S. Department of Health
and Human Services
Published by: National Center
for Health Statistics Staff; avail-
able through the Government
Printing Office, 1990

Where's What: Sources of
Information for Federal
Investigators
By Murphy, Harry J.
Published by: Warner Books,
1976

Wisconsin Municipal Records
Manual
By Fox, Michael J. and
McDonough, Kathleen A.
Published by: State Historical
Society of Wisconsin: Wisconsin
Department of Development,
1980
LCCN: 81-110916

Periodicals

ADOPTEE/ BIRTHPARENT SEARCH PUBLICATIONS

A POEM
Adoptee-Birthparent Searches (ABS)
234 N. 2nd Street
Jeannette, PA 15644

ATM Reunion Registry
Adoption Triangle Ministries
1105 Cape Coral Parkway E.
Suite G
Cape Coral, FL 33904-9175

Adoptologist
Kansas City Adult Adoptees Organization
Box 15225
Kansas City, MO 64106

AIS Newsletter
Adoptees in Search (AIS)
P.O. Box 41016
Bethesda, MD 20824
(301) 656-8555;
Fax (301) 652-2106

ALMA Searchlight
Adoptees' Liberty Movement Association (ALMA)
P.O. Box 727
Radio City Station
New York, NY 10101-0727
(212) 581-1568;
Fax (212) 765-2861

Concerned United Birthparents—Communicator
Concerned United Birthparents, Inc. (CUB)
2000 Walker Street
Des Moines, IA 50317-5255
(800) 822-2777; (515) 263-9558

Consultant
Independent Search

Consultants (ISC)
P.O. Box 10192
Costa Mesa, CA 92627

Midwest Searching Magazine
P.O. Box 122
Oakland City, IN 47660

Missing Persons—Registry
(Newsletter)
International Soundex Reunion Registry
P.O. Box 2312
Carson City, NV 89702
(702) 882-7755

MPB/Searching
P.O. Box 290333
Nashville, TN 37229-0333

Network News
Adoptee-Birthparent Support Network (ABSN)
3421 M Street NW; No. 328
Washington, DC 20007
(202) 686-4611; Fax (301) 774-1741

The OASIS Lobstick
Organized Adoption Search Information Services (OASIS)
P.O. Box 53-0761
Miami Shores, FL 33153
(305) 948-8933

Operation Identity Newsletter
Operation Identity
13101 Black Stone Road NE
Albuquerque, NM 87111
(505) 293-3144

Origins (Newsletter)
Origins
P.O. Box 556
Whippany, NJ 07981-0556
(201) 428-9683

Parent Finder Newsletter
Parent Finders
P.O. Box 12031

Edmonton, AB, Canada T5J 3L2
(403) 466-3335

People Searching News
P.O. Box 22611
Ft. Lauderdale, FL 33335
(305) 370-7100
ISSN: 1047-6598

Reunions, The Magazine
P.O. Box 11727
Milwaukee, WI 53211-1727
(414) 263-4567

Searchers' Digest
P.O. Box 50219
Jacksonville Beach, FL 32240

There are many additional publications available from adoption/birthparent associations. You can find some of these through the associations and others listed on the Internet.

COMPETITIVE AND BUSINESS INTELLIGENCE PUBLICATIONS

Business Intelligence Newsletter
(This is an online newsletter.)
ION Incorporated
2111 East Baseline; Suite F7
Tempe, AZ 85283
(800) 257-1048

Competitive Information System Development
Washington Researchers Publishing
Box 19005
20th Street Station
Washington, DC 20036-9005
(202) 333-3533

**Competitive Intelligence
Review**
(Society of Competitive
Intelligence Professionals
Newsletter)
John Wiley and Sons, Inc.
Subscription Department
605 Third Avenue
New York, NY 10158
(212) 850-6000
Fax (212) 850-6799
ISSN: 1058-0247

Pointblank Press
Certified Corporate Services
3313 B. Bloor Street West; Unit 3
Toronto, Ontario M8X 1E7
Canada
(416) 760-3181

Note that there are also competitive intelligence magazines and reports for specific industries.

FUNDRAISING/
PROSPECT RESEARCH
PUBLICATIONS

501 (C) (3) Monthly Letter
American Association for
Corporate Contributions
601 Trap Street
Old Courthouse
Ontanagon, MI 49953
(906) 884-2397

AHP News
Association for Healthcare
Philanthropy
313 Park Avenue; Suite 400
Falls Church, VA 22046
(703) 532-6243
Fax (703) 532-7170

**American Prospect Research
Association Newsletter**
American Prospect Research
Association (APRA)
1730 North Lynn Street; Suite 502
Arlington, VA 22209
(703) 525-1191
Fax (703) 276-8196

CASE Currents
Council for Advancement and
Support of Education
11 Dupont Circle; Suite 400
Washington, DC 20036-1207
(202) 358-5900
Fax (202) 387-4973

**Chronicle of Philanthropy
Chronicle of Higher Education**
1255 23rd Street, NW; Suite 775
Washington, DC 20037
(202) 466-1200
Fax (202) 296-2691

Corporate Giving Watch
Taft Corp.
12300 Twinbrook Parkway; #450
Rockville, MD 20852
(202) 966-7086

Dimensions
National Catholic Development
Conference
86 Front Street
Hempstead, NY 11550
(516) 481-6000; Fax (516) 489-9287

DMFA Forum
Direct Mail Fundraisers
Association
445 West 45th Street
New York, NY 10036
(212) 489-4929

Donor Briefing
Business Publishers, Inc.
951 Pershing Drive
Silver Spring, MD 20910-4464
(301) 587-6300

FRI Monthly Portfolio
Fund Raising Institute
P.O. Box 365
Ambler, PA 19002
(215) 646-7019

FRM Weekly
Hoke Communications, Inc.
224 Seventh Street
Garden City, NY 11530
(516) 746-6700

Foundation Giving Watch
Taft Corp.

12300 Twinbrook Parkway; #450
Rockville, MD 20852
(202) 966-7086

Foundation News
Council on Foundations, Inc.
1828 L Street, NW
Washington, DC 20036-5168
(202) 466-6512

Fund for Animals
Fund for Animals
200 West 57th Street
New York, NY 10019
(212) 246-2096

Fund Raising Forum
National Catholic Development
Conference
86 Front Street
Hempstead, NY 11550
(516) 481-6000
Fax (516) 489-9287

Fund Raising Management
Hoke Communications, Inc.
224 Seventh Street
Garden City, NY 11530
(516) 746-6700

Giving USA Update
American Association of Fund-
Raising Counsel (AAFRC)
25 W. 43rd Street; Suite 820
New York, NY 10036
(212) 354-5799
Fax (212) 768-1795

**Grassroots Fundraising
Journal**
Grassroots Fundraising Journal
517 Union Avenue; #206
Knoxville, TN 37902
(615) 687-6624

**Healthcare Fund Raising
Newsletter: A summary of
healthcare fund raising
activities**
Health Resources Publishing
Brinley Professional Plaza
3100 Highway 38
P.O. Box 1442
Wall Township, NJ 07719-1442
(201) 681-1133

Intermed Journal
Dooley Foundation-
Intermed-U.S.A.
420 Lexington Avenue
New York, NY 10170
(212) 687-3620

KRC Letter
KRC Letter
P.O. Box 53
Hastings-on-Hudson, NY 10706
(914) 478-0888

*Medical Research Funding
Bulletin*
Science Support Center
P.O. Box 7507
FDR Station
New York, NY 10150

Member Exchange
National Catholic Development
Conference
86 Front Street
Hempstead, NY 11550
(516) 481-6000
Fax (516) 489-9287

Monitor
National Catholic Development
Conference
86 Front Street
Hempstead, NY 11550
(516) 481-6000; Fax (516) 489-9287

National Fund Raiser
Barnes Associates Inc.
603 Douglas Boulevard
Roseville, CA 95678
(800) 231-4157; (916) 786-7471
Fax (916) 782-2145

New Jersey Notes
Mitchell Guide Publications
P.O. Box 613
Belle Mead, NJ 08502
(201) 359-2215

*Non Profit Organization
Resource Review*
NPO Management Services, Inc.
P.O. Box A-6
Cathedral Station
New York, NY 10002
(212) 678-7077

Non-Profit Times
Non-Profit Times
P.O. Box 408
Hopewell, NJ 08525
(609) 520-8300

Nonprofit Colorado
Colorado Association of Nonprofit
Organizations
1245 East Colfax #411
Denver, CO 80218
(303) 832-5710

Nonprofit Insights
Whitaker Newsletters Inc.
313 South Avenue
Fanwood, NJ 07023-1324
(908) 889-6336
Fax (908) 889-6339
(Available online through
NewsNet, Inc.)

Nonprofit World Report
Society for Nonprofit
Organizations
6314 Odana Road; Suite 1
Madison, WI 53719
(608) 274-9777

Notebook
Association of Volunteer Bureaus
801 North Fairfax Street
Alexandria, VA 22314

NSFRE Journal
National Society of Fund Raising
Executives (NSFRE)
1101 King Street; Suite 700
Alexandria, VA 22314
(703) 684-0410
Fax (703) 684-0540

NSFRE News
National Society of Fund Raising
Executives (NSFRE)
1101 King Street; Suite 700
Alexandria, VA 22314
(703) 684-0410
Fax (703) 684-0540

Philanthropic Digest
Brakeley
John Price Jones, Inc.
5010 Wisconsin Avenue
NW; #118

Washington, DC 20016
(202) 785-4829

Philanthropic Trends Digest
Douglas M. Lawson
Association, Inc.
39 East 51st Street
New York, NY 10022
(212) 759-5660

Philanthropy Monthly
Non-Profit Report, Inc.
2 Bennitt Street
P.O. Box 989
New Milford, CT 06776
(203) 354-7132

Philanthropy Resource Letter
Cerise Communications Co.
1821 San Ramon Avenue
Berkeley, CA 94707
(415) 525-4300

Religious Funding Monitor
Taft Corp.
12300 Twinbrook Parkway; #450
Rockville, MD 20852
(202) 966-7086

Smith Funding Report
SFR, Inc.
11605 Summer Oak Drive
Germantown, MD 20874
(301) 540-3931

Week in Review
National Association of
Independent Colleges and
Universities
122 C Street, NW; Suite 750
Washington, DC 20001-2190
(202) 347-7512
Fax (202) 628-2513

GENEALOGICAL
RESEARCH
PUBLICATIONS

AUSTRIA

ADLER-Jahrbuch (in German)
Genealogical and Heraldic
Society (ADLER)

Heraldisch-Genealogische
Gesellschaft
1 Haarhof 4 A
A-1014 Vienna, Austria

**ADLER-Zeitschrift fur
Genealogie und Heraldik**
(in German)
Genealogical and Heraldic
Society (ADLER)
Heraldisch-Genealogische
Gesellschaft
1 Haarhof 4 A
A-1014 Vienna, Austria

BELGIUM

Genealogie and Computer
Vlaamse Vereniging voor
Familiekunde
Centrum voor
Familiegeschiedenis
Van Heybeeckstraat 3, Antwerp-
Merksem, Belgium
ISSN: 0771-713X

CANADA

Heraldry in Canada
(in French and English)
Heraldry Society of Canada (HSC)
Societe Heraldique
du Canada (SHC)
P.O. Box 8467; Station T
Ottawa, Ontario,
Canada K1G 3H9
(613) 993-6783

Newsleaf
Ontario Genealogical Society
40 Orchard View Boulevard
Suite 251
Toronto, Ontario,
Canada M4R 1B9
(416) 489-0734
Fax (416) 489-9803
ISSN: 0380-1616

DENMARK

Heraldisk Tidsskrift (in
Danish, Norwegian, and Swedish)
Societas Heraldica Scandinavica
(SHS)

Heraldisk Selskab (HS)
c/o Ole Rostock
Sigmundsvej 8, DK-2880
Bagsvaerd, Denmark
42980756

ISRAEL

Sharsheret Hadorot
(in English and Hebrew)
Israel Genealogical Society (IGS)
50 Harav Uziel Street
96424 Jerusalem, Israel
(2) 424147
ISSN: 0792-5751

NETHERLANDS

Misjpoge
Dutch Society for Jewish
Genealogy (DSJG)
Nederlandse Kring voor Joodse
Genealogie (NKJG)
DA Costalaan 21
NL-3743 HT Baarn, Netherlands
(21) 5414094

SWITZERLAND

Archives Heraldiques Suisses
(in English, French, German,
and Italian)
Swiss Heraldry Society (SHS)
Societe Suisse d'Heraldique
c/o Gregor Brunner
Burgstrasse 32
CH-8706 Meilen, Switzerland
(1) 9231077; Fax 55 423597
ISSN: 0004-0673

UNITED KINGDOM

Coat of Arms
Heraldry Society (HS)
44/45 Museum Street
London WC1A 1LY, England
(71) 4302172

Computers in Genealogy
Society of Genealogists
14 Charterhouse Buildings
Goswell Road
London EC1M 7BA, England
071-251-8799
ISSN: 0263-3248

Double Tressure
Heraldry Society of Scotland
(HSS)
Societe Ecossaise d'Heraldique
25 Craigentinny Crescent
Edinburgh EH7 6QA, Scotland
(31) 6572791

Family History
The Institute of Heraldic &
Genealogical Studies
79-82 Northgate
Canterbury, Kent, England
CT1 1BA
44 227 768664

**Family History News and
Digest**
Federation of Family History
Societies (FFHS)
c/o Pauline A. Saul
Birmingham and Midland
Institute
Kingsley Norris Room
Margaret Street
Birmingham, West Midlands B3
3BS, England
(74) 3365505

Fraueyn as Banglaneyn
Isle of Man Family History
Society (IMFHS)
5 Selbourne Drive Douglas
Isle of Man, England
(624) 622188

Heraldry Gazette
Heraldry Society (HS)
44/45 Museum Street
London WC1A 1LY, England
(71) 4302172

**Heraldry Society of Ireland
Newsletter**
Heraldry Society of Ireland (HSI)
Cumann Araltais na h Eireann
San Elmo, Vico Road
Dorkey, Dublin, Ireland
(1) 2859722

The Irish Genealogist
Irish Genealogical Research
Society (IGRS)
c/o The Irish Club
83 Eaton Square
London SW1W 9AJ, England

Irish Herald
Heraldry Society of Ireland (HSI)
Cumann Araltais na h Eireann
San Elmo, Vico Road
Dorkey, Dublin, Ireland
(1) 2859722

UNITED STATES

A Tale of Mid-Cities
Mid-Cities Genealogical Society
(MCGS)
P.O. Box 407
Bedford, TX 76095-0407
(817) 267-8023

American Elm
Western Massachusetts
Genealogical Society
P.O. Box 80206
Forest Park Station
Springfield, MA 01108

Ancestree
Logan County Genealogical
Society (LCGS)
P.O. Box 1959
Logan, WV 25601
(304) 239-3202

Ancestry
Palm Beach County Genealogical
Society
P.O. Box 1746
West Palm Beach, FL 33402
(407) 832-3279

The Ancient City Genealogist
St. Augustine Genealogical
Society (SAGS)
c/o St. Johns County Public
Library
1960 N. Ponce de Leon Boulevard
St. Augustine, FL 32084
(904) 829-1933

Antepasados
Los Californianos (LC)
P.O. Box 1693
San Leandro, CA 94577-0169
(510) 276-5429

Appalachian Families
Mountain Press Research Center
P.O. Box 400

Signal Mountain, TN 37377-0400
(615) 886-6369

The Archivist
Genealogical Society of Bergen
County
P.O. Box 432
Midland Park, NJ 07432

Backtracker
Northwest Arkansas Genealogical
Society
P.O. Box 796
Rogers, AR 72757

Between the Lakes
Interlaken Historical Society
(IHS)
Main Street
Interlaken, NY 14847
(607) 532-4430

*Blue Water Family
Backgrounds*
St. Clair County Family History
Group
1115 6th Street
Port Huron, MI 48060

Bluegrass Roots
Kentucky Genealogical Society
(KGS)
P.O. Box 153
Frankfort, KY 40602
(502) 223-7541

Branches and Twigs
Genealogical Society of Vermont
46 Chestnut Street
Brattleboro, VT 05301

*Branching Out from St. Clair
County Illinois*
Marissa Historical and
Genealogical Society (MHGS)
P.O. Box 47
Marissa, IL 62257-0047
(618) 295-2562

Bulletin
Jewish Genealogical Society of
Westchester
94 Beverly Road
New Rochelle, NY 10804
(914) 576-2748

Bulletin
Yakima Valley Genealogical
Society (YVGS)
P.O. Box 445
Yakima, WA 98907
(509) 248-1328

The Carriage
Jessamine County Historical and
Genealogical Society (JCHGS)
504 West Maple Street
Nicholasville, KY 40356
(606) 885-4871

*Central Georgia Genealogical
Society Quarterly*
Central Georgia Genealogical
Society, Inc.
P.O. Box 2024
Warner Robins, GA 31099-2024
(912) 923-7662
ISSN: 0738-8209

Chronicles
Jewish Genealogical Society of
Philadelphia
332 Harrison Avenue
Elkins Park, PA 19117-2662
(215) 635-3263

The Circuit Rider
Sangamon County Genealogical
Society (SCGS)
P.O. Box 1829
Springfield, IL 62705
(217) 529-0542

*Clark County Genealogical
Society—Newsletter*
Clark County Genealogical
Society & Library
P.O. Box 2728
Vancouver, WA 98668-2728
(206) 693-6436

The Cleveland Kol
Jewish Genealogical Society of
Cleveland
996 Eastlawn Drive
Highland Heights, OH 44143
(216) 449-2326

Clinton Trials
Genealogists of Clinton County
Historical Society

P.O. Box 23
St. Johns, MI 48879-0023
(517) 224-4315

Connecticut Ancestry
Stamford Genealogical Society
(SGS)
P.O. Box 249
Stamford, CT 06904
(203) 328-5173

Connections
Pontiac Area Historical and
Genealogical Society
P.O. Box 430901
Pontiac, MI 48343-0901

**Court House Records of
Garland County, Arkansas**
Melting Pot Genealogical Society
(MPGS)
P.O. Box 936
Hot Springs, AR 71902
(501) 262-4975

Crossroads
Orphan Train Heritage Society of
America (OTHSA)
4912 Trout Farm Road
Springdale, AR 72762
(501) 756-2780
Fax (501) 756-0769
ISSN: 1044-5544

Descend-O-Gram
Sons and Daughters of the First
Settlers of Newbury,
Massachusetts (SDFSNM)
P.O. Box 444
Newburyport, MA 01950

Descender
Montgomery County Genealogical
Society (MCGS)
P.O. Box 444
Coffeyville, KS 67337
(316) 251-0716

DeSoto Descendants
Genealogical Society of DeSoto
County
P.O. Box 632
Hernando, MS 38632-9230
(601) 429-7013

The Dinghy
Pentref Press
P.O. Box 398
Machias, ME 04654
(207) 255-4114
ISSN: 0899-7322

DOROT
Jewish Genealogical Society of
New York
P.O. Box 6398
New York, NY 10128
(212) 330-8257

The Eaglet
Polish Genealogical Society of
Michigan (PGSM)
Detroit Public Library
Burton Historical Collection
5201 Woodward Avenue
Detroit, MI 48202
(313) 842-3044

**Effingham County
Genealogical Society Journal**
P.O. Box 1166
Effingham, IL 62401-1166
(217) 342-4711

ESOG News
Essex Society of Genealogists
(ESOG)
P.O. Box 313
Lynnfield, MA 01940
(508) 657-7232

The Essex Genealogist
Essex Society of Genealogists
(ESOG)
P.O. Box 313
Lynnfield, MA 01940

**Estill County Historical and
Genealogical Society (ECHGS)
Newsletter**
Estill County Historical and
Genealogical Society (ECHGS)
P.O. Box 221
Ravenna, KY 40472
(606) 723-7238

Everton's Genealogical Helper
Everton Publishers, Inc.
P.O. Box 368
Logan, UT 84323-0368

(800) 443-6325; (801) 752-6022
Fax (801) 752-0425

Family Finder
Genealogical Association of
English-Speaking Researchers in
Europe (GAESRE)
HQ USAREUR
CMR 420; Box 142
APO, NY 09063
ISSN: 1040-4821

Family Gatherings
Jewish Genealogical Society of
Broward County
P.O. Box 17251
Ft. Lauderdale, FL 33318
(305) 472-5455

Family History Capers
Genealogical Society of
Washtenaw County
P.O. Box 7155
Ann Arbor, MI 48107-7155
(313) 663-2825

Family Ties
Holland Genealogical Society
c/o Herrick Public Library
300 River Avenue
Holland, MI 49424

Family Tree Talk
Muskegon County Genealogical
Society
Hackley Public Library
316 West Webster
Muskegon, MI 49440
(616) 894-2234

Family Vines
Manitowoc County Genealogical
Society (MCGS)
P.O. Box 1745
Manitowoc, WI 54221-1745
(414) 682-8391

Fayette Connection
Fayette County Genealogical
Society (FCGS)
P.O. Box 342
Washington Court House
OH 43160
(614) 335-0266

FEEFHS Newsletter
Federation of East European
Family History Societies
(FEEFHS)
P.O. Box 21346
Salt Lake City, UT 84121
(801) 278-4586

FGS Forum
Federation of Genealogical
Societies (FGS)
P.O. Box 3385
Salt Lake City, UT 84110-3385
(801) 240-3997

FHGS Newsletter
Flint Hills Genealogical Society
(FHGS)
P.O. Box 555
Emporia, KS 66801
(316) 342-0933

*Florida Genealogical Society
Newsletter*
Florida Genealogical Society
P.O. Box 18624
Tampa, FL 33629-8624
(813) 254-3045

Footprints
Ft. Worth Genealogical Society
(FWGS)
P.O. Box 9767
Ft. Worth, TX 76147-2767

Footprints in Marion County
Marion County Genealogical and
Historical Society (MCGS)
P.O. Box 342
Salem, IL 62881

Footsteps
Ft. Worth Genealogical Society
(FWGS)
P.O. Box 9767
Ft. Worth, TX 76147-2767

Fort Norfolk Courier
Norfolk Historical Society (NHS)
P.O. Box 6367
Norfolk, VA 23508-0367
(804) 625-1720

Franklintonian
Franklin County Genealogical

Society (FCGS)
P.O. Box 2503
Columbus, OH 43216-2503
(614) 469-1300

Freeborn County Tracer
Freeborn County Genealogical
Society (FCGS)
P.O. Box 403
Albert Lea, MN 56007

Fulton County Folk Finder
Fulton County Historical Society
(FCHS)
37 East 375 North
Rochester, IN 46975
(219) 223-4436

*Fulton County Historical and
Genealogical Society
(FCHGS) Newsletter*
Fulton County Historical and
Genealogical Society (FCHGS)
45 North Park Drive
Canton, IL 61520
(309) 647-0771

*Fulton-Hickman
Genealogical Journal*
Fulton County Genealogical
Society (FCGS)
P.O. Box 31
Fulton, KY 42041

Geborener Deutscher
(A newsletter for German-born
adoptees and their
birth-adoptive families)
805 Alvarado Drive NE
Albuquerque, NM 87108-1648
(505) 268-1310

Gemini
Twin Tiers Genealogical Society
P.O. Box 763
Elmira, NY 14902

Genealogical Aids Bulletin
Miami Valley Genealogical
Society (MVGS)
P.O. Box 1364
Dayton, OH 45401-1364
(513) 698-5540

Genealogical Computing
Ancestry Incorporated
P.O. Box 476
Salt Lake City, UT 84110-0476
(801) 531-1790
Fax (801) 531-1798
ISSN: 0277-5913
(Available online through
CompuServe Information
Service)

Genealogical Gazette
Southwest Georgia Genealogical
Society (SGGS)
P.O. Box 4672
Albany, GA 31706
(912) 435-9659

*Genealogical Society
Newsletter*
Genealogical Society
1020 Illinois
Sidney, NE 69162

*Genealogical Society of Old
Tryon County (GSOTC)
Bulletin*
Genealogical Society of Old
Tryon County (GSOTC)
P.O. Box 938
Forest City, NC 28043
(704) 245-4460

Generations Magazine
Genealogy Council of the
Jewish Historical Society of
Maryland
15 Lloyd Street
Baltimore, MD 21202
(301) 732-6400

The Generator
St. Marys Genealogical Society
P.O. Box 1109
Leonardtown, MD 20650
(301) 769-2304

German American Genealogy
Immigrant Genealogical Society
(IGS)
1310B Magnolia Boulevard
P.O. Box 7369
Burbank, CA 91510-7369
(818) 848-3122
Fax (818) 716-6300

The German Connection
German Research Association
(GRA)
P.O. Box 711600
San Diego, CA 92171-1600
(619) 453-6198
ISSN: 8755-1756

Germanna
Memorial Foundation of
Germanna Colonies in Virginia
P.O. Box 693
Culpeper, VA 22701
(703) 825-1919
Fax (703) 825-3878

GGSA Bulletin
German Genealogical Society of
America (GGSA)
P.O. Box 291818
Los Angeles, CA 90029-8818
(909) 593-0509

GGSQ
Georgia Genealogical Society
(GGS)
P.O. Box 38066
Atlanta, GA 30334

**Gleanings from the West
Fields**
Genealogical Society of the West
Fields (GSWF)
Westfield Memorial Library
550 East Broad Street
Westfield, NJ 07090
(908) 789-4090

**Gratiot County Pages from the
Past**
Gratiot County Historical and
Genealogical Society
1012 Iowa
Alma, MI 48801
(517) 463-5256

Greenmead Gazette
Livonia Historical Society (LHS)
20501 Newburgh
Livonia, MI 48152
(313) 477-7375

GSMC Record
Genealogical Society of Monroe
County, Michigan

P.O. Box 1428
Monroe, MI 48161

Ha-Gesher
Jewish Genealogical Society of
Dayton
P.O. Box 338
Dayton, OH 45406
(513) 277-3995

Hacker's Creek Journal
Hacker's Creek Pioneer
Descendants
P.O. Box 37
Jane Lew, WV 26378
(304) 269-7091

Hallockville Happenings
Hallockville Museum Farm
163 Sound Avenue
Riverhead, NY 11901
(516) 298-5292

Heir-Lines
North Oakland Genealogical
Society (NOGS)
825 Joslyn Road
Lake Orion, MI 48362

Henry County Genie
Henry County Genealogical
Society (HCGS)
P.O. Box 346
Kewanee, IL 61443
(309) 853-4189

The Herald
Montgomery County Genealogical
Society (MCGS)
P.O. Box 867
Conroe, TX 77305-0867
(409) 756-8625

Heraldry
Hereditary Order of Armigerous
Augustans (OAA)
P.O. Box P
Torrance, CA 90508-0210
(213) 320-7766
Fax (213) 530-7530

Heritage
Historical and Genealogical
Society of Indiana County
200 South 6th Street

Indiana, PA 15701-2999
(412) 463-9600

The Heritage of Wake County
Wake County Genealogical Society
P.O. Box 17713
Raleigh, NC 27619
(919) 772-6899

Historical Observer
Middlesex County Historical
Society (MCHS)
151 Main Street
Middletown, CT 06457
(203) 346-0746

The Hudson Green
Hudson Chapter, the Ohio
Genealogical Society
Hudson Library and
Historical Society
Dept. G
22 Aurora Street
Hudson, OH 44236-2947

**Huxford Genealogical Society
Magazine**
Huxford Genealogical Society
(HGS)
P.O. Box 595
Homerville, GA 31634
(912) 487-2310

**I Remember When
Whiteside County Genealogists
(WCG)**
P.O. Box 145
Sterling, IL 61081

Illiana Genealogist
Illiana Genealogical and
Historical Society (IGHS)
P.O. Box 207
Danville, IL 61834-0207
(217) 431-8733

Illinois Mennonite Heritage
Illinois Mennonite Historical and
Genealogical Society (IMHGS)
P.O. Box 819
Metamora, IL 61548
(309) 367-2551

**Illinois State Genealogical
Society Quarterly**

Illinois State Genealogical Society
P.O. Box 10195
Springfield, IL 62791
(217) 789-1968
ISSN: 0046-8622

Immigration Digest
Genealogical Institute (GI)
P.O. Box 22045
Salt Lake City, UT 84122
(801) 257-6174

Indian Awareness Center Newsletter
Fulton County Historical Society (FCHS)
37 East 375 North
Rochester, IN 46975
(219) 223-4436

International Society for British Genealogy and Family History—Newsletter
International Society for British Genealogy and Family History (ISBGFH)
P.O. Box 3115
Salt Lake City, UT 84110-3115
(801) 240-4314
ISSN: 0736-8054

Iredell County Tracks
Genealogical Society of Iredell County (GSIC)
P.O. Box 946
Statesville, NC 28687
(704) 878-5384

Irish Genealogy
Irish Genealogical Society (IGS)
21 Hanson Avenue
Somerville, MA 02143
(617) 666-0877

Iroquois Stalker
Iroquois County Genealogical Society (ICGS)
Old Courthouse Museum
2nd and Cherry Streets
Watseka, IL 60970
(815) 432-2215

Historic Jasper (HJ)
Jasper Area History
P.O. Box 525

Jasper, IN 47547-0525
(812) 482-6873

JCGS Newsletter
Jackson County Genealogical Society
c/o Jackson District Library
244 West Michigan
Jackson, MI 49201
(517) 787-8105

Johnston County Genealogical Society Newsletter
Johnston County Genealogical Society
305 Market Street
Smithfield, NC 27577
(919) 934-8146

Jots from the Point
Western Pennsylvania Genealogical Society (WPGS)
Historical Society of Western Pennsylvania Building
4338 Bigelow Road
Pittsburgh, PA 15213-2695
(412) 681-5533

Journal of Genealogical Society of Okaloosa County
Genealogical Society of Okaloosa County (GSOC)
P.O. Box 1175
Ft. Walton Beach, FL 32549
(904) 862-8388

Journal of Heraldic Studies
Heraldry Society of the United States of America (HSUSA)
P.O. Box 386
Torrance, CA 90508
(213) 326-8603
Fax (213) 530-7530

Journal of the Kanawha Valley Genealogical Society
Kanawha Valley Genealogical Society (KVGS)
P.O. Box 8555
South Charleston, WV 25303
(304) 342-2757

Journey into the Past
Graves County Genealogical Society (GCGS)

P.O. Box 245
Mayfield, KY 42066
(502) 674-5750

Keyhole to the West
Genealogical Society of Southwestern Pennsylvania
P.O. Box 894
Washington, PA 15301-0894

Kinfolks
Southwest Louisiana Genealogical Society (SWLGS)
P.O. Box 5652
Lake Charles, LA 70606-5652

La Voix des Prairies
Evangeline Genealogical and Historical Society (EGHS)
P.O. Box 664
Ville Platte, LA 70586

Lapeer Legacy
Lapeer County Genealogical Society (LCGS)
Marguerite de Angeli Branch Library
921 West Nepessing Street
Lapeer, MI 48446

Laurel Messenger
Historical and Genealogical Society of Somerset County
RD 2; Box 238
Somerset, PA 15501
(814) 445-6077
Fax (814) 445-6077

Lexicon
Jackson County Genealogical Society
c/o Jackson District Library
244 West Michigan
Jackson, MI 49201
(517) 787-8105

LGS Newsletter
Louisville Genealogical Society
P.O. Box 5164
Louisville, KY 40205
(502) 425-4656

The Licking Lantern
Licking County Genealogical Society (LCGS)

P.O. Box 4037
Newark, OH 43055
(614) 345-3571

Lifelines
Northern New York American-
Canadian Genealogical Society
(NNYACGS)
P.O. Box 1256
Plattsburgh, NY 12901

Lineage
Jewish Genealogy Society of
Long Island
37 Westcliff Drive
Dix Hills, NY 11746
(516) 549-9532

Lines and By-Lines
Louisville Genealogical Society
(LGS)
P.O. Box 5164
Louisville, KY 40205
(502) 425-4656

Lives and Times
Smyrna Historical and
Genealogical Society (SHAGS)
825 Austin Drive
Smyrna, GA 30082-3305
(404) 435-7549

Longhunter
Southern Kentucky Genealogical
Society (SKGS)
P.O. Box 1782
Bowling Green, KY 42102-1782
(502) 843-9452

**Louisiana Genealogical
Register**
Louisiana Genealogical and
Historical Society (LGHS)
P.O. Box 3454
Baton Rouge, LA 70821
(504) 766-1555

MCGHS Newsletter
Marshall County Genealogical
and Historical Society
P.O. Box 373
Benton, KY 42025
(502) 527-7918

MCHS Newsletter
Madison County Historical
Society (MCHS)
435 Main Street
P.O. Box 415
Oneida, NY 13421
(315) 363-4136

MCIGS Connections
McHenry County Illinois
Genealogical Society (MCIGS)
P.O. Box 184
Crystal Lake, IL 60039-0184
(815) 385-0686

The Megaphone
Meigs County Genealogical
Society (MCGS)
34465 Crew Road
Pomeroy, OH 45769
(614) 992-7874

Mennonite Heritage
Illinois Mennonite Historical
and Genealogical Society
(IMHGS)
P.O. Box 819
Metamora, IL 61548
(309) 367-2551

MGC Newsletter
Michigan Genealogical Council
(MGC)
P.O. Box 30007
Lansing, MI 48909

MGS Newsletter
Minnesota Genealogical Society
(MGS)
P.O. Box 16069
St. Paul, MN 55116
(612) 645-3671

Middle Tennessee Genealogy
Middle Tennessee Genealogical
Society
P.O. Box 190625
Nashville, TN 37219-0625

**Mills County Genealogical
Society**
Mills County Genealogical
Society (MCGS)
Glenwood Public Library
109 North Vine

Glenwood, IA 51534
(712) 527-5252

Minnesota Genealogist
Minnesota Genealogical Society
(MGS)
P.O. Box 16069
St. Paul, MN 55116
(612) 645-3671

Mirror
Lancaster Mennonite Historical
Society (LMHS)
2215 Millstream Road
Lancaster, PA 17602-1499
(717) 393-9745
ISSN: 0738-7237

MISHPACHA
Jewish Genealogy Society of
Greater Washington (JGSGW)
P.O. Box 412
Vienna, VA 22183-0412

**Monroe County Genealogical
Society News**
Monroe County Genealogical
Society (MCGS)
Route 3
Albia, IA 52531
(515) 932-5477

Monroe County Historian
Monroe County Historical
Society and Museum (MCHS)
202 East 6th Street
Bloomington, IN 47408
(812) 332-2517

Morasha Heritage
Jewish Genealogical Society of
Illinois (JGSI)
1025 Antique Lane
Northbrook, IL 60062
(708) 577-7453

**Moultrie County Heritage
Quarterly**
Moultrie County Historical and
Genealogical Society (MCHGS)
P.O. Box 588
Sullivan, IL 61951
(217) 728-4085

Muscogiana: Journal of the
Muscogee Genealogical Society
Muscogee Genealogical Society
(MGS)
P.O. Box 761
Columbus, GA 31902
(706) 649-0780

The Muskingum
Muskingum County Genealogical
Society (MCGS)
P.O. Box 3066
Zanesville, OH 43702
(614) 796-2221

Nassau County Historical
Society Journal
Nassau County Historical Society
(NCHS)
P.O. Box 207
Garden City, NY 11530
(516) 747-1141

Natchez Trace Newsletter
Natchez Trace Genealogical
Society (NTGS)
P.O. Box 420
Florence, AL 35631-0420

Natchez Trace Traveler
Natchez Trace Genealogical
Society (NTGS)
P.O. Box 420
Florence, AL 35631-0420

National Genealogical
Society—Newsletter
National Genealogical Society
(NGS)
4527 17th Street North
Arlington, VA 22207-2399
(703) 525-0050
Fax (703) 525-0052

New England Genealogy
Institute of Family History and
Genealogy (IFHG)
21 Hanson Avenue
Somerville, MA 02143
(617) 666-0877

New England Historical and
Genealogical Register
99-101 Newbury Street
Boston, MA 02116

(617) 536-5740
Fax (617) 536-7307

The New Hampshire
Genealogical Record
New Hampshire Society of
Genealogists (NHSOG)
P.O. Box 2316
Concord, NH 03302-2316
(603) 432-8137
Fax (603) 437-1808

The New Hampshire Society of
Genealogists Newsletter
New Hampshire Society of
Genealogists (NHSOG)
P.O. Box 2316
Concord, NH 03302-2316
(603) 432-8137
Fax (603) 437-1808

New Orleans Genesis
Genealogical Research Society of
New Orleans (GRSNO)
P.O. Box 51791
New Orleans, LA 70151
(504) 581-3153

The New York Genealogical
and Biographical Record
New York Genealogical and
Biographical Society (NYGBS)
122 East 58th Street
New York, NY 10022-1939
(212) 755-8532

News of the Family History
Library
Family History Department of
the Church of Jesus Christ of
Latter-Day Saints
50 East North Temple
Salt Lake City, UT 84150
(801) 240-2331
Fax (801) 240-5551

The Newsletter
Genealogy Unlimited Society
2511 Churchill Drive
Valdosta, GA 31602
(912) 244-0464

Newsnotes
Genealogy Society of Fayette and
Raleigh Counties (GSFRC)

P.O. Box 68
Oak Hill, WV 25901

Nexus
New England Historic
Genealogical Society (NEHGS)
99-101 Newbury Street
Boston, MA 02116
(617) 536-5740
Fax (617) 536-7307

Noble News
Noble County Genealogical
Society (NCGS)
109 North York Street
Albion, IN 46701
(219) 636-7197
Fax (219) 636-3321

North Carolina Genealogical
Society Journal
North Carolina Genealogical
Society (NCGS)
P.O. Box 1492
Raleigh, NC 27602

North Central North Dakota
Genealogical Record
Mouse River Loop Genealogical
Society (MRLGS)
P.O. Box 1391
Minot, ND 58702-1391
(701) 839-2827

Northampton Notes
Northampton County Historical
and Genealogical Society
(NCHGS)
101 South 4th Street
Easton, PA 18042
(215) 253-1222

Northwest Trail Tracer
Genealogical Society, Northwest
Territory
c/o Donna Beeson
Vincennes University
Lewis Library—LRC
Vincennes, IN 47591
(812) 885-4330

Norwegian Tracks
Vesterheim Genealogical Center
(VGC)
415 West Main Street

Madison, WI 53703
(608) 255-2224
Fax (608) 255-6842

Noticias Para Los Californianos
Los Californianos (LC)
P.O. Box 1693
San Leandro, CA 94577-0169
(510) 276-5429

O'Lochlainns Personal Journal of Irish Families
Irish Genealogical Foundation (IGF)
P.O. Box 7575
Kansas City, MO 64116
(816) 454-2410
Fax (816) 454-2410

Oak Leaves
Warren County Historical and Genealogical Society
P.O. Box 313
Belvidere, NJ 07823
(908) 475-4246

Oakland County Genealogical Society—Acorns to Oaks
Oakland County Genealogical Society (OCGS)
P.O. Box 1094
Birmingham, MI 48012
(313) 357-3193

The Ohio Genealogical Society Newsletter
Ohio Genealogical Society (OGS)
P.O. Box 2625
Mansfield, OH 44906-0625
(419) 522-9077

Ohio Records and Pioneer Families
Ohio Genealogical Society (OGS)
P.O. Box 2625
Mansfield, OH 44906-0625
(419) 522-9077

Ohio's Last Frontier
Williams County Genealogical Society
P.O. Box 293
Bryan, OH 43506

Old and New
Stoughton Historical Society (SHS)
P.O. Box 542
Stoughton, MA 02072
(617) 344-5456

On the Trail
Ohio Genealogical Society, Brown County Chapter
P.O. Box 83
Georgetown, OH 45121-0083
(513) 444-3521

The Orangeburg German-Swiss Newsletter
Orangeburg German-Swiss Genealogical Society
P.O. Box 974
Orangeburg, SC 29116-0974
(803) 534-3917

Our Missing Links
Kosciusko County Historical Society (KCHS)
P.O. Box 1071
Warsaw, IN 46581
(219) 269-1078

Pastfinder
Southwestern Michigan Genealogical Society
P.O. Box 573
St. Joseph, MI 49085
(616) 983-7002

Pathways and Passages
Polish Genealogical Society of Connecticut
8 Lyle Road
New Britain, CT 06053
(203) 229-8873; (203) 223-5596

Pea River Trails
Pea River Historical and Genealogical Society (PRHGS)
P.O. Box 628
Enterprise, AL 36331
(205) 393-2901

PENN in Hand
Genealogical Society of Pennsylvania (GSP)
1300 Locust Street
Philadelphia, PA 19107
(215) 545-0391

Pennsylvania Genealogical Magazine
Genealogical Society of Pennsylvania (GSP)
1300 Locust Street
Philadelphia, PA 19107
(215) 545-0391

Pennsylvania Mennonite Heritage
Lancaster Mennonite Historical Society (LMHS)
2215 Millstream Road
Lancaster, PA 17602-1499
(717) 393-9745
ISSN: 0148-4036

The Pibroch
Saint Andrew's Society of the State of New York
71 West 23rd Street; Room 1006
New York, NY 10010
(212) 807-1730
Fax (212) 807-1877

Pinellas Genealogist
Pinellas Genealogy Society
8476 15th Way North
St. Petersburg, FL 33702
(813) 576-4899

Pioneer Record
Midland Genealogical Society
c/o Grace A. Dow Memorial Library
1710 West St. Andrews Drive
Midland, MI 48640

Pioneer Trails
Jackson County Genealogical Society (JCGS)
P.O. Box 2145
Independence, MO 64055

Pioneer Wagon
Jackson County Genealogical Society (JCGS)
P.O. Box 2145
Independence, MO 64055

Pointers
Pursuing Our Italian Names Together (POINT)
P.O. Box 2977
Palos Verdes, CA 90274

Polish Genealogical Society of America—Bulletin
Polish Genealogical Society of American (PGSA)
984 North Milwaukee Avenue
Chicago, IL 60622

Polish Genealogical Society of America—Journal
Polish Genealogical Society of American (PGSA)
984 North Milwaukee Avenue
Chicago, IL 60622
ISSN: 0735-9349

Poweshiek County, Iowa Searcher
Poweshiek County Historical and Genealogical Society (PCHGS)
206 North Mill Street
P.O. Box 280
Montezuma, IA 50171
(515) 623-3322

Prairie Trails Journal
Odell Prairie Trails Historical and Genealogical Society (OPTHGS)
P.O. Box 82
Odell, IL 60460
(815) 998-2324

Preble's Pride
Preble County Genealogical Society
c/o Preble County District Library
301 North Barron Street
Eaton, OH 45320
(513) 456-4331; Fax (513) 456-4774

Quarterlies
Hart County Historical Society (HCHS)
P.O. Box 606
Munfordville, KY 42765
(502) 524-0101

The Report
Ohio Genealogical Society
34 Sturges Avenue
P.O. Box 2625
Mansfield, OH 44906-0625
(419) 522-9077

Richmond County Record
Society of Richmond County, North Carolina Descendants

P.O. Box 848
Rockingham, NC 28379
(919) 997-6641

Roots-Key
Jewish Genealogical Society of Los Angeles
P.O. Box 55443
Sherman Oaks, CA 91413-0443
(818) 991-5864

Rota-Gene
International Genealogical Fellowship of Rotarians
5721 Antietam Drive
Sarasota, FL 34231
(813) 924-9170
ISSN: 0730-5168

Saga
Scandinavian-American Genealogical Society (SAGS)
P.O. Box 16069
St. Paul, MN 55116-0069
(612) 645-3671

SCCGS Quarterly
St. Clair County Genealogical Society (SCCGS)
P.O. Box 431
Belleville, IL 62222
(618) 227-0848

Scott County Genealogical Newsletter
Scott County Genealogical Society (SCGS)
Scott County Public Library
East Main
Georgetown, KY 40324
(502) 863-3566

Scott County Iowan
Scott County Iowa Genealogical Society
P.O. Box 3132
Davenport, IA 52808-3132

Search
Jewish Genealogical Society of Illinois (JGSI)
1025 Antique Lane
Northbrook, IL 60062
(708) 577-7453

Searchers and Researchers
Ellis County Genealogical Society (ECGS)
P.O. Box 479
Waxahachie, TX 75165
(214) 330-7637

The Second Boat
Pentref Press
P.O. Box 398
Machias, ME 04654
(207) 255-4114
ISSN: 0274-6441

Seedling Patch
Lawrence County Historical and Genealogical Society
Lawrence County Court House, Basement
Bedford, IN 47421
(812) 275-4141

Shelby County Ancestors
Shelby County Historical and Genealogical Society (SCHGS)
151 South Washington
P.O. Box 286
Shelbyville, IL 62565
(217) 774-2260

Shelby County Historical Society Quarterly
Shelby County Historical Society (SCHS)
1854 Courthouse
P.O. Box 457
Columbiana, AL 35051
(205) 669-3912

SLVGS Newsletter
St. Lawrence Valley Genealogical Society (SLVGS)
P.O. Box 341
Culton, NY 13625-0341

Smoke Signals
Fort Assiniboine Genealogy Society
P.O. Box 321
Havre, MT 59501
(406) 265-9641

Southern Genealogists Exchange Society (SGES) Journal

Southern Genealogist's
Exchange Society (SGES)
P.O. Box 2801
Jacksonville, FL 32203
(904) 387-9142

SPGS Newsletter
South Plains Genealogical
Society (SPGS)
P.O. Box 6607
Lubbock, TX 79493

Splinters from the Tree
Pasadena Genealogy Society
(PGS)
P.O. Box 94774
Pasadena, CA 91109-4774
(818) 794-7973

Steppin' Stones
Shiawassee County Genealogical
Society
P.O. Box 841
Owosso, MI 48867
(517) 725-8549

Stripes
Texas State Genealogical Society
Route 4; Box 56
Sulphur Springs, TX 75482
(903) 885-3523

*Tarentum Genealogical
Society Newsletter*
Tarentum Genealogical Society
Community Library of
Allegheny Valley
315 East 6th Avenue
Tarentum, PA 15084
(412) 226-0770

Tayerer Landsman
Jewish Genealogical Society of
South Florida
1501 Cayman Way; Apt. F2
Coconut Creek, FL 33066
(305) 979-6926

Taylor County in Profile
Taylor County Historical and
Genealogical Society (TCHGS)
P.O. Box 522
Grafton, WV 26354

Thea Kiki
Kankakee Valley Genealogical
Society
P.O. Box 442
Bourbonnais, IL 60914
(815) 933-5529
Fax (815) 933-2516

Timbertown Log
Saginaw Genealogical Society
(SGS)
Saginaw Public Library
505 Janes
Saginaw, MI 48605
(517) 755-0904

Traces
South Central Kentucky
Historical and Genealogical
Society (SCKHGS)
P.O. Box 157
Glasgow, KY 42142-0157
(502) 651-5511

Trails West
Parker County Genealogical
Society
1214 Charles
Weatherford, TX 76086
(817) 594-2767

TSGS Newsletter
Texas State Genealogical Society
Route 4; Box 56
Sulphur Springs, TX 75482
(903) 885-3523

The Tumbleweeds
Hyde County Historical and
Genealogical Society (HCHGS)
HC 2; Box 112
Highmore, SD 57345
(605) 852-2376; (605) 852-2251

*Van Buren County Historical
Society Journal*
Van Buren County Historical
Society (VBCHS)
P.O. Box 126
Spencer, TN 38585
(615) 946-2121

*Van Buren Historical Society
Newsletter*
Van Buren County Historical

Society (VBCHS)
P.O. Box 126
Spencer, TN 38585
(615) 946-2121

Vinton County Heritage
Vinton County Historical and
Genealogical Society (VCHS)
P.O. Box 306
Hamden, OH 45634
(614) 384-2467

W.R.H.S. News
Western Reserve Historical
Society (WRHS)
10825 East Boulevard
Cleveland, OH 44106
(216) 721-5722
Fax (216) 721-0645

Wagoneer
Northwest Genealogical Society
(NWGS)
P.O. Box 6
Alliance, NE 69301

WCGS Bulletin
Weakley County Genealogical
Society (WCGS)
P.O. Box 894
Martin, TN 38237

Webster's Wagon Wheel
Webster County Historical and
Genealogical Society (WCHGS)
300 East Leiper Street
Dixon, KY 42409
(502) 639-9171

Westchester Connections
Westchester County Genealogical
Society
P.O. Box 518
White Plains, NY 10603

*Wetzel County Genealogical
Society Quarterly*
Wetzel County Genealogical
Society
P.O. Box 464
New Martinsville, WV 26155

White County Heritage
White County Historical Society
P.O. Box 537

Searcy, AR 72143
(501) 268-8726
ISSN: 0043-4906

Windsor Historical Society News
Windsor Historical Society (WHS)
96 Palisado Avenue
Windsor, CT 06095
(203) 688-3813

Wisconsin Slovak
Wisconsin Slovak Historical
Society (WSHS)
P.O. Box 164
Cudahy, WI 53110-0164
(414) 747-1757

WNYG Journal
Western New York Genealogical
Society (WNYGS)
P.O. Box 338
Hamburg, NY 14075

WSGS Newsletter
Wisconsin State Genealogical
Society (WSGS)
2109 20th Avenue
Monroe, WI 53566
(608) 325-2609

Wymondak Messenger
Tri-State Genealogy Association
c/o Public Library
905 5th Avenue
Belle Fourche, SD 57717
(605) 892-4019

Yesterday's Tuckaways
Hopkins County Genealogical
Society
P.O. Box 51
Madisonville, KY 42431

York County Genealogical Society Journal
York County Genealogical Society
(YCGS)
P.O. Box 2242
Ogunquit, ME 03907
(207) 646-3753

Z'chor
Jewish Genealogical Society of
Pittsburgh

2127-31 5th Avenue
Pittsburgh, PA 15219
(412) 471-0772
Fax (412) 471-1004

ZichronNote
San Francisco Bay Area Jewish
Genealogical Society (SFBAJGS)
3916 Louis Road
Palo Alto, CA 94303-4541
(415) 424-1622

VENEZUELA

Boletin (in Spanish)
Venezuelan Institute of
Genealogy (VIG)
Instituto Venezolano de
Genealogia (IVG)
Palacio de las Academias
Apartado Postal 60706
Caracas 1060-A, Venezuela
(2) 2635217

*Note that there are many
additional newsletters and
publications produced by
genealogical associations. Not
all have been included here.*

INVESTIGATIVE JOURNALISM & INVESTIGATIVE PUBLICATIONS

CIJ Eye Opener
Centre for Investigative
Journalism
Journal Department
Carleton University
Ottawa, Ontario ON K1S 5B6
Canada
(613) 788-7424
Fax (613) 788-5604

Centre for Investigative Journalism Bulletin
Centre for Investigative
Journalism
Journal Department
Carleton University

Ottawa, Ontario ON K1S 5B6,
Canada
(613) 788-7424
Fax (613) 788-5604

FREEDOM Magazine: Investigative Reporting in the Public Interest
Church of Scientology
International
6331 Hollywood Boulevard
Suite 1200
Los Angeles, CA 90028-6329
(213) 960-3500
Fax (213) 960-3508
Fax (213) 960-3509

Hastings Communications and Entertainment Law Journal (Comm—Ent)
University of California at San
Francisco
Hastings College of the Law
200 McAllister Street
San Francisco, CA 94102-4978
(415) 565-4731
ISSN: 1061-6578, 0193-8398
(Available online through West
Services, Inc.; also available on
CD-ROM)

The IRE Journal
Investigative Reporters and
Editors, Inc. (IRE)
University of Missouri
100 Neff Hall
School of Journalism
Columbia, MO 65211
(314) 882-2042
Fax (314) 882-5431
ISSN: 0164-7016

The Legal Investigator
3304 Crescent Drive
Des Moines, IA 50312

Muckraker: Journal of the Center for Investigative Reporting
Center for Investigative
Reporting (CIR)
530 Howard Street; 2nd Floor
San Francisco, CA 94105-3007
(800)733-0015; (415) 543-1200
Fax (415) 543-8311

Private Investigators'
Connection
Thomas Publications
P.O. Box 33244
Austin, TX 78764

Rights and Liabilities of
Publishers, Broadcasters, and
Reporters
Shepard's—McGraw-Hill, Inc.
Box 35300
Colorado Springs, CO 80935-3530
(800) 525-2474

Uplink
Investigative Reporters and
Editors (IRE)
University of Missouri
100 Neff Hall
Columbia, MO 65211
(314) 882-2042
Fax (314) 882-5431

MAILING LISTS/
DIRECT MARKETING
PUBLICATIONS

Admarks
Chicago Association of Direct
Marketing (CADM)
600 South Federal Street
Chicago, IL 60605
(312) 922-6222

Dateline: DMA (in English,
French, Japanese, and Spanish)
Direct Marketing Association
(DMA)
11 West 42nd Street
New York, NY 10036-8096
(212) 768-7277
Fax (212) 768-4546

Direct Line: The DMA
Newsletter
Direct Marketing Association
(DMA)
11 West 42nd Street
New York, NY 10036-8096
(212) 768-7277
Fax (212) 768-4546
ISSN: 0743-7625

Direct Marketing Magazine:
Using Direct Response
Advertising to Enhance
Marketing Database
Hoke Communications, Inc.
224 7th Street
Garden City, NY 11530
(800) 229-6700; (516) 746-6700
Fax (516) 294-8141
ISSN: 0012-3188
(Available online through
LEXIS-NEXIS)

Direct Marketing News
C D M N Publishing
1200 Markham Road; Suite 301
Scarborough, Ontario M1H 3C3
Canada,
(416) 439-4083
ISSN: 1187-7111

Direct Response: The Digest of
Direct Marketing
Creative Direct Marketing Group
P.O. Box 2100
Rolling Hills Estates, CA 90274
(213) 212-5727
Fax (213) 212-5773

DM News
Mill Hollow Corporation
19 West 21st Street
New York, NY 10010
(212) 741-2095
Fax (212) 633-9367
(Available online through
LEXIS-NEXIS)

DMA News
Direct Marketing Association
(DMA)
Haymarket House
1 Oxenden Street
London SW1Y 4EE, England
(71) 3212525; (71) 3210191

DMA Washington Report:
Federal and State Regulatory
Issues of Concern
Direct Marketing Association
(DMA)
11 West 42nd Street
New York, NY 10036-8096
(212) 768-7277
Fax (212) 768-4546

EDMA-Flash
European Direct Marketing
Association (EDMA)
36, rue du Gouvernement
Provisoire, B-1000 Brussels
Belgium
(2) 2176309; Fax (2) 2176985

Marketing AdVents
Direct Marketing Association of
Washington (DMAW)
655 15th Street NW; Suite 300
Washington, DC 20005-5798
(202) 393-3629; Fax (202) 628-2113

The Mirror
Direct Marketing Association
of Detroit
30800 Telegraph Road; Suite 1724
Birmingham, MI 48025
(313) 258-8803

Target Marketing: The
Leading Magazine for
Integrated Database
Marketing
North American Publishing Co.
401 North Broad Street
Philadelphia, PA 19108
(215) 238-5300
ISSN: 0889-5333

ONLINE RESEARCH
AND DATABASE
PUBLICATIONS

Business Information Markets
(Year)
SIMBA—Communications Trends
213 Danbury Road
P.O. Box 7430
Wilton, CT 06897-7430
(203) 834-0033

Connections
Association of Independent
Information Professionals
Administrative Services Office
245 Fifth Avenue; Suite 2103
New York, NY 10016
(212) 779-1855
Fax (212) 481-3071

DATABASE
Online Inc.
462 Danbury Road
Wilton, CT 06897-2126
(800) 248-8466; (203) 761-1466
Fax (203) 761-1444
ISSN: 0162-4105

Database
(in Japanese)
Japan Database Industry
Association (DINA)
3-2, Nishishinjuku 2-chome
Shinjuku-ku,
Tokyo 163-03, Japan
(3) 33477107; Fax (3) 33475300

DataBase Alert
Knowledge Industry
Publications, Inc.
701 Westchester Avenue
White Plains, NY 10604
(914) 328-9157
ISSN: 0737-951X
(Available online through BRS
Online Products) (KIPD)

Database Review
DataBase Associates
Box 215
Morgan Hill, CA 95038-0215
(408) 779-0436
ISSN: 1042-2595

EFFector Online
Electronic Frontier Foundation
155 2nd Street
Cambridge, MA 02141
(617) 864-0665
Fax (617) 864-0866
ISSN: 11062-9242
(Available online on the Internet)

EMedia Professional
Online Inc.
462 Danbury Road
Wilton, CT 06897-2126
(800) 248-8466; (203) 761-1466
Fax (203) 761-1444

Friday Memo
Information Industry
Association
555 New Jersey Avenue NW

Suite 800
Washington, DC 20001
(202) 639-8262
(Available online through
NewsNet) (PB15)

**Infodb: The Leading Technical
Journal for Database Users**
DataBase Associates
Box 215
Morgan Hill, CA 95038-0215
(408) 779-0436
ISSN: 0891-6004

Information Broker
Burwell Enterprises, Inc.
3724 F.M. 1960 W.; Suite 214
Houston, TX 77068
(713) 537-9051
Fax (713) 537-8332

Information Searcher
Datasearch, Inc.
14 Hadden Road
Scarsdale, NY 10583
(914) 723-3156
ISSN: 1055-3916

**Information Technology and
Libraries**
Library and Information
Technology Association (LITA)
50 East Huron Street
Chicago, IL 60611-2795
(800) 545-2433; (312) 280-4270
Fax (312) 280-3257
ISSN: 0730-9295

Information Today
Learned Information, Inc.
143 Old Marlton Pike
Medford, NJ 08055-8707
(609) 654-6266
Fax (609) 654-4309
ISSN: 8755-6286

**InformationWEEK: The
Newsmagazine for
Information Management**
CMP Publications, Inc.
600 Community Drive
Manhasset, NY 11030
(516) 365-4600
Fax (516) 562-5472
ISSN: 8750-6874

**Link Review of Interactive
Services**
Link Resources Corporation
79 5th Avenue; 12th Floor
New York, NY 10003
(212) 627-1500;
Fax (212) 620-3099
(Available online through
NewsNet Inc., Information Access
Company (IAC), Predicasts, Inc.
PTS Newsletter Database)

**Link-Up: The Newsmagazine
for Users of Online Services
and CD-ROM**
Learned Information, Inc.
143 Old Marlton Pike
Medford, NJ 08055-8707
(609) 654-6266
Fax (609) 654-4309
ISSN: 0739-988X; LCCN: TK5105
(Available online through
LEXIS-NEXIS)

Login
Netherlands Association of Users
of Online Information Systems
(NAUOIS)
Nederlandse Vereniging van
Gebruikers van Online
Informatie-Systemen (VOGIN)
c/o Mr. P.J.C. Rosenbrand
COBIDOC BV
St. Athoniesbreestraat 16II,
NL-1011 HB Amsterdam,
Netherlands
(20) 6223955; Fax (20) 6222556
ISSN: 0920-0290

**Monitor (Oxford): An
Analytical Review of Current
Events in the Online and
Electronic Publishing
Industry**
Learned Information (Europe) Ltd.
Woodside, Hinksey Hill
Oxford OX1 5AU, England
0865-730275
ISSN: 0260-6666

**Netguide: The Guide to Online
Services and the Internet**
C M P Publications, Inc.
600 Community Drive

Manhasset, NY 11030
(516) 562-7308

OLBG—Info: Mitteilungsblatt
der Online-Benutzergruppe in
der DGD
Deutsche Gesellschaft fuer
Dokumentation e.V.
Hanauerlandstr. 126-128
60314 Frankfurt, Germany
069-740805
ISSN: 0172-732X

ONLINE
Online Inc.
462 Danbury Road
Wilton, CT 06897
(203) 761-1466
Fax (203) 761-1444
ISSN: 0146-5422
LCCN: Z699.A1

Online
The "On-Line Database" Gazette
P.O. Box 360368
Melbourne, Florida 32937

Online & CD-ROM Review: The
International Journal of
Online & Optical
Information Systems
Learned Information, Inc.
143 Old Marlton Pike
Medford, NJ 08055-8750
(609) 654-6266
LCCN: Z699.A1

Online Access
Chicago Fine Print, Inc.
920 N. Franklin; Suite 203
Chicago, IL 60610-3119
(312) 573-1700
ISSN: 0898-2015

Online Currents
Enterprise Information
Management Pty. Ltd.
6-217 Eastern Valley Way
Willoughby, N.S.W. 2068, Australia
02-958-7099
ISSN: 0816-956X

Online Files: Comparative
Cost Analysis: A Unique

Guide to the Costs of
Searching the World's Major
Online Databases Effective
Technology Marketing Ltd.
Enterprise House
Wilton Road
Humberston, Great Grimsby
DB36 4AS, England
0472-210707
ISSN: 0967-6090

Online Newsletter
Information Intelligence Inc.
Box 31098
Phoenix, AZ 85046
(800) 228-9982
(Available online through
DataStar, Knight-Ridder
Information, Inc., Dow Jones
News/Retrieval, European Space
Agency, and NewsNet)

Online Product News
Worldwide Videotex
Box 3273
Boynton Beach, FL 33424-3273
(407) 738-2276
(Available online through
NewsNet)

Searcher: The Magazine for
Database Professionals
Learned Information, Inc.
143 Old Marlton Pike
Medford, NJ 08055
(609) 654-6266
ISSN: 1070-4795

Worldwide Databases
Worldwide Videotex
P.O. Box 3273
Boynton Beach, FL 33424-3273
(407) 738-2276
Fax (407) 738-2275
(Available online through
Information Access Company
(IAC), Predicasts, Inc., PTS,
Newsletter Database,
NewsNet Inc.)

Library associations sometimes
include articles about databases
or searching in their publications.
Most database vendors also produce

newsletters, documentation and
other publications that can provide
information about searching their
databases.

PRE-EMPLOYMENT SCREENING AND RECRUITMENT PUBLICATIONS

BNA's Employee Relations
Weekly
The Bureau of National Affairs,
Inc. (BNA)
1231 25th Street, NW
Washington, DC 20037
(800) 862-4636; (202) 452-4132
Fax (202) 452-4062
(Available online through HRIN)

Croner's Employment Law
Croner Publications Ltd.
Subsidiary of: Wolters
Kluwer N.V.
Croner House
London Road
Kingston, Surrey KT2 6SR
England
081-547-3333

Employee Development
Bulletin: Practice and Policy
in Training and Development;
Recruitment, Selection and
Retention
Eclipse Group Ltd.
18-20 Highbury Place
London N5 1QP, England
0171-354-5858
ISSN: 1351-055X

Employer Advocate: Warnings
and Recommendations That
Help You Lead and Manage
Better Independent Small
Business Employers of
America
520 South Pierce; Suite 224
Mason City, IA 50401
(800) 728-3187; (515) 424-3187
Fax (515) 424-1673

Employment at Will Reporter
New England Legal Publishers
Box 425
Weston, MA 02193
(617) 891-6200

Employment Law Counselor
Business Laws, Inc. (BLI)
11630 Chillicothe Road
Chesterland, OH 44026
(800) 759-0929; (216) 729-7996
Fax (216) 729-0645
ISSN: 1052-2964

Executive Recruiter News
Kennedy Publications
Templeton Road
Fitzwilliam, NH 03447
(800) 531-0007; (603) 585-3101
Fax (603) 585-6401
ISSN: 0271-0781

Federal Staffing Digest
Superintendent of Documents
U.S. Government Printing Office
Box 371954
Pittsburgh, PA 15250-7954
(202) 606-0960
ISSN: 1053-4652

Fordyce Letter
Kimberly Organization
Box 31011
Des Peres, MO 63131
(314) 965-3883
ISSN: 0733-0324

*Human Resource
Measurements: Perspectives on
Testing and Hiring Procedures*
Wonderlic Personnel Text Inc.
1509 North Milwaukee Avenue
Libertyville, IL 60048
(800) 323-3742; (708) 680-4900
Fax (708) 680-9492

*Individual Employment
Rights*
The Bureau of National Affairs,
Inc.
1231 25th Street NW
Washington, DC 20037
(800) 372-1033; (202) 452-4200
(Available online through
Human Resources Information

Network (CDD, HDD); LEXIS-
NEXIS, West Services, Inc.
(File FLB-CS, LRR-IERN)

*Journal of Career Planning
& Employment: The
International Magazine of
Placement and Recruitment*
College Placement Council, Inc.
62 Highland Avenue
Bethlehem, PA 18017
(215) 868-1421

*The Recruiting & Search
Report*
Kenneth J. Cole
P.O. Box 9433
Panama City Beach, FL 32410
(904) 235-3733

Recruiting Trends
Remy Publishing Company
350 W. Hubbard Street; Suite 440
Chicago, IL 60610
(800) 542-6670; (312) 464-0300
Fax (312) 464-0166

Workforce Strategies
c/o Mark Dibner, Vice President
9435 Key West Avenue
Rockville, MD 20850
(919) 549-8873
ISSN: 1062-8991

*There are many additional
publications that are specialized by
industry, such as those for the
healthcare industry, banking, the
legal profession, and the sciences.*

PRIVACY AND
COMPUTER SECURITY
PUBLICATIONS

*Canada Privacy
Commissioner Annual Report*
Privacy Commissioner; Canada
112 Kent Street; 3rd Floor
Ottawa, ON K1A 1H3, Canada
(613) 995-2410
ISSN: 0825-7361

Cipher Newsletter
Technical Committee on Security
& Privacy
IEEE Computer Society
1730 Massachusetts Avenue NW
Washington, DC 20036-1992
(202) 371-0101
Fax (202) 728-9614

Civil Liberties Alert
American Civil Liberties Union
Foundation (ACLU)
132 West 43rd Street
New York, NY 10036
(212) 944-9800
Fax (212) 354-5290
ISSN: 0009-790X

Civil Liberty Newsletter
Australian Civil Liberties Union
(ACLU)
P.O. Box 1137
Carlton, VIC 3053, Australia
(3) 476302

*Computer Security and
Privacy Abstracts*
Techgnosis Ltd.
Blade House
Battersea Road
Stockport, Cheshire SK4 3AE,
England
(061) 442-2639
ISSN: 0958-1413

Computer Security Digest
Computer Protection
Systems, Inc.
150 N. Main Street
Plymouth, MI 48170
(313) 459-8787
Fax (313) 459-2720
ISSN: 0882-1453

The CPSR Newsletter
Computer Professionals for Social
Responsibility (CPSR)
P.O. Box 717
Palo Alto, CA 94302
(415) 322-3778
Fax (415) 322-4748

EFFector Online
Electronic Frontier Foundation
155 2nd Street

Cambridge, MA 02141
(617) 864-0665
Fax (617) 864-0866
(Available online on the Internet)
ISSN: 11062-9242

EPIC Alert
Electronic Privacy Information
Center
666 Pennsylvania Avenue SE
Suite 301
Washington, DC 20003
(202) 544-9240
Fax (202) 547-5482

**Federal Information
Disclosure, 2-E**
Shepard's—McGraw-Hill, Inc.
Box 35300
Colorado Springs, CO 80935-3530
(800) 525-2474

Financial Privacy Report
Box 1277
1129 E. Cliff Road
Burnsville, MN 55337
(612) 895-8757
ISSN: 1059-0013

Gray Areas
Gray Areas, Inc.
Box 808
Broomall, PA 19008-0808
(215) 353-8238
ISSN: 1062-5712

**Hastings Communications
and Entertainment Law
Journal (Comm—Ent)**
University of California
at San Francisco
Hastings College of the Law
200 McAllister Street
San Francisco, CA 94102-4978
(415) 565-4731
ISSN: 1061-6578
(Available online through West
Services, Inc., as well as on
CD-ROM)

**Informatization and the
Public Sector: An
International Journal on the
Development, Adoption, Use
and Effects of Information**

Technologies
I O S Press
Van Diemenstr. 94
1013 CN Amsterdam,
Netherlands
31-20-6382189
ISSN: 0925-5052

L D R C Bulletin
Libel Defense Resource Center
404 Park Avenue South
16th Floor
New York, NY 10016
(212) 889-2306
ISSN: 0737-8130

**Litigation Under the Federal
Open Government Laws**
American Civil Liberties Union
Foundation
122 Maryland Avenue NE
Washington, DC 20002
(202) 544-1681
ISSN: 1068-7149

**National Association to
Protect Individual Rights
Newsletter**
National Association to Protect
Individual Rights
P.O. Box 90030
Washington, DC 20090-0030
(703) 242-8671
Fax (703) 242-8390

Privacy
Social Issues Resources Series
Box 2348
Boca Raton, FL 33427-2348
(407) 994-0079
ISSN: 0272-9989

Privacy & Security Review
Thin Man & Associates
133 E. de la Guerra, No. 143
Santa Barbara, CA 93101
(805) 963-1500
Fax (805) 963-9898

Privacy and Security 2001
Ross Engineering, Inc.
504 Shaw Road, No. 222
Sterling, VA 20166
(703) 318-8600

**Privacy Journal: An
Independent Monthly on
Privacy in a Computer Age**
Robert Ellis Smith
P.O. Box 28577
Providence, RI 02908
(401) 274-7861
ISSN: 0145-7659
(Available online through
NewsNet Inc.)

Privacy Law and Practice
Matthew Bender & Co., Inc.
11 Penn Plaza
New York, NY 10001
(212) 967-7707

Privacy Times
Privacy Times, Inc.
P.O. Box 21501
Washington, DC 20009
(202) 829-3660
Fax (202) 526-2415

Private Citizen News
Private Citizen, Inc. (PCI)
P.O. Box 233
Naperville, IL 60566
(708) 393-1555

**Rights and Liabilities of
Publishers, Broadcasters, and
Reporters**
Shepard's—McGraw-Hill, Inc.
Box 35300
Colorado Springs, CO 80935-3530
(800) 525-2474

**Texas Bill of Rights: A
Commentary and Litigation
Manual**
Butterworth Legal Publishers
(Salem)
Subsidiary of: Reed Elsevier plc
8 Industrial Way; Building C
Salem, NH 03079
(800) 548-4001

**Washington Credit Letter
Privacy Report**
Capitol Reports, Inc.
1750 Pennsylvania Avenue NW
Suite 1107
Washington, DC 20006
(202) 393-1480

PRIVATE INVESTIGATION PUBLICATIONS

The Advisor
Ohio Association of Security and
Investigation Services
5310 E. Main Street; No. 100
Columbus, OH 43213
(614) 759-7435;
Fax (614) 759-7420

CALI Newsletter
California Association of Licensed
Investigators
1408 Claremont Way
Sacramento, CA 92582

The Eagle: An Independent
Newsletter of Security,
Investigation, and Counter-
Espionage
International Security &
Detective Alliance—I S D A
755 Bronx
Toledo, OH 43609
(419) 382-0967

The Eye Newsletter
Private Investigators Association
of Virginia (PIAV)
P.O. Box 104
Burke, VA 22015
(703) 273-1200

Investigative News
Marathon Press
Martinique Drive
Chino Hills, CA 91709

The Investigator's Journal
P.I. Publications
P.O. Box 11628
Jacksonville, FL 32239-1628

Investigator's Online News
Investigators' Online Network
(ION Incorporated)
2111 East Baseline; Suite F7
Tempe, AZ 85283
(800) 257-1048

The Legal Investigator
National Association of Legal

Investigators
3304 Crescent Drive
Des Moines, IA 50312

P I Magazine
(America's private investigation
journal)
P.O. Box 6303
Corpus Christi, TX 78466-6303
(512) 888-6164

PI Magazine
755 Bronx
Toledo, OH 43609

Private Investigator's
Connection
Thomas Publishing
Box 33244
Austin, TX 78764
(512) 832-0355

WAD News
World Association of Detectives
(WAD)
P.O. Box 1049
Severna Park, MD 21146
(800) 962-0516; (301) 544-0119
Fax (301) 544-6181

PROPERTY MANAGEMENT PUBLICATIONS

Canadian Property
Management
R K Communications Inc.
33 Fraser Avenue; Suite 208
Toronto, ON M6K 3J9 Canada
(416) 588-6220

CPM Aspects
(Certified Property Manager
Aspects)
Institute of Real Estate
Management
P.O. Box 109025
Chicago, IL 60610-9025
(312) 329-6055

Journal of Property
Management

Institute of Real Estate
Management
P.O. Box 109025
Chicago, IL 60610
(312) 661-1930
Fax (312) 661-0217

Professional Apartment
Management
Brownstone Publishers, Inc.
149 5th Avenue; 16th Floor
New York, NY 10010-6801
(800) 643-8095; (212) 473-8200

Property Management
M C B University Press Ltd.
60-62 Toller Lane
Bradford, W. Yorks BD8 9BY
England
0274-499821

Property Management
Association—Bulletin
Property Management
Association (PMA)
8811 Colesville Road; Suite G106
Silver Spring, MD 20910
(301) 587-6543
Fax (301) 589-2017

Property Management
Monthly: Serving the Decision
Makers of Income Producing
Properties
The Adler Group, Inc.
8601 Georgia Avenue; 4th Floor
Silver Spring, MD 20910
(301) 588-0681
Fax (301) 588-6314

Property Management News
K-Rey Publishing Inc.
789 W. Pender Street; Suite 920
Vancouver, BC V6C 1H2 Canada
(604) 669-7671

The Property Professional
National Property Management
Association
380 Main Street; Suite 290
Dunedin, FL 34698
(813) 736-3788
Fax (813) 736-6707

Organizations

ADOPTEE/ BIRTHPARENT SEARCH ORGANIZATIONS

AUSTRALIA

Adoption Jigsaw SA
48 Watson Avenue
Broadview, South Australia 5083
Adoption Jigsaw WA, Inc.
P.O. Box 252; Hillarys
Perth, West Australia 6025
09-388-1922

Association of Relinquishing
Mothers, WA, Inc.
P.O. Box 60
Tuart Hill, West Australia 6060

Australian Relinquishing Mothers
51 North Terrace
Hackney, South Australia 5069
08-362-2418

Child Migrants Trust
228 Canning Street
North Carlton
Melbourne, Victoria, 3054

AUSTRIA

Osterreichisches Rotes Kreuz
Suchdienst
Gusshausstrasse 3
A-1041 Wien

BELGIUM

Vereniging voor Kind en Adoptiegezin, VZW
Sulferbergstraat 38
8000 Brugge

CANADA

National Organizations and National Headquarters

Adoptions and Operational Services
Adoption Unit
Ministry of Community and
Social Services
2 Bloor Street W.; 24th Floor
Toronto, Ontario M7A 1E9
(416) 327-4730

Adoptions Canada—A Private Adoptions Registry
National Headquarters
P.O. Box 637
430 Birch Street
Southhampton, Ontario N0H 2L0
(519) 389-4645; (519) 797-3363

American Adoption Congress (AAC)
Canadian Region (All of Canada)
P.O. Box 4853
Edmonton, Alberta T6E 5G7
(403) 433-4524

Parent Finders, National Headquarters
3998 Bayridge Avenue
W. Vancouver, BC V7V 3J5
(604) 926-1096; (604) 980-6005

Society for Truth in Adoption (TRIAD) National Office
P.O. Box 5922; Station B
Victoria, BC V8R 6S8
(604) 385-7884

DENMARK

Lillian Molin
Folkets Alle 37
2000 Frederiksberg

FRANCE

Service Social d'Aide aux Emigrants
Association Reconnue D'utilite
Publique
SIEGE SOCIAL
72, rue Regnault
F-75640 Paris Cedex 13

GERMANY

Deutsches Rotes Kreuz
Generalsekretariat
Suchdienst Munchen
Zentrale Auskunfts—und
Dokumentationsstelle
Infanteriestrabe 7 A
80797 Munchen
Frau Ingrid Baer, Direktorin

Internationaler Sozialdienst (Deutscher Zweig) e.V.
Am Stockborn 5-7
60439 Frankfurt/Main

NETHERLANDS

Adoption Centre
University of Utrecht
Heidelberglaan 1
3584 CS Utrecht

Stichting International Social Service
Laan Copes van Cattenburch 139
NL-2585 GA's-Gravenhage

NEW ZEALAND

Adoption Jigsaw, Inc.
P.O. Box 28-037
Remuera, Aukland 5

Aotearoa Birthmothers Support Group
Wellesley Street
P.O. Box 5479
Auckland, New Zealand
(9) 3660752; (9) 3602204

Hutt Adoption Search and Support
P.O. Box 38304
Petone, New Zealand

SOUTH AFRICA

Child Welfare Society
P.O. Box 2539
2000 Johannesburg

SPAIN

Servicio Social Internacional
Consejo Superior de Protection
de Menores
Condesa de Venadito 34
28027 Madrid

SWITZERLAND

Fondation Suisse Du Service Social International
10, rue A. Vincent
CH-1201 Geneva, Switzerland
022-731-67-00
Fax 022-731-67-65

UNITED KINGDOM

Channel Islands

C.L.A.I.R.E.
En Evant
17 Magnolia Gardens
Bel Royale, Jersey JE3 1JW
England

GRO (General Register Office)
Trafalgar Road
Birkdale; Southport
Merseyside PR8 2HH

Ireland

Barnardos Adoption Advice Service
244/246 Harold's Cross Road
Dublin 6

Scotland

Campaign for Adoption Reform in Europe
St. Stephan's Manse
33 Camperdown Street
Broughty Ferry
Dundee DD5 3AA

Family Care (and Scottish Birth-Link Register)
21 Castle Street
Edinburgh EH2 3DN
General Register Office
New Register House
Edinburgh EH1 3YT

Wales

Adoption Wales Helpline
011-44-122-257-5711

UNITED STATES

National Organizations and National Headquarters

Adoptees' Liberty Movement Association (ALMA) Headquarters
P.O. Box 727
Radio City Station
New York, NY 10101-0727
(212) 581-1568;
Fax (212) 765-2861

Adoption Forum Headquarters
525 South Fourth Street; #3465
Philadelphia, PA 19147-1570

Adoption Information Exchange Headquarters
P.O. Box 1917
Matthews, NC 28106

American Adoption Congress (AAC)
1000 Connecticut Avenue, NW
Suite #9
Washington, DC 20036
(202) 483-3399

American WWII Orphans Network
P.O. Box 4369
Bellingham, WA 98227
(206) 733-1678

BirthParent Connection
P.O. Box 230643
Encinitas, CA 92023-0643

Birthparent Support Network (BSN) Headquarters
P.O. Box 120
North White Plains, NY 10603

Concerned United Birthparents, Inc. (CUB)
2000 Walker Street
Des Moines, IA 50317-5255
(800) 822-2777; (515) 263-9558

Council for Equal Rights in Adoption (CERA)
401 E. 74 Street; #17-D
New York, NY 10021

National Indian Child Welfare Association
3611 SW Hood Street; Suite 201
Portland, OR 97201
(503) 222-4044; Fax (503) 222-4007

National Organization for Birthfather's and Adoption Reform (NOBAR)
P.O. Box 50
Punta Gorda, FL 33951
(813) 637-7477

Organized Adoption Search Information Services (OASIS) National Headquarters
P.O. Box 53-0761
Miami Shores, FL 33153
(305) 948-8933

Orphan Train Heritage Society of America
Route 4; Box 565
Springdale, AR 72764

Orphan Voyage National Headquarters
2141 Road 2300
Cedaredge, CO 81413
(303) 856-3937

PURE, Inc.
Searchelp U.S.A. &
TRIADOPTION Publications
P.O. Box 638
Westminster, CA 92684
1-800-USEARCH

The Researchers Clearinghouse
P.O. Box 22363
Ft. Lauderdale, FL 33335

Please note that large organizations such as Adoptees' Liberty Movement Association (ALMA) and Concerned United Birthparents, Inc. (CUB) have many local chapters. Contact national headquarters to inquire about a chapter near you.

Regional Organizations

**Adoptee-Birthparent
Support Network (ABSN)**
(serves Washington, DC,
Virginia, & Maryland)
3421 M Street, NW; Suite 328
Washington, DC 20007-3552

*Although there are many local
adoptee/birthparent associations
and societies, there was not space
to list them all here. There are
many sites on the Internet that
list these, however, so you should
have little trouble finding one in
your area.*

ASSET SEARCH
ORGANIZATIONS

**The Asset Search Industry
Association (ASIA)**
2000 L Street NW; Suite 200
Washington, DC 20036
(202) 416-1616

*Asset search experts may also be
found in Legal Research
Associations, Private Investigators
Associations, and Writers and
Reporters Organizations, within
this chapter.*

FUNDRAISING/
PROSPECT RESEARCH
ORGANIZATIONS

**American Association of
Fund-Raising Counsel
(AAFRC)**
25 West 43rd Street; Suite 820
New York, NY 10036
(212) 354-5799; Fax (212) 768-1795

**American Prospect Research
Association (APRA)**
1730 N. Lynn Street; Suite 502
Arlington, VA 22209
(703) 525-1191; Fax (703) 276-8196

**Association for Healthcare
Philanthropy**
313 Park Avenue; Suite 400
Falls Church, VA 22046
(703) 532-6243; Fax (703) 532-7170

**Council for Advancement
and Support of Education**
11 Dupont Circle; Suite 400
Washington, DC 20036-1207
(202) 358-5900; Fax (202) 387-4973

**Direct Mail Fundraisers
Association**
445 West 45th Street
New York, NY 10036
(212) 489-4929

**Foundation for Independent
Higher Education**
5 Landmark Square; Suite 330
Stamford, CT 06901-2502
(203) 353-1544; Fax (203) 353-0931

Independent Sector
1828 L Street, NW; Suite 1200
Washington, DC 20036
(202) 223-8100

**International Fund-Raising
Association (IFRA)**
(214) 699-7900; Fax (214) 235-1468

**Massachusetts Chapter,
National Society of Fund
Raising Executives**
170 Linden Street; Suite 1-C
Wellesley, MA 02181
(617) 237-8045

**National Association of
Independent Colleges and
Universities**
122 C Street, NW; Suite 750
Washington, DC 20001-2190
(202) 347-7512; Fax (202) 628-2513

**National Catholic
Development Conference**
86 Front Street
Hempstead, NY 11550
(516) 481-6000; Fax (516) 489-9287

**National Society of Fund
Raising Executives (NSFRE)**

1101 King Street; Suite 700
Alexandria, VA 22314
(703) 684-0410; Fax (703) 684-0540

**National Society of Fund
Raising Executives (NSFRE)**
Austin Chapter
Austin, TX 78767
(512) 323-1990

**National Society of Fund
Raising Executives (NSFRE)**
Massachusetts Chapter
170 Linden Street; Suite 1-C
Wellesley, MA 02181
(617) 237-8045

Utah Society of Fund Raisers
P.O. Box 581078
Salt Lake City, UT 84158-1078

GENEALOGICAL
RESEARCH
ORGANIZATIONS

AUSTRALIA

**Australasian Federation of
Family History Organizations
(AFFHO)**
120 Kent Street
Sydney, NSW 2000, Australia
(2) 2473953; Fax (2) 2414872

AUSTRIA

**Genealogical and Heraldic
Society (ADLER)**
Heraldisch-Genealogische
Gesellschaft
1 Haarhof 4 A
A-1014 Vienna, Austria

CANADA

**Heraldry Society of Canada
(HSC)**
Societe Heraldique du Canada
(SHC)
P.O. Box 8467; Station T
Ottawa, Ontario
Canada K1G 3H9
(613) 993-6783

Alberta

**Alberta Family Histories
Society**
P.O. Box 30270, Station B
Calgary, Alberta T2M 4P1
Alberta Genealogical Society
Box 3151; Station A
Edmonton, Alberta T5J 2G7

**Brooks and District
Genealogy Society**
Box 1538
Brooks, Alberta T0J 0J0

**Calgary PC Computer User
Society**
Calgary Genealogy Special
Interest Group
Box 61206
Brentwood Centre
Calgary, Alberta T2L 2K6
(403) 251-5540

Historical Society of Alberta
Box 4035
Station C
Calgary, Alberta T2T 5M9

British Columbia

**Abbotsford Genealogical
Club**
1913 Westbury Crescent
Abbotsford, BC V2S 1B9

**British Columbia
Genealogical Society**
P.O. Box 94371
Richmond, BC V6Y 2A8

**British Columbia Historical
Association**
3450 West 20th Avenue
Vancouver, BC

**Chase & District Family
History Association**
P.O. Box 64
Anglemont, BC V0E 1A0

**Cowichan Valley
Genealogical Society**
7361 Bell-McKinnon Road; RR #4
Duncan, BC V9L 3W8

**Kamloops Family History
Society**
P.O. Box 1162
Kamloops, BC V2C 6H3

**Kelowna & District
Genealogical Society**
Box 501; Station A
Kelowna, BC V1Y 7A1

Langley Genealogical Society
21107-88th Avenue
Langley, BC V3A 6X5

**Matsqui-Sumas-Abbotsford
Museum Society**
2313 Ware Street
Abbotsford, BC V2S 3C6

**Nanaimo Family History
Society**
P.O. Box 1027
Nanaimo, BC V9R 5Z2

Powell River Genealogy Group
P.O. Box 446
Powell River, BC V8A 5C2

**Prince George Family
History Society**
P.O. Box 1056
Prince George, BC V2L 4V2

**Provincial Archives of
British Columbia**
655 Belleville Street
Victoria, BC V8V 1X4

**Revelstoke & District
Historical Association**
P.O. Box 1908
Revelstoke, BC V0E 2S0

Revelstoke Genealogy Club
P.O. Box 309
Revelstoke, BC V0E 2S0

**Vernon & District Family
History Society**
P.O. Box 1447
Vernon, BC

Victoria Genealogical Society
P.O. Box 4171, Station A
Victoria, BC V8X 3X8

Manitoba

Manitoba Historical Society
147 James Avenue
Winnipeg, Manitoba

**Thompson Historical
Heritage & Museum Society**
P.O. Box 762
Thompson, Manitoba R8N 1N5

New Brunswick

**Cahiers de la Societe
Historique Acadienne**
Box 2263, Station A
Moncton, NB E1C 8J1

**Carleton County Historical
Society**
128 Connell Street, P.O. Box 828
Woodstock, NB E0J 2B0
(506) 328-9706

**Central Miramichi
Historical Society**
Box 38
Doaktown, NB E0C 1G0

**Charlotte County
Historical Society**
123 Frederick Street
P.O. Box 130
St. Andrews, NB E0G 2X0

**Charlotte County
Historical Society**
78 Prince William Street
St. Stephen, NB E3L 1S3

**Kings County Historical
Society & Museum**
Centennial Building
Centennial Drive
Hampton, NB E0G 1Z0
(506) 832-6009

**New Brunswick Genealogical
Society**
P.O. Box 3235; Station B
Fredericton, NB E3A 5G9

**Restigouche Genealogical
Society**
Dalhousie Centennial Library

405 Adelaide Street
P.O. Box 293
Dalhousie, NB E0K 1B0
(506) 684-5156

**Societe d'Histoire de la
Riviere Saint-Jean**
715 Priestman
Fredericton, NB E3B 5W7

Societe Historique Acadienne
P.O. Box 2363; Station A
Moncton, NB E1C 8J3

Societe Historique de Kent
C.P. 697
Bouctouche, NB E0A 1G0

**Societe Historique de la
Vallee de Memramcoo**
Societe Historique de Clair
P.O. Box 119
Clair, NB E0L 1B0

**Societe Historique du Comte
de Restigouche**
C.P. 534
Campbelltown, NB E3N 3G9

**Societe Historique du
Madawaska**
C.P. 474
Edmundston, NB E3B 3L1

**Societe Historique
Nicolas-Denys**
Centre Universitaire
Shippagan, NB E0B 2P0
(506) 336-4761

**United Empire Loyalists
Association**
54 MacKay Drive
Fredericton, NB E3A 3S2

Newfoundland

**Bay St. George Heritage
Association**
P.O. Box 314, Stephenville,
Newfoundland, A2N 2Z5

**Newfoundland & Labrador
Genealogical Society**
Colonial Building

Military Road
St. John's, Newfoundland A1C 2C9

**Wessex Society of
Newfoundland**
c/o Dr. W. Gordon Handcock
Department of Geography
Memorial University
St. John's, Newfoundland A1C 5S7

Nova Scotia

Bedford Heritage
P.O. Box 704
Bedford, NS B4A 3H5

Canso Historical Society
RR #1, Hazel Hill
Canso, NS B0H 1H0

**Cape Breton Genealogical
Society**
P.O. Box 53
Sydney, NS B1P 6G9

East Hants Historical Society
RR #1, Maitland, NS B0N 1T0

**Federation of Museums,
Heritage & Historical Society**
5516 Spring Garden Road
Suite 305
Halifax, NS B3J 1G6

**Federation of Nova Scotia
Heritage**
5515 Spring Garden Road
Suite 305
Halifax, NS B3J 1G6

**Genealogical Association of
Nova Scotia**
P.O. Box 641; Station M
Halifax, NS B3J 2T3

**Genealogical Association of
Royal Nova Scotia Historical
Society**
Box 895
Armdale, NS B3L 4K5

**Heritage Association of
Antigonish**
Box 1492
Antigonish, NS B2G 2L7

**North Cumberland Historical
Society**
RR #3
Pugwash, NS B0K 1L0

North Shore Archives Society
Fraser Cultural Centre
Tatamagouche, NS B0K 1V0

**Pictou County Genealogical
Society**
Box 1210, Pictou, NS B0K 1H0

**Port Hastings Historical
Society**
Box 115
Port Hastings, NS B0E 2T0

**Royal Nova Scotia Historical
Society**
6016 University Avenue
Halifax, NS B3H 1W4

**Royal Nova Scotia Historical
Society**
Box 895
Armdale, NS B3L 4K5

**Shelburne County
Genealogical Society**
Box 43
Shelburne, NS B0T 1W0

**Societe Historique Acadienne
de la Baie**
Saint-Marie
Universite Sainte-Anne
Pointe-de-l'Eglise
NS B0W 1M0

**Societe Historique Acadienne
de Pubnico-Oues**
Pubnico-Ouest le Centre
Yarmouth, NS B0W 2M0

Societe Saint-Pierre
Les Trois Pignons
C.P. 430
Cheticamp, NS B0E 1H0

**South Shore Genealogical
Society**
Box 901
Lunenburg, NS B0J 2C0

West Hants Historical Society
140 Chestnut Street
Windsor, NS B0N 2T0

**Yarmouth County Historical
Society**
Box 39
Yarmouth
NS B5A 4B1

Ontario

**Association for Canadian
Archivists**
Room 349
395 Wellington Street
Ottawa, Ontario K1A 0N3

**Baptist Federation of
Canada**
Box 1298
Brantford, Ontario N3T 5T6

**Canadian Historical
Association**
395 Wellington Street
Ottawa, Ontario K1A 0N3

Canadian Jewish Congress
4600 Bathurst Street
Toronto, Ontario M2R 3V3

**Glengarry Genealogical
Society**
R.R. 1
Lancaster, Ontario K0C 1N0

Heraldry Society of Canada
P.O. Box 8467
Station T
Ottawa, Ontario K1G 3H9

**Norfolk County Historical
Society**
Genealogical Committee
Eva Brook Donnely Museum
Simcoe, Ontario

Ontario Genealogical Society
40 Orchard View Boulevard
Suite 240
Toronto, Ontario M4R 1B9

Ontario Genealogical Society
40 Orchard View Boulevard

Suite 253
Toronto, Ontario M4R 1B9

**Simcoe County Historical
Society**
Genealogical Section
Box 144
Barrie, Ontario L4M 4S9

**Societe de Genealogie
d'Ottawa-Hull**
316, rue Dalhousie
Ottawa, Ontario K1N 7E7

**United Empire Loyalists
Association of Canada**
National Headquarters
50 Baldwin Street
Toronto, Ontario
(416) 591-1783

Prince Edward Island

**Prince Edward Island
Genealogical Society**
P.O. Box 2744
Charlottetown, PEI C1A 8C4

**Prince Edward Island
Museum and Heritage
Foundation**
2 Kent Street
Charlottetown, PEI C1A 1M6
(902) 892-9127

**Societe Historique Acadienne
de l'ile-du-Prince-Edouard**
C.P. 88
Summerside, PEI C1N 4P6

Quebec

L'Arbre Historique Enr.
610 Prevost
Trois-Rivieres, Quebec G8Y 4A5

**Quebec Family Histories
Society**
P.O. Box 1026
Pointe Claire, Quebec H9S 4H9

**Societe de Genealogie de l'est
du Quebec**
C.P. 253
Rimouski, Quebec G5L 7C1

**Societe de Genealogie de la
Mauricie**
C.P. 901
Trois-Rivieres, Quebec F9A 5K2

**Societe de Genealogie de
Lanaudiere**
C.P. 221, Joliette, Quebec J6E 3Z2

**Societe de Genealogie de
Quebec**
C.P. 9066
Ste-Foy, Quebec G1V 4A8

**Societe de Genealogie de
Quebec**
Case postale 2234
Quebec, Quebec G1K 7N8

**Societe de Genealogie de
Salaberry-de-Val**
75, St-Jean-Baptiste
Salaberry-de-Val., Quebec J6T 1Z6

**Societe de Genealogie des
Laurentides**
C.P. 31, St-Jerome, Quebec J7Z 5T7

**Societe Genealgique
Canadienne-Francaise**
C.P. 335, Place d'Armes
Montreal, Quebec H2Y 3H1

**Societe Genealogique de
Saguenay**
C.P. 814
Chicoutimi, Quebec G7H 5E8

**Societe Genealogique des
Cantons de l'Est**
C.P. 635
Sherbrooke, Quebec J1H 5K5

**Societe Genealogique et
Historique**
de Trois-Pistoles
C.P. 1478
Trois-Pistole, Quebec G0L 4K0

Saskatchewan

**Saskatchewan Genealogical
Society**
Box 1894
Regina, SK S4P 3E1

Many local branches of these societies may also be found throughout Canada. You can find listings of these on the Internet, or by contacting other offices of these societies.

CHILE

Chilean Institute of Genealogical Research (CIGR)
Instituto Chileno de
Investigaciones Genealogicas
(ICIG)
Correo Central, Casilla 1386
Santiago, Chile

DENMARK

Societas Heraldica Scandinavica (SHS)
Heraldisk Selskab (HS)
c/o Ole Rostock Sigmundsvej 8
DK-2880 Bagsvaerd, Denmark
42980756

DOMINICAN REPUBLIC

Dominican Institute of Genealogy (DIG)
Instituto Dominicano de
Genealogia (IDG)
El Recodo 8
Bella Vista
Apartado Postal 407-2
Santo Domingo
Dominican Republic
(809) 532-0438; (809) 532-6965
Fax (809) 535-7891

GERMANY

Deutschen Arbeitsgemeinschaft Genealogischer Verbande (DAGV)
NW Personenstandsarchiv
Rheinland
Schlosstrasse 12
50321 Bruhl, Germany
(2232) 42948

Zentralstelle fur Personen— und Familiengeschichte (ZPF)
Birkenweg 13

88046 Friedrichsdorf, Germany
(6172) 78263

ISRAEL

Israel Genealogical Society (IGS)
50 Harav Uziel Street
96424 Jerusalem, Israel
(2) 424147

LUXEMBOURG

Academie Internationale
d'Heraldique (AIH)
95 rue de Luxembourg
L-8140 Bridel, Luxembourg

NEW ZEALAND

Commonwealth Heraldry Board (CHB)
Conseil de la Science Heraldique
du Commonwealth
P.O. Box 23-056
Papatoetoe, New Zealand
(9) 2787415

PORTUGAL

Associacao Portuguesa de Genealogia
Rua Marques da Fronteira, 127, 2.∫
P-1000 Lisboa, Portugal

SPAIN

Asociacion de Hidalgos
Calle Atocha 94, Madrid ESPA—A

SWITZERLAND

Swiss Heraldry Society (SHS)
Societe Suisse d'Heraldique
Burgstrasse 32
CH-8706 Meilen, Switzerland
(1) 9231077; Fax 55 423597

UNITED KINGDOM

England

Association of Genealogists and Record Agents (AGRA)

29 Badgers Close
Horsham, West Sussex RH12 5RU
England

Federation of Family History Societies (FFHS)
Birmingham and Midland
Institute
Kingsley Norris Room
Margaret Street
Birmingham, West Midlands B3
3BS, England
(74) 3365505

Heraldry Society (HS)
44/45 Museum Street
London WC1A 1LY
England
(71) 4302172

The Institute of Heraldic & Genealogical Studies
79-82 Northgate
Canterbury, Kent
England
CT1 1BA
44 227 768664

Irish Genealogical Research Society (IGRS)
c/o The Irish Club
83 Eaton Square
London SW1W 9AJ, England

Isle of Man Family History Society (IMFHS)
5 Selbourne Drive Douglas
Isle of Man, England
(624) 622188

Society of Genealogists (SG)
14 Charterhouse Buildings
Goswell Road, London EC1M
7BA, England
(71) 2518799

Ireland

Heraldry Society of Ireland (HSI)
Cumann Araltais na h Eireann
San Elmo, Vico Road
Dorkey, Dublin, Ireland
(1) 2859722

Ulster Historical Foundation (UHF)
Balmoral Building
12 College Square East
Belfast BT1 6DD
Northern Ireland
(232) 332288
Fax (232) 239885

Scotland

Anglo Scottish Family History Society
2 Beech Road
Salford M6 5FJ, U.K.

Association for Scottish Genealogists and Record Agents (ASGRA)
51/53 Mortonhall Road
Edinburgh, Scotland, EH9 2HN

Central Scotland Family History Society
5 Ochil Gardens
Dunning
Perthshire PH2 0SR, U.K.

Glasgow and West Scotland Family History Society
11 Gartcows Crescent
Falkirk FK1 5QY, U.K.

Heraldry Society of Scotland (HSS)
Societe Ecossaise d'Heraldique
25 Craigentinny Crescent
Edinburgh EH7 6QA, Scotland
(31) 6572791

Highland Family History Society
c/o Reference Room
Public Library
Farroline Park
Inverness IV1 1NH, U.K.

International Commission for Orders of Chivalry (ICOC)
Commission Internationale
d'Etudes des Ordres de
Chevalerie
1-3 Gloucester Lane
Edinburgh EH3 6ED, Scotland

Largs and North Ayrshire Family History Society
4 Burnside Road
Largs
Ayrshire KA30 9BU, U.K.

North East Scotland Family History Society
The Family History Shop
164 King Street
Aberdeen AB2 3BD, U.K.
0224 646323

Scots Ancestry Research Society
29b Albany Street
Edinburgh EH1 3QN, U.K.

The Scottish Genealogical Society
15 Victoria Terrace
Edinburgh EH1 2JL, U.K.
031 220 3677

Scottish Record Society (SRS)
c/o Scottish History Department
9 University Gardens
University of Glasgow
Glasgow G12 8QQ, Scotland
(41) 3398855

Tay Valley Family History Society
179 Princess Street
Dundee
Tayside DD4 6DQ, U.K.

UNITED STATES

Ark-La-Tex Genealogical Association (ALTGA)
P.O. Box 4462
Shreveport, LA 71134-0462
(318) 687-3673; (318) 687-9823

Tri-State Genealogical Society
c/o Willard Library
21 1st Avenue
Evansville, IN 47710
(812) 425-4309

Tri-State Genealogical Society
P.O. Box 1053

East Liverpool, OH 43920
(216) 385-2048

Tri-State Genealogy Association
c/o Public Library
905 5th Avenue
Belle Fourche, SD 57717
(605) 892-4019

Tri-State Corners Genealogical Society (TSCGS)
Lydia Bruun Public Library
Falls City, NE 68355
(402) 245-2913

There are so many local genealogical associations throughout the United States there was not room to list them here. You should be able to find listings of them on the Internet.

VENEZUELA

Venezuelan Institute of Genealogy (VIG)
Instituto Venezolano de
Genealogia (IVG)
Palacio de las Academias
Apartado Postal 60706
Caracas 1060-A
Venezuela
(2) 2635217

Please note that family groups were not included in this list.

LEGAL RESEARCH ASSOCIATIONS

American Association of Law Libraries
53 West Jackson Boulevard; #940
School of Law Library
Chicago, IL 60604
(312) 939-4764

American Legal Studies Association
Northeastern University
305 Cusing Hall

Boston, MC 02115
(617) 437-5211
Fax (617) 437-2942

National Association of Legal Investigators
P.O. Box 516
Newport, OR 97365
(503) 265-6966; Fax (503) 444-1344

National Center for Automated Information Research (NCAIR)
165 E. 72nd Street; Suite 1B
New York, NY 10021
(212) 249-0760

National Federation of Paralegal Associations, Inc. (NFPA)
P.O. Box 33108
Kansas City, MO 64114
(816) 941-4000; Fax (816) 941-2725

MAILING LIST/ DIRECT MARKETING ASSOCIATIONS

ARGENTINA

Asociacion de Marketing Directo de Argentina
Lavalle 1711
1354 Buenos Aires, Argentina
(1) 35-9973

AUSTRALIA

Australian Direct Marketing Association
G.P.O. Box 3982/10F
52-58 Clarance Street; 10th Floor
Sydney, NSW 2000 Australia
(2) 29-2914; Fax (2) 62-2435

BELGIUM

Association du Marketing Direct
Rue de Stalle 142/1180
Brussels, Belgium
(2) 332-0375; Fax (2) 332-1070

Groupement de la Vente Par Correspondance
Rue de la Science, 3/1040
Brussels, Belgium
(2) 537-3060; Fax (2) 539-4026

Flemish Direct Marketing Association
Bierbeekstraat #14/3030
Heverlee, Belgium
(16) 233109

European Direct Marketing Association (EDMA)
36, rue du Gouvernement
Provisoire, B-1000 Brussels,
Belgium
(2) 2176309; Fax (2) 2176985

BRAZIL

Associacao Brasileira de Marketing Direto
Avenida Angelica 1391
ler Andar, Sala A
Sao Paulo SP CEP 01227, Brazil
(11) 826-3458

CANADA

Canadian Direct Marketing Association
1 Concorde Gate; Suite 607
Don Mills, Ontario
M3C 3N6, Canada
(416) 391-2362

Mid-Western Direct Marketers Association
1340 Church Avenue
Winnipeg, Manitoba R2X 1G4,
Canada
(204) 633-5700; Fax (204) 694-4398

DENMARK

The Danish Direct Marketing Club
Dansk Markedsforing Forund
Vesterbrogade #24
DK-1620 Copenhagen, Denmark
(35) 378055

FINLAND

Finnish Direct Marketing

Association (FDMA)
Suomen Suoramarkkinointiliitto
(SSML)
Henry Fordin Katu 5M
SF-00150 Helsinki, Finland
(0) 663744; Fax (0) 663772

FRANCE

Union Francaise de la Publicite Directe
60, rue La Boetie
75008 Paris, France
(1) 42 56-38 86; Fax (1) 45-639195

GERMANY

Bundesverband Des Duetsschen Versandhandels E.V.
Johann-Klotz Strasse 12
D-6000 Frankfurt
Main 71, Germany
Hauptgeschaftsfuhrer
(69) 675047

DDV—Deutscher Direktmarketing Verband e.v.
Schiersteiner Strasse 20
D-6200 Wiesbaden, Germany
(6121) 843061
Fax (6121) 807921

HONG KONG

Hong Kong Direct Mail & Marketing Association
G.P.O. Box 7416
Hong Kong
(5) 68-11-77
Fax (5) 88-41-381

ITALY

Associazione Italiana per Il Direct Marketing (AIDIM)
Corso Venezia 16/20121
Milan, Italy
(2) 7601534

Associazione Nationale FRA Aziende Di Vendita per Corrispondenza
Via Melchiore Gioia 70/20125
Milan, Italy
(2) 688-4525

JAPAN

**Japan Direct Mail
Association (JDMA)**
Dai Hachi Kojimachi Building,
3F/4-5
Kojimachi, Chiyoda-ku
Tokyo 102, Japan
(3) 239-4062; Fax (3) 584-3909

**Japan Direct Marketing
Association (JADMA)**
Nihon Tsushin Hanbai Kyokai
32, Mori Building; 6th Floor; 3-
4-30
Shiba-Koen, Minato-ku
Tokyo 105, Japan
(3) 434-4700; Fax (3) 434-4700

**Nihon Direct Marketing
Association (NDMA)**
2-2-15 Minami Aoyama
Wion Aoyama 337
Minato-ku, Tokyo 107 Japan
(3) 487-1307; Fax (3) 584-0108

MEXICO

**Asociacion Mexicana por
Correo Directo**
Avenida Toluca 725
Mexico DF 11000, Mexico
(905) 655-7900
Fax (905) 655-7145

NETHERLANDS

**Direct Marketing Instituut
Nederland (DMIN)**
Weerdestein 96, NL-1083 GG
Amsterdam, Netherlands
(20) 6429595; Fax (20) 6440199

Nederlandse Postorderbond
Lange Voorhout 86
2514 EJ Den Haag
Netherlands
(70) 652837

NEW ZEALAND

**New Zealand Direct
Marketing Association**
P.O. Box 937
Auckland, New Zealand
(9) 499-329

SINGAPORE

**Direct Marketing Association
of Singapore**
450 Alexandra Road
#10-00 Inchcape Hov, Singapore
0611
(65) 4750220; Fax (65) 4758586

SOUTH AFRICA

**The South African Direct
Marketing Association**
P.O. Box 85370
Emmerentia 2029
Republic of South Africa
(21) 25 2690; Fax (21) 419-5780

SPAIN

**Asociacion Espanola de
Marketing Directo**
Provenza, 238
Barcelona 08008, Spain
(3) 323-4061; (3) 323-4408
Fax (3) 254-0795

SWEDEN

**Swedish Direct Marketing
Association**
P.O. Box 14038
104-40 Stockholm, Sweden
(8) 661-39-10; Fax (8) 662-7612

SWITZERLAND

**European Direct Marketing
Association**
4, Rue de la Scie
CH-1207, Geneva, Switzerland
(22) 7863386; Fax (22) 7359-880

UNITED KINGDOM

**Association of Mail Order
Publishers**
1 New Burlington Street
London, W1X 1FD, England
(1) 437-0706; Fax (1) 287-3956

**The British Direct Marketing
Association**
Grosvenor Gardens House
35 Grosvenor Gardens

London, SW1W 0BS, England
(1) 630-7322; Fax (1) 828-7125

**Direct Marketing Association
(DMA)**
Haymarket House
1 Oxenden Street
London SW1Y 4EE, England
(71) 3212525; (71) 3210191

**Direct Mail Producers
Association**
34 Grand Avenue
London N10 3BP, England
(1) 883-9854
Fax (1) 444-6475

**Irish Direct Marketing
Association**
1/2 Upper O'Connell Street
Dublin 1, Ireland
(1) 615512
Fax (1) 612026

UNITED STATES

**Direct Marketing Association
(DMA)**
11 West 42nd Street
New York, NY 10036-8096
(212) 768-7277
Fax (212) 768-4546

**Direct Marketing Association
Catalog Council (DMACC)**
11 West 42nd Street
New York, NY 1003608096
(212) 768-7277; Fax (212) 768-4546

**Direct Marketing Credit
Association (DMCA)**
c/o Sandy Freund
Newfield Publications
P.O. Box 857
Shelton, CT 06484-0857
(203) 944-2534
Fax (203) 944-2500

URUGUAY

**Asociacion de Diregentes de
Marketing Del Uruguay**
Itvzaingo 1324
Escritorio 304
Montevideo, Uruguay
(598) 959578

ORGANIZATIONS INVOLVED IN PRIVACY RIGHTS, COMPUTER PRIVACY, OR FREEDOM OF INFORMATION

Always Causing Legal Unrest
P.O. Box 2085
Rancho Cordova, CA 95741-2085
(408) 427-2858

American Civil Liberties Union (ACLU)
132 West 43rd Street
New York, NY 10036
(212) 944-9800; Fax (212) 354-5290

American Society of Access Professionals (ASAP)
7910 Woodmont Avenue
Bethesda, MD 20814-3015
(301) 913-0030

Australian Civil Liberties Union (ACLU)
P.O. Box 1137
Carlton, VIC 3053, Australia
(3) 476302

Computer Professionals for Social Responsibility (CPSR)
P.O. Box 717
Palo Alto, CA 94302
(415) 322-3778; Fax (415) 322-4748

Electronic Frontier Foundation
c/o On Technology
155 2nd Street
Cambridge, MA 02141
(617) 864-0665

Electronic Privacy Information Center
666 Pennsylvania Avenue SE
Suite 301
Washington, DC 20003
(202) 544-9240
Fax (202) 547-5482

Federal Trade Commission (FTC)
(Regulates Credit Reporting practices)

Free Press Association (FPA)
P.O. Box 15548
Columbus, OH 43215
(614) 291-1441

IEEE Computer Society Security and Privacy Committee
1730 Massachusetts Avenue NW
Washington, DC 20036
(202) 371-0101
Fax (202) 728-9614

LibertyTree Network (LTN)
134 98th Avenue
Oakland, CA 94603
(800) 972-8733; (510) 568-6047
Fax (510) 568-6040

National Association to Protect Individual Rights
P.O. Box 90030
Washington, DC 20090-0030
(703) 242-8671; Fax (703) 242-8390

National Center for Freedom of Information Studies (NCFIS)
Loyola University of Chicago
820 North Michigan Avenue
Chicago, IL 60611
(312) 915-6548; Fax (312) 915-7095

National Consumers League (NCL)
815 15th Street NW; Suite 928
Washington, DC 20005
(202) 639-8140

National Council for Civil Liberties
21 Tabard Street
London SE1 4LA, England
(71) 4033888
Fax (71) 4075354

Privacy Rights Clearinghouse
University of San Diego
School of Law
Center for Public Interest Law
5998 Alcala Park
San Diego, CA 92110-2492
(619) 260-4806
Internet: http://pwa.acusd.edu:80/~prc/

Private Citizen, Inc. (PCI)
P.O. Box 233
Naperville, IL 60566
(800) CUT-JUNK; (708) 393-1555

United States Privacy Council (USPC)
P.O. Box 15060
Washington, DC 20003
(202) 829-3660

PRIVATE INVESTIGATORS ASSOCIATIONS

American Academy of Forensic Sciences
P.O. Box 669
Colorado Springs, CO 80901
(719) 636-1100

Arizona Association of Licensed Private Investigators
6825 South 45th Way
Phoenix, AZ 85040

Associated Licensed Detectives of New York State
233 Broadway
New York, NY 10279
(212) 962-4054

Association of British Investigators (ABI)
10 Bonner Hill Road
Kingston upon Thames, London
KT1 3EP, England
(81) 5463368; Fax (81) 5467701

Buckeye State Association of Private Investigators
P.O. Box 711
Sunbury, OH 43074-0711

California Association of Licensed Investigators
1408 Claremont Way
Sacramento, CA 95822
(916) 456-9908; Fax (916) 456-0245

Council of International Investigators Inc. (CII)
P.O. Box 266

Palmer, MA 01069-0266
(800) 852-5073; (413) 283-7003
Fax (413) 283-2900

**Indiana Association of
Private Detectives, Inc.**
618 South Melvenia
Indianapolis, IN 46219
(317) 353-2264

**International Association of
Arson Investigators**
25 Newton Street
Box 600
Marlboro, MA 01752

**International Association of
Computer Crime Investigators**
150 North Main Street
Plymouth, MI 48170
(313) 459-8787

**International Association of
Credit Card Investigators**
P.O. Box 813
Novato, CA 94947

International Police Congress
8740 SW 158th Street
Miami, FL 33157
(305) 238-1147

**International Security and
Detective Alliance**
P.O. Box 6303
Corpus Christi, TX 78466-6303
(512) 888-6164

**Investigative & Security
Society of Hawaii**
1000 Bishop Street; #608
Honolulu, HI 96813
(808) 526-2002

**Investigative Online
Network (ION Incorporated)**
2111 East Baseline; Suite F7
Tempe, AZ 85283
(800) 257-1048; (602) 730-8088
Fax (602) 730-8103

**Louisiana Association of
Private Security Agencies &
Private Investigators**
P.O. Box 50230

New Orleans, LA 70150
(504) 488-4405

**Maryland Investigation &
Security Association**
3241 Rhode Island Avenue
Mt. Rainer, MD 20712

**Massachusetts Association of
Licensed Detective Agencies**
399 Washington Street
Weymouth, MA 02188

**Michigan Association of
Private Detective and
Security Agencies**
27208 Southfield Road; Suite 3
Lathrup Village, MI 48076
(313) 557-4530

**National Association of Auto
Theft Investigations**
255 South Vernon
Dearborn, MI 48124

**National Association of Fire
Investigators**
53 West Jackson Boulevard
Chicago, IL 60604

**National Association of
Investigative Specialists**
P.O. Box 33244
Austin, TX 78764
(512) 928-8190
Fax (512) 928-4544

**National Association of
Investigative Specialists
(NAIS)**
P.O. Box 33244
Austin, TX 78764
(512) 928-8190; Fax (512) 928-4544

**National Association of Legal
Investigators, Inc.**
2801 Fleur Drive
Des Moines, IA 50321

**National Association of
Traffic Accident
Reconstructionists and
Investigators (NATARI)**
P.O. Box 61208
King of Prussia, PA 19406

(215) 992-9817
Fax (215) 992-9817

**National Council of
Investigation and Security
Services**
P.O. Box 449
Severna Park, MD 21146
(800) 445-8408; (410) 647-3227
Fax (410) 544-6181

**Nevada Association of
Private Investigators and
Security Services**
1711 South Highland F
Las Vegas, NV 89102
(703) 387-9028

**New Hampshire Association
of Private Detectives and
Security Services**
P.O. Box 280
Union, NH 03887
(603) 473-8285

**North Carolina Association
of Private Investigators**
P.O. Box 18164
Charlotte, NC 28218-8164

**Ohio Association of Security
and Investigation Services**
5310 E. Main Street; No. 100
Columbus, OH 43213
(614) 759-7435
Fax (614) 759-7420

**Oklahoma Private
Investigators Association**
508 West Vanament; Suite 100J
Yukon, OK 73099
(405) 354-1292

**Private Detective Association
of New Jersey, Inc.**
415 Route 18; Suite 278
East Brunswick, NJ 08816
(201) 238-5080

**Private Investigator
Business Owners Association
of Virginia (PIBOAVA)**
P.O. Box 7600
Alexandria, VA 22307
(703) 360-4848

Private Investigators
Association of Virginia
P.O. Box 7600
Alexandria, VA 22307
(703) 360-4348

Private Investigators
Association of Virginia
(PIAV)
P. O. Box 104
Burke, VA 22015
(703) 273-1200

Private Investigators
Association of Florida
P.O. Box 300332
Fern Park
FL 32730

Professional INV-SEC
Association
7311 Tyler Avenue
Falls Church
VA 22042

Professional Private
Investigators Association of
Colorado
P.O. Box 24244
Denver, CO 80224

Tennessee Association of
Private Investigators
P.O. Box 80251
Chattanooga, TN 37411

United States Private
Security and Detective
Association
P.O. Box 6303
Corpus Christi, TX 78411

Vermont Association of
Licensed Detectives, Inc.
P.O. Box 862
Burlington, VT 05402
(207) 623-0083

World Association of
Detectives (WAD)
P.O. Box 1049
Severna Park, MD 21146
(800) 962-0516
(410) 544-0119
Fax (410) 544-6181

PROCESS SERVER ASSOCIATIONS

National Association of
Professional Process Servers
P.O. Box 4547
Portland, OR 97208
(503) 222-4180; Fax (503) 222-3950

National Association of
Private Process Servers
P.O. Box 8202
Northfield, IL 60093
(312) 973-7712

PROFESSIONAL RESEARCH ASSOCIATIONS THAT ARE KNOWLEDGEABLE ABOUT ONLINE SEARCHING

African-American Library
and Information Science
Association (AALISA)
UCLA Center for Afro-American
Studies Library
405 Hilgard Avenue
44 Haines Hall
Los Angeles, CA 90024-1545
(310) 825-6060; Fax (310) 206-3421

American Library
Association
50 East Huron Street
Chicago, IL 50511-2795
(312) 944-6780; Fax (312) 440-9374

American Society for
Information Science (ASIS)
8720 Georgia Avenue; Suite 501
Silver Spring, MD 20910-3602
(301) 495-0900; Fax (202) 495-0810

ASLIB (Association of
Special Libraries and
Information Bureaux)
20/24 Old Street
London EC1V9AP, England
(71) 253-4488

Association for Library and
Information Science
Education (ALISE)
4101 Lake Boone Trail
Suite 201
Raleigh, NC 27607
(919) 787-5181; Fax (919) 787-4916

Association of Independent
Information Professionals
(AIIP)
Administrative Services Office
245 Fifth Avenue; Suite 2103
New York, NY 10016
(212) 779-1855
Fax (212) 481-3071
CompuServe: 73263,34

Canadian Association for
Information Science (CAIS)
University of Toronto
140 St. George Street
Toronto, Canada
M5S 1A1
(416) 978-8876

Canadian Association of
Special Libraries and
Information Science (CASLIS)
c/o Canadian Library Association
200 Elgin Street; Suite 602
Ottawa, Ontario
Canada K2P 1L5
(613) 232-9625; Fax (613) 563-9895

European Information
Researchers Network
(EIRENE)
Manchester Business School
Booth Street West
Manchester, M15 6PB

United Kingdom Health
Sciences Libraries
Consortium (HSLC)
3600 Market Street; Suite 550
Philadelphia, PA 19104-2646
(215) 222-1532; Fax (215) 222-0416

Information Industry
Association
555 New Jersey Avenue NW
Suite 800
Washington, DC 20001
(202) 639-8262; Fax (202) 638-4403

International Association of
Aquatic and Marine Science
Libraries and Information
Centers (IAMSLIC)
c/o Harbor Branch
Oceanographic Institute Library
5600 U.S. 1 N.
Ft. Pierce, FL 34946
(407) 465-2400
Fax (407) 465-2446

Japan Database Industry
Association (DINA)
3-2, Nishishinjuku 2-chome
Shinjuku-ku, Tokyo 163-03,
Japan
(3) 33477107
Fax (3) 33475300

Map Online Users Group
(MOUG)
Map Library
University of South Carolina
Columbia, SC 29208
(803) 777-2802

Library and Information
Technology Association
(LITA)
50 East Huron Street
Chicago, IL 60611-2795
(800) 545-2433; (312) 280-4270
Fax (312) 280-3257

National Association of
Investigative Specialists
(NAIS)
Computer/Database Records
Committee
Computer Research Committee
P.O. Box 33244
Austin, TX 78764
(512) 928-8190
Fax (512) 928-4544

National Center for
Automated Information
Research (NCAIR)
165 East 72nd Street; Suite 1B
New York, NY 10021
(212) 249-0760

Netherlands Association of
Users of Online Information
Systems (NAUOIS)

Nederlandse Vereniging van
Gebruikers van Online
Informatie-Systemen (VOGIN)
c/o Mr. P.J.C. Rosenbrand
COBIDOC BV
St. Athoniesbreestraat 16II
NL-1011 HB Amsterdam,
Netherlands
(20) 6223955; Fax (20) 6222556

New England Online Users
Group
P.O. Box 753
Cambridge, MA 02139-0007

Society of Competitive
Intelligence Professionals
(SCIP)
1700 Diagonal Road; Suite 520
Alexandria, VA 22314
(703) 739-0696
Fax (703) 739-2524

South African Institute for
Librarianship and
Information Science (SAILIS)
Suid-Afrikaanse Instituut vir
Biblioteek en Inligtingwese
P.O. Box 36575
Menlo Park, Pretoria 0102

Republic of South Africa
(12) 3464967; Fax (12) 3462020

Southern California Online
User's Group (SCOUG)
c/o Seek Information Service,
Inc.
1600 Victory Boulevard
Glendale, CA 91201
(818) 242-2793
Fax (818) 242-2876

Special Libraries Association
(SLA)
1700 18th Street NW
Washington, DC 20009
(202) 234-4700
Fax (202) 265-9317

United Kingdom Online User
Group (UKOLUG)
Institute of Information
Scientists
44-45 Museum Street

London WC1A 1LY, England
(71) 8318003; Fax (71) 4301270

PROPERTY
MANAGEMENT
ORGANIZATIONS

National Property
Management Association
(NPMA)
380 Main Street; Suite 290
Dunedin, FL 34698
(813) 736-3788; Fax (813) 736-6707
(Contact this organization for the
location of a chapter near you.)

Property Management
Association (PMA)
8811 Colesville Road; Suite G106
Silver Spring, MD 20910
(301) 587-6543; Fax (301) 589-2017

PUBLIC RECORDS
RESEARCH
ORGANIZATIONS

Association of Public Data
Users (APDU)
87 Prospect Avenue
Princeton, NJ 08544
(609) 258-6025; Fax (609) 258-3943

National Archives and
Records Administration
Volunteer Association
NE Office of Public Programs
Room G-8
National Archives
8th at Pennsylvania NW
Washington, DC 20408
(202) 501-5205

National Public Records
Research Association (NPRRA)
P.O. Box 10329
Tallahassee, FL 32302

Public Record Retriever
Network (PRRN)
Carl Ernst

BRB Publications, Inc.
4653 S. Lakeshore; #3
Tempe, AZ 85282
(800) 929-3811

*Public records search experts may
also be found in Adoptee/
Birthparent Search Organizations,
Legal Research Associations,
Private Investigators Associations,
and Writers and Reports
Organizations, within this chapter.*

SKIP-TRACERS AND COLLECTION AGENCY ASSOCIATIONS

**American Collectors
Association (ACA)**
ASAE Building
4040 West 70th Street
Minneapolis, MN 55435-4199
(612) 926-6547; Fax (612) 926-1624
(You may also contact this association for information on local
chapters.)

**American Recovery
Association, Inc.**
P.O. Box 6788
New Orleans, LA 70174
(504) 367-0711; Fax (504) 392-2612

**Association of Professional
Collectors (APC)**
Executive Square
4480 Gen. DeGaulle Drive
Suite 111
New Orleans, LA 70131
(504) 394-8933

**National Association of
Investigative Specialists
(NAIS)**
P.O. Box 33244
Austin, TX 78764
(512) 928-8190; Fax (512) 928-4544

**National Consumer Credit
Consultants (NCCC)**
2840 W. Arthur Avenue
Chicago, IL 60645-5222
(312) 465-0090

**North Dakota Collectors
Association**
c/o Credit Bureau of Jamestown,
North Dakota
Box 1805
Jamestown, ND 58402
(701) 252-6770;
Fax (701) 252-6772

**Puerto Rico Association of
Collection Agencies**
P.O. Box 1169
Bayamon, PR 00960-1169
(809) 740-1710; Fax (809) 740-7638

TENANT SCREENING ASSOCIATIONS

**National Association of
Screening Agencies (NASA)**
c/o Index Companies
14232 Marsh Lane; #331
Dallas, TX 75234
(800) 624-0647; (214) 247-7878

WRITERS AND REPORTERS ORGANIZATIONS

**Center for Investigative
Reporting (CIR)**
530 Howard Street; 2nd Floor
San Francisco, CA 94105-3007
(800)733-0015; (415) 543-1200
Fax (415) 543-8311

**China Biographic Literature
Society**
21 Dongsi 12th Lane
Beijing 100708
People's Republic of China
(1) 4032266

Free Press Association (FPA)
P.O. Box 15548
Columbus, OH 43215
(614) 291-1441

**International Association of
Crime Writers (IACW)**
Asociacion Internacional de

Escritores Policiacos (AIEP)
Benjamin Hill 242-244
Colonia Condesa, Mexico City,
DF, Mexico
(5) 2713621; Fax (5) 2713621
**International Security and
Detective Alliance (ISDA)**
P.O. Box 6303
Corpus Christi, TX 78466-6303
(512) 888-6164

**Investigative Reporters and
Editors (IRE)**
University of Missouri
100 Neff Hall
Columbia, MO 65211
(314) 882-2042; Fax (314) 882-5431

**National Biographical
Association (NBA)**
c/o Universal Intelligence Data
Bank of America
U.S. Federal Building
Rooms 201-201A
301 W. Lexington Street
Independence, MO 64050
(816) 833-0033; Fax (816) 833-2125

**New York Genealogical and
Biographical Society (NYGBS)**
122 E. 58th Street
New York, NY 10022-1939
(212) 755-8532

APPENDICES

Databases That Include Biographies

The '88 Vote: Campaign for the White House
ABC News InterActive
7 West 66th Street; 4th Floor
New York, NY 10023
(212) 456-4060;
Fax (212) 887-3205

CD-ROM: ABC News InterActive

Academic Index
Refer to Appendix N for Information Access Company (IAC)

Online: Knight-Ridder Information, Inc. (as File 88); CompuServe Knowledge Index (as EDUC5); DataStar (as ACAD)

CD-ROM: Information Access Company (IAC)

AFP-DOC sur CD-ROM
Refer to Appendix N for Agence France-Presse (AFP)

CD-ROM: Chadwyck-Healey Ltd.

The African American Experience: A History on CD-ROM
Quanta Press, Inc.
1313 Fifth Street SE; Suite 223A
Minneapolis, MN 55414
(612) 379-3956;
Fax (612) 623-4570

CD-ROM: Quanta Press, Inc.

AGORA-DOCUMENTAIRE (ADOC)
Refer to Appendix N for Agence France-Presse (AFP)

Online: Europeenne de Donnees (ADOC)

Almanac of American Politics
National Journal Inc.
1501 M Street, NW
Washington, DC 20036
(800) 424-2921; (202) 857-1400
Fax (202) 833-8069

Online: NEXIS (as AMPOL) and Legi-Slate, Inc.

AP Political Service
Associated Press Political Service
The Associated Press (AP)
50 Rockefeller Plaza
New York, NY 10020
(212) 621-1585;
Fax (212) 621-5488

Online: DataTimes Corporation (as APOLI); LEXIS (as APOLIT, CAMPGN—campaign coverage since 1980, BIO—candidate biographies); and NEXIS (ALLAP, APBIO, CAMPGN)

Attivita dei Deputati
Camera dei Deputati d'Italia, Servizio per la Documentazione Automatica (SDA)
Piazza Montecitorio
I-00186 Rome, Italy
06 6760

Online: Camera dei Deputati d'Italia, Servizio per la Documentazione Automatica (SDA)

Audio Notes: Beethoven's String Quartet No. 14
Time Warner Interactive
2210 West Olive Avenue
Burbank, CA 91505
(800) 482-3766; (818) 955-9999
Fax (818) 955-6499

CD-ROM: Time Warner Interactive

Audio Notes: The Orchestra
Refer to the preceding Audio Notes: Beethoven's String Quartet No. 14

CD-ROM: Time Warner Interactive

Australian Architecture Database (ARCH)
Stanton Library
234 Miller Street
North Sydney, NSW 2060, Australia
02 9555889; Fax 02 9545512

Online: AUSINET (as ARCH)

Australian Historic Records Register (AHRR)
National Library of Australia
Parkes Place
Canberra, ACT 2600, Australia
062 621111; Fax 062 571703

Online: OZLINE: Australian Information Network (AHRR)

AUSTROM (Australian Social Science Law and Education Databases)
Royal Melbourne Institute of Technology (RMIT)
INFORMIT
RMIT Libraries
G.P.O. Box 2476V
Melbourne, VIC 3001, Australia
03 0265667; Fax 03 663 3047

CD-ROM: Royal Melbourne Institute of Technology (RMIT), INFORMIT, RMIT Libraries

Base de Dados Mope
*Refer to Appendix N for Lda
Mope*
Online: Lda Mope

BASELINE
*Refer to Appendix N for
BASELINE II INC.*
Online: BASELINE II INC. and
LEXIS

BIODOC
Database SC
44 Av. Rene Gobert
B-1180 Brussels, Belgium
02 3740185; Fax 02 3740185
Online: Europeenne de Donnees

Biografias (BIOG)
Secretaria General Tecnica,
Ministerio de Cultura de
Espana
Plaza del Rey 1
E-28071 Madrid, Spain
01 4292444

Online: Ministerio de Cultura
de Espana, Secretaria General
Tecnica, Puntos de Informacion
Cultural (PIC)

**Biographical Directory of
the United States Congress
1774-1989**
Staff Directories, Ltd.
P.O. Box 62
Mount Vernon, VA 22121-0062
(703) 739-0900;
Fax (703) 739-0234
CD-ROM: Staff Directories, Ltd.

**Biography & Genealogy
Master Index CD-ROM**
*Refer to Appendix N for Gale
Research Inc.*
CD-ROM: Gale Research Inc.

Biography Index
*Refer to Appendix N for
H.W. Wilson Company*
Online: WILSONLINE, CDP
Online (as Wilson Biography
Index), OCLC EPIC, OCLC
FirstSearch Catalog, CDP After

Dark (Wilson Biography Index)
and CDP COLLEAGUE (as
Wilson Biography Index)
CD-ROM: H.W. Wilson
Company, WILSONDISC, and
SilverPlatter Information, Inc.

**Biography Master Index
(BMI)**
*Refer to Appendix N for Gale
Research, Inc.*
Online: Knight-Ridder
Information, Inc. (as File 287)

**Bowker Biographical
Directory**
*Refer to Appendix N for Reed
Reference Publishing Group*
Online: Knight-Ridder
Information, Inc. (as File 236)

**Canadian Business and
Current Affairs (CBCA)**
Micromedia Ltd.
20 Victoria Street
Toronto, ON, Canada M5C 2N8
(800) 387-2689; (416) 362-5211
Fax (416) 362-6161

Online: CAN/OLE (as CBCA);
Knight-Ridder Information, Inc.
(as File 262); CompuServe
Knowledge Index (as MAGA2);
and Infomart Online (as XCBA)
CD-ROM: Knight-Ridder
Information, Inc.,
DIALOG OnDisc

Canadian Who's Who Online
University of Toronto Press
10 St. Mary Street; Suite 700
Toronto, ON, Canada M4Y 2W8
(416) 978-8651;
Fax (416) 978-4738
Online: Info Globe Online
(as WHO)

CCIDOC
Centre de Creation Industrielle
(CCI), Service Documentation
Centre Georges Pompidou
F-75191 Paris Cedex 4, France
01 42771233
Online: Centre de Creation

Industrielle (CCI), Service
Documentation

Cinemania
*Refer to Appendix N for
Microsoft Corporation*
CD-ROM: Microsoft Corporation

**The Complete Marquis Who's
Who Plus**
*Refer to Appendix N for Reed
Reference Publishing Group*
CD-ROM: Bowker Electronic
Publishing

COSMOS 3
Teikoku Databank, Ltd.
5-20, Minami Aoyama 2-Chome
Minato-ku
Tokyo 107, Japan
03 34044311; Fax 03 34044339
Online: COSMOSNET

Demografiska Databasen
Umea Universitet
S-901 87 Umea, Sweden
90 166740; Fax 90 166958
Online: Umea Universitet

DiscLit: American Authors
Macmillan Publishing Co., G.K.
Hall & Co.
866 Third Avenue
New York, NY 10022
(212) 702-6789
CD-ROM: OCLC Online
Computer Library Center, Inc.

DiscLit: British Authors
Macmillan Publishing Co., G.K.
Hall & Co.
866 Third Avenue
New York, NY 10022
(212) 702-6789
CD-ROM: OCLC Online
Computer Library Center, Inc.

DiscLit: World Authors
Macmillan Publishing Co., G.K.
Hall & Co.
866 Third Avenue
New York, NY 10022
(212) 702-6789

CD-ROM: OCLC Online
Computer Library Center, Inc.

DISCovering Authors
*Refer to Appendix N for Gale
Research, Inc.*
CD-ROM: Gale Research Inc.

**DISCovering Authors: British
Edition**
*Refer to Appendix N for Gale
Research, Inc.*
CD-ROM: Gale Research Inc.

**DISCovering Authors:
Canadian Edition**
*Refer to Appendix N for Gale
Research, Inc.*
CD-ROM: Gale Research Inc.

**DISCovering Multicultural
America CD-ROM**
*Refer to Appendix N for Gale
Research, Inc.*
CD-ROM: Gale Research Inc.

**Eadweard Muybridge:
Motion Studies**
Voyager
1351 Pacific Coast Highway
Santa Monica, CA 90401
(800) 446-2001; (310) 451-1383
(446) 443-2001;
Fax (310) 394-2156
CD-ROM: The Voyager Company

**The Electronic Encyclopedia
of World War II**
Marshall Cavendish Corporation
2415 Jerusalem Street
P.O. Box 587
North Bellmore, NY 11710
(800) 821-9881; (516) 826-4200
Fax (516) 785-8133
CD-ROM: Marshall Cavendish
Corporation

**Encyclopedia of
Judaism/Dictionary of
Jewish Biography**
Davka Corporation
7074 North Western Avenue
Chicago, IL 60645

(800) 621-8227; (312) 465-4070
Fax (312) 292-9298
CD-ROM: Davka Corporation

**European Monarchs on
CD-ROM**
Quanta Press, Inc.
1313 Fifth Street SE; Suite 223A
Minneapolis, MN 55414
(612) 379-3956;
Fax (612) 623-4570
CD-ROM: Quanta Press, Inc.

Gale Biographies
*Refer to Appendix N for Gale
Research, Inc.*
Online: NEXIS (as GALBIO)

Gospel Library CD
Infobases, Inc.
1875 South State Street; No. 3100
Orem, UT 84058
(800) 537-7823
CD-ROM: Infobases, Inc.

Heritage & Environment
Royal Melbourne Institute of
Technology (RMIT)
INFORMIT
RMIT Libraries
G.P.O. Box 2476V
Melbourne, VIC 3001, Australia
03 0265667; Fax 03 663 3047
CD-ROM: Royal Melbourne
Institute of Technology (RMIT),
INFORMIT, RMIT Libraries

**Igor Stravinsky: The Rite of
Spring**
Robert Winter
UCLA Music Department
2539 Schoenberg Hall Annex
405 Hilgard Avenue
Los Angeles, CA 90025
(213) 825-4761
CD-ROM: The Voyager Company

**Important Personalities in
Eastern Europe**
American Directory Corporation
P.O. Box 7426
New York, NY 10116
(718) 797-4311; Fax (718) 596-4852

CD-ROM: American Directory
Corporation

In the Holy Land
ABC News InterActive
7 West 66th Street; 4th Floor
New York, NY 10023
(212) 456-4060;
Fax (212) 887-3205
CD-ROM: ABC News InterActive

**Information on the Great
Barrier Reef**
Great Barrier Reef Marine Park
Authority
P.O. Box 1379
Townsville, QLD 4810, Australia
077 818811; Fax 077 726093
Online: AUSTRALIS (as REEF)

**Instant Computer
Arbitration Search**
*Refer to Appendix N for LRP
Publications*
Online: LRP Publications

Jazz Giants
Philips Interactive Media of
America (PIMA)
11111 Santa Monica Boulevard
Los Angeles, CA 90025
(310) 444-6619;
Fax (310) 478-4810
CD-ROM: Philips Interactive
Media of America (PIMA)

Junior DISCovering Authors
*Refer to Appendix N for Gale
Research, Inc.*
CD-ROM: Gale Research Inc.

Kojien Japanese Dictionary
Iwanami Shoten
2-5-5 Hitotsubashi
Chiyoda-ku
Tokyo, Japan
03 32654111
CD-ROM: Iwanami Shoten

**L'Elite et les Institutions
Sovietiques**
Le Monde
7, rue des Italiens

F-75427 Paris Cedex 9, France
01 42479744; 01 45230681 Fax

Online: Europeenne de Donnees

LDS Historical Library CD
Infobases, Inc.
1875 South State Street;
No. 3100
Orem, UT 84058
(800) 537-7823

CD-ROM: Infobases, Inc.

Legal Resource Index (LRI)
*Refer to Appendix N for
Information Access Company (IAC)*

Online: Knight-Ridder
Information, Inc. (as File 150);
CompuServe Knowledge Index (as
LEGA1); LEXIS (as LGLIND);
WESTLAW (as LRI); DataStar (as
LAWS); CARL Systems Network

LEGI-SLATE
*Refer to Appendix N for
Legi-Slate, Inc.*

(Available by subscription)

**Los Angeles Times
Biographical Stories
(LATBIO)**
Los Angeles Times
A Division of Times Mirror
Company
Times Mirror Square
Los Angeles, CA 90053

Online: LEXIS-NEXIS

**Louis Armstrong: An
American Songbook**
Philips Interactive Media of
America (PIMA)
11111 Santa Monica Boulevard
Los Angeles, CA 90025
(310) 444-6619;
Fax (310) 478-4810

CD-ROM: Philips Interactive
Media of America (PIMA)

**Ludwig van Beethoven's
Symphony No. 9**
Robert Winter
UCLA Music Department
2539 Schoenberg Hall Annex

405 Hilgard Avenue
Los Angeles, CA 90025
(213) 825-4761

CD-ROM: The Voyager Company

Marquis Who's Who (MWW)
*Refer to Appendix N for Reed
Reference Publishing Group*

Online: Knight-Ridder Information,
Inc. (as File 234); CompuServe
Knowledge Index (as REFR2)

Marquis Who's Who Plus
*Refer to Appendix N for Reed
Reference Publishing Group*

CD-ROM: Bowker Electronic
Publishing

Martin Luther King Jr.
ABC News InterActive
7 West 66th Street; 4th Floor
New York, NY 10023
(212) 456-4060;
Fax (212) 887-3205

CD-ROM: ABC News InterActive

Masterplots II CD-ROM
Salem Press, Inc.
131 North El Molino; Suite 350
Pasadena, CA 91101
(800) 221-1592; (818) 584-0106
Fax (818) 584-1525

CD-ROM: EBSCO Publishing

Microsoft Complete Baseball
*Refer to Appendix N for
Microsoft Corporation*

CD-ROM: Microsoft Corporation

Monarch Notes on CD-ROM
Simon & Schuster
Consumer Group
1230 Avenue of the Americas
New York, NY 10020
(212) 592-7000

CD-ROM: Bureau of Electronic
Publishing, Inc.

Mozart: A Musical Biography
Philips Interactive Media of
America (PIMA)
11111 Santa Monica Boulevard
Los Angeles, CA 90025

(310) 444-6619;
Fax (310) 478-4810

CD-ROM: Philips Interactive
Media of America (PIMA)

**The New York Times
Biographical File**
The New York Times Company
New York Times
On-Line Services
1719A Route 10
Parsippany, NJ 07054
(201) 267-2268;
Fax (201) 267-3464

Online: NEXIS (as NYTBIO)

**The New York Times
Biography (Government)**
The New York Times Company
New York Times
On-Line Services
1719A Route 10
Parsippany, NJ 07054
(201) 267-2268;
Fax (201) 267-3464

Online: NEXIS (as GOVBIO)

**The NewsBank Electronic
Information System**
NewsBank, inc.
58 Pine Street
New Canaan, CT 06840
(800) 762-8182; (203) 966-1100
Fax (203) 966-6254

CD-ROM: NewsBank, inc.

Newsearch
*Refer to Appendix N for
Information Access Company
(IAC)*

Online: Knight-Ridder
Information, Inc. (as File 211);
CompuServe Knowledge Index
(as NEWS1)

**Newspaper & Periodical
Abstracts (UMI)**
620 South Third Street
Louisville, KY 40202-2475
(800) 626-2823; (502) 583-4111
Fax (502) 589-5572
Online: Knight-Ridder
Information, Inc. (as File 484),

OCLC EPIC; OCLC; FirstSearch Catalog; Infomart Online; CARL Systems Network (planned); CitaDel Service

NOMINE
Refer to Appendix N for LEXIS-NEXIS

Online: LEXIS and NEXIS (as NOMINE)

The Olympics Factbook
Refer to Appendix N for Gale Research, Inc.

Online: NEXIS (as OLYFAC); PRODIGY (as an OLYMPICS database)

Pavarotti: O Sole Mio
Philips Interactive Media of America (PIMA)
11111 Santa Monica Boulevard
Los Angeles, CA 90025
(310) 444-6619;
Fax (310) 478-4810

CD-ROM: Philips Interactive Media of America (PIMA)

Political Profile
Refer to Appendix L for Prodigy Services Company

Online: PRODIGY

The Presidents: It All Started With George
National Geographic Society, Educational Services
Washington, DC 20036
(800) 368-2728;
(301) 921-1330
Fax (301) 921-1575

CD-ROM: National Geographic Society, Educational Services

Prospector's Choice
The Taft Group
12300 Twinbrook Parkway
Suite 520
Rockville, MD 20852
(301) 816-0210

CD-ROM: The Taft Group

The Published Ellen G. White Writings
Ellen G. White Estate
12501 Old Columbia Pike
Silver Spring, MD 20904
(301) 680-6552

CD-ROM: Ellen G. White Estate

Reuter Country Reports
Refer to Appendix N for Reuters Ltd.

Online: Reuters Ltd.

SciTech Reference Plus
Refer to Appendix N for Reed Reference Publishing Group

CD-ROM: Bowker Electronic Publishing

The Sporting News Multimedia Pro Football Guide
The Sporting News Publishing Company
1212 North Lindbergh Boulevard
St. Louis, MO 63132
(314) 997-7111

CD-ROM: Compton's NewMedia

Sports Illustrated CD-ROM Sports Almanac
Time Inc.
Time-Life Building
New York, NY 10020
(212) 522-1212;
Fax (212) 333-4066

CD-ROM: Time Warner Interactive

Time Man of the Year CD-ROM
Refer to Appendix N for Time Inc.

CD-ROM: Compact Publishing, Inc.

Total Baseball
Creative Multimedia Corporation
514 N.W. 11th Avenue; Suite 203
Portland, OR 97209
(503) 241-4351;
Fax (503) 241-4370

CD-ROM: Creative Multimedia Corporation

Twelve Roads to Gettysburg
Hawks Interactive Systems
445 Breton, S.E.; Suite 137
Kentwood, MI 49512
(616) 956-0284

CD-ROM: Hawks Interactive Systems

U.S. Presidents
Quanta Press, Inc.
1313 Fifth Street SE; Suite 223A
Minneapolis, MN 55414
(612) 379-3956;
Fax (612) 623-4570

CD-ROM: Quanta Press, Inc.

USA Wars: Civil War
Quanta Press, Inc.
1313 Fifth Street SE; Suite 223A
Minneapolis, MN 55414
(612) 379-3956;
Fax (612) 623-4570

CD-ROM: Quanta Press, Inc.

USA Wars: Korea
Quanta Press, Inc.
1313 Fifth Street SE; Suite 223A
Minneapolis, MN 55414
(612) 379-3956;
Fax (612) 623-4570

CD-ROM: Quanta Press, Inc.

USA Wars: World War II
Quanta Press, Inc.
1313 Fifth Street SE; Suite 223A
Minneapolis, MN 55414
(612) 379-3956;
Fax (612) 623-4570

CD-ROM: Quanta Press, Inc.

VideoHound Multimedia
Refer to Appendix N for Gale Research, Inc.

CD-ROM: Gale Research Inc.

The Washington Post
Biographical Stories
The Washington Post News Research Center
1150 15th Street, NW; 5th Floor
Washington, DC 20071
(202) 334-7341

Online: NEXIS (WPBIO)

Who's Who in Germany
Verlag Schmidt-Roemhild
Redaktion WER IST WER
P.O. Box 103952
D-45039 Essen, Germany
492018130112;
Fax 492018130108

Online: GENIOS
Wirtschaftsdatenbanken
(as WIW)

**Who's Who in Russia and the
Commonwealth of
Independent States; Who's
Who Directory; Russian
Information; Communications
Agency (RUSSICA)**
Spartakovskaya St. 13
107066 Moscow, Russia
095 9325610
Fax 095 9326300

Online: SovInfoLink and
Gesellschaft fur
Betriebswirtschaftliche
Information mbH (GBI)
(SOWHO); NEXIS
(as WHORUS); MagnaTex
COMMUNICATE!

Who's Who in Technology
*Refer to Appendix N for
Gale Research, Inc.*

Online: QUESTEL•ORBIT
(as WHOT)

**Wilson Author Biographies
on Disc**
*Refer to Appendix N for
H.W. Wilson Company*

CD-ROM: H.W. Wilson Company,
WILSONDISC

Winning Elections
Political Publishing Company
P.O. Box 17274
Alexandria, VA 22302
(703) 549-7586
Fax (703) 549-8059

CD-ROM: Wayzata
Technology Inc.

**World Biographical
Dictionary of Artists on
CD-ROM**
K.G. Saur Verlag
GmbH & Co. KG
Heilmanstr. 17
Postfach 711009
D-8000 Munich 71, Germany
089 791040
Fax 089 7910499

CD-ROM: Bowker Electronic
Publishing

**World Biographical Index on
CD-ROM**
K.G. Saur Verlag
GmbH & Co. KG
Heilmanstr. 17
Postfach 711009
D-8000 Munich 71, Germany
089 791040
Fax 089 7910499

CD-ROM: Bowker Electronic
Publishing

*Please note that general
encyclopedias have been omitted
from this section, as they have
been listed in Appendix F. Some
specialized encyclopedias are
listed here. Professional directories, some of which contain
biographical information,
are in Appendix D.*

Book Directory Databases

Archivio Libri Italiani su Calcolatore Elettronico (ALICE)
Editrice Bibliografica srl
Viale Vittorio Veneto 24
I-20124 Milan, Italy

Online and CD-ROM: CILEA
(Consorzio Interuniversitario
Lombardo per l'Elaborazione
(Automatica)

Australian Books in Print (ABIP)
D.W. Thorpe
18 Salmon Street
Port Melbourne, VIC 3207,
Australia
03 6451511; Fax 03 6453981

Online: AUSINET (as ABIP)

Australian National Bibliography (ANB)
National Library of Australia
Parkes Place
Canberra, ACT 2600, Australia
062 621111; Fax 062 571703

Online: OZLINE: Australian
Information Network (as ANB)

BIBLIODATA
Die Deutsche Bibliothek
Zeppelinallee 4-8
D-60325 Frankfurt am Main 1,
Germany
069 75661; Fax 069 7566476

Online: STN International (as
BIBLIODATA)

BNB on CD-ROM
British Library, National
Bibliographic Service
Boston Spa
Wetherby, Yorks LS23 7BQ,
England
0937 546600; Fax 0937 546586

CD-ROM: Chadwyck-Healey Ltd.

BNBMARC (British Library, National Bibliographic Service)
Boston Spa
Wetherby, Yorks LS23 7BQ,
England
0937 546600; Fax 0937 546586

Online: BLAISE-LINE

Bookbase
IDD Verlag fur Internationale
Dokumentation
Werner Flach KG
Heddernheimer Landstr. 78a
D-6000 Frankfurt am Main 50,
Germany
069 577777

Online: FIZ Technik (BOOK)

BookFind-CD
Book Data Limited
Northumberland House
2 King Street
Twickenham TW1 3RZ, England
081-892 2272; Fax 081-892 9109

CD-ROM: Book Data Limited

BookFind-CD World Edition
Book Data Limited
Northumberland House
2 King Street
Twickenham TW1 3RZ, England
081-892 2272; Fax 081-892 9109

CD-ROM: Book Data Limited

BOOKLINE: UTOPIA
Bancroft-Parkman, Inc.
Bookline
P.O. Box 1236
Washington, CT 06793

Online: Bancroft-Parkman,
Inc., Bookline

Booklink (The Online Database and Book Order Service)
Library Wholesale Services

11910-U Parklawn Drive
Rockville, MD 20852
(800) 423-2665; (202) 298-8015

Online: Booklink (Library
Wholesale Services)

BookQuest
ABACIS, Inc.
15 Southwest Park
Westwood, MA 02090
(800) 627-2216; (410) 581-0394
Fax (410) 581-0398

Online: The Faxon Company,
Faxon Quest

BookQuest for Small Press
ABACIS, Inc.
15 Southwest Park
Westwood, MA 02090
(800) 627-2216; (410) 581-0394
Fax (410) 581-0398

Online: The Faxon Company,
Faxon Quest

Books in Print Online (BIP)
*Refer to Appendix N for Reed
Reference Publishing Group*

Online: CDP Online (as BBIP);
CDP After Dark (as BBIP); CDP
COLLEAGUE (as BBIP);
Knight-Ridder Information, Inc.
(File 470); and CompuServe
Knowledge Index (as BOOK1)

Books in Print Plus
*Refer to Appendix N for Reed
Reference Publishing Group*

CD-ROM: Bowker Electronic
Publishing

Books in Print with Book Reviews Plus
*Refer to Appendix N for Reed
Reference Publishing Group*

CD-ROM: Bowker Electronic Publishing

Books Master File
U.S. Library of Congress, Cataloging Distribution Service Washington, DC 20541-5017 (202) 707-6100; Fax (202) 707-1334

CD-ROM: U.S. Library of Congress, Cataloging Distribution Service

Books out-of-Print Plus
Refer to Appendix N for Reed Reference Publishing Group

CD-ROM: Bowker Electronic Publishing

British Books in Print (BBIP)
J. Whitaker & Sons, Ltd.
12 Dyott Street
London WC1A 1DF, England
071-836 8911

Online: Knight-Ridder Information, Inc. (as File 430); BLAISE-LINE

CD-ROM: J. Whitaker & Sons, Ltd.

Brodart Interactive Access System
Brodart Co.
500 Arch Street
Williamsport, PA 17705
(800) 233-8467; (717) 326-2461

Online: Brodart Co.

Canadian Books in Print
University of Toronto Press
10 St. Mary Street; Suite 700
Toronto, ON, Canada M4Y 2W8
(416) 978-8651;
Fax (416) 978-4738

Online: Info Globe Online

CCB: Belgian Union Catalogue
National Conference of University Chief Librarians
Manager Ladeuzeplein 21
B-3000 Leuven, Belgium
32 16 284619; Fax 32 16 294097
CD-ROM: Brepols Publishers

CD-CATSS
ISM Library Information Services
3300 Bloor Street W; 16th Floor, West Tower
Etobicoke, ON, Canada M8X 2X2
(416) 236-7171; Fax (416) 236-7489

CD-ROM: ISM Library Information Services

CDMARC Bibliographic
U.S. Library of Congress, Cataloging Distribution Service Washington, DC 20541-5017 (202) 707-6100;
Fax (202) 707-1334

CD-ROM: U.S. Library of Congress, Cataloging Distribution Service

Children's Reference Plus
Refer to Appendix N for Reed Reference Publishing Group

CD-ROM: Bowker Electronic Publishing

Cumulative Book Index (CBI)
Refer to Appendix N for H.W. Wilson Company

Online: WILSONLINE; CDP Online; (Wilson Cumulative Book Index, planned)

CD-ROM: H.W. Wilson Company, WILSONDISC, and SilverPlatter Information, Inc.

Deutsche Bibliographie Aktuell CD-ROM
Buchhandler Vereinigung GmbH
Grosser Hirschgraben 17-21
Postfach 100442
D-6000 Frankfurt am Main 1, Germany
069 13060

CD-ROM: Bowker Electronic Publishing

Dutch Collective Catalogus van Belgie
National Conference of University Chief Librarians
Mgr. Ladeuzeplein 21
B-3000 Leuven, Belgium
32 16 284619; Fax 32 16 294097

CD-ROM: Brepols Publishers

Eighteenth Century Short Title Catalogue
British Library, Humanities and Social Sciences
Great Russell Street
London WC1B 3DG,
England
071-323 7607

CD-ROM: Research Publications International and Research Libraries Information Network (RLIN)

Eighteenth Century Short Title Catalogue (ESTC)
British Library, Humanities and Social Sciences
Great Russell Street
London WC1B 3DG, England
071-323 7607

Online: BLAISE-LINE; Research Libraries Information Network (RLIN)

Electre-Biblio
Editions du Cercle de la Librairie
35, rue Gregoire de Tours
F-75006 Paris, France
01 43291000; Fax 01 43296895

Online: Editions du Cercle de la Librairie

French Catalogue Collectif de Belgique
National Conference of University Chief Librarians
Mgr. Ladeuzeplein 21
B-3000 Leuven, Belgium
32 16 284619; Fax 32 16 294097

CD-ROM: Brepols Publishers

Gale Literary Index CD-ROM
Refer to Appendix N for Gale Research, Inc.

CD-ROM: Gale Research Inc.

German Books in Print
Buchhandler Vereinigung GmbH
Grosser Hirschgraben 17-21
Postfach 100442
D-6000 Frankfurt am Main 1,

Germany
069 13060

CD-ROM: Bowker Electronic
Publishing

German Books Out of Print
K.G. Saur Verlag GmbH & Co. KG
Heilmanstr. 17
Postfach 711009
D-8000 Munich 71, Germany
089 791040

CD-ROM: Bowker Electronic
Publishing

**German National Bibliography
on CD-ROM**
Buchhandler Vereinigung GmbH
Grosser Hirschgraben 17-21
Postfach 100442
D-6000 Frankfurt am Main 1,
Germany
069 13060

CD-ROM: Bowker Electronic
Publishing

Global Books in Print Plus
*Refer to Appendix N for Reed
Reference Publishing Group*

CD-ROM: Bowker Electronic
Publishing

Ingram Books in Print Plus
*Refer to Appendix N for Reed
Reference Publishing Group*

CD-ROM: Bowker Electronic
Publishing

**Ingram Books in Print with
Book Reviews Plus**
*Refer to Appendix N for Reed
Reference Publishing Group*

CD-ROM: Bowker Electronic
Publishing

**International Books in Print
on CD-ROM**
K.G. Saur Verlag GmbH & Co. KG
Heilmanstr. 17
Postfach 711009
D-8000 Munich 71, Germany
089 791040

CD-ROM: Bowker Electronic
Publishing

Italian Books in Print
Editrice Bibliografica srl
Viale Vittorio Veneto 24
I-20124 Milan, Italy

Online and CD-ROM: CILEA
(Consorzio Interuniversitario
Lombardo per l'Elaborazione
(Automatica)

**LibraryDisc: MARC for
Schools**
CASPR, Inc.
635 Vaqueros Avenue
Sunnyvale, CA 94086
(800) 852-2777; (408) 522-9800
Fax (408) 522-9806

CD-ROM: CASPR, Inc.

**Libros en Venta en His-
panoamerica y Espana Plus**
*Refer to Appendix N for Reed
Reference Publishing Group*

CD-ROM: Bowker Electronic
Publishing

**Near East National Union List
(NENUL)**
U.S. Library of Congress
Information System
101 Independence Avenue, SE
Washington, DC 20540
(202) 707-5114

Online: U.S. Library of Congress
Information System

New Titles On-Line (NTO)
Blackwell North America, Inc.
6024 S.W. Jean Road; Building G
Lake Oswego, OR 97035
(800) 547-6426; (503) 684-1140
Fax (503) 639-2481

Online: Blackwell North
America, Inc.

**NIPS (Nippan Information
Processing System)**
Nippon Shuppan Hanbai, Inc.
4-3, Surugadai
Kanda, Chiyoda-ku
Tokyo 101, Japan
Fax 03 32331111; 03 32928521

Online: Japan Computer
Technology Co. Ltd.

**Out-of-Print Scientific,
Medical and Technical Books
Online (OP SMTB ONLINE)**
John P. Coll, Books
P.O. Box 5626
Berkeley, CA 94705-0626
(510) 845-8475

Online: John P. Coll, Books
(free of charge)

**Russian Books in Print Plus
with Books out of Print**
Bowker-Saur Ltd.
Maypole House
Maypole Road
East Grinstead
W. Sussex RH19 1HH, England
0342 330100

CD-ROM: Bowker Electronic
Publishing

SciTech Reference Plus
*Refer to Appendix N for Reed
Reference Publishing Group*

CD-ROM: Bowker Electronic
Publishing

Spanish Books in Print Plus
*Refer to Appendix N for Reed
Reference Publishing Group*

CD-ROM: Bowker Electronic
Publishing

U.S. Copyrights
Knight-Ridder Information, Inc.
3460 Hillview Avenue
Palo Alto, CA 94304
(800) 334-2564; (415) 858-3785
(334) 668-9215; Fax (415) 858-
7069

Online: Knight-Ridder
Information, Inc. (as File 120)

**Universal Terminalized
On-line Printing and
Investigative Aid**
Bancroft-Parkman, Inc., Bookline
P.O. Box 1236
Washington, CT 06793

Online: Bancroft-Parkman, Inc.,
Bookline

Business Credit and Company Financial Databases Including Personal Information

ABC Netherlands
ABC voor Handel en Industrie
C.V.
P.O. Box 190
NL-2000 AD Haarlem,
Netherlands
023 319031; Fax 023 327033

Online: Gesellschaft fur
Betriebswirtschaftliche
Information mbH (GBI)
(ABCNL)

Advertising Red Books Plus
National Register Publishing
(NRP)
*Refer to Appendix N for Reed
Reference Publishing Group*

CD-ROM: Bowker Electronic
Publishing

American Business Directory
American Business Information,
Inc. (ABI)
5711 South 86th Circle
P.O. Box 27347
Omaha, NE 68127
(402) 593-4500; Fax (402) 331-
1505

Online: American Business
Information, Inc. (ABI); American
Business Lists; Knight-Ridder
Information, Inc. as American
Business Directory (File 531), as
well as a subset of this database
in American Business 20 Plus
Companies (File 532)

**American Business
20 Plus Companies**
American Business
Information, Inc. (ABI)

5711 South 86th Circle
P.O. Box 27347
Omaha, NE 68127
(402) 593-4500
Fax (402) 331-1505

Online: American Business
Information, Inc. (ABI);
American Business Lists;
Knight-Ridder Information, Inc.
as part of American Business
Directory (File 531), as well as
in American Business 20 Plus
Companies (File 532)

Analysis
FT Analysis
Ibex House
42/47 Minories
London EC3 1DY, England
071-702 0991
Fax 071-702 2067

**Annual Reports Abstracts
(ARA)**
*Refer to Appendix N for
Information Access Company
(IAC)*

Online: DataStar (as PTAR);
Knight-Ridder Information, Inc.
(as File 17)

**Asia-Pacific Dun's Market
Identifiers**
Dun & Bradstreet (Australia)
Pty. Ltd.
P.O. Box 7405
St. Kilda Road
Melbourne, VIC 3004, Australia
03 8283333; Fax 03 8283300

Online: Knight-Ridder
Information, Inc. (as File 522)

**Australian Business
Compendium**
Read Only Memory Pty. Ltd.
127 Lawrence Street
Alexandria, NSW 2011, Australia
02 5503938

CD-ROM: Laser Design &
Training (LDT)

**The Bankers' Almanac
Database**
Reed Information Services
Windsor Court
East Grinstead House
East Grinstead, West Sussex
RH19 1XA, England
0342 326972; Fax 0342 335612

Online: KOMPASS Online (Reed
Information Services Ltd.)

CD-ROM: Reed Information
Services; KOMPASS CD

Base de Dados Mope
*Refer to Appendix N for Lda
Mope*

Online: Lda Mope

BELGI
Belgian Companies
EURO DB
18, Place de l'Universite
B-1348 Louvain-la-Neuve
Belgium
010 476711

Online: QUESTEL•ORBIT

BISNES Plus
*Refer to Appendix N for
INFOTRADE N.V.*

Online: INFOTRADE N.V.

Business America on CD-ROM
Refer to Appendix N for American Business Information, Inc. (ABI)

Available on CD-ROM from American Business Information, Inc. (ABI)

Business & Company Profile
Refer to Appendix N for Information Access Company (IAC)

CD-ROM: Information Access Company (IAC)

The Business Elite
Database America
100 Paragon Drive
Montvale, NJ 07645-0419
(800) 478-0318

CD-ROM: Database America

Business Who's Who of Australia (BWWA)
Riddell Information Services Pty. Ltd.
100 William Street
Sydney, NSW 2011, Australia
02 3682100; Fax 02 3682150

Online: AUSINET (BWWA)

CD-ROM: Riddell Information Services Pty. Ltd.

Canadian Corporations (CANCORP)
Micromedia Ltd.
20 Victoria Street
Toronto, ON, Canada M5C 2N8
(800) 387-2689; (416) 362-5211
Fax (416) 362-6161

Online: Knight-Ridder Information, Inc. (as File 491, CANCORP Canadian Corporations); Infomart Online (as CANCORP); DataStar (CNCO: CANCORP Canadian Company Financials); LEXIS (CNCORP)

Canadian Dun's Market Identifiers (CDMI)
Dun & Bradstreet Canada
5770 Hurontario Street
Mississauga, ON
Canada L5R 3G5

(800) 232-1026; (905) 568-6000
(232) 265-3867; Fax (905) 568-6279

Online: Knight-Ridder Information, Inc. (as File 520: D & B—Canadian Dun's Market Identifier); NIFTY-Serve (as CDMI); DataStar (as DNCA, Dun & Bradstreet Canada); WESTLAW; CompuServe Information Service

Canadian Federal Corporations and Directors
Southam Electronic Publishing
1450 Don Mills Road
Don Mills, ON, Canada M3B 2X7
(416) 445-6641
Fax (416) 445-3508

Online: Infomart Online (as DCFC)

Canadian Financial Database (CFD)
Refer to Appendix N for Globe Information Services

Online: Info Globe Online (as CFD)

CCN Business Information Database
Refer to Appendix N for CCN Business Information Ltd.

Online: CCN Business Information Ltd.

CD/Corporate: European Mergers and Acquisitions
OneSource Information Services
150 Cambridge Park Drive
Cambridge, MA 02140
(800) 554-5501; (617) 441-7000
Fax (617) 225-7058

CD-ROM: OneSource Information Services

CD/Corporate: SEC Filings
Disclosure Incorporated
5161 River Road
Bethesda, MD 20816
(800) 945-3647; (301) 951-1300
Fax (301) 657-1962

CD-ROM: OneSource Information Services

CD/Corporate: U.K. Private Companies
OneSource Information Services
Lotus Park
The Causeway
Staines
Middlesex TW18 3AG, England
0784 445186; Fax 0784 469344

CD-ROM: OneSource Information Services

CD/Corporate: U.K. Public Companies
OneSource Information Services
Lotus Park
The Causeway
Staines
Middlesex TW18 3AG, England
0784 445186; Fax 0784 469344

CD-ROM: OneSource Information Services

CD/Corporate: U.S. Mergers and Acquisitions
OneSource Information Services
150 Cambridge Park Drive
Cambridge, MA 02140
(800) 554-5501; (617) 441-7000
Fax (617) 225-7058

CD-ROM: OneSource Information Services

CD/Corporate: U.S. Private Plus
CD/Private Plus
OneSource Information Services
150 Cambridge Park Drive
Cambridge, MA 02140
(800) 554-5501; (617) 441-7000
Fax (617) 225-7058

CD-ROM: OneSource Information Services

CD/Corporate: U.S. Public Companies
OneSource Information Services
150 Cambridge Park Drive
Cambridge, MA 02140
(800) 554-5501; (617) 441-7000
Fax (617) 225-7058

CD-ROM: OneSource Information Services

CD-Direct: The Danish Marketing Database

Kobmandsstandens
Oplysningsbureau A/S
Gammel Mnt. 4
DK-1117 Copenhagen K, Denmark
33 111200; Fax 33 111629

CD-ROM: Kobmandsstandens
Oplysningsbureau A/S

CD/Investment: International Equities

OneSource Information Services
150 Cambridge Park Drive
Cambridge, MA 02140
(800) 554-5501; (617) 441-7000
Fax (617) 225-7058

CD-ROM: OneSource
Information Services

CD/Notes: U.S. Private Profiles

OneSource Information Services
150 Cambridge Park Drive
Cambridge, MA 02140
(800) 554-5501; (617) 441-7000
Fax (617) 225-7058

CD-ROM: OneSource
Information Services

CD/Notes: U.S. Public Profiles

OneSource Information Services
150 Cambridge Park Drive
Cambridge, MA 02140
(800) 554-5501; (617) 441-7000
Fax (617) 225-7058

CD-ROM: OneSource
Information Services

CDA/Spectrum Institutional Ownership

*Refer to Appendix N for CDA
Investment Technologies, Inc.*

Online: CDA Investment
Technologies, Inc.

COMLINE Japanese Corporate Directory

COMLINE Business Data, Inc.
1-12-5 Hamamatsucho, Minto-ku
Tokyo 105, Japan
03 5401 4567; Fax 03 5401 2345

Online: DataStar (JPCO);
NEXIS

Compact D/Canada

Micromedia Ltd.
20 Victoria Street
Toronto, ON, Canada M5C 2N8
(800) 387-2689
(416) 362-5211
Fax (416) 362-6161

CD-ROM: Disclosure
Incorporated, Compact
Disclosure

Compact D/SEC

Disclosure Incorporated
5161 River Road
Bethesda, MD 20816
(800) 945-3647; (301) 951-1300
Fax (301) 657-1962

CD-ROM: Disclosure
Incorporated

Compact D/'33

'33 Act Disclosure Database
Disclosure Incorporated
5161 River Road
Bethesda, MD 20816
(800) 945-3647; (301) 951-1300
Fax (301) 657-1962

CD-ROM: Disclosure
Incorporated

Companies International

*Refer to Appendix N for
Gale Research, Inc.*

CD-ROM: Gale Research Inc.

Company Credit Reports (CCR)

Teikoku Databank, Ltd.
5-20, Minami Aoyama 2-Chome
Minato-ku
Tokyo 107, Japan
03 34044311; Fax 03 34044339

Online: COSMOSNET

Company Intelligence

*Refer to Appendix N for
Information Access Company
(IAC)*

Online: Knight-Ridder
Information, Inc. (as File 479);

NEXIS (as CI, CIUS, CIINTL);
and DataStar (as INCO)

Company Profile

*Refer to Appendix N for
Information Access Company
(IAC)*

Online: CARL Systems Network

CD-ROM: Information Access
Company (IAC); also available
as part of the General Business
File CD-ROM product

COMPMARK

*Refer to Appendix N for
Standard & Poor's*

Online: Standard & Poor's

COMPUSTAT PC Plus Corporate Text

Standard & Poor's Compustat
7400 South Alton Court
Englewood, CO 80112
(800) 525-8640; (303) 771-6510
Fax (303) 740-4687

CD-ROM: Standard & Poor's
Compustat

COMPUSTAT PC Plus Standard & Poor's Stock Reports

Standard & Poor's Compustat
7400 South Alton Court
Englewood, CO 80112
(800) 525-8640; (303) 771-6510
Fax (303) 740-4687

CD-ROM: Standard & Poor's
Compustat

Corporate Affiliations OnDisc (Who Owns Whom)

National Register Publishing
(NRP)
*Refer to Appendix N for Reed
Reference Publishing Group*

CD-ROM: Knight-Ridder
Information, Inc.;
DIALOG OnDisc

Corporate Affiliations Online (Who Owns Whom)

National Register Publishing
(NRP)

Refer to Appendix N for Reed Reference Publishing Group

Online: Knight-Ridder Information, Inc. (as File 513); CompuServe Information Service (AFFILIATIONS)

Corporate Affiliations Plus
National Register Publishing (NRP)
Refer to Appendix N for Reed Reference Publishing Group

CD-ROM: Bowker Electronic Publishing

Corporate Canada Online
Refer to Appendix N for Globe Information Services

Online: Info Globe Online (CCO); Dow Jones News/Retrieval (as CANADA)

The Corporate Directory of U.S. Public Companies
Walker's Western Research
1650 Borel Place; Suite 130
San Mateo, CA 94402
(800) 258-3747; (415) 341-1110
Fax (415) 341-2351

CD-ROM: Walker's Western Research and Gale Research Inc.

Corporate Technology Database (CTD)
(CorpTech Database)
Corporate Technology
Information Services, Inc.
(CorpTech)
12 Alfred Street; Suite 200
Woburn, MA 01801-9998
(800) 333-8036; (617) 932-3939
Fax (617) 932-6335

Online: ORBIT•QUESTEL (as CORP); DataStar (as CTCO); Knowledge Express

Credit Analysis Reference Disc
Standard & Poor's Ratings Group
25 Broadway
New York, NY 10004
(212) 208-8830

CD-ROM: Standard & Poor's Ratings Group

Creditreform-Datenbank (CREFO)
Verband der Vereine
Creditreform e.V. (VC)
Hellersbergstr. 12
Postfach 101553
D-41415 Neuss, Germany
02101 109210; Fax 02131 109225

Online: Verband der Vereine
Creditreform e.V. (VC); DataStar (as DVVC); Gesellschaft fur Betriebswirtschaftliche Information mbH (GBI) (CREFO); GENIOS Wirtschaftsdatenbanken (VC)

DATEX
Datex Services Ltd.
P.O. Box 30-988
Lower Hutt, New Zealand
04 5693293; Fax 04 5697997

Online: Kiwinet (as DATX)

DBRISK (DunsPrint France)
Refer to Appendix N for Dun & Bradstreet France S.A.

Online: Dun & Bradstreet France S.A.

DDR Companies
DB Research GmbH,
Information Resources Center
Postfach 100611
D-60006 Frankfurt am Main 1, Germany
069 71007408; Fax 069 71007322

Online: FIZ Technik (DDRF)

Disclosure/Spectrum Ownership Database
Refer to Appendix N for Disclosure Incorporated

Online: Knight-Ridder Information, Inc. (as File 540)

Dun & Bradstreet Dunserve II (DBII)
Refer to Appendix N for Dun & Bradstreet Canada

Online: Infomart Online (DBII)

Dun & Bradstreet Eastern Europe
Refer to Appendix N for Dun & Bradstreet Ltd.

Online: DataStar (as DNEE)

Dun & Bradstreet European Marketing File
Dun & Bradstreet Ltd.
2nd Floor; Arndale House
Arndale Centre
Cannon Street
Manchester M43AQ, England
61 4555119; Fax 61 8342488

Online: DataStar (DBZZ)

Dun & Bradstreet Guide to Canadian Manufacturers (DBGCM)
Refer to Appendix N for Dun & Bradstreet Canada

Online: Infomart Online

Dun & Bradstreet Swiss Company Information
Dun & Bradstreet AG
Schoeneggstr. 5
8026 Zurich, Switzerland
Fax 01 2410230; 01 2425307

Online: DataStar (as SWCO)

Dun & Bradstreet United States (DBUS)
Refer to Appendix N for Dun & Bradstreet Canada

Online: Infomart Online

Dun's Family Tree Service
Refer to Appendix N for Dun & Bradstreet Business Credit Services

Online: WESTLAW; NewsNet, Inc.

Dun's Market Identifiers (DMI)
Dun & Bradstreet Information Services
Three Sylvan Way
Parsippany, NJ 07054-3896
(800) 223-1026; (201) 605-6000
Fax (201) 605-6921

Online: Knight-Ridder Information, Inc. (as File 516: D & B—Dun's Market Identifiers

Online); DataStar (as DBUS: Dun's Marketing Identifiers USA); Dow Jones News/Retrieval (as DMI); CompuServe Information Service (DUNS)

Dun's Middle Market Disc
Dun & Bradstreet Information Services
Three Sylvan Way
Parsippany, NJ 07054-3896
(800) 223-1026; (201) 605-6000
Fax (201) 605-6921

CD-ROM: Dun & Bradstreet Information Services

Dun's Million Dollar Directory (MDD)
Dun & Bradstreet Information Services
Three Sylvan Way
Parsippany, NJ 07054-3896
(800) 223-1026; (201) 605-6000
Fax (201) 605-6921

Online: Knight-Ridder Information, Inc. (as File 517: D & B—Dun's Million Dollar Directory); NIFTY-Serve (as MDD)

Dun's Million Dollar Disc
Dun & Bradstreet Information Services
Three Sylvan Way
Parsippany, NJ 07054-3896
(800) 223-1026; (201) 605-6000
Fax (201) 605-6921

CD-ROM: Dun & Bradstreet Information Services

Dun's Underwriting Guide
Refer to Appendix N for Dun & Bradstreet Business Credit Services

Online: Dun & Bradstreet Business Credit Services

Duns Asia/Pacific Key Business Enterprises
Dun & Bradstreet (Australia) Pty. Ltd.
P.O. Box 7405
St. Kilda Road
Melbourne, VIC 3004, Australia
03 8283333; Fax 03 8283300

CD-ROM: Riddell Information Services Pty. Ltd.

Duns Legal Search
Refer to Appendix N for Dun & Bradstreet Business Credit Services

Online: Dun & Bradstreet Business Credit Services

Dunsmarketing
Dun & Bradstreet France Marketing (DBFM)
Refer to Appendix N for Dun & Bradstreet France S.A.

Online: QUESTEL•ORBIT (as DBFM)

DunsPrint Canada
Refer to Appendix N for Dun & Bradstreet Canada

Online: Dun & Bradstreet Canada

DunsPrint Worldwide
Refer to Appendix N for Dun & Bradstreet Ltd.

Holmers Farm Way
High Wycombe, Bucks. HP12 4UL, England
0494 422000; Fax 0494 422260

Online: Dun & Bradstreet Ltd.

EDGAR Plus
Refer to Appendix N for Disclosure Incorporated

Online: Disclosure Incorporated

The Electric Utility Encyclopedia
Oil Pipeline Research Institute, Inc.
P.O. Box 1433
Manhattan Beach, CA 90266
(310) 372-0722; Fax (310) 374-0259

CD-ROM: Oil Pipeline Research Institute, Inc.

EMMA (Easy Mailing and Marketing Applications)
ICC Marketing Services Ltd.
Field House
72 Oldfield Road
Hampton, Middlesex TW12

2HQ, England
081-783 0788; Fax 081-783 1940

CD-ROM: CD-ROM Publishing Company

EURIDILE
France Institut National de la Propriete Industrielle (INPI)
26 bis, rue de Leningrad
F-75800 Paris Cedex 8, France
01 42945260; Fax 01 42940216

Online: O.R. Telematique

Euro Kompass CD
Reed Information Services
Windsor Court
East Grinstead House
East Grinstead, West Sussex
RH19 1XA, England
0342 326972; Fax 0342 335612

CD-ROM: Reed Information Services

European Analysis
FT Analysis
Ibex House
42/47 Minories
London EC3 1DY, England
071-702 0991; Fax 071-702 2067

Online: ARK Information Services

European Dun's Market Identifiers (EDMI)
Dun & Bradstreet International
International Marketing Services
430 Mountain Avenue
Murray Hill, NJ 07974
(800) 223-1026; (908) 665-5000

Online: Knight-Ridder Information, Inc. (as File 521: D & B—European Dun's Market Identifiers); ESA-IRS (162: Dun's European Marketing Online); NIFTY-Serve (EDMI); WESTLAW; and CompuServe Information Service

Exchange Offers/ Debt Tender Offers
Refer to Appendix N for Securities Data Company, Inc.

Online: Securities Data Company, Inc., Financial Database System

EXTEL Cards
Extel Financial Ltd.
Fitzroy House
13-17 Epworth Street
London EC2A 4DL, England
071-251 3333; Fax 071-251 2725

Online: DataStar (EXTL); Knight-Ridder Information, Inc. (as File 500: EXTEL International Financial Cards; and 501: EXTEL International News Cards); LEXIS (Extel Cards); FT PRO-FILE (Extel Financial Cards)

FAME (Financial Analysis Made Easy)
Jordan & Sons Ltd.
21 St. Thomas Street
Bristol BS1 6JS, England
0272 230600; Fax 0272 230063

CD-ROM: Jordan & Sons Ltd.

FBR Asian Company Profiles
*Refer to Appendix N for
F.B.R. Data Base Inc.*

Online: Knight-Ridder Information, Inc. (as File 505)

**FIB Database
(Firmen-Info-Bank)**
*Refer to Appendix N for AZ
Direct Marketing*

Online: AZ Direct Marketing; Bertelsmann GmbH; Gesellschaft fur Betriebswirtschaftliche Information mbH (GBI) (FIB); GENIOS Wirtschaftsdatenbanken (FIB)

The Financial Elite
Database America
100 Paragon Drive
Montvale, JN 07645-0419
(800) 478-0318

CD-ROM: Database America

FINDAS
Financial Data Service
DATABANK S.p.A
Via dei Piatti 11
I-20123 Milan, Italy
02 809556; Fax 02 8056495

Online: DATABANK S.p.A.

Forbes Annual Directory
Forbes Inc.
60 Fifth Avenue
New York, NY 10011
(212) 620-2200

Online: LEXIS (FORBAD)

FP Corporate Survey
The Financial Post Datagroup
333 King Street East
Toronto, ON, Canada M5A 4N2
(416) 350-6440; Fax (416) 350-6501

Online: Infomart Online

French Companies Full Financials
SNRC-WYSMULLER (S & W)
4, quai Jean Moulin
F-69001 Lyon Cedex, France
720 07702; Fax 720 79818

Online: DataStar (FRFF, FREF)

Gale Business Resources CD-ROM
*Refer to Appendix N for
Gale Research, Inc.*

CD-ROM: Gale Research Inc.

General BusinessFile
*Refer to Appendix N for
Information Access Company
(IAC)*

CD-ROM: Information Access Company (IAC)

Germany's Top 300
Frankfurter Allgemeine Zeitung GmbH (FAZ),
Informationsdienste
P.O. Box 100808
Hellerhofstr. 9
D-60327 Frankfurt, Germany
06196 960601; Fax 06196 960649

Online: GENIOS Wirtschaftsdatenbanken (T300)

Global Report
(Citibank Global Report)
Citicorp
77 Water Street; 2nd Floor
New York, NY 10043
(800) 842-8405; (212) 898-7425
Fax (212) 742-8769

Online: FAME Information Services, Inc.; Info Globe Online; CompuServe Information Service (GLOREP)

High-Tech Texas
*Refer to Appendix N for Texas
Innovation Network System
(TINS)*

Online: Texas Innovation Network System (TINS); Knowledge Express

Hoover's Handbook of American Business
The Reference Press, Inc.
6448 Highway 290 E; Suite E-104
Austin, TX 78723
(512) 454-7778
Fax (512) 454-9401

Online: LEXIS (HVR); America Online; Bloomberg Financial Markets

Hoover's Handbook of American Business: Multimedia Business 500
The Reference Press, Inc.
6448 Highway 290 E; Suite E-104
Austin, TX 78723
(512) 454-7778
Fax (512) 454-9401

CD-ROM: The Reference Press, Inc.

Hoover's Handbook of World Business
The Reference Press, Inc.
6448 Highway 290 E; Suite E-104
Austin, TX 78723
(512) 454-7778
Fax (512) 454-9401

Online: LEXIS (HVRWLD); America Online; Bloomberg Financial Markets

Hoover's Masterlist of Major U.S. Companies on CD-ROM: Best Businesses
The Reference Press, Inc.
6448 Highway 290 E; Suite E-104
Austin, TX 78723
(512) 454-7778; Fax (512) 454-9401
CD-ROM: The Reference Press, Inc.

Hoppenstedt Austria
Refer to Appendix N for Verlag Hoppenstedt GmbH

Online: DataStar (HOAU); Gesellschaft fur Betriebswirtschaftliche Information mbH (GBI) (AUST); NEXIS (HOPAUS); Austria Presse Agentur (APA)

CD-ROM: Verlag Hoppenstedt GmbH, Wirtschaftsdatenbank

Hoppenstedt Benelux
Refer to Appendix N for ABC voor Handel en Industrie C.V.

Online: DataStar (BNLU); ABC voor Handel en Industrie C.V.; Gesellschaft fur Betriebswirtschaftliche Information mbH (GBI)

Hoppenstedt Directory of German Companies
(Hoppenstedt Companies)
Refer to Appendix N for Verlag Hoppenstedt GmbH

CD-ROM: Verlag Hoppenstedt GmbH, Wirtschaftsdatenbank

Hoppenstedt Germany
Hoppenstedt Companies
Refer to Appendix N for Verlag Hoppenstedt GmbH

Online: DataStar (HOPE); Knight-Ridder Information, Inc. (as File 529: Hoppenstedt Directory of German Companies); GENIOS Wirtschaftsdatenbanken (HOPP); Gesellschaft fur Betriebswirtschaftliche Information mbH (GBI) (HOPE); FT PROFILE (Hoppenstedt German Company Information); QUESTEL•ORBIT (HOPGER)

ICC Full Text Accounts
ICC Information Group Ltd.
ICC Online Services Division
Field House
72 Oldfield Road
Hampton, Middlesex TW12 2HQ, England
081-783 1122; Fax 081-783 0049

Online: Knight-Ridder Information, Inc. (as File 564, ICC British Company Annual Reports); DataStar (ICAC, ICC Full Text Company Reports & Accounts); FT PROFILE (ICF, ICC Full Text U.K. and European Accounts); NEXIS (ICCCO); also online as part of: M.A.I.D (Market Analysis and Information Database)

IMSWorld Pharmaceutical Company Profiles
IMSWorld Publications Ltd.
7 Harewood Avenue
London NW1 6JB, England
071-393 5100; Fax 071-393 5900

Online: DataStar (IPCP)

CD-ROM: IMSWorld Publications Ltd.

IMSWorld Pharmaceutical Directory
IMSWorld Publications Ltd.
7 Harewood Avenue
London NW1 6JB, England
071-393 5100; Fax 071-393 5900

Online: DataStar (IPDI, IPWE)

IMSWorld World Market Manual
IMSWorld Publications Ltd.
7 Harewood Avenue
London NW1 6JB, England
071-393 5100; Fax 071-393 5900

CD-ROM: IMSWorld Publications Ltd.

INFOCHECK
The Infocheck Group, Ltd.
Godmersham Park, Godmersham
Canterbury, Kent CT4 7DT, England
0227 81300; Fax 0227 813100

Online: The Infocheck Group, Ltd.; DataStar (CHCK, Infocheck UK Company Financial Datasheets)

INFOTRADE Belgian Company Financial Data
Refer to Appendix N for INFOTRADE N.V.

Online: DataStar (BECO); also online as part of: BISNES Plus

Insiderline
Refer to Appendix N for Disclosure Incorporated

Online: Disclosure Incorporated

Insurance Profiles
OneSource Information Services
150 Cambridge Park Drive
Cambridge, MA 02140
(800) 554-5501
(617) 441-7000
Fax (617) 225-7058

CD-ROM: OneSource Information Services

International Dun's Market Identifiers (IDMI)
Dun & Bradstreet International
International Marketing Services
430 Mountain Avenue
Murray Hill, NJ 07974
(800) 223-1026
(908) 665-5000

Online: Knight-Ridder Information, Inc. (as File 518: D & B—International Dun's Market Identifiers); NIFTY-Serve (IDMI); Dow Jones News/Retrieval (DMI); WESTLAW; CompuServe Information Service

Italian Company Profiles
Refer to Appendix N for DATABANK S.p.A

Online: DataStar (as ITFF)

Japanese Company Factfinder: Teikoku Databank
Teikoku Databank, Ltd.
5-20, Minami Aoyama 2-Chome
Minato-ku
Tokyo 107, Japan
03 34044311; Fax 03 34044339

CD-ROM: Knight-Ridder Information, Inc.; DIALOG OnDisc

Jordans Company Information
Refer to Appendix N for Jordan & Sons Ltd.

Online: Jordan & Sons Ltd.; FT PROFILE (JDN); DataStar (JORD, Jordanwatch); Waterlow Signature (The Registered Companies Database)

KOMPASS CD: U.K.
Reed Information Services
Windsor Court
East Grinstead House
East Grinstead, West Sussex
RH19 1XA, England
0342 326972
Fax 0342 335612

CD-ROM: Reed Information Services; KOMPASS CD

KOMPASS EUROPE
Reed Information Services
Windsor Court
East Grinstead House
East Grinstead, West Sussex
RH19 1XA, England
0342 326972; Fax 0342 335612

Online: Knight-Ridder Information, Inc. (as File 590); KOMPASS Online (Reed Information Services Ltd.)

Kompass Far East (ISEN)
Israel National Center of Scientific and Technological Information, (COSTI)
84 Hachashmonaim Street
67011 Tel-Aviv, Israel
3 297781; Fax 3 492033

Online: Israel National Center of Scientific and Technological Information (COSTI); KOBR, KOMA, KOPH, KOSI, KOSK, KOTH)

KOMPASS UK
Reed Information Services
Windsor Court
East Grinstead House
East Grinstead, West Sussex
RH19 1XA, England
0342 326972
Fax 0342 335612

Online: Knight-Ridder Information, Inc. (as File 591); KOMPASS Online (Reed Information Services Ltd.)

Kreditschutzverband von 1870 (KSVA)
Kreditschutzverband von 1870
Zelinkagasse 10
A-1010 Vienna, Austria
01 53484 6; Fax 01 53484 380

Online: DataStar (KSVA); Austria Presse Agentur (APA); Gesellschaft fur Betriebswirtschaftliche Information mbH (GBI); Kreditschutzverband von 1870; Laser D SEC
Refer to Appendix N for Disclosure Incorporated

CD-ROM: Disclosure Incorporated

Luxembourgs ABC voor Handel en Industrie
(Luxembourgs ABC for Trade and Industry)
Refer to Appendix N for ABC voor Handel en Industrie C.V.

Online: ABC voor Handel en Industrie C.V.; Gesellschaft fur Betriebswirtschaftliche Information mbH (GBI) (ABCLUX); DataStar; also online as part of: Hoppenstedt Benelux

M & A Filings
Prentice Hall Legal & Financial Services (PHL&FS)
Refer to Appendix M for CDB Infotek, which acquired this company

Online: Knight-Ridder Information, Inc. (as File 548)

M&A (Mergers & Acquisitions)
MLR Publishing Co.
229 South 18th Street; 3rd Floor
Philadelphia, PA 19103
(800) 637-4464; (215) 790-7000
Fax (215) 790-7005

Online: ADP Network Services, Inc.

The M&A Adviser Data Base ADP/MLR
MLR Publishing Co.
229 South 18th Street; 3rd Floor

Philadelphia, PA 19103
(800) 637-4464; (215) 790-7000
Fax (215) 790-7005

Online: ADP Network Services, Inc.

M.A.I.D. (Market Analysis and Information Database)
M.A.I.D. Systems Ltd.
M.A.I.D. House
18 Dufferin Street
London EC1Y 8PD, England
071-253 6900; Fax 071-253 0060

Online: MAID Systems Ltd.

Mergers and Acquisitions Database
The Infocheck Group, Ltd.
Godmersham Park, Godmersham
Canterbury, Kent CT4 7DT, England
0227 81300; Fax 0227 813100

Online: The Infocheck Group, Ltd.

Moody's Company Data
Moody's Investors Service, Inc.
99 Church Street
New York, NY 10007
(800) 342-5647; (212) 553-0546
Fax (212) 553-4700

CD-ROM: Moody's Investors Service, Inc.

Moody's International Company Data
Moody's Investors Service, Inc.
99 Church Street
New York, NY 10007
(800) 342-5647; (212) 553-0546
Fax (212) 553-4700

CD-ROM: Moody's Investors Service, Inc.

Multimedia Business 500
The Reference Press, Inc.
6448 Highway 290 E; Suite E-104
Austin, TX 78723
(512) 454-7778; Fax (512) 454-9401

CD-ROM: Allegro New Media

National Directory of Minority-Owned Business Firms
Business Research Services, Inc.
4201 Connecticut Avenue, NW

Suite 610
Washington, DC 20008
(800) 845-8420; (202) 364-6473
(845) 325-8720; Fax (202) 686-3228

Online: Business Research
Services, Inc.

NEEDS-COMPANY
Nihon Keizai Shimbun, Inc.
(NIKKEI), Databank Bureau
1-9-5 Otemachi, Chiyoda-ku
Tokyo 100, Japan
03 52942407
Fax 03 52942411

Online: NEEDS (NIKKEI
Economic Electronic Databank
System)

**OPRI Natural Gas Pipeline
Encyclopedia**
Oil Pipeline Research
Institute, Inc.
P.O. Box 1433
Manhattan Beach, CA 90266
(310) 372-0722; Fax (310) 374-0259

CD-ROM: Oil Pipeline Research
Institute, Inc.

**The Petroleum Pipeline
Encyclopedia**
Oil Pipeline Research
Institute, Inc.
P.O. Box 1433
Manhattan Beach, CA 90266
(310) 372-0722; Fax (310) 374-0259

CD-ROM: Oil Pipeline Research
Institute, Inc.

Profile Canada
Micromedia Ltd.
20 Victoria Street
Toronto, ON, Canada M5C 2N8
(800) 387-2689; (416) 362-5211
Fax (416) 362-6161

CD-ROM: Micromedia Ltd.

Prospector's Choice
The Taft Group
12300 Twinbrook Parkway
Suite 520
Rockville, MD 20852
(301) 816-0210

CD-ROM: The Taft Group

**REACH: Review and
Analysis of Companies in
Holland**
DELWEL Uitgeverij B.V.
Alexanderstr. 26
Postbus 19110
NL-2500 Gravenhage,
Netherlands
070 3624800
Fax 070 3605606

CD-ROM: DELWEL Uitgeverij B.V.

SEC Online
*Refer to Appendix N for
Disclosure Incorporated*

Online: I/PLUS Direct;
Knight-Ridder Information, Inc.
(as Files 541, 542, 543 and 544);
LEXIS; WESTLAW;
Information America (IA);
Dow Jones News/Retrieval
(SEC); Disclosure Incorporated;
SEC Online; Bridge Information
Systems, Inc.; Telescan, Inc.;
Track Data Corporation (TDC);
Bloomberg Financial Markets;
Knowledge Express

SEC Online on SilverPlatter
*Refer to Appendix N for
Disclosure Incorporated*

CD-ROM: SilverPlatter
Information, Inc.

**Soliditet On-Line Service
(SOS)**
Kobmandsstandens
Oplysningsbureau A/S
Gammel Mnt. 4
DK-1117 Copenhagen K,
Denmark
33 111200; Fax 33 111629

Online: Kobmandsstandens
Oplysningsbureau A/S

**Standard & Poor's Corporate
Descriptions**
*Refer to Appendix N for
Standard & Poor's*

Online: LEXIS (SPDESC);
NEXIS (SPDESC); NewsNet,
Inc. (SP03E); CompuServe
Knowledge Index (CORP3)

**Standard & Poor's Corporate
Descriptions plus News**
*Refer to Appendix N for
Standard & Poor's*

Online: Knight-Ridder
Information, Inc. (as File 133)

**Standard & Poor's Corporate
FirstFacts**
*Refer to Appendix N for
Standard & Poor's*

Online: NewsNet, Inc. (SP02E)

**Standard & Poor's
Corporations**
*Refer to Appendix N for
Standard & Poor's*

CD-ROM: DIALOG OnDisc

Standard & Poor's Daily News
*Refer to Appendix N for
Standard & Poor's*

Online: Knight-Ridder
Information, Inc. (as File 132);
CompuServe Knowledge Index
(CORP1); LEXIS; NEXIS
(SPNEWS); NewsNet, Inc. (SP01)

**Standard & Poor's Register—
Corporate**
*Refer to Appendix N for
Standard & Poor's*

Online: Knight-Ridder Infor-
mation, Inc. (as File 527); Compu-
Serve Knowledge Index (CORP6);
LEXIS; NEXIS (SPCORP)

**Taiwan On-Line Business
Data Services**
*Refer to Appendix N for F.B.R.
Data Base Inc.*

Online: F.B.R. Data Base Inc.;
also online as part of: FBR Asian
Company Profiles (company directory only); Global Scan (credit
reports only)

Teikoku Japanese Companies
Teikoku Databank, Ltd.
5-20, Minami Aoyama 2-Chome
Minato-ku
Tokyo 107, Japan
03 34044311; Fax 03 34044339

Online: Knight-Ridder
Information, Inc. (as File 502);
Nikkei Telecom; DataStar
(TOKU); COSMOSNET;
G-Search Corporation

TELE INFORM 1
*Refer to Appendix N for
O.R. Telematique*
Online: O.R. Telematique

TSR-BIGS
Tokyo Shoko Research, Ltd. (TSR)
Shinichi Building, 9-6, 1-Chome
Shinbashi, Minato-ku
Tokyo 105, Japan
033 5742211

Online: NIFTY-Serve

U.K. Company Factfinder
ICC Information Group Ltd.
ICC Online Services Division
Field House
72 Oldfield Road
Hampton, Middlesex TW12
2HQ, England
081-783 1122; Fax 081-783 0049

CD-ROM: Knight-Ridder
Information, Inc.;
DIALOG OnDisc

UK Corporations CD
ICC Information Group Ltd.
ICC Online Services Division
Field House
72 Oldfield Road
Hampton, Middlesex TW12
2HQ, England
081-783 1122
Fax 081-783 0049

CD-ROM: SilverPlatter
Information, Inc.

U.S. Businesses
*Refer to Appendix N for
American Business
Information, Inc. (ABI)*

Online: American Business
Information, Inc. (ABI);
American Business Lists;
Knight-Ridder Information, Inc.
(as American Business Directory

File 531, as well as a subset of
this database in American
Business 20 Plus Companies—
File 532)

U.S. Manufacturers
*Refer to Appendix N for
American Business Information,
Inc. (ABI)*

Online: American Business
Information, Inc. (ABI);
American Business Lists

Vickers Bond Data
*Refer to Appendix N for Vickers
Stock Research Corporation*

Online: Vickers Stock Research
Corporation; NEXIS (VICINS);
also online as part of LEXIS
Financial Information Service

**Vickers Institutional Stock
System**
*Refer to Appendix N for Vickers
Stock Research Corporation*

Online: Quotron Systems, Inc.
(Vickers Holdings, Vickers
Insider Trading); Vickers Stock
Research Corporation; Track
Data Corporation (TDC);
NEXIS (VICSEC); also online as
part of LEXIS Financial
Information Service

**World Aviation Directory &
Buyer's Guide CD-ROM**
McGraw-Hill Aviation
Week Group
1200 G Street, NW
Suite 200
Washington, DC 20005
(800) 636-3438; (202) 383-2399
Fax (202) 383-2442

CD-ROM: McGraw-Hill Aviation
Week Group

World Energy CD-ROM
Longman Group UK Ltd.,
Longman Information &
Reference
Westgate House; 6th Floor
The High Harlow

Essex CM20 1YR, England
0279 442601
Fax 0279 444501

CD-ROM: Microinfo Ltd.

Worldscope
Disclosure/Worldscope
W/D Partners
1000 Lafayette Boulevard
Bridgeport, CT 06604
(203) 330-5261
Fax (203) 330-5001

Online: Dow Jones
News/Retrieval; Bridge
Information Systems, Inc.;
FactSet Data Systems, Inc.;
LEXIS (WLDSCP); Randall-
Helms International, Inc.;
also online as part of: M.A.I.D.
(Market Analysis and
Information Database)

CD-ROM: W/D Partners

**Worldscope Corporate
Snapshots**
*Refer to Appendix N for
Disclosure Incorporated*

Online: OCLC FirstSearch
Catalog (WORLDSCOPE)

Professional and Staff Directory Databases

Ag Ed Network
ARI Network Services, Inc.
330 East Kilbourn Avenue
Milwaukee, WI 53202
(800) 558-9044; (414) 278-7676
(558) 242-6001; Fax (414) 283-4357

Online: ARI Network Services, Inc.

Albi Avvocati e Procuratori
Corte Suprema di Cassazione
d'Italia
Centro Elettronico di
Documentazione (CED)
Via Damiano Chiesa 24
I-00136 Rome, Italy
06 33081; Fax 06 3308338

Online: Centro Elettronico di
Documentazione (CED)

Artists in Canada
National Gallery of Canada
Library
P.O. Box 427; Station A
Ottawa, ON, Canada K1N 9N4
(613) 990-0588; Fax (613) 990-9818

Online: Canadian Heritage
Information Network (CHIN)

**Aviation Compendium
(AvComp)**
Flightline Electronic Publishing,
Inc.
1804 Mountainview Drive
Wayne, PA 19087-5533
(800) 842-1716; (215) 296-9205

CD-ROM: Flightline Electronic
Publishing, Inc.

BASELINE
*Refer to Appendix N for
BASELINE II INC.*

Online: BASELINE II INC.

BEST Biotech
Longman Cartermill Inc.
1615 Thames Street
Baltimore, MD 21231
(800) 237-8621; (410) 563-2378
Fax (410) 563-5389

Online: Cartermill Inc.

BEST Great Britain
*Refer to Appendix N for
Longman Cartermill Ltd.*

Online: Longman Cartermill Ltd.

**BEST Great Britain on
CD-ROM**
*Refer to Appendix N for
Longman Cartermill Ltd.*

CD-ROM: Longman Cartermill Ltd.

Boardlink Plus!
*Refer to Appendix N for Gale
Research, Inc.*

CD-ROM: Gale Research Inc.

**California State Government
Directory**
California Journal, Inc.
1901 K Street
Sacramento, CA 95816
(916) 444-2840

Online: State Net (Information
for Public Affairs, Inc.)

**Canadian Journalism
Database (CJD)**
University of Western Ontario
Graduate School of Journalism
Middlesex College
London, ON, Canada N6A 5B7
(519) 661-3383; Fax (519) 661-3848

Online: QL Systems Limited (CJD)

Canadian Register CD-ROM
University of Western Ontario
Social Science Computing
Laboratory (SSCL)
Information Services
London, ON, Canada N6A 5C2
(519) 661-2152; Fax (519) 661-3868

CD-ROM: University of Western
Ontario, Social Science
Computing Laboratory (SSCL),
Information Services

**Canadian Register of
Research and Researchers in
the Social Sciences**
University of Western Ontario
Social Science Computing
Laboratory (SSCL)
Information Services
London, ON, Canada N6A 5C2
(519) 661-2152; Fax (519) 661-3868

Online: CAN/OLE (as CANREG)

The Capital Source
National Journal Inc.
1501 M Street, NW
Washington, DC 20036
(800) 424-2921; (202) 857-1400
Fax (202) 833-8069

Online: NEXIS (as CAPTAL)

**Commonwealth Executive
Responsibilities**
Info-One International Pty. Ltd.
Level 3
2 Elizabeth Plaza
North Sydney, NSW 2060,
Australia
02 9595075; Fax 02 9295127

Online: Info-One International
Pty. Ltd. (a LAWPAC file)

Consultants and Consulting Organizations Directory (CCOD)
Refer to Appendix N for Gale Research, Inc.

Online: HRIN, The Human Resource Information Network (CCOD)

Contemporary Authors on CD (CA on CD)
Refer to Appendix N for Gale Research, Inc.

CD-ROM: Gale Research Inc.

COSMOS 3
Teikoku Databank, Ltd.
5-20, Minami Aoyama 2-Chome
Minato-ku
Tokyo 107, Japan
03 34044311
03 34044339

Online: COSMOSNET

CQ Member Profiles
Refer to Appendix N for Congressional Quarterly Inc. (CQ)

Online: CQ Washington Alert Service (as MEMBERS)

CQ Weekly Report
Congressional Quarterly Weekly Report
Refer to Appendix N for Congressional Quarterly Inc. (CQ)

Online: CQ Washington Alert Service (WR); DataTimes Corporation (CQWEEK)

Deutsche Unternehmensberater
German Consultants
Bundesverband Deutscher Unternehmensberater BDU e.V
Friedrich Wilhelm-Str. 2
D-53113 Bonn
Germany
228 238055
Fax 228 230625

Online: GENIOS Wirtschaftsdatenbanken (as BDUB)

Directories of Physicists and Astronomers
American Institute of Physics (AIP)
Robert Ubell Associates
111 8th Avenue; Suite 1503
New York, NY 10011
(212) 645-3303
Fax (212) 463-8645

Online: American Institute of Physics (AIP); PINET (Physics INformation NETwork)

Directors Database
CCN Business Information Ltd.
Abbey House
Abbeyfield Road
Lenton, Nottingham NG7 2SW, England
0602 863864; Fax 0602 863592

Online: CCN Business Information Ltd.

Directory of Directors Electronic Edition
(Financial Post Directory of Directors)
The Financial Post Datagroup
333 King Street East
Toronto, ON, Canada M5A 4N2
(416) 350-6440; Fax (416) 350-6501

Online: Infomart Online; NEXIS (as FPDIR)

Dirigeants
Refer to Appendix N for O.R. Telematique

Online: O.R. Telematique

The Electric Utility Encyclopedia
Oil Pipeline Research Institute, Inc.
P.O. Box 1433
Manhattan Beach, CA 90266
(310) 372-0722; Fax (310) 374-0259

CD-ROM: Oil Pipeline Research Institute, Inc.

Executive Affiliations
Refer to Appendix M for Information America (IA)

Online: Information America (IA)

ExpertNet
ExpertNet, Ltd.
2519 Royal Ridge Drive
Crete, IL 60417
(800) 888-8318; (708) 672-3078

Online: WESTLAW (EXPNET)

Federal Political and Government Directory
Info-One International Pty. Ltd.
Level 3, 2 Elizabeth Plaza
North Sydney, NSW 2060, Australia
02 9595075; Fax 02 9295127

Online: Info-One International Pty. Ltd.

The Federal Tax Directory
Tax Analysts
140 Wendy Hill Drive
Alpharetta, GA 30201
(800) 955-3444; (703) 533-4400

Online: LEXIS

George Eastman House Interactive Catalog
International Museum of Photography
George Eastman House
900 East Avenue
Rochester, NY 14607
(716) 271-3361
Fax (716) 271-3970

Online: International Museum of Photography

Hoppenstedt Austria
Refer to Appendix N for Verlag Hoppenstedt GmbH

Online: DataStar (HOAU); Gesellschaft fur Betriebswirtschaftliche Information mbH (GBI) (AUST); NEXIS (HOPAUS); Austria Presse Agentur (APA)

Labor Arbitration Information System (LAIS)
Refer to Appendix N for LRP Publications

Online: HRIN, The Human Resource Information Network (LAIS); LRP Publications

LEXIS State Corporation
Information Library (INCORP)
Refer to Appendix N for LEXIS-NEXIS

Online: LEXIS (as INCORP)

Lloyd's Ship Owners, Managers, and Parent Companies File
Lloyd's Maritime Information
Services Ltd. (LMIS)
1 Singer Street
London EC2A 4LQ, England
071-490 1720; Fax 071-250 3142

Online: Lloyd's Maritime
Information Services Ltd.
(LMIS)

Management Experten-Nachweis (MANEX)
Management Experts
Gesellschaft fur
Betriebswirtschaftliche
Information mbH (GBI)
Freischutzstr. 96
Postfach 810360
D-8000 Munich 81, Germany
089 9570064; Fax 089 954229

Online: Gesellschaft fur
Betriebswirtschaftliche
Information mbH (GBI)
(MANEX)

Martindale-Hubbell Law Directory on CD-ROM
Martindale-Hubbell, Inc.
Refer to Appendix N for Reed Reference Publishing Group

CD-ROM: Bowker Electronic
Publishing

Martindale-Hubbell Law Directory Online
Martindale-Hubbell, Inc.
Refer to Appendix N for Reed Reference Publishing Group

Online: LEXIS (as MARHUB)

Medical Reference on Research CD-ROM
Longman Group UK Ltd.
Longman Information &
Reference

Westgate House; 6th Floor
The High Harlow
Essex CM20 1YR, England
0279 442601; Fax 0279 444501

CD-ROM: Microinfo Ltd.

Member Profile Report
Refer to Appendix N for LEXIS-NEXIS

Online: LEXIS and NEXIS
(as MEMBR)

Military Personnel/Base LOCATOR
Staff Directories, Ltd.
P.O. Box 62
Mount Vernon, VA 22121-0062
(703) 739-0900; Fax (703) 739-0234

CD-ROM: Staff Directories, Ltd.

NAME
Centre de Recherche
Documentaire (CREDOC)
Rue de la Montagne
34 B.P. 11
B-1000 Brussels, Belgium
02 5116941; Fax 02 5133195

Online: BELINDIS (as NAME)

New South Wales Political and Government Directory
Political Reference Service Pty.
Ltd.
Civic Square
P.O. Box 607
Canberra, ACT 2608, Australia
062 476950; Fax 062 488169

Online: Info-One International
Pty. Ltd.

NNDC Address List
Brookhaven National Laboratory
Chemistry Department
Upton, NY 11973-5000
(516) 282-3629; Fax (516) 282-5751

Online: National Nuclear Data
Center (NNDC)

The Official American Board of American Specialties (ABMS)
Refer to Appendix N for Reed Reference Publishing Group

CD-ROM: Bowker Electronic
Publishing

OPRI Natural Gas Pipeline Encyclopedia
Oil Pipeline Research
Institute, Inc.
P.O. Box 1433
Manhattan Beach, CA 90266
(310) 372-0722; Fax (310) 374-0259

CD-ROM: Oil Pipeline Research
Institute, Inc.

PARAD Online
Bonnier Business
Publishing Group
AffarsData
P.O. Box 3188
S-103 63 Stockholm, Sweden
08 7365919; Fax 08 7231390

Online: AffarsData (Bonnier
Business Publishing)

PDQ (Physician Data Query)
U.S. National Cancer Institute
International Cancer
Information Center (ICIC)
Building 82; Room 107
Bethesda, MD 20892
(301) 496-7406
Fax (301) 480-8105

Online: DIMDI

CD-ROM: SilverPlatter
Information, Inc.

The Petroleum Pipeline Encyclopedia
Oil Pipeline Research Institute, Inc.
P.O. Box 1433
Manhattan Beach, CA 90266
(310) 372-0722; Fax (310) 374-0259

CD-ROM: Oil Pipeline Research
Institute, Inc.

PHN AIDS Network
Public Health Foundation (PHF)
Public Health Network (PHN)
1220 L Street, NW; Suite 350
Washington, DC 20005
(202) 898-5600; Fax (202) 898-5609

Online: CompuServe Information
Service

Prentice Hall Law & Business Directory of Bankruptcy Attorneys
Prentice Hall Law & Business
Refer to Appendix M for CDB Infotek, which acquired this company

Online: WESTLAW (as BKR-DIR); LEXIS (as BKRDIR)

Prentice Hall Law & Business Directory of Corporate Counsel
Prentice Hall Law & Business
Refer to Appendix M for CDB Infotek, which acquired this company

Online: WESTLAW
(as CORP-DIR)

Q-NET (The On-Line Quality Information Network)
Timeplace, Inc.
460 Totten Pond Road
Waltham, MA 02154
(800) 544-4023; (617) 890-4636
Fax (617) 890-7274

Online: Timeplace, Inc.

Resource People/Personnes Ressources
Canadian Centre for
Occupational Health and Safety
(CCOHS)
250 Main Street East
Hamilton, ON, Canada L8N 1H6
(800) 668-4284; (905) 570-8094
Fax (905) 572-2206

Online: CCINFOline

Staff Directories on CD-ROM
Staff Directories, Ltd.
P.O. Box 62
Mount Vernon, VA 22121-0062
(703) 739-0900; Fax (703) 739-0234

CD-ROM: Staff Directories, Ltd.

Standard & Poor's Register— Biographical
Refer to Appendix N for Standard & Poor's

Online: Knight-Ridder
Information, Inc. (as File 526);

CompuServe Knowledge Index
(as CORP5); LEXIS and NEXIS
(as SPBIO)

Technical Advisory Service for Attorneys (TASA)
Technical Advisory Service, Inc.
1166 DeKalb Pike
Blue Bell, PA 19422
(800) 523-2319
(215) 275-8272
Fax (215) 643-5557

Online: WESTLAW (as TASA)

United Kingdom Reference on Research CD-ROM
Longman Group UK Ltd.
Longman Information
& Reference
Westgate House; 6th Floor
The High Harlow
Essex CM20 1YR, England
0279 442601
Fax 0279 444501

CD-ROM: Microinfo Ltd.

West's Legal Directory
Refer to Appendix N for West Publishing

Online: WESTLAW
(as WLD, WLD-CORPCO,
WLD-LFM, WLD-GOV,
WLD-LS, WLD-PRI,
WLD-CANADA, WLS-AALS,
WL); on the Internet at:
http://www.westpub.com/WLDInfo/WLD.htm

Who's Who in European Business and Industry
WHO'S WHO Edition GmbH
Sturmerweg 7
D-82211 Herrsching, Germany
8152 1061
Fax 8152 1093

Online: GENIOS
Wirtschaftsdatenbanken
(as WHO)

Other Directory Databases Containing Employee Information

1x1 German Buyers' Guide
Einkaufs-1x1 der Deutschen
Industrie (E1x1).
Deutscher Addressbuchverlag fur
Wirtschaft und Verkehr GmbH
Arheilger Weg 17
D-64380 Rossdorf 1, Germany
6154 699500; Fax 06154 6995490

Online: DataStar (E1x1: German
Buyers Guide); FIZ Technik

**ABC Belge pour le Commerce
et l'Industrie**
*Refer to Appendix N for
ABC Belge pour le Commerce
et l'Industrie B.V.*

Online: ABC Belge pour le
Commerce et l'Industrie B.V.

**ABC der Deutschen Wirtschaft
(German Buyers' and Sellers'
Guide) (Info Bonds)**
ABC der Deutschen Wirtschaft
Verlagsgesellschaft mbH
ABC Publishing Group
P.O. Box 100262
D-64202 Darmstadt, Germany
6151 3892-0; Fax 6151 33164

CD-ROM: ABC der Deutschen
Wirtschaft Verlagsgesellschaft
mbH

**ABC Europe Production
Europex**
Europe Export Edition GmbH
P.O. Box 100262
D-64202 Darmstadt 1, Germany
06151 38920; Fax 06151 33164

Online: DataStar (as EURE); FIZ
Technik (as ABC EUROPA)

ABC EUROPEX
Europ Export Edition GmbH
P.O. Box 100262
D-64202 Darmstadt 1, Germany
06151 38920; Fax 06151 33164

CD-ROM: Europ Export Edition
GmbH

**ABC Germany (ABC der
Deutschen Wirtschaft;
German Buyers' and Sellers'
Guide; Info Bonds)**
ABC der Deutschen Wirtschaft
Verlagsgesellschaft mbH
ABC Publishing Group
P.O. Box 100262
D-64202 Darmstadt, Germany
6151 3892-0; Fax 6151 33164

Online: DataStar (as ABCE);
FIZ Technik (as ABCE)

**ABC Luxembourgeois pour le
Commerce et l'Industrie**
*Refer to Appendix N for
ABC Belge pour le Commerce
et l'Industrie B.V.*

Online: ABC Belge pour le
Commerce et l'Industrie B.V.

ABC Netherlands
*Refer to Appendix N for ABC voor
Handel en Industrie C.V.*

Online: Gesellschaft fur
Betriebswirtschaftliche
Information mbH (GBI) (ABCNL)

**ABC voor Handel en Industrie
(ABC for Trade and Industry)**
*Refer to Appendix N for ABC voor
Handel en Industrie C.V.*

Online: ABC voor Handel en
Industrie C.V.; also online as
part of: Hoppenstedt Benelux

**ABC/Dienstverleners
(Dutch Directory of
Business Services) (ABC
Services)**
*Refer to Appendix N for ABC
voor Handel en Industrie C.V.*

Online: ABC voor Handel en
Industrie C.V.; also online as
part of: Hoppenstedt Benelux

**Ag.ROUND (Australian
Agriculture and Natural
Resources on CD-ROM)**
Australia Commonwealth
Scientific and Industrial
Research Organization,
(CSIRO)
CSIRO Information Services
314 Albert Street, P.O. Box 89
East Melbourne, VIC 3002,
Australia
03 4187333; Fax 03 4190459

CD-ROM: Info-One
International Pty. Ltd.

**American Library Directory
(ALD)**
*Refer to Appendix N for Reed
Reference Publishing Group*

Online: Knight-Ridder
Information, Inc. (as File 460)

**Archaeological Sites Data
Base (AZSITE)**
Arizona State Museum
University of Arizona

Tucson, AZ 85721
(602) 621-6275

Online: Arizona State Museum

Asia-Pacific Kompass CD
Kompass International
Management Corporation
Rutistr. 38
CH-8044 Zurich, Switzerland
01 8203495; Fax 01 8203653

CD-ROM: Reed Information
Services

**Australian Energy Research
in Progress (ERIP)**
Energy Research and
Development Corporation
G.P.O. Box 629
Canberra, ACT 2601, Australia
616 274 4800; Fax 616 274 4801

Online: OZLINE: Australian
Information Network

**Australian Rural Research in
Progress (ARRIP)**
Australia Commonwealth
Scientific and Industrial
Research Organization, (CSIRO)
CSIRO Information Services
314 Albert Street
P.O. Box 89
East Melbourne, VIC 3002,
Australia
03 4187333; Fax 03 4190459

Online: OZLINE: Australian
Information Network

**Belgisch ABC voor Handel en
Industrie**
*Refer to Appendix N for ABC
voor Handel en Industrie C.V.*

Online: ABC voor Handel en
Industrie C.V. and Gesellschaft
fur Betriebswirtschaftliche
Information mbH (GBI) (ABC-
BEL); also online as part of:
Hoppenstedt Benelux

BioScan
Oryx Press
4041 North Central Avenue
Suite 700
Phoenix, AZ 85012-3397

(800) 279-6799; (602) 265-2651
Fax (602) 265-6250

Online: Knowledge Express

**BizEkon News—Soviet
Business Directory**
BizEkon Companies in the C.I.S.
Russian Information and
Communications Agency
(RUSSICA)
Spartakovskaya St. 13
107066 Moscow, Russia
095 9325610; Fax 095 9326300

Online: SovInfoLink;
Gesellschaft fur
Betriebswirtschaftliche
Information mbH (GBI) (SOBIZ);
LEXIS (as SOVCO); MagnaTex
COMMUNICATE!; also online as
part of: Soviet News

**Burrelle's Media Directory
on Disc**
*Refer to Appendix N for
Burrelle's Information Services*

CD-ROM: SilverPlatter
Information, Inc.

Canadian Trade Index
Southam Electronic Publishing
1450 Don Mills Road
Don Mills, ON, Canada M3B 2X7
(416) 445-6641; Fax (416) 445-3508

Online: Infomart Online
(as CTIX)

CCINFOdisc: Core Series B2
OSH InterData
Canadian Centre for
Occupational Health and Safety
(CCOHS)
250 Main Street E.
Hamilton, ON, Canada L8N 1H6
(800) 668-4284; (905) 570-8094
Fax (905) 572-2206

CD-ROM: Canadian Centre for
Occupational Health and Safety
(CCOHS), CCINFOdisc

**China's Research and
Development Institutes
(RDIDB)**
AsiaInfo Services, Inc.

2474 Manana Drive; Suite 121
Dallas, TX 75220
(214) 351-3091; Fax (214) 351-4861

CD-ROM: AsiaInfo Services, Inc.

**Chinese Machinery and
Electronics Enterprises and
Their Products Information
DB Ondisc**
China Educational Publications
Import and Export Corporation
15 XueYuanLu
Beijing 100083, People's
Republic of China
01 2023014; Fax 01 2010821

CD-ROM: China Educational
Publications Import and Export
Corporation

COTRAITEL
Association Cotraitel
Immeuble du Mas d'Alco
254, rue Michel Teule
B.P. 6076
F-34030 Montpellier Cedex 1,
France
Fax 67 618100; 67 618110

Online: Association Cotraitel

**Current Research in Britain
(CRIB)**
*Refer to Appendix N for Longman
Cartermill Ltd. Technology Centre*

CD-ROM: Longman
Cartermill Ltd.

Der Runde Herold
Herold Business Data GmbH
Schleierg. 18
A-1100 Vienna, Austria
0222 60141
Fax 0222 601418

CD-ROM: Herold Business Data
GmbH

Directory of Nursing Homes
HCIA Inc.
300 East Lombard Street
Baltimore, MD 21202
(800) 568-3282; (410) 576-9600
Fax (410) 539-5220

Online: HRIN, The Human
Resource Information Network

Directory of U.S. Importers and Exporters
Journal of Commerce, Inc.
Two World Trade Center
27th Floor
New York, NY 10048-0662
(212) 837-7000; Fax (212) 837-7070

CD-ROM: Knight-Ridder Information, Inc.; DIALOG OnDisc

DTIC Manpower and Training Research Information System (MATRIS)
U.S. Defense Technical Information Center (DTIC)
Building No. 5
Cameron Station
Alexandria, VA 22304-6145
(703) 274-7709; Fax (703) 274-9307

Online: U.S. Defense Technical Information Center (DTIC); Defense RDT&E OnLine System (DROLS)

Dun & Bradstreet Germany
Dun & Bradstreet Ltd.
Holmers Farm Way
High Wycombe, Bucks
HP12 4UL, England
0494 422000; Fax 0494 422260

Online: DataStar (as DBWG); QUESTEL•ORBIT (as DBGR)

Dun & Bradstreet Italy
Dun & Bradstreet Ltd.
Holmers Farm Way
High Wycombe, Bucks
HP12 4UL, England
0494 422000; Fax 0494 422260

Online: DataStar (as DBIT); QUESTEL•ORBIT (as DBIT)

Dun & Bradstreet United Kingdom
Dun & Bradstreet Ltd.
Holmers Farm Way
High Wycombe, Bucks
HP12 4UL, England
0494 422000; Fax 0494 422260

Online: DataStar (as DBGB); QUESTEL•ORBIT (as DBUK)

Dun's Business Update
Dun & Bradstreet Information Services
Three Sylvan Way
Parsippany, NJ 07054-3896
(800) 223-1026; (201) 605-6000
Fax (201) 605-6921

Online: Knight-Ridder Information, Inc. (as File 514)

Encyclopedia of Associations (EA)
Refer to Appendix N for Gale Research, Inc.

Online: Knight-Ridder Information, Inc. (as File 114); OCLC EPIC; OCLC FirstSearch Catalog

Encyclopedia of Associations CD-ROM
Refer to Appendix N for Gale Research, Inc.

CD-ROM: SilverPlatter Information, Inc.

Encyclopedia of Associations: National Organizations of the U.S.
Refer to Appendix N for Gale Research, Inc.

CD-ROM: Gale Research Inc.

ESSOR
Union Francaise des Annuaires Professionnels (UFAP)
13, ave. Hennequin, B.P. 36
F-78192 Trappes Cedex, France
1 30506148; Fax 1 30504827

Online: QUESTEL•ORBIT (as ESSOR)

EUDISED R & D Data Base (European Documentation and Information System for Education)
Council of Europe
European Documentation and Information System for Education (EUDISED)
F-67075 Strasbourg Cedex, France
88 412000; Fax 88 412788
Online: ESA-IRS (24)

EURISTOTE
Commission of the European Communities (CEC)
P.O. Box 2373
L-1023 Luxembourg, Luxembourg
34981200

Online: ECHO

European Book World on CD-ROM
Anderson Rand
Scott's Bindery
Russell Court
Cambridge CB2 1HL, England
44 223 566640

CD-ROM: Anderson Rand

The Executive Desk Register (EDR)
Demand Research Corporation
625 North Michigan Avenue
Chicago, IL 60611
(312) 664-6500

Online: Delphi Internet Services Corporation; America Online

Finnish Export Companies
Finnish Foreign Trade Association
Information Department
Arkadiankatu 4-6 B
P.O. Box 908
SF-00101 Helsinki, Finland
90 69591; Fax 90 6940028

Online: Gesellschaft fur Betriebswirtschaftliche Information mbH (GBI) (FINEX)

Foundation Directory
The Foundation Center
79 Fifth Avenue
New York, NY 10003-3050
(212) 620-4230; Fax (212) 691-1828

Online: Knight-Ridder Information, Inc. (as File 26)

French Companies (TELE-FIRM) (Directory of French Companies)
Association TELEFIRM
Chambre de Commerce et

d'Industrie de Paris (CCIP)
27 Avenue de Friedland
F-75382 Paris Cedex 8, France
01 42897219; Fax 01 42897286

Online: DataStar (as FRCO)

FUNDED!
IGW Canada Inc.
4500 16 Avenue NW; Suite 300
Calgary, AB, Canada T3B OM6
(800) 668-1017
(403) 247-9506
Fax (403) 247-9915

CD-ROM: IGW Canada Inc.

Harvest Database
Harvest Information Services
18-19 Long Lane
London EC1A 9HE, England
071-606 4533; Fax 071-226 6083

Online: Harvest Information
Services

**Health Devices Sourcebook
(ECRI)**
5200 Butler Pike
Plymouth Meeting, PA 19462
(610) 825-6000
Fax (610) 834-1275

Online: Knight-Ridder
Information, Inc. (as File 188)

Holland Exports
*Refer to Appendix N for ABC
voor Handel en Industrie C.V.*

Online: ABC voor Handel en
Industrie C.V.; also online as
part of: Hoppenstedt Benelux

**Hoppenstedt German
Machinery Building Industry**
*Refer to Appendix N for
Verlag Hoppenstedt GmbH*

Online: Gesellschaft fur
Betriebswirtschaftliche
Information mbH (GBI) (HUCO)

I-EXPORT
Chambre de Commerce et
d'Industrie de Paris (CCIP),
Direction de l'Information
Economique (DIE)
2, rue de Viarmes

F-75001 Paris, France
01 45083643; Fax 01 45083610

Online: Chambre de Commerce
et d'Industrie de Paris (CCIP),
Business Information
Department; also online as part
of TELEXPORT

INRS-Recherche
Institut National de Recherche
et de Securite
Service de Documentation
30, rue Olivier Noyer
F-75680 Paris Cedex 14, France
01 40443093; Fax 01 40443099

Online: Europeenne de Donnees

**International ABC Aerospace
Directory**
Jane's Information Group
1340 Braddock Place; Suite 300
P.O. Box 1436
Alexandria, VA 22313-2036
(703) 683-3700; Fax (703) 836-0029

CD-ROM: Jane's
Information Group

Inventario Musical (IMUS)
Ministerio de Cultura de Espana
Instituto Nacional de las Artes
Escenicas y de la Musica
Centro de Documentacion
Teatral
Capitan Haya 44
28020 Madrid, Spain
01 5723311

Online: Ministerio de Cultura de
Espana; Secretaria General
Tecnica, Puntos de Informacion
Cultural (PIC)

**Inventory of Marriage &
Family Literature**
National Council on Family
Relations (NCFR)
3989 Central Avenue, NE
Suite 550
Minneapolis, MN 55421
(612) 781-9331; Fax (612) 781-9348

Online: CDP Online (NCFR);
CDP After Dark (NCFR);
Knight-Ridder Information, Inc.
(as File 291); HRIN, The Human

Resource Information Network
(as FAMRES); CDP
COLLEAGUE (NCRF)

**Investor's Guide and Mutual
Fund Directory**
The Association of No-Load
Funds
Mutual Fund Education Alliance
1900 Erie Street; Suite 120
Kansas City, MO 64116
(816) 471-1454

Online: CompuServe Information
Service (NOLOAD)

Jane's AFV Retrofit Systems
Jane's Armoured Fighting
Vehicles Retrofit Systems
Jane's Information Group
1340 Braddock Place; Suite 300
P.O. Box 1436
Alexandria, VA 22313-2036
(703) 683-3700
Fax (703) 836-0029

CD-ROM: Jane's
Information Group

Jane's All the World's Aircraft
Jane's Information Group
1340 Braddock Place; Suite 300
P.O. Box 1436
Alexandria, VA 22313-2036
(703) 683-3700
Fax (703) 836-0029

CD-ROM: Jane's
Information Group

Jane's Armour & Artillery
Jane's Information Group
1340 Braddock Place; Suite 300
P.O. Box 1436
Alexandria, VA 22313-2036
(703) 683-3700
Fax (703) 836-0029

CD-ROM: Jane's
Information Group

Jane's Avionics
Jane's Information Group
1340 Braddock Place; Suite 300
P.O. Box 1436
Alexandria, VA 22313-2036
(703) 683-3700
Fax (703) 836-0029

CD-ROM: Jane's Information Group

Jane's Battlefield Surveillance Systems
Jane's Information Group
1340 Braddock Place; Suite 300
P.O. Box 1436
Alexandria, VA 22313-2036
(703) 683-3700
Fax (703) 836-0029

CD-ROM: Jane's Information Group

Jane's C3I Systems
Jane's Command, Control Communications & Intelligence Systems
Jane's Information Group
1340 Braddock Place; Suite 300
P.O. Box 1436
Alexandria, VA 22313-2036
(703) 683-3700
Fax (703) 836-0029

CD-ROM: Jane's Information Group

Jane's Fighting Ships
Jane's Information Group
1340 Braddock Place; Suite 300
P.O. Box 1436
Alexandria, VA 22313-2036
(703) 683-3700
Fax (703) 836-0029

CD-ROM: Jane's Information Group

Jane's Infantry Weapons
Jane's Information Group
1340 Braddock Place; Suite 300
P.O. Box 1436
Alexandria, VA 22313-2036
(703) 683-3700; Fax (703) 836-0029

CD-ROM: Jane's Information Group

Jane's Land-Based Air Defense
Jane's Information Group
1340 Braddock Place; Suite 300
P.O. Box 1436
Alexandria, VA 22313-2036
(703) 683-3700
Fax (703) 836-0029

CD-ROM: Jane's Information Group

Jane's Military Communications
Jane's Information Group
1340 Braddock Place; Suite 300
P.O. Box 1436
Alexandria, VA 22313-2036
(703) 683-3700
Fax (703) 836-0029

CD-ROM: Jane's Information Group

Jane's Military Training Systems
Jane's Information Group
1340 Braddock Place; Suite 300
P.O. Box 1436
Alexandria, VA 22313-2036
(703) 683-3700
Fax (703) 836-0029

CD-ROM: Jane's Information Group

Jane's Military Vehicles and Logistics
Jane's Information Group
1340 Braddock Place; Suite 300
P.O. Box 1436
Alexandria, VA 22313-2036
(703) 683-3700
Fax (703) 836-0029

CD-ROM: Jane's Information Group

Jane's Radar & Electronic Warfare Systems
Jane's Information Group
1340 Braddock Place; Suite 300
P.O. Box 1436
Alexandria, VA 22313-2036
(703) 683-3700; Fax (703) 836-0029

CD-ROM: Jane's Information Group

Jane's Underwater Warfare Systems
Jane's Information Group
1340 Braddock Place; Suite 300
P.O. Box 1436
Alexandria, VA 22313-2036
(703) 683-3700
Fax (703) 836-0029

CD-ROM: Jane's Information Group

Japanese Government and Public Research in Progress
Japan Information Center of Science and Technology (JICST)
5-2, Nagatacho, 2-Chome, Chiyoda-ku
C.P.O. Box 1478
Tokyo 100, Japan
03 35816411; Fax 03 35816446

Online: STN International (as JGRIP)

Kompass Asia/Pacific
Kompass International Management Corporation
Rutistr. 38
CH-8044 Zurich, Switzerland
01 8203495; Fax 01 8203653

Online: Knight-Ridder Information, Inc. (as File 592)

Kompass Canada
Micromedia Ltd.
20 Victoria Street
Toronto, ON, Canada M5C 2N8
(800) 387-2689; (416) 362-5211
Fax (416) 362-6161

Online: Infomart Online (as KCAN); Knight-Ridder Information, Inc. (as File 594)

CD-ROM: Micromedia Ltd.

KOMPASS EUROPE
Reed Information Services
Windsor Court
East Grinstead House
East Grinstead
West Sussex RH19 1XA, England
0342 326972; Fax 0342 335612

Online: Knight-Ridder Information, Inc. (as File 590); KOMPASS Online (Reed Information Services Ltd.)

Kompass Far East (ISEN)
Israel National Center of Scientific and Technological Information, (COSTI)
84 Hachashmonaim Street

67011 Tel-Aviv, Israel
Fax 3 297781; 3 492033

Online: Israel National Center of
Scientific and Technological
Information (COSTI); (KOBR,
KOMA, KOPH, KOSI, KOSK,
KOTH)

Kompass France on Disc
Kompass France S.A.
66, quai de Marechal Joffre
F-92415 Courbevoie Cedex, France
Fax 01 41165100; 01 41165118

CD-ROM: Bureau van Dijk,
SA (BvD)

KOMPASS-FRANCE
Kompass France S.A.
66, quai de Marechal Joffre
F-92415 Courbevoie Cedex,
France
01 41165100; Fax 01 41165118

Online: Kompass France S.A.

KOMPASS Israel
Kompass Israel Ltd.
118 Ahad Haam Street
64253 Tel-Aviv, Israel
03 5619374; Fax 03 5614914

Online: Knight-Ridder
Information, Inc. (planned);
Infomart Online (as KISR)

KOMPASS Online
Bonnier Information Services
Saltmatargatan 8; Box 3223
S-10364 Stockholm, Sweden
08 229120; Fax 08 311898

Online: AffarsData (Bonnier
Business Publishing)

Kompass Poland
EUROSTART Sp. z o.o.
ul. Nagorskiego 3
60-408 Poznan, Poland
Fax 48 61475264; 48 61475448

Online: KOLIBER

**LEXIS State Corporation
Information Library (INCORP)**
*Refer to Appendix N for
LEXIS-NEXIS*
Online: LEXIS (as INCORP)

**Longman/Microinfo World
Research Database
(World Research Database
on CD-ROM)**
Longman Group UK Ltd.
Longman Information &
Reference
Westgate House; 6th Floor
The High Harlow
Essex CM20 1YR, England
0279 442601
Fax 0279 444501

CD-ROM: Microinfo Ltd.

**Morningstar Mutual Funds
OnDisc**
Morningstar
225 West Wacker Drive
Suite 400
Chicago, IL 60606
(800) 876-5005; (312) 696-6000
Fax (312) 696-6001

CD-ROM: Morningstar

Nordres
Teknillisen Korkeakoulun
Kirjasto
Otaniementie 9
FIN-02150 Espoo, Finland
0 4514120
Fax 0 4514132

Online: Teknillinen Korkeakoulu
Laskentakeskus; also available
as part of the TENTUU CD-ROM

Ofertas de Tecnologia
Instituto de la Pequena y
Mediana Empresa Industrial
(IMPI)
Paseo de la Castellana 141
E-28046 Madrid, Spain
01 5829300
Fax 01 5712831

Online: Instituto de la Pequena
y Mediana Empresa Industrial
(IMPI)

**Research Centers and
Services Directory (RCSD)**
*Refer to Appendix N for
Gale Research, Inc.*

Online: Knight-Ridder
Information, Inc. (as File 115)

RESPROC
Canada Department of Energy
Mines and Resources
Canada Centre for Mineral and
Energy Technology (CANMET)
Library & Documentation
Services Division
555 Booth Street
Ottawa, ON, Canada K1A 0G1
(613) 943-8773
Fax (613) 952-2587

Online: QL Systems Limited
(RESM)

**SANI (Italian National
Register of Companies)**
CERVED International S.A.
85-87, Boulevard Clovis
B-1040 Bruxelles, Belgium
02 2801777; Fax 02 2303453

Online: CERVED International,
S.A.

SIEPPO/Kirjastot
Helsingin Yliopiston Kirjasto
Science Library
University of Helsinki
P.O. Box 26
FIN-00014 Helsinki, Finland
08 07084114; Fax 08 07084441

Online: Helsingin Yliopiston
Laskentakeskus

**Sportwissenschaftliche
Forschungsprojekte
(SPOFOR)**
Bundesinstitut fur
Sportwissenschaft (BISp)
Fachbereich
Kulturwissenschafter und
Fachinformation
Carl-Diem-Weg 4
D-50933 Cologne, Germany
0221 49790; Fax 0221 495164

Online: DIMDI

Sveriges Handelskanlendera
Bonnier Information Services
Saltmatargatan 8; Box 3223
S-10364 Stockholm, Sweden
08 229120
Fax 08 311898

Online: Bonniers Foretagsinfo AB

TEKTRAN
Technology Transfer Automated
Retrieval System
U.S. Department of Agriculture
Agricultural Research Service
(ARS)
Room 415; Building 005;
BARC-West
Beltsville, MD 20705
(301) 504-5345
Fax (301) 504-5060

Online: U.S. Department of
Agriculture, Agricultural
Research Service (ARS); Office
of Cooperative Interactions
(OCI); Knowledge Express

TELE INFORM 2
*Refer to Appendix N for
O.R. Telematique*

Online: O.R. Telematique

**The Telephone Industry
Directory**
Phillips Business Information,
Inc. (PBI)
7811 Montrose Road
Potomac, MD 20854-3363
(301) 340-2100
Fax (301) 424-7261

Online: NewsNet, Inc.
(as TE83E)

Thomas Register
Thomas Publishing Company
Thomas Online
One Penn Plaza
250 West 34th Street
New York, NY 10119
(212) 290-7291
Fax (212) 290-7362

CD-ROM: Knight-Ridder
Information, Inc.,
DIALOG OnDisc

Thomas Register Online
Thomas Publishing Company
Thomas Online
One Penn Plaza
250 West 34th Street
New York, NY 10119
(212) 290-7291
Fax (212) 290-7362

Online: Knight-Ridder
Information, Inc. (as File 535);
CompuServe Information
Service (THOMAS, Thomas
Companies & Products Online)

**Verbande, Behorden,
Organisationen der
Wirtschaft (VBO)
(Hoppenstedt German Trade
Associations)**
*Refer to Appendix N for
Verlag Hoppenstedt GmbH*

Online: Gesellschaft fur
Betriebswirtschaftliche
Information mbH (GBI);
GENIOS
Wirtschaftsdatenbanken

CD-ROM: Verlag Hoppenstedt
GmbH, Wirtschaftsdatenbank

Who is Who
B. Breidenstein GmbH
Untermainkai 83
D-6000 Frankfurt am Main 1,
Germany
069 230905
Fax 069 235279

Online: FIZ Technik (as WHOI)

**Yearbook of International
Organizations on CD-ROM**
K.G. Saur Verlag GmbH & Co. KG
Heilmanstr. 17
Postfach 711009
D-8000 Munich 71, Germany
089 791040
Fax 089 7910499

CD-ROM: Bowker Electronic
Publishing

*Please note that many other
databases contain the names of
executives, researchers, or other
personnel. Financial and
Business Credit Databases
often contain the names of executives and directors. These can
be found in Appendix C.
Professional Directory
Databases are in Appendix D,
and personnel names can also
be found within them.*

General Encyclopedia Databases

Academic American Encyclopedia (AAE)
Grolier Electronic Publishing, Inc.
Sherman Turnpike
Danbury, CT 06816
(800) 356-5590; (203) 797-3500
Fax (203) 797-3197

Online: CompuServe Information Service(as ENCYCLOPEDIA); Delphi Internet Services Corporation (as GROLIER); Dow Jones News/Retrieval (as ENCYC); GEnie; PRODIG; Fort Worth Star-Telegram; StarText; CARL Systems Network

The ATTICA Writers Reference Bookshelf
ATTICA Cybernetics Ltd.
Unit 2, Kings Meadow
Ferry Hinksey Road
Oxford OX2 ODP, England
0865 791346; Fax 0865 794561

CD-ROM: ATTICA Cybernetics Ltd.

Compton's Multimedia Encyclopedia
Compton's NewMedia
2320 Camino Vida Roble
Carlsbad, CA 92009
(800) 533-0130; (619) 929-2500

CD-ROM: Compton's NewMedia

The Concise Columbia Electronic Encyclopedia
Columbia University Press
562 West 113th Street
New York, NY 10025
(212) 666-1000; Fax (212) 316-9422

Online: OCLC FirstSearch Catalog

Everyman's Encyclopaedia
J.M. Dent & Sons Ltd.
91 Chapham High Street
London SW4A 7TA, England
071-622 9933; Fax 071-627 3361

Online: Knight-Ridder Information, Inc. (as File 182); CompuServe Knowledge Index (as REFR7)

Information Finder
World Book Publishing
525 West Monroe Street
20th Floor
Chicago, IL 60661
(800) 621-8202; (312) 258-3700
Fax (312) 258-3950

CD-ROM: World Book Publishing

Lexikodisc
Bertelsmann Electronic Publishing
Neumarkter Street 18
81664 Muchen, Germany
49 8943189727; 49 8943189743

CD-ROM: Bertelsmann Electronic Publishing

Microsoft Encarta Multimedia Encyclopedia
Refer to Appendix N for Microsoft Corp.

CD-ROM: Microsoft Corporation

The New Grolier Multimedia Encyclopedia
Grolier Electronic Publishing, Inc.
Sherman Turnpike
Danbury, CT 06816
(800) 356-5590; (203) 797-3500
Fax (203) 797-3197

CD-ROM: Grolier Electronic Publishing, Inc.

The New Illustrated Information Finder
World Book Publishing
525 West Monroe Street
20th Floor
Chicago, IL 60661
(800) 621-8202; (312) 258-3700
Fax (312) 258-3950

CD-ROM: World Book Publishing

Schole
Boston University
School of Education
605 Commonwealth Avenue
Boston, MA 02215
(617) 353-3295

Online: Delphi Internet Services Corporation

The Software Toolworks Illustrated Encyclopedia
Grolier Electronic Publishing, Inc.
Sherman Turnpike
Danbury, CT 06816
(800) 356-5590; (203) 797-3500
Fax (203) 797-3197

CD-ROM: The Software Toolworks, Inc.

Magazine, Newsletter, Newspaper, and Periodical Directory Databases

BBC Monitoring Summary of World Broadcasts
British Broadcasting Corporation (BBC), BBC Monitoring
Caversham Park
Reading RG4 8TZ, England
0734 463823; Fax 0734 461105

Online: NEXIS (BBCSWB); FT PROFILE (SWB); British Broadcasting Corporation (BBC); BBC Monitoring; DataStar (BBCM); also online as part of: LEXIS Country Information Service; Reuter TEXTLINE

BiblioData Fulltext Sources Online
BiblioData
P.O. Box 61
Needham Heights, MA 02194
(617) 444-1154; Fax (617) 449-4584

Online: DataStar (FULL)

Broadcast News on CD-ROM
Journal Graphics Inc.
1535 Grant Street
Denver, CO 80203
(800) 825-5746; (303) 831-9000
Fax (303) 831-8901

CD-ROM: Research Publications International

Burrelle's Broadcast Database and Burrelle's TV Transcripts
Refer to Appendix N for Burrelle's Information Services

Burrelle's Broadcast Database is available online through Burrelle's Information Services, and a subset, Burrelle's TV

Transcripts, is available online through DataTimes Corporation.

Burrelle's Media Directory on Disc
Refer to Appendix N for Burrelle's Information Services

CD-ROM: SilverPlatter Information, Inc.

The Business Library
Refer to Appendix N for Dow Jones News / Retrieval

Online: Dow Jones News/Retrieval

Business Periodicals Global
University Microfilms International (UMI)
300 North Zeeb Road
Ann Arbor, MI 48106
(800) 521-0600; (313) 761-4700
(521) 343-5299; Fax (313) 761-1203

CD-ROM: University Microfilms International (UMI), UMI Ondisc

Changing Times
News Multimedia
P.O. Box 481
Virginia Street
London E1 9BD, England
071-782 3982

CD-ROM: News Multimedia

CMP Publications Communications File
CMP Publications, Inc.
600 Community Drive
Manhasset, NY 11030
(516) 562-5000; Fax (516) 562-5718

Online: DataTimes Corporation; CommunicationsWeek is also available online through NewsNet, Inc. (as TE23) and NEXIS (as COMMWK); CommunicationsWeek International is also available online through NewsNet, Inc. (as TE28); Information Week is also available online through NewsNet, Inc. (as TE34) and NEXIS (as INFOWK)

CMP Publications Computers File
CMP Publications, Inc.
600 Community Drive
Manhasset, NY 11030
(516) 562-5000; Fax (516) 562-5718

Online: DataTimes Corporation; Computer Reseller News is also available online through NewsNet, Inc. (as EC07) and NEXIS (as CRN); Network Computing is also available online through NewsNet, Inc. (as EC86); Open Systems Today is also available online through NewsNet, Inc. (as EC06); VAR-BUSINESS is also available online through NewsNet, Inc. (as EC08) and DataTimes Corporation (as VRB)

CMP Publications Electronics File
CMP Publications, Inc.
600 Community Drive
Manhasset, NY 11030
(516) 562-5000; Fax (516) 562-5718

Online: DataTimes Corporation;

Electronic Buyers' News is also available online through NewsNet, Inc. (as EC12); Electronic Engineering Times is also available online with NewsNet, Inc. (as EC14); Electronic WorldNews is also available online through NewsNet, Inc. (as EC13)

CMP Publications Travel File
CMP Publications, Inc.
600 Community Drive
Manhasset, NY 11030
(516) 562-5000; Fax (516) 562-5718

Online: DataTimes Corporation; Tour & Travel News is also available online through NewsNet, Inc. (TR09)

CNN News Transcripts
Cable News Network (CNN)
1 CNN Center
Atlanta, GA 30303-2705
(404) 827-2491

Online: DataTimes Corporation; NEXIS (CNN)

CNN Newsroom Global View
Compact Publishing, Inc.
5141 MacArthur Boulevard
P.O. Box 40310
Washington, DC 20016
(800) 964-1518; (202) 244-4770
Fax (202) 244-6363

CD-ROM: Compact Publishing, Inc.

Computer ASAP
Refer to Appendix N for Information Access Company (IAC)

Online: CompuServe Information Service (COMPDB); Knight-Ridder Information, Inc. (as File 675); also online as part of The Computer Database

Ethnic NewsWatch
SoftLine Information, Inc.
65 Broad Street
Stamford, CT 06901
(800) 524-7922; (203) 975-8292
Fax (203) 975-8347

Online: NEXIS and LEXIS (ENW)

Gale Database of Publications and Broadcast Media
Refer to Appendix N for Gale Research, Inc.

Online: Knight-Ridder Information, Inc. (as File 469)

General Periodicals Research II
University Microfilms International (UMI)
300 North Zeeb Road
Ann Arbor, MI 48106
(800) 521-0600; (313) 761-4700
(521) 343-5299; Fax (313) 761-1203

CD-ROM: University Microfilms International (UMI), UMI Ondisc

The MacNeil/Lehrer Newshour
MacNeil-Lehrer-Gannett Productions
356 West 58th Street
New York, NY 10019
(212) 560-2000

Online: NEXIS (MACLEH)

Magazine ASAP
Refer to Appendix N for Information Access Company (IAC)

Online: Knight-Ridder Information, Inc. (as File 647); NEXIS (as ASAP); CompuServe Information Service (as MDP); and DataStar (as MAGS)

Magazine Express
University Microfilms International (UMI)
300 North Zeeb Road
Ann Arbor, MI 48106
(800) 521-0600; (313) 761-4700
(521) 343-5299; Fax (313) 761-1203

CD-ROM: University Microfilms International (UMI)

McGraw-Hill Publications Online
McGraw-Hill, Inc.
Princeton-Hightstown Road

Hightstown, NJ 08520
(609) 426-5000; Fax (609) 426-7352

Online: Knight-Ridder Information, Inc. (as File 624); Dow Jones News/Retrieval

MEDIATHEK
Media-Service GmbH (MS)
Bahnhofstr. 1
D-6084 Gernsheim, Germany
06258 3073; 06258 51536

Online: GENIOS Wirtschaftsdatenbanken (MEDI)

NARIC Guide to Disability and Rehabilitation Periodicals
U.S. National Institute on Disability and Rehabilitation Research, (NIDRR)
National Rehabilitation Information Center (NARIC)
8455 Colesville Road; Suite 935
Silver Spring, MD 20910-3319
(800) 346-2742; (301) 588-9284
Fax (301) 587-1967

Online: ABLE INFORM

Network Earth Forum
Turner Broadcasting System (TBS)
1 CNN Plaza
Atlanta, GA 30348
(404) 827-1700

Online: America Online

NewsCom Communications Solutions
2801 Ponce de Leon Boulevard
Suite 1050
Coral Gables, FL 33134
(800) 601-NEWS; (305) 448-8411
Fax (305) 443-6538

Newsletter Database
Refer to Appendix N for Information Access Company (IAC)

Online: DataStar (PTBN); Knight-Ridder Information, Inc. (as File 636); Dow Jones News/Retrieval); STN International (NLDB)

Newsletters in Print (NIP)
Refer to Appendix N for
Gale Research, Inc.

Online: HRIN, The Human
Resource Information Network
(NIP)

PIMS UK Media Directory
PIMS UK Ltd.
PIMS House
Mildmay Avenue
London N1 4RS, England
71 2261000
71 7041360

Online: PIMS UK Ltd.

**PROMT (Predicasts
Overview of Markets and
Technology)**
Refer to Appendix N for
Information Access Company
(IAC)

Online: DataStar (PTSP);
Knight-Ridder Information, Inc.
(as File 16); NIFTY-Serve
(PROMT); NEXIS; I/PLUS
Direct; QUESTEL•ORBIT
(PROMT); FT PROFILE
(PROMT); GENIOS
Wirtschaftsdatenbanken
(PROM); STN International

Reuter TEXTLINE
Reuters Ltd.
85 Fleet Street
London EC4P 4AJ, England
071 250 1122; 080 001 0701
080 365 7674; Fax 071 696 8761

Online: DataStar (TXLN, TX88,
TXYY, and TXLD); Knight-
Ridder Information, Inc.
(File 799, 772, and 771:
Textline Global News)

Reuter Transcript Report
Reuters Information Services Inc.
1333 H Street, NW; Suite 410
Washington, DC 20005
(202) 898-8300

Online: Reuters Ltd.; CQ
Washington Alert Service;
NEXIS

Standard Periodical Directory
Oxbridge Communications, Inc.
150 Fifth Avenue
New York, NY 10011
(800) 955-0231; (212) 741-0231
Fax (212) 741-0231

CD-ROM: Oxbridge
Communications, Inc.

Time Almanac
Refer to Appendix N for
Time Inc.

CD-ROM: Compact
Publishing, Inc.

Time Publications
Refer to Appendix N for
Time Inc.

Online: Knight-Ridder
Information, Inc. (as File 746)

Trade & Industry ASAP
Refer to Appendix N for
Information Access Company
(IAC)

Online: Knight-Ridder
Information, Inc. (as File 648);
NEXIS (ASAP); DataStar
(INDY, Trade & Industry
Database)

TRANSCRIPT
Journal Graphics Inc.
1535 Grant Street
Denver, CO 80203
(800) 825-5746; (303) 831-9000
Fax (303) 831-8901

Online: CompuServe
Information Service
(TRANSCRIPT); CARL
Systems Network

**Ulrich's International
Periodicals Directory Online**
Bowker's International Serials
Database (BISD)
Refer to Appendix N for Reed
Reference Publishing Group

Online: Knight-Ridder
Information, Inc. (as File 480);
ESA-IRS (as 103: Ulrich's
Periodicals)

Ulrich's Plus
Bowker's International Serials
Database (BISD)
Refer to Appendix N for Reed
Reference Publishing Group

CD-ROM: Bowker Electronic
Publishing

Wall $treet Week (WSW)
Maryland Center for Public
Broadcasting
11767 Owings Mills Boulevard
Baltimore, MD 21117
(410) 356-5600

Online: Dow Jones
News/Retrieval (WSW)

Quotation, Speech, and Transcript Databases

The '88 Vote: Campaign for the White House
ABC News InterActive
7 West 66th Street; 4th Floor
New York, NY 10023
(212) 456-4060; Fax (212) 887-3205

CD-ROM: ABC News InterActive

3500 Good Quotes for Speakers
Sylvia Lieberman
2325 Ocean Avenue
Brooklyn, NY 11229
(718) 339-8642

Online: NEXIS (as GQUOTE)

25,001 Jokes, Anecdotes, and Funny Quotes
National Information Services
Corporation (NISC)
Wyman Towers; Suite 6
3100 St. Paul Street
Baltimore, MD 21218
(410) 243-0797; Fax (410) 243-0982

CD-ROM: National Information
Services Corporation (NISC),
NISC DISC

ABC News Transcripts
Capital Cities/ABC, Inc.
ABC News
47 West 66th Street
New York, NY 10023

Online: NEXIS (as ABCNEW)

American Banker News Service
American Banker—Bond Buyer
One State Street Plaza; 31st Floor
New York, NY 10004
(800) 356-4763; (212) 803-8366
Fax (212) 943-2214

Online: Knight-Ridder
Information, Inc.
(as BANKNEWS)

The ATTICA Writers Reference Bookshelf
ATTICA Cybernetics Ltd
Unit 2, Kings Meadow
Ferry Hinksey Road
Oxford OX2 ODP, England
0865 791346; Fax 0865 794561

CD-ROM: ATTICA
Cybernetics Ltd

BBC Monitoring Summary of World Broadcasts
British Broadcasting
Corporation (BBC)
BBC Monitoring
Caversham Park
Reading RG4 8TZ, England
0734 463823; Fax 0734 461105

Online: NEXIS (as BBCSWB);
FT PROFILE (as SWB); British
Broadcasting Corporation (BBC);
BBC Monitoring; DataStar (as
BBCM); and as part of: LEXIS
Country Information Service;
Reuter TEXTLINE

BONMOT
Sinnspruche, Aphorismen und
Lebenweischeiten
Gesellschaft fur
Betriebswirtschaftliche
Information mbH (GBI)
Freischutzstr. 96
Postfach 810360
D-8000 Munich 81, Germany
089 9570064

Online: Gesellschaft fur
Betriebswirtschaftliche

Information mbH (GBI)
(as BONMOT)

Broadcast News on CD-ROM
Journal Graphics Inc.
1535 Grant Street
Denver, CO 80203
(800) 825-5746; (303) 831-9000
Fax (303) 831-8901

CD-ROM: Research Publications
International

The Budget Database
*Refer to Appendix N for Globe
Information Services*

Online: Info Globe Online (BUD)

Burrelle's Broadcast Database
*Refer to Appendix N for
Burrelle's Information Services*

Online: Burrelle's Information
Services

Burrelle's TV Transcripts
*Refer to Appendix N for
Burrelle's Information Services*

Online: DataTimes Corporation

Canada Budget Database
QL Systems Limited
901 St. Andrew's Tower
275 Sparks Street
Ottawa, ON, Canada K1R 7X9
(800) 387-0899; (613) 238-3499
Fax (613) 238-7597

Online: QL Systems Limited
(C86-C93, F87-F93)

**Canadian Journalism
Database (CJD)**
University of Western Ontario

Graduate School of Journalism
Middlesex College
London, ON, Canada N6A 5B7
(519) 661-3383; Fax (519) 661-3848

Online: QL Systems Limited
(CJD)

Clinton: Portrait of Victory
Epicenter Communications
180 Harbor Drive; Suite 215
Sausalito, CA 94965
(415) 332-0808

CD-ROM: Time Warner
Interactive

CNN News Transcripts
Cable News Network (CNN)
1 CNN Center
Atlanta, GA 30303-2705
(404) 827-2491

Online: DataTimes Corporation;
NEXIS (as CNN)

CNN Newsroom Global View
Compact Publishing, Inc.
5141 MacArthur Boulevard
P.O. Box 40310
Washington, DC 20016
(202) 244-4778; Fax (202) 244-6363

CD-ROM: Compact
Publishing, Inc.

**The Columbia Granger's
World of Poetry**
Columbia University Press
562 West 113th Street
New York, NY 10025
(212) 666-1000; Fax (212) 316-9422

CD-ROM: Columbia
University Press

Congressional Activities
Oliphant Washington News
Service (OWS)
1819 H Street, NW; Suite 330
Washington, DC 20006-3677
(703) 764-0935

Online: NewsNet, Inc. (as GT20)

Congressional Record
U.S. Government Printing Office
(GPO)
Office of Electronic Information

Dissemination Services
Washington, DC 20401
(202) 512-1530; Fax (202) 512-1262

Online: LEXIS-NEXIS (as
RECORD); WESTLAW (as CR),
and as part of: LEGI-SLATE

**Congressional Record
Abstracts (CRECORD)**
National Standards Association,
Inc. (NSA)
1200 Quince Orchard Boulevard
Gaithersburg, MD 20878
(800) 638-8094; (301) 590-2300
Fax (301) 990-8378

Online: Knight-Ridder
Information, Inc. (as File 135);
U.S. Library of Congress
Information System

CQ Weekly Report
Congressional Quarterly
Weekly Report
*Refer to Appendix N for
Congressional Quarterly Inc. (CQ)*

Online: CQ Washington Alert
Service (as WR); DataTimes
Corporation (as CQWEEK)

Department of the Army News
U.S. Department of the Army
Office of the Chief of Public
Affairs (OCPA)
The Pentagon, Room 2E 626
Washington, DC 20310
(212) 695-3001; Fax (202) 697-2159

Online: Dialcom

The Executive Speaker
The Executive Speaker (TES)
P.O. Box 292437
Dayton, OH 45429
(513) 294-8493; Fax (513) 294-6044

Online: NEXIS (as EXECSP)

FDA Electronic Bulletin Board
U.S. Food and Drug
Administration
5600 Fishers Lane
Rockville, MD 20857
(301) 443-3285

Online: Dialcom

**Federal and Provincial
Budgets Database**
*Refer to Appendix N for
Globe Information Services*

Online: Info Globe Online (BUD)

Federal News CD-ROM
Federal News Service
620 National Press Building
Washington, DC 20045
(202) 347-1400; Fax (202) 626-8947

CD-ROM: National Information
Services Corporation (NISC);
NISC DISC

Federal News Service (FNS)
Federal News Service
620 National Press Building
Washington, DC 20045
(202) 347-1400; Fax (202) 626-8947

Online: NEXIS (as FEDNEW);
Knight-Ridder Information, Inc.
(as File 660)

**Federal News Service
Kremlin Transcripts**
Federal News Service
620 National Press Building
Washington, DC 20045
(202) 347-1400; Fax (202) 626-8947

Available online as part of:
Federal News Service

**Federal News Service
Washington Transcripts**
Federal News Service
620 National Press Building
Washington, DC 20045
(202) 347-1400; Fax (202) 626-8947

Online: NewsNet, Inc. (as
FN01W and FN04); also online
as part of: Federal News Service

**Gale's Quotations: Who Said
What**
*Refer to Appendix N for
Gale Research, Inc.*

CD-ROM: Gale Research Inc.

General Meetings Speeches
Das Wertpapier
Verlagsgesellschaft mbH
Humboldstr. 9

D-4000 Dusseldorf 1, Germany
221 669750

Online: Gesellschaft fur
Betriebswirtschaftliche
Information mbH (GBI)

**Hansard and Political
Statements Monitor**
Political Reference Service
Pty. Ltd.
Civic Square
P.O. Box 607
Canberra, ACT 2608, Australia
062 476950
Fax 062 488169

Online: Info-One International
Pty. Ltd.

Health Care Reform Hotfile
*Refer to Appendix N for
LEXIS-NEXIS*

Online: LEXIS and NEXIS
(as Health)

History of the World
Bureau of Electronic
Publishing, Inc.
141 New Road
Parsippany, NJ 07054
(800) 828-4766; (201) 808-2700
Fax (201) 857-3031

CD-ROM: Bureau of Electronic
Publishing, Inc.

**The Hutchinson Multimedia
Encyclopedia**
Helicon
42 Hythe Bridge Street
Oxford OX1 2EP, England
0865 204204
Fax 0865 204205

CD-ROM: Helicon

LOGOS
La Documentation Francaise,
Banque d'Information Politique
et d'Actualite (BIPA)
8, ave. de l'Opera
F-75001 Paris, France
01 42961422
Fax 01 42613784

Online: QUESTEL•ORBIT
(as LOGOS)

**The MacNeil/Lehrer
Newshour**
MacNeil-Lehrer-Gannett
Productions
356 West 58th Street
New York, NY 10019
(212) 560-2000

Online: NEXIS (as MACLEH)

Martin Luther King Jr
ABC News InterActive
7 West 66th Street; 4th Floor
New York, NY 10023
(212) 456-4060; Fax (212) 887-3205

CD-ROM: ABC News
InterActive

Microsoft Bookshelf
*Refer to Appendix N for
Microsoft Corp.*

CD-ROM: Microsoft Corporation

The New York Times Ondisc
The New York Times Company
New York Times
On-Line Services
1719A Route 10
Parsippany, NJ 07054
(201) 267-2268; Fax (201) 267-3464

CD-ROM: University Microfilms
International (UMI);
UMI Ondisc

**Origins: Catholic
Documentary Service**
Catholic News Service
3211 Fourth Street, NE
Washington, DC 20017
(202) 541-3250; Fax (202) 541-3255

Online: NewsNet, Inc. (as CN03)

PR On-Line
Stephen K. Cook & Company, Inc.
1090 Vermont Avenue, NW
Suite 800
Washington, DC 20005
(202) 347-8918; (202) 347-8920

Online: Stephen K. Cook &
Company, Inc.

**The Presidents: It All Started
With George**
National Geographic Society

Educational Services
Washington, DC 20036
(800) 368-2728; (301) 921-1330
Fax (301) 921-1575

CD-ROM: National Geographic
Society, Educational Services

**Proverbs & Quotes for All
Occasions**
National Information Services
Corporation (NISC)
Wyman Towers; Suite 6
3100 St. Paul Street
Baltimore, MD 21218
(410) 243-0797;
Fax (410) 243-0982

CD-ROM: National Information
Services Corporation (NISC);
NISC DISC

Quotations Database
Oxford University Press
Electronic Publishing
Walton Street
Oxford OX2 6DP, England
0865 267979

Online: Knight-Ridder
Information, Inc. (as File 175);
CompuServe Knowledge Index
(as REFR1)

RAPID
Commission of the European
Communities (CEC)
200, rue de la Loi
B-1049 Brussels, Belgium
02 2950001; Fax 02 2960624

Online: EUROBASES

Reuter Transcript Report
Reuters Information
Services Inc.
1333 H Street, NW; Suite 410
Washington, DC 20005
(202) 898-8300

Online: Reuters Ltd.; CQ
Washington Alert Service;
NEXIS

Reuter Washington Report
Reuters Information
Services Inc.

1333 H Street, NW; Suite 410
Washington, DC 20005
(202) 898-8300

Online: Reuters Ltd.; NEXIS

**Speaker's Lifetime Treasury
on CD-ROM**
National Information Services
Corporation (NISC)
Wyman Towers; Suite 6
3100 Street Paul Street
Baltimore, MD 21218
(410) 243-0797
Fax (410) 243-0982

CD-ROM: National Information
Services Corporation (NISC);
NISC DISC

Strategic Defense
Phillips Business Information,
Inc. (PBI)
7811 Montrose Road
Potomac, MD 20854-3363
(301) 340-2100
Fax (301) 424-7261

Online: NewsNet, Inc. (as DE13)
and as part of Newsletter
Database

**SWB Political and Economic
Reports**
British Broadcasting
Corporation (BBC)
Broadcasting House
Portland Place
London W1A 1AA, England
071-580 4468

Online: FT PROFILE (as BBC
SWB) and as part of: Reuter
TEXTLINE

**Technology Entertainment
Design 2 (TED2)**
Voyager
1351 Pacific Coast Highway
Santa Monica, CA 90401
(800) 446-2001; (310) 451-1383
(446) 443-2001
Fax (310) 394-2156

CD-ROM: The Voyager Company

Time Traveler CD
Orange Cherry New Media

390 Westchester Avenue
Pound Ridge, NY 10576
(800) 672-6002; (914) 764-4104

CD-ROM: Orange Cherry
New Media

TRANSCRIPT
Journal Graphics Inc.
1535 Grant Street
Denver, CO 80203
(800) 825-5746; (303) 831-9000
Fax (303) 831-8901

Online: CompuServe
Information Service (GO
TRANSCRIPT); CARL Systems
Network

**United Nations Conference
on Environment and
Development (UNCED)**
United Nations Conference on
Environment and Development
160 Route de Florissant
P.O. Box 80
CH-1231 Conches, Switzerland
022 7891676; Fax 022 7893536

Online: International
Telecommunication Union (ITU)

The Wall Street Transcript
WARNDEX
The Wall Street Transcript
99 Wall Street
New York, NY 10005
(212) 747-9500

Online: DataTimes Corporation

Wall $treet Week (WSW)
Maryland Center for Public
Broadcasting
11767 Owings Mills Boulevard
Baltimore, MD 21117
(410) 356-5600

Online: Dow Jones
News/Retrieval (as WSW)

Telephone Directories

1 Million Health & Medical Industry Reference Directory
Refer to Appendix N for American Business Information, Inc. (ABI)

Available on CD-ROM from American Business Information, Inc. (ABI)

11 Million Businesses Phone Directory
Refer to Appendix N for American Business Information, Inc. (ABI)

Available on CD-ROM from American Business Information, Inc. (ABI)

70 Million Households Phone Book
Refer to Appendix N for American Business Information, Inc. (ABI)

Available on CD-ROM from American Business Information, Inc. (ABI)

Academy OnLine
Quality Education Data (QED) Database
Quality Education Data, Inc. (QED)
1600 Broadway; 12th Floor
Denver, CO 80202-4912
(800) 525-5811; (303) 860-1832
Fax (303) 860-0238

Online: Quality Education Data, Inc. (QED).

Address Make
Data Disc Systems, Inc.
2-16-2 Sotokanda
Chiyoda-ku
Tokyo 101, Japan

03 32579334; 03 32579338
CD-ROM: Data Disc Systems, Inc.

American Yellow Pages
Refer to Appendix N for American Business Information, Inc. (ABI)

Available on CD-ROM from American Business Information, Inc. (ABI)

The Bankers' Almanac Database
Reed Information Services
Windsor Court
East Grinstead House
East Grinstead, West Sussex
RH19 1XA, England
0342 326972; Fax 0342 335612

Online: KOMPASS Online (Reed Information Services Ltd.)

Base de Dados Mope
Refer to Appendix N for Lda Mope

Online: lMope

Biz*File
Refer to Appendix N for American Business Information, Inc. (ABI)

Online: CompuServe Information Service

Calling All Businesses
Database America
100 Paragon Drive
Montvale, JN 07645-0419
(800) 478-0318

CD-ROM: Database America

Canada Phone
Pro CD, Inc.
222 Rosewood Drive
Danvers, MA 01923-4510

(508) 750-0000; Fax (508) 750-0070
CD-ROM: Pro CD, Inc.

Canadian Businesses
Refer to Appendix N for American Business Information, Inc. (ABI)

Online: American Business Information, Inc. (ABI); American Business Lists

CONQUEST/DIRECT
Strategic Mapping Inc.
70 Seaview Avenue
P.O. Box 10250
Stamford, CT 06904
(800) 866-2255; (203) 353-7295
Fax (203) 353-7276

Available on CD-ROM from Strategic Mapping Inc.

Direct Phone
Pro CD, Inc.
222 Rosewood Drive
Danvers, MA 01923-4510
(508) 750-0000; Fax (508) 750-0070

CD-ROM: Pro CD, Inc.

Electronic White Pages (EWP)
DirectoryNet, Inc.
600 Morgan Falls Road; Suite 100
Atlanta, GA 30350
(800) 733-1212; (404) 512-5090
Fax (404) 512-5091

Online: DirectoryNet, Inc.

EUROPAGES
Euredit S.A.
9, ave. de Friedland
F-75008 Paris, France
01 42893466; Fax 42893473

CD-ROM: Euredit S.A.

EuroPages
Pro CD, Inc.

222 Rosewood Drive
Danvers, MA 01923-4510
(508) 750-0000; Fax (508) 750-0070

Available on CD-ROM from
Pro CD, Inc.

FONE*Data
Mailer's Software
970 Calle Negocio
San Clemente, CA 92673-6201
(800) 800-6245; (714) 492-7000
Fax (714) 492-7086

Available on CD-ROM from
Mailer's Software

Free Phone
Pro CD, Inc.
222 Rosewood Drive
Danvers, MA 01923-4510
(508) 750-0000; Fax (508) 750-0070

CD-ROM: Pro CD, Inc.

Home Phone
Pro CD, Inc.
222 Rosewood Drive
Danvers, MA 01923-4510
(508) 750-0000; Fax (508) 750-0070

CD-ROM: Pro CD, Inc.

infodirect Disc
Pro CD, Inc.
222 Rosewood Drive
Danvers, MA 01923-4510
(508) 750-0000; Fax (508) 750-0070

CD-ROM: Pro CD, Inc.

**International Communications
Database on CD-ROM**
Telex-Verlag Jaeger Waldmann
GmbH
P.O. Box 111454
D-64295 Darmstadt, Germany
06151 33020; Fax 06151 330250

Available on CD-ROM from
Telex-Verlag Jaeger Waldmann
GmbH

Italian Yellow Pages
SEAT
SS 148 Pontina, KM. 29,100
I-00040 Pomezia (Rome), Italy
06 910981; Fax 06 9105111

Available on CD-ROM from SEAT

JW CommDisc International
Telex-Verlag Jaeger Waldmann
GmbH
P.O. Box 111454
D-64295 Darmstadt, Germany
06151 33020; Fax 06151 330250

Available on CD-ROM from
Telex-Verlag Jaeger Waldmann
GmbH

Kompass Far East
Israel National Center of
Scientific and Technological
Information, (COSTI)
84 Hachashmonaim Street
67011 Tel-Aviv, Israel
3 297781; 3 492033

Online: Israel National Center of
Scientific and Technological
Information

Mailer's BUSINESS Database
Mailer's Software
970 Calle Negocio
San Clemente, CA 92673-6201
(800) 800-6245; (714) 492-7000
Fax (714) 492-7086

Available on CD-ROM from
Mailer's Software

Main Street U.S.A.
Database America
100 Paragon Drive
Montvale, JN 07645-0419
(800) 478-0318

CD-ROM: Database America

MetroNet
Metromail
An R.R. Donnelley & Sons Company
360 East 22nd Street
Lombard, IL 60148-4989
(800) 638-7623

Online: Metromail

MetroSearch
Metromail
An R.R. Donnelley & Sons
Company
360 East 22nd Street
Lombard, IL 60148-4989
(800) 638-7623

CD-ROM: Metromail

**The North American
Facsimile (Fax)**
Quanta Press, Inc.
1313 Fifth Street SE; Suite 223A
Minneapolis, MN 55414
(612) 379-3956; Fax (612) 623-4570

Available on CD-ROM from
Quanta Press, Inc.

**NYNEX Fast Track Digital
Directory**
NYNEX Information Resources
Company
100 Church Street
9th Floor
New York, NY 10007-2670
(800) 338-0646; (212) 513-9876

Available on CD-ROM from
NYNEX Information Resources
Company

**NYNEX Fast Track Digital
Directory: Directory
Assistance Version**
NYNEX Information Resources
Company
100 Church Street; 9th Floor
New York, NY 10007-2670
(800) 338-0646; (212) 513-9876

CD-ROM: NYNEX Information
Resources Company

**NYNEX Fast Track Digital
Directory: National Directory**
NYNEX Information Resources
Company
100 Church Street; 9th Floor
New York, NY 10007-2670
(800) 338-0646
(212) 513-9876

CD-ROM: NYNEX Information
Resources Company; Regional
versions are also available for
Mid-Atlantic, Mid-Central,
Southeast, Deep South, West
Central, Southwest, Far West,
West Coast, and Northeast

OzOnDisc
Read Only Memory Pty. Ltd.
127 Lawrence Street
Alexandria, NSW 2011, Australia
02 5503938

Available on CD-ROM from Laser Design & Training (LDT)

People Finder
Information America (IA)
One Georgia Center
600 West Peachtree Street, NW
Atlanta, GA 30308
(800) 235-4008; (404) 892-1800
Fax (404) 875-8192

Online: Information America (IA)

Phone*File
Metromail Corporation
360 E. 22nd Street
Lombard, IL 60148-4989
(708) 620-3012

Online: CompuServe
Information Service

PhoneDisc Business
Digital Directory Assistance,
Inc. (DDA)
5161 River Road; Building 6
Bethesda, MD 20816
(800) 284-8353; (617) 639-2900
Fax (800) 284-8355

Available on CD-ROM from
Digital Directory Assistance,
Inc. (DDA)

PhoneDisc California
Digital Directory Assistance,
Inc. (DDA)
5161 River Road; Building 6
Bethesda, MD 20816
(800) 284-8353; (617) 639-2900
Fax (800) 284-8355

Available on CD-ROM from
Digital Directory Assistance,
Inc. (DDA)

PhoneDisc New York and New England
Digital Directory Assistance,
Inc. (DDA)
5161 River Road; Building 6
Bethesda, MD 20816
(800) 284-8353; (301) 657-8548
Fax (301) 652-7810

Available on CD-ROM from

Digital Directory Assistance,
Inc. (DDA)

PhoneDisc PowerFinder
Digital Directory Assistance, Inc.
(DDA)
5161 River Road; Building 6
Bethesda, MD 20816
(800) 284-8353; (301) 657-8548
Fax (301) 652-7810

Available on CD-ROM from
Digital Directory Assistance, Inc.
(DDA)

PhoneDisc QuickRef
Digital Directory Assistance, Inc.
(DDA)
5161 River Road; Building 6
Bethesda, MD 20816
(800) 284-8353; (617) 639-2900
Fax (800) 284-8355

Available on CD-ROM from
Digital Directory Assistance, Inc.
(DDA)

PhoneDisc Residential
Digital Directory Assistance, Inc.
(DDA)
5161 River Road; Building 6
Bethesda, MD 20816
(800) 284-8353; (617) 639-2900
Fax (800) 284-8355

Available on CD-ROM from
Digital Directory Assistance, Inc.
(DDA)

PhoneDisc Reverse
Digital Directory Assistance, Inc.
(DDA)
5161 River Road; Building 6
Bethesda, MD 20816
(800) 284-8353; (617) 639-2900
Fax (800) 284-8355

CD-ROM: Digital Directory
Assistance, Inc. (DDA)

PhoneDisc USA Business
Digital Directory Assistance, Inc.
(DDA)
5161 River Road; Building 6
Bethesda, MD 20816
(800) 284-8353; (617) 639-2900
Fax (800) 284-8355

CD-ROM: Digital Directory
Assistance, Inc. (DDA)

PhoneDisc USA Residential
Digital Directory Assistance, Inc.
(DDA)
5161 River Road; Building 6
Bethesda, MD 20816
(800) 284-8353; (617) 639-2900
Fax (800) 284-8355

CD-ROM: Digital Directory
Assistance, Inc. (DDA)

ProSearch—NorthEast
Pro CD, Inc.
222 Rosewood Drive
Danvers, MA 01923-4510
(508) 750-0000; Fax (508) 750-0070

CD-ROM: Pro CD, Inc.

Research Centers and Services Directory (RCSD)
Refer to Appendix N for Gale Research, Inc.

Online: Knight-Ridder
Information, Inc. (as File 115)

Select Phone
Pro CD, Inc.
222 Rosewood Drive
Danvers, MA 01923-4510
(508) 750-0000; Fax (508) 750-0070

Online: American Online

CD-ROM: Pro CD, Inc.

The Software Toolworks Reference Library
The Software Toolworks, Inc.
60 Leveroni Court
Novato, CA 94949
(800) 231-3088; (415) 883-3000
Fax (415) 883-3303

CD-ROM: The Software
Toolworks, Inc.

STELA
Moscow City Telephone Network
Referral-Information Center
Novy Arbat Avenue 2
121019 Moscow, Russia
095 2038618; 095 2022413

Online: Moscow City Telephone
Network; Referral-Information

Center; also available on
diskette.

**Teleauskunft 1188, Teil
Datex-J und Telefax-
Teilnehmer**
Deutsche Telekom Medien GmbH
P.O. Box 160211
D-60065 Frankfurt, Germany
069 2682348; Fax 069 2682464

CD-ROM: Dataware
Technologies GmbH

**The Telephone Industry
Directory**
Phillips Business Information,
Inc. (PBI)
7811 Montrose Road
Potomac, MD 20854-3363
(301) 340-2100; Fax (301) 424-7261

Online: NewsNet, Inc.

TwixTel
Twix Equipment AG
Gewerbestr. 12
CH-8132 Zurich, Switzerland
01 9842211; Fax 01 9843337

CD-ROM: Twix Equipment AG

U.S. West SearchDisc
Pro CD, Inc.
222 Rosewood Drive
Danvers, MA 01923-4510
(508) 750-0000; Fax (508) 750-0070

CD-ROM: Pro CD, Inc.

*Please note that those business
telephone directories that include
sales figures or other financial
information have been included
in Appendix C, Business Credit
and Company Financial
Databases.*

Adoption Registries

CANADA

Alberta

Post Adoption Registry
9th Floor; South Tower
Seventh Street Plaza
10030 107 Street
Edmonton, Alberta T5J 3E4
(403) 427-6387

British Columbia

Adoption Reunion Registry
Family Services of Greater
Vancouver #205
3369 Fraser Street
Vancouver, BC V5V 4C2
(604) 875-9434

Adoption Reunion Registry
202-1600 West 6th Avenue
Vancouver, BC V6J 1R3
(800) 665-1899; (604) 736-7917

**Parent Finders National
Reunion Registry**
Parent Finders, National
Headquarters
3998 Bayridge Avenue
W. Vancouver, BC V7V 3J5
(604) 926-1096; (604) 980-6005

**Society for Truth in Adoption
(TRIAD) National Registry**
National Office
Box 5922; Station B
Victoria, BC V8R 6S8
(604) 385-7884

Manitoba

**Adoption Registry
Coordinator**
270 Osborne Street North

Winnipeg, Manitoba R3C 1V7
(204) 945-4562

**Child and Family Services
Registry**
200 185 Carlton Street
Winnipeg, Manitoba
(204) 942-7987

Ontario

**Adoptions Canada—A
Private Adoptions Registry**
P.O. Box 637
430 Birch Street
Southhampton, Ontario N0H 2L0
(519) 389-4645

**Canadian Adoption Reunion
Register (CARR)**
63 Welland Avenue
Toronto Ontario M4T 2H9
(416) 516-2134

Saskatchewan

Post-Adoption Services
2240 Albert Street
Regina, Saskatchewan S4S 3V7
(306) 787-3654

UNITED KINGDOM

England

Adopt-A-Link
60 Downside Road
Surrey, England, SM2 5HP
(081) 642-7064

Child Migrants Trust
8 Kingston Road
West Bridgford

Nottingham NG2 7AQ

**International Social Service
of Great Britain**
39 Cramer House
39 Brixton Road
London SW9 6DD

**National Organization for
Counseling Adoptees &
Parents (NORCAP)**
3 New High Street
Headington, Oxford OX3 5AJ
44 (1865) 750554

**Searchline & Adoption
Contact Register**
7 Okeford Road
Broadstonem Dorset BH18 8BA
+44 (1202) 693102

**TRACE (Transatlantic
Children's Endeavors)**
The Coach House
Between 28/30 Langley Avenue
Surbiton, Surrey KT6 6QP

War Babes
15 Plough Avenue
South Woodgate
Birmingham B32 3TQ

Scotland

Scottish Birth-Link Register
21 Castle Street
Edinburgh EH2 3DN

UNITED STATES

Arkansas

**Arkansas Mutual Consent
Voluntary Adoption Registry**

Department of Human Services
Division of Children and Family
Services
Permanency Planning Unit
P.O. Box 1437
Little Rock, Arkansas 72203-1437

California

**California Department of
Social Services**
Adoptions Branch
744 P Street, M.S. 19/68
Sacramento, California 97814
(916) 322-5973

**Home for Unwed Mothers
Registry**
BirthParent Connection
P.O. Box 230643
Encinitas, CA 92023-0643

Colorado

**Colorado Voluntary Adoption
Registry**
Colorado State Department of
Health
4210 E. 11th Avenue
Denver CO 80220
(303) 331-4887

**Orphan Voyage Reunion
Registry**
2141 Road 2300
Cedaredge, CO 81413
(303) 856-3937

Connecticut

**Department of Children and
Youth Services**
170 Sigourney Street
Hartford, CT 06105
(203) 566-8742

**National Adoption Reunion
Registry**
P.O. Box 2494
Danbury, CT 06813-2494

Florida

ATM Reunion Registry
1105 Cape Coral Parkway East

Suite G
Cape Coral, FL 33904-9175
(813) 542-1342; Fax (813) 549-9393

**Florida Adoption Registry
Vital Statistics Registry**
P. O. Box. 2197
Jacksonville, FL 32232
(904) 488-8000

**HRS Children Youth &
Family Services**
Building 7; Room 102
Tallahassee, FL 32399-0700

Georgia

**Georgia—Georgia State
Reunion Registry**
State Adoption Unit
878 Peachtree Street NE
Room 501
Atlanta, GA 30309
(404) 894-4454

Idaho

**Department of Health and
Welfare**
Division of Family and
Children's Services
Statehouse Mail
Boise, ID 33720
(208) 338-7000

Illinois

Illinois Adoption Registry
Illinois Department of Public
Health
Division of Vital Records—
Adoption Registry
605 West Jefferson Street
Springfield, IL 62702
(217) 782-6553

**Yesterday's Children
National Adoption Registry**
Advocating Legislation for
Adoption Reform Movement
(A.L.A.R.M.) Network
Representative
1755 West Wabansia Avenue
Chicago, IL 60622-1415
(312) 545-6900

Indiana

**Indiana Department Of
Health**
Indiana Adoption History Program
(317) 466-3900

**Indiana State Board of
Health**
330 West Michigan Street
Indianapolis, IN 46202
(317) 633-0274

Reunion Registry of Indiana
P.O. Box 361
South Bend, IN 46624

Iowa

Iowa Reunion Registry
P.O. Box 8
Blairsburg, IA 50034

Kentucky

Cabinet for Human Resources
Department for Social Services
275 East Main Street
6th Floor West
Frankfort, KY 40621
(502) 564-2136

Louisiana

Louisiana Voluntary Registry
Department of Health and
Human Resources
P.O. Box 3318
Baton Rouge, LA 70821
(504) 342-4041

Maine

**Maine State Adoption
Reunion Registry**
Office of Vital Statistics
Department of Human Services
Station 11
221 State Street
Augusta, ME 04333
(207) 289-3181

Maryland

Mutual Consent Voluntary

Adoption Registry
Social Services Administration
311 West Saratoga Street
Baltimore, MD 21201
(301) 333-0237

Michigan

Adoption Identity Movement Registry
1434 Southlawn Drive, SW
P.O. Box 9265
Grand Rapids, MI 49509-4354
(616) 531-1380

Michigan Reunion Registry
P.O. Box 3007
300 S. Capitol Avenue
Lansing, MI 48909

Quebec Quest Reunion Registry
P.O. Box 4532
Union, MI 49130

Truths in the Adoption Triad Registry
2462 Kansas
Saginaw, MI 48601
(517) 777-6666

Minnesota

Leaf/Minnesota Reunion Registry & Support
23247 Lofton Court North
Scandia, MN 55073

Minnesota Reunion Registry
State Registrar
Vital Statistics
Department of Health
717 Delaware SW
Minneapolis, MN 55440
(612) 296-5316
(Fed into the INTERNATIONAL SOUNDEX REUNION REGISTRY)

Missouri

Adoption Information Registry
Missouri Division of Family Services

P.O. Box 88
Jefferson City, MO 65103

Montana

Montana Adoption Reunion Registry
4104 Barbara Lane
Missoula, MT 59803
(406) 251-4158

Nevada

INTERNATIONAL SOUNDEX REUNION REGISTRY
P.O. Box 2312
Carson City, NV 89702
(702) 882-7755

Nevada Reunion Registry State Reunion Registry
Department of Human Resources
251 Jeanell Drive
Capitol Mall Complex
Carson City, NV 89710
Welfare Division
2527 North Carson Street
Carson City, NV 89710

New Jersey

Department of Human Services
Division of Youth and Family Services
1 South Montgomery Street
CN 717
Trenton, NJ 08625
(609) 633-3991

New Jersey Reunion Registry
Bureau of Resource Development
Box 510
Trenton, NJ 08625
(609) 292-8816

New York

Adoption Information Registry
New York State Health Department

Corning Tower; Room 208
Empire State Plaza
Albany, NY 12237
(518) 474-2800

Ohio

Ohio Reunion Registry
(614) 644-5635

Oklahoma

Voluntary Adoption Reunion Registry
P.O. Box 25352
Oklahoma City, OK 73125
(405) 521-4373

Oregon

Department of Human Resources
Children's Services Division
198 Commercial Street, SE
Salem, OR 97310-0450
(503) 378-4452

Rhode Island

Reunion Registry
State of Rhode Island and Providence Plantations
Family Court, Juvenile Division
One Dorrance Plaza
Providence, RI 02903
(401) 277-3352

South Carolina

Adoption Reunion Register
Department of Social Services
P.O. Box 1520
Columbia, SC 29202-1520
(803) 734-6095

South Dakota

Department of Social Services

Tennessee

Department of Human Services
P.O. Box 2960

Austin, TX 78769
(512) 450-3302

**Missing Persons Bureau
Mutual Consent Registry**
U.F.O.
P.O. Box 290333
Nashville, TN 37229-0333

Utah

Adoption Reunion Registry
Department of Health
Vital Statistics
288 North 1460 West
Salt Lake City, UT 84116
(801) 538-3916

Vermont

**Department of Social and
Rehabilitation Services**
Division of Social Services
Adoption Unit
103 South Main Street
Waterbury, VT 05676
(808) 241-2131

West Virginia

**West Virginia Mutual
Consent Voluntary Adoption
Registry**
Children's Home Society of WV
P.O. Box 2942
Charleston, WV 25330

**AOL/Prodigy ADOPTION
REGISTRY**
America Online's Adoption
Registry can be found on
America Online, using the keyword "Adoption." This registry is
now linked with Prodigy's
Adoption Registry. You do not
need to have access to America
Online or Prodigy to be placed
on the registry. A form for joining the AOL Registry can also be
found on the Internet, at:

**ftp://ftp.netcom.com/pub/km/
kmc/adoption/AOL_registry.
form**

Major Bulletin Board Vendors

America Online, Inc.
8619 Westwood Center Drive
Vienna, VA 22182-2285
(800) 827-6364; (703) 448-8700

AT&T EasyLink & FYI News Service
FYI News Service
5501 LBJ Freeway; Room 1015
Dallas, TX 75240
(800) 242-6005

CompuServe Information Services
5000 Arlington Centre Boulevard
P.O. Box 20212
Columbus, OH 43220
(800) 848-8199; (614) 457-8600
Fax (614) 457-0348

CompuServe Knowledge Index
Refer to CompuServe Information Services

Delphi Internet Services Corporation
1030 Massachusetts Avenue
4th Floor
Cambridge, MA 02138-5302
(800) 695-4005; (617) 491-3393
Fax (617) 491-6642

GE Information Services (GEIS), GEnie
401 North Washington Boulevard
Rockville, MD 20850
(800) 638-9636; (301) 340-4000

Internet
The Internet is the largest bulletin board system in the world. According to *Online Access* magazine, every day 25 million people in 200 countries access the Internet (and these numbers are ever increasing). There are so many vendors that provide access to the Internet that there are actu-

ally Internet sites that have been built just to index all of the lists of Internet access providers. Three examples that point to many lists of Internet access providers are:

http://thelist.com/

http://www.netusa.net/

http://www.best.be/iap/

and there is even a list of lists of providers:

http://www.tagsys.com:80/ Provider/ListOfLists.html

One of these lists claims over 3,000 Internet service providers already (as of July 1996), and more are springing up every day. One can hardly open a magazine or newspaper without encountering another vendor offering Internet access, so if you're not already connected, you should have little difficulty finding an Internet access provider. Furthermore, there is so much competition that it pays to periodically comparison shop to make sure that you've got the best deal available in your area.
None of the Internet access providers control or regulate the Internet. New bulletin boards (referred to on the Internet as Usenet newsgroups) and other services may be added, changed, moved or deleted at any time, so it is not my intention to document all of the bulletin boards here (which as of July 1996 exceeded 14,000 according to Alta Vista!). Internet Web pages have been designed to help you navigate and search for Usenet newsgroups that would be of interest to you.

Two such Internet sites are:

http://sunsite.unc.edu:80/ usenet-b/home.html

http://scwww.ucs.indiana. edu:80/NetRsc/usenet.html

In order to find on the Internet Usenet newsgroups (i.e., bulletin boards) that interest you, I recommend sites such as these, as well as learning to use Internet navigation tools such as:

Alta Vista:
http://www.altavista.digital.com
excite:
http://www.excite.com/
Lycos:
http://www.infoseek.com/
Yahoo!:
http://www.yahoo.com/ search.html

all of which provide the ability to restrict your search to Usenet newsgroups alone. You could also subscribe to magazines such as *Online Access* or the plethora of others that highlight new Internet developments and services each month, or use *The Internet Yellow Pages,* or one of the hundreds of other Internet books now on the market.

Prodigy Services Company
445 Hamilton Avenue
White Plains, NY 10601
(800) 776-3449; (914) 448-8000

Please note that there are quite literally thousands of both public and private bulletin boards available, and more are added each day. This list serves only to highlight the major bulletin board vendors.

Public Records Producers and Vendors

Although there are many other companies that offer public records, tenant and employee screening, and related services, the following list is an attempt to identify only those companies that are producers of proprietary databases of this type, which are available online or on CD-ROM.

Accufax
5801 E. 41st Street; Suite 800
Tulsa, OK 74145
P.O. Box 35563
Tulsa, OK 74153
(800) 256-8898; (918) 627-2226
Fax (918) 622-9453
Accufax maintains a proprietary tenant database covering Arkansas, Kansas, Missouri, and Oklahoma.

Accusearch of Texas Inc.
2727 Allen Parkway; Suite 1200
Houston, TX 77019
P.O. Box 3248
Houston, TX 77253-3248
(800) 833-05778; (713) 529-3383
Fax (713) 864-7639
Accusearch of Texas maintains several proprietary databases. They offer a database of bankruptcies, corporate/trade names, and Uniform Commercial Code filings (UCCs) for Texas, another database of UCCs for Bexar, Dallas, Harris, and Tarrant Counties in Texas, as well as a database of real estate/assessor records and corporate/trade names for Harris County, Texas.

Accu-Source, Inc.
11500 N. Stemmons #182

Dallas, TX 75229
(800) 243-0794; (214) 241-0437
Fax (214) 241-8668
Accu-Source maintains a proprietary database of criminal records for Dallas County, Texas, and a national database for aviation and vessels.

ACXIOM Corp.
301 Industrial Boulevard
Conway, AR 72032
(501) 329-6836; Fax (501) 329-3950
This is mainly a mailing list house, but they offer a tool, AcxiTrack, which has been designed as a skip tracing tool.

American Information Network (AIN)
1258 Cleveland Avenue NW
Canton, OH 44703
(800) 779-6938; (330) 484-6272

American Professional Data Network (APDN)
P.O. Box 58
Bradford, AR 72020
(800) 759-9977; (501) 344-2544
Fax (501) 344-2315
Primarily offering pre-employment screening services, APDN also offers SAFESCAN fraud protection, and APDN Termination and Work Record Verification Database.

AMS
(A subsidiary of Agency Management Services)
3001 E. Bypass
College Station, TX 77842-0076
P.O. Box 30001

College Station, TX 77842-3001
(800) 683-8553; (409) 693-6122
Fax (409) 693-5480
This is reported to be one of the largest providers of motor vehicle record information in the country.

Aristotle Industries
205 Pennsylvania Avenue SE
Washington, DC 20003
(800) 296-2747; (202) 543-8345
Fax (202) 543-6407
Maintains a nationwide database of registered voters, enhanced by listed phone numbers, postal corrections, census information, age, and voting history.

Avert, Inc.
301 Reminton Street
Fort Collins, CO 80524
(800) 367-5933; (303) 484-7722
Fax (303) 221-1526
Offers an online employee screening database, including confirmation of education, workers' compensation claims, reference checks, driving record, criminal histories, credit histories, and Social Security number verification.

Background Information Services
1800 30th Street; Suite 213
Boulder, CO 80301
(800) 433-6010; (303) 442-3960
Fax (303) 442-1004
This company offers a proprietary database containing civil and criminal records from district and county courts for most of Colorado.

Cambridge Statistical Research Associates (CSRA)
23 Rocky Knoll
Irvine, CA 92715
(714) 509-9900; Fax (714) 509-9119

CSRA maintains a nationwide death index, by name and Social Security number.

CARFax
3975 Fair Ridge Drive; Suite 200N
Fairfax, VA 20003
(800) 444-0145; (703) 934-2664
Fax (703) 273-5195

CARFax maintains a vehicle title history database for Arkansas, Florida, Illinois, Indiana, Iowa, Kansas, Kentucky, Mississippi, Missouri, Oklahoma, Texas, Washington, and Wyoming.

CDB Infotek
6 Hutton Center Drive
Santa Ana, CA 92707
(800) 427-3747; (714) 708-2000
Fax (714) 708-1000

CDB Infotek is one of the premiere online public records vendors, and is still growing, as evidenced by their recent purchase of Prentice Hall Online (PHO), and the Charles E. Simon Company (a provider of SEC information on publicly held companies). CDB Infotek offers a wide variety of databases and search tools, many of which are proprietary.

Commercial Information Systems, Inc.
4747 SW Kelly; Suite 110
Portland, OR 97201-4221
(800) 454-6575; (503) 222-7422
Fax (503) 222-7405

Maintains several proprietary databases, including real estate/ assessor records for Idaho, Oregon, and Washington, corporate/trade name, UCC, and motor vehicle records for Oregon and Washington, bankruptcy and workers' compensation records for Oregon, and motor vehicle records for Idaho and Oregon.

CompuServe
Although most widely known as a bulletin board service, CompuServe does serve as a gateway to several public records databases, including one for Uniform Commercial Code filings in Florida, corporate/trade names in Florida and New Jersey, motor vehicle records for Florida, Secretary of State records for Texas, and national SEC records, along with other financial offerings. (Refer to Appendix L for Major Bulletin Board Vendors for the CompuServe address.)

Control Data Systems Canada Ltd.
130 Albert Street; Suite 1100
Ottawa, Ontario K1P 5G4
(613) 598-0211; Fax (613) 563-1716

Maintains a proprietary database of corporate/trade names for Canada and trademarks/ patents for Canada.

Courthouse Data Inc.
550 Pharr Road; Suite 833
Atlanta, GA 30305
(800) 633-3961; (404) 266-0831
Fax (404) 364-9184

Maintains a proprietary database of corporate/trade names for Georgia.

Courthouse Records, Inc.
12375 East Cornell Avenue
Aurora, CO 80014
(303) 695-1111; Fax (303) 695-0182

CD-ROM products include: Real property market information for many areas. Typical data on disc includes owner name, as well as property information and improvements. Tax Assessor maps are also available on compact disc, for certain counties in Colorado and Oregon.

CT Corporation System
1633 Broadway; Floor 23
New York, NY 10019

(800) 624-0909; (212) 664-1666
Fax (212) 247-2882

Offers an online proprietary database of UCCs, litigation, judgments, and tax liens for Arizona, California, Colorado, Connecticut, Illinois, Maryland, Michigan, Nevada, New York, Oregon, Pennsylvania, and Texas.

DAC Services (aka Transportation Information Service)
4110 South 100 East Avenue
Tulsa, OK 74146
(800) 331-9175; (918) 664-9991
Fax (918) 664-4366

Maintains several proprietary databases, including one with education and employment records, another with motor vehicle records, and another with criminal records; all of these are national. They also maintain a database of work workers' compensation records for Arkansas, Colorado, Florida, Illinois, Indiana, Iowa, Kansas, Maine, Maryland, Massachusetts, Michigan, North Dakota, New Mexico, Ohio, Oklahoma, Oregon, and Texas.

Dallas Computer Services Inc.
10000 North Central Expressway
Suite 704
Dallas, TX 75231
(800) 394-3274; (214) 360-5800
Fax (214) 360-5806

Maintains a proprietary database containing motor vehicle records for Texas, a unique name search feature, and various other public records offerings.

DAMAR Real Estate Information Service
3610 Central Avenue
Riverside, CA 92506
(800) 345-7334

Maintains real estate records online.

Data Control Corporation
2501 West Burbank Boulevard
Burbank, CA 91505-2347
(818) 557-2347; Fax (818) 563-4300

Maintains a proprietary database containing death records from the Social Security Administration and elsewhere.

Data Resource Group, Inc.
P.O. Box 26816
Tempe, AZ 85285
(800) 828-4144; (602) 275-7886
Fax (602) 275-4683

Maintains a proprietary database containing forcible detainer and vacating status records for use in tenant screening.

Database Technologies, Inc. (DBT Online)
100 East Sample Road
Pompano Beach, FL 33064
(800) 279-7710; (954) 781-2756
Fax (954) 943-9726

Their AutoTrack Plus system provides driving and vehicle records, and they also offer a national locator tool.

DataQuick Information Systems, Inc.
9171 Towne Centre Drive, 6th Floor
San Diego, CA 92122
(800) 863-INFO; (619) 455-6900
Fax (619) 455-6522

Maintains a proprietary database containing real estate/assessor records for Arizona and California. Also offers assessor parcel maps for California on CD-ROM.

DATEQ Information Network Inc.
5555 Triangle Parkway; Suite 400
Norcross, GA 30092
(404) 446-8282; Fax (404) 449-5866

Maintains proprietary databases containing motor vehicle records nationally, and insurance claims.

Employment Research Services
a.k.a. Rental Research Services

11300 Minnetonka Mills Road
Minnetonka, MN 55305-5151
(800) 328-0333; (612) 935-5700
Fax (612) 935-9212

Maintains a proprietary database containing evictions and landlord records for Minnesota, Cass County, North Dakota, Douglas, Pierce, and St. Croix Counties, Wisconsin

Environmental Data Resources Inc.
3530 Post Road
Southport, CT 06490
(800) 352-0050; (203) 255-6606
Fax (800) 231-6802
Fax (203) 255-1976

Maintains a proprietary database containing data on environmental liabilities associated with companies and properties.

Experian REDI Property Data
3610 Central Avenue; Suite 400
Riverside, CA 92506
(800) 345-7334
(714) 276-3600

Maintains a proprietary database containing real estate/ assessor records for 31 states, and assessor maps on CD-ROM.

Fidelifacts Metropolitan Inc.
50 Broadway
New York, NY 10004
(800) 678-0007; (212) 425-1520
Fax (212) 248-5619

Maintains a proprietary database containing criminal records in Connecticut, New Jersey, New York, and nationally.

Finance & Commerce Daily aka Dolan Media Company
615 South 7th Street
Minneapolis, MN 55415
(800) 297-4348
(612) 333-4244
Fax (612) 333-3243

Maintains a proprietary database containing bankruptcies, litigation, judgments, and tax

liens for Illinois, Indiana, Iowa, Kansas, Kentucky, Michigan, Minnesota, Missouri, Nebraska, Ohio, and Wisconsin

General Information Services (GIS)—a division of Policy Management Systems Corporation
P.O. Box 10
Columbia, SC 29204
(803) 735-4498; (803) 735-4000
Fax (803) 735-5313

Maintains a proprietary database containing motor vehicle insurance claims, and another containing undisclosed driver information.

Hollingsworth Information Services Inc.
aka Hollingsworth Court Reporting
10761 Perkins Road; Suite A
Baton Rouge, LA 70810
(504) 769-3386; Fax (504) 769-1814

Maintains several proprietary databases, including corporate/ trade names, UCC records, litigation, judgments, and tax liens, and a cross-index to officers and agents for a corporation; all of these records are for Louisiana and Mississippi.

The Info*Center Inc.
940 North St. Extension
Feeding Hills, MA 01030-1336
(800) 462-3033; (413) 786-7987
Fax (413) 789-0435

Maintains a proprietary database containing landlord data for Connecticut, Maine, Massachusetts, New Mexico, New York, and Rhode Island. Another database includes criminal records for Connecticut, Maine, and Rhode Island.

Information America (IA) (owned by West Publishing)
One Georgia Center
600 West Peachtree Street, NW
Atlanta, GA 30308
(800) 235-4008; (404) 892-1800

Fax (800) 845-6319
Fax (404) 875-8192

Information America is one of the largest public records vendors in the U.S. They offer many proprietary databases and searches.

Information Resource Services Company (IRSC), Inc.
3777 North Harbor Boulevard
Fullerton, CA 92635-1356
(800) 640-4772; (800) 841-1990
(714) 526-8485; Fax (714) 738-9106

IRSC offers a wide variety of public records databases, many of which are proprietary.

**Informus Corp.
(formerly Mississippi Business Information, Inc.)**
P.O. 1639
Madison, MS 39130
(601) 853-4636

Intelligence Network Inc.
P.O. Box 727
Clearwater, FL 34615
(800) 562-4007; (813) 449-0072
Fax (813) 448-0949

Maintains a proprietary database containing motor vehicle records for Florida.

LEXIS-NEXIS
(Refer to Appendix N for Other Database Vendors)

Lloyd's Maritime Information Services
1200 Summer Street
Stamford, CT 06905
(800) 423-8672; (203) 359-8383
Fax (203) 358-0437

Maintains a proprietary database containing records of ship characteristics and ownership, nationally.

**Marine Index Bureau
(a subsidiary of MIB Services Inc.)**
67 Scotch Road
Ewing, NJ 08628
(800) 929-0654; (609) 882-8909
Fax (609) 882-9282

Maintains a proprietary database containing education and employment information for maritime personnel. Injury and related claims histories are included.

Merlin Investigations
a.k.a. Merlin Information Services
408 Bryant Circle; Suite K
Ojai, CA 93023
(800) 367-6646; (805) 640-0284
Fax (805) 640-0851

Maintains a proprietary database containing corporate/trade names, UCCs, licenses, registrations and permits for California, and another containing litigation, judgments, and tax liens for Southern California.

Minnesota Driving Records (MDR)
10600 University Avenue NW
Coon Rapids, MN 55448
(800) 644-6877; (612) 755-1164
Fax (612) 755-0903

Maintains a proprietary database containing motor vehicle records for Minnesota.

Minnesota Secured Transaction Reports
459 Rice Street
St. Paul, MN 55103
P.O. Box 65607
St. Paul, MN 55165-0607
(800) 331-8806; (612) 227-7575
Fax (612) 292-0134

Maintains a proprietary database containing UCCs for Minnesota.

Mississippi Business Information Inc.
2068 Main Street
Madison, MS 39110
P.O. Box 1639
Madison, MN 39130-1639
(601) 853-4636; Fax (601) 856-9008

Maintains a proprietary database containing various types of public records for Mississippi.

Motznik Computer Services Inc.
8301 Briarwood Street; Suite 100
Anchorage, AK 99518-3332
(907) 344-6254

Maintains proprietary databases containing various types of public records and motor vehicle records for Alaska.

National Credit Information (NCI) Network
7721 Hamilton Avenue
Cincinnati, OH 45231
P.O. Box 31221
Cincinnati, OH 45231-0221
(513) 522-3832
Fax (513) 522-1702

Maintains a proprietary database containing tenant records.

National Fraud Investigation Center
922 East Butler Pike
Ambler, PA 19002
(800) 999-5658; (215) 540-9340
Fax (215) 540-9344

Maintains several proprietary databases containing criminal records including bank fraud, insurance fraud, organized crime, and casino fraud.

New Mexico Technet Inc.
4100 Osuna NE; Suite 103
Albuquerque, NM 87109-4442
(505) 345-6555
Fax (505) 345-6559

Maintains a proprietary database containing many types of public records and motor vehicle records for New Mexico.

Offsite Public Record Assess (OPRA)
5 South Fitzhugh Street; Suite 225
Rochester, NY 14614
(716) 454-7390
Fax (716) 454-7409

Maintains proprietary databases containing real estate/assessor records, UCCs, litigation, judgments, and tax liens for Monroe County, New York, bankruptcies for Western and Northern districts of New York, and UCCs, litigation, judgments, and tax liens for Erie County, New York

Ohio Professional Electronic Network (OPEN)
1650 Lake Shore Drive; Suite 180
Columbus, OH 43204
(800) 366-0106

Offers access to UCC transactions filed with the Ohio Secretary of State.

Oregon State Legislative Administration Committee
S424 State Capitol
Salem, OR 97310
(503) 378-8194

PACER
(800) 676-6856

This government service provides direct online access to court records. It is available in many states, and the records available are constantly expanding. A call to the toll-free number listed here will direct you to your nearest PACER location.

Plat System Services Inc.
5955 Golden Valley Road, #210
Golden Valley, MN 55422
(612) 544-0012
Fax (612) 544-0617

Maintains proprietary databases containing real estate / assessor records for Minneapolis / St. Paul, Minnesota

Pollock & Co.
P.O. Box 310224
Newington, CT 06131
(203) 667-1490

Offers driving records, criminal records, workers' compensation reports, and other public records

Prentice Hall Online
Refer to CDB Infotek, earlier in this Appendix.

Property Data Center Inc.
7100 East Belleview; Suite 110
Greenwood Village, CO 80111
(303) 850-9586
Fax (303) 850-9637

Maintains a proprietary database containing real estate / assessor records for Colorado.

PRR Inc.
607 Marquette Avenue; Suite 500
Minneapolis, MN 55402
(800) 533-8897
(612) 332-2427
Fax (612) 334-5932

Maintains a proprietary database containing bankruptcies for Indiana, Iowa, Kansas, Michigan, Minnesota, Missouri, Nebraska, Ohio, and Wisconsin, and another database containing litigation, judgments, and tax liens for Indiana, Iowa, Minnesota, Nebraska, Ohio, and Wisconsin.

Public Data Corporation
80 Broad Street; Floor 24
New York, NY 10004
(212) 797-9800
Fax (212) 797-9881

Maintains a proprietary database containing many types of public records for New York, New York.

Rapid Information Services
1176 Capital CR SE
Tallahassee, FL 32301
(800) 777-6655
Fax (800) 456-5143

Online searches include: driving records available nationwide; VIN searches, license plate searches, and vehicle ownership searches for the state of Florida; Florida workers' compensation histories; consumer credit reports

The Registry
11140 Rockville Pike; Suite 1200
Rockville, MD 20852
(800) 999-0350
(301) 881-3400
Fax (301) 984-7312

Maintains a proprietary database

containing evictions and landlord records for the District of Columbia, Maryland, New Jersey, New York, Pennsylvania, and Virginia. Another database contains criminal records, nationally.

Resident Evaluation Service, Inc.
2755 South Locust Street
Suite 209
Denver, CO 8222-7132
(800) 752-8575
(303) 758-8575
Fax (303) 757-5573

Maintains a proprietary database containing tenant records for Colorado and New Mexico.

Rhino Referral Systems
104 Westmark Boulevard
#2-C
Lafayette, LA 70506
P.O. Box 30723
Lafayette, LA 70593-0723
(800) 984-9918
(318) 981-9918

Maintains a proprietary database containing evictions and complaints against tenants in Louisiana.

Search Network Ltd.
Two Corporate Place; Suite 100
1501 S. 42nd Street
West Des Moines, IA 50265
(800) 383-5050
(515) 223-1153
Fax (800) 383-5060
Fax (515) 223-2814

Maintains a proprietary database containing UCC records for Iowa, Kansas, and Missouri.

Superior On-Line Data LP
300 Phillips Boulevard; Suite 500
Trenton, N 08618
P.O. Box 8787
Trenton, NJ 08650-0787
(800) 848-0489
(609) 883-7000
Fax (800) 883-0677
Fax (609) 883-0677

Maintains a proprietary database

(Casey) containing bankruptcies, litigation, judgments, and tax liens for Delaware, New Jersey, New York, Pennsylvania, corporate/ trade names for New York, and UCCs for Pennsylvania

Trans Registry Limited (TRL)
11140 Rockville Pike; #1200
Rockville, MD 20852
(301) 881-3400; Fax (301) 984-7312

Links the tenant history and court record databases of thousands of member companies.

TransUnion Business Division
20 Constance Court
Hauppauge, NY 11788-4200
(516) 582-2692
Fax (516) 582-2767

Maintains a proprietary database containing business litigation for New Jersey and New York.

Verifacts Inc.
7326 27th Street West
Suite C
Tacoma, WA 98466-4637
(800) 458-5665
(206) 565-9109
Fax (800) 799-5885
Fax (206) 566-1231

Maintains a proprietary data-base containing evictions and landlord records for Arizona, California, Idaho, Nevada, Oregon, and Washington.

Other Database Vendors

There are hundreds of online database vendors and hundreds more who produce CD-ROM databases. The following list represents only a small sampling of these vendors. It is my intention to include the major vendors who offer a broad base of databases, as well as the vendors whose databases I have found to be most helpful researching information on individuals (in addition to those listed in Appendix L and Appendix M).

For a comprehensive list of databases and database vendors, I heartily recommend the *Gale Directory of Databases,* available in print and on CD-ROM. I have found the CD-ROM version invaluable in searching out sources of information both for this book, as well as in my research work.

ABC Belge pour le Commerce et l'Industrie B.V.
Avenue de l'Heliport 21
B-1210 Brussels, Belgium
02 2184414; Fax 02 2194271

ABC voor Handel en Industrie C.V.
P.O. Box 190
NL-2000 AD Haarlem
Netherlands
023 319031; Fax 023 327033

ABLE INFORM Bulletin Board System
U.S. National Institute on Disability and Rehabilitation Research (NIDRR)
8455 Colesville Road; Suite 935
Silver Spring, MD 20910-3319

(800) 346-2742; (301) 589-3563
Fax (301) 587-1697

ADP Data Services
42 Broadway; 17th Floor
Suite 1730
New York, NY 10004
(212) 908-5400

ADP Financial Services (UK) Ltd.
ADP House
2 Pine Trees
Chertsey Lane
Staines, Middlesex TW18 3DS, England
0784 451355

ADP Network Services, Inc.
175 Jackson Plaza
Ann Arbor, MI 48106
(800) 521-3166; (313) 769-6800
Fax (313) 995-6458

AffarsData
Bonnier Business Publishing Group
P.O. Box 3188
S-103 63 Stockholm, Sweden
08 7365919; Fax 08 7231390

Agence France-Presse (AFP)
13, place de la Bourse, B.P. 20
F-75061 Paris Cedex 2, France
01 40414867; 40414632

Agricultural Research Service (ARS)
U.S. Department of Agriculture
Office of Cooperative Interactions (OCI)
Room 404, Building 005, BARC-West
Beltsville, MD 20705
(301) 344-4045

Alberta Treasury, Statistics
Park Plaza; 6th Floor
10611—98 Avenue
Edmonton, AB, Canada T5K 2R7
(403) 427-3099; Fax (403) 427-0409

America Online
Refer to Appendix L

American Business Information, Inc. (ABI)
American Business Lists—Online
5711 S. 86th Circle, P.O. Box 27347
Omaha, NE 68127
(402) 593-4593; Fax (402) 331-6681

American Business Lists
Refer to American Business Information, Inc.

American Directory Corporation
P.O. Box 7426
New York, NY 10116
(718) 797-4311; Fax (718) 596-4852

American Institute of Physics (AIP)
PINET (Physics INformation NETwork)
500 Sunnyside Boulevard
Woodbury, NY 11797-2999
(516) 576-2262; Fax (516) 349-9704

ARI Network Services, Inc.
330 E. Kilbourn Avenue
Milwaukee, WI 53202
(800) 558-9044; (800) 242-6001
(414) 278-7676; Fax (414) 283-4357

Arizona State Museum
Department of Archaeology
Boston University
675 Commonwealth Avenue
Boston, MA 02215
(617) 353-3415

ARK Information Services
10 Barley Mow Passage
Chiswick
London W4 4PH, England
081-944 9539; Fax 081-994 6380

Aslib, The Association for Information Management
Information House
20-24 Old Street
London EC1V 9AP, England
071-253 4488; Fax 071-430 0514

Association Cotraitel
Immeuble du Mas d'Alco
254, rue Michel Teule
B.P. 6076
F-34030 Montpelier Cedex 1, France
67 618100; Fax 67 678110

Association TELEXPORT
92 bis, rue Cardinet
F-75017 Paris, France
01 47631415; Fax 01 42679969

ATTICA Cybernetics Ltd.
Unit 2, Kings Meadow
Ferry Hinksey Road
Oxford OX2 ODP, England
0865 791346; Fax 0865 794561

AUSINET
310 Ferntree Gully Road
Clayton, VIC 3168, Australia
03 5415600; Fax 03 5422671

Australian Bureau of Statistics (ABS)
Cameron Offices
P.O. Box 10
Belconnen, ACT 2616, Australia
06 2525853; Fax 06 2531809

Austria Presse Agentur (APA)
Gunoldstr. 14
A-1199 Vienna, Austria
01 3605; Fax 01 3605

AZ Direct Marketing
Bertelsmann GmbH
Carl-Bertelsmann-Str. 161
D-33311 Gutersloh, Germany
05241 803285
Fax 05241 26987

Bancroft-Parkman, Inc.
Bancroft-Parkman, Inc.
P.O. Box 1236
Washington, CT 06793
(212) 737-2715; Fax (203) 868-0080

BASELINE II INC.
838 Broadway
New York, NY 10003
(800) 254-8235; (212) 254-8235
Fax (212) 529-3330
BASELINE offers several databases which are very useful in researching anyone in the entertainment industry.

BBC Monitoring
British Broadcasting Corporation (BBC)
Caversham Park
Reading RG4 8TZ, England
0734 463823; Fax 0734 461105

BELINDIS
Belgium Ministere des Affaires Economiques
Centre de Traitement de l'Information
30, rue J.A. de Mot
B-1040 Brussels, Belgium
02 2336111; Fax 02 2304619

Bertelsmann Information Service GmbH
Landsberger Str. 191a
D-80686 Munich, Germany
089 5795220; Fax 089 5795244

BISNES Plus
Refer to INFOTRADE N.V.

Blackwell North America, Inc.
6024 S.W. Jean Road; Building G
Lake Oswego, OR 97035
(800) 547-6426; (503) 684-1140
Fax (503) 639-2481

BLAISE-LINE
British Library
National Bibliographic Service
Boston Spa
Wetherby, W. Yorks, LS23 7BQ
England
0937 546585
Fax 0937 546586

Bloomberg Financial Markets
499 Park Avenue
New York, NY 10022
(212) 318-2000

Bonniers Foretagsinfo AB
Sveavagen 84
Box 3303
S-10366 Stockholm, Sweden
8 6740100; Fax 8 6121290

Booklink
Library Wholesale Services
11910-U Parklawn Drive
Rockville, MD 20852
(800) 423-2665; (202) 298-8015

Bowker Electronic Publishing
Reed Reference Publishing Group
121 Chanlon Road
New Providence, NJ 07974
(800) 521-8110; (908) 464-6800
Fax (908) 665-3528

Bridge Information Systems, Inc.
717 Office Parkway
St. Louis, MO 63141
(800) 325-3282; (314) 567-8100
Fax (314) 432-5391

British Broadcasting Corporation (BBC)
BBC Monitoring
Caversham Park
Reading RG4 8TZ, England
0734 463823
Fax 0734 461105

Brodart Co.
500 Arch Street
Williamsport, PA 17705
(800) 233-8467; (800) 666-9162
(717) 326-2461
Fax (717) 326-1479

Burrelle's Information Services
75 East Northfield Road
Livingston, NJ 07039-9873
(800) 631-1160; (201) 992-6600
Fax (201) 992-5122
Burrelle's offers transcripts from radio and television broadcasts.

**Business Information
Department**
*Refer to Chambre de Commerce
et d'Industrie de Paris (CCIP)*

**Business Research Services,
Inc.**
4201 Connecticut Avenue, NW
Suite 610
Washington, DC 20008
(800) 845-8420; (202) 364-6473
(845) 325-8720
Fax (202) 686-3228

**BYGGDOK (Institutet for
Byggdokumentation)**
Halsingegatan 47
S-113 31 Stockholm, Sweden
08 340170; Fax 08 324859

CACI Marketing Systems
1100 N. Glebe Road; Suite 200
Arlington, VA 22201-4714
(800) 292-2224; (703) 841-7800
Fax (703) 243-6272

Camera dei Deputati d'Italia
Servizio per la Documentazione
Automatica (SDA)
Piazza Montecitorio
I-00186 Rome, Italy
06 6760

**Canadian Heritage
Information Network (CHIN)**
Canada Department of
Canadian Heritage
Journal Tower South; 12th Floor
365 Laurier Avenue W
Ottawa, ON, Canada K1A 0C8
(613) 992-3333; Fax (613) 952-2318

CAN/OLE
Canada Institute for Scientific
and Technical Information (CISTI)
Electronic Products and Services
Montreal Road
Ottawa, ON, Canada K1A 0S2
(613) 993-1210; Fax (613) 952-8244

CARL Systems Network
CARL Corporation
3801 E. Florida Avenue; Suite 300
Denver, CO 80203
(303) 758-3030; Fax (303) 758-0606

Cartermill Inc.
1615 Thames Street
Baltimore, MD 21231
(800) 237-8621
Fax (410) 563-5389

Catalyst
53 Brown Road
Ithaca, NY 14850-1262
(800) 234-0425; (607) 257-5757
Fax (607) 266-0425

CCINFOline
Canadian Centre for
Occupational Health and Safety
(CCOHS)
250 Main Street E
Hamilton, ON, Canada L8N 1H6
(800) 668-4284; (905) 570-8094
Fax (905) 572-2206

**CCN Business Information
Ltd.**
Abbey House
Abbeyfield Road
Lenton, Nottingham NG7 2SW
England
0602 410888; Fax 0602 643377

**CD Plus Technologies
(Formerly BRS)**
333 7th Avenue
New York, NY 10001
(800) 950-2035; (212) 563-3006
Fax (212) 563-3784
*CD Plus Technologies offers
hundreds of databases across
various disciplines.*

**CDA Investment
Technologies, Inc.**
1355 Piccard Drive
Rockville, MD 20850
(301) 975-9600
Fax (301) 590-1350

CDA/Investnet
3265 Meridian Parkway
Suite 130
Fort Lauderdale, FL 33331
(305) 384-1500
Fax (305) 384-1540

CDP After Dark
Refer to CD Plus Technologies

CDP COLLEAGUE
Refer to CD Plus Technologies

CDP Online
Refer to CD Plus Technologies

**Centre de l'Industrie
Francaise des Travaux Publics**
3, rue de Berri
F-75008 Paris, France
01 45631144; Fax 01 45610447

**Centro Elettronico di
Documentazione (CED)**
Corte Suprema di Cassazione
d'Italia
Via Damiano Chiesa 24
I-00136 Rome, Italy
06 35081; Fax 06 3598338

CERVED International, S.A.
85-87, Boulevard Clovis
B-1040 Bruxelles, Belgium
02 2801777; Fax 02 2303453

**Chambre de Commerce et
d'Industrie de Paris (CCIP)**
Business Information Department
2, rue de Viarmes
F-75001 Paris, France
01 45083643; Fax 45083610

**CILEA (Consorzio
Interuniversitario Lombardo
per l'Elaborazione,
Automatica)**
Via R. Sanzio 4
I-20090 Segrate/Milan, Italy
02 2132541

Cineman Syndicate
7 Charles Court
Middletown, NY 10940
(914)692-4572; Fax (914)692-8311

Claritas
201 N. Union Street
Alexandria, VA 22314
(800) 284-4868; (703) 683-8300
Fax (703) 683-8309

John P. Coll Books
P.O. Box 5626
Berkeley, CA 94705-0626
(510) 845-8475

Colorado State Data Center
1313 Sherman Street; Room 521
Denver, CO 80203
(303) 866-3120
Fax (303) 866-2251

**CompuServe Information
Service**
Refer to Appendix L

**CompuServe Knowledge
Index**
Refer to Appendix L

The Computer Database
*Refer to Information Access
Company (IAC)*

Computer Sports World
1005 Elm Street
Boulder City, NV 89005
(800) 321-5562; (702) 294-0191
Fax (702) 294-1322

**Congressional Information
Service, Inc.**
4520 East-West Highway
Suite 800
Bethesda, MD 20814-3389
(800) 638-8380; (301) 654-1550
Fax (301) 654-4033

**Congressional Quarterly Inc.
(CQ)**
CQ Washington Alert Service
1414 22nd Street, NW
Washington, DC 20037
(800) 432-2250; (202) 887-6253
CQ is a legislative tracking system.

**Stephen K. Cook &
Company, Inc.**
1090 Vermont Avenue, NW
Suite 800
Washington, DC 20005
(202) 347-8918
Fax (202) 347-8920

COSMOSNET
Teikoku Databank, Ltd.
5-20, Minami Aoyama 2-Chome
Minato-ku
Tokyo 107, Japan
03 34044311; Fax 03 34044339

CQ Washington Alert Service
*Refer to Congressional Quarterly
Inc. (CQ)*

DATABANK S.p.A
Via dei Piatti 11
I-20123 Milan, Italy
02 809556; Fax 02 865579

DataStar
*Refer to Knight-Ridder
Information, Inc. DataStar offers
hundreds of online database
from numerous producers.*

Datastream International Ltd.
Monmouth House
58-64 City Rd.
London EC1Y 2AL, England
071 250-3000; Fax 071-253 0171

DataTimes Corporation
Parkway Plaza; Suite 450
1400 Quail Springs Parkway
Oklahoma City, OK 73134
(800) 642-2525; (405) 751-6400
Fax (405) 755-8028
*DataTimes is primarily a news
database, offering newspapers,
newswires, journals, and news
transcripts from around the world.*

**Defense RDT&E OnLine
System (DROLS)**
U.S. Defense Technical
Information Center (DTIC)
Building No. 5, Cameron Station
Alexandria, VA 22304-6145
(800) 841-9553; (703) 274-7709

**Delphi Internet Services
Corporation**
Refer to Appendix L

Dialcom
2560 N. 1st Street
P.O. Box 49019
San Jose, CA 95161
(800) 435-7342; (409) 922-0250
Fax (710) 825-9601

**DIMDI (Deutsches Institut fur
Medizinische Dokumentation
und Information)**
Weisshausstr. 27

Postfach 420580
D-50899 Cologne, Germany
0221 47241; Fax 0221 411429

DirectoryNet, Inc.
600 Morgan Falls Road; Suite 100
Atlanta, GA 30350
(800) 733-1212; (404) 512-5090
Fax (404) 512-5091

Disclosure Incorporated
5161 River Road
Bethesda, MD 20816
(800) 945-3647; (301) 951-1300
Fax (301) 657-1962
*Disclosure Incorporated offers
corporate business and financial
information, through both online
and CD-ROM databases. Many of
Disclosure's databases are offered
through other vendors as well.*

Dow Jones News/Retrieval
Dow Jones & Company, Inc.
P.O. Box 300
Princeton, NJ 08543-0300
(609) 520-4000; Fax (609) 520-4660
*Dow Jones offers many news data-
bases, as well as business financial databases, and databases
covering other other disciplines.*

DRI/McGraw-Hill
Data Products Division
24 Hartwell Avenue
Lexington, MA 02173
(617) 863-5100

**Dun & Bradstreet Business
Credit Services**
One Diamond Hill Road
Murray Hill, NJ 07974-0027
(800) 362-3425; (908) 665-5000
*Dun & Bradstreet offers finan-
cial information on businesses
throughout the U.S., as well as
Canada, Europe, and other parts
of the world.*

Dun & Bradstreet Canada
5770 Hurontario Street
Mississauga, ON, Canada L5R 3G5
(800) 232-1026; (800) 265-3867
(905) 568-6000; Fax (905) 568-6279

Dun & Bradstreet France S.A.
17, Avenue de Choisy
Le Palatino
F-75643 Paris Cedex 13, France
01 40770707; Fax 01 45839234

Dun & Bradstreet Ltd.
Holmers Farm Way
High Wycombe, Bucks. HP12 4UL
England
0494 422000
Fax 0494 422260

ECHO
Echo Communications Group, Inc.
97 Perry Street; Suite 13
New York, NY 10014
(212) 255-3839

Editions du Cercle de la Librairie
35, rue Gregoire de Tours
F-75006 Paris, France
01 44412800; Fax 01 43296895

ESA-IRS
European Space Agency (ESA),
Information Retrieval
Service (IRS)
ESRIN, Via Galileo Galilei
I-00044 Frascati (Rome), Italy
06 941801; Fax 06 94180361

EUROBASES
European Commission, Office for
Official Publications
200, rue de la Loi
B-1049 Brussels, Belgium
02 2950001; Fax 02 2960624

Europeenne de Donnees
164 Ter, rue d'Aguesseau
F-92100 Boulogne-Billancourt,
France
1 46052929
Fax 1 46054255

FactSet Data Systems, Inc.
One Greenwich Plaza
Greenwich, CT 06830
(203) 863-1500

FAME Information Services, Inc.
77 Water Street

New York, NY 10005
(212) 898-7800; Fax (212) 742-8956

The Faxon Company
15 Southwest Park
Westwood, MA 02090
(800) 766-0039; (617) 329-3350
Fax (617) 326-5484

FBR Asian Company Profiles
Refer to F.B.R. Data Base Inc.

F.B.R. Data Base Inc.
P.O. Box 11530
Taipei, Taiwan
886-2-875 4355
Fax 886-2-875 4360

Federal News Service
620 National Press Building
Washington, DC 20045
(202) 347-1400; Fax (202) 626-8947

Financial Database System
Securities Data Company, Inc.
1180 Raymond Boulevard
5th Floor
Newark, NJ 07102
(201) 622-3100; Fax (201) 622-1421

FIZ Technik (Fachinformationszentrum Technik)
Ostbahnhofstr. 13
D-60314 Frankfurt am Main 60,
Germany
069 43080225

Fort Worth Star-Telegram
StarText
400 W. 7th Street
Fort Worth, TX 76102
(817) 390-7905; Fax (817) 390-7797

FT PROFILE
P.O. Box 12
Sunbury-on-Thames, Middlesex
TW16 7UD, England
0932 761444; Fax 0932 781425

FT Profile offers a broad base of databases crossing many disciplines.

Gale Research Inc.
835 Penobscot Building

Detroit, MI 48226-4094
(800) 347-4253; (313) 961-2242
Fax (313) 961-6815

GBI
Refer to Gesellschaft fur Betriebswirtschaftliche Information mbH

GE Information Services (GEIS)
401 North Washington Boulevard
Rockville, MD 20850
(301) 340-4572; Fax (301) 294-5501

GE Information Services offers a wide variety of databases from various producers, addressing many topics.

GEnie
Refer to Appendix L

GENIOS Wirtschaftsdatenbanken
Handelsblatt GmbH
Kasernenstr. 67
Postfach 10 11 02
D-4000 Dusseldorf 1, Germany
0211 8871524; Fax 0211 8871520

Gesellschaft fur Betriebswirtschaftliche Information mbH (GBI)
Freischutzstr. 96
D-81927 Munich, Germany
089 9570064; Fax 089 954229

This is a German database vendor offering a wide variety of databases covering topics and interests from around the world.

The Glimpse Corporation
1101 King Street; Suite 601
Alexandria, VA 22314
(703) 838-5529

Global Meeting Line, Inc.
1345 Oak Ridge Turnpike
Suite 357
Oak Ridge, TN 37830
(615) 482-6451; Fax (615) 483-7494

Globe Information Services
444 Front Street West

Toronto, ON, Canada M5V 2S9
(800) 268-9128; (800) 456-9190
(416) 585-5250; Fax (416) 585-5249
*This Canadian database vendor
offers a variety of business and
news databases.*

G-Search Corporation
Loop-X Building; 7th Floor
3-9-15, Kaigan, Minato-ku
Tokyo 108, Japan
03 55424381; Fax 03 54424391

**Handelsblatt GmbH, GENIOS
Wirtschaftsdatenbanken**
Kasernenstr. 67
P.O.Box 101102
D-40213 Dusseldorf 1, Germany
0211 8871524; Fax 0211 8871520
*This German database vendor
offers hundreds of databases
from many disciplines.*

Harvest Information Services
18-19 Long Lane
London EC1A 9HE, England
071-606 4533; Fax 071-226 6083

**Helsingin Yliopiston
Laskentakeskus**
Teollisuuskatu 23
PO Box 26
FIN-00014 Helsinki, Finland
0 708851; Fax 0 7084441

Hispanic Business, Inc.
360 S. Hope Avenue; Suite 300C
Santa Barbara, CA 93105
(805) 682-5843; Fax (805) 687-4546

Hoppenstedt Benelux
*Refer to ABC voor Handel en
Industrie C.V.*

**HRIN, The Human Resource
Information Network**
1200 Quince Orchard Boulevard
Gaithersburg, MD 20878
(800) 638-8094; (301) 590-2300
Fax (301) 590-2301

**Huang Kwan & Associates
Limited**
Java Commercial Centre

Room 1605
128 Java Road
Hong Kong
852 811 0079; Fax 852 811 8103

IDD Information Services
Two World Trade Center
New York, NY 10048
(212) 432-0045; Fax (212) 432-0192
*IDD offers several proprietary
databases containing corporate
financial information.*

Info Globe Online
*Refer to Globe Information
Services*

**Info-One International Pty.
Ltd.**
Level 3, 2 Elizabeth Plaza
North Sydney, NSW 2060
Australia
02 9595075; Fax 02 9295127
*This Australian database vendor
offers many legal and legislative
databases.*

The Infocheck Group, Ltd.
Godmersham Park, Godmersham
Canterbury, Kent CT4 7DT,
England
0227 81300; Fax 0227 813100

Infomart Online
1450 Don Mills Road
Don Mills, ON, Canada M3B 2X7
(800) 668-9215; (416) 442-2198
Fax (416) 445-3508
*Infomart Online is primarily a
news database vendor in Canada.*

**Information Access Company
(IAC)**
362 Lakeside Drive
Foster City, CA 94404
(800) 321-6388; (415) 378-5000
Fax (415) 358-4759

Information America
Refer to Appendix M

**Information Intelligence, Inc.
(III)**
P.O. Box 31098

Phoenix, AZ 85046
(800) 228-9982; (602) 996-2283

INFOTRADE N.V.
A. Gossetlaan 32a
B-1702 Groot-Bijgaarden, Belgium
02 4666480; Fax 02 4666970

**Instituto Brasileiro de
Informacao em Ciencia e
Tecnologia (IBICT)**
SAS, Quadra 5, Lote 6, Bloco H
70070-000 Brasilia, DF, Brazil
061 2176111; Fax 061 2262677

**Instituto de la Pequena y
Mediana Empresa Industrial
(IMPI)**
Paseo de la Castellana 141
28046 Madrid, Spain
01 5829300; Fax 01 5712831

**International Museum of
Photography**
George Eastman House
900 East Avenue
Rochester, NY 14607
(716) 271-3361; Fax (716) 271-3970

**International Society of
Appraisers (ISA)**
500 N. Michigan Avenue; No. 1400
Chicago, IL 60611-3703
(312) 661-1700; Fax (312) 661-0769

I/PLUS Direct
Thomson Financial Services, Inc.
11 Farnsworth Street
Boston, MA 02210
(800) 662-7878; (617) 345-2000
Fax (617) 330-1986

**Israel National Center of
Scientific and Technological
Information, (COSTI)**
P.O. Box 43074
61430 Tel-Aviv, Israel
03 492037; Fax 03 492033

**Istituto Centrale di Statistica
(ISTAT)**
Via Cesare Balbo 16
I-00100 Rome, Italy
06 46731

Jordan & Sons Ltd.
21 St. Thomas Street
Bristol BS1 6JS, England
0272 230600; Fax 0272 230063

kiNexus, Inc.
640 N. LaSalle Street; Suite 560
Chicago, IL 60610
(800) 828-0422; (312) 335-0787
Fax (312) 642-0616

Kiwinet
National Library of New Zealand
Corner Molesworth & Aitken
Streets
P.O. Box 12-264
Wellington, New Zealand
04 4743000; Fax 04 4743042

Knight-Ridder Information, Inc.
3460 Hillview Avenue
Palo Alto, CA 94304
(800) 334-2564; (800) 387-2689
(415) 858-3785; Fax (415) 858-7069
Knight-Ridder offers approximately 400 online databases from various producers, as well as offering CD-ROM databases.

Knowledge Express
Knowledge Express Data Systems
900 West Valley Road; Suite 401
Wayne, PA 19087
(800) 248-2469; (610) 293-9712
Fax (610) 687-2704

**Kobmandsstandens
Oplysningsbureau A/S**
Gammel Mnt. 4
DK-1117 Copenhagen K, Denmark
33 111200; Fax 33 111629

KOLIBER
EUROSTART Sp. z o.o.
ul. Nagorskiego 3
60-408 Poznan, Poland
48 61475264; Fax 48 61475448

Kompass France S.A.
66, quai du Marechal Joffre
F-92415 Courbevoie Cedex,
France
01 41165100; Fax 01 41165118

KOMPASS Online
Reed Information Services Ltd.
Windsor Court
East Grinstead House
East Grinstead, W. Sussex RH19
1XA, England
0342 326972; Fax 0342 335612

Kreditschutzverband von 1870
Zelinkagasse 10
A-1010 Vienna, Austria
01 53484 6; Fax 01 53484 380

LA ONLINE
1332 Hermosa Avenue; Suite 7
Hermosa Beach, CA 90254
(310) 372-9364; Fax (310) 374-6588

Lda Mope
Rua de Santa Marta
43 E/F; 4th Floor
1100 Lisbon, Portugal
1 3522996; Fax 1 3520418

Legi-Slate, Inc.
777 N. Capital Street; 9th Floor
Washington, DC 20002
(800) 366-6363; (202) 898-2319
(202) 898-2300; Fax (202) 842-4748

Legi-Tech
1029 J Street; Suite 450
Sacramento, CA 95814
(916) 447-1886; Fax (916) 447-1109
Legi-Tech is a legislative tracking service.

LEXIS
Refer to LEXIS-NEXIS

**LEXIS-NEXIS
(Formerly Mead Data
Central, Inc. (MDC))**
9443 Springboro Pike
P.O. Box 933, Dayton, OH 45401
(800) 227-4908; (513) 865-6800
Fax (513) 865-6909
LEXIS-NEXIS offers online news, entertainment, and legal databases, as well as public records.

**Lloyd's Maritime Information
Services Inc. (LMIS)**
MARDATA

1200 Summer Street
Stamford, CT 06905
(800) 423-8672; (203) 359-8383
Fax (203) 358-0437

Longman Cartermill Ltd.
Technology Centre
St. Andrews
Fife KY16 9EA, Scotland
0334 77660; Fax 0334 77180

LRP Publications
747 Dresher Road
P.O. Box 980
Horsham, PA 19044
(215) 784-0860; Fax (215) 784-9639

**MagnaTex International,
Inc., COMMUNICATE!**
1173 Rockrimmon Road
Stamford, CT 06903
(800) 777-9246; Fax (203) 329-3763

**M.A.I.D. Systems Ltd.
(Market Analysis and
Information Database)**
M.A.I.D. House
18 Dufferin Street
London EC1Y 8PD, England
071-253 6900; Fax 071-253 0060

MECC
6160 Summit Drive N
Minneapolis, MN 55430-4003
(800) 685-6322; (612) 569-1500
Fax (612) 569-1551

**MEDLARS Management
Section**
U.S. National Library of
Medicine (NLM)
8600 Rockville Pike
Bethesda, MD 20894
(800) 638-8480; (301) 496-6193

Metromail Corporation
360 E. 22nd Street
Lombard, IL 60148-4989
(708) 620-3012

Microsoft Corporation
One Microsoft Way
Redmond, WA 98052-6394
(800) 426-9400; (206) 882-8080
Fax (206) 883-8101

MILITRAN, Inc.
P.O. Box 490
Southeastern, PA 19399-0490
(800) 426-9954; (215) 687-3900
Fax (215) 687-6814

Ministerio de Cultura de Espana, Secretaria General Tecnica, Puntos de Informacion Cultural (PIC)
Plaza del Ray 1
28071 Madrid, Spain
01 5325089; Fax 01 5319212
This Spanish database vendor offers many databases covering various topics.

Moscow City Telephone Network
Referral-Information Center
Novy Arbat Avenue 2
121019 Moscow, Russia
095 2038618; Fax 095 2022413

National Information Services Corporation (NISC)
Wyman Towers; Suite 6
3100 St. Paul Street
Baltimore, MD 21218
(410) 243-0797; Fax (410) 243-0982

National Library of Canada
DOBIS Client Information Centre
395 Wellington Street
Ottawa, ON, Canada K1A ON4
(800) 665-6045; (819) 997-7227

National Nuclear Data Center (NNDC)
Brookhaven National Laboratory
Building 197D, Upton, NY 11973
(516) 282-2901; Fax (516) 282-2806

The National Resume Bank
3637 4th Street N; Suite 330
St. Petersburg, FL 33704
(813) 896-3694

National Science Council
Science and Technology
Information Center Network
(STICNET)
P.O. Box 91-37
Taipei, Taiwan
02 7377631; Fax 02 7377663

NEEDS (NIKKEI Economic Electronic Databank System)
Nihon Keizai Shimbun, Inc.
(NIKKEI)
1-9-5 Otemachi, Chiyoda-ky
Tokyo 100, Japan
03 52942407; Fax 03 52942411

NewsNet, Inc.
945 Haverford Road
Bryn Mawr, PA 19010
(800) 345-1301; (215) 527-8030
Fax (215) 527-0338
NewsNet is primarily a news database vendor.

NEXIS
Refer to LEXIS-NEXIS

NIFTY-Serve
NIFTY Corporation
26-1, Minami-oi 6-chome
Shinagawa-ku
Tokyo 140, Japan
03 54715800; Fax 03 5471 5890
This Japanese database vendor offers news from around the world in their databases.

NIKKEI Economic Electronic Databank System (NEEDS)
Nihon Keizai Shimbun, Inc.
(NIKKEI)
1-9-5 Otemachi, Chiyoda-ky
Tokyo 100, Japan
03 52942407; Fax 03 52942411

Nikkei Telecom
1-9-5 Ohtemachi, Tokyo 100, Japan
Fax 03 32700251

North American Publishing Company
401 N. Broad Street
Philadelphia, PA 19108
(215) 238-5300; Fax (215) 238-5283

OCLC EPIC
Refer to OCLC Online Computer Library Center, Inc.

OCLC FirstSearch Catalog
Refer to OCLC Online Computer Library Center, Inc.

OCLC Online Computer Library Center, Inc.
6565 Frantz Road
Dublin, OH 43017
(800) 848-5878; (800) 848-8286
(614) 764-6000
Fax (614) 764-6096
OCLC offers a broad base of databases covering various topics.

Office of Cooperative Interactions (OCI)
Refer to Agricultural Research Service (ARS)

OneSource Information Services
150 Cambridge Park Drive
Cambridge, MA 02140
(800) 554-5501; (617) 441-7000
Fax (617) 225-7058

OPTIM Corporation
99 Metcalf Street; 3rd Floor
Ottawa, ON, Canada K1P 6L7
(800) 267-8462; (613) 232-3766

OZLINE: Australian Information Network
National Library of Australia
Parkes Place
Canberra, ACT 2600, Australia
6 2621531; Fax 6 2731180

Personnel Research Associates
49 Oakridge Rd.
Verona, NJ 07044
(201) 239-6154
Fax (201) 239-1013

PIMS UK Ltd.
PIMS House
Mildmay Avenue
London N1 4RS, England
071-226 1000
Fax 071-704 1360

PINET (Physics INformation NETwork)
American Institute of Physics
(AIP)
500 Sunnyside Boulevard
Woodbury, NY 11797-2999
(516) 576-2262
Fax (516) 349-9704

PRODIGY
Refer to Appendix L

Publications and Communications, Inc.
12416 Hymeadow Drive
Austin, TX 78750
(800) 678-9724; (512) 250-9023
Fax (512) 331-3900

QL Systems Limited
901 St. Andrew's Tower
275 Sparks Street
Ottawa, ON, Canada K1R 7X9
(800) 387-0899; (613) 238-3499
Fax (613) 238-7597
This Canadian database vendor offers a wide variety of legal, legislative, and news databases.

Quality Education Data, Inc. (QED)
1600 Broadway; Suite 1200
Denver, CO 80202-4912
(800) 525-5811; (303) 860-1832
Fax (303) 860-0238

Quanta Press, Inc.
1313 Fifth Street SE; Suite 223A
Minneapolis, MN 55414
(612) 379-3956
Fax (612) 623-4570

QUESTEL•ORBIT
Le Capitole
55, Avenue des Champs Pierreux
F-92029 Nanterre Cedex, France
01 46145660
Fax 01 46145511
This French database vendor offers a broad base of databases for many disciplines.

Quotron Systems, Inc.
77 Water Street; 9th Floor
New York, NY 10005
(800) 366-6610; (212) 898-7000
Fax (212) 363-1351

Randall-Helms International, Inc.
19 Center Street
Chatham, NJ 07928
(201) 635-0510; Fax (201) 635-8330

Reed Reference Publishing Group
R.R. Bowker
121 Chanlon Road
New Providence, NJ 07974
(800) 521-8110; (908) 464-6800
Fax (908) 665-3528

Reuter TEXTLINE
Refer to Reuters Ltd.

Reuters Information Services (Canada) Ltd.
Exchange Tower; Suite 1900
2 First Canadian Place
Toronto, ON, Canada M5X 1E3
(800) 387-1588; (416) 364-5361
Most of the dozens of databases offered by Reuters center around business and financial information.

Reuters Ltd.
85 Fleet Street
London EC4P 4AJ, England
071-250 1122
Most of the dozens of databases offered by Reuters center around business and financial information.

Russian Information and Communications Agency (RUSSICA)
Spartakovskaya Street 13
107066 Moscow, Russia
095 9325610
Fax 095 9326300

SARITEL S.p.A.
Via Aurelio Saffi 18
C.P. 512
I-10138 Torino, Italy
011 33301

SEC Online
Disclosure Incorporated
201 Moreland Road; Suite 2
Hauppauge, NY 11788
(516) 864-7200; Fax (516) 864-7215

Securities Data Company, Inc.
1180 Raymond Boulevard
5th Floor

Newark, NJ 07102
(201) 622-3100

Sema Group InfoData AB, Rattsbanken
Box 34101
S-100 26 Stockholm, Sweden
08 7385000; Fax 08 6950524
This Swedish database vendor offers many databases for the legal community.

Silverplatter Information, Inc.
100 River Ridge Drive
Norwood, MA 02062-5026
(800) 343-0064; (617) 769-2599
Fax (617) 769-8763
Silverplatter is a vendor of numerous CD-ROM products, including many containing business financial information.

Simmons Market Research Bureau, Inc. (SMRB)
420 Lexington Avenue
New York, NY 10170
(212) 916-8900; Fax (212) 916-8918

Slater Hall Information Products (SHIP)
1301 Pennsylvania Avenue, NW
Suite 507
Washington, DC 20004
(202) 393-2666; Fax (202)638-2248

Soviet News
Refer to Russian Information and Communications Agency (RUSSICA)

SovInfoLink
Russian Information and Communications Agency (RUSSICA)
Spartakovskaya Street 13
107066 Moscow, Russia
095 9325610; Fax 095 9326300

Space-Time Research Pty. Ltd.
668 Burwood Road
Hawthorn East, VIC 3123, Australia
03 8133211; 03 8824029

Sportel Communications Network
P.O. Box 1182
Las Vegas, NV 89125
(800) 634-3112; (702) 871-6529

The Sporting News Publishing Company
1212 North Lindbergh Boulevard
St. Louis, MO 63132
(314) 997-7111

The Sports Network (TSN)
701 Mason's Mill Business Park
Huntingdon Valley, PA 19006
(215) 947-2400; Fax (215) 938-8466

SportsTicker
Harborside Financial Center
600 Plaza Two
Jersey City, NJ 07311-3992
(201) 309-1200; Fax (201) 860-9742

Standard & Poor's
25 Broadway; 14th Floor
New York, NY 10004
(212) 208-8300; Fax (212) 412-0498

StarText
Fort Worth Star-Telegram
400 W. 7th Street
Fort Worth, TX 76102
(817) 390-7905; Fax (817) 390-7797

State Net
Information for Public Affairs, Inc. (IPA)
2101 K Street
Sacramento, CA 95816-4920
(916) 444-0840

STN International
FIZ Karlsruhe
P.O. Box 2465
D-76012 Karlsruhe 1, Germany
07247 808555; Fax 07247 808131
STN offers many databases geared toward the scientific community, and others in a wide variety of topics.

Strategic Mapping Inc.
70 Seaview Avenue
P.O. Box 10250
Stamford, CT 06904

(800) 866-2255; (203) 353-7295
Fax (203) 353-7276

STSC, Inc.
2115 E. Jefferson Street
Rockville, MD 20852
(800) 592-0050; (301) 984-5000

SUNIST (Serveur Universitaire National pour l'Information Scientifique et Technique)
CNUSC-SUNIST
950 rue de Saint Priest BP 7229
34184 Montpelier cdex 4
67 14 14 14; Fax 67 52 37 63

Teknillinen Korkeakoulu Laskentakeskus
Otakaari 1
FIN-02150 Espoo, Finland
0 4514112; Fax 0 4514132

O.R. Telematique
7, rue de Sens
Rochecorbon
F-37210 Vouvray, France
047 626262; Fax 047 525281

Telerate Systems Inc.
Harborside Financial Center
600 Plaza Two
Jersey City, NJ 07311
(201) 860-4000

Telescan, Inc.
10550 Richmond Avenue
Suite 250
Houston, TX 77042-5019
(800) 324-8246; (713) 952-1060
Fax (713) 952-7138

TETRAD Computer Applications Limited
3873 Airport Way
P.O. Box 9754
Bellingham, WA 98227-9754
(800) 663-1334; (206) 734-3318
Fax (206) 734-4005

Texas Innovation Network System (TINS)
3500 W. Balcones Center Drive
Austin, TX 78759
(800) 645-8324; (512) 338-3283
Fax (512) 338-3336

Time Inc.
Time-Life Building
New York, NY 10020
(212) 522-1212; Fax (212) 333-4066

Timeplace, Inc.
460 Totten Pond Road
Waltham, MA 02154
(800) 544-4023; (617) 890-4636
Fax (617) 890-7274

Track Data Corporation (TDC)
61 Broadway; Suite 2301
New York, NY 10006
(800) 223-0113; (212) 943-4555
Fax (212) 943-3963

Track Data Corporation (TDC)
95 Rockwell Place
Brooklyn, NY 11217
(718) 522-0222; Fax (718) 522-6847

U.S. Bureau of the Census
Data User Services Division
Washington, DC 20233-8300
(301)763-4100; Fax (301)763-4794

U.S. Defense Technical Information Center (DTIC)
Defense RDT&E OnLine
System (DROLS)
Building No. 5, Cameron Station
Alexandria, VA 22304-6145
(800) 841-9553; (703) 274-7709

U.S. Department of Agriculture
Agricultural Research Service (ARS)
Office of Cooperative Interactions (OCI)
Room 404; Building 005,
BARC-West
Beltsville, MD 20705
(301) 344-4045

U.S. Library of Congress Information System
101 Independence Avenue, SE
Washington, DC 20540
(202) 707-5114

U.S. Statistics, Inc.
1101 King Street; Suite 601
P.O. Box 816

Alexandria, VA 22314
(703) 979-9699; Fax (703) 548-4585

**University of Alaska,
Anchorage**
Alaska Center for International
Business (ACIB)
4201 Tudor Centre Drive
Suite 120
Anchorage, AK 99508
(907) 561-2322
Fax (901) 561-1541

University of Durham
Unit 3P
Mountjoy Research Centre
Durham DH1 3SW, England
091 3742468; Fax 091 3844971

**Urban Decision Systems, Inc.
(UDS)**
4676 Admiralty Way; Suite 624
Marina Del Rey, CA 90292-6607
(800) 633-9568; (213) 820-8931
Fax (213) 826-0933

**Verband der Vereine
Creditreform e.V. (VC)**
Hellersbergstr. 12
Postfach 101552
D-4040 Neuss, Germany
02101 109210; Fax 02131 109225

Verlag Hoppenstedt GmbH,
Wirtschaftsdatenbank
Havelstrasse 9
Postfach 100139
D64201 Darmstadt, Germany
06151 3800; Fax 06151 380360

**Vickers Stock Research
Corporation**
226 New York Avenue
Huntington, NY 11743
(800) 645-5043; (800) 832-5280
(516) 423-7710; Fax (516) 423-7715

**Waterlow Signature
(The Registered Companies
Database)**
Waterlow Information Services
Limited
Classic House
174-180 Old Street
London EC1V 9BP, England

071-250 3350; (080) 181 377
Fax 071-608 0867

The WEFA Group
401 City Line Avenue; Suite 300
Bala Cynwyd, PA 19004-1780
(215) 667-6000; Fax (215 660-6477

West Publishing
620 Opperman Drive
Eagan, MN 55123
(800) 328-9352; (612) 687-7000
Fax (612) 687-7302
*WESTLAW is the online service
offered by West Publishing, which
has now merged with Information
America. WESTLAW's databases
include coverage of law, news,
and business financial information. They also offer the public
records databases of Prentice Hall
Online. Refer to Appendix M.*

WESTLAW
Refer to West Publishing

H.W. Wilson Company
950 University Avenue
Bronx, NY 10452
(800) 367-6770; (718) 588-8400
Fax (718) 590-1617

WILSONLINE
*WILSONLINE offers many data-
bases, including several reference
works, and databases addressing
various topics. Refer to H.W.
Wilson Company*

Companies and Associations That Can Help to Remove Your Name from Mailing Lists

---

Buyer's Choice
(800) 664-MAIL

Direct Marketing Association
Telephone Preference Service
P.O. Box 9014
Farmingdale, NY 11735

Reuben H. Donnelley Corp.
399 Knollwood Road
White Plains, NY 10603
(914) 421-5700

Haines & Company Inc
Criss-Cross Directory
8050 Freedom Avenue NW
North Canton, OH 44720

R.L. Polk & Company
List Compilation & Directory
(800) 873-7655

Private Citizen, Inc. (PCI)
P.O. Box 233
Naperville, IL 60566
(800) CUT-JUNK; (708) 393-1555

Stop Junk Mail Association
3020 Bridgeway, #150
Sausalito, CA
(800) 827-5540

Have I Missed Anything?

If there are sources that I've missed, or anything that you think should be covered that you did not find in *Naked in Cyberspace*, please send your comments and updates to:

Carole A. Lane

3915 Mission Avenue #7-109

Oceanside, CA 92054-7801

(619) 721-5500

CompuServe: 75260,2251

Internet: calane@cerfnet.com

Index

T

The Taft Group, foundation and grants databases, 117
Taiwan On-Line Business Data Services, 90
Talk Show Guest Directory, 111
talk shows
  locating experts, 104
  transcripts, 176
TargetScan CD-ROM, 355
Tasmanian Pioneers Index, 238, 336
tax liens
  asset searches, 93
  bank records and, 191
  public records and, 260, 268-270
tax records
  See also IRS (Internal Revenue Service)
  corporate, 259
  types of, 239-240
Taxpayers for Government Reform, 160
TBS television program, 176
Technical Advisory Service for Attorneys, 105
technical papers, 188
telemarketing calls, 164-165
telephone directories
  America Online "White Pages," 25, 146
  CompuServe "Phone File," 25
  in computerized databases, 5-6, 56, 60
  demographic data, 357
  Internet resources, 146-147
  online databases, 143-146, 465-468
  prospect research and, 116
  searches, 273-274
  usage restrictions, 17, 145
Telephone Preference Service, Direct Marketing Association, 165
telephone records, private investigation, 119-120
TELESPORT database, 297
television
  accessing broadcast transcripts, 10, 27, 176-177
  death announcements, 237
  job opportunities, 81
  writers, 105
Television Programming Source Books, 290
Telran legislative tracking service, 347, 351
tenant screening
  associations, 417
  property management, 85-87
  services, 206
TenantNet, Online Resource for Residential Tenant's Rights, 86
Territorial Vital Records, 238
TETRAD Computer Applications Limited, 356
Texas, divorce records, 260
Texas Innovation Network System (TINS), Texas Faculty Profiles, 106
Texas Voluntary Adoption Registry, 284
"This Day in Sports" feature, Reuters Sports News, 296
Thomas, Clarence (Judge), 346
thumbnail images, 181
Timber Yield Tax, 239
TIME, 182
Time Almanac, 183
Time International, Time Publications, 295
TIME magazine, Time Publications, 295

Time Publications, 172, 295
Time Traveler CD, 185
The Times of London News Service, 182
Tiny Tafel format, genealogical records
Tomei, Marissa, 133-134
"Tonight Show," 288
Toolworks Reference Library, The Software Toolworks, 188
Top 10 Archive, Late Night with David Letterman, 190
Trade & Industry ASAP database, 178
trade associations, 155
Trans Registry Limited (TRL), 86
Trans Union Credit Information Company, Business Litigation Database, 94
TRANSCRIPT database, 176
transcripts
  from legal cases, 110, 254
  online databases with, 461-464
  from talk shows, 111
Transportation Information Services, Inc., 278
TransUnion Corporation
  accessing, 198
  contacting, 207
trash, revealing information, 42, 192
Travaux Publics de France, 78, 81
TREVI, 218-219
Trump, Donald, 95
TV + Films Web site, 300
TV Guide Entertainment Network, 296
TV Guide Online, 296
typographical errors, 53

U

UCC
  See Uniform Commercial Code (UCC) filings
UK+Ireland Genealogy Index, 337
Ulin, Jeff, 293, 294
Ultimate TV Show List, 300
Ultimate White Pages, 146
Umea Universitet, 237
unclaimed assets (Verifind), 206
Uniform Child Custody Act, 256
Uniform Commercial Code (UCC) filings
  asset searches, 91, 95
  bank records and, 191, 194
  in business credit databases, 195
  contents of, 270
  financial statements and, 240
unique names, 55
United Kingdom
  adoption search organizations, 404
  census records, 358
  genealogical research organizations, 409-410
  genealogical research publications, 384-385
United Nations Crime and Justice Information Network (UNCJIN), 222
United States
  adoption search organizations, 404-405
  genealogical research organizations, 410
  genealogical research publications, 385-395
  removing your name from mailing lists, 165
United States Bureau of Census, 353, 355
United States federal court decisions, adoption legislation, 285

United States Library of Congress Information Systems, 107
United States National Cancer Institute, 242
United States National Healthcare Reform Initiative, 243
United States Toll-free Number directory, 25
universities, Web sites, 58, 113
  See also colleges; students
University of Durham, U.K., 358
University of Houston Libraries, Scholarly Journals Distributed Via the World Wide Web, 175
University of St. Gallen Student Association, Switzerland, 147
University of Sussex (UK) telephone directory, 150
unlisted telephone numbers, 144, 156
UPI (United Press International) newswires, 170
UPMC (University of Pittsburgh Medical Center) Telephone Directory, 149-152
Urban Decision Systems, Inc. (UDS), 355
Uruguay, mailing list/direct marketing associations, 412
U.S. Census of Population and Housing, 356
U.S. Coast Guard, watercraft ownership records, 274-275
U.S. Department of Justice
  criminal justice databases, 211
  identifying foreign resources, 219
  publications, 220
  Web site, 223
U.S. Department of Labor, 71, 79
U.S. Department of State, Bureau of Consular Affairs, 219
U.S. Employment Discrimination Law, 73
U.S. Employment Law, 73
U.S. Food and Drug Administration, 222
U.S. Library of Congress Information System, 56
U.S. military personnel, 78
U.S. National Archives, 341
U.S. National Central Bureau, 215, 219
U.S. News and World Report, 182
U.S. Newswire, 344
U.S. Postal Service
  document retrieval, 275
  mailing lists and, 155, 160, 272
U.S. Presidents biographical database, 345
U.S. Resume, 77
U.S. Securities and Exchange Commission, 94
U.S. Statistics, Inc., 356
USA GeoGraph II—Multimedia Edition CD-ROM, 354
USA GeoGraph II—Spanish Edition CD-ROM, 354
USA Today, 182
USA Wars: Vietnam CD-ROM database, 235
USA Wars: World War II database, 185
USCD Science and Engineering Library— People and Organizations page, 60
Use Fuel Tax, 239
Usenet newsgroups
  adoptee/birthparent classified ads, 26
  alt. quotations, 189
  celebrities, 299
  described, 21

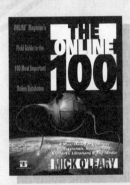

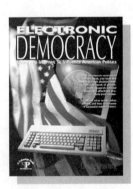